INTERNATIONAL CRIMINAL LAW

ANTONIO CASSESE

OXFORD
UNIVERSITY PRESS

OXFORD
UNIVERSITY PRESS

Great Clarendon Street, Oxford OX2 6DP

Oxford University Press is a department of the University of Oxford.
It furthers the Universityís objective of excellence in research, scholarship,
and education by publishing worldwide in

Oxford New York

Auckland Bangkok Buenos Aires Cape Town Chennai
Dar es Salaam Delhi Hong Kong Istanbul Karachi Kolkata
Kuala Lumpur Madrid Melbourne Mexico City Mumbai Nairobi
S„o Paulo Shanghai Taipei Tokyo Toronto

Oxford is a registered trade mark of Oxford University Press
in the UK and in certain other countries

Published in the United States
by Oxford University Press Inc., New York

First published 2003

British Library Cataloguing in Publication Data
Data available

Library of Congress Cataloging in Publication Data
Data applied for

ISBN 0-19-925911-9 (pbk)
ISBN 0-19-926128-8 (cloth)

3 5 7 9 10 8 6 4

Typeset in Adobe Minion
by RefineCatch Limited, Bungay, Suffolk
Printed in Great Britain by
Ashford Colour Press Ltd, Gosport, Hampshire

Sedulo curavi, humanas actiones non ridere, non lugere, neque detestari, sed intelligere: atque adeo humanos affectus, ut sunt amor, odium, ira, invidia, gloria, misericordia, et reliquae animi commotiones, non ut humanae naturae vitia, sed ut proprietates contemplatus sum, quae ad ipsam ita pertinent, ut ad naturam aëris aestus, frigus, tempestas, tonitru, et alia hujusmodi, quae, tametsi incommoda sunt, necessaria tamen sunt, certasque habent causas, per quas eorum naturam intelligere conamur, et Mens eorum vera contemplatione aeque gaudet, ac earum rerum cognitione, quae sensibus gratae sunt.

Spinoza, *Tractatus politicus* (1677), I, §4, 28–37*

* 'I sedulously endeavoured neither to deride nor to pity nor to loathe human actions, but only to understand them. Thus I have regarded human passions—such as love, hatred, wrath, envy, glory, mercy and other commotions of human soul—not as vices of human nature, but as qualitities that pertain to it, just as warm, cold, tempest, thunder and similar phenomena pertain to weather. Even when they are uncomfortable they are nevertheless necessary. They are grounded on specific causes. Through these causes we try to understand their nature. And our mind draws from their true apprehension and understanding as much pleasure as from what is agreeable to our senses.'

CONTENTS

PREFACE

In this book I have endeavoured to distil from an immense array of cases, both national and international, as well as the relatively few available treaties, the fundamental rules proscribing inadmissible conduct as international crimes, and outlining international proceedings for the prosecution and punishment of such crimes.

Offences prohibited as international crimes, in particular war crimes, have for long been stigmatized. Their alleged perpetrators have been brought to trial on a great many occasions. Nonetheless, strikingly this subject matter has never been dealt with in a systematic manner by scholars. Now that the two ad hoc International Tribunals (for the former Yugoslavia and Rwanda) have proved able effectively and fairly to dispense justice and the International Criminal Court is about to commence fulfilling its long awaited mission, it is time for commentators to offer a fairly complete, if concise, outline of international criminal law. This has been my purpose. I have tried succinctly to expound the fundamentals of both substantive and procedural international criminal law. In so doing, I also have made an effort to conceptualize as much as possible, that is, give what I hope is a coherent theoretical framework to the patchwork of disparate rules, principles, concepts, and legal constructs that at present make up international criminal law.

I am keenly aware that this first attempt is destined to be replaced fairly soon by more extensive and in-depth treatment of this complex matter. I would be content if this book could serve as a general introduction, for both students and practitioners, to this fascinating branch of international law and as a stimulus to other scholars or practitioners to delve deeper into its notions.

I have cited all the national or international cases that seemed to me to be relevant to a particular matter under discussion. The purpose of my mentioning cases was not only to support a specific proposition by reference to the jurisprudence relating thereto, or to show how courts have applied a rule of law, or what interpretation they have placed on it. I have also aimed to point to the historical and human dimension of cases. For this purpose, I have tried as far as possible to recount the facts behind the court's legal findings. For, one should never forget that this body of law, more than any other, results from a myriad of small or great tragedies. Each crime is a tragedy, for the victims and their relatives, the witnesses, the community to which they belong, and even the perpetrator, who, when brought to trial, will endure the ordeal of criminal proceedings and, if found guilty, may suffer greatly, in the form of deprivation of life, at worst, or of personal liberty, at best. Law, it is well known, filters and rarefies the halo of horror and suffering surrounding crimes. As a consequence, when one reads a law book or a judgment, one is led almost to forget the violent and cruel origin of criminal law prescriptions. That origin, however, remains the rationale and underpinning of those prescriptions. One ought not to become oblivious to it. To recall it may serve as a reminder of the true historical source of criminal law. This branch of law, more than any other, is about human folly, human wickedness, and human aggressiveness. It deals with the darkest side of our nature. It also deals with how society confronts violence and viciousness and seeks to stem them as far as possible so as 'to make gentle the life on this world'. Of course the lawyer can do very little, for he is enjoined by his professional ethics neither to loathe nor to pity human conduct. He is required to remain impassive and simply extract from the chaos of conflicting standards of behaviour those that seem to him to be imposed by law.

To provide the English-speaking reader with details of cases in other languages, I have relied extensively upon, besides the most significant older or more recent cases in English, relevant judgments in Dutch, French, German, Italian, and Spanish. Translations are mine, unless indicated to the contrary. In order not to divert attention from the essentials, I have cited in footnotes the cases or passages that are of relatively minor importance. The reader may therefore ignore footnotes without missing the gist of the reasoning.

The reader interested in consulting the treaties and other documents cited in this book may use the Oxford University Press companion web site. I am grateful to I. Pierangeli Borletti for skilfully helping me set up this website.

I am beholden to a few friends or colleagues who kindly read and made insightful comments on some chapters: M. Delmas-Marty, S. Manacorda, F. Mantovani, M. Papa, B. Swart. Other friends (P. Gaeta, John R. W. D. Jones, G. Mettraux, and S. Zappalà) read the whole book and offered helpful criticisms and suggestions. Of course, the responsibility for any misapprehension that may remain rests solely with me.

As I am keenly aware of how vast this subject matter is and how easy it is to overlook significant cases or miss inaccuracies, I would be grateful for any comments, suggestions or critical remarks, which should be sent to me via the 'contact and comments' link on the companion web site: **www.oup.com/uk/best.textbooks/law/cassese_internationalcriminallaw**

ABBREVIATIONS

AILC	American International Law Cases
AJCL	*American Journal of Comparative Law*
AJIL	*American Journal of International Law*
Ambos, *Der 'Allgemeine Teil'*	Ambos, K., *Der Allgemeine Teil des Völkerstrafrechts—Ansätze einer Dogmatisierung* (Berlin: Duncker & Humblot, 2002)
Ascensio, Decaux, Pellet, *Droit international pénal*	Ascensio, H., Decaux, E., and Pellet, A. (eds), *Droit international pénal* (Paris: Pedone, 2000)
Ashworth, *Principles*	Ashworth, A., *Principles of Criminal Law*, 3rd edn (Oxford: Oxford University Press, 1999)
Bassiouni and Nanda, *A Treatise*	Bassiouni M. C., and Nanda V. P. (eds), *A Treatise on International Criminal Law*, 2 vols (Springfield: Thomas, 1973)
BILC	British International Law Cases
British Military Manual	The War Office, *The Law of War on Land* (being Part III of the Manual of Military Law) (London: War Office, 1958)
Bull. Crim.	*Bulletin des arrêts de la Cour de Cassation*, Chambre criminelle (Paris)
BYIL	*British Yearbook of International Law*
Cassese, Delmas-Marty, *Juridictions nationales*	Cassese A., and Delmas-Marty M. (eds), *Juridictions nationales et crimes internationaux* (Paris: PUF, 2002)
Cassese, Delmas-Marty, *Crimes internationaux*	Cassese A., and Delmas-Marty M. (eds), *Crimes internationaux et juridictions internationales* (Paris: PUF, 2002)
Cassese, Gaeta, and Jones, *ICC Commentary*	Cassese, A., Gaeta, P., Jones, J. R. W. D. (eds), *The Rome Statute of the International Criminal Court—A Commentary* (Oxford: Oxford University Press, 2002)
CLForum	Criminal Law Forum
CLR	*Columbia Law Review*
CrimLR	*Criminal Law Review*
CSCE	Conference on Security and Co-operation in Europe
Donnedieu de Vabres, *Procès*	Donnedieu de Vabres, H., 'Le procès de Nuremberg devant les principes modernes du droit pénal international', 70 HR (1947–I), 477–582
Donnedieu de Vabres, *Traité*	Donnedieu de Vabres, H., *Traité de droit criminel et de législation pénale comparée*, 3rd edn (Paris: Sirey, 1947)

Entscheidungen	*Entscheidungen des Obersten Gerichtshofes für die Britische Zone—Entscheidungen in Strafsachen*, 3 vols (Berlin and Hamburg: Walter de Gruyter, 1949–51)
EJIL	*European Journal of International Law*
Fischer, Kress, Lüder, *International and National Prosecution*	Fischer, H., Kress, C., Lüder, S. R. (eds), *International and National Prosecution of Crimes under International Law—Current Developments* (Berlin: Berlin Verlag Arno Spitz, 2001)
Fletcher, *Basic Concepts*	Fletcher, G. P., *Basic Concepts of Criminal Law* (New York and Oxford: Oxford University Press, 1998)
Fletcher, *Rethinking*	Fletcher, G. P., *Rethinking Criminal Law* (Boston and Toronto: Little, Brown & Co., 1974)
Friedman	Friedman, L., *The Law of War—A Documentary History*, 2 vols (New York: Random House, 1972)
FRUS	Papers relating to the Foreign Relations of the United States
FRY	Federal Republic of Yugoslavia (Serbia and Montenegro)
GA	General Assembly of the United Nations
Glaser, *Culpabilité*	Glaser S., 'Culpabilité en droit international pénal', 99 HR (1960–I), 473–591
Glaser, *Introduction*	Glaser S., *Introduction à l'étude du droit international pénal* (Bruxelles, Paris : Bruylant-Recueil Sirey, 1954)
GP	*Giustizia penale*
HILJ	*Harvard International Law Journal*
HLR	*Harvard Law Review*
HR	*Recueil des Cours de l'Académie de droit international de La Haye*
IACHR	Inter-American Commission of Human Rights
ICC	International Criminal Court
ICJ	International Court of Justice
ICLQ	*International and Comparative Law Quarterly*
ICTR	International Criminal Tribunal for Rwanda
ICTY	International Criminal Tribunal for the former Yugoslavia
ILR	*International Law Reports*
IMTFE	International Military Tribunal for the Far East, Tokyo
IMT	International Military Tribunal for the Major War Criminals, Nuremberg
IMT Tokyo	R. J. Pritchard and S. Magbanua Zaide (eds) *The Tokyo War Crimes Trial* (The Complete Transcripts of the Proceedings of the International Military Tribunal for the Far East), (New York and London: Garland Publishing House, 1981)

International Conference on Military Trials	*Report of Robert H. Jackson, United States Representative to the International Conference on Military Trials, London 1945* (Washington DC: Department of State, 1949)
IRRC	*International Review of the Red Cross*
IYHR	*Israeli Yearbook on Human Rights*
IYIL	*Italian Yearbook of International Law*
JAIL	*Japanese Annual of International Law*
JCP	*Juris-classeur périodique (la semaine juridique)*, France
Jescheck, *Entwicklung*	Jescheck, H. H., 'Die Entwicklung des Völkerstrafrechts nach Nürnberg', *Schweizerische Zeitschrift für Strafrecht* (1957), 217–48
Jescheck, *Protection*	Jescheck, H. H., 'La protection pénale des Conventions internationales humanitaires', 24 *Revue internationale de droit pénal* (1953), 13–67
Jescheck, *Verantwortlichkeit*	Jescheck, H. H., *Die Verantwortlichkeit der Staatsorgane nach Völkerstrafrecht: eine Studie zu den Nürnberger Prozessen* (Bonn: Ludwig Röhrscheid Verlag, 1952)
Justiz und NS-Verbrechen	*Justiz und NS-Verbrechen, Sammlung Deutscher Strafurteile wegen Nationalsozialistischer Tötungsverbrechen 1945–1966*, 22 vols (Amsterdam: University Press Amsterdam, 1968–75), also available on CD-Rom
Kelsen, *Principles*	Kelsen, H., *Principles of International Law* (New York: Rinehart & Co., 1952)
Kirk McDonald, Swaak-Goldman, *Substantive and Procedural Aspects*	Kirk McDonald G., and Swaak-Goldman O. (eds), *Substantive and Procedural Aspects of International Criminal Law—The Experience of International and National Courts*, vol. I (The Hague, London, Boston: Kluwer Law International, 2000)
LJIL	*Leiden Journal of International Law*
LRTWC	*Law Reports of Trials of War Criminals*, 15 vols (London: UN War Crimes Commission, 1949)
Mantovani	Mantovani, F., *Diritto penale*, 4th edn (Padua: Cedam, 2001)
May and others, *ICTY Procedure and Evidence*	R. May and others (eds), *Essays on ICTY Procedure and Evidence—In Honour of G. Kirk McDonald* (The Hague: Kluwer, 2001)
Mettraux, *Landmark Decisions*	Mettraux G. (ed.), *International Criminal Law before National Courts—A Collection of Landmark Decisions* (Oxford: Oxford University Press, 2003, forthcoming)
NederJ	*Nederlandse Jurisprudentie*

NAM	Non-Aligned Movement
NILR	*Netherlands International Law Review*
NSDAP	German national socialist (Nazi) party
NSKK	German national socialist (Nazi) commandos
PCIJ	Permanent Court of International Justice
Pradel	Pradel, J., *Droit pénal comparé* (Paris: Dalloz, 1995)
PrepCom	Preparatory Committee on the Establishment of an International Criminal Court
Quintano Ripollés, *Tratado*	Quintano Ripollés, A., *Tratado de derecho penal internacional e internacional penal*, vol. I (Madrid: CSIC, Istituto 'Francisco de Vitoria', 1955)
RDPC	*Revue de droit pénal et de criminologie*
RGDIP	*Revue générale de droit international public*
RDMDG	*Revue de droit militaire et de droit de la guerre*
Röling, *The Law of War*	Röling, B. V. A., 'The Law of War and the National Jurisdiction since 1945', 100 HR (1960–II), 329–453
RPE	Rules of Procedure and Evidence
SA	Sturm Abteilung (Nazi paramilitary force)
Sassòli and Bouvier	M. Sassòli and A. Bouvier (eds), *How Does Law Protect in War? Cases, Documents and Teaching Materials*, (Geneva: ICRC, 1999)
SC	UN Security Council
SS	Schutz Staffel (Nazi elite corps)
Smith and Hogan	Smith and Hogan, *Criminal Law*, 9th edn (London: Butterworths, 1999)
Trial of the Major War Criminals	*Trial of the Major War Criminals Before the International Military Tribunal, Nuremberg 14 November 1945–1 October 1946* (Nuremberg, 1947)
Triffterer, *ICC Commentary*	Triffterer, O. (ed.), *Commentary on the Rome Statute of the International Criminal Court* (Baden-Baden: Nomos, 1999)
TWC	*Trials of War Criminals before the Nürnberg Military Tribunals under Control Council Law no. 10*, 12 vols (Washington, DC: US Govt Printing Office, 1950)
UNMIK	United Nations Interim Administration in Kosovo
UNTAET	United Nations Transitional Administration in East Timor
US Restatement Third	The American Law Institute, Restatement of the Law Third, *Restatement of the Law—The Foreign Relations Law of the United States*, vol. I (St. Paul, Minn.: American Law Institute Publishers, 1987)

Verhandlungen	*Verhandlungen des Reichstags I. Wahlperiode 1920*, Band 368, *Anlagen zu den Stenographischen Berichten Nr 2254 bis 2628* (Berlin: Julius Sittenfeld, 1924): contains the original text of the cases tried by the German Supreme Court at Leipzig
YIHL	*Yearbook of International Humanitarian Law*
YILC	*Yearbook of the International Law Commission*

TABLE OF CASES

TABLE OF TREATIES AND CONVENTIONS

TABLE OF NATIONAL LEGISLATION

TABLE OF INTERNATIONAL INSTRUMENTS

TABLE OF STATUTES OF INTERNATIONAL TRIBUNALS

PART I

INTRODUCTION

1

THE REACTION OF THE INTERNATIONAL COMMUNITY TO ATROCITIES

This book examines the *judicial response* of both national and international courts to the commission of those serious violations of international standards on human rights or humanitarian law that reach the legal threshold of international crimes. It is nonetheless appropriate briefly to consider the more general question of how the international community at present reacts to atrocities. By this means the prosecution and punishment by courts of those crimes are placed in their proper perspective. In addition it is hoped that the reader will thereby be able to appraise both the merits and the limitations of the judicial response.

1.1 THE FAILURE OF INTERNATIONAL SANCTIONS BY STATES

It has become a truism that, after the demise of the Cold War, the growing disparity between rich and poor, increasing poverty and hopelessness, as well as nationalism, religious fundamentalism, and ethnic and religious hatred, have spawned violence, ethnic cleansing, and bloodshed. Internal conflicts have mushroomed. One of the striking features of the present-day international community, however, is the failure of the collective bodies to discharge their function of preventing or punishing large-scale and serious violations of human rights amounting to international crimes. The UN Security Council is mandated, under Chapter VII of the UN Charter, to deal with threats to, or breaches of, international peace and security. Often such threats or breaches may and indeed do result from, among other things, serious crimes. In recent years, however, the Security Council has, more than ever before, proved unable to resolve major international crises and keep up with the staggering increase in global violence. No one can contest its inability to react promptly and effectively, and to put a stop to massacres amounting to serious threats to the peace or breaches of the peace in Somalia, the former Yugoslavia including Kosovo, Sierra Leone, Ethiopia and Eritrea, Indonesia, the Middle East, and so on.

The failure to command respect for international law relates not only to the resort to force proper. It also concerns the adoption of *economic sanctions*, which in principle was conceived of as a fallback position for the Security Council, but in practice has become one of the major means available to international organs to impose peace and security and, if need be, induce compliance with international rules. These sanctions, however, normally prove ineffective or carry little weight; frequently they are unfair and counterproductive. Although they are intended as a reaction to wrongdoings done by the State officials responsible for the international delinquencies, they target the State as such and therefore often end up adversely affecting, or at any rate having a negative knock-on effect on, the civilian population or other innocent persons.

As stressed above, under the UN Charter the Security Council is competent only to deal with international crises likely to jeopardize or endanger international peace and security. The Security Council is not expected to handle relatively 'minor' conflicts, which consequently fall within the province of the States concerned. In other words, the settlement of crises resulting from gross human rights violations amounting to crimes may often be left to the States directly affected by the friction or conflict. (Of course the SC can step in when the situation arises solely *within* a State but nonetheless is of such a nature as to threaten international peace and security, i.e. because of spill-over effects such as floods of refugees, or because the atrocities are inflaming world public opinion, as in Rwanda and Kosovo, thereby destabilizing the region or international public order.)

In addition, individual States have had scant, if any, resort to one particular legal weapon which is available as a response to gross violations of human rights and other atrocities, namely, *peaceful reprisals*, currently termed *countermeasures*. (These include the suspension or termination of commercial treaties or treaties granting special rights to nationals of the offending State, trade embargoes, freezing or seizure of assets belonging to the foreign State or to its nationals, etc.)

Why do States refrain from taking countermeasures against gross violations of international law? The reason is simple: States tend to resort to countermeasures only when their own interests are at stake and other States have harmed those interests by breaching international law. In other words, States tend to react to the breach of *reciprocal* obligations by other States.[1] In contrast, they are inclined to turn a deaf ear to breaches of international obligations enshrining basic values such as peace, human dignity, and protection of ethnic, religious, or racial groups against extermination, etc. These are what one may call *community obligations*.[2] They exhibit two basic features: first, they are incumbent upon each and every member of the world community towards all other members; and, secondly, any other member of that community has a correlative right to demand fulfilment of these obligations and, in cases of breach, may be entitled to resort to countermeasures. Plainly, the gross breaches of inter-

[1] On the notion of reciprocal obligations see B. Simma, 'From Bilateralism to Community Interest in International Law', 250 HR (1994–VI), 230–3; A. Cassese, *International Law* (Oxford: Oxford University Press, 2001), at 13–15.

[2] See Simma, op. cit., at 233–84; Cassese, op. cit., at 15–17.

national law we are discussing are normally breaches of precisely such community obligations. A strong reaction by States to these breaches presupposes the existence of a community interest to put a stop to them. However, the community interest in their fulfilment remains potential rather than real. States continue to pursue short-term national interests rather than global human values. It follows that they are disinclined to intervene in order to stop blatant infringements of community values. That is to say, community obligations, which reflect progress in the world community towards a *Kantian* model, remain an ideal whereas, in fact, States tend to cling to the *Grotian*, traditional paradigm.[3]

1.2 OTHER RESPONSES TO ATROCITIES

Faced with the problem of how to stem rampant violence in the world community, and given the failure of international collective or individual 'sanctions', a gradual trend has emerged to resort to a variety of fallback solutions. Various reactions, mechanisms, and devices can be discerned.

1.2.1 GENERAL

States, groups, and individuals may react in many different ways to gross atrocities and international crimes. Whenever a collective, institutional response is lacking, or is held by the victim community to be utterly insufficient, there is often resort to *revenge*. Revenge is undoubtedly a primitive form of justice, a private system of law enforcement, already condemned in the Bible (in Genesis, 4: 8–13, it is God, or in other words the centralized authority, that punishes Cain for the murder of his brother Abel and, in addition, enjoins all others not to kill or attack him for the murder). It has an altogether different foundation from justice: an implacable logic of hatred and retaliation. Revenge can only be the last resort for persons who have been denied due process, as is shown by what occurred after the First World War in the case of the Armenians (who took justice into their own hands to punish in 1921–2 those whom they regarded as responsible for the Armenian genocide of 1915).

Another possible response, often resorted to, is *forgetting* through the granting of amnesties or by allowing crimes which have never been judged to slide into oblivion. Forgetting beguiles future dictators or authoritarian leaders into counting on impunity. In addition, forgetting means that the victims are murdered twice: first, when they are exterminated physically, and thereafter when they are forgotten. Furthermore, the memory of massacres and other atrocities is never really buried along with the victims. Like an open wound, it lingers and, if untreated, festers. Clearly, when large-scale atrocities are perpetrated in a State, an end must be put to the ensuing predicament.

Conversely, *bringing alleged culprits to trial* or at any rate *before a public quasi-judicial*

[3] See Cassese, op. cit, at 18 (and references given there).

authority has the following merits. First, trials or public proceedings establish individual responsibility over the collective assignment of guilt. Secondly, they dissipate the call for revenge, because, when the courts or other public bodies mete out the right punishment to the perpetrator, the victim's call for retribution is met. Thirdly, by dint of the dispensation of justice, victims may be prepared to be reconciled with their erstwhile tormentors, because they know that the latter have now paid for their actions. And, fourthly, a reliable record of atrocities is established, so that future generations may be made fully aware of the events, and remember the victims.

1.2.3 SPECIFIC RESPONSES

A. The exercise by State courts of jurisdiction on grounds of territoriality or nationality

The normal response to atrocities, albeit 'more honoured in the breach than in the observance', is to bring the alleged perpetrators to justice in the courts of the State where the crimes were perpetrated, or of the State of nationality of the alleged perpetrator. This response does not target the State for blame, bur rather the individuals (State officials or persons acting in a private capacity) who allegedly perpetrated the atrocities. This is in contrast to the approach taken when international enforcement agencies seek to impose respect for international values upon the State where atrocities have been committed, in which situation the State itself is stigmatized and sanctioned.

Gradually also the State of which the victims have the nationality (under the *passive nationality* principle) have begun to exercise jurisdiction, especially with regard to war crimes (see 3.1–4). However, initially there was resistance to such assertion of jurisdiction, particularly if the crime had been committed in the State of active nationality or on the high seas, as evidenced by the famous *Lotus* case, decided in 1927 by the Permanent Court of International Justice (France had opposed the exercise of the passive nationality principle by Turkey for a common crime committed on the high seas, but the Court found it was wrong). Another significant case is *Shimoda.* Since neither the State of active nationality (that is the USA) nor any international body had pronounced upon the lawfulness of the atomic bombing of Hiroshima and Nagasaki, in *Shimoda* in 1963 a group of survivors sued the Japanese Government before the Tokyo District Court (the forum of the territorial State and of passive nationality). They claimed compensation for damages (no issue of criminal liability was raised; this was patently a case of civil litigation). They argued that they could not sue either President Truman or the US Government before the courts of the USA, because in the US legal system both the highest executive organs of the State, including the President, and the State itself were covered by the doctrine of sovereign immunity whereby neither the State nor State officials may incur liability for damages for unlawful acts performed in their official capacity, a doctrine similar in effect to the principle in England that 'the King can do no wrong'. The plaintiffs thus contended before the Tokyo court that they had had to turn to Japanese courts for justice. It was their submission that by the peace treaty of 1952 with the USA the Japanese Government had unlawfully waived its rights and claims and those of its nationals, against the US Government, including claims for compensation for the illegal atomic bombing. The Court pronounced the atomic bombing illegal, although in the final analysis it held against the complainants.[4]

Another interesting case is *Yunis*. The defendant was a citizen of Lebanon accused of participating in the hijacking of a Jordanian airliner that resulted in the passengers (including several Americans) being held hostage. He was brought to trial in the US after being arrested at sea by the US authorities. Yunis challenged the jurisdiction of the US courts, arguing that there was no nexus between the hijacking and US territory (the aircraft did not fly over US airspace or have contact with US territory). In its judgment of 12 February 1988, the District Court of Columbia dismissed the defendant's motion and affirmed US jurisdiction. It held:

> Not only is the United States acting on behalf of the world community to punish alleged offenders of crimes that threatened the very foundations of world order, but the United States has its own interest in protecting its nationals.[5]

B. The assumption by national courts of the task of dealing with atrocities perpetrated abroad

In some countries, courts have been prepared to substitute themselves for national or territorial courts, whenever the latter courts fail to take proceedings against persons suspected or accused of serious international crimes.

The most important case in this respect is *Eichmann*. In its judgment of 29 May 1962, the Supreme Court of Israel dismissed the submissions of the appellant, Eichmann, who claimed that Israeli courts lacked jurisdiction over his alleged crimes because there was no territorial or personal link between those crimes and Israel. In its concluding remarks, the Court held as follows:

> Not only do all the crimes attributed to the appellant bear an international character, but their harmful and murderous effects were so embracing and widespread as to shake the international community to its very foundations. The State of Israel therefore was entitled, pursuant to the principle of universal jurisdiction and in the capacity of a guardian of international law and an agent for its enforcement, to try the appellant. That being the case, no importance attaches to the fact that the State of Israel did not exist when the offences were committed.[6]

As we shall see *infra* (15.5), more recently the courts of a number of States, chiefly Spain, Belgium, and to some extent Germany, faced with the failure of the territorial or national State to prosecute and punish international crimes, have begun to replace

4 Text of the judgment (in English) in L. Friedman (ed.), *The Law of War—A Documentary History* (New York, 1972), vol. ii, at 1688–1702.

5 See 681 F. Supp. 896 (DDC), at 903.

6 See ILR, 36, at 304. It should be noted that Israel was also very influenced by the fact that it was the home of the Jews and the Jews were the victims of the crimes. So there was obviously a clear link between the crimes and the State of Israel, i.e. a sort of passive nationality was de facto an alternative basis for jurisdiction.

those States in fulfilling the prosecutorial function. They have asserted criminal jurisdiction over international crimes committed abroad by foreigners against other foreigners (see, for instance, such celebrated cases as *Pinochet*, *Bouterse*, *Hissène Habré*, *Cavallo* etc.).[7] It is notable that the trend towards asserting national jurisdiction over extraterritorial crimes accelerated greatly after the establishment of the ICTY and the ICTR. These two international tribunals have given a remarkable push to the institution of national criminal proceedings, and in particular have revitalized the repressive system established by the four 1949 Geneva Conventions, which have for more than forty years remained a dead letter.

The country whose national courts have taken the most vigorous action against crimes committed abroad is—perhaps surprisingly, given its occasionally isolationist tendencies and sceptical attitude towards international law—the United States, although this action has been taken in *civil, not criminal*, proceedings. In 1980 civil liberties lawyers, in a landmark case (*Filartiga* v. *Peña-Inala*), persuaded the federal courts to take from the shelf, dust off, and apply a statute passed in 1789, perhaps originally intended to deal with piracy. This is the Alien Torts Claim Act, under which 'The [US] district courts shall have original jurisdiction of any civil action by an alien for a tort only, committed in violation of the law of nations or a treaty of the United States'. The US courts have applied this statute to gross violations of human rights perpetrated abroad by foreign State officials against American nationals, thus obliging the culprits to pay compensation for those violations.[8]

No one can deny the significance of these decisions. In most (albeit not all) of these cases, the US courts filled the gap existing both at the international level (no international collective body took action, nor did other States intervene against the State to which the offending officials belonged) and at the domestic level (no authority of the territorial State stepped in). The courts therefore acted on behalf of the international community at large and vindicated rights pertaining to human dignity. In so doing, they proclaimed in judicial decisions some fundamental human values.

However, one should be mindful of the limits of this approach. First, as pointed out above, these are civil cases, where the alleged perpetrator of serious crime is ordered only to pay *compensation*; the defendant is not *convicted* of any crime, even though the evidence discloses—albeit by proof to the civil 'balance of probabilities' standard and not to the criminal 'beyond a reasonable doubt' standard—the commission of appalling crimes 'committed in violation of the law of nations'. In addition, the defendant is often abroad when the decision is issued and can easily avoid paying damages as

[7] For references see *infra*, 15.5.1(B) and 16.3.2.

[8] Since 1980, the US courts have pronounced in this way on torture in Paraguay (the celebrated *Filartiga* case), political assassination ordered by the Chilean authorities (*Letelier*), torture and racial discrimination for economic gain in Argentina (*Siderman de Blake*), torture, arbitrary arrest, and forced disappearance in Argentina (*Forti* v. *Suarez-Mason*), torture, summary execution, and forced disappearances in the Philippines (*Marcos*), atrocities in Bosnia and Herzegovina (*Kadić* v. *Karadžić*, and *Vucković*), torture and arbitrary detention in Haiti (*Avril*), torture in Guatemala (*Gramajo*), torture in Ethiopia (*Negewo*), the terrorist bombing of a Pan Am aircraft over Lockerbie in Scotland (*Al-Megrahi and Fhimah*) and atrocities in Salvador (*Garcìa and Vides Casanova*).

ordered by the Court. The decision therefore ends up being purely symbolic. Secondly, as these are cases involving purely civil litigation, and as the defendant is normally absent, no in-depth examination of the evidence takes place. Thirdly, this judicial trend has occurred in one country only. There is a danger that the courts of this country will set themselves up as universal judges of atrocities committed abroad. This type of 'humanitarian imperialism' may give rise to concern. On its own this might not be a problem, if it did not go hand in hand with the tendency of the US Government to take upon itself the task of policing the world.

C. Making international treaties imposing upon contracting States the obligation to exercise jurisdiction

Often States have considered it advisable to strengthen national criminal jurisdiction over international crimes by drafting multilateral treaties concerning matters such as war crimes, torture, and terrorism. These treaties impose an obligation on contracting States to pass legislation for the exercise of criminal jurisdiction (often in the form of universal jurisdiction) over such crimes. The four Geneva Conventions of 1949, as updated by the two Additional Protocols of 1977, as well as the 1984 UN Convention against Torture and various conventions on terrorism come to mind. They provide that the courts of each contracting State can, and indeed *must*, exercise jurisdiction over crimes perpetrated on their territory or abroad, when the alleged offender is on their territory (so-called *forum deprehensionis*). If they choose not to prosecute the alleged offender, they must surrender him to any other State concerned (*aut dedere aut prosequi* principle) or, as in the case of the four Geneva Conventions, they must bring the alleged offender to trial, or otherwise hand him over to a State concerned (*aut judicare aut dedere*).

It is on the strength of one of these treaties, the Torture Convention, that in *Pinochet* the House of Lords held that the UK courts had jurisdiction over the crimes of torture allegedly committed by Pinochet and could therefore extradite him to Spain (judgment of 24 March 1999, so-called *Pinochet 3*). It is also by virtue of this Convention that the former Chadian dictator Hissène Habré was arrested and brought to trial in Senegal for the alleged torture of Chadians (although he was subsequently released, on rather legalistic grounds) (see *Hissène Habré*), and French courts asserted jurisdiction over a case concerning a Rwandan priest accused of torture, as well as crimes against humanity and genocide (see *Munyeshyaka*, at 7).[9]

Unfortunately, the application of these treaties by national courts remains sporadic. In addition, it is sometimes subject to the vagaries of political interest.

D. The establishment of Truth and Reconciliation Commissions

Under certain historical circumstances (when a repressive political regime that perpetrated massive violations of human rights including crimes against humanity, after

[9] See also *Ilnitskiy Vladimir and others* (at 450).

collapsing or being ousted from power, is replaced by a democratic government bent on promoting reconciliation while not prepared to brush aside past abuses) there is an important alternative option to the ignominy and jeopardy of criminal proceedings. This is fact-finding followed by forgiveness, through the establishment of *Truth and Reconciliation Commissions.* These commissions have been set up since the early 1980s in many Latin American countries (Argentina, Bolivia, Chile, Uruguay, El Salvador, Haiti, etc., as well as in such African countries as Uganda and South Africa), some as a result of UN action or with UN support. They normally consist of State organs charged with: (i) gathering evidence about gross violations (in particular, through testimony of victims and, if possible, confessions of perpetrators), (ii) investigating the general social, economic, and political causes of the violations, (iii) compiling a public report containing a detailed account of the findings, with possible recommendations. The South African Commission (1995–8) stands out, for, in addition to those tasks, it was endowed with quasi-judicial powers. In particular, it exhibited some significant and novel features: (i) it had the power to grant amnesty to individual perpetrators on condition that they had made full disclosure of crimes 'associated with a political objective' and, if possible, had also testified on crimes perpetrated by others and, if need be, had paid compensation to the victims; (ii) it was empowered to recommend the criminal prosecution of perpetrators brought before it, as an alternative to granting amnesty or simply hearing the case; (iii) it had powers of subpoena and search and seizure, thereby being able to carry out thorough investigations, and the power directly to question witnesses, including those implicated in violations, who had not applied for amnesty; (iv) the hearings were public, thus enabling the public to become cognizant of facts before the issuance of the Commission's final report; and (v) it created a significant witness protection programme, which enabled witnesses to come forward with information the possession of which might otherwise have put them at risk.

The advantages of these Commissions as a way of reacting to atrocities are evident: they (i) further understanding in lieu of vengeance, reparation in lieu of retaliation, and reconciliation instead of victimization; (ii) promote a kind of historical catharsis, through public exposure of crimes; (iii) delve into the historical, social, and political roots of the crimes; (iv) establish a historical record of the atrocities committed; and (v) prevent or render superfluous long trials against thousands of alleged perpetrators.

Nonetheless, the flaws of most of these Commissions should not be underestimated. In many cases they have proved unable to bring about true reconciliation. In addition, even when they have identified the culprits (a relatively rare occurrence), the crimes they have committed are usually cancelled through amnesty laws, or else the offenders are granted pardons exempting them from the punishment for the crime perpetrated. Even the fairer and much more effective Commission established in South Africa in 1995 did not always bring about real and lasting reconciliation. In many cases the Commission pardoned the authors of horrific crimes, whether Afrikaners or members of the ANC. Thus it sparked much resentment and anger among the victims and their relatives, who desired retribution, or at least ordinary criminal justice.

E. The establishment of international criminal tribunals or so-called internationalized or mixed courts

Another way of reacting to atrocities is by the establishment of international criminal tribunals entrusted with the task of trying those responsible for serious atrocities and other international crimes. In 1993, one of the decisions taken by the UN Security Council, which had been unable to stop the war in the former Yugoslavia while States were unwilling to take action such as air strikes, was to set up the International Criminal Tribunal for the former Yugoslavia (ICTY). The following year it established the International Criminal Tribunal for Rwanda (ICTR). In 1998, the Statute of the International Criminal Court (ICC) was adopted in Rome, and in 2002 the UN and Sierra Leone entered into an agreement for the establishment of the Special Court for Sierra Leone. In addition, both in Kosovo and in East Timor international organizations set up mixed courts, that is courts composed of both local and international judges (see *infra*, 20.5). It is hoped that such courts will also be set up in Cambodia.

F. The promotion of the extraterritorial jurisdiction of international courts and human rights monitoring bodies, over serious violations of human rights

A significant reaction to the proliferation of callous and atrocious crimes in the world has led to an interesting development: international bodies have gradually extended, by way of interpretation, the territorial reach of international obligations concerning respect for human rights, incumbent upon States. In this way, such bodies have come to assert a right to pronounce on and, if need be, condemn or stigmatize massive violations committed by a State or its officials *abroad*, i.e. outside the territorial jurisdiction traditionally considered as delimiting the State's responsibilities.

To put this development in context, it should be noted that when States undertake obligations in the area of human rights, they tend to view those obligations as applying only to individuals within their own territory. In other words, they construe these obligations as having a strictly *territorial* scope. This, for instance, was the interpretation most commentators tended to place on Article 2 of the UN Covenant on Civil and Political Rights, whereby 'Each State Party . . . undertakes to respect and to ensure to all individuals within its territory and subject to its jurisdiction the rights recognized in the present Covenant'.

However, international bodies responsible for scrutinizing compliance with human rights standards have increasingly interpreted these obligations as also having *extra-territorial* scope. In other words, the States that are bound by international obligations concerning human rights are obliged to respect those obligations not only when their State officials act on the State's own territory, but also when they take action abroad.

Thus, for example, in 1995 the UN Human Rights Committee, in commenting on the report submitted by the USA, noted that it could not share the view of the US

Government that the UN Covenant on Civil and Political Rights lacked extraterritorial reach under all circumstances. Such a view—it went on to point out—is 'contrary to the consistent interpretation of the Committee on this subject that, in special circumstances, persons may fall under the subject matter jurisdiction of a State party even when outside that State territory'.[10] More specifically, in *Delia Saldías de Lopez* v. *Uruguay*, the Committee had already ruled that Uruguay had violated the Covenant when its security forces had abducted and tortured in Argentina a Uruguayan citizen living there. It held that indeed a State is also accountable for human rights violations perpetrated by its agents abroad.[11]

In an important case, *Loizidou* v. *Turkey*, the European Court of Human Rights carried this doctrine even further. The question had arisen of whether the denial by Turkish armed forces stationed in Northern Cyprus of access by the applicant (a Cypriot) to her property in Northern Cyprus, if imputable to Turkey, fell under Turkey's jurisdiction pursuant to Article 1 of the European Convention on Human Rights. The Court gave an affirmative answer. In its decision on preliminary objections, it held that a State could be held responsible for violations of human rights committed by its officials abroad. In its decision on the merits, the Court then ruled that what mattered for establishing whether Turkey was responsible was the question of whether Turkey had effective or overall control of the armed forces stationed in an area outside its national territory.[12] However, in a recent decision in *Banković and*

[10] UN Doc. CCPR/C/79/Add 50 (1995), §19.

[11] It pointed out that: 'The reference in Article 1 of the Optional Protocol to "individuals subject to its jurisdiction" does not affect the above conclusion [that the Covenant also covered crimes perpetrated by Uruguayans acting on foreign soil] because the reference in that Article is not to the place where the violations occurred, but rather to the relationship between the individuals and the State in relation to a violation of any of the rights set forth in the Covenant, wherever they occurred. Article 2.1 of the Covenant places an obligation upon a State party to respect and to ensure rights "to all individuals within its territory and subject to its jurisdiction", but it does not imply that the State party concerned cannot be held accountable for violations of rights under the Covenant which its agents commit upon the territory of another State, whether with the acquiescence of the Government of that State or in opposition to it . . . In line with this, it would be unconscionable to so interpret the responsibility under Article 2 of the Covenant as to permit a State party to perpetrate violations of the Covenant on the territory of another State, which violations it could not perpetrate on its own territory'. (Decision of 29 July 1981 (Communication No. 52/1979), in Human Rights Committee, *Selected Decisions (Second to Sixteenth Sessions)* (1985) 91, §§12.2–12.3.)

[12] It noted that: '[T]he Court recalls that, although Article 1 sets limits on the reach of the Convention, the concept of "jurisdiction" under this provision is not restricted to the national territory of the High Contracting Parties. According to its established case law, for example, the Court has held that the extradition or expulsion of a person by a Contracting State may give rise to an issue under Article 3, and hence engage the responsibility of that State under the Convention . . . In addition, the responsibility of Contracting Parties can be involved because of acts of their authorities, whether performed within or outside national boundaries, which produce effects outside their own territory.

'Bearing in mind the object and purpose of the Convention, the responsibility of a Contracting Party may also arise when as a consequence of military action—whether lawful or unlawful—it exercises effective control of an area outside its national territory. The obligation to secure, in such an area, the rights and freedoms set out in the Convention derives from the fact of such control whether it be exercised directly, through its armed forces, or through a subordinate local administration.

'In this connection the respondent Government have acknowledged that the applicant's loss of control of her property stems from the occupation of the northern part of Cyprus by Turkish troops and the *others*, the Court has somewhat restricted the scope of its doctrine of the extraterritorial reach of the Convention's provisions, by insisting among other things on the *regional* dimension of such reach.[13]

The Inter-American Commission of Human Rights spelled out the doctrine forcefully in *Coard* v. *US*. The question at issue was whether the USA could be held responsible for violating the 1948 American Declaration of the Rights and Duties of Man for allegedly holding incommunicado and mistreating 17 Grenadian nationals in Grenada in October 1983, when US and Caribbean armed forces invaded the island, deposing the 'revolutionary government'. In its report of 29 September 1999, the Commission replied in the affirmative. (Its task was however facilitated by the fact that the American Declaration, like the 1948 Universal Declaration, does not contain a clause stipulating that its provisions apply only to persons subject to the jurisdiction of the relevant State.)[14]

It should be noted that this case law is consistent with the object and purpose of human rights obligations, which aim to protect individuals against arbitrariness, abuse, and violence, regardless of where the State's actions were carried out.

It follows from the above that States must respect human rights obligations not only on their own territory but also abroad. In exercising authority abroad, they must respect the human rights of all individuals subject to their authority. In this context, 'exercise of authority' means not only the display of sovereign or other powers

establishment there of the [Turkish Republic of Northern Cyprus]. Furthermore, it has not been disputed that the applicant was prevented by Turkish troops from gaining access to her property.

'It follows that such acts are capable of falling within Turkish "jurisdiction" within the meaning of Article 1 of the Convention.' (ECHR (1995) Series A, No. 310, at §62; *Merits*, ECHR, 18 December 1996, *Reports* (1996–VI) 2230, at §57.)

13 The Court noted that: 'the case-law of the Court demonstrates that its recognition of the exercise of extraterritorial jurisdiction by a Contracting State is exceptional: it has done so when the respondent State, through the effective control of the relevant territory and its inhabitants abroad as a consequence of military occupation or through consent, invitation or acquiescence of the Government of that territory, exercises all or some of the public powers normally to be exercised by that Government' (§71). The Court dismissed the applicants' submissions as 'tantamount to arguing that anyone adversely affected by an act imputable to a Contracting State, wherever in the world that act may have been committed or its consequences felt, is thereby brought within the jurisdiction of that state for the purpose of Article 1 of the [European] Convention [on Human Rights]' (§75). The Court concluded that the European Convention 'is a multilateral treaty operating . . . in an essentially regional context and notably in the legal space (*espace juridique*) of the Contracting States. The FRY [Federal Republic of Yugoslavia] clearly does not fall within this legal space. The Convention was not designed to be applied throughout the world, even in respect of the conduct of Contracting States. Accordingly, the desirability of avoiding a gap or vacuum in human rights' protection has so far been relied on by the Court in favour of establishing jurisdiction only when the territory in question was one that, but for the specific circumstances, would normally be covered by the Convention.' (§80.)

14 The Commission noted that: 'Given that individual rights inhere simply by virtue of a person's humanity, each American State is obliged to uphold the protected rights of any person subject to its jurisdiction. While this most commonly refers to persons within a State's territory, it may, under given circumstances, refer to conduct with an extraterritorial locus where the person concerned is present in the territory of one State, but subject to the control of another State—usually through the acts of the latter's agents abroad. In principle, the inquiry turns not on the presumed victim's nationality or presence within a particular geographic area, but on whether, under the specific circumstances, the State observed the rights of a person subject to its authority and control.' (Case No. 10.951, Report No. 109/99, 29 September 1999, §37.)

(law-making, law-enforcement, administrative powers, etc.) but *any* exercise of power, however limited in time (for instance, the use of belligerent force in an armed conflict, which of course would be covered by international humanitarian law).

SELECT BIBLIOGRAPHY

N. Kritz (ed.), *Transnational Justice: How Emerging Democracies Reckon with Former Regimes*, 3 vols (Washington: US Institute for Peace Press, 1995); N. Roht-Arriaza (ed.), *Impunity and Human Rights in International Law and Practice* (New York and Oxford: Oxford University Press, 1995); H. Steiner, 'Introduction', in Harvard Law School Human Rights Program and World Peace Foundation, *Truth Commissions: A Comparative Assessment* (Cambridge, Ma.: Harvard Law School, 1997); M. Minow, *Between Vengeance and Forgiveness* (Boston, Ma.: Beacon Press, 1998); W. M. Reisman, 'Compensation for Human Rights Violations: The Practice of the Past Decade in the Americas', in A. Randelzhofer and C. Tomuschat (eds), *State Responsibility and the Individual* (The Hague, London, Boston: Nijhoff, 1999), 63–108. P. Ricoeur, *La mémoire, l'histoire, l'oubli* (Paris: Seuil, 2000), 626–630; T. Todorov, *Mémoire du Mal, Tentation du Bien* (Paris: Laffont, 2000), 125–59, 224–30, 284–93; idem, 'Les limites de la justice', in Cassese and Delmas-Marty (eds), *Crimes internationaux*, 39–48.

2

FUNDAMENTALS OF INTERNATIONAL CRIMINAL LAW

2.1 THE NOTION OF INTERNATIONAL CRIMINAL LAW

International criminal law is a body of international rules designed both to proscribe international crimes and to impose upon States the obligation to prosecute and punish at least some of those crimes. It also regulates international proceedings for prosecuting and trying persons accused of such crimes. The first limb of this body makes up *substantive* law. This is the set of rules indicating what acts amount to international crimes, the subjective elements required for such acts to be regarded as prohibited, the possible circumstances under which persons accused of such crimes may nevertheless not be held criminally liable, as well as on what conditions States may or must, under international rules, prosecute or bring to trial persons accused of one of those crimes. The set of rules regulating international proceedings, that is *procedural* criminal law, governs the action by prosecuting authorities and the various stages of *international* trials.

Traditionally, especially in the French, German, Italian, and Spanish legal tradition, one assigns to another branch of law, called 'criminal international law' (*droit pénal international*), the whole area concerning the role of national courts in international criminality, that is the grounds of jurisdiction asserted by national courts to adjudicate international crimes, the law applied by national courts to pronounce upon such crimes, as well as interstate judicial co-operation for the repression of criminal offences including extradition. Instead, it is suggested here that a modern conception of international law should also take into account various fundamental questions relating to the role played by national courts in international criminal law, on the grounds that: (i) national courts have powerfully contributed to the development of international criminal law, as we shall soon see; (ii) at present international courts and tribunals duly take into account national case law and the way national courts apply the relevant law when pronouncing upon international crimes; (iii) international courts must perforce rely upon State co-operation if they wish to fulfil their mandate effectively (see *infra*, 19.4 and 22.23); hence the issue of co-operation of States between themselves in the area of international crimes, as well as with international criminal courts is central to this branch of law; (iv) the fact that the International Criminal Court (ICC) is grounded on the principle of complementarity (see *infra*, 19.7), that is, only adjudicates cases when national courts are unable or unwilling to pronounce upon them, makes it imperative for the ICC to be fully cognizant of the legal framework of national courts' judicial action when they sit in judgment over international crimes.

Consequently, in this book we will also discuss the legal grounds of jurisdiction over international crimes, asserted by *national* courts, the possible obstacles to national adjudication of those crimes, as well as other problems relating to co-operation between States and between States and international courts and tribunals.

2.2 GENERAL FEATURES OF INTERNATIONAL CRIMINAL LAW

International criminal law is a branch of *public international law*. The rules making up this body of law emanate from sources of international law (treaties, customary law, etc.).[1] Hence, they are subject, among other things, to the principles of interpretation proper to that law. However, one should not be unmindful of some unique features of international criminal law.

First, it is a *relatively new branch of international law*. The list of international crimes, that is of the acts for whose accomplishment international law makes the authors criminally responsible, has come into being by gradual accretion. Initially, in the late nineteenth century, and for a long time, only war crimes were punishable. (Piracy, traditionally considered an international crime, is not discussed in this book for, in addition to having become obsolete, it does not meet the requirements of international crimes proper; see *infra*, 2.3) It is only since the Second World War that new categories of crimes have developed, while that of war crimes has been restated: in 1945 and 1946, the Statutes of the International Military Tribunal at Nuremberg (IMT) and the International Military Tribunal for the Far East (IMTFE), respectively, were adopted, laying down new classes of international criminality. Thus, in 1945 crimes against humanity and against peace were added, followed in 1948 by genocide as a special subcategory of crimes against humanity (soon to become an autonomous class of crimes), and then in the 1980s, by torture as a discrete crime. Recently, international terrorism has been criminalized, subject to certain conditions. As for rules on international criminal proceedings, they were first laid down in the Statutes of the IMT and the IMTFE, then in those of the ICTY and the ICTR and more recently in the Rome Statute of the ICC. Nonetheless they are still scant and, what is even more important, they only pertain to the specific criminal court for which they have been adopted, that is, they have no general scope. A

[1] For a succinct survey of these sources, I take the liberty of referring the reader to my book, *International Law*, cit., 117–61.

fully-fledged corpus of generally applicable international procedural rules is only gradually evolving.

Secondly, international criminal law is still a very *rudimentary* branch of law. The gradual broadening of substantive criminal law has been a complex process. Among other things, when a new class of crime has emerged, its constituent elements (the objective and subjective conditions of the crime, or, in other words, *actus reus* and *mens rea*) have not been immediately clear. Nor has any scale of penalties been laid down in international rules. This process can be easily explained. Three main features of the formation of international criminal law stand out.

The first is that, for a long time, either treaties or (more seldom) customary rules have confined themselves to *prohibiting* certain acts (for instance, killing prisoners of war or civilians), without however adding anything on the criminal consequences of such acts; in other words, they simply laid down prohibitions without providing for the criminal nature of breaches of such prohibitions, let alone the conditions for their criminal repression and punishment.

Furthermore, when international law has moved on to criminalize some categories of act (war crimes, crimes against humanity, etc.), it has left to *national courts* the task of prosecuting and punishing the alleged perpetrators of those acts. As a consequence, municipal courts of each State have applied their procedural rules (legal provisions on jurisdiction and on the conduct of criminal proceedings) and rules on 'the general part' of substantive criminal law, that is, on the definition and character of the objective and subjective elements of crimes, on defences, etc. Among other things, very often national courts, faced with the *indeterminacy* of most criminal rules, have found it necessary to flesh them out and give them legal precision. They have thus refined notions initially left rather loose and woolly by treaty or customary law.

Finally (and this is the third of the features referred to above), when international criminal courts were set up (first in 1945–7, then in 1993–4 and more recently in 1998), they did indeed lay down in their Statutes the various classes of crimes to be punished; however, these classes were conceived of and couched merely as offences over which each court had jurisdiction. In other words, the crimes were not enumerated as in a criminal code, but simply as a specification of the jurisdictional authority of the relevant court. The value and scope of those enumerations was therefore only germane to the court's jurisdiction and did not purport to have a general reach.

Given these characteristics of the evolution of international criminal law, it should not be surprising that even the recent addition of the sets of written rules referred to above has not proved sufficient for building a coherent legal system, as is shown by the heavy reliance by the newly created *international* courts upon customary rules or unwritten general principles.

As for *procedural* law, it was scantily delineated in the Statutes of the IMT and the Tokyo Tribunal. Only recently has it been fortified, when the UN Security Council passed such international instruments as the Statutes of the ICTY, in 1993 and the ICTR, in 1994 and subsequently the judges of these two tribunals adopted their respective Rules of Procedure and Evidence (RPE). Then, in 1998, States agreed upon the Statute of the ICC and the Rules of Procedure and Evidence for the Court. Nonetheless, even procedural law remains at a rather underdeveloped stage.

Thirdly, international criminal law presents the unique characteristic that, more than any other segment of international law, it simultaneously *derives its origin from* and continuously *draws upon* both *human rights law* and *national criminal law.*

Human rights law, essentially consisting of international treaties and conventions on the matter, as well as the case law of international bodies such as the European Court of Human Rights, has contributed to the development of criminal law in many respects. Thus, it has expanded or strengthened, or created grater sensitivity to, the values to be protected through the prohibition of attacks on such values (human dignity, the need to safeguard life and limb as far as possible, etc.). Furthermore, human rights law lays down the fundamental rights of suspects and accused persons, of victims and witnesses; it also sets out the basic safeguards of fair trial. In short, this increasingly important segment of law has significantly impregnated the whole area of international criminal law.

In addition, most customary rules of international criminal law have primarily evolved from *municipal case law* relating to international crimes (chiefly war crimes). This element as well as the paucity of international treaty rules on the matter explain why international criminal law to a great extent results from the gradual *transposition* on to the international level of rules and legal constructs proper to national criminal law or to national trial proceedings. The grafting of municipal law notions and rules on to international law has not however been a smooth process. National legal orders do not contain a uniform regulation of criminal law. On the contrary, they are split into many different systems, from among which two principal ones emerge: that prevailing in common law countries (the UK, the USA, Australia, Canada, many African and Asian countries), and that obtaining in civil law countries, chiefly based on a legal system of Roman-German origin (they include States of continental Europe, such as France, Germany, Italy, Belgium, the countries of Northern Europe such as Norway, Sweden, Denmark, as well as Latin American countries, and many African and Asian States including for instance China). The heterogeneous and composite origin of many international rules and institutions of both substantive and procedural criminal law, *a real patchwork of normative standards*, complicates matters, as we shall see.[2]

[2] This, as already noted above, in particular applies to the so-called 'general part of criminal law', that is the set of rules regulating the subjective elements of crimes, the various forms or categories of criminal liability (for instance, joint responsibility for common criminal purpose, aiding and abetting, and so on), conditions excluding criminal liability, etc. It was only natural for each national court pronouncing on war crimes or crimes against humanity to apply the general notions of criminal law prevailing in that country. As a result, one is confronted with hundreds of national cases where judges have relied upon different conceptions of, or approaches to, the 'general part', or have even resorted to the national definition of some subjective or objective elements of the relevant international crime. For instance, in *Fröhlich*, a British Court of Appeal (established in Germany under Control Council Law no. 10), to satisfy itself that the offence of the accused (a German charged with and convicted by a Court of first instance of killing four Russian prisoners of war) amounted to a war crime consisting of murder, applied the German notion of 'murder' (at 280–2).

It follows that international criminal law is an essentially *hybrid branch of law*: it is public international law impregnated with notions, principles, and legal constructs derived from national criminal law and human rights law. However, the recent establishment of international criminal tribunals, and in particular of the ICC, has given a stupendous impulse to the evolution of a corpus of international criminal rules proper. It can therefore be safely maintained that we are now heading for the formation of a fully fledged body of law in this area.

A fourth major feature of international criminal law, in particular of substantive criminal law, which is closely bound up with the feature to which I have just drawn attention, ought to be emphasized. This law has a *twofold relationship* with the general body of public international law.

The first relationship is one of *mutual subsidiarity or support*. Strikingly, most of the offences that international criminal law proscribes and for the perpetration of which it endeavours to punish the individuals that allegedly committed them, also are regarded by international law as particularly serious violations *by States*: they are international delinquencies entailing the 'aggravated responsibility' of the State on whose behalf the perpetrators may have acted.[3] This holds true not only for genocide, crimes against humanity, torture, terrorism, but also for war crimes. Thus, when one of these crimes is committed by an individual not acting in a private capacity, a dual responsibility may follow: criminal liability of the individual, falling under international criminal law, and State responsibility, regulated by international rules on this matter.[4] Admittedly, there is at present a tendency in the international community to give pride of place to the former category of responsibility whilst playing down or neglecting the latter. Political motivations underpin this trend, chiefly the inclination of States to avoid invoking the aggravated responsibility of other States except when they are prompted to do so out of self-interest or on strong political grounds. It is nevertheless a fact that theoretically both legal avenues remain open and may be utilized, as is shown by the proceedings for genocide recently instituted by some States before the International Court of Justice[5] while at the same time genocide trials are taking place before the ICTY.[6]

[3] On the notion of 'aggravated State responsibility' see Cassese, cit., at 200–11.

[4] It is notable that the four Geneva Conventions of 1949, while they institute a special legal regime for the criminal repression of 'grave breaches' of the Conventions, at the same time provide for the 'State responsibility' of contracting Parties for the case of commission of such 'grave breaches'. See for instance Articles 129–30 of the Third Convention (on Prisoners of War), concerning the penal sanctions for 'grave breaches' and Article 131 on State responsibility. (Under the latter provision, 'No High Contracting Party shall be allowed to absolve itself or any other High Contracting Party of any liability incurred by itself or by another High Contracting Party in respect of breaches referred to in the preceding Article'.)

[5] See the case brought by Bosnia and Herzegovina against the Federal Republic of Yugoslavia (*Application of the Convention on the Prevention and Punishment of Genocide*).

[6] See, for instance, the judgment in *Krstić* (2 August 2001) as well as the indictments against *Milošević* (of 8 October 2001 and 22 November 2001), as well as the revised indictment against *Kazadžić* of 28 April 2000.

The second relationship between public international law and international criminal law is more complex. Two somewhat *conflicting philosophies* underlie each area of law. International criminal law aims at protecting society against the most harmful transgressions of legal standards of behaviour perpetrated by individuals (whether they be State agents or persons acting in a private capacity). It therefore aims at the punishment of the authors of those transgressions, while however safeguarding the rights of suspects or accused persons from any arbitrary prosecution and punishment. It follows among other things that one of the mainstays of international criminal law is the *exigency* that its prohibitions be as clear, detailed, and specific as possible. Furthermore no one should be punished for conduct that was not considered as criminal at the time when it was taken. In short, any person suspected or accused of a crime is entitled to a set of significant rights protecting him from possible abuse by the prosecuting authorities.

Public international law, on the other hand, pursues, in essence, the purpose of reconciling as much as possible the conflicting interests and concerns of sovereign States (without however neglecting the interests and exigencies of individuals and non-state entities). True, part of general international law is concerned with both the violations by States of the most fundamental legal standards and the ensuing State responsibility. This area of international law is, however, relatively less conspicuous than the corresponding segment of international criminal law. In fact, the thrust of general international law is legally to regulate and facilitate a minimum of peaceful international intercourse between States, much more than calling to account States for their breaches of law. To put it differently, the *normative* role of law is more important and effective than its *repressive* function. What is even more important from our present viewpoint is that, in order to take account of the conflicting interests and preoccupations of States, the law-making process is often actuated by dint of gradual evolution of general and often *loose* rules through custom or even so-called 'soft law' (that is, standards and guidelines devoid of legally binding force). Often even treaties do not lay down unambiguous and specific provisions; this happens whenever the need to reconcile conflicting State interests makes it necessary to agree upon vague formulas. In short, the need for detailed, clear, and unambiguous legal regulation is less strong in the general area of public international law than in the specific area of criminal law, where this need becomes of crucial relevance, given that the fundamental rights of suspects or accused persons are at stake.

The inherent requirements underlying international criminal law (not less than any national body of criminal law) may therefore collide with the traditional characteristics of public international law, which, as we have just stated, still relies to a large extent upon custom. In this respect international criminal law bears a strong resemblance to the criminal law of such common law countries as England, where next to statutory offences there exist many common law offences, developed through judicial precedents. However, there the existence of a huge wealth of judicial precedents built up over centuries, and above all the hierarchical structure of the judiciary coupled with the doctrine of 'judicial precedent' (whereby each court is bound by the decisions of courts above), as well as the extrapolation by legal scholars of general principles from that copious case law, tend to a large extent to meet the exigencies of legal certainty and foreseeability proper to any system of criminal law.[7]

The contrast between the relative indeterminacy and 'malleability' of international criminal rules deriving from their largely customary nature, and the imperative requirement that criminal rules be clear and specific, results in the *role of national or international courts* being conspicuously crucial. It falls to courts, both national and international, to try to cast light on, and give legal precision to, rules of customary nature, whenever their content and purport is still surrounded by uncertainty, as well as to spell out and elaborate upon the frequently terse content of treaty provisions. In particular, courts play an indispensable role for (i) the ascertainment of the existence and contents of customary rules, (ii) the interpretation and clarification of treaty provisions, and (iii) the elaboration, based on general principles, of legal categories and constructs indispensable for the application of international criminal rules. It is mainly due to judicial decisions that international criminal law is progressing so rapidly.[8]

Closely bound up with the characteristic just underlined is another major trait of current international criminal law. More than other branches of public international law, but like those legal areas where rapid changes in technology impose speedy normative updating (for instance, the law of the environment or the law of international trade) *international criminal law is changing very quickly*. This is because unfortunately, in the world community there is an increase in the perpetration of atrocities, whether or not linked to armed conflict. There is, therefore, a widely felt need to respond to them by among other things criminal repression. However, what is even more striking in this branch of law is that legal change (i) goes hand in hand

[7] In 1923 the great British international lawyer J. L. Brierly contested the analogy of international criminal law with English law. In commenting on the notion that an international criminal court to be established would be much in the position of any English court under the English system of building up the law by precedents, he stated that this analogy did not hold: 'For the greater part of English criminal law is now statutory; and in any case the discretionary powers which our law, statutory or not, allows to a judge in defining the constitution of a crime or fixing the sentence is not in the least comparable in extent to the extraordinarily wide discretion which would have to be entrusted to an international criminal court attempting to apply and develop such laws of war as exist at present.' (J. L. Brierly, 'Do we Need an International Criminal Court?', 8 BYIL (1923), at 86–7.)

[8] These characteristic features of this body of law, have in some respects a negative connotation, while other features may prove advantageous. The drawback is that the rights of the accused risk being jeopardized by the *normative flux* that still characterizes this branch of international law. It is chiefly for courts to endeavour as far as possible to safeguard the rights of the accused from any unwarranted deviation from the fundamental principles of criminal law and human rights law. The advantage of the unique nature of international criminal law is that change and adaptation to evolving historical circumstances occur more easily and smoothly than in legal systems based on codes and other forms of written law. In this respect courts may become instrumental in reconciling the demands for change with the requirement of respect for the rights of the accused.

with increasing sophistication of the legal system (we are now moving from a rudimentary jumble of rules and principles to a fairly consistent body of law) and (ii) is accompanied by a gradual shift in its philosophical underpinning: in particular, a shift from the doctrine of *substantive justice* (whereby the need to protect society requires the punishment of harmful actions even if such actions had not been previously criminalized) to that of *strict legality* (whereby the need to protect individuals' human rights, in particular to safeguard individuals from arbitrary action of the executive or judicial powers, requires that no one may be punished for any action not considered criminal when performed). On this matter see *infra*, 7.3.

Finally, let me stress a significant characteristic of international criminal law, which, however, is *not* unique to it. Like most national legal systems, international rules criminalize not only conduct causing *harm* to others (for example, murder, rape, torture, destruction of hospitals, shelling of innocent civilians) but also conduct creating an *unacceptable risk* of harm. The rationale behind this legal regulation is that—as in this area criminal conduct is normally of great magnitude and seriously offends against fundamental values—international humanitarian and criminal rules aim not only at protecting persons as far as possible from unlawful conduct, but also at criminalizing any actions that may carry a serious risk of causing grave harm, that is those rules also have a *preventative* role. This feature of international criminal law manifests itself in three major ways: (i) by also criminalizing the early stage or the preparation of crimes that are then committed, (ii) by the prohibition of so-called inchoate crimes (or preliminary criminal offences), (iii) by the prohibition of specific conduct likely to cause serious risk.[9]

[9] As for the first aspect, suffice it to stress that international criminal law among other things prohibits *planning*. As for inchoate crimes, it may be sufficient to recall that international rules criminalize *attempt* and (in the case of at least the most serious crime, genocide), *conspiracy* and *incitement* (see *infra*, 9.10–11). All these inchoate offences that constitute the preparatory stage of other offences may be punished even if the crime they are intended to bring about does not in fact occur. Criminalization of these offences is a way of preventing them from occurring, to the extent possible, that is, preventing the perpetration of the crime to which they intend to lead. By criminalizing such conduct, international rules endeavour to forestall the danger that the execution of those offences may cause major harm. They also serve to stigmatize attempting, inciting or conspiring as criminal *in itself*. Thus the message is conveyed that people should not only not commit crimes but also not incite, conspire or attempt such crimes; if they do so, they will be labelled as criminals and punished accordingly. (For this reason, some have criticized these crimes, especially conspiracy, as 'thought crimes', but this is inaccurate as each offence requires some overt conduct in addition to the *mens rea* requirement.)

With regard to the third of the elements referred to, it may be pointed out that criminalization of risk occurs any time a criminal rule envisages, among the possible subjective elements of criminal conduct, recklessness or *dolus eventualis* (see *infra*, 8.2–4). Such criminalization may also specifically derive from the specific content of individual provisions. For instance, Article 7 of the Geneva Convention of 1929 on Prisoners of War provided, among other things, that 'As soon as possible after their capture, prisoners of war shall be evacuated to depots sufficiently removed from the fighting zone for them to be out of danger . . . Prisoners shall not be unnecessarily exposed to danger while awaiting evacuation from a

2.3 THE NOTION OF INTERNATIONAL CRIMES

International crimes are breaches of international rules entailing the personal criminal liability of the individuals concerned (as opposed to the responsibility of the State of which the individuals may act as organs).

Before considering the various categories of such crimes, it should be specified that international crimes may be held *cumulatively* to embrace the following:

1. Violations of international *customary* rules (as well as treaty provisions, where such provisions exist and either codify or spell out customary law or have contributed to its formation).

2. Rules intended to protect *values* considered important by the whole international community and consequently binding all States and individuals. These values are not propounded by scholars or thought up by starry-eyed philosophers. Rather, they are laid down, although not always spelled out in so many words, in international instruments, the most important of which are the 1945 UN Charter, the 1948 Universal Declaration of Human Rights, the 1950 European Convention on Human Rights, the two 1966 UN Covenants on Civil and Political Rights, and on Economic, Social and Cultural Rights, the American Convention on Human Rights of 1969, the UN Declaration on Friendly Relations of 1970, the 1981 African Charter on Human and Peoples' Rights. Other treaties also enshrine these values, although from another viewpoint: they do not proclaim the values directly, but prohibit conduct that infringes them: for instance, the 1948 Convention on Genocide, the 1949 Geneva Conventions on the protection of victims of armed conflict and their two Additional Protocols of 1977, the 1984 Convention against Torture, and the various treaties providing for the prosecution and repression of specific forms of terrorism.

3. Furthermore, there is a universal interest in repressing these crimes. Subject to certain conditions their alleged authors may in principle be prosecuted and punished *by any State*, regardless of any territorial or nationality link with the perpetrator or the victim.

4. Finally, if the perpetrator has acted in an official capacity, i.e. as a *de jure* or de facto State official, the State on whose behalf he has performed the prohibited act is

fighting zone'. (At present a rule corresponding to that provision is Article 23 of the Third Geneva Convention of 1949.)

In 1947 a Dutch Court Martial in Indonesia applied this provision in *Koshiro*. The accused, an officer in the Japanese Navy in charge of Japanese forces at Makassar in the Netherlands East Indies, was charged with among other things unnecessarily exposing a large number of Allied prisoners of war to danger, in that in 1944 a large ammunition depot had been built by the prisoners of war at a distance of about fifty yards from the prisoner of war camp, and stocked with ammunition (the air-raid shelters constructed in the camp were inadequate). The Court Martial found the accused guilty of the charge. The district in which the camp and the depot were situated was several times the immediate target for Allied planes, and as a result 'the ammunition depot might have been hit, with disastrous consequences for the prisoners' (at 211).

barred from claiming enjoyment of immunity from the civil or criminal jurisdiction of foreign States, accruing under customary law to State officials acting in the exercise of their functions (although, if the State official belongs to a category such as head of State, foreign minister or diplomatic agent and is still serving, then he enjoys complete personal immunity: see *Pinochet*,[10] *Fidel Castro* (Legal Grounds 1–4), and the *Congo* v. *Belgium* case, §§57–61).

Under this definition international crimes include war crimes, crimes against humanity, genocide, torture (as distinct from torture as one of the categories of war crimes or crimes against humanity), aggression, and some extreme forms of terrorism (serious acts of State-sponsored or -tolerated international terrorism). By contrast, the notion at issue does not embrace other classes.

First of all, it does not encompass piracy (a phenomenon that was important and conspicuous in the seventeenth to the nineteenth centuries). Indeed, as I have tried to show elsewhere,[11] piracy was (and is) not punished for the sake of protecting a *community* value: all States were (and still are) authorized to seize, capture, and bring to trial pirates in order to safeguard their *joint interest* to fight a common danger and a consequent (real or potential) damage. This is to some extent supported by the fact that when piracy was committed *on behalf of a State* (and was then called 'privateering'), there was not universal jurisdiction over it. That shows that the conduct amounting to piracy—which was identical to the conduct amounting to 'privateering'—was not considered so abhorrent that it was an international crime. After all, piracy could be just a simple matter of theft on the high seas but of course it more usually involved more nasty conduct, like making sailors walk the plank, murder, torture, etc. Probably it was simply because piracy *by definition* occurred outside any State's territorial jurisdiction that a useful repressive mechanism evolved of allowing all or any State to bring pirates to justice.

Secondly, the notion of international crimes does not include illicit traffic in narcotic drugs and psychotropic substances, the unlawful arms trade, smuggling of nuclear and other potentially deadly materials, or money laundering. For one thing, this broad range of crimes is only provided for in international *treaties* or *resolutions* of international organizations, not in customary law. For another, normally it is private individuals or criminal organizations which perpetrate these offences; States fight against them, often by joint official action. In other words, as a rule these offences are committed *against* States. Usually they do not involve States as such or, if they involve State agents, these agents typically act for private gain, perpetrating what national legislation normally regards as ordinary crimes.

10 See *Pinochet* (House of Lords, judgment of 24 March 1999), speeches of Lord Browne-Wilkinson (at 112–15), Lord Hope of Craighead (at 145–52), Lord Saville of Newdigate (at 169–70), Lord Millet (171–91) and of Lord Phillips of Worth Matravers (at 181–90).

11 See Cassese, cit., at 15, well as my paper on 'When May Senior State Officials Be Tried for International Crimes? Some comments on the *Congo* v. *Belgium* Case', 13 EJIL (2002), at 857–8.

The list of international crimes also does not include apartheid, provided for in a Convention of 1973 (which entered into force in 1976). It would seem that this offence has not yet reached the status of a customary law crime, probably because it was held that it was limited in time and space. Moreover, the 101 States parties to the Convention do not include any Western country: only two major segments of the international community (developing and Eastern European countries) have agreed to label apartheid as an international crime, whereas another grouping, that of Western States, has refused to take the same view. There is therefore a case for maintaining that under customary international law apartheid, although probably prohibited as a State delinquency, is not however regarded as a crime entailing the criminal liability of individuals. Nevertheless, the fact that Article 7(1)(j) of the Statute of the ICC grants the Court jurisdiction over apartheid and Article 7(2)(h) provides a definition of this crime, might gradually facilitate the formation of a customary rule. This development could occur if and when cases concerning 'inhumane acts' 'committed in the context of an institutionalized regime of systematic oppression and domination by one racial group over any other racial group or groups and committed with the intention of maintaining that regime' are ever brought before the Court.

2.4 SOURCES OF INTERNATIONAL CRIMINAL LAW

What are the law-making processes from which one can draw the rules making up international criminal law to be applied by *international* criminal courts?

An attempt will be made here to answer this question. The problem of the extent to which the same sources may be used by *national* courts and within what constraints will, however, be left open. In many respects each national legal system provides for its own mechanism for the implementation of international rules. In particular, each system lays down the conditions under which international rules of criminal law may be applied (for instance, in some States, in order for courts to be authorized to pronounce on some international crimes, it is necessary for the legislature to have passed the appropriate legislation defining the crimes and granting courts jurisdiction over them; see *infra*, 16.3.2). In consequence, the system of sources drawn upon by national courts for the purpose of trying persons accused of international crimes is to a large extent bound up with the general manner in which the national system puts international rules into effect. That is not to say that sources of international criminal law vary from State to State; it is simply to say that the way national courts apply this body of law may vary. For instance, courts of all States may and do apply both treaties and international customary law as well as general principles of international law. Nonetheless, depending on the rank of each category of international rules within the national legal system and their status *vis-à-vis* national legislation, treaty rules may prevail over, or be prevailed over, by national laws. (Of course, when courts make national laws conflicting with international rules and the national laws take precedence over the international rules, the State may incur international responsibility for a breach of those rules.)

Since international criminal law is but a branch of public international law, the sources of law from which one may derive the relevant rules (i) are *those proper to international law*, and (ii) must be resorted to in the *hierarchical order* dictated by international law.

Hence, one may draw upon primary sources (treaties, customary law), secondary sources (that is, rules produced by sources envisaged in customary rules or treaty provisions), general principles of international criminal law or general principles of law, or in the final analysis such subsidiary sources as general principles of law recognised by the community of States. The order in which one may use such sources (and which at present is to a large extent codified in Article 21 of the ICC Statute), is as follows: one should first of all look for treaty rules or for rules laid down in such international instruments as binding resolutions of the UN Security Council (as is the case for the ICTY and the ICTR), when these treaty rules or resolutions contain the provisions conferring jurisdiction on the court or tribunal and setting out the procedure. When such rules are lacking or contain gaps, one should resort to customary law or to treaties implicitly or explicitly referred to in the aforementioned rules. When even this set of general or treaty rules is of no avail, one should apply general principles of international criminal law (which may be inferred, by a process of induction and generalization, from treaty provisions or customary rules) or, as a fallback, general principles of law. If one still does not find the applicable rule, one may have resort to general principles of criminal law common to the nations of the world.

Let us now consider these various sources in some detail.

2.4.1 THE STATUTES OF COURTS AND TRIBUNALS

Chief among the texts deriving from the Statutes of courts and tribunals are the London Agreement of 8 August 1945, setting out the substantive and procedural law of the IMT of Nuremberg, and the 1998 Statute of the ICC, a long and elaborate instrument that lays down both a list of crimes subject to the jurisdiction of the Court and some general principles of international criminal law, and in addition sets forth the main elements of the proceedings before the Court.

Other international instruments endowed with legally binding force and regulating international tribunals are the resolutions passed respectively in 1993 and 1994 by the UN Security Council to adopt the Statutes of the ICTY and the ICTR. These resolutions, taken on the strength of Chapter VII of the UN Charter, are legally binding on all UN member States pursuant to Article 25 of the UN Charter. They constitute 'secondary' international legislation (in that they have been adopted by virtue of provisions contained in a treaty, the UN Charter).

For the interpretation of these instruments one must rely upon the rules of interpretation laid down in the Vienna Convention on the Law of Treaties. Indeed, in many respects these resolutions, and their annexed Statutes, may be equated with international treaties. The ICTY Appeals Chamber upheld this view in a number of decisions.[12]

2.4.2 OTHER TREATIES

Often some provisions of the Statutes of courts and tribunals refer, if only implicitly, to international treaties. For instance, Article 2 of the ICTY Statute, conferring on the Tribunal jurisdiction over grave breaches of the Geneva Conventions of 1949, explicitly refers to these Geneva Conventions with regard to the notion of 'protected persons' and 'protected property'. Article 4 of the ICTR Statute, granting jurisdiction over violations of Article 3 (which is common to the Geneva Conventions) and the Second Additional Protocol, admittedly incorporates only the main provisions of common Article 3 and the Additional Protocol; nevertheless, for its interpretation the Tribunal may need to look at the provisions of the Conventions or of the Protocol.

International treaties may come into play from another viewpoint. By definition treaties are only binding upon the contracting States and any international body they may establish. Nonetheless, they may also be taken into account, whenever this is legally admissible, as evidence of the crystallization of customary rules.

Of course, given the overriding importance of the *nullum crimen* principle (see *infra*, 7.3–7.4), an international court is not allowed to apply treaties other than that conferring on it jurisdiction over certain categories of crimes, if such treaties provide for *other* categories of crimes. For instance, if the Statute of a court or tribunal grants jurisdiction over crimes against humanity and genocide only, the court or tribunal may not have recourse to a treaty prohibiting war crimes and try an accused for such class of crimes.

Treaties relevant to our subject matter are those laying down substantive rules of international humanitarian law (for instance, the Regulations annexed to the Fourth Hague Convention of 1907, the four Geneva Conventions of 1949, the two Geneva Additional Protocols of 1977, various recent treaties prohibiting the use of certain specific weapons,[13] and so on), that is, rules the serious violation of which may amount to war crimes. Other treaties refer to other international crimes: for instance, the 1948 Convention on Genocide (the fundamental provisions of which have subsequently turned into customary law); the 1984 Convention against Torture, various international treaties on terrorism, etc.

[12] See for instance *Tadić* (*Interlocutory Appeal*) (§§71–93) as well as *Tadić* (*Appeal*) (§§282–6 and 287–305). An ICTY Trial Chamber rightly held in *Slobodan Milošević* (*decision on preliminary motions*) that 'the Statute of the International Tribunal is interpreted as a treaty' (§47).

[13] See for instance the 1925 Geneva Protocol for the Prohibition of the Use in War of Asphyxiating, Poisonous or Other Gases, and of Bacteriological Methods of Warfare, or the 1980 UN Convention on Prohibitions on Restrictions on the Use of Certain Conventional Weapons which may be deemed to be excessively injurious or to have Indiscriminate Effects, or the 1997 Ottowa Convention on the Prohibition of the Use, Stockpiling, Production and Transfer of Anti-personnel Mines and their Destruction.

The rules for *interpreting* treaties are those laid down Articles 31–3 of the 1969 Vienna Convention on the Law of Treaties, which is declaratory of customary international rules on the construction of both treaties and, arguably, of other written rules as well.

2.4.3 CUSTOMARY LAW

As pointed out above, written rules on our subject matter (belonging either to treaties or to other international instruments endowed with normative force, such as binding resolutions of the UN Security Council) are not numerous. Hence, one has frequently to rely upon customary rules or general principles either to clarify the content of treaty provisions or to fill gaps in these provisions. Resort to customary law may also prove necessary for the purpose of pinpointing general principles of criminal law, whenever the application of such principles becomes necessary (see below).

What has been said above, with regard to treaties and the *nullum crimen* principle, also holds true for customary law. A court or tribunal may not apply a customary rule criminalizing conduct that does not fall within one of the categories of crimes over which it has jurisdiction under its Statute.

As noted above, both customary rules and principles may normally be drawn or inferred from case law, which to a very large extent emanates from *national* courts. As each State court tends to apply the general notions of national criminal law even when adjudicating international crimes, it often proves arduous to find views and concepts that are so uniform and consistent as to evidence the formation of an international customary rule. The same holds true for principles.

In addition, differences originating from *different legal approaches* may influence the appraisal by an international judge of the significance of case law. Judges trained in common law systems naturally tend to attach great importance to cases as 'precedents' and are inclined to apply such 'precedents' without asking themselves whether they evince the formation of, or crystallize, an international customary rule, or instead testify to the proper interpretation of a treaty or customary rule offered by another court. On the other hand, judges from civil law countries, where judicial precedents have lesser weight and criminal codes enjoy great legal status, tend to play down judicial decisions, or at least to first ask themselves, before relying upon such decisions, what legal status should be attached to them in international proceedings. This difference in cultural background and legal training of international judges often leads to different legal decisions.

Many examples may be cited of cases where national or international courts have taken into consideration case law (plus, if need be, treaties and other international instruments) to establish whether a customary rule had evolved on a specific matter. For instance, in *Furundžija* an ICTY Trial Chamber held that a rule on the definition of rape had come into being at the customary law level.[14] In a case decided in 1950 the Brussels Court Martial had already ruled that torture in time of armed conflict was prohibited by a customary international law rule.[15]

In many cases courts have resorted to customary law to determine the content and scope of an international rule that made a crime punishable without however properly defining the prohibited conduct. For instance, in *Kupreškić and others* an ICTY Trial Chamber had to carefully consider treaties and cases to establish what the prohibition of *persecution* as a crime against humanity meant (§§567–626).[16]

In *Tadić* (*Appeal*) the ICTY Appeals Chamber had to establish whether the doctrine of acting in pursuance of a common criminal purpose covered the case where one of the perpetrators committed an act that, while outside the common design, was nevertheless a foreseeable consequence of pursuing that common purpose or design. After considering various national cases and two international treaties, as well as the legislation of a number of civil law and common law countries, the Court gave an affirmative answer. It noted, however, that since there was no uniformity in the national legislation in the major legal systems of the world (§§204–25), the Chamber could not consider that a general rule had been generated by the general principles of criminal

[14] After noting that rape was prohibited in treaty law, it pronounced as follows: 'The prohibition of rape and serious sexual assault in armed conflict has also evolved in customary international law. It has gradually crystallised out of the express prohibition of rape in Article 44 of the [1863] Lieber Code and the general provisions contained in Article 46 of the Regulations annexed to Hague Convention IV, read in conjunction with the "Martens clause" laid down in the preamble to the Convention. While rape and sexual assaults were not specifically prosecuted by the Nuremberg Tribunal, rape was expressly classified as a crime against humanity under Article II(1)(c) of Control Council Law no. 10. The Tokyo International Military Tribunal convicted Generals Toyoda and Matsui of command responsibility for violations of the laws or customs of war committed by their soldiers in Nanking, which included widespread rapes and sexual assaults. The former Foreign Minister of Japan, Hirota, was also convicted for these atrocities. This decision and that of the United States Military Commission in *Yamashita*, along with the ripening of the fundamental prohibition of "outrages upon personal dignity" laid down in common Article 3 into customary international law, has contributed to the evolution of universally accepted norms of international law prohibiting rape as well as serious sexual assault. These norms are applicable in any armed conflict. It is indisputable that rape and other serious sexual assaults in armed conflict entail the criminal liability of the perpetrators.' (§§168–9.)

[15] In *K.W.* German officers had been accused of ill-treating civilians in occupied Belgium. After noting that Article 46 of the Hague Regulations imposed upon the Occupant to respect the life of individuals but did not expressly forbid acts of violence or cruelty, the Court Martial held that a customary rule had evolved on the matter. To this effect it relied upon the celebrated Martens Clause as well as Article 5 of the Universal Declaration of Human Rights, concluding that 'hanging a human being by his hands tied behind his back from a pulley specially rigged for the purpose' was torture, whereas 'blows to the face, delivered so repeatedly and violently that they caused it to swell up and, in several cases, broke some teeth' amounted to cruel treatment (at 566). See also *Auditeur* v. *K.* (at 654).

[16] The Court found that under customary law persecution must contain the following elements: (i) the elements required for all crimes against humanity under the ICTY Statute (namely, to be part of a widespread or systematic attack on the civilian population, etc.); (ii) to be a gross or blatant denial of a fundamental right reaching the same level of gravity as the other acts prohibited under Article 5 of the ICTY Statute (on crimes against humanity); and (iii) to be based on discriminatory grounds (§627). Similarly, in *Kunarac and others* an ICTY Trial Chamber held that 'at the time relevant to the indictment', *enslavement* as a crime against humanity was prohibited by customary international law 'as the exercise of any or all of the powers attaching to the right of ownership over a person' (§539). It reached this conclusion after a long survey of treaties and national and international cases (§§518–38).

law recognized by the nations of the world (§225). Rather, the law on the matter was customary in nature:

> the consistency and cogency of the case law and the treaties referred to above, as well as their consonance with the general principles on criminal responsibility laid down in the [ICTY] Statute and general international criminal law and in national legislation, warrant the conclusion that the case law reflects customary rules of international criminal law. (§226.)

In the same case the Chamber upheld the Prosecutor's submissions that the ICTY Statute did not contain a requirement that crimes against humanity could not be committed for purely personal motives. The Court undertook a careful examination of 'case law as evidence of customary international law' (§§248–69) and concluded that 'the relevant case law and the spirit of international rules concerning crimes against humanity make it clear that under customary law, "purely personal motives" do not acquire any relevance for establishing whether or not a crime against humanity has been perpetrated' (§270).[17]

In some cases courts reached the conclusion that, contrary to the submissions of one of the parties, a specific matter was not governed by customary international rules. Thus, for instance, in *Tadić* (*Appeal*) the ICTY Appeals Chamber held that:

> customary international law, as it results from the gradual development of international instruments and national case law into general rules, does not presuppose a discriminatory or persecutory intent for all crimes against humanity. (§§288–92.)

Conversely, as pointed out above, in some cases international or national courts, following an approach akin to that of common law courts, did not take into consideration case law for the purpose of determining whether it had brought about the crystallization of an international customary rule. Rather, they viewed and used case law as a set of precedents that could be of assistance in establishing the applicable law. (One should, however, note that on a typical common law approach, precedents are *binding*, not merely of assistance. *Obiter dicta* are of assistance, but by definition they are not precedents.)[18]

[17] In other words, the Appeals Chamber held *for* the Prosecution on the Prosecutor's Cross-Appeal that a crime against humanity *could* be committed for purely personal motives, since whether the crime is committed for purely personal reasons or not is irrelevant.

In *Slobodan Milošević* (*Decision on Preliminary Motions*) an ICTY Trial Chamber concluded that the provision of the ICTY Statute whereby the 'official position' of an accused does not relieve him of criminal responsibility reflected customary international law, as evidenced by numerous treaty provisions on the matter, the adoption by a very large majority of the ICC Statute at the Rome Diplomatic Conference, the adoption by the ILC of the Draft Code of Crimes against the Peace and Security of Mankind, as well as case law (§§26–33).

[18] For instance, in *Kvočka and others* an ICTY Trial Chamber, when discussing the issue of how to distinguish co-perpetrators from aiders and abettors in the case of participation by a number of persons in a joint criminal enterprise, merely relied upon case law as such ('A number of cases assist the Trial Chamber in its assessment of the level of participation required to incur criminal responsibility as either a co-perpetrator or an aider and abettor in a criminal endeavour in which several participants are involved': §290; and see §§291–312).

Perhaps, in *Kvočka and others*, the Chamber was trying to discover the content of international customary law but did not say in so many words that that was what it was doing.

2.4.4 GENERAL PRINCIPLES OF INTERNATIONAL CRIMINAL LAW AND GENERAL PRINCIPLES OF INTERNATIONAL LAW

General principles of international criminal law include principles specific to criminal law, such as the principles of legality (see *infra*, 7.3), and of specificity (see *infra*, 7.4.1), the presumption of innocence (see *infra*, 21.2), the principle of equality of arms (see *infra*, 21.4.1), etc.[19] The application of these principles at the international level normally results from their gradual transposition over time from national legal systems on to the international order. They are now firmly embedded in the international legal system.

General principles of international law consist of principles inherent in the international legal system. Hence, their identification does not require an in-depth comparative survey of all the major legal systems of the world, but can be carried out by way of generalization and induction from the main features of the international legal order.

By way of illustration, mention may first be made of *Furundžija*. In that case, after surveying international treaties and case law to establish whether there existed any rule of customary international law defining rape, Trial Chamber II embarked upon an examination of national legislation in order to identify a possible common definition of that offence. It concluded that such a common definition did exist, except for one point (whether or not the sexual penetration of the mouth by the male sexual organ amounted to rape), on which a major discrepancy in the various legal systems could be discerned. The Tribunal—it would seem, somewhat contradictorily—held that at this stage it was appropriate to look for 'general principles of international criminal law or, if such principles are of no avail, to the general principles of international law' (§182). It then applied the 'general principle of respect for human dignity' both as a principle underpinning international humanitarian law and human rights law, and as a principle permeating the whole body of international law (§183). It also applied the general principle *nullum crimen sine lege* (§184), probably as a general principle of criminal law.

Arguably a more consistent and compelling approach was taken in *Kupreškić*

[19] Trial Chamber II of the ICTY, in *Delalić et al.* in 1998 mentioned the *nullum crimen sine lege* and the *nulla poena sine lege* principles, noting that they 'are well recognised in the world's major criminal justice systems as being fundamental principles of criminality' (§402). The Chamber also referred to another 'fundamental principle', namely 'the prohibition against ex post facto criminal laws with its derivative rule of non-retroactive application of criminal laws and criminal sanctions' as well as 'the requirement of specificity and the prohibition of ambiguity in criminal legislation' (ibid.). The Chamber then pointed out that: 'the above principles of legality exist and are recognised in all the world's major criminal justice systems' (§403). However, the Chamber warned, '[i]t is not certain to what extent they have been admitted as part of international legal practice, separate and apart from the existence of the national legal systems. This is essentially because of the different methods of criminalisation of conduct in national and international criminal justice systems' (§403).

et al.[20] The Tribunal applied general criteria, when dealing with the question of determining how a double conviction for a single criminal action should be reflected in sentencing.[21]

2.4.5 GENERAL PRINCIPLES OF CRIMINAL LAW RECOGNIZED BY THE COMMUNITY OF NATIONS

While the general principles just mentioned may be inferred from the whole system of international criminal law or of international law, the principles we will now discuss may be drawn from a comparative survey of the principal legal systems of the world. Their enunciation is therefore grounded not merely on interpretation and generalization, but rather on a comparative law approach.

This source is subsidiary in nature; hence, recourse to it can only be made if reliance upon the other sources (treaties, custom, general principles of international law, rules produced through a secondary source) has turned out to be of no avail. It is at this stage that the search for general principles shared by the major legal systems of the community of nations may be initiated. This is precisely the approach taken in Article 21 of the ICC Statute. Pursuant to this provision resort to the general principles under discussion is the *extrema ratio* for the ICC.

Clearly, a principle of criminal law may belong to this class only if a court finds that it is shared by common law and civil law systems as well as other legal systems such as those of the Islamic world, some Asian countries such as China and Japan, and the African continent. (It is more and more frequently being pointed out in the legal

20 In that case Trial Chamber II held that: '[A]ny time the Statute [of the ICTY] does not regulate a specific matter, and the *Report of the Secretary-General* [submitted to the Security Council and endorsed by it as a document accompanying the resolution establishing the Tribunal] does not prove to be of any assistance in the interpretation of the Statute, it falls to the International Tribunal to draw upon (i) rules of customary international law or (ii) general principles of international criminal law; or, lacking such principles, (iii) general principles of criminal law common to the major legal systems of the world; or, lacking such principles, (iv) general principles of law consonant with the basic requirements of international justice' (§591).

21 After finding that no general principle could be garnered from the various legal systems, the Tribunal stated the following: 'Faced with this discrepancy in municipal legal systems, the Trial Chamber considers that a fair solution can be derived both from the object and purpose of the provisions of the Statute as well as the general concepts underlying the Statute and from 'the general principles of justice applied by jurists and practised by military courts' referred to by the International Military Tribunal at Nuremberg' (§717).

The Trial Chamber came back to the same problem when it dealt with the issue of how a Trial Chamber should act in the case of an erroneous legal classification of facts by the Prosecutor. It carefully examined various legal systems for the purpose of establishing whether principles of criminal law common to the major legal systems of the world exist on the matter (§§728–37). The Chamber concluded that no such principle could be found and added: 'It therefore falls to the Trial Chamber to endeavour to look for a general principle of law consonant with the fundamental features and the basic requirements of international criminal justice' (§738).

It then set out two basic, potentially conflicting, requirements (that 'the rights of the accused be fully safeguarded' and that 'the Prosecutor and, more generally, the International Tribunal be in a position to exercise all the powers expressly or implicitly deriving from the Statute or inherent in their functions, that are necessary for them to fulfil their mission efficiently and in the interests of justice': §§738–9). The Trial Chamber concluded that a careful balancing of these two requirements, as delineated by it, enabled a satisfactory legal solution to be attained (§§742–8). One could note that, in actual practice, rather than applying a general principle or conception of law, the Trial Chamber outlined—others could say crafted—a principle based on such general concepts as fair trial and equality of arms.

literature that limiting comparative legal analysis to civil law and common law systems alone is too restrictive).[22]

International courts have sounded a note of warning about resorting to general principles. They have emphasized that one ought not to transpose legal constructs typical of national legal systems into international law, whenever these constructs do not harmonize with the specific features of the international legal system. The ICTY has taken this approach. Arguably it was in 1998 that a Trial Chamber in *Furundžija* set out the more articulate delineation of the limitations inherent in resort to general principles. After mentioning the need to look for 'principles of criminal law common to the major legal systems of the world' (§177), Trial Chamber II went on to specify the following:

> Whenever international criminal rules do not define a notion of criminal law, reliance upon national legislation is justified, subject to the following conditions: (i) unless indicated by an international rule, reference should not be made to one national legal system only, say that of common-law or that of civil-law States. Rather, international courts must draw upon the general concepts and legal institutions common to all the major legal systems of the world. This presupposes a process of identification of the common denominators in these legal systems so as to pinpoint the basic notions they share; (ii) since 'international trials exhibit a number of features that differentiate them from national criminal proceedings' [reference is made here to Judge Cassese's Separate and Dissenting Opinion in *Erdemović*, 7 October 1997], account must be taken of the specificity of international criminal proceedings when utilising national law notions. In this way a mechanical importation or transposition from national law into international criminal proceedings is avoided, as well as the attendant distortions of the unique traits of such proceedings. (§178.)[23]

International courts have often relied upon these principles. For instance, the ICTY has had the opportunity to resort to this subsidiary source of law in a number of cases. In some cases the ICTY found that there existed general principles common to the major legal systems of the world, and accordingly applied them.

[22] This distinction (still to a large extent upheld in such standard works as R. David and C. Juaffret Spinosi, *Les grands systèmes de droit contemporains*, 10th edn (Paris, 1992); as is well known, David divided the legal world into four families: common law, civil law, socialist law, other conceptions of law), is held to be on the wane by such writers as, for instance, Gordely, 'Common Law and Civil Law: eine überholte Unterscheidung', 3 *Zeitschrift für Europäisches Privatrecht* (1993), 498 ff.; Glenn, 'La civilization de la common law', 45 *Revue internationale de droit comparé* (1993), 599 ff.; B. S. Markesinis (ed.), *The Gradual Convergence: Foreign Ideas, Foreign Influences, and English Law on the Eve of the 21st Century* (Oxford: Clarendon Press, 1994).

Recently a distinguished author (U. Mattei, 'Three Patterns of Law: Taxonomy and Change in the World's Legal Systems', 45 *American J. of Comparative Law* (1997), 5–44) has suggested a tripartite scheme: in his view there exist three patterns of law, according to the relative prevalence of 'the rule of professional law', 'the rule of political law' and 'the rule of traditional law'. The 'rule of professional law', which predominates in the Western world (North America, western Europe, South Africa, and Oceania) can be subdivided, in his opinion, into three subsystems: common law, civil law, and mixed systems (such as Scotland, Louisiana, Quebec, South Africa) including the Scandinavian countries (ibid., 41–2).

[23] The same Trial Chamber conclusively enshrined this notion in *Kupreškić et al.* (§677 and see also §539). It held that '[I]t is now clear that to fill possible gaps in international customary and treaty law, international and national criminal courts may draw upon general principles of criminal law as they derive from the convergence of the principal penal systems of the world. Where necessary, the Trial Chamber shall use such principles to fill any *lacunae* in the Statute of the International Tribunal and in customary law' (§677; see also §539).

Thus, in *Erdemović* (sentencing judgment of 29 November 1996), Trial Chamber I, in discussing the defences of duress, state of necessity, and superior order, held that 'a rigorous and restrictive approach' to this matter should be taken, adding that such approach was in line with the 'general principles of law as expressed in numerous national laws and case law' (§19). However, it actually relied only on French law and case law (see ibid., n. 13).

In the same case the Trial Chamber set about looking for the scale of penalties applicable for crimes against humanity. It found that among the various elements to be taken into account were 'the penalties associated with [crimes against humanity] under international law and national laws, which are expressions of general principles of law recognised by all nations' (§26). After a brief survey of international practice, it pointed out that '[a]s in international law, the States which included crimes against humanity in their national laws provided that the commission of such crimes would entail the imposition of the most severe penalties permitted in their respective systems' (§30).

However, the Trial Chamber did not give any specific indication of these laws. It then concluded as follows:

> The Trial Chamber thus notes that there is a general principle of law common to all nations whereby the severest penalties apply for crimes against humanity in national legal systems. It thus concludes that there exists in international law a standard according to which a crime against humanity is one of extreme gravity demanding the most severe penalties when no mitigating circumstances are present. (§31.)[24]

It may be respectfully noted that the Court not only failed to indicate on what national laws it had relied but also omitted to specify whether it had taken into account, in addition to general criminal legislation, national laws on war crimes as well as those on genocide, to establish whether these last laws provide for penalties as serious as those attaching to crimes against humanity. It would therefore seem that the legal proposition set out by the Court does not carry the weight it could have, had it been supported by convincing legal reasoning.

In *Furundžija*, Trial Chamber II was faced with the problem of the definition of one of the categories of war crimes and crimes against humanity, namely rape. After going through international treaties and having considered the relevant case law for the purpose of establishing if it evinced the formation of a customary rule on the matter, the Tribunal stated that no elements other than the few resulting from such examination could be

> drawn from international treaty or customary law, nor is resort to general principles of international criminal law or to general principles of international law of any avail. The Trial

24 Subsequently, after surveying the general practice regarding prison sentences in the case law of the former Yugoslavia, the Court found that reference to this practice was 'in fact a reflection of the general principle of law internationally recognised by the community of nations whereby the most severe penalties may be imposed for crimes against humanity' (§40).

Chamber therefore considers that, to arrive at an accurate definition of rape based on the criminal law principle of specificity . . . it is necessary to look for principles of criminal law common to the major legal systems of the world. (§177.)

After undertaking this examination, the Court reached the conclusion that 'in spite of inevitable discrepancies, most legal systems in the common and civil law worlds consider rape to be the forcible sexual penetration of the human body by the penis or the forcible insertion of any other object into either the vagina or the anus' (§181). (However, on one point, namely whether forced oral penetration could be defined rape or sexual assault, the Court found that there was no uniformity in national legislation.)[25]

Far more numerous are the cases where the ICTY has ruled out the existence of a general principle of law recognised by all nations.[26]

[25] In *Kupreškić and others*, Trial Chamber II took into consideration the question of general principles on a number of occasions. Thus it considered whether there were 'principles of criminal law common to the major systems of the world' outlining the 'criteria for deciding whether there has been a violation of one or more provisions' when the same conduct can be regarded as breaching more than one provision of criminal law (the question of *cumulation of offences*), and concluded that such criteria did exist (§§680–95).

In *Blaškić*, Trial Chamber I held that the principle on the various forms of individual criminal responsibility laid down in Article 7(1) of the ICTY Statute was consonant 'with the general principles of criminal law' as well as international customary law (§264). Subsequently, in appraising the various elements to be considered for the determination of the appropriate penalty, the Chamber held that the 'principle of proportionality' [of the penalty to the gravity of the crime] is a 'general principle of criminal law' (§796).

[26] Thus, in *Tadić*, Trial Chamber II rightly excluded a principle whereby *unus testis nullus testis* (one witness is no witness), i.e. a principle requiring corroboration of evidence. It found that this principle was not even universally upheld in civil law systems (§§256, 535–9). In *Erdemović* (appeals judgment of 7 October 1997), Judges McDonald and Vohrah in their Joint Separate Opinion, as well as Judge Li in his Separate and Dissenting Opinion, held that there was no general principle on the question of whether duress can serve as a defence to the killing of innocent civilians (§§46–58 and 4, respectively). Judge Cassese, in his Dissenting Opinion, contended, on the basis of the international case law, that no *special* rule excluding duress as a defence in a case of *murder* had evolved in international criminal law and that, in the absence of such a special rule, the Tribunal had to apply the general rule, which was to recognize duress as a defence without specifying to which crimes it applied and to which crimes it did not. Consequently, and subject to the strict requirements enumerated in his dissent, duress could be admitted as a complete defence even to the crime of killing innocent persons: see §§11–49).

Similarly, in *Tadić* (appeals judgment of 15 July 1999) the Appeals Chamber held that the criminal doctrine of acting in pursuance of a common purpose, although rooted in the national law of many States, did not amount to a general principle common to the major legal systems of the world (§§224–5). In *Kupreškić and others*, Trial Chamber II looked for general principles common to the major systems of the world on the question of how a *double conviction* for a single action must be reflected in sentencing, and concluded that no such principles could be discerned (§§713–16). It reached the same negative conclusion in another area: the specific question of 'how a Trial Chamber should proceed when certain legal ingredients of a charge [made by the Prosecutor] have not been proved but the evidence shows that, if the facts were differently characterised, an international crime under the jurisdiction of the Tribunal would nevertheless have been perpetrated' (§§728–38). The Court therefore held that, lacking a general principle common to the major legal systems of the world, it fell to it 'to endeavour to look for a general principle of law consonant with the fundamental features and the basic requirements of international criminal justice' (§738).

It is also notable that in *Aleksovski*, the Appeals Chamber pointed out that the principle of *stare decisis*, or binding precedent, tended to underpin the general trend of both common and civil law. However, the Appeals Chamber rightly held that in the event the issue was to be settled in light not of a general principle common to the systems of the world, but of international law (§98).

2.4.6 REGULATIONS AND OTHER RULES OF INTERNATIONAL LAW

International proceedings are normally governed by 'Rules of procedure and evidence' that may be adopted by the international Court itself, by virtue of a provision contained in the Court's Statute (this is the case of the ICTY and the ICTR). The adoption of such Rules is thus provided for in an international instrument (the Court's Statute) adopted on the strength and by virtue of an international treaty (the UN Charter). It follows that the passing of such rules of procedure amounts to 'tertiary legislation.'

In the case of the ICC, under Article 51(1) and (2) it is the Assembly of States Parties that adopts the Rules of Procedure and Evidence by a two-thirds majority. However, under Article 51(3), 'in urgent cases where the Rules [of Procedure and Evidence] do not provide for a specific situation before the Court, the judges may, by a two-thirds majority, draw up provisional Rules to be applied until adopted, amended or rejected at the next ordinary or special session of the Assembly of the States Parties'. Clearly, in this case, the law-making process leading to the adoption of the Rules constitutes a 'secondary' source of law, for it is envisaged in a treaty (the ICC Statute).

This set of rules must not conflict either with the primary (or 'secondary') legislation governing the same matter (the Statute of the ICTY, the ICTR, and the ICC) or with rules and principles laid down in customary law. In case of inconsistency, a court should refrain from applying the relevant regulation or rule of procedure, or else it must construe and apply them in such a manner that they prove consonant with the overriding rules.[27]

As for the principles of interpretation, once again they should be those upheld in international law and codified in the Vienna Convention on the Law of Treaties: see to this effect the judgment of the ICTY Appeals Chamber in *Jelisić* (*Appeal*), where the Court rightly relied upon the Vienna Convention to construe a Rule (98 *bis* (B)) of the RPE (§35).

2.4.7 THE ROLE OF JUDICIAL DECISIONS AND THE OPINION OF SCHOLARS

As stated above, judicial decisions—even of the same court—per se do not constitute a source of international criminal law. Formally speaking they may only amount to a

[27] In *Blaškić* (*subpoena*) the ICTY Appeals Chamber asked itself whether the term 'subpoena' used in Rule 54 of the RPE should be understood 'to mean an injunction accompanied by a threat of penalty in case of non-compliance', or instead should be taken to designate a binding order not necessarily implying the assertion of a power to imprison or fine. The Court held that, since under customary international law tribunals were not empowered to issue to States subpoenas capable of being enforced by a penalty, the term was to be given a narrow interpretation: it was to be construed as indicating compulsory orders, which, only when addressed to individuals acting in their private capacity, could imply the possible imposition of a penalty (§§21, 24–5 and 38).

'subsidiary means for the determination of international rules of law (see Article 38(1)(d) of the ICJ Statute, which reflects customary international law).

Nevertheless, given the characteristics of international criminal law (see *supra*, 2.2) one should set great store by national or international judicial decisions. They may prove of crucial importance not only for ascertaining whether a customary rule has evolved, but also as a means for establishing the most appropriate interpretation to be placed on a treaty rule.

In *Aleksovski* (*Appeal*), the ICTY Appeals Chamber held that it could depart from a previous decision by the same Appeals Chamber if it had cogent reasons for so doing (at §§92–111). One may wonder whether the Chamber purported to establish a form of precedent at the Tribunal. The objection is possible that this would be trying to pull oneself up by one's own boot-straps: one cannot establish a doctrine of precedent *by precedent*, for it would be tautological. In any event, that decision was not really precedent. According to the traditional and strict doctrine of precedent, one court has to follow another court's decision, if the prior decision dealt with the same issue, whether it has cogent reasons for departing from it or not. It would therefore seem that according to the *Aleksovski* approach, one Appeals Chamber's decision is only really *persuasive authority* for another Appeals Chamber.

However a decision by an Appeals Chamber *in the very same case* (e.g. the Appeals Chamber directing a Trial Chamber to do x or y) is binding on the Trial Chamber. That, however, is not really a matter of precedent but rather of the hierarchy of power between the appellate and trial levels: the Appeals Chamber has the power to 'order' the Trial Chamber to act in a certain way as a matter of the division of labour between them and their respective powers.

Legal literature, although it carries less weight that case law, may significantly contribute to the elucidation of international rules.

2.5 THE HISTORICAL EVOLUTION OF INTERNATIONAL CRIMES

Traditionally, individuals have been subject to the exclusive (judicial and executive) jurisdiction of the State on whose territory they live. Hence, their possible violations of international rules (for example, ill-treatment of foreigners, attacks on foreign diplomats, wrongful expulsion of foreigners by State officials, etc.) were prosecuted and punished by the competent authorities of the State where these acts had been performed (under the doctrine of territorial jurisdiction). Clearly, such prosecution and punishment only occurred if the State authorities were entitled to do so under their national legislation, and provided they were willing so to proceed. If they did not, the State of which the victim had the nationality was authorized to internationally claim from the delinquent State that it either punish the perpetrators or pay compensation. As what was involved was the responsibility of the State (for failure to bring to trial and punish the offenders), the individuals who had *materially* breached international rules could not be called to account by the foreign State, unless they were their nationals (think of the case of a Russian killing a Russian diplomat in Berlin). In particular, if the international wrongful act had been performed by one or more State officials (for instance, in that they had wrongfully refrained from instituting criminal proceedings against the material offender or had wilfully instigated him to commit the offence), they were entitled abroad to immunity in that they had acted in an official capacity. Hence, if they travelled to the territory of the aggrieved State and were arrested and brought to trial, they were entitled to claim immunity from jurisdiction as well as from substantive law (if they had the status of heads of State, senior members of cabinet, or diplomats, they could also invoke personal immunities and inviolability; in consequence, they could not even be arrested let alone put in the dock).

A few exceptions existed. One of them was piracy, a practice that was widespread in the seventeenth and eighteenth centuries, and has recently regained some importance, albeit limited to one area of the world, East Asia. (An authoritative definition of piracy can now be found in Article 101 of the 1982 Convention on the Law of the Sea.)[28] All States of the world were empowered to search for and prosecute pirates, regardless of the nationality of the victims and of whether the proceeding State had been directly damaged by piracy. The pirates were regarded as enemies of humanity (*hostes humani generis*) in that they hampered the freedom of the high seas and infringed private property.

Another exception was constituted by war crimes. This category of international crimes gradually emerged in the second half of the nineteenth century. Together with piracy (which however is a much older category), it constituted the first exception to the concept of collective responsibility prevailing in the international community.

Two factors gave great impulse and a significant contribution to the emergence of this class of crimes. The first was the codification of the customary law of warfare, as it was then called, at both a private or semi-private level and at State level. At the private level, there emerged the famous Lieber Code, in 1863[29] (which, issued by Army order no. 100 of President Lincoln, as 'Instructions for the Government of the United States in the Field', was applied during the American Civil War, 1861–5). Also notable was the adoption by the Institut de Droit international of the important Oxford Manual, in 1880.[30] At the State level, a remarkable impulse was given by the Hague codification

28 'Piracy consists of any of the following acts:
(a) any illegal acts of violence or detention, or any act of depredation, committed for private ends by the crew or the passengers of a private ship, or a private aircraft, and directed
  (i) on the high seas, against another ship or aircraft, or against persons or property on board such ship or aircraft;
  (ii) against a ship, aircraft, persons or property in a place outside the jurisdiction of any State;
(b) any act or voluntary participation in the operation of a ship or of an aircraft with knowledge of facts making it a pirate ship or aircraft,
(c) any act of inciting or of intentionally facilitating an act described in subparagraph (a) and (b).'

29 Text in Friedman, I, 158–86.

30 See *Les Lois de la Guerre sur Terre, Manuel publié par l'Institut de Droit International* (Brussels and Leipzig: C. Muquardt, 1880).

(1899–1907). Secondly, there were some important trials, held at the end of the American Civil War, notably *Henry Wirz* (a case of serious ill-treatment of prisoners of war), heard by a US Military Commission (1865), and then many cases brought in 1902 before US Courts-Martial during the US armed conflict against insurgents in the Philippines (which Spain had ceded by treaty to the USA in 1898). One may mention in particular *General Jacob H. Smith* (about a superior order to deny quarter), the case of *Major Edwin F. Glenn* (concerning an order to torture a detained enemy), that of *Lieutenant Preston Brown* (about the killing of an unarmed prisoner of war), and *Augustine de La Pena* (again a case of torture of an enemy detained person). US courts held many other trials in relation to crimes committed in armed conflict.[31]

Traditionally such crimes were defined as violations of the laws of warfare committed by combatants in international armed conflicts. War crimes entailed that (i) individuals acting as State officials (chiefly low-ranking servicemen) could be brought to trial and punished for alleged violations of the laws of warfare;[32] (ii) they could be punished, not only by their own State, but also by the enemy belligerent. The exceptional character of war (a pathological occurrence in international dealings, leading to utterly inhuman behaviour) warranted this deviation from traditional law (which, as already pointed out above, granted to any State official acting in an official capacity immunity from prosecution by foreign States). For many years it was primarily the adversary that before the end of the hostilities as well as thereafter carried out the prosecution and punishment of those guilty of war crimes, on the basis of the principle of 'passive nationality' (the victims of breaches were nationals of the State conducting the trial).[33] Characteristically, the 1912 British *Manual on Land Warfare*

[31] See the numerous cases cited in W. Winthrop, *Military Law and Precedents*, 2nd edn (Buffalo, NY: William S. Helm & Co., 1920), 839–62.

[32] The contrary view of A. Verdross, *Völkerrecht* (Berlin: Springer Verlag, 1937) at 298 was (and is) wrong. (According to the distinguished Austrian international lawyer, 'punishment [of authors of war crimes] must be ruled out when the action was not performed on one's own impulse, but must be exclusively attributed to the State of which the person is a national (*Heimatstaat*)'.) H. Kelsen (*Peace through Law* (Chapel Hill: University of North Carolina Press, 1944, at 97) shared Verdross's view.

[33] According to the authoritative *History of the United Nations War Crimes Commission and the Development of the Laws of War*, compiled by the 'United Nations War Crimes Commission' (London: His Majesty's Stationery Office, 1948, at 29) 'The right of the belligerent to punish as war criminals persons who violate the laws or customs of war is a well-recognized principle of international law. It is the right of which a belligerent may effectively avail himself during the war in cases when such offenders fall into his hands, or after he has occupied all or part of enemy territory and is thus in the position to seize war criminals who happen to be there. . . . And although the Treaty of Peace brings to an end the right to prosecute war criminals, no rule of international law prevents the victorious belligerent from imposing upon the defeated State the obligation, as one of the provisions of the armistice or of the Peace Treaty, to surrender for trial persons accused of war crimes.'

This view, also shared by H. Kelsen (*Peace through Law*, cit., at 108–10) does not seem, however, to reflect the status of traditional international law. As was conclusively demonstrated by A. Mérignhac ('De la sanction des infractions au droit des gens commises, au cours de la guerre européenne, par les empires du centre', 24 RGDIP (1917), 28–56) and L. Renault ('De l'application du droit pénal aux faits de la guerre', ibid., 25 (1918), 5–29), State practice shows that belligerents are entitled to prosecute and punish their servicemen as well as enemy military both during the armed conflict and after the end of hostilities.

stipulated that 'war crimes is the technical expression for such an act of enemy soldiers and enemy civilians as may be visited by punishment on capture of the offenders'.[34] However, an important exception can be seen in the numerous war crimes trials held in 1902 by US Courts Martial for offences committed by Americans in the armed conflict in the Philippines (1901).

Since the First World War the prosecution was also effected by allies, on the basis either of the principle of territoriality (the crime was committed on their territory), or of passive nationality (it was sufficient for the victim to have the nationality of an allied country). Although various national legislations also made provision for punishment on the basis of the principle of 'active nationality' (the law-breaker had the nationality of the prosecuting State), in practice scant use was made of this principle, for obvious reasons.

The creation of the IMT and the subsequent trial at Nuremberg of the major German criminals (followed in 1946 by the Tokyo Trial), marked a crucial turning point. First, two new categories of crime were envisaged: crimes against peace and crimes against humanity. Secondly, until 1945 (with the exception of the provisions of the 1919 Treaty of Versailles relating to the German Emperor, which however remained a dead letter), senior State officials had never been held personally responsible for their wrongdoings. Until that time States alone could be called to account by other States, plus servicemen (normally low-ranking people) accused of misconduct during international wars. In 1945, for the first time in history, the principle was laid down—and carried through, in contrast to what had happened in 1919—that other State representatives (high-ranking officers, politicians, prominent administrators or financiers, as well as men in charge of official State propaganda) could also be made answerable for gross misconduct in time of armed conflict. Those men were no longer protected by State sovereignty; they could be brought to trial before organs—representative if not of the international community at least of the large group of the allied victors—and punished by foreign States. (However, the idea propounded by such distinguished international lawyers as the American Hyde[35] and the Austrian Kelsen,[36] that the international Court should consist of neutral nationals, was not upheld, clearly for political reasons, that is, because the victors wished to be and remain in control of the trials.) For the first time the basic principle was proclaimed that, faced with the alternative of complying with either national legal commands or international standards, State officials and individuals must opt for the latter. As the IMT forcefully stated, 'the very essence of the Charter [instituting the IMT] is that individuals have international duties which transcend the national obligations of obedience imposed by the individual State' (at 223).

34 Col. J. E. Edmons and Prof. L. Oppenheim, *Land Warfare, An Exposition of the Laws and Usages of War on land for the Guidance of Officers of His Majesty's Army* (London: His Majesty's Stationery Office, 1912), at 95, para. 441.

35 C. C. Hyde, 'Punishment of War Criminals', *Proceedings of the ASIL* (1943), at 43–4.

36 H. Kelsen, *Peace through Law*, cit., at 111–16.

After the adoption, in 1948, of the Convention on Genocide (which laid down genocide as a discrete crime), the 1949 Geneva Conventions marked a great advance as regards the extension both of substantive law (new categories of war crimes were added: they were termed 'grave breaches of the Geneva Conventions') and of procedural law (they set up a very advanced system for repressing violations by States; see *infra*, 15.5.1(A)). The relevant provisions represented a momentous departure from customary law, for the Conventions also laid down the principle of universality of jurisdiction (a contracting State could bring to trial a person held in its custody and accused of a 'grave breach', regardless of his nationality, of the nationality of the victim, and of the place where the alleged offence had been committed). It is probable that the exceedingly bold character of this regulation contributed to its remaining ineffective for many years.

The Geneva Conventions were followed by the two Additional Protocols in 1977, the Convention against Torture in 1984 (which significantly contributed to the emergence of torture as a distinct crime), and a string of treaties against terrorism since the 1970s (which contributed to the evolution of an international crime of terrorism).

Later on, as the ICTY Appeals Chamber authoritatively held in *Tadić* (*Interlocutory Appeal*) (§§94–137), the notion of war crimes was gradually extended to serious violations of international humanitarian rules governing *internal* armed conflict.

SELECT BIBLIOGRAPHY

BASIC NOTIONS OF INTERNATIONAL CRIMINAL LAW

Jescheck, *Verantwortlichkeit*, 149–282, 302–420; A. Quintano Ripollés, *Tratado*, I, 149–255; G. Dahm, *Zur Problematik des Völkerstrafrechts*, (Göttingen: Vandenhaeck und Ruprecht, 1956), 14–67; S. Glaser, *Introduction*, 3–10; Y. Dinstein, 'International Criminal Law', 5 IYHR (1975), 55–87; Jescheck, 'Development, Present State and Future Prospects of International Criminal Law', 2 RIDP (1981), 337–63; A. Eser, 'Common Goals and Different Ways in International Criminal Law: Reflections from a European Perspective', 31 *Harvard Int. Law Journal* (1990), 117–27; M. Delmas-Marty, *Pour un droit commun* (Paris: Jeuil 1994), 121–202; S.R. Ratner, 'The Schizophrenias of International Criminal Law', 33 *Texas Int. Law Journal* (1998), 237–56; J. Crawford, 'International Law and International Crimes: Comments on a Developing Relationship', in *Cooperazione fra Stati e Giustizia Penale Internazionale* (Naples: Editoriale Scientifica, 1999), 147–58; J. I. Charney, 'Progress in International Criminal Law?', 93 AJIL (1999), 452–64; G. Mettraux, 'Using Human Rights Law for the Purpose of Defining Criminal Offences—the Practice of the International Criminal Tribunal in the Former Yugoslavia', in M. Henzelin and R. Roth (eds), *Le droit pénal à l'épreuve de l'internationalisation* (Paris, Geneva, Bruxelles: L. G. D. J, Georg, Bruylant, 2002), 183–216. Mantovani, 983–98.

SOURCES OF INTERNATIONAL CRIMINAL LAW

Quintano Ripollés, *Tratado*, 51–141; S. Glaser, 'Les pouvoirs du juge en droit international pénal', 74–5 *Revue pénale suisse* (1959), 77–93; C. Tomuschat, 'La cristallisation coutumière', in Ascencio, Decaux, Pellet (eds), *Droit international pénal*, 23–35; A. Mahiou, 'Le processus de codification', ibid., 37–53; B. Simma and A. Paulus, 'Le rôle relatif des différentes sources du droit international (dont les principes généraux du droit)', ibid., 55–69; P.-M. Dupuy, 'Normes internationales pénales et droit impératif (*jus cogens*)', ibid., 71–80; T. Meron, 'International Criminalization of Internal Atrocities', AJIL (1995), 554–7.

PART II

SUBSTANTIVE CRIMINAL LAW

SECTION I

INTERNATIONAL CRIMES

3

WAR CRIMES

3.1 THE NOTION

War crimes are *serious violations* of customary or, whenever applicable, treaty rules belonging to the corpus of the international humanitarian law of armed conflict. As the Appeals Chamber of the ICTY stated in *Tadić* (*Interlocutory Appeal*), (i) war crimes must consist of 'a serious infringement' of an international rule, that is to say 'must constitute a breach of a rule protecting important values, and the breach must involve grave consequences for the victim'; (ii) the rule violated must either belong to the corpus of customary law or be part of an applicable treaty; (iii) 'the violation must entail, under customary or conventional law, the individual criminal responsibility of the person breaching the rule' (§94); in other words, the conduct constituting a serious breach of international law must be criminalized.

In the same decision the Appeals Chamber gave the following example of a non-serious violation: 'the fact of a combatant simply appropriating a loaf of bread in an occupied village' would not amount to such a breach, 'although it may be regarded as falling foul of the basic principle laid down in Art. 46(1) of the [1907] Hague Regulations [on Land Warfare] (and the corresponding rule of customary international law) whereby "private property must be respected" by any army occupying an enemy territory' (§94).

War crimes may be perpetrated in the course of either *international* or *internal* armed conflicts, that is, civil wars or large-scale and protracted armed clashes breaking out within a sovereign State. Traditionally war crimes were held to embrace only violations of international rules regulating war proper, that is international armed conflicts and not civil wars. Particularly after the ICTY Appeals Chamber decision in *Tadić* (*Interlocutory Appeal*) of 1995 (see *infra*, 3.3), it is now widely accepted that serious infringements of customary or applicable treaty law on internal armed conflicts must also be regarded as amounting to war crimes proper. As evidence of this new trend, suffice it to mention Article 8(2)(c–f) of the ICC Statute.

War crimes are serious violations of the international humanitarian law of armed conflict, a vast body of substantive rules comprising what are traditionally called 'the law of the Hague' and 'the law of Geneva'.

The former set of rules includes many Hague Conventions of 1899 or 1907 on international warfare. These rules provide for the various categories of lawful combatants, and regulate both combat actions (means and methods of warfare) and the treatment of persons who do not take part in armed hostilities (civilians, wounded, and the sick) or no longer take part in them (chiefly prisoners of war). The so-called 'law of Geneva' comprises the various Geneva Conventions (at present the four Conventions of 1949 plus the two Additional Protocols of 1977), and is essentially designed to regulate the treatment of persons who do not, or no longer, take part in the armed conflict. However, the Third Geneva Convention of 1949 also regulates the various classes of lawful combatants, thereby updating the Hague rules; in addition the First Additional Protocol of 1977 to some extent updates those rules of the Hague law which deal with means and methods of combat, for the sake of sparing civilians as far as possible from armed hostilities. It is thus clear that the traditional distinction between the two sets of rules is fading away; even assuming it has not become obsolete, its purpose now is largely descriptive.

War crimes may be perpetrated *by military personnel against enemy servicemen or civilians*, or *by civilians against* either *members of the enemy armed forces* or *enemy civilians* (for instance, in occupied territory). Conversely, crimes committed by servicemen against their own military (whatever their nationality) do not constitute war crimes, as clarified in *Pilz* by the Dutch Special Court of Cassation[1] as well as in *Motosuke*, by a Temporary Court Martial of the Netherlands East Indies, at Amboina.[2] Such offences may nonetheless fall within the ambit of the military law of the relevant belligerent.

[1] A young Dutchman in the occupied Netherlands had enlisted in the German army and while attempting to escape from his unit had been fired upon and wounded. Pilz, a German doctor serving in the German army with the rank of *Hauptstürmführer*, prevented medical and other aid or assistance being given by a doctor and hospital orderly to the wounded Dutchman, and in addition, 'in abuse of his authority as a superior', had 'ordered or instructed a subordinate to kill the wounded [man] by means of a firearm' (at 1210), as a result of which the Dutchman had died. The Court held that the offence was not a war crime, for 'the wounded person was part of the occupying army and the nationality of this person is therefore irrelevant, given that, by entering the military service of the occupying forces, he removed himself from the protection of international law and placed himself under the laws of the occupying power' (at 1210): consequently, the offence constituted a crime 'within the province of the internal law of Germany' (at 1211).

[2] Motosuke, a Japanese officer, had been accused, among other things, of having ordered the execution by shooting of a Dutch national named Barends, who, during the occupation of Ceram by Japanese armed forces, had joined the Gunkes, a corps of volunteer combatants composed mainly of Indonesian natives serving with the Japanese army. The Court held that by joining the Japanese forces, Barends had lost his nationality. His killing by Japanese forces was not considered a war crime (at 682–4).

3.2 THE NEED FOR A LINK BETWEEN THE OFFENCE AND AN (INTERNATIONAL OR INTERNAL) ARMED CONFLICT

Criminal offences, to amount to war crimes, must also have a link with an international or internal armed conflict. Many courts, chiefly the ICTY[3] and the ICTR,[4] have restated this proposition, which can be easily deduced from the whole body of international humanitarian law of armed conflict. This applies in particular to offences committed by civilians, although courts have also required the link or nexus with an armed conflict in the case of crimes perpetrated by members of the military. (In this respect a case worth mentioning is *Lehnigk and Schuster*, decided by the Italian Court of Assize of S. Maria Capua Vetere in 1994.)[5]

Special attention should be paid to crimes committed by civilians *against other civilians*. They may constitute war crimes, provided there is a link or connection between the offence and the armed conflict. If such a link is absent, the breach does not amount to a war crime, but simply constitutes an 'ordinary' criminal offence under the law applicable in the relevant territory. The Swiss Appellate Military Tribunal aptly confirmed this proposition in *Niyonteze*, in 2000;[6] as did the Tribunal Militaire de Cassation in its decision of 27 April 2001 on the same case (§9).

[3] See *Tadić* (Trial Chamber), at §573; *Delalić and others* (§193).

[4] See *Akayesu* (§§630–4, 638–44), *Kayishema and Ruzindana* (§§185–9, 590–624), *Musema* (§§259–62, 275, and 974). In all these cases the Court eventually found that the link required was lacking.

[5] In October 1943, after Italy had declared war against Germany and while the German troops were pulling out as a result of the military advance of the Allied forces in Southern Italy, a German unit including the two accused killed 22 Italian civilians who had taken shelter in a farm, to avoid being caught in the adverse consequences of the armed conflict under way. In the case brought against the two Germans *in absentia* (in Germany one of the two accused had been acquitted because the crime was covered by a statute of limitation, while the legal condition of the other was unclear, although criminal proceedings had been instituted against him). The Italian Court first asked itself whether the crime with which the two accused were charged should be regarded as ordinary murder or 'murder against the laws and customs of war', or in other words a war crime (at 8). In this respect the Court stated that a murder may amount to war crime only if it was proved that there exists 'an objective link [of the offence] with the demands of war' or, in other words, if the offence had 'a war-like nature', namely it had a link with war and did not 'prove to be generically linked to war' (at 9). The Court then dwelled at length on the facts and concluded that what some witnesses had stated (namely that the German unit had killed the civilians in the farm, in the dark, because they had seen light signals from the farm and feared that there could be partisans or enemy troops) was not correct; the killing was not carried out as a response to, or out of fear of, enemy action, and did not serve any military purpose; indeed the Germans had killed the civilians only out of 'intolerance and hatred for the Italian people' (at 26–30); hence, the murder was not linked to war and could not be classified as a war crime (at 30). That these conclusions totally lack legal merit is patent: the Court undisputedly misinterpreted the laws of war. Clearly, even assuming that the killing only resulted from hatred, it still was a war crime: subjective motives do not have legal relevance in this context.

[6] The accused was a Rwandan arrested in Switzerland and accused of having instigated, and in some cases ordered, the murder of civilians in Rwanda in 1994 in his capacity as mayor of a local 'community' (*commune*). The Tribunal could not apply the Genocide Convention since Switzerland had not yet ratified it. The Tribunal held, therefore, that it would apply the laws of warfare and the provisions of the Geneva Conventions applicable to internal armed conflicts as well as the Second Protocol of 1977. Faced with the question whether

3.3 ESTABLISHING WHETHER A SERIOUS VIOLATION OF INTERNATIONAL HUMANITARIAN LAW HAS BEEN CRIMINALIZED

As pointed out above, in order for a serious violation of international humanitarian law to become a war crime, it is necessary that the violation be criminalized. The question then becomes one of how to determine whether this is the case.

The point of departure is the observation that the failure of the relevant rules of international humanitarian law to provide for any courts or criminal proceedings in the event of the rule being breached is not determinative of the issue. What matters is that criminal or military courts have in fact adjudicated breaches of international humanitarian law. Various courts rightly held this view: for instance, the IMT in *Göring and others* (at 220–1), a US Military Tribunal sitting at Nuremberg in *List and others* (the so-called *Hostages* case) (at 635), and in *Ohlendorf and others* (the so-called *Einsatzgruppen* case) (at 658), as well as the US Supreme Court in *Ex parte Quirin* (at 465).

A second, general and preliminary, remark concerns the need to avoid the following simplistic proposition: to determine whether a particular act may be termed a war crime, one need only establish that the act breaches international humanitarian law, since all violations of the laws of war are war crimes under national law and military manuals. The Judge Advocate at a Canadian Military Court pronouncing in 1946 on a war crime in *Johann Neitz* took this view. After noting that, under Canadian law, a war crime was any 'violation of the laws and usages of war committed during any war in which Canada had been or may be engaged at any time', the Judge Advocate added: 'The test of criminal responsibility is therefore not properly applicable, and the issue upon any charge is not "did the accused commit a crime?" as we understand the word "crime" under our criminal law, but "did he violate the laws and usages of war"?' (at 195–6).

This approach is not convincing, as not all violations of international humanitarian

a civilian could be held responsible for war crimes where he had instigated or ordered the murder of other civilians, the Tribunal held that 'Anyone, whether military or civilian, who attacks a civilian protected by the Geneva Conventions . . . breaches these Conventions and consequently falls under Article 109 of the Swiss Penal Military Code [providing for the punishment of war crimes]. This Appellate Tribunal thus differs from the judgments of the ICTR, which require a close link between the breach and an armed conflict and confine the application of the Geneva Conventions to persons discharging functions within the armed forces or the civilian government (*Musema* §§259[–62] and *Akayesu* §§642–3). Nevertheless this Tribunal considers that in any case there must exist a link between the breach and an armed conflict. If, within the framework of a civil war, where civilians of the two sides are both protected by the Geneva Conventions, a protected person commits a breach against another protected person, it is necessary to establish a link between this act and the armed conflict. If such link is lacking, the breach does not constitute a war crime but an ordinary offence (*infraction de droit commun*)' (at 39–40). In the case at bar, the Tribunal found this link in the fact that the accused was the mayor of the *commune*, and exercised *de jure* and de facto authority over the local citizens; it was thus in his capacity as a 'public official' or civil servant that he committed the crimes (at 40–1).

law amount to war crimes, as pointed out in *Tadić* (*Interlocutory Appeal*) (§94). In short, to establish whether a breach of that body of law, in addition to giving rise to State responsibility (if the act was performed by a State agent), is also criminalized, the simple equation, breach of international humanitarian law equals a war crime, may not suffice, in light of case law and the general principles of criminal justice, in particular the principle of legality (*nullum crimen sine lege*).

These points having been established, several situations need to be distinguished. First, it may be that a violation has been consistently considered a war crime by national or international courts (this is, for example, true of the most blatant violations, such as unlawfully killing prisoners of war or innocent civilians, shelling hospitals, refusing quarter, killing shipwrecked or wounded persons, and so on). The existence of war crimes cases on a particular matter may sometimes be considered sufficient for holding the breach to be a war crime. However, strictly speaking the existence of a few (possibly isolated) war crimes cases may not be enough. It would be better if it were possible to show that the breach is considered a war crime under customary international law, in which case there would have to be widespread evidence that States customarily prosecute such breaches as war crimes and that they do so because they believe themselves to be acting under a binding rule of international law (*opinio juris*).

A second possible instance is that a breach is termed a war crime by the Statute of an international tribunal. In this case, even if the breach has never been brought before a national or international tribunal, it may justifiably be regarded as a war crime—or, at least, as a war crime falling under the jurisdiction of that international tribunal.

A third, and more difficult, category is when the case law and statutes of international tribunals are absent or silent on the matter.[7] In such a case, how is one to determine whether violating a prohibition of international humanitarian law amounts to a war crime? In light of the case law (see *List and others* (*Hostages* case), *John G. Schultz*, *Tadić* (*Interlocutory Appeal*), and *Blaškić*, to which I will presently return) and the general principles of international criminal law, one is entitled, in seeking an answer to the question, to examine: (i) military manuals, (ii) the national legislation of States belonging to the major legal systems of the world, or, if these elements are lacking, (iii) the general principles of criminal justice common to nations of the world, as set out in international instruments, acts, resolutions and the like; and (iv) the legislation and judicial practice of the State to which the accused belongs or on whose territory the crime has allegedly been committed.

Let us now take a look at how courts have gone about this matter.

In *List and others* (the *Hostages* case) the defendants were high-ranking officers in the German armed forces charged with war crimes and crimes against humanity. (They were accused of offences committed by troops under their command during

[7] An example is the prohibition on the use of weapons that are inherently indiscriminate or cause unnecessary suffering.

the occupation of Greece, Yugoslavia, Albania, and Norway, these offences mainly being reprisal killings, purportedly carried out in an attempt to maintain order in the occupied territories in the face of guerrilla opposition, or wanton destruction of property not justified by military necessity.) They claimed that Control Council Law no. 10, on the basis of which they stood accused, was an *ex post facto* act and retroactive in nature. The Tribunal rejected the contention, holding that the crimes defined in that Law were crimes under pre-existing rules of international law, 'some by conventional law and some by customary law'. It went on to state that the war crimes at issue were such under the Hague Regulations of 1907 and then added:

> In any event, the practices and usages of war which gradually ripened into recognized customs with which belligerents were bound to comply, recognized the crimes specified herein as crimes subject to punishment. It is not essential that a crime be specifically defined and charged in accordance with a particular ordinance, statute or treaty if it is made a crime by international convention, recognized customs and usages or war, or the general principles of criminal justice common to civilized nations generally. (At 634–5.)

The Tribunal then noted that the acts at issue were traditionally punished, adding that, although no courts had been established nor penalties provided for the commission of these crimes, 'this is not fatal to their validity. The acts prohibited are without deterrent effect unless they are punishable as crimes' (at 635).

It was the Appeals Chamber of the ICTY that best addressed the issue under discussion, in *Tadić* (*Interlocutory Appeal*). The question in dispute was whether the accused could be held criminally liable for breaches of international humanitarian law allegedly committed in an internal armed conflict; in other words, whether he could be held responsible for war crimes perpetrated in a civil war. The Appeals Chamber first considered whether there were customary rules of international humanitarian law governing internal armed conflicts, and answered in the affirmative (§§96–127). It then asked itself whether violations of those rules could entail individual criminal responsibility. For this purpose, the Court examined national cases, military manuals, national legislation, and resolutions of the UN Security Council. It concluded in the affirmative (§§128–34) and then added that in the case at issue this conclusion was fully warranted 'from the point of view of substantive justice and equity', because violations of international humanitarian law in internal armed conflicts were punished as criminal offences in the countries concerned, that is both the old Socialist Federal Republic of Yugoslavia and in Bosnia and Herzegovina; as the Court noted, 'Nationals of the former Yugoslavia as well as, at present, those of Bosnia-Herzegovina were therefore aware, or should have been aware, that they were amenable to the jurisdiction of their national criminal courts in cases of violation of international humanitarian law' (§135; see also §136).

An ICTY Trial Chamber returned to the question in *Blaškić*. The defence contended that violations of common Article 3 of the four 1949 Geneva Conventions (on internal armed conflict) did not entail criminal liability. The Trial Chamber dismissed this contention by noting, first, that those violations were envisaged in Article 3 of the

ICTY Statute, conferring jurisdiction on the Tribunal, and secondly, that the criminal code of Yugoslavia, taken over in 1992 as the criminal code of Bosnia and Herzegovina (the place where the alleged offences had been committed), provided that war crimes committed either in international or in internal armed conflicts involved the criminal liability of the perpetrator (§176). The question was also dealt with, albeit in less compelling terms, by a US Court of Military Appeals in *John G. Schultz*.[8]

[8] The accused, a former captain of the US Air Force who had returned to civilian life, in 1950, in Japan, had killed two Japanese pedestrians. He was tried by a US General Court Martial on charges of involuntary manslaughter and drunken driving, in violation of Articles of War (respectively 93 and 96). The Judge Advocate General of the Air Force appealed the case on, among other grounds, the issue of whether the Court Martial had jurisdiction over the accused and the offences charged. The Court of Appeals, having found that the accused was neither a 'retainer to the camp' nor a 'person accompanying or serving with the US Armies', hence not amenable to a US Court Martial's jurisdiction on these grounds, asked itself whether he fell under the category of 'any other person who by the law of war is subject to trial by military tribunals'. To answer this question it noted, among other things, that US jurisdiction extended to two types of offences: first, crimes committed against the civilian population made 'punishable by the penal codes of all civilized nations', namely war crimes; secondly, 'crimes condemned by local statute which the military occupying power must take cognizance of inasmuch as the civil authority is superseded by the military'. The Court first looked into the first category, to establish whether the offence at issue fell within such category. Having reached a negative conclusion, it turned to the second category, and concluded that the offence came within its purview. Let us now briefly see how the Court discussed the class of war crimes in a lengthy *obiter dictum*.

The Court noted that this category 'finds its basis in the customs and usages of civilized nations'. It then went on to say that, 'In deciding whether a given offence constitutes a crime under the common law of war, we have no single source which will provide a ready answer. This law is nowhere precisely codified. We note, however, that certain crimes are universally recognized as properly punishable under the law of war. These include murder, manslaughter, robbery, rape, larceny, arson, maiming, assaults, burglary, and forgery . . . The test bringing these offences within the common law of war has been their almost universal acceptance as crimes by the nations of the world. This test is consistent with the rule, already noted, that the common law of war has its sources in the principles, customs, and usages of civilized nations. We know of no authority for the proposition that the list of crimes denounced above is either all-inclusive or unchanging. By definition, the law of war must be a concept which changes with the practice of war and the customs of nations. It is neither formalized nor static . . . It is therefore no obstacle to finding a particular offence to be a violation of the law of war that it has not yet been precisely labelled as such. On the other hand, of course, we are not free to add offences at will. In deciding whether an offence comes within the common law of war, we must consider the international attitude towards that offence. The power to define such offences is derived from Articles of War 12 and 15 . . . and it is no objection that Congress has not codified that branch of international law or defined the acts which that law condemns . . . The accused was convicted, in substance, of homicide through negligent operation of a motor vehicle. By the court's findings, there is indicated an intent to find the accused guilty of a crime of a lesser degree than involuntary manslaughter. The question before us is whether the common law of war includes such an offence. We note first that all the crimes which, historically, have been treated as violations of the law of war include an element of *animus criminalis*. Negligent homicide or vehicular homicide, as the term is commonly used, does not include such an element. This is, however, not necessarily determinative. We shall assume that a crime may become a violation of the law of war if universally recognized as an offence even though it contains no element of specific criminal intent. A careful perusal of the penal codes of most civilized nations leads us to the conclusion that homicide involving less than culpable negligence is not universally recognized as an offence. Even in those American jurisdictions—still relatively few in number—which have given statutory recognition to either negligent homicide or vehicular homicide, the degree of negligence required is often held to be "culpable" or "gross"—the same as that required for involuntary manslaughter. Imposing criminal liability for less than culpable negligence is a relatively new concept in criminal law and has not, as yet, been given universal acceptance by civilized nations' (at 114–16).

3.4 THE OBJECTIVE ELEMENTS OF THE CRIME

3.4.1 GENERAL

In order to identify the main legal features of the prohibited conduct, it is necessary to consider in each case the content of the substantive rule that has been allegedly breached. This should not be surprising. No authoritative and legally binding list of war crimes exists in customary law. (An enumeration can only be found in the Statute of the ICC, under Article 8, which is not, however, intended to codify customary law.) It should also be noted, more generally, that the principle *nullum crimen sine lege* (traditionally cherished in national legal systems, particularly those of civil law countries) is upheld in international criminal law only in a limited way (see *infra*, 7.3 and 7.4.1). Hence in each case the objective element of the crime can only be inferred from the substantive rule of international humanitarian law allegedly violated. For a subcategory of war crimes, namely those acts that are provided for in terms and defined by the 1949 Geneva Conventions and Additional Protocol I of 1977 as 'grave breaches', a further requirement is provided for: such acts must be committed within the context of an international armed conflict. (However, as the ICTY Appeals Chamber held in *Tadić* (*Interlocutory Appeal*), a customary rule is *in statu nascendi*, that is in the process of forming, whereby 'grave breaches' can also be perpetrated in internal armed conflicts; according to Judge Abi-Saab's Separate Opinion delivered in that case, such a rule has already evolved.)

3.4.2 CLASSES OF WAR CRIMES

War crimes can be classified under different headings. The following classification is based on some objective criteria, and may prove useful, although of course it only serves descriptive purposes: (i) war crimes committed in *international* armed conflicts (that is, between two or more States, or between a State and a national liberation movement, pursuant to Article 1(4) of the First Additional Protocol of 1977), and (ii) war crimes perpetrated in *internal* armed conflicts (that is, large-scale armed hostilities, other than internal disturbances and tensions, or riots or isolated or sporadic acts of armed violence, between State authorities and rebels, or between two or more organized armed groups within a State). Traditionally States and courts have held that war crimes may only be committed during wars proper. Violations of international law committed in the course of internal armed conflicts were not criminalized. Thus, a glaring and preposterous disparity existed. As stated above, in 1995, a seminal judgment of the ICTY Appeals Chamber in *Tadić* (*Interlocutory Appeal*) (§§97–137) signalled a significant advance: the Appeals Chamber held that war crimes could be committed not only in international armed conflicts but also in internal armed conflicts. Since then the view has been generally upheld and the ICC Statute definitively consecrates it in Article 8(2)(c)–(f).

Both classes include the following:

1. Crimes committed *against persons not taking part, or no longer taking part, in armed hostilities.* In practice by far the most numerous crimes are committed against civilians,[9] or armed resistance movements in occupied territory,[10] and include sexual violence against women.[11] In particular, they are perpetrated against persons detained in internment or concentration camps.[12] They are also committed against prisoners of war.[13]

In the case of international armed conflicts, these crimes are termed 'grave breaches' against one of the 'protected persons' (wounded, shipwrecked persons, prisoners of war, civilians on the territory of the Detaining Power or subject to the belligerent occupation of an Occupying Power) or 'protected objects' provided for in the 1949 Geneva Conventions as well as the First Additional Protocol. These Conventions stipulate that 'grave breaches' of the same Conventions are also subject to 'universal jurisdiction'. Grave breaches are defined in the following provisions: Articles 50, 51, 130, and 147 of the First, Second, Third, and Fourth Geneva Conventions, respectively, as well as in Article 85 of the First Additional Protocol. They include wilful killing, torture or inhuman treatment, including biological experiments, wilfully causing great suffering or serious injury to body or health, extensive

9 See for instance *von Falkenhausen and others* (at 867–93), *Bellmer* (at 541–4), *Lages* (at 2–3), *Wagener and others* (at 148), *Sch. O.* (at 305–7), *Sergeant W.* (decision of 18 May 1966, at 1–3; decision of 14 July 1966, at 2). For fairly recent cases see for instance *Major Malinky Shmuel and others* (at 10–137), *Calley* (at 1164–84), *Tzofan and others* (*Yehuda Meir* case) at 724–46, *Sablić and others* (at 37–135).

10 See for instance the *SIPO Brussels* case (at 11518–26), *Allers and others* (at 225–47).

11 In this respect it is worth mentioning two cases brought after the Second World War before the Dutch Temporary Court Martial in Batavia (Indonesia). The first is *Washio Awochi.* The accused, a Japanese civilian who managed a club for Japanese civilians in Indonesia, had procured or arranged the procurement of girls and women for the club's visitors, forcing them into prostitution; they were not free to leave the part of the club where they had been confined. The Court held that the defendant was guilty of the war crime of 'forcing into prostitution' and sentenced him to 10 years' imprisonment (at 1–15). In *Takeuchi Hiroe* the accused, a Japanese national, had used violence or threats of violence against a young Indonesian woman, and had forced her to have sexual intercourse with him. The Court found him guilty of the war crime of rape and sentenced him to five years' imprisonment (at 1–5).

See also some cases of rape brought before the ICTY: *Furundžija* (§§165–89) and *Kunarac and others* (§§436–64 and 630–87, 717–45, 785–98, 806–22).

12 Among the numerous cases on this matter one may recall various ones concerning the ill-treatment of persons detained in the concentration camps instituted in Poland, such as Auschwitz (see *Mulka and others*), in Germany, at Dachau (see *Martin Gottfried and others*), by the German occupying troops in Majdanek (see *Götzfrid*, at 2–70), in camps in Belgium (see for instance *Köpperlmann* as well as *K.W.* (at 565–7) and *K.* (at 653–5), in Amersfoort (Netherlands) (see for instance *Kotälla*), or in Bolzano (Italy) (see for instance, *Mittermair*, at 2–5, *Mitterstieler*, at 2–7, *Lanz*, at 2–4, *Cologna*, at 2–9, *Koppelstätter and others*, at 3–7) or in the Italian camp of Fossoli (see *Gutweniger*, at 2–4), or in internment camps in the former Yugoslavia (see for instance *Sarić*, 2–6). Such crimes may even be perpetrated by internees against other internees (see for instance *Ternek*, at 3–11, and *Enigster*, at 5–26).

13 See for instance some cases brought after the First World War before the Leipzig Supreme Court: *Heynen* (at 2543–7), *Müller* (at 2549–52) and *Neumann* (at 2553–6). See also other cases, relating to the Second World War: *Mälzer* (at 53–5), *Feurstein and others* (at 1–26), *Krauch and others* (at 668–80), *Weiss and Mundo* (at 149), *Gozawa Sadaichi and others* (at 195–228), *General Seeger and others* (*Vosges* case), at 17–22; *St. Die* case, at 58–61; *La Grande Fosse* case, at 23–7; *Essen lynching* case, at 88–92.

destruction and appropriation of property, not justified by military necessity and carried out unlawfully and wantonly.

In the case of internal armed conflict,[14] the same violations are prohibited and may amount to a war crime if they are serious, but may not be termed 'grave breaches'. In this connection reference should be made to Article 3 common to the four 1949 Geneva Conventions, Additional Protocol II (especially Article 4 thereof),[15] as well as Article 4 of the ICTR Statute.[16]

2. Crimes against enemy combatants or civilians, committed by resorting to *prohibited methods of warfare.*

Examples include intentionally directing attacks against the civilian population in the combat area or individual civilians in the combat area not taking part in hostilities; committing acts or threats of violence the primary purpose of which is to spread terror among the civilian population; intentionally launching an indiscriminate attack affecting the civilian population or civilian objects in the knowledge that such attack will cause excessive loss of life, injury to civilians, or damage to civilian objects; intentionally making non-defended localities or demilitarized zones the object of attack; intentionally making a person the object of attack in the knowledge that he is *hors de combat*; intentionally attacking medical buildings, material, medical units and transport, and personnel; intentionally using starvation of civilians, as a method of warfare by depriving civilians of objects indispensable to their survival, including wilfully impeding relief supplies; intentionally launching an attack in the knowledge that such attack will cause widespread, long-term, and severe damage to the natural environment; utilizing the presence of civilians or other protected persons with a view to rendering certain points, areas, or military forces immune from military operations; declaring that no quarter will be given, that is, that enemy combatants will be killed and not taken prisoner.

3. Crimes against enemy combatants and civilians, involving the use of *prohibited means of warfare.*

Examples include employing weapons, projectiles, and materials which are of a nature to cause superfluous injury or unnecessary suffering; employing poison or poisoned weapons, or asphyxiating, poisonous, or other gases, and all analogous liquids, materials, or devices; using chemical or bacteriological weapons; employing expanding bullets, or weapons the primary effect of which is to injure by fragments not detectable by X-rays, or blinding laser weapons (according to the definition of the

[14] For a case where a court has endeavoured to define the notion of 'internal armed conflict' see *Ministère public and Centre pour l'égalité des chances et la lutte contre le racism* v. *C. and B.* (at 5–7). Other cases where courts had to pronounce on whether or not the conflict was internal, include: *Osvaldo Romo Mena* (decision of the Supreme Court of Chile of 26 October 1995, at 3, and decision of 9 September 1998, at 2–5), *Chilean state of emergency* case (at 1–3), *G.* (Swiss Military Tribunal, at 7).

[15] For a case where a court has held that Additional Protocol II was applicable, see *Applicability of the Second Additional Protocol to the Conflict in Chechnya*, (*Chechnya* case) (at 2–3). See also *Constitutional Conformity of Protocol II* (§25).

[16] For a case of war crimes in civil war, see *Nwaoga* (at 494–5).

1995 Protocol IV to the Convention on Prohibitions or Restrictions on the Use of Certain Conventional Weapons Which May be Deemed to be Excessively Injurious or to Have Indiscriminate Effects, adopted at Geneva on 10 October 1980, the latter are 'laser weapons specifically designed, as their sole combat function or as one of their combat functions, to cause permanent blindness to un-enhanced vision, that is to the naked eye or to the eye with corrective eyesight devices'); employing booby-traps or land mines indiscriminately, that is, in such a way as to hit both combatants and civilians alike, or anti-personnel mines which are not detectable; employing napalm and other incendiary weapons in a manner prohibited by the 1980 Protocol III to the aforementioned Convention (for instance, by making a military objective 'located within a concentration of civilians the object of attack by air-delivered incendiary weapons').

4. Crimes *against specially protected persons and objects* (such as medical personnel units or transport, personnel participating in relief actions, humanitarian organizations such as the Red Cross, or Red Crescent, or Red Lion and Sun units, UN personnel belonging to peace-keeping missions, etc.).

5. Crimes consisting of *improperly using protected signs and emblems* (such as a flag of truce; the distinctive emblems of the Red Cross, or Red Crescent, or Red Lion and Sun; perfidious use of a national flag or of military uniform and insignia, etc.).

3.5 THE SUBJECTIVE ELEMENT OF THE CRIME

The subjective—or mental—element (*mens rea*) of the crime is sometimes specified by the international rule prohibiting a certain conduct.

Thus, for instance, Article 130 of the Third Geneva Convention of 1949 (on prisoners of war) enumerates among the 'grave breaches' of the Convention the 'wilful killing [of prisoners of war], torture or inhuman treatment, including biological experiments' as well as 'wilfully causing great suffering or serious injury to body or health' of a prisoners of war, or 'wilfully depriving a prisoner of war of the rights of fair and regular trial prescribed in [the] Convention'. The word 'wilful' obviously denotes *criminal intent*, namely the intention to bring about the consequences of the act prohibited by the international rule (for instance, in the case of 'wilful killing' proof must be produced of the intention to cause the death of the victim; in the case of 'wilfully causing great suffering' it must be proved that the perpetrator had the intention to cause great suffering, etc.). The same holds true for other similar provisions, such as Article 147 of the Fourth Geneva Convention (on civilians) as well as provisions of other treaties, such as Article 15 of the 1999 Second Hague Protocol for the Protection of Cultural Property in the Event of Armed Conflict. (This provision, in enumerating the serious violations of the Protocol entailing individual criminal liability, makes such liability contingent upon the fact that the author of the 'offence' has perpetrated it 'intentionally'.)

One can also mention Article 85(3) of the First Additional Protocol of 1977. This provision subordinates the criminalization of such acts as attacking civilians or undefended localities, or demilitarized zones, or perfidiously using the distinctive emblem of the Red Cross, Red Crescent or Red Lion and Sun, to three conditions: (i) the acts must be committed 'wilfully'; (ii) they must be carried out in violation of the relevant provisions of the Protocol; and (iii) they must cause death or serious injury to body or health. Thus, the provisions clearly require intent or at least *recklessness* (so-called *dolus eventualis*), which exists whenever somebody, although aware of the likely pernicious consequences of his conduct, knowingly takes the risk of bringing about such consequences (see *infra*, 8.3). For other acts, the same provision also requires '*knowledge*' as a condition of criminal liability. This, for instance, applies to 'launching an indiscriminate attack affecting the civilian population or civilian objects in the knowledge that such attack will cause excessive loss of life, injury to civilians or damage to civilian objects' (Article 85(3)(b)); or to 'launching an attack against works or installations containing dangerous forces in the knowledge that such attack will cause excessive loss of life, injury to civilians or damage to civilian objects' (Article 85(3)(c)). As we shall see (*infra*, 8.2.1), in criminal law 'knowledge' normally is part of 'intent' (*dolus*) and refers to awareness of the circumstances forming part of the definition of the crime. However, in the context of the provision at issue, 'knowledge' must be interpreted to mean 'predictability of the likely consequences of the action' (recklessness or *dolus eventualis*). Therefore, for an act such as that just mentioned to be regarded as a war crime, evidence must be produced not only of the intention to launch an attack, for instance an attack on a military objective normally used by civilians (e.g. a bridge, a road, etc.), but also of the foreseeability that the attack is likely to cause excessive loss of life or injury to civilians or civilian objects. In other instances, international rules require knowledge in the sense of awareness of a circumstance of fact, as part of criminal intent (*dolus*). Thus, Article 85(3)(e) of the same Protocol makes it a crime to wilfully attack a person 'in the knowledge that he is *hors de combat*'.

When international rules do not provide, even implicitly, for a subjective element, it would seem appropriate to hold that what is required is the intent or, depending upon the circumstances, recklessness as prescribed in most legal systems of the world for the underlying offence (murder, rape, torture, destruction of private property, pillage, etc.).

Generally speaking, it appears admissible to contend that, for at least some limited categories of war crimes, gross or *culpable negligence* (*culpa gravis*) may be sufficient, that is, the author of the crime, although aware of the risk involved in his conduct, is nevertheless convinced that the prohibited consequence will not occur (whereas in the case of 'recklessness' or *dolus eventualis* the author knowingly takes the risk); see *infra*, 8.4. Indeed, the consequent broadening of the range of acts amenable to international prosecution is in keeping with the general object and purpose of international humanitarian law. This modality of *mens rea* may for instance apply to cases of command responsibility (see *infra*, 10.4), where the commander should have known that war crimes were being committed by his subordinates. Also, it could be contended that it may apply to such cases as wanton destruction of private property; in contrast, it may seem difficult to consider culpable negligence a sufficient subjective element of the crime in cases involving the taking of human life.

3.6 THE DEFINITION OF WAR CRIMES IN THE STATUTE OF THE ICC

Generally speaking, the Rome Statute appears to be praiseworthy in many respects as far as substantive criminal law is concerned. Many crimes have been defined with the required degree of specificity, and the general principles of criminal liability have been set out in detail.

As far as war crimes more specifically are concerned, it is no doubt commendable that they have been regulated in such a detailed manner. Furthermore, the notion of war crimes has rightly been extended to offences committed in time of internal armed conflict. However, in some areas the relevant provision of the Rome Statute, Article 8, marks a retrograde step with respect to existing international law.

First of all, there is a perplexing phrase, 'within the established framework of international law', that appears in Article 8(2)(b) and (e), dealing with crimes likely to be perpetrated while in combat (that is, crimes involving the wrongful use of means or methods of combat), respectively in international armed conflicts and in non-international armed conflicts. These two provisions are worded as follows:

> [For the purpose of this Statute 'war crimes' means] Other serious violations of the laws and customs applicable in international armed conflict [in armed conflicts not of an international character: litt (e)], *within the established framework of international law*, namely, any of the following acts.

As in the other provisions of Article 8 no mention is made of 'the established framework of international law'. One could argue that there is only one possible explanation of this odd phrase: the offences listed in the two aforementioned provisions are to be considered as war crimes for the purpose of the Statute only if they are regarded as such by customary international law. In other words, whilst for the other classes of war crimes the Statute confines itself to setting out the content of the prohibited conduct, and the relevant provision can thus be directly and immediately applied by the Court, in the case of the two provisions under consideration things are different. The Court may consider that the conduct envisaged in these provisions amounts to a war crime only if and to the extent that general international law already regards the offence as a war crime. It would follow, for example, that 'declaring that no quarter will be given' (Article 8(2)(b)(xii)) will no doubt be taken to amount to a war crime, because indisputably denial of quarter is prohibited by customary international law and, if effected, amounts to a war crime. By contrast offences such as 'The transfer, directly or indirectly, by the Occupying Power of parts of its own civilian population into the territory it occupies, or the deportation or transfer of all or parts of the population of the occupied territory within or outside this territory' (Article 8(2)(b)(viii)) cannot *ipso facto* be regarded as war crimes. The Court will first have to establish whether: (i) under general international law they are considered as breaches of the international humanitarian law of armed conflict and, in addition, (ii) whether under customary international law their commission amounts to a war crime.

If the above explanation were to be regarded as sound, it would follow that for two broad categories of war crimes the Statute does not set out a self-contained legal regime, but presupposes a mandatory examination, by the Court, on a case by case basis, of the current status of general international law. This method, while commendable in some respects, may however entail that the Statute's provisions eventually constitute only a tentative and interim regulation of the matter, for the final say rests with the Court's determination. Whether or not such a regulation is considered satisfactory, in any event it seems indisputable that it has been designed to leave greater freedom to sovereign States or, to put it differently, to make the net of international prohibitions less tight and stringent.

Secondly, the legal regulation of means of warfare seems to be narrower than that laid down in customary international law.

The use in international armed conflict of modern weapons which are contrary to the two basic principles prohibiting those weapons which (a) cause superfluous injury or unnecessary suffering, or (b) are inherently indiscriminate, is not banned per se and therefore does not amount to a crime under the ICC Statute. The ban will only take effect, and its possible breach amount to a crime, if an amendment to this end is made to the Statute pursuant to Articles 121 and 123. In practice, as it is extremely unlikely that such amendment will ever be agreed upon, those weapons may eventually be regarded as lawful. Thus, in the event the two principles are deprived of their overarching legal value. This seems all the more questionable because even bacteriological weapons, which undoubtedly are already prohibited by general international law, might be used without entailing the commission of a crime falling under the jurisdiction of the Court. (It would seem that the use of this category of weapons is not covered by the ban on 'asphyxiating, poisonous or other gases and all analogous liquids, materials or devices', contained in Article 8(2)(b)(xviii) and clearly relating to chemical weapons only.)

A similar criticism may be made of the sub-article on damage to the environment, 'Intentionally launching an attack in the knowledge that such attack will cause . . . widespread, long-term and severe damage to the natural environment which would be clearly excessive in relation to the concrete and direct overall military advantage anticipated' (Article 8(2)(b)(iv)). Article 55(1) of Additional Protocol I—to which any article on environmental war crimes must accord 'precedential' value—provides:

> Care shall be taken in warfare to protect the natural environment against widespread, long-term and severe damage. This protection includes a prohibition on the use of methods or means of warfare which are intended or may be expected to cause such damage to the natural environment and thereby to prejudice the health or survival of the population.

Article 55 makes no mention of the 'excessive' or disproportionate character of the attack nor of 'anticipated military advantage' (let alone of the 'direct overall military advantage anticipated', a phrase that gives belligerents a very great latitude and renders judicial scrutiny almost impossible). Moreover, in paragraph 2 it prohibits reprisals by way of attack against the natural environment. Article 8 of the ICC Statute therefore takes a huge leap backwards by allowing the defence that 'widespread, long-term and severe damage to the natural environment' caused by the perpetrator—not just damage, but widespread, long-term and severe damage, intentionally caused—was not 'clearly excessive' (perhaps it was excessive, but not 'clearly excessive') in relation to the concrete and direct overall military advantage anticipated. This seems indefensible.

Thirdly, one may entertain some misgivings concerning the distinction, upheld in Article 8, between the regulation of *international* armed conflict, on the one side, and *internal* conflicts on the other. Insofar as Article 8 separates the law applicable to the former category of armed conflict from that applicable to the latter category, it is somewhat retrograde, as the current trend has been to abolish the distinction and to have simply one corpus of law applicable to all conflicts. It can be confusing—and unjust—to have one law for international armed conflict and another for internal armed conflict.

More specific flaws may be discerned. For instance, while for crimes in internal armed conflicts perpetrated against adversaries *hors de combat* (combatants who have laid down their weapons, the wounded, the sick, civilians) the relevant provision (Article 8(2)(c)) refers to a low threshold of armed conflict ('an armed conflict not of an international character', excluding 'situations of internal disturbances and tensions, such as riots, isolated and sporadic acts of violence or other acts of a similar nature'), as for the threshold required by the provision for crimes committed in combat, it is provided (in Article 8(2)(f)), that the relevant provisions apply 'to armed conflicts that take place in the territory of a State when there is *protracted* armed conflict between governmental authorities and organized groups or between such groups' (emphasis added). It follows that for a crime belonging to the second class to be perpetrated, an added requirement is envisaged, namely that the internal armed clash be 'protracted'. It would seem that the main reason for this distinction is that in the first class, there already existed a set of provisions laid down in Article 3 common to the four Geneva Conventions and that furthermore these provisions are held to have turned into customary international law. In contrast, no previous treaty or customary rule existed regulating method of combat in internal armed conflict. While making progress in this area, the majority of States gathered at the Rome Conference have preferred, so the explanation goes, to tread gingerly so as to take due account of States' concerns. Assuming that this explanation is correct, nonetheless the fact remains that a dichotomy has been created, which appears contrary to the fundamental object and purpose of international humanitarian law.

Furthermore, the prohibited use of weapons in internal armed conflicts is not regarded as a war crime. This regulation does not reflect the current status of general international law. As the Appeals Chamber of the ICTY stressed in *Tadić* (*Interlocutory Appeal*), in modern warfare it no longer makes sense to distinguish between international and internal armed conflicts:

> Why protect civilians from belligerent violence, or ban rape, torture or the wanton destruction of hospitals, churches, museums or private property, as well as *proscribe weapons causing unnecessary suffering* when two sovereign States are engaged in war, and yet refrain from enacting the same bans or providing the same protection when armed violence has erupted 'only' within the territory of a sovereign State? (§97, emphasis added.)

The Appeals Chamber rightly answered this question by finding that the prohibition of weapons causing unnecessary suffering, as well as the specific ban on chemical weapons, also applies to internal armed conflicts (§§119–24).

The above restrictions on modern regulation of armed conflict are compounded by two more factors: (i) allowance has been made for superior orders to relieve subordinates of their responsibility for the execution of orders involving the commission of war crimes; (ii) Article 124 allows States to declare, upon becoming parties to the Statute, that the Court's jurisdiction over war crimes committed by their nationals or on their territory shall not become operative for a period of seven years.[17]

One is therefore left with the impression that the framers have been eager to shield their servicemen as much as possible from being brought to trial for, and possibly convicted of, war crimes.

In sum, a tentative appraisal of the provisions on war crimes of the Rome Statute cannot but be chequered: in many respects the Statute marks a great advance in international criminal law, in others it proves instead faulty; in particular, it is marred by being too obsequious to State sovereignty.

SELECT BIBLIOGRAPHY

H. Lauterpacht, 'The Law of Nations and the Punishment of War Crimes' 21 BYIL (1944) 58–95; T. Taylor, *Nuremberg and Vietnam: an American Tragedy* (Chicago: Quadrangle Books, 1970); M. Bothe, K. J. Partsch, and W. A. Solf, *New Rules for Victims of Armed Conflicts. Commentary on the Two Protocols Additional to the Geneva Conventions of 1949* (The Hague, Boston, London: Martinus Nijhoff, 1982); D. Plattner, 'The Penal Repression of Violations of International Humanitarian Law Applicable in Non-International Armed Conflict', 278 IRRC (1990) 409 ff.; H. McCoubrey, 'War Crimes: The Criminal Jurisprudence of Armed Conflict', 31 RDMDG 1992, 167–87; T.

[17] One should also note an odd provision, which applies to all the crimes envisaged in the Rome Statute. While children may be conscripted or enlisted as from the age of 15 (Article 8(2)(b)(xxvi), and (e)(vii)), the Court has no jurisdiction over persons under the age of 18 at the commission of the crime (Art. 26). Thus a person between 15 and 17 is regarded as a lawful combatant and may commit a crime without being brought to court and punished. A commander could therefore recruit minors into his army expressly for the purpose of forming terrorist units whose members would be immune from prosecution. Moreover, in modern warfare, particularly in developing countries, young persons are more and more involved in armed hostilities and thus increasingly in a position to commit war crimes and crimes against humanity.

Meron, 'International Criminalization of Internal Atrocities', in AJIL 89 (1995), 554–7; Y. Dinstein and M. Tabory (eds), *War Crimes in International Law* (The Hague, Boston, London: Nijhoff, 1996); T. L. H. McCormack and G. J. Simpson (eds), *The Law of War Crimes* (The Hague, London, Boston: Kluwer, 1997); T. Meron, 'War Crimes Law Comes of Age', 92 AJIL (1998), 462–8; K. D. Askin, 'Crimes within the Jurisdiction of the International Criminal Court', in 10 *CLForum* (1999), 50–7; W. J. Fenrick, 'Should Crimes against Humanity Replace War Crimes?', 37 *Columbia Journal of Transnational Law* (1999), 767 ff.; D. Robinson and H. von Hebel, 'War Crimes in Internal Conflicts: Article 8 of the ICC Statute', 2 YIHL (1999), 193 ff.; G. Abi-Saab and R. Abi-Saab, 'Les crimes de guerre', in Ascensio, Decaux, and Pellet, *Droit international pénal* 265–85; H. Fischer, 'The Jurisdiction of the International Criminal Court for War Crimes: Some Observations Concerning Differences between the Statute of the Court and War Crimes Provisions in Other Treaties', in *Festschrift für K. Ipsen* (Munich: Beck, 2000), 77–101; idem, 'Grave Breaches of the 1949 Geneva Conventions', in Kirk McDonald and Swaak-Goldman (eds), *Substantive and Procedural Aspects*, 67–93; G. Aldrich, 'Violations of the Laws and Customs of War', ibid., 99–111; H. Fujita, 'Application of International Humanitarian Law to Internal Armed Conflict', in T. L. H. McCormack *et al.* (eds), *A Century of War and Peace* (The Hague, London, Boston: Kluwer, 2001), 139–54; K. Kittichaisaree, *International Criminal Law* (Oxford University Press, 2001), 129–205; C. Kress, 'War Crimes Committed in Non-International Armed Conflicts and the Emerging System of International Criminal Justice', 30 IYHR (2001), 103 ff. M. Bennouna, 'The Characterization of the Armed Conflict in the Practice of the ICTY', in R. May *et al.*, *Essays on ICTY Procedure and Evidence* (The Hague, Boston: Kluwer, 2001), 55–64; P. Gaeta, 'War Crimes Trials before Italian Criminal Courts: New Trends', in Fischer, Kress, and Lüder (eds), *International and National Prosecution*, 751–68; M. Bothe, 'War Crimes', in Cassese, Gaeta, and Jones, *ICC Commentary*, 379–426.

4

CRIMES AGAINST HUMANITY

4.1 THE NOTION

Under general international law the category of crimes against humanity is sweeping but sufficiently well defined. It covers actions that share a set of common features:

1. They are *particularly odious offences* in that they constitute a serious attack on human dignity or a grave humiliation or degradation of one or more human beings.

2. They *are not isolated or sporadic events*, but are part either of a governmental policy, or of a *widespread* or *systematic* practice of atrocities tolerated, condoned, or acquiesced in by a government or a de facto authority. Clearly, it is required that a single crime be an instance of a repetition of similar crimes or be part of a string of such crimes (widespread practice), or that it be the manifestation of a policy or a plan drawn up, or inspired by, State authorities or by the leading officials of a de facto state-like organization, or of an organized political group (systematic practice).

3. They are prohibited and may consequently be punished *regardless of whether they are perpetrated in time of war or peace.* While in 1945 a link or nexus with an armed conflict was required, at present customary law no longer attaches any importance to such requirement.

4. The victims of the crime may be *civilians* or, in the case of crimes committed during armed conflict, persons who do not take part (or no longer take part) in armed hostilities, as well as, under *customary* international law (but not under the Statute of the ICTY, ICTR, and the ICC), *enemy combatants.*

Before embarking upon a detailed exposition of the history of the notion and the various classes of crimes, it may be fitting to note that to a large extent many concepts underlying this category of crimes derive from, or overlap with, those of human rights law (the rights to life, not to be tortured, to liberty and security of the person, etc.), laid down in provisions of international human rights instruments (e.g. the Universal Declaration of Human Rights, the European Convention on Human Rights, the UN Covenant on Civil and Political Rights). Indeed, while international criminal law concerning war crimes largely derives from, or is closely linked with, international humanitarian law, international criminal law concerning crimes against humanity is to a great extent predicated upon international human rights law. International humanitarian law (which traditionally regulates warfare between States), and international human rights law (which regulates what States may do to their own citizens and, more generally, to individuals under their control), are in essence two distinct bodies of law, each arising from separate concerns and considerations. The former is rooted in notions of *reciprocity*—one need not be a great humanist to be in favour of laws of war for international conflicts, as it is simple self-interest for a State to ensure that its soldiers are treated well in exchange for treating enemy soldiers well and that its civilians are spared the horrors of war. The latter is more geared to *community concerns*, as it intends to protect human beings per se regardless of their national or other allegiance. From this perspective, laws governing internal conflict are more akin to crimes against humanity than to war crimes, as the protections in, for example, common Article 3 stem from human rights concerns for the individual rather than self-interested concerns of States to have reciprocal laws governing warfare. (The question of reciprocity does not arise in an internal conflict.)

Let us now return to the *systematic nature* of the crimes. That this feature is a necessary ingredient of the objective element of the crimes may be inferred from the first provisions setting out a list of crimes against humanity. They clearly if implicitly required that the offence, to constitute an attack on humanity, be of extreme gravity and not be limited to a sporadic event but be part of a pattern of misconduct. Subsequent case law has consistently borne out that this is a major feature of the crimes.

In 1949, in *Albrecht*, the Dutch Special Court of Cassation delivered one of the first decisions on crimes against humanity, after the Nuremberg Judgment of the International Military Tribunal. The defendant, a German *Sturmscharführer* (commander of a storm company) of the *Waffen SS* (*Schütz Staffeln*) (German State Security Police), had been accused of killing a Dutch national and ill-treating five others. The Court was called upon to decide if the offences perpetrated by Albrecht were to be regarded as war crimes or as crimes against humanity. It opted for the first category, adding that they could not be also classified as crimes against humanity. Addressing this last class of crimes the Court stated that:

> [C]rimes of this category are characterised either by their seriousness and their savagery (*barbaarsheid*), or by their magnitude, or by the circumstance that they were part of a system designed to spread terror (*een systeem van terreurhandelingen*), or that they were a link in a deliberately pursued policy against certain groups of the population. (At 750.)

A judgment of the Dutch Court of Cassation in 1981 substantially supported this view (see *Menten* at 362–3). The link or connection with a systematic policy of a government or a de facto authority was emphasised by the German Supreme Court in the British zone of occupation, in the numerous and significant decisions on crimes against humanity it delivered in the years 1948–52. By way of illustration, one may mention *J. and R.* In 1950 the Court of Assizes of Hamburg summed up the case law in *Veit Harlan.*[1]

However, when the atrocities are part of a government policy, the perpetrators need not identify themselves with this policy, as the District Court of Tel Aviv held in 1951 in *Enigster* (a case concerning a Jew imprisoned in a Nazi concentration camp, who persecuted his fellow Jewish inmates). The District Court of Tel Aviv rightly stated that:

> a person who was himself persecuted and confined in the same camps as his victims can, from the legal point of view, be guilty of a crime against humanity if he performs inhumane acts against his fellow prisoners. In contrast to a war criminal, the perpetrator of a crime against humanity does not have to be a man who identified himself with the persecuting regime or its evil intention. (At 542.)

In sum, murder, extermination, torture, rape, political, racial, or religious persecution and other inhumane acts reach the threshold of crimes against humanity only if they are part of a practice. Isolated inhumane acts of this nature may constitute grave infringements of human rights or, depending on the circumstances, war crimes, but fall short of meriting the stigma attaching to crimes against humanity. On the other hand, an individual may be guilty of crimes against humanity even if he perpetrates one or two of the offences mentioned above, or engages in one such offence against only a few civilians, provided those offences are part of a consistent pattern of misbehaviour by a number of persons linked to that offender (for example, because they engage in armed action on the same side, or because they are parties to a common plan, or for any other similar reason).

[1] In *J. and R.*, a trial court had sentenced for crimes against humanity a German who had denounced to the police two other Germans for listening to a foreign radio, which amounted under German law to national treason; as a consequence the two persons had been arrested and sentenced to imprisonment; they had died as a result of harsh prison conditions. The Supreme Court overruled the acquittal pronounced by the trial court and the Appeals Court. It pointed out, among other things, that the aggressive behaviour of the agent and the inhuman injury to the victim had to be objectively connected with the Nazi system of violence and tyranny. 'This connection does not need . . . to lie in support for the tyranny, but may, for example, also consist of the use of the system of violence and tyranny. [Furthermore], the agent need not act systematically; it is sufficient that his single action be connected with the system and thereby lose the character of an isolated occurrence.' The Court went on to explain that the denunciation by the accused was closely linked with the arbitrary and violent Nazi system, that there existed no freedom, and the State suppressed any deviant behaviour by violence and harsh punishment. The denunciation at issue had been intended to achieve the handing over of two persons to an arbitrary police system based on terror: hence 'he who caused such a consequence through his denunciation, objectively committed a crime against humanity' (at 167–71).

Veit Harlan dealt with a charge of complicity in a crime against humanity. (The accused, a film director, had contributed to the persecution of Jews by his film *Jud Süss*, produced in 1940.) The Court of Assizes, basing itself on numerous judicial precedents on the matter, gave the following definition of crimes against humanity: 'One must regard as a crime against humanity any conscious and willed attack that, in connection with the Nazi system of violence and arbitrariness, harmfully interferes with the life and existence of a person or his relationships with his social sphere, or interferes with his assets and values, thereby offending against his human dignity as well as humanity as such (*die Menschheit als solche*)' (at 52).

4.2 THE ORIGIN OF THE NOTION

The notion of crimes against humanity was propounded for the first time in 1915, on the occasion of mass killings of Armenians in the Ottoman Empire. On 28 May 1915 the French, British, and Russian Governments decided to react strongly. They therefore jointly issued a declaration stating that

In view of these new *crimes* of Turkey *against humanity and civilisation*, the Allied governments announce publicly to the *Sublime Porte* that they will hold personally responsible [for] these crimes all members of the Ottoman Government and those of their agents who are implicated in such massacres.[2]

It is relevant that the expression 'crimes against humanity' was not in the original proposal emanating from the Russian Foreign Minister, Sazonov. He had suggested instead a protest against 'crimes against Christianity and civilisation'. However, the French Foreign Minister Delcassé took issue with the reference to crimes against Christianity. He feared that the Muslim populations under French and British colonial domination might take umbrage at that expression, because it excluded them; consequently, they might feel discriminated against. Hence, he proposed, instead of 'crimes against Christianity', 'crimes against humanity'. This proposal was accepted by the Russian and British Foreign Ministers, and passed into the joint Declaration.[3] It would seem that the three States were neither aware of, nor interested in, the general philosophical implications of the phrase they had used. Indeed, they did not ask themselves, nor did they try to establish in practice, whether by 'humanity' they meant 'all human beings' or rather 'the feelings of humanity shared by men and women of modern nations' or even 'the concept of humanity propounded by ancient and modern philosophy'. It is probable that they were only intent on solving a

[2] Emphasis added. For the full text of the note, see the dispatch of the US Ambassador in France, Sharp, to the US Secretary of State, Bryan, of 28 May 1915, in *Papers Relating to the Foreign Relations of the United States, 1915, Supplement* (Washington: US Government Printing Office, 1928), at 981.

[3] See the Russian despatch of 11 May 1915, published in A. Beylerian, *Les Grandes Puissances, l'Empire Ottoman et les Arméniens dans les archives françaises (1914–1918)—Recueil de documents* (Paris, 1983), p. 23 (doc. no. 29). The Russian draft referred to 'crimes against Christianity and civilisation' ('*crimes de la Turquie contre la chretienté et la civilisation*'). The French Foreign Minister, Delcassé, changed the expression to 'crimes against humanity' ('*crimes contre l'humanité*'), in addition to making another, minor change (ibid., p. 23, footnotes with an asterisk).

The political reasons for this change, in particular for dropping any reference to Christianity, were set out by the French Ministry in a Note of 20 May 1915 to the British Embassy (ibid., p. 26, doc. 34: 'L'intérêt qu'il y a à ménager le sentiment des populations musulmanes qui vivent sous la souveraineté de la France et de l'Angleterre fera sans doute estimer au gouvernement britannique comme au gouvernement français qu'il convient de s'abstenir de spécifier que l'intérêt des deux puissances paraît ne se porter que du côté des éléments chrétiens'). The two French suggestions were eventually accepted by Great Britain and Russia and the text of the Note was changed accordingly.

short-term political problem, as is shown by the fact that there was no practical follow-up to their joint protest.[4]

In any event, various initiatives to act diplomatically on behalf of humanity subsequently failed.[5]

Similarly, the special Commission set up after the First World War proposed in its report to the Versailles Conference that an international criminal tribunal be created and that its jurisdiction extend to 'offences against the laws of humanity'.[6] However, the 'Memorandum of Reservations' submitted by the two distinguished representatives of the United States, Robert Lansing and James Brown Scott, paralysed any action by the Conference. They emphasized that while war crimes should be punished because 'the laws and customs of war are a standard certain' (at 64), the 'laws and principles of humanity are not certain, varying with time, place and circumstance, and according, it may be, to the conscience of the individual judge. There is no fixed and universal standard of humanity' (at 73). This, the US delegates thought, 'if for no other reason, should exclude them from consideration in a court of justice, especially one charged with the administration of criminal law' (at 64). As a result of the American opposition, no provision was made for crimes against humanity.

During the Second World War, the Allies became aware that some of the most heinous acts of barbarity perpetrated by the Germans were not prohibited by traditional international law. The laws of warfare only proscribed violations involving the adversary or the enemy populations, whereas the Germans had also performed inhuman acts for political or racial reasons against their own citizens (Jews, trade union members, social democrats, communists, gypsies, members of the church) as well as other persons not covered by the laws of warfare.[7] In addition, in 1945 such

[4] On 11 August 1915, during the massacre of Armenians, the American Ambassador to Turkey, Morgenthau, had proposed to the US Secretary of State, Robert Lansing, among other things, that 'The United States Government on behalf of humanity urgently request the Turkish Government to cease at once the present campaign and to permit the survivors to return to their homes if not in the war zones, or else to receive proper treatment'. However, the Secretary of State did not adopt this suggestion, contenting himself instead merely with asking whether the protest of the German Ambassador to the Turkish Government had 'improved conditions'. See *Papers Relating to the Foreign Relations of the United States*, cit., at 986.

[5] The Peace Treaty of Sèvres of 10 August 1920 provided in Article 230 that the 'Ottoman Government' undertake to hand over to the Allies the persons requested by these Powers as responsible for the massacres perpetrated, during the war, on territories which constituted part of the Ottoman Empire; the Allies reserved the right to 'designate' the tribunal which would try those persons. However, the Treaty was never ratified, and its replacement, the Peace Treaty of Lausanne, of 24 July 1923, provided for an amnesty for crimes committed between 1914 and 1922.

[6] See 'Report presented to the preliminary Peace Conference by the Commission on the Responsibility of the Authors of the War and on the Enforcement of Penalties', in Carnegie Endowment for International Peace, Division of International Law, Pamphlet No. 32, *Violations of the Laws and Customs of War, Report of Majority and Dissenting Reports of American and Japanese Members of the Commission of Responsibilities, Conference of Paris 1919* (Oxford: Clarendon Press, 1919), pp. 25–6.

[7] For instance, citizens of the Allies (e.g. French Jews under the Vichy regime (1940–4)); nationals of States not formally under German occupation and, therefore, not protected by the international rules safeguarding the civilian population of occupied territories: this applied to Austria, annexed by Germany in 1938, and Czechoslovakia (following the Munich Treaty in 1938, the Sudeten territory was annexed by Germany, and

acts as mere persecution for political or racial purposes were not prohibited, even if perpetrated against civilians of occupied territories.

In 1945, at the strong insistence of the USA, the Allies decided that a better course of action than simply to execute all the major war criminals would be to bring them to trial. The London Agreement embodying the Charter of the IMT included a provision under which the Tribunal was to try and punish persons guilty, among other things, of 'crimes against humanity'. These were defined as:

murder, extermination, enslavement, deportation, and other inhumane acts committed against any civilian population, before or during the war, or persecutions on political, racial, or religious grounds in execution of or connexion with any crimes within the jurisdiction of the Tribunal [i.e. either 'crimes against peace' or 'war crimes'], whether or not in violation of the domestic law of the country where perpetrated.

One major shortcoming of this definition is that it closely linked crimes against humanity to the other two categories of offences. Article 6(c) indeed required, for crimes against humanity to come under the jurisdiction of the IMT, that they be perpetrated 'in execution of or in connection with' war crimes or crimes against peace. This link was not spelled out, but it was clear that it was only within the context of a war or of the unleashing of unlawful aggression that these crimes could be prosecuted and punished. As was rightly remarked by Schwelb,[8] this association meant that only those criminal activities were punished which 'directly affected the interests of other States' (either because these activities were connected with a war of aggression or a conspiracy to wage such a war, or because they were bound up with war crimes, that is crimes against enemy combatants or enemy civilians). Plainly, in 1945 the Allies did not feel that they should 'legislate' in such a way as to prohibit inhuman acts regardless of their consequences or implications for third States.

the rest of the country became the so-called Protectorate of Bohemia and Moravia, in 1939). The Germans also harassed and murdered stateless Jews and gypsies.

[8] E. Schwelb, 'Crimes Against Humanity', 23 BYIL (1946), at 207.

The concept of humanity upheld in international criminal law with particular reference to crimes against humanity, is best illustrated in a French case that is however not connected with criminal law: the *Dwarf* case. In 1991 the mayor of a small French municipality (Morsang-sur-Orge) prohibited a public show in a disco consisting of spectators 'throwing a dwarf' (*attraction de lancer de nains*). The company that employed the dwarf appealed to the Versailles Administrative Tribunal, claiming that all necessary security measures had been taken to protect the dwarf's health and that it was entirely on his own volition that he took part in the spectacle upon renumeration. The Tribunal quashed the mayor's decision and made the municipality pay compensation to the company. On appeal, in 1995 the Council of State (*Conseil d'Etat*) overturned the Tribunal's decision. It held that the dwarf could not rely upon the principles of freedom of work and freedom of trade and industry. In its view the municipal authorities were authorized to ensure public order (*ordre public*) and 'respect for the dignity of human beings is a component of public order'; the local authorities were therefore entitled to prohibit a show that infringed respect for human dignity. As the court put it, 'the show of "throwing the dwarf", that consisted in allowing spectators to throw a dwarf, led to utilize as a projectile a physically handicapped person, presented as such; . . . by its very object, such a show infringed on the dignity of human beings; . . . hence the municipal authorities vested with enforcement powers were authorized to prohibit such a show even in the absence of special local circumstances, and even if protective measures had been taken to ensure the security of that person, and the dwarf voluntarily participated in the show upon payment.' (At 1.)

Despite this limitation, the creation of the new category marked a great advance. First, it indicated that the international community was widening the category of acts considered of 'meta-national' concern. This category came to include all actions running contrary to those basic values that are, or should be, considered inherent in any human being (in the notion, humanity did not mean 'mankind' or 'human race' but 'the quality' or concept of human being). Secondly, inasmuch as crimes against humanity were made punishable even if perpetrated in accordance with domestic laws, the 1945 Charter showed that in some special circumstances there were limits to the 'omnipotence of the State' (to quote the British Chief Prosecutor, Sir Hartley Shawcross) and that 'the individual human being, the ultimate unit of all law, is not disentitled to the protection of mankind when the State tramples upon his rights in a manner which outrages the conscience of mankind'.[9]

It has been explicitly or implicitly held by a number of courts that Article 6(c) of the London Agreement simply crystallized or codified a nascent rule of general international law which prohibited crimes against humanity. It seems more correct to contend that that provision constituted *new* law. This explains both the limitations to which the new notion was subjected (and to which reference has already been made above) and the extreme caution and indeed reticence of the IMT.

The reticence and what could be viewed as the embarrassment of the IMT on the matter are striking. Six points, in particular, should be stressed. First, the IMT tackled the issue of *ex post facto* law only with regard to crimes against peace (in particular aggression) whereas it did not pronounce at all upon the no less delicate question of whether or not crimes against humanity constituted a new category of offence. Secondly, when dealing with *ex post facto* law, the IMT was rather reticent and indeed vague, as is apparent from, *inter alia*, the glaring discrepancy between the English and the French text of the judgment,[10] both authoritative. Thirdly, probably aware of the novelty of that class of crimes, the IMT tended to find that some defendants accused of various classes of crimes were guilty both of war crimes and of crimes against humanity (this was the case with 14 defendants): in other words, the Tribunal tended not to clearly identify the distinction between the two classes but preferred instead to find that in many cases the defendant was answerable for both. Fourthly, the IMT held that no evidence had been produced to the effect that crimes against humanity had been committed *before* the war, in execution of or in connection with German

[9] Sir Hartley Shawcross, in *Speeches of the Chief Prosecutors at the Close of the Case Against the Individual Defendants* (London: HM Stationery Office, Cmd. 6964, 1946), at 63.

[10] In the English text, the IMT stated that 'the maxim *nullum crimen sine lege* is not a limitation of sovereignty, *but is in general a principle of justice*' (at 219; emphasis added), while in the French text it is stated that '*Nullum crimen sine lege* ne limite pas la souveraineté des États; *elle ne formule qu'une règle généralement suivie*' (at 231; emphasis added). Furthermore, the phrase in the English text, 'On this view of the case alone, it would appear that the maxim has no application to the present facts' (at 219) does not appear in the French text.

aggression.[11] The IMT thus markedly narrowed the scope, *in casu*, of the category of crimes against humanity, although it asserted that it did so on grounds linked to the evidence produced. Fifthly, in the only two cases where the IMT found a defendant guilty exclusively of crimes against humanity (Streicher and von Schirach), the Tribunal did not specify the nature, content, and scope of the link between crimes against humanity and war crimes (in the case of Streicher) or crimes against humanity and aggression (in the case of von Schirach); rather, the Tribunal confined itself to a generic reference to the connection between the classes of crimes, without any further elaboration. Finally, it is striking that in the part of the judgment referring to Streicher, the English text is markedly different from the French. In the English text it is stated that 'Streicher's incitement to murder and extermination at the time when Jews in the East were being killed under the most horrible conditions clearly constitutes persecution on political and racial grounds in connection with War Crimes, as defined in the Charter, and constitutes a crime against humanity' (at 304). By contrast, in the French text it is stated that Streicher's persecution of Jews was itself a war crime as well as a crime against humanity.[12] Clearly, this wording reflects the position of the French Chief Prosecutor, François de Menthon,[13] as well as the reservations and misgivings of the French Judge, Donnedieu de Vabres. The latter in 1947 set forth his views in scholarly papers in which he argued that crimes against humanity simultaneously constituted war crimes and hence, the Tribunal did not breach the *nullum crimen, nulla poena sine lege* principle.[14]

It appears, therefore, that in all probability the IMT applied new law, or substantially new law, when it found some defendants guilty of crimes against humanity

[11] The tribunal stated the following: 'To constitute crimes against humanity, the acts relied on before the outbreak of war must have been in execution of, or in connection with, any crime within the jurisdiction of the Tribunal. The Tribunal is of the opinion that revolting and horrible as many of these crimes were, it has not been satisfactorily proved that they were done in execution of, or in connection with, any such crime. The Tribunal therefore cannot make a general declaration that the acts before 1939 were crimes against humanity within the meaning of the Charter' (at 254).

[12] 'Le fait que Streicher poussait au meurtre et à l'extermination, à l'époque même où, dans l'Est, les Juifs étaient massacrés dans les conditions les plus horribles, réalise "la persécution pour des motifs politiques et raciaux" prévue parmi les crimes de guerre définis par le Statut, et constitue également un crime contre l'Humanité' (at 324).

[13] See his opening statement, of 17 January 1946, in IMT, vol. 5, at 371. The French Prosecutor stated that 'This horrible accumulation and maze of Crimes against Humanity both include and go beyond the two more precise juridical notions of Crimes against Peace and War Crimes. But I think—and I will revert later separately to Crimes against Peace and War Crimes—that this body of Crimes against Humanity constitutes, in the last analysis, nothing less than the perpetration for political ends and in a systematic manner, of common law crimes such as theft, looting, ill treatment, enslavement, murders, and assassinations, crimes that are provided for and punishable under the penal laws of all civilized states. No general objection of a juridical nature, therefore, appears to hamper your task of justice.

'Moreover, the Nazis accused would have no ground to argue on alleged lack of written texts to justify the penal qualification that you will apply to their crimes.'

[14] See H. Donnedieu de Vabres, 'Le Jugement de Nuremberg et le principe de légalité des délits et des peines', in 27 *Revue de droit pénal et de criminologie* (1946–47), pp. 826–7. See also his Hague Academy lectures: 'Le procès de Nuremberg devant les principes modernes du droit pénal international', HR (1947–I), 525–7 (see in particular n. 1 at 526).

alone or of these crimes in conjunction with others. However, this was not in breach of a general norm that strictly prohibited retroactive criminal law. As we shall see (*infra*, 7.3), immediately after the Second World War, the *nullum crimen sine lege* principle could be regarded as a moral maxim destined to yield to superior exigencies whenever it would have been contrary to justice not to hold persons accountable for appalling atrocities. The strict legal prohibition of *ex post facto* law had not yet found expression in international law; at least, it did not appear to comprise a general principle of law universally accepted by all States. The IMT set out the view that 'the maxim *nullum crimen sine lege* . . . is in general a principle of justice' allowing the punishment of actions not proscribed by law at the time of their commission, when it would be 'unjust' for such wrongs to be 'allowed to go unpunished' (at 219).[15]

In the wake of the major war trials, momentous changes in international law took place. On 11 December 1946 the UN GA unanimously adopted a resolution 'affirming' the principles of the Charter of the Nuremberg International Tribunal and its judgment. On 13 February 1946 it passed resolution 3(1) recommending the extradition and punishment of persons accused of the crimes provided for in the Nuremberg Charter. These resolutions show that the category of crimes against humanity was in the process of becoming part of customary international law.[16]

[15] However, as pointed out above, the IMT expressed this view only with regard to aggressive war; in addition it hastened to add (at 219–23) that in any event, under international law, such wars were already regarded as criminal before the outbreak of the Second World War.

Interestingly, the first of the two propositions referred to in the text was repeatedly set forth, with specific regard to crimes against humanity, by the German Supreme Court in the British Occupied Zone. According to this Court, '[r]etroactive punishment is unjust when the action, at the time of its commission, falls foul not only of a positive rule of criminal law, but also of the moral law (*Sittengesetz*). This is not the case for crimes against humanity. In the view of any morally-oriented person, serious injustice (*schweres Unrecht*) was perpetrated, the punishment of which would have been a legal obligation of the State. The subsequent cure of such dereliction of a duty through retroactive punishment is in keeping with justice. This also does not entail any violation of legal security (*Rechtssicherheit*) but rather the re-establishment of its basis and presuppositions' (Judgment of 4 May 1948, case against *Bl.*, at 5).

See also the following judgments: 15 February 1949, *B. and A.* case, at 297; 18 October 1949, *H.* case, at 232–3; 12 July 1949, *N.* case, at 335; 11 September 1950, at 135.

Other judgments include elaborate reasoning concerning the distinction to be drawn between law enacted by the Occupying Powers and German law: see, for example, *G.* case, 21 March 1950, at 362–4; *M. et al.* case, at 378–81 (this judgment contains important reasoning in support of the view that crimes against humanity could be punished retroactively: see 380–1).

[16] Strikingly, the French Court of Cassation, in *Sobanski Wladyslav* (also called the *Boudarel* case), in 1993 placed an aberrant interpretation on the second resolution and the Charter of the IMT, to which the resolution referred. It held that the resolution and Article 6 of the Tribunal's Statute only related to 'offences perpetrated on behalf of the Axis European States', hence it could not apply to atrocities committed elsewhere. The specific question brought to the Court revolved around the scope of the French law of 26 December 1964. (Under this law, crimes against humanity by their nature are not covered by any statute of limitation; the law stated that such crimes were those referred to in the UN resolution of 13 February 1946 which in turn adverted to the definition set out in the Statute of the Tribunal.) In the case at bar the question was whether such law applied to the accused Boudarel, a French serviceman who after deserting the French army had sided with the Viet Minh and allegedly committed atrocities against French prisoners of war in 1952–4. By interpreting the GA resolution and the IMT Statute as recalled above, and consequently by also

A number of international instruments were then drawn up embodying the prohibition of crimes against humanity, certain of which improved and extended the London Agreement, for instance, the Peace Treaties with Italy, Romania, Hungary, Bulgaria, and Finland, each of which included terms providing for the punishment of these crimes.[17]

In particular, after 1945 the link between crimes against humanity and war was gradually dropped. This is evidenced by Article II(1)(c) of such 'multinational' legislation as Control Council Law no. 10 passed by the four victorious Powers four months after the London Agreement, that is on 20 December 1945, by national legislation (such as the Canadian[18] and the French[19] criminal codes), case law,[20] as well as international treaties such as the 1948 Genocide Convention, the 1968 Convention on the Non-Applicability of Statutory Limitations to War Crimes and Crimes against Humanity, and the 1973 Convention on Apartheid. This evolution gradually led to the abandonment of the nexus between crimes against humanity and war: at present, customary international law bans crimes against humanity whether they are committed in time of war or peace.[21] The same holds true for the Rome Statute for an ICC,

restrictively construing the French law of 1964, the Court concluded that the law did not apply to the accused, who consequently could not be tried. According to the Court, his alleged crimes were covered by a law of 1966 granting amnesty for all crimes committed in Indochina before 1 October 1957 (at 354–5).

To refute the legal grounds set forth in the judgment, it may suffice to quote the sort of 'authentic interpretation' of Article 6 of the IMT Statute, propounded by Robert H. Jackson, the protagonist of the London Conference that led to the adoption, on 8 August 1945, of that Statute. After the Conference he wrote that 'The most serious disagreement [at the Conference], and one on which the United States declined to recede from its position even if it meant the failure of the Conference, concerned the definition of crimes. The Soviet Delegation proposed and until the last meeting pressed a definition which, in our view, had the effect of declaring certain acts crimes only when committed by the Nazis. The United States contended that the criminal character of such acts could not depend on who committed them and that international crimes could only be defined in broad terms applicable to statesmen of any nation guilty of the proscribed conduct. At the final meeting the Soviet qualifications were dropped and agreement was reached on a generic definition acceptable to all' (*International Conference on Military Trials*, at vii–viii).

17 See for instance Article 45 of the Peace Treaty with Italy, Article 6 of the Treaty with Romania, and Article 5 of that with Bulgaria.

18 Para. 7 (3.76) of the Canadian Criminal Code provides that: "[C]rimes against humanity" means murder, extermination, enslavement, deportation, persecution or any other inhumane act or omission that is committed against any civilian population or any identifiable group of persons, whether or not it constitutes a contravention of the law in force at the time and in the place of its commission, and that, at that time and in that place, constitutes a contravention of customary international law or conventional international law or is criminal according to the general principles of law recognized by the community of nations'.

19 Article 212–1, para. 1 of the French Criminal Code (enacted by Law no. 92–1336 of 16 December 1992, modified by Law no. 93–913 of 19 July 1993), which entered into force on 1 March 1994, provides that: 'La déportation, la réduction en esclavage ou la pratique massive et systématique d'exécutions sommaires, d'enlèvements de personnes suivis de leur disparition, de la torture ou d'actes inhumains, inspirés par des motifs politiques, philosophiques, raciaux ou religieux et organisés en exécution d'un plan concerté a l'encontre d'un groupe de population civile sont punies de la réclusion criminelle à perpétuité'.

20 See e.g. the *Einsatzgruppen* case, at 49; *Altstötter and others* (*Justice* case), at 974. See, however, the *Flick* case, at 1213 and the *Weizaecker* case, at 112.

21 See on this point the *dictum* of the ICTY Appeals Chamber in its Decision of 2 October 1995 in *Tadić* (*Interlocutory Appeal*), §141.

which confirms the rupture of the link between crimes against humanity and armed conflict.

On the other hand, some treaties and other binding international instruments enshrining the Statutes of international courts and tribunals also restrict the scope of customary rules; or, to be more accurate (because strictly speaking those Statutes do not lay down substantive rules of criminal law but only provide for the definition of those crimes over which each relevant court or tribunal is endowed with jurisdiction), such treaties and other instruments may *indirectly contribute* to the restriction of the customary rules. Thus, as we shall see (*infra*, 4.6), the Statutes of the ICTY (1993), the ICTR (1994), and the ICC (1998) provide that the crimes at issue can only be committed *against civilians*, whereas in some respects customary law upholds a broader notion of victims of such crimes.

4.3 THE OBJECTIVE ELEMENT OF THE CRIME

The conduct prohibited was loosely described in the London Agreement of 1945, and similarly in Control Council Law no. 10 and the Statutes of the Tokyo International Tribunal, as well the ICTY and the ICTR. Gradually case law has contributed to defining the legal contours of the *actus reus*, and in the event the various categories have been largely spelled out in the ICC Statute, Article 7 of which may be held to either crystallize nascent notions or to codify the bulk of existing customary law.

At present, the following classes of offences make up crimes against humanity:

1. *Murder*, that is, intentional killing, whether or not premeditated.

2. *Extermination*, that is mass or large-scale killing, as well as 'the intentional infliction of conditions of life, *inter alia* the deprivation of access to food and medicine, calculated to bring about the destruction of part of a population' (Article 7(2)(b) of the ICC Statute).

The ICTR has defined the notion of extermination in a few cases: *Akayesu* (§§591–2), *Kambanda* (§§141–7), *Kayishema and Ruzindana* (§§141–7), *Rutaganda* (§§82–4), *Musema* (§§217–19). The ICTR has held that the requisite elements of the offence are as follows: (i) the accused or his subordinate participated in the killing of certain named or described persons; (ii) the act or omission was unlawful and intentional; (iii) the unlawful act or omission must be part of a widespread or systematic attack; and (iv) the attack must be against the civilian population. This definition does not seem to be satisfactory, for it is loose and does not indicate the unique objective features of the crime.

A Chamber of the ICTY offered a better definition in *Krstić*. It held that:

> for the crime of extermination to be established, in addition to the general requirements for a crime against humanity, there must be evidence that a particular population was targeted

and that its members were killed or otherwise subjected to conditions of life calculated to bring about the destruction of a numerically significant part of the population. (§503.)

The Trial Chamber also specified that 'In accordance with the *Tadić* (*Appeal*) judgment, . . . it is unnecessary that the victims were discriminated against for political, social or religious grounds'(§499).

In the same case the Trial Chamber found that the accused was guilty of extermination, as follows:

Although there is evidence that a small number of killings in Potocari [in the Srebrenica enclave] and afterwards involved women, children and elderly, virtually all of the persons killed in the aftermath of the fall of Srebrenica were Bosnian Muslim males of military age. The screening process at Potocari, the gathering of those men at detention sites, their transportation to execution sites, the opportunistic killings of members of the column along the Bratunac-Milici road as they were apprehended, demonstrate beyond any doubt that all of the military aged Bosnian Muslim males that were captured or fell otherwise in the hands of the Serb forces were systematically executed. The result was that the majority of the military aged Bosnian Muslim males who fled Srebrenica in July 1995 were killed. A crime of extermination was committed at Srebrenica. (§§504–5.)

It is submitted that one ought not to exclude from this class of crimes extermination carried out by groups of terrorists *for the purpose of spreading terror*. (Of course, the necessary condition that the terrorist attack exterminating a group of persons be part of a widespread or systematic attack, must be fulfilled.)

3. *Enslavement*. This notion was gradually elaborated upon by case law, notably by two US Military Tribunals sitting at Nuremberg, in the *Milch* case (at 773–91) and in *Pohl and others* (at 970), and then refined by a Trial Chamber of the ICTY in *Kunarac and others* (§§515–43). According to the ICC Statute, which crystallizes a nascent notion, enslavement 'means the exercise of any or all of the powers attaching to the right of ownership over a person and includes the exercise of such power in the course of trafficking in persons, in particular women and children' (Article 7(2)(c)). The ICTY Trial Chamber in *Kunarac and others* convincingly propounded a set of elements that clarify this definition. It stated the following:

Under this definition, indications of enslavement include elements of control and ownership; the restriction or control of an individual's autonomy, freedom of choice or freedom of movement; and, often, the accruing of some gain to the perpetrator. The consent or free will of the victim is absent. It is often rendered impossible or irrelevant by, for example, the threat or use of force or other forms of coercion; the fear of violence, deception or false promises; the abuse of power; the victim's position of vulnerability; detention or captivity, psychological oppression or socio-economic conditions. Further indications of enslavement include exploitation; the exaction of forced or compulsory labour or service, often without remuneration and often, though not necessarily, involving physical hardship; sex; prostitution; and human trafficking. With respect to forced or compulsory labour or service, international law, including some of the provisions of Geneva Convention IV and the Additional Protocols, make clear that not all labour or service by protected persons, including civilians, in armed conflicts, is prohibited—strict conditions are, however, set for such labour or service. The 'acquisition' or 'disposal' of someone for monetary or other compensation, is not a requirement for enslavement. Doing so, however, is a prime example of the exercise of the right of ownership over someone. The duration of the suspected exercise of powers attaching to the right of ownership is another factor that may be considered when determining whether someone was enslaved; however, its importance in any given case will depend on the existence of other indications of enslavement. Detaining or keeping someone in captivity, without more, would, depending on the circumstances of a case, usually not constitute enslavement.

The Trial Chamber is therefore in general agreement with the factors put forward by the Prosecutor, to be taken into consideration in determining whether enslavement was committed. These are the control of someone's movement, control of physical environment, psychological control, measures taken to prevent or deter escape, force, threat of force or coercion, duration, assertion of exclusivity, subjection to cruel treatment and abuse, control of sexuality and forced labour. The Prosecutor also submitted that the mere ability to buy, sell, trade or inherit a person or his or her labours or services could be a relevant factor. The Trial Chamber considers that the *mere ability* to do so is insufficient, such actions actually occurring could be a relevant factor. (§§542–3.)

In addition, the Trial Chamber set out clearly the reasons for which it found two of the defendants guilty of enslavement.[22]

4. *Deportation or forcible transfer of population*, that is the 'forced displacement of the persons concerned by expulsion or other coercive acts from the area in which they are lawfully present, without grounds permitted under international law' (Article 7(2)(d)).

[22] It found that Kunarac (the leader of a permanent reconnaissance group of about fifteen men, belonging to the Serbian Bosnian army) in 1992, together with another soldier, DP6, kept two young girls for about six months in an abandoned house, constantly raping them, and denied them any control over their lives during their stay there. 'They had to obey all orders, they had to do household chores and they had no realistic option whatsoever to flee the house . . . or to escape their assailants. They were subjected to other mistreatments, such as Kunarac inviting a soldier into the house so that he could rape [one of the girls] for 100 Deutschmark if he so wished. On another occasion, Kunarac tried to rape [one of the girls] while in his hospital bed, in front of other soldiers. The two women were treated as the personal property of Kunarac and DP6.' (See §742 and, more generally, §§728–45.) The Trial Chamber found that the other accused, Kovač, had also engaged in enslavement of various women. It found that on different occasions he had detained various girls in his apartment, for periods varying in length, each time raping, humiliating and degrading the girls. Each time the girls were beaten, threatened, psychologically oppressed and kept in constant fear; they could not and did not leave the apartment without one of the men occupying the apartment with Kovač accompanying them. When the men were away, the girls would be locked inside the apartment with no way to get out. 'Only when the men were there would the door of the apartment be left open. Notwithstanding the fact that the door may have been open while the men were there . . . the girls were also psychologically unable to leave, as they would have had nowhere to go had they attempted to flee. They were aware of the risks involved if they were recaptured. While they were detained in Radomir Kovač's apartment, the girls were required to take care of the household chores, the cooking and the cleaning' (see §§750–1 and, more generally, 746–82). On one occasion the accused even sold two girls, whom he had detained for some time in his apartment, for 500 Deutschmarks to two unidentified Montenegrin soldiers (§§775–80). The Trial Chamber concluded that Kovač exercised de facto ownership over the girls he kept in his apartment. 'For all practical purposes, he possessed them, owned them and had complete control over their movements, and he treated them as his property . . . Kovač exercised the above powers over the girls intentionally' (§781).

A Trial Chamber of the ICTY emphasized in *Krstić* that:

Both deportation and forcible transfer relate to involuntary and unlawful evacuation of individuals from the territory in which they reside. Yet the two are not synonymous in customary international law. Deportation presumes transfer beyond State borders, whereas forcible transfer relates to displacement within a State. (§521.)

In that case the Trial Chamber found that, on 12–13 July 1995, about 25,000 Bosnian Muslim civilians were forcibly bussed outside the enclave of Srebrenica to the territory under Bosnian Muslim control, always within the same State (Bosnia and Herzegovina). The transfer was compulsory and was carried out 'in furtherance of a well organised policy whose purpose was to expel the Bosnian Muslim population from the enclave'. The Chamber concluded that the civilians transported from Srebrenica were not subjected to deportation but to forcible transfer, a crime against humanity (§§527–32).

5. *Imprisonment* or other severe deprivation of physical liberty in violation of fundamental rules of international law.

A Trial Chamber of the ICTY, in *Kordić and Čerkez*, was the first international court to offer a definition of imprisonment. It held that imprisonment as a crime against humanity must 'be understood as arbitrary imprisonment, that is to say, the deprivation of liberty of the individual without due process of law, as part of a widespread or systematic attack directed against a civilian population' (§§302–3).

6. *Torture*, that is 'the intentional infliction of severe pain or suffering, whether physical or mental, upon a person in the custody or under the control of the accused', except when pain or suffering is inherent in or incidental to lawful sanctions (Article 7(2)(e) of the ICC Statute).

In *Delalić and others* Trial Chamber II of the International Tribunal noted that the definition of torture contained in the 1984 Torture Convention was broader than, and included, that laid down in the 1975 Declaration of the United Nations General Assembly and in the 1985 Inter-American Convention, and considered it to reflect a consensus which the Trial Chamber regarded as 'representative of customary international law' (§459). Another Trial Chamber of the ICTY, ruling in *Furundžija*, shared that conclusion, although on different legal grounds. It held that, as shown by the broad convergence of international instruments and international jurisprudence, there was general acceptance of the main elements contained in the definition set out in Article 1 of the Torture Convention. It considered, however, that some specific elements pertained to torture as considered from the specific viewpoint of international criminal law relating to armed conflicts. It held that torture as a crime committed in an armed conflict must contain the following elements:

it (i) consists of the infliction, by act or omission, of severe pain or suffering, whether physical or mental; in addition, (ii) this act or omission must be intentional; (iii) it must aim at obtaining information or a confession, or at punishing, intimidating, humiliating or coercing the victim or a third person, or at discriminating, on any ground, against the victim or a third person; (iv) it must be linked to an armed conflict; (v) at least one of the persons involved in the torture process must be a public official or must at any rate act in a non-private capacity, e.g. as a *de facto* organ of a State or any other authority-wielding entity.

The Trial Chamber went on to note the following:

As is apparent from this enumeration of criteria, the Trial Chamber considers that among the possible purposes of torture one must also include that of humiliating the victim. This proposition is warranted by the general spirit of international humanitarian law: the primary purpose of this body of law is to safeguard human dignity. The proposition is also supported by some general provisions of such important international treaties as the Geneva Conventions and Additional Protocols, which consistently aim at protecting persons not taking part, or no longer taking part, in the hostilities from 'outrages upon personal dignity'. The notion of humiliation is, in any event close to the notion of intimidation, which is explicitly referred to in the Torture Convention's definition of torture. (§162.)

Subsequently, in *Kunarac and others*, another Trial Chamber of the ICTY broadened that definition. Starting from the correct assumption that one ought to distinguish between the definition of torture under international human rights law and that applicable under international criminal law, the Trial Chamber held among other things that 'the presence of a State official or of any other authority-wielding person in the torture process is not necessary for the offence to be regarded as torture under international humanitarian law' (§496). Another Trial Chamber shared this view in *Kvočka and others* (§§137–41).[23]

7. *Sexual violence.* This class of offence includes: (i) *rape*, a category of crime that was not defined in international law until a Trial Chamber of the ICTR set out a rather terse definition in *Akayesu* (rape is 'a physical invasion of a sexual nature, committed under circumstances which are coercive', §597), taken up by a Trial Chamber of the

[23] It is worth examining, as a case study, the finding of torture made in *Furundžija*. In that case, the Chamber was satisfied that the accused, an officer of the special forces (the so-called 'Jokers') of the Bosnian Croat armed forces (HVO), was guilty of torturing the victim, Witness A, a Muslim woman who had been detained by the Bosnian Croats. He 'was present in the large room and interrogated Witness A, whilst she was in a state of nudity. As she was being interrogated, Accused B [another officer, not on trial, for he was in hiding] rubbed his knife on the inner thighs of Witness A and threatened to cut out her private parts if she did not tell the truth in answer to the interrogation by the accused. The accused did not stop his interrogation, which eventually culminated in his threatening to confront Witness A with another person, meaning Witness D and that she would then confess to the allegations against her. To this extent, the interrogation by the accused and the activities of Accused B became one process. The physical attacks, as well as the threats to inflict severe injury, caused severe physical and mental suffering to Witness A. The intention of the accused, as well as Accused B, was to obtain information which they believed would benefit the HVO. They therefore questioned Witness A about the activities of members of Witness A's family and certain other named individuals, her relationship with certain HVO soldiers and details of her alleged involvement with the ABiH [Bosnian Muslim armed forces]. The Trial Chamber has found that the accused was also present in the pantry where the second phase of the interrogation of Witness A occurred. Witness D was taken there for a confrontation with Witness A to make her confess as "promised" by the accused in the large room. Both Witness A and Witness D were interrogated by the accused and hit on the feet with a baton by Accused B in the course of this questioning. Accused B again assaulted Witness A who was still naked, before an audience of soldiers' (§§264–7).

ICTY in *Delalić and others* (§479). Subsequently two ICTY Trial Chambers delivered important judgments, respectively in *Furundžija* and *Kunarać and others*;[24] (ii) *sexual slavery*; (iii) *enforced prostitution*; (iv) *forced pregnancy*, namely 'the unlawful confinement of a woman forcibly made pregnant, with the intent of affecting the ethnic composition of any population or carrying out other grave violations of international law' (Article 7(2)(f) of the Rome Statute for an ICC); (v) *enforced sterilization*; and (vi) any other form of *sexual violence of comparable gravity*.

8. *Persecution* against any identifiable group or collectivity on political, racial, national ethnic, cultural, religious, gender, or other grounds, that are universally recognized as impermissible under international law; persecution 'means the intentional and severe deprivation of fundamental rights contrary to international law by reason of the identity of the group or collectivity' (Article 7(2)(g) of the Rome Statute for an ICC).

A Trial Chamber of the ICTY propounded an elaborate definition of this crime in *Kupreškić and others*.[25]

24 In *Furundžija*, the Trial Chamber held that neither international customary or treaty law, nor general principles of international criminal law, nor general principles of international law offered any possible definition of rape. It therefore resorted to the principles of criminal law common to the major legal systems of the world, deriving them, with caution, from national laws. It concluded that the objective elements of rape are as follows: '(i) the sexual penetration, however slight: (a) of the vagina or anus of the victim by the penis of the perpetrator or any other object used by the perpetrator; or (b) of the mouth of the victim by the penis of the perpetrator; (ii) by coercion or force or threat of force against the victim or a third person' (§185). Subsequently, in *Kunarac and others*, another Trial Chamber of the same ICTY placed a different interpretation on one of the elements of the definition set out in *Furundžija*, that is the element of 'coercion, or force, or threat of force'. According to this Trial Chamber that element must be taken to mean that there is rape whenever sexual autonomy is violated, or in other terms the person subjected to the act has not freely agreed to it or is otherwise not a voluntary participant. Therefore, that element may be set out as follows: 'sexual penetration occurs without the consent of the victim. Consent for this purpose must be consent given voluntarily, as a result of the victim's free will, assessed in the context of the surrounding circumstances' (§460, and see §§438–60).

It would appear that the two definitions are in substance equivalent, for 'coercion, or force, or threat of force' in essence imply or means 'lack of consent'.

25 The Trial Chamber held that 'in order for persecution to amount to a crime against humanity it is not enough to define a core assortment of acts and to leave peripheral acts in a state of uncertainty. There must be clearly defined limits on the types of acts which qualify as persecution. Although the realm of human rights is dynamic and expansive, not every denial of a human right may constitute a crime against humanity. Accordingly, it can be said that at a minimum, acts of persecution must be of an equal gravity or severity to the other acts enumerated under Article 5 [of the ICTY Statute, concerning crimes against humanity]. This legal criterion has already been resorted to, for instance, in the *Flick* case. It ought to be emphasised, however, that if the analysis based on this criterion relates only to the level of seriousness of the act, it does not provide guidance on what types of acts can constitute persecution. The *ejusdem generis* criterion can be used as a supplementary tool, to establish whether certain acts which generally speaking fall under the proscriptions of Article 5(h), reach the level of gravity required by this provision. The only conclusion to be drawn from its application is that only gross or blatant denials of fundamental human rights can constitute crimes against humanity . . . in order to identify those rights whose infringement may constitute persecution, more defined parameters for the definition of human dignity can be found in international standards on human rights such as those laid down in the Universal Declaration on Human Rights of 1948, the two United Nations Covenants on Human Rights of 1966 and other international instruments on human rights or on humanitarian law. Drawing upon the various provisions of these texts it proves possible to *identify a set of fundamental rights*

The Trial Chamber found that in the case at issue the defendants were guilty of persecution. It found that 'the "deliberate and systematic killing of Bosnian Muslim civilians" as well as their "organised detention and expulsion from Ahmici [the village where the crimes were committed]" can constitute persecution. This is because these acts qualify as murder, imprisonment, and deportation, which are explicitly mentioned in the Statute under Article 5' (§629). The Trial Chamber also found that the comprehensive destruction of Bosnian Muslim homes and property constituted 'a gross or blatant denial of fundamental human rights', and, being committed on discriminatory grounds, amounted to persecution (§§630–1).

9. *Enforced disappearance of persons*, namely 'the arrest, detention or abduction of persons by, or with the authorization, support or acquiescence of, a State or a political organization, followed by a refusal to acknowledge that deprivation of freedom or to give information on the fate or whereabouts of those persons, with the intention of removing them from the protection of the law for a prolonged period of time' (Article 7(2)(i) of the Rome Statute for an ICC). It may be noted that with respect to this crime the ICC Statute has not codified existing customary law but contributed to the crystallization of a nascent rule, evolved primarily out of treaty law (that is, the numerous treaties on human rights prohibiting various acts falling under this heading) as well as the case law of the Inter-American Commission and Court of Human Rights, in addition to a number of UN General Assembly resolutions. These various strands have gradually contributed to the formation of a customary rule prohibiting enforced disappearance of persons. The ICC Statute has upheld and codified the criminalization of this conduct.

10. *Other inhumane acts of a similar character and gravity*, intentionally causing great suffering, or serious injury to body or to mental or physical health. This notion, harking back to Article 6(c) of the Nuremberg Statute, and subsequently interpreted in such cases as *Ternek*[26] has been restated in Article 7(1)(k) of the ICC Statute, which to a large extent codifies and in some respects develops customary international law.

appertaining to any human being, the gross infringement of which may amount, depending on the surrounding circumstances, to a crime against humanity. Persecution consists of a severe attack on those rights, and aims to exclude a person from society on discriminatory grounds. The Trial Chamber therefore defines persecution as *the gross or blatant denial, on discriminatory grounds, of a fundamental right, laid down in international customary or treaty law, reaching the same level of gravity as the other acts prohibited in Article 5* . . . acts of persecution must be evaluated not in isolation but in context, by looking at their cumulative effect. Although individual acts may not be inhumane, their overall consequences must offend humanity in such a way that they may be termed "inhumane". This delimitation also suffices to satisfy the principle of legality, as inhumane acts are clearly proscribed by the Statute . . . the Trial Chamber does not exclude the possibility that a single act may constitute persecution. In such a case, there must be clear evidence of the discriminatory intent . . . In sum, a charge of persecution must contain the following elements: (a) those elements required for all crimes against humanity under the Statute; (b) a gross or blatant denial of a fundamental right reaching the same level of gravity as the other acts prohibited under Article 5; (c) discriminatory grounds' (§§616–27).

[26] The District Court of Tel-Aviv held in a decision of 14 December 1951 that the definition of 'other inhumane acts', was to apply only to such other inhumane acts as resembled in their nature and their gravity those specified in the definition (at §7 or p. 538).

In *Kupreškic and others* an ICTY Trial Chamber dwelt on the interpretation of this loose clause.[27]

4.4 THE SUBJECTIVE ELEMENT OF THE CRIME

Courts have insisted on three points. First, *intent*, that is the intention to bring about a certain result, is normally required for an accused to be found guilty of crimes against humanity.

Secondly, in the case of an accused who, acting as an agent of a system, does not directly and immediately cause the inhumane acts, it is not necessary that he anticipate all the specific consequences of his misconduct; it is sufficient for him to be *aware of the risk* that his action might bring about serious consequences for the victims, on account of the violence and arbitrariness of the system to which he delivers the victim. (This point was particularly stressed by the German Supreme Court in the British Occupied Zone, with particular reference to cases of denunciation of Jews or political opponents to the police or Gestapo, for instance in *T. and K.*, in which the accused had been charged with burning down a synagogue in 1938 (at 198–202).[28]

Thirdly, the agent must be *cognisant of the link* between his misconduct and a policy

[27] The Trial Chamber stated that: 'There is a concern that this category lacks precision and is too general to provide a safe yardstick for the work of the Tribunal and hence, that it is contrary to the principle of the "specificity" of criminal law. It is thus imperative to establish what is included within this category. The phrase "other inhumane acts" was deliberately designed as a residual category, as it was felt to be undesirable for this category to be exhaustively enumerated. An exhaustive categorization would merely create opportunities for evasion of the letter of the prohibition . . . In interpreting the expression at issue, resort to the *ejusdem generis* rule of interpretation does not prove to be of great assistance. Under this rule, that expression would cover *actions similar* to those specifically provided for . . . Less broad parameters for the interpretation of "other inhumane acts" can instead be identified in international standards on human rights such as those laid down in the Universal Declaration on Human Rights of 1948 and the two United Nations Covenants on Human Rights of 1966. Drawing upon the various provisions of these texts, it is possible to identify a set of basic rights appertaining to human beings, the infringement of which may amount, depending on the accompanying circumstances, to a crime against humanity. Thus, for example, serious forms of cruel or degrading treatment of persons belonging to a particular ethnic, religious, political or racial group, or serious widespread or systematic manifestations of cruel or humiliating or degrading treatment with a discriminatory or persecutory intent no doubt amount to crimes against humanity: inhuman or degrading treatment is prohibited by the United Nations Covenant on Civil and Political Rights (Article 7), the European Convention on Human Rights, of 1950 (Article 3), the American Convention on Human Rights of 1969 (Article 5) and the 1984 Convention against Torture (Article 1). Similarly, the expression at issue undoubtedly embraces the forcible transfer of groups of civilians (which is to some extent covered by Article 49 of the IVth Convention of 1949 and Article 17(1) of the Additional Protocol II of 1977), enforced prostitution (indisputably a serious attack on human dignity pursuant to most international instruments on human rights), as well as the enforced disappearance of persons (prohibited by General Assembly Resolution 47/133 of 18 December 1992 and the Inter-American Convention of 9 June 1994). Plainly, all these, and other similar acts, must be carried out in a systematic manner and on a large scale. In other words, they must be as serious as the other classes of crimes provided for in the other provisions of Article 5. Once the legal parameters for determining the content of the category of "inhumane acts" are identified, resort to the *ejusdem generis* rule for the purpose of comparing and assessing the gravity of the prohibited act may be warranted' (§§563–6).

[28] See also *Finta*, decisions by the Ontario Court of Appeal (at 1–153) and the Supreme Court of Canada (at 701–877).

or systematic practice. As the ICTY Appeals Chamber held in *Tadić* (*Appeal*), the perpetrator needs to know that there is an attack on the civilian population and that his acts comprise part of the attack (§248), or, as held in *Blaškić*, he at least needs to be aware of the risk that his act is part of the attack, and then takes that risk (§§247, 251). This does not, however, entail that he needs to know the details of the attack (*Kunarac and others*, §434).

Finally, it is worth mentioning that courts have not required, as part of the *mens rea*, that the perpetrator should have a specifically racist or inhuman frame of mind.[29]

To sum up, the requisite subjective element or *mens rea* in crimes against humanity is not simply limited to the *criminal intent* (or *recklessness*) *required for the underlying offence* (murder, extermination, deportation, rape, torture, persecution, etc.). The viciousness of these crimes goes far beyond the underlying offence, however wicked or despicable it may be. This additional element—which helps to distinguish crimes against humanity from war crimes—consists of awareness of the broader context into which this crime fits, that is *knowledge that the offences are part of a systematic policy* or of widespread and large-scale abuses. In addition, when these crimes take the form of persecution, another mental element is required: a persecutory or discriminatory animus. The intent must be to subject a person or group to discrimination, ill-treatment, or harassment, so as to bring about great suffering or injury to that person or group on religious, political, or other such grounds. This added element for persecution amounts to a *special criminal intent* (*dol spécial*).

Furthermore, in some cases the subjective element may be *culpable negligence* (see *infra*, 8.4), as admitted in *Hinselmann and others* (at 58–60) (see thereon 8.4). In some German cases it was held that instead mere negligence or *Fahrlässigkeit* was not sufficient (see, for instance, *R.*, at 45–9).

[29] On this point, a number of cases brought before the German Supreme Court in the British Occupied Zone are also relevant. Most of these cases concern denunciations by Germans to the police or military authorities of Jews or political opponents, with the consequence that the denounced persons were arrested and imprisoned or severely ill-treated; some such cases concern the burning of synagogues in 1938.

In the *Sch.* case, a person had in 1943 denounced his landlord to the Gestapo for his statements against Hitler; as a result the man had been arrested and sentenced to death. It is notable that the German Supreme Court held that the existence of a link or nexus between an offence against humanity and a general policy or a systematic practice of abuses did not necessarily imply that the author of the crime against humanity intended by his action to further or promote the violent and brutal practice of the regime within which the crime had been committed. Nor was it required that the agent should approve the final result of his action. In other words, the Court simply required an *objective link* between that act and the policy or practice as well as the awareness of the policy or practice; not necessarily the intention to commit the crime for the purpose of pursuing that policy or practice, or a state of mind which approved the outcome of the crime (at 124). In *K.* (at 50) the German Supreme Court in the British Occupied Zone held that for the *mens rea* in a crime against humanity to exist, it is not necessary for the agent to have acted 'out of inhumane convictions'.

The *Barbie* (at 137–41 and 331–7) and *Touvier* (337) cases, brought before the French Court of Cassation, confirm this approach.

4.5 THE POSSIBLE AUTHORS OF THE CRIME

Normally it is State organs, i.e. individuals acting in an official capacity, such as military commanders, servicemen, etc. who perpetrate crimes against humanity. Is this a *necessary element* of crimes against humanity, that is, *must* the offence be perpetrated by organs or agents of a State or a governmental authority or on behalf of such bodies, or may crimes against humanity be committed by individuals not acting in an official capacity? In the latter case, must the offence be approved or at least condoned or countenanced by a governmental body for it to amount to a crime against humanity?

The case law seems to indicate that crimes against humanity may be committed by individuals acting in their private capacity, provided they act in unison, as it were, with a general state policy and find support for their misdeeds in such policy. This is clearly shown by the numerous cases brought after 1945 before the German Supreme Court in the British Occupied Zone and concerning denunciations to the German authorities of Jews or political opponents by private German individuals.[30]

An interesting problem that may arise is whether crimes against humanity may be committed by State officials acting in a private capacity and without formal approval of their superior authorities. It would seem that in such cases some sort of explicit or implicit approval or endorsement by State or governmental authorities is required, or else that it is necessary for the offence to be clearly encouraged by a general governmental policy, or at least to *fit clearly within such a policy*. This is best illustrated by the *Weller* case. This case, which seems to have been unknown until it was cited by the ICTY in *Kupreškić* (§555), gave rise to six different judgments by German courts after the Second World War. Given its significance (and its historical value as well), it may be useful to dwell on it at some length.

The facts, as set out in almost all the six judgments, are as follows. In early 1940, in the small German town of Mönchengladbach (near Düsseldorf), various Jewish families were obliged to move together into one house; eventually 16 persons lived there. One night, in May 1940, three (probably drunken) persons broke into the house. One of them was the accused Weller, a member of the SS, who was in civilian clothing; another wore the SA uniform, and the third wore the blue uniform of the German Navy. They obliged all 16 inhabitants to assemble in their night clothes in the basement, then went to the kitchen, where they summoned the 16 persons, one by one. There, 11 (or 10, according to some of the judgments) of the 16 inhabitants of the house were beaten with a 'heavy leather whip' and verbally abused. The next day the injured parties reported to the Jewish community (*Jüdische Gemeinde*), which turned

30 See for instance the judgments in *B.*, decision of 25 May 1948 (at 6–10), in *P.*, decision of 20 May 1948 (at 11–18), in *V.*, decision of 22 June 1948 (at 20–5), in *R.*, decision of 27 July 1948 (at 46–9), in *K.*, decision of 27 July 1948 (at 49–52), in *M.*, decision of 28 September 1948 (at 91–5), in *H.*, decision of 20 April 1949 (at 385–91), in *P.*, decision of 10 May 1949 (at 17–19), in *Ehel. M.*, decision of 24 May 1949 (at 67–9), in *A.*, decision of 6 September 1949 (at 144–7), in *S.*, decision of 15 May 1950 (at 56–7).

to the local Gestapo. The head of the Gestapo informed the wronged Jews that 'Weller's and the other persons' actions were an isolated event, which would in no way be approved' (judgment of the 16 June 1948, at 3). Thereafter Weller was summoned by the Gestapo and strongly taken to task by the district leader of the NSDAP (the national socialist party). It is not clear (nor was it established by the various German courts dealing with the case after 1945) whether in 1940 Weller had in fact been fined 20RM for bodily harm, as alleged, instead of imprisonment for not less than two months (this being the penalty which was usually imposed by German law for bodily harm).[31] After the war, the case was brought before the District Court (*Landgericht*) of Mönchengladbach. The court found Weller guilty of grievous bodily harm and sentenced him to 18 months' imprisonment. While admitting that he had acted out of racist motives, the court ruled that his action could nevertheless not be regarded as a crime against humanity. In this connection the court held that three requirements were to be met for such a crime to exist: (i) a significant breach of human dignity (this the court held to have been established in the case at issue, and lay in the ill treatment of Jews); (ii) the racial motivation of the offence (this could also be found in this case); and (iii) the action must be perpetrated 'by abusing the authority of the State or of the police' (at 7–12). The court found that this third element was lacking. It held that a crime against humanity must be 'either systematically organized by the government or carried out with its approval' (at 10). In the case at issue, one was faced with the 'occasional persecution of various persons by one person', not with abuses perpetrated by the 'holder of political power or at least by a person acting under the protection of or with the approval of [those holding] political power' (ibid.). In short, the necessary 'link between crimes against humanity and State authority' was lacking.

On appeal, the case was passed on, 'to ensure uniform jurisprudence' (at 5), by the Court of Appeal in Düsseldorf to the Supreme Court (*Oberster Gerichtshof*) for the British Occupied Zone. This court overturned the decision of the District Court and held that the offence did indeed constitute a crime against humanity. According to the Supreme Court, it was sufficient for the attack on human dignity to be *connected* to the national socialist system of power and hegemony (at 7–9). It should be noted that the same Supreme Court when it was again seized with the case (the Prosecutor contending that the sentence newly passed by the Court of Assize was too light), emphasized that the offence amounted to a crime against humanity, although it had been committed by Weller 'on his own initiative and out of racial hatred' (*eigenmächtig und aus Rassendünkel*) (decision of 10 October 1949, at 2, or 150). The court also pointed out that the 'punishment' (fine of 20DM) allegedly inflicted in 1940 and on which the accused so much insisted, was a measure that,

[31] As a matter of history this case seems astonishing. The Nuremberg laws had been passed years before and it is well known that by 1940 the Jews had no rights whatsoever. The fact that they could turn to the local *Gestapo* for comfort seems almost unbelievable.

assuming it had been taken, 'would not serve justice, but only scorn the victims' (at 5, or 153).[32]

4.6 THE POSSIBLE VICTIMS OF THE CRIME

Article 6(c) of the London Agreement clearly prohibited two distinct categories of crimes: (i) inhumane acts such as murder, extermination, enslavement, and deportation of *any* civilian population, i.e. *any group of civilians* whatever their nationality, and (ii) persecution on political, racial, or religious grounds. Since the customary international law of crimes against humanity that has emerged is largely based on Article 6(c), it is fitting to look into the fundamental elements of that provision.

It is apparent from the wording of Article 6(c) that the *actus reus* is different for these two classes of crimes. Murder, extermination, and other 'inhumane acts' largely constitute offences already covered by all national legal systems and also, are committed against civilians. 'Persecutions' embrace actions that may not be prohibited by national legal systems. In other words, such actions may take the form of acts other than murder, extermination, enslavement, or deportation. Furthermore, since no mention is made of the possible victims of persecutions, or rather, as it is not specified that such persecutions should target 'any civilian population', the inference is warranted that not only any civilian group but also members of the armed forces may be the victims of this class of crimes.

For the purposes of our discussion, it is useful to deal separately with each of the two classes of crimes against humanity.

[32] The Supreme Court pointed out the following: 'The national-socialist leadership often, and quite readily, utilized for its criminal goals and plans actions which appeared to have, or actually had, originated from quite personal decisions. This was true even of actions that were outwardly disapproved of, perhaps because it was felt that some sort of consideration should be shown and it was inappropriate openly to admit such actions . . . The link, in this sense, with the national-socialist system of power and tyranny does in the case at issue manifestly exist. The State and the party had long before the action at issue made Jews out to be sub-humans, not worthy to be respected as human beings . . . Also the action of the accused fitted into the numerous persecutory measures which then affected the Jews in Germany, or could at any time affect them. As the trial court established, the accused, influenced by official propaganda, acted from racial hatred (*Rassendünkel*). In the decision [of the Düsseldorf Court of Appeal] . . . it is rightly pointed out that the link with the national-socialist system of power and tyranny exists not only in the case of those actions which are ordered and approved by the holders of hegemony. That link also exists when those actions can only be explained by the atmosphere and condition (*Stimmung und Lage*) created by the authorities in power. The trial court was wrong when it attached decisive value to the fact that after his action the accused was "rebuked" and that even the Gestapo disapproved of the excess as an isolated infringement. This action nevertheless fitted into the persecution of Jews carried out by the State and the party. This is proved by the fact that the accused, assuming he was the subject of an order for summary punishment (*Strafbefehl*) or a criminal measure (*Strafverfügung*) for the payment of 20RM—a matter that in any case has not been clarified—was in any event not held criminally accountable in a manner commensurate to the gravity of his guilt . . . Given the gravity of the abuse, the harm caused to the victims brought about consequences extending beyond the single individuals and affecting the whole of humanity' (at 206–7).

4.6.1 'MURDER-TYPE' CRIMES AGAINST HUMANITY

'Murder-type' crimes against humanity embrace crimes that are perpetrated 'against *any civilian* population'. The words 'any' and 'civilian' need careful interpretation. As for 'any', it is apparent, both from the text of the provision and from the legislative history of Article 6(c), that it was intended to cover civilians other than those associated with the enemy, who were already protected by the traditional rules of the law of warfare. In other words, by using 'any', the draftsmen intended to protect the civilian population of the State committing crimes against humanity, as well as civilians of its allied countries or of countries under its control, although formally under no military occupation.

As for the word 'civilian', it is apparent that it was intended to refer to persons other than lawful combatants, *whether or not* such persons were civilians fighting alongside enemy military forces. In other words, this phrase does not cover the categories of lawful belligerents envisaged in the Regulations annexed to the Fourth Hague Convention of 1899/1907 (subsequently supplemented by Article 4 of the Third Geneva Convention of 1949 and Articles 43–4 of the First Additional Protocol of 1977). The rationale for the relatively limited scope of Article 6(c) is that *enemy* combatants were already protected by the traditional laws of warfare, while it was deemed unlikely that a belligerent might commit atrocities against *its own* servicemen or those of *allied* countries. In any event, such atrocities, if any, would come under the jurisdiction of the Courts Martial of the country concerned; in other words, they would fall within the scope of *national* legislation.

Nonetheless, after the Second World War courts gradually inclined towards placing a liberal interpretation on the term 'civilians'. For instance, the Supreme Court of Germany in the British Occupied Zone propounded a broad construction of Article 6(c). This court held in at least three cases that military persons could be the victims of crimes against humanity even in situations where the crime did not take the form of persecution. In other words, the court held that the crime at issue could be perpetrated against military personnel even if the offence was not one of those envisaged in the second part of Article 6(c) or in the corresponding second part of Article II(1)(c) of Control Council Law no. 10. As a consequence, the court substantially broadened the notion of 'any civilian population' included in the first part of that provision. These three cases will be briefly summarized.

In a decision of 27 July 1948 in *R.*, the court pronounced upon the guilt of a member of the NSDAP (*Nazionalsozialistische Deutsche Arbeiterpartei*, or Nazi party) and the NSKK (*Nazionalsozialistiche Kommando Korps*, or Nazi commandos) who in 1944 had denounced a non-commissioned officer in uniform and member of the NSDAP and of the SA, for insulting the leadership of the NSDAP. As a result of this denunciation, the victim had been brought to trial three times and eventually sentenced to death (the sentence had not been carried out because in the interim the Russians had occupied Germany). The court held that the denunciation could constitute a crime against humanity if it could be proved that the agent had intended to hand over the victim to the 'uncontrollable power structure of the [Nazi] party and State', knowing that as a consequence of his denunciation, the victim was likely to be caught up in an arbitrary and violent system (at 47).

In 1948, in *P. and others* the same court applied the notion of crimes against humanity to members of the military. In the night following Germany's partial capitulation (5 May 1945), four German marines had tried to escape from Denmark back to Germany. The next day they were caught by Danes and delivered to the German troops, who court martialled and sentenced three of them to death for desertion; on the very day of the general capitulation of Germany (10 May 1945), the three were executed. The German Supreme Court found that the five members of the Court Martial were guilty of complicity in a crime against humanity. According to the Supreme Court, the glaring discrepancy between the offence and the punishment proved that the execution of the three marines had constituted a clear manifestation of the Nazis' brutal and intimidatory justice, which denied the very essence of humanity in blind deference to the superior exigencies of the Nazi State. In this case as well, there had taken place 'an intolerable degradation of the victims to mere means for the pursuit of a goal, hence the depersonalisation and reification of human beings' (at 220); consequently, by sentencing to death those marines, the members of the Court Martial had also injured humanity as a whole. With regard to the wording of the relevant provision on crimes against humanity (namely, Article II(1)(c) of Control Council Law no. 10, which referred only to offences 'against civilian populations'), the court observed the following:

> Whoever notes the expressly emphasized illustrative character of the instances and classes of instance mentioned there, cannot come to the conclusion that action between soldiers may not constitute crimes against humanity. [Admittedly], a single and isolated excess would not constitute a crime against humanity pursuant to the legal notion of such crimes. [However], it has already been shown [in the judgment] that the action at issue *can* belong to the criminal system and criminal tendency of the Nazi era. For the offence to be a crime against humanity, it is not necessary that the action should support or sustain Nazi tyranny, or that the accused should intend so to act. (At 228.)

Finally, in its decision of 18 October 1949 in the *H.* case, the court dealt with a case in which a German presiding judge had presided over two trials by a naval Court Martial (*Bordkriegsgericht*) against two officers of the German Navy: one against a commander of submarines who had been charged with criticizing Hitler in 1944, the other against a lieutenant-commander of the German naval forces, charged with procuring two foreign identity cards for himself and his wife in 1944. The judge had initially sentenced both officers to death (the first had been executed, while the sentence against the second had been commuted by Hitler to ten years' imprisonment). The Supreme Court held that the judge could be held guilty of crimes against humanity to the extent that his action was undertaken deliberately in connection with the Nazi system of violence and terror (at 233–4, 238, 241–4).

It should be added that in 1985 the French Court of Cassation in *Barbie* held that the victims of crimes against humanity could include 'the opponents of . . . [a] policy [of ideological supremacy, manifesting itself in inhumane acts and persecution committed in a systematic manner], whatever the form of their "opposition"' (at 137 and 139–40).

After the Second World War other courts tended instead to place a strict interpretation on the term 'civilians' and consequently to rule out from the notion of victims of crimes against humanity persons who belonged, or had belonged, to the military. Notable in this respect is *Neddermeier*, brought before a British Court of Appeal established under Control Council Law no. 10.[33]

The trend towards loosening the strict requirement that the victims be civilians also continued however in more recent times. It is significant that the ICTY has placed a liberal interpretation on the narrow notion of victims of crimes against humanity set out in Article 5 of its Statute (according to which those crimes can only be committed against 'any civilian population'). In its decision in *Mrkšić and others.* (rendered under Rule 61 of the Rules of Procedure and Evidence), the court held that crimes against humanity could be committed even where the victims at one time bore arms. In *Kupreškić et al.*, a Trial Chamber held that 'the presence of those actively involved in the conflict should not prevent the characterization of a population as civilian and those actively involved in a resistance movement can qualify as victims of crimes against humanity'. In *Kunarac and others*, an ICTY Trial Chamber held that:

> as a minimum, the perpetrator must have known or considered the possibility that the victim of his crime was a civilian . . . in case of doubt as to whether a person is a civilian, that person shall be considered to be a civilian. The Prosecution must show that the perpetrator could not reasonably have believed that the victim was a member of the armed forces. (§435.)

A different issue that arose in cases brought before the United States Military Tribunals sitting at Nuremberg is whether victims of extermination through euthanasia as a crime against humanity may be nationals of the State concerned, or whether such victims must perforce be foreigners. In these cases some defendants had been accused of participating in euthanasia programmes for the chronically disabled or terminally ill. The Tribunals wrongly held that euthanasia amounted to a crime against humanity only if carried out against *foreigners*, i.e. non-nationals of the State practising euthanasia. In *Karl Brandt*, the Tribunal found that the defendant had

[33] The accused had been convicted by the High Court of Brunswick of crimes against humanity, pursuant to Article II(1)(c) of Control Council Law no. 10. The court had found that he had caused a number of Polish workers to be beaten (the Poles, originally brought to Germany as prisoners of war, had subsequently been compelled to sign agreements to surrender such status and be treated as civilians). Before the Appeal Court the Defence claimed among other things that the offence did not amount to a crime against humanity because 'there was no element of cruelty'. The Prosecution admitted that, if the victims of ill-treatment were to be considered as prisoners of war, a conviction under the label of war crimes 'could be substituted' for the conviction for crimes against humanity. The court held that the victims had the status of prisoners of war 'and not civilians'. It consequently set aside the conviction for crimes against humanity and substituted for it that for war crimes (at 58–60).

participated in a programme for the extermination of disabled persons, and that this programme had quickly been extended to Jews and then to concentration camp inmates (those inmates deemed to be unfit for labour were ruthlessly weeded out and sent to extermination camps in great numbers). The Tribunal stressed that it was difficult to believe Brandt's assertion that he was not implicated in the extermination of Jews or of concentration camp inmates; however, even if it were true, 'the evidence [was] conclusive that almost at the outset of the programme *non-German nationals* were selected for euthanasia and extermination' (at 197–8).

The same Tribunal also took this restrictive (and undisputedly fallacious) view in *Greifelt and others* (at 654–5).

4.6.2 'PERSECUTION-TYPE' CRIMES AGAINST HUMANITY

As stated above, it is apparent from Article 6(c) that in the case of *persecution*, the victims of crimes against humanity need not necessarily be civilians; they may also include military personnel. There is an obvious rationale for this regulation: traditional laws of warfare, while they protected servicemen against such illegal actions by the enemy as treachery and use of prohibited means or methods of warfare, did not safeguard them against persecution either by the enemy, or by the Allies or by the very authorities to which military personnel belonged.

The textual and logical construction of Article 6(c) was confirmed implicitly in *Pilz* by the Dutch Special Court of Cassation and explicitly by French courts in *Barbie* and *Touvier*.

As recalled above, *Pilz* was a German medical doctor serving with the German army occupying the Netherlands. He had prevented a young Dutchman, who had enlisted in the German army and been wounded while attempting to escape from his unit, from being treated and had then ordered a subordinate to kill the Dutchman. The Dutch Special Court of Cassation held that the offence did not amount to a war crime, because the victim, even if still a Dutch national, belonged to the German army. It then asked itself whether it could amount to a crime against humanity, and answered in the negative, noting that the victim 'was not part of the civilian population of occupied territory, nor [could] the acts with which he [was] charged be seen as forming part of a system of persecution on political, racial or religious grounds' (at 1211). Clearly, it can be deduced from this reasoning that had the victim, a member of the military, been the object of persecution on one of those grounds, the offence might have amounted to a crime against humanity.

In *Barbie*, in a decision rendered on 20 December 1985 the French Court of Cassation held that crimes against humanity in the form of persecution had been perpetrated against members of the French Resistance movements (at 136). Subsequently the Paris Court of Appeal took the same view in a judgment of 9 July 1986, again in *Barbie*, followed by the Chambre d'accusation of the same Court of Appeal in a judgment of 13 April 1992 in *Touvier* (at 352). In this last decision the Chambre d'accusation held that:

Jews and members of the Resistance persecuted in a systematic manner in the name of a State practising a policy of ideological supremacy, the former by reason of their membership of a racial or religious community, the latter by reason of their opposition to that policy, can equally be the victims of crimes against humanity. (At 352.)

4.6.3 THE GRADUAL BROADENING OF THE CATEGORY OF VICTIMS

It is submitted that as a result of the gradual disappearance in customary international law of the nexus between crimes against humanity and armed conflict, so too has the emphasis on civilians as the exclusive class of victims of such crimes dwindled, if not disappeared. For if crimes against humanity may be committed *in time of peace* as well, it no longer makes sense to require that such crimes be perpetrated against civilians alone. Why should members of military forces be excluded, since they in any case would not be protected by international humanitarian law in the absence of any armed conflict? Plainly in times of peace military personnel too may become the object of crimes against humanity at the hand of their own authorities. By the same token, *in time of armed hostilities*, there is no longer any reason for excluding servicemen, whether or not *hors de combat* (wounded, sick, or prisoners of war), from protection against crimes against humanity (chiefly persecution), whether committed by their own authorities, by allied forces, or by the enemy.

This broadening of the category of persons safeguarded by the relevant rules of customary international law is consonant with the overall trend in international humanitarian law toward expanding the scope of protection of the basic values of human dignity, regardless of the legal status of those entitled to such protection. This trend has manifested itself in, *inter alia*, the adoption of international treaties protecting human rights and treaties prohibiting crimes such as genocide, apartheid, or torture, in the adoption of some significant resolutions by the United Nations General Assembly, and in certain pronouncements of the International Court of Justice. Nowadays, international human rights standards also clearly protect individuals against abuses and misdeeds of *their own* governmental authorities. It follows that there no longer exists any substantial reason for refusing to apply the notion of crimes against humanity to vicious and inhumane actions undertaken on a large scale by governments against the human dignity of their own military or the military personnel of allies or other non-enemy countries (or even of the enemy). It is worth noting that, had this expansion of the notion of crimes against humanity not occurred, a strict interpretation of the notion of civilians would lead in times of armed conflict to a questionable result. Some categories of combatants who, in modern armed conflicts (particularly in internal conflicts) often find themselves in a twilight area, would remain unprotected—or scantily protected—against serious atrocities. Consider, for example, members of paramilitary forces or members of police forces who occasionally or sporadically take part in hostilities. These are persons whose legal status may be uncertain, as one may not be sure whether they are to be regarded as combatants or civilians. It could therefore follow that, under a strict and traditional interpretation of the crimes at issue, and assuming that these persons were at the same time regarded as combatants, they would ultimately be unprotected by the prohibition against such crimes.

By way of conclusion on this point, the proposition is warranted that the scope of the *customary* rules on crimes against humanity is much broader than normally admitted. Private individuals may also perpetrate those crimes (provided the governmental authorities approve of or condone their action or their action fits into a widespread or systematic practice of official misconduct). Furthermore, the victims of those crimes (or, at least of the crimes belonging to the subclass of persecutory crimes) may embrace both civilians and combatants. In addition, such victims need not have the nationality of an enemy country but may belong to the country whose authorities order, approve, or condone the pattern of misbehaviour amounting to crimes against humanity.

4.7 CUSTOMARY INTERNATIONAL LAW AND ARTICLE 7 OF THE ICC STATUTE

Let us now ask ourselves whether Article 7 of the ICC Statute, contemplating crimes against humanity as one of the categories of criminal conduct over which the Court has jurisdiction, departs from or instead restates customary international law.

A comparison between the notion of crimes against humanity laid down in customary international law and that set out in Article 7 shows that by and large, the latter is based on the former. However, many differences may be discerned. In some respects, Article 7 elaborates upon and clarifies customary international law. In some respects it is narrower than customary international law; in others, Article 7 instead broadens the scope of customary international law.

4.7.1 AREAS WHERE ARTICLE 7 SETS FORTH ELEMENTS OF CUSTOMARY INTERNATIONAL LAW

Article 7 specifies and elaborates upon customary international law in many respects. First, it specifies that a crime against humanity must be committed 'with knowledge of the attack'. The provision thus makes it clear that the requisite *mens rea* must include the awareness that the individual criminal act is part of a widespread or systematic attack on a civilian population.

Secondly, Article 7 clarifies the objective elements of some of the underlying offences, by making explicit notions that, until set out in this Article, were only implicit and could therefore be determined only by way of interpretation. These notions are further elaborated upon in the 'Elements of Crimes' adopted by the Preparatory Commission.[34]

Finally one should emphasize that the 'Elements of Crime' have clarified an important aspect of *mens rea.* In commenting on the need for the offender to have knowledge of a widespread or systematic attack on a civilian population, it is stated there that: 'However, the last element should not be interpreted as requiring proof that the perpetrator had knowledge of all characteristics of the attack or the precise details of the plan or policy of the State or organization. In the case of an emerging widespread or systematic attack on a civilian population, the intent clause of the last element indicates that this mental element is satisfied if the perpetrator intended to further such attack'.

[34] This applies to the following notions: (i) 'Extermination', which, pursuant to Article 7(2)(b), 'includes the intentional infliction of conditions of life, inter alia, the deprivation of access to food and medicine, calculated to bring about the destruction of part of a population'; (ii) 'Enslavement', which under Article 7(2)(c) refers to 'the exercise of any or all the powers attaching to the right of ownership over a person and includes the exercise of such power in the course of trafficking in persons, in particular women and children'. This notion is made more specific in the 'Elements of Crime', where it is stated that the conduct at issue takes place when 'the perpetrator exercised any or all of the powers attaching to the right of ownership over one or more persons, such as purchasing, selling, lending or bartering such a person or persons, or by imposing on them a similar deprivation of liberty', and it is added (in a footnote) that deprivation of liberty may include 'exacting forced labour or otherwise reducing a person to a servile status'; (iii) 'Deportation or forcible transfer of population', which under Article 7(2)(d) is defined as 'forced displacement of the persons concerned by expulsion or other coercive acts from the area in which they are lawfully present, without grounds permitted under international law'. In the 'Elements of Crime' the important specification is added that the persons deported or forcibly transferred 'were lawfully present in the area from which they were so deported or transferred' and that 'the perpetrator was aware of the factual circumstances that established the lawfulness of such presence'; (iv) 'Torture': Article 7(2)(e) sets out a definition of torture that is broader than that laid down in customary international law, with regard to torture as an international crime per se (instead of torture as one of the classes of crimes against humanity) as established by Trial Chamber II of the ICTY in *Kunarac and others.* In general international law, for the international crime of torture to have occurred, it is necessary, amongst other things, that a public official be involved, either as the perpetrator or as one of the participants or accomplices. By contrast, under Article 7, torture may amount to a crime against humanity even if committed by civilians against other civilians without any involvement of public officials or military personnel. Indeed, Article 7(2)(e) defines torture as 'the intentional infliction of severe pain or suffering, whether physical or mental, upon a person in the custody or under the control of the accused'. Consequently, as long as the single act of torture is part of a widespread or systematic practice, even torture inflicted without any participation of a public official is punishable as a crime against humanity. The only involvement of public authorities is required by the 'Elements of Crime': it is necessary for the widespread or systematic practice constituting the general context of the crime to take place 'pursuant to or in furtherance of a State or organizational policy' of torture; (v) 'Imprisonment', which under Article 7(1)(e) embraces 'other severe deprivation of physical liberty in violation of fundamental rules of international law'; (vi) 'Rape', which under Article 7(1)(g) is not the sole form of sexual violence punishable under international law; as spelled out by Trial Chamber II of the ICTY in *Furundžija,* in addition to the violent physical penetration of the victim's body, other forms of serious sexual violence are criminalized by international law: 'sexual slavery, enforced prostitution . . . enforced sterilization, or any other form of sexual violence of comparable gravity'; 'Other inhumane acts' are defined in Article 7(1)(k) as acts 'of a similar character [to those listed in Article 7(1), from (a) to (j)] intentionally causing great suffering, or serious injury to body or to mental or physical health'.

4.7.2 AREAS WHERE ARTICLE 7 IS NARROWER THAN CUSTOMARY INTERNATIONAL LAW

In some respects, Article 7 departs from customary law by setting out a notion of crimes against humanity at odds with that body of law. On this score, three points must be noted.

First, Article 7(1) defines the victim or target of crimes against humanity as 'any civilian population'. This provision, which thus adopts a position similar to that taken in the statutes of the ICTY (Article 5) and the ICTR (Article 6), excludes non-civilians (i.e. the military) from the class of victims of the crimes under discussion. Thus, any of the acts enumerated in Article 7(1)(c) to (k), if perpetrated against an enemy combatant, would only amount to a war crime or a grave breach of the 1949 Geneva Conventions. The question arises of whether the term 'civilian population' includes belligerents *hors de combat* who have laid down their weapons, either because they are wounded or because they have been captured. As we have seen above, the case law of the ICTY has answered this question in the affirmative. It would seem to be consonant with the humanitarian object and purpose of Article 7 to suggest the same solution with regard to this provision.

Secondly, Article 7, in defining 'attack directed against any civilian population' narrows the scope of the notion of 'widespread or systematic practice' required as a context of a specific offence, for the offence to amount to a crime against humanity. Indeed, in paragraph 2(a) that provision stipulates that 'attack' means 'a course of conduct involving the multiple commission of acts referred to in paragraph 1 against any civilian population, pursuant to or in furtherance of a State or organizational policy to commit such attack'. It would seem that the Statute requires that the offender, in committing a crime against humanity, pursue or promote such a practice. It would follow that any practice simply tolerated or condoned by a State or an organization would not constitute an attack on the civilian population or a widespread or systematic practice. For instance, in the case of murder, or rape, or forced pregnancy, why should it be required that the general practice constitute a policy pursued by a State or an organization? Would it not be sufficient for the practice to be accepted, or tolerated, or acquiesced in by the State or the organization, for those offences to constitute crimes against humanity? Clearly, this requirement goes beyond what is required under international customary law and unduly restricts the notion under discussion. The 'Elements of Crime' make this restriction even more explicit and broader. There it is stated that 'the policy to commit such attack' 'requires that the State or organization *actively promote or encourage* such an attack against a civilian population' (emphasis added).

Thirdly, Article 7 is less liberal than customary international law with regard to one element of the definition of persecution. Under Article 7(1)(h), persecution, in order to fall under the jurisdiction of the ICC, must be perpetrated 'in connection with any act referred to in this paragraph or any crime within the jurisdiction of the Court'. It would seem that under customary international law, no such link is required. In other words, it is not necessary for persecution to consist of (a) conduct defined as a war crime or a crime against humanity or linked to any such crime, plus (b) a discriminatory intent. Under general international law, persecution may also consist of *acts not punishable as war crimes or crimes against humanity*, as long as such acts (a) result in egregious violations of fundamental human rights, (b) are part of a widespread or systematic practice, and (c) are committed with a discriminatory intent. Instead, Article 7(1)(h) imposes a further burden on the Prosecution: it must be proved that, in addition to discriminatory acts based on one of the grounds described in this provision, the *actus reus* must consist of one of the acts prohibited in Article 7(1) or a war crime or genocide (or aggression, if this crime is eventually accepted as falling under the jurisdiction of the Court), or must be 'connected' with such acts or crimes. Besides adding a requirement not provided for in general international law, Article 7 uses the phrase 'in connection with' which is unclear and susceptible to many interpretations.

4.7.3 AREAS WHERE ARTICLE 7 IS BROADER THAN CUSTOMARY INTERNATIONAL LAW

Article 7 expands general international law in at least two respects.

First, it broadens the classes of conduct amounting to crimes against humanity. Thus, it includes within this category 'forced pregnancy' (Article 7(1)(g) and (2)(f)); 'enforced disappearance of persons' (Article 7(1)(i) and (2)(i)); and 'the crime of apartheid' (Article 7(1)(j) and (2)(h)).

Secondly, in dealing with the crime of persecution, it greatly expands the category of discriminatory grounds. While under customary international law these grounds may be political, racial, ethnic, or religious, Article 7(1)(h) adds 'cultural' grounds, 'gender as defined in paragraph 3 [of the same provision]', as well as 'other grounds that are universally recognized as impermissible under international law.'

SELECT BIBLIOGRAPHY

CUSTOMARY INTERNATIONAL LAW

E. Schwelb, 'Crimes against Humanity', 23 BYBIL (1946), 178–226; J. Graven, 'Les crimes contre l'humanité', 76 HR (1950–I), 429–610; G. Levasseur, 'Les crimes contre l'humanité et le problème de leur prescription,' 93 *Journal du droit international* (1966), 259–84; C. Lombois, 'Crimes contre l'humanité, crimes de guerre', 4 RSCDPC (1987), 937–42; R. S. Clark, 'Crimes against Humanity', in G. Ginsburg and V. N. Kudriavtsev (eds), *The Nuremberg Trial and International Law* (1990), 177–212; C. Bassiouni, *Crimes against Humanity in International Criminal Law*, 2nd edn, vol. III (Dordrecht: Nijhoff, 1999); E. Zoller, 'La définition des crimes contre l'humanité', 120 *Journal du droit international* (1993), 549–68; P. Truche, 'Le crime contre l'humanité', 18 *Droits* (1993), 19–29; M. Delmas-Marty, 'Le crime contre l'humanité, les droits de l'homme et l'irréductible humain', 11 *RSCDPC* (1994), 477–90; A. Becker, *Der Tatbestand des Verbrechens gegen die Menschlichkeit: Überlegungen zur Problematik eines völkerrechtlichen Strafrechts* (Berlin: Duncker & Humblot, 1996); Y. Dinstein, 'Crimes against Humanity', in J. Makarczyk (ed.), *Theory of International Law at the Threshold of the 21st Century—Essays in Honour of K. Skubiszewki* (The Hague, London, and Boston: Kluwer Law International, 1997), 891–908; H. Fujita, 'Les crimes contre l'humanité dans les procès de Nuremberg et de Tokyo', 34 *Kobe University Law Review* (2000), 1–15.

ICTY AND ICTR

J. Rikhof, 'Crimes against Humanity, Customary International Law and the International Tribunals for Bosnia and Rwanda', 6 *National Journal of Constitutional Law* (1995), 231; F. Lattanzi, 'Crimes against Humanity in the Jurisprudence of the International Criminal Tribunals for the former Yugoslavia and Rwanda', in H. Fischer, C. Kress, S. R. Lüder (eds), *International and National Prosecution of Crimes Under International Law* (Berlin: Verlag Arno Spitz GmbH, 2001), 473–504; G. Mettraux, 'Crimes Against Humanity in the Jurisprudence of the International Criminal Tribunals for the Former Yugoslavia and for Rwanda', 43 *Harvard Int. Law Journal* (2002), 237–316.

ARTICLE 7 OF THE ICC STATUTE

D. Donat-Cattin, in F. Lattanzi (ed.), *Comments*, 49–77; D. Robinson, 'Defining "Crimes against Humanity" at the Rome Conference', 93 *AJIL* (1999), 43–57; M. Boot, R. Dixon, and C. K. Hall, in O. Triffterer (ed.), *Commentary on the Rome Statute* (1999), 117–72; K. D. Askin, 'Crimes within the Jurisdiction of the International Criminal Court', 10 *CLForum* (1999), 40–9; R. S. Clark, 'Crimes against Humanity and the Rome Statute of the International Criminal Court', in M. Politi and G. Nesi (eds), *The Rome Statute of the International Criminal Court* (Ashgate: Burlington, VT, 2001), 75–93; K. Kittichaisaree, *International Criminal Law* (Oxford; Oxford University Press, 2001), 85–128.

5

GENOCIDE

5.1 THE NOTION

Genocide, that is, the *intentional killing, destruction, or extermination of groups or members of a group as such*, was first envisaged merely as a sub-category of crimes against humanity. Neither Article 6(c) of the Charter of the IMT nor Article II(1)(c) of Control Council Law no. 10 explicitly envisaged genocide as a separate category of these crimes. However, the wording of the relevant provisions clearly shows that those crimes encompassed genocide. The IMT and the Tokyo International Tribunal did not explicitly mention genocide; in dealing with the extermination of Jews and other ethnic or religious groups, they mostly referred to the crime of persecution.

However, genocide was discussed in a few other cases: in particular *Hoess*, decided by a Polish court in 1948 (at 25) and *Greifelt and others*, decided in 1948 by a United States Military Tribunal sitting at Nuremberg (at 17).

Genocide acquired autonomous significance as a specific crime in 1948, when the UN GA adopted the Genocide Convention. The Convention has numerous merits. Among other things, (i) it sets out a careful definition of the crime; (ii) it punishes other acts connected with genocide (conspiracy, complicity, etc.); (iii) prohibits genocide regardless of whether it is perpetrated in time of war or peace; (iv) considers genocide both as a crime involving the criminal responsibility of the perpetrator (and other participants), and as an international delinquency entailing the responsibility of the State whose authorities engage, or otherwise participate, in the commission of genocide (this international wrongful act may be the subject of an international dispute and in any case entails all the consequences of international wrongdoings).

However, one should be mindful of the flaws or omissions of the Convention. These are the most blatant ones:

1. The definition of genocide does not embrace cultural genocide (that is, the destruction of the language and culture of a group).[1] Similarly, genocide does not encompass the extermination of a group on political grounds. This was a deliberate omission. One may wonder whether the elimination of political groups fits with the notion of genocide. Killing all the communists in a country is extermination, but is it

[1] See for instance the decision of the High Court of Australia in *Kruger* v. *Commonwealth* (at 32).

genocide? Many would think not. Cultural genocide is also difficult because it is rather nebulous. For these reasons, political, cultural (and economic) genocide were excluded from the Convention. The Convention confined itself to the physical destruction of groups to which persons in most instances belong 'involuntarily' and, often, by birth (clearly, in the case of religious groups, membership may be voluntary).

2. The four classes of protected groups are not defined, nor are criteria for their definition provided.

3. The enforcement mechanism envisaged in the Convention is ineffective (in Article IV the Convention contemplates trials before the courts of the State on the territory of which genocide has occurred, or before a future 'international penal tribunal'. This is a flaw because it is the territorial State authorities (or persons supported by such authorities) that normally tend to commit acts of genocide; so national prosecutors will be reluctant to bring prosecutions; furthermore, no international penal tribunal existed at the time, nor for 50 years afterwards. Furthermore Article VIII provides that any contracting party 'may call upon the competent organs of the United Nations to take such action' under the Charter 'as they consider appropriate' for the prevention or suppression of genocide, whereas Article IX confers on the ICJ jurisdiction over disputes between States concerning the interpretation, application, or fulfilment of the Convention).

Indeed, at the *enforcement* level the Convention has long proved a failure. Only once did a United Nations body pronounce on a specific instance of genocide: this occurred in the case of *Sabra and Shatila*, when the UN GA characterized the massacre perpetrated there by Christian falangist troops as 'an act of genocide' in its resolution 37/123 D of 16 December 1982. Subsequently in 1993 for the first time a State brought a case of genocide before the International Court of Justice: *Bosnia and Herzegovina* v. *Federal Republic of Yugoslavia (Serbia and Montenegro).*

Strikingly, only few cases of genocide have been brought before national criminal courts: chief among them is *Eichmann* (decided in 1961 by the District Court of Jerusalem and subsequently by the Israeli Supreme Court). Eichmann was tried for crimes against the Jewish people, an offence under Israeli law which incorporated all the elements of the definition of genocide.

After the establishment of the ICTY, some national courts began to institute criminal proceedings against persons accused of serious crimes in the former Yugoslavia. German courts have thus pronounced on some cases of genocide: *Jorgić*, decided in 1997 by the Higher State Court (*Oberlandsgericht*) of Düsseldorf[2] and confirmed by

[2] See *Jorgic* (Judgment of 26 September 1997, in 3 *Strafrecht* 215/98). The Court found the defendant guilty of genocide and sentenced him to life imprisonment. The most significant part of the judgment is that relating to *mens rea*. The Court held that the intent to destroy a group 'means destroying the group as a social unit in its specificity, uniqueness and feeling of belonging: the biological-physical destruction of the group is not required' (section III, para. 1). The Court's findings about the factual and psychological elements from which one can infer the existence of 'intent' are extremely interesting.

the Federal High Court (*Bundesgerichtshof*) in 1999, followed by the Constitutional Court in 2000; *Sokolović* and *Kušljić* in 2001.

By contrast, much headway has been made both at the *normative* level and at the level of prosecution and punishment of genocide by *international* criminal tribunals.

At the norm-setting level, some major advances stand out. The major substantive provisions of the Convention have gradually turned into customary international law. In its Advisory Opinion on *Reservations to the Convention on Genocide*, the Court held that 'the principles underlying the Convention are principles which are recognized by civilized nations as binding on States, even without any conventional obligation' (at 24). It is notable that the UN Secretary-General took the same view of the customary status of the Genocide Convention (or, more accurately, of the substantive principles it lays down), a view that was endorsed implicitly by the UN Security Council,[3] and explicitly by the ICTR in *Akayesu* (§495) and by the ICTY in *Krstić* (§541).

In addition, at the level of *State* responsibility it is now widely recognized that customary rules on genocide impose *erga omnes* obligations, that is, lay down obligations towards all other member States of the international community, and at the same time confer on any State the right to require that acts of genocide be discontinued. Finally, those rules now form part of *jus cogens* or the body of peremptory norms, that is, they may not be derogated from by international agreement (nor *a fortiori* by national legislation).

Genocide having been provided for in the Statutes of both the ICTY and the ICTR as well as the ICC, the first two courts have had the opportunity to try quite a few persons accused of this crime, and have delivered important judgments on the matter (the ICTR, particularly in *Akayesu* (§§204–28) and *Kayishema and Ruzindana* (§§41–9), and the ICTY in *Jelisić* (§§78–83) and *Krstić* (§§539–69)).

5.2 THE OBJECTIVE ELEMENT OF THE CRIME

Article IV of the Genocide Convention, and the corresponding rule of customary law, clearly defines the conduct that may amount to genocide: (i) *killing* members (hence more than one member) of a national or ethnical, racial, or religious group; (ii) causing *serious bodily or mental harm* to members of the group; (iii) deliberately inflicting on the group *conditions of life calculated to bring about its physical destruction* in whole or in part; (iv) imposing *measures intended to prevent birth* within the group; or (v) *forcibly transferring children* of the group to another group.

It would seem that Article IV does not cover the conduct currently termed in non-technical language 'ethnic cleansing', that is the forcible expulsion of civilians belonging to a particular group from an area, a village, or a town. (In the course of the drafting of the Genocide Convention, Syria proposed an amendment designed to add

[3] See Report of the Secretary-General Pursuant to Para. 2 of Security Council Resolution 808 (1993), UN Doc. S/25704, at para. 45.

a sixth class of acts of genocide: 'Imposing measures intended to oblige members of a group to abandon their homes in order to escape the threat of subsequent ill-treatment'. However, the draftsmen rejected this proposal.)[4]

Some courts have indeed excluded the forced expulsion of persons belonging to a particular ethnic, racial, or religious group from the notion of genocide.[5] However, in other cases courts have asserted that that expulsion, under certain circumstances, could be held to amount to genocide.[6] Probably the better view is that upheld by the

4 For the Syrian proposal see UN Doc. A/C6/234.

5 See for instance *Jelišić*, Judgment of 14 December 1999 (§§107–8). The Prosecution had alleged that Jelišić had contributed to the campaign of ethnic cleansing in Brčko in eastern Bosnia and had, for a period, acted as the principal executioner at the Luka camp 'with the intent to destroy, in whole or in part, a racial, ethnic or religious group' (*Jelišić*, Trial Chamber, oral ruling, 19 October 1999). The Prosecution asserted that the accused demonstrated considerable authority, that he had received instructions to kill as many Muslims as possible and that his genocidal intent could be shown by the accused's own words as was reported to the judges by the witnesses. In this regard, they characterized Jelišić as 'an effective and enthusiastic participant in the genocidal campaign' and noted, in addition, that the group targeted by Jelišić was significant, 'not only because it included all the dignitaries of the Bosnian Muslim community in the region but also because of its size'. The Trial Chamber ruled, however, that Jelišić could not be found guilty of the crime of genocide. Although he had pleaded guilty to both war crimes and crimes against humanity, with respect to the crime of genocide, the Trial Chamber issued the following pronouncement: 'In conclusion, the acts of Goran Jelišić are not the physical expression of an affirmed resolve to destroy in whole or in part a group as such. All things considered, the Prosecutor has not established beyond all reasonable doubt that genocide was committed in Brčko during the period covered by the indictment. Furthermore, the behaviour of the accused appears to indicate that, although he obviously singled out Muslims, he killed arbitrarily rather than with the clear intention to destroy a group. The Trial Chamber therefore concludes that it has not been proved beyond all reasonable doubt that the accused was motivated by the *dolus specialis* of the crime of genocide. The benefit of the doubt must always go to the accused and, consequently, Goran Jelišić must be found not guilty on this count.'

On ethnic cleansing it is also worth mentioning the decision delivered on 31 August 2001 by the Supreme Court of Kosovo in *Vuckovic*: 'Indeed, the essential characteristic of the criminal act of genocide is the intended destruction of a national, ethnical, racial or religious group. However, the appealed verdict only considered that the accused, forcefully expelling population from their houses in unbearable living conditions, was ready to accept the consequence that the part or entire group of Albanian population of these villages will be exterminated. Such motivation does not characterize the intent to destroy an ethnic group in whole or in part. More generally, according to the Supreme Court, the exactions committed by the Milošević regime in 1999 cannot be qualified as criminal acts of genocide, since their purpose was not the destruction of the Albanian ethnic group in whole or in part, but its forceful departure from Kosovo as a result of a systematic campaign of terror including murders, rapes, arsons and severe mistreatments' (at 2–3).

See also *Kušljić* (decision of the German *Bundesgerichtshof* of 21 February 2001), at 7–10.

6 In the confirmation of the second indictment of 16 November 1995 (pertaining to the fall of the UN safe area of Srebrenica) against Radovan Karadžić and Ratko Mladić, for instance, Judge Riad expressly characterized 'ethnic cleansing' as a form of genocide: 'After Srebrenica fell to besieging Serbian forces in July 1995 a terrible massacre of the Muslim population appears to have taken place . . . These executions were committed in the context of a broader policy of 'ethnic cleansing' which is directed against the Bosnian Muslim population and which also includes massive deportations. This policy aims at creating new borders by violently changing the national or religious composition of the population. As a result of this policy, the Muslim population of Srebrenica was totally banished from the area . . . The policy of 'ethnic cleansing' referred to above presents, in its ultimate manifestation, genocidal characteristics.' (*The Prosecutor* v. *Karadžić and Mladić*, confirmation of indictment (IT-95-18-I) of 16 November 1995).

An ICTY Trial Chamber observed in the *Karadžić and Mladić* Rule 61 Decision that the character of the acts in question may permit the inference of genocidal intent: *Karadžić and Mladić*, Rule 61 Decision of 11 July 1996, at para. 94. See also *Nikolić*, Rule 61 Decision, ICTY Trial Chamber, 20 October 1995, §34.

However, a subsequent judgment of the Trial Chamber suggests a retreat from the Trial Chamber's abovementioned and relatively expansive stance (see *Jelišić*, *infra*).

German Constitutional Court in *Jorgić*, namely that 'systematic expulsion can be a method of destruction and therefore an indication, though not the sole substantiation, of an intention to destroy' (at §24). (A similar view was propounded by an ICTY Trial Chamber in *Krstić* (at §§589–98).)

Although, as stated above, genocide emerged as a subcategory of crimes against humanity, it soon acquired autonomous status and contents. This is among other things proved by the fact that international rules do not require the existence of a widespread or systematic practice as a legal ingredient of the crime of genocide. This conclusion is, of course, material at the procedural level, for it implies that the prosecutor in a national or international trial need not lead evidence on that practice. In reality, genocidal acts are hardly conceivable as isolated or sporadic events. Normally they are part of a widespread practice (often tolerated, approved, or at least condoned or acquiesced in by governmental authorities), or even if of a governmental policy. These circumstances remain, however, factual events, not provided for as legal requirements of the crime. Thus, in principle, the killing of, say, five or ten members of a religious, ethnic, national, or racial group with the intention of destroying, in whole or in part, the group, may amount to genocide even if it is an isolated act. The problem however arises of how to prove the genocidal intent. Since such special intent is normally deduced from the factual circumstances, in the instance just mentioned it may turn out to be extremely difficult to prove it. If instead the genocidal act is part of a whole pattern of conduct taking place in the same State (or region or geographical area), or, *a fortiori*, of a policy planned or pursued by the governmental authorities (or by the leading officials of an organized political or military group), then it may become easier to deduce the intent from the facts of the case. Thus, the question of 'widespread' or 'systematic' practice may eventually acquire importance from an *evidentiary* viewpoint, not as a legal ingredient of the crime.

The major problems concerning the objective element of genocide relate to the *notion of the group* victim of the crime as well as the *identification of the four groups* enumerated in the rule (national, ethnical, racial, religious). The former problem may be framed as follows: what do the Convention and the corresponding customary rule mean by 'group'? In other words, when can one state with certainty that one is faced with a group protected by the Convention? The latter question, which is obviously closely related to the former, is: by what standards or criteria can one identify each of the four groups? Can one rely upon an objective test for each group? If so, where does one find such a test?

The case law of the ICTR and ICTY has contributed considerably to clarifying these various elements. As we shall see, these two Tribunals have taken a stand on these matters.

The importance of *Akayesu* in particular needs to be stressed. In this case, an ICTR Trial Chamber not only emphasized that genocide is the most grave international crime or, as it put it, 'the crime of crimes' (§16), but also, and more importantly, made a significant contribution to the elaboration of the notion of genocide, elucidating a number of points that deserve to be briefly underlined.

The Trial Chamber set out a definition of 'group'. In its view, this word, in the provisions on genocide, refers only to 'stable groups',

> constituted in a permanent fashion and membership of which is determined by birth, with the exclusion of the more 'mobile' groups which one joins through individual voluntary commitment, such as political and economic groups. Therefore, a common criterion in the four types of groups protected by the Genocide Convention is that membership in such groups would seem to be normally not challengeable by its members, who belong to it automatically, by birth, in a continuous and often irremediable manner. (§511.)

According to the Trial Chamber, the groups protected against genocide should not be limited to the four groups envisaged in the relevant rules, but—in order to respect the intention of the drafters of the Genocide Convention, who clearly intended to protect any identifiable group—should include 'any stable and permanent group' (§516). This proposition without further elaboration appears unconvincing, given that the framers of the Convention, as clearly expressed in the text of that instrument, evinced an intention to protect only the four groups explicitly indicated there. The Chamber then propounded a definition of each of the four groups envisaged in the relevant rules. It defined 'national groups' as 'a collection of people who are perceived to share a legal bond of common citizenship, coupled with reciprocity of rights and duties' (§512), an 'ethnic group' as 'a group whose members share a common language or culture' (§513), a 'racial group' as a group 'based on the hereditary physical traits often identified with a geographical region, irrespective of linguistic, cultural, national or religious factors' (§514), and a 'religious group' as a group 'whose members share the same religion, denomination or mode of worship'(§515).

It should be noted that in the particular case of the genocide of Tutsis by Hutus in Rwanda, the question of how to identify a protected group played a major role. Indeed, these two groups shared language, religion, and culture, lived in the same areas and in addition there was a high rate of mixed marriages. The ICTR, in *Akayesu* solved the problem by noting that:

> in Rwanda, in 1994, the Tutsi constituted a group referred to as 'ethnic' in official classifications. Thus, the identity cards at the time included a reference to '*ubwoko*' in Kinyarwnda or '*ethnie*' (ethnic group) in French which, depending on the case, referred to the designation Hutu or Tutsi, for example . . . [In addition] all the Rwandan witnesses who appeared before it [the Trial Chamber] invariably answered spontaneously and without hesitation the questions of the Prosecutor regarding their ethnic identity. (§702.)

It would thus seem that for the Trial Chamber the question of whether or not a multitude of persons made up a group protected by the rules against genocide was primarily a question of fact: the court had to establish whether (i) those persons were *in fact treated* as belonging to one of those protected groups, and in addition (ii) they *considered themselves* as belonging to one of such groups.

One may find the same admixture of objective and subjective criteria in *Kayishema and Ruzindana*. There an ICTR Trial Chamber stated that:

An ethnic group is one whose members share a common language and culture: or a group which distinguishes itself, as such (self-identification); or a group identified as such by others, including perpetrators of the crimes (identification by others). A racial group is based on hereditary physical traits often identified with geography. A religious group includes denomination or mode of worship or a group sharing common beliefs. (§98.)

In *Rutaganda* the ICTR pushed the *subjective standard* even further. It noted that:

The concepts of national, ethnical, racial and religious groups have been researched extensively and . . . at present, there are no generally and internationally accepted precise definitions thereof. Each of these concepts must be assessed in the light of a particular political, social and cultural context. Moreover, the Chamber notes that for the purposes of applying the Genocide Convention, membership of a group is, in essence, a subjective rather than an objective concept. The victim is perceived by the perpetrator of genocide as belonging to a group slated for destruction. In some instances, the victim may perceive himself/herself as belonging to the said group. (§56.)

Also two ICTY Trial Chambers shared this subjective approach, in *Jelisić* (§§70–1) and *Krstić* (§§556–7 and 559–60).

The various classes of action falling under genocide were to a large extent spelled out in *Akayesu*. The Trial Chamber advanced a definition of each of the various forms of conduct constituting the *actus reus* of genocide, namely: (i) killing members of the group ('killing' must be interpreted as 'murder', i.e. voluntary or intentional killing (§§500–1)); (ii) causing serious bodily or mental harm (these terms 'do not necessarily mean that the harm is permanent and irremediable': §§502–4); (iii) deliberately inflicting on the group conditions of life calculated to bring about its physical destruction (in the view of the Trial Chamber, this expression includes among other things, 'subjecting a group of people to a subsistence diet, systematic expulsion from homes and the reduction of essential medical services below minimum requirement[s]': §§505–6); (iv) imposing measures intended to prevent births within the group (these measures would consist of 'sexual mutilation, the practice of sterilization, forced birth control [and the] separation of the sexes and prohibition of marriages' (§507); (v) in addition, the measures at issue may be not only physical but also mental (§508)), and may include forcibly transferring children of the group to another group (§509).

Another interesting problem relating to *actus reus* is whether genocide may also include the killing, with the required intent, of only *one single member* of a protected group. In *Akayesu* the Trial Chamber, when dealing with the constituent elements of genocide, held the view that there may be genocide even if one of the acts prohibited by the relevant rules on this matter is committed 'against one' member of a group (§521). Arguably this broad interpretation is not consistent with the text of the norms on genocide, which speak instead of 'members of a group'.

5.3 THE SUBJECTIVE ELEMENT OF THE CRIME

The *mental* or subjective requirement for genocide as a crime involving international criminal liability is provided for in Article II, paragraph 1 (and in the corresponding customary rule): the 'intent to destroy, in whole or in part, a national, ethnical, racial or religious group'. Genocide is a typical crime based on the 'depersonalization of the victim' that is a crime where the victim is not targeted on account of his or her individual qualities or characteristics, but only because he or she is a member of a group. As the German Federal Court of Justice rightly held in *Jorgić* in 1999, in the case of genocide the perpetrators do not target a person 'in his capacity as an individual'; they 'do not see the victim as a human being but only as a member of the persecuted group' (at 401).[7]

This intent amounts to *dolus specialis*, that is, to an *aggravated criminal intention*, required *in addition* to the criminal intent accompanying the underlying offence (killing; causing serious bodily or mental harm; inflicting conditions of life calculated to physically destroy the group; imposing measures designed to prevent births within the group; forcibly transferring children). It logically follows that other categories of mental element are excluded: recklessness (or *dolus eventualis*) and gross negligence.

The ICTR Trial Chambers have contributed greatly to elucidating the subjective element of genocide. In *Akayesu*, an ICTR Trial Chamber held that the commission of genocide required 'a special intent or *dolus specialis*'. 'Special intent' is defined by the ICTR as 'the specific intention, required as a constitutive element of the crime, which demands that the perpetrator clearly seeks to produce the act charged' (§498). The Trial Chamber added that intent 'is a mental factor which is difficult, even impossible to determine. This is the reason why, in the absence of a confession from the accused, his intent can be inferred from a certain number of presumptions of fact' (§523).

The interpretation given in *Akayesu* has to a very large extent been followed by the Trial Chambers of the ICTR: in *Kayishema and Ruzindana* (§§87–118) as well as in *Rutaganda* (§§44–63) and in *Musema* where the Tribunal in particular considered the issues of complicity and conspiracy in genocide (§§884–941). (In three other cases concerning genocide the accused had pleaded guilty and therefore the Trial Chamber

[7] In the same case the German Constitutional Court took the following view: 'The Higher State Court and Federal Constitutional Court take the view that para. 220(a) of the StGB [the German Criminal Code] protects the group. They have unanimously interpreted the intention of StGB para. 220a as meaning that the destruction of the group as a social entity in its specificity and particularity and sense of togetherness, or even geographically limited part of the group, need not extend to its physical and biological extermination . . . It is enough if the culprit takes upon himself the intent of the central controlling structure that inevitably must be in place for the elements of the crime to be met, even if toward a part of the group . . . the statutory definition of genocide defends a supra-individual object of legal protection, i.e. the social existence of the group . . . The text of the law does not therefore compel the interpretation that the culprit's intent must be to exterminate physically at least a substantial number of the members of the group . . . the intent can be deduced as a rule from the circumstances of an attack carried out under a structurally organized central control on the group, of which the culprit is aware, and which he wills' (§§19–22).

only dealt with sentencing: see *Kambanda* (sentence of 4 September 1998), *Serushago* (sentence of 5 February 1999), and *Ruggiu* (sentence of 1 June 2000).)

In *Krstić*, Trial Chamber I of the ICTY made a considerable contribution, in various respects, to the definition of *mens rea* (as well as *actus reus*) of genocide. As in that case the Prosecution accused the defendant of genocide for having planned and participated in the massacre in a limited locality (the area of Srebrenica), of between 7,000 and 8,000 Bosnian Muslims, all of them men of military age, two questions arose. First, was the 'protected group' constituted by the 'Bosnian Muslims of Srebrenica' or instead by 'Bosnian Muslims'? Secondly, as customary law requires for genocide the intent to destroy (in whole or) in part a group, was this intent present in this case where only men of military age were systematically massacred? The Chamber answered the first query by noting that the group was that of Bosnian Muslims, and the Bosnian Muslims of Srebrenica constituted 'a part of the protected group under Article 4' of the Genocide Convention (§560) (which the Chamber held to be declaratory of customary international law). The Chamber added that 'the intent to eradicate a group within a limited geographical area such as the region of a country or even a municipality' could be characterized as genocide (§589). It then pointed out the following:

> the intent to destroy a group, even if only in part, means seeking to destroy a distinct part of the group as opposed to an accumulation of isolated individuals within it. Although the perpetrators of genocide need not seek to destroy the entire group protected by the Convention, they must view the part of the group they wish to destroy as a distinct entity which must be eliminated as such. A campaign resulting in the killings, in different places spread over a broad geographical area, of a finite number of members of a protected group might not thus qualify as genocide, despite the high total number of casualties, because it would not show an intent by the perpetrators to target the very existence of the group as such. Conversely, the killing of all members of the part of a group located within a small geographical area, although resulting in a lesser number of victims, would qualify as genocide if carried out with the intent to destroy the part of the group as such located in this small geographical area. Indeed, the physical destruction may target only a part of the geographically limited part of the larger group because the perpetrators of the genocide regard the intended destruction as sufficient to annihilate the group as a distinct entity in the geographic area at issue. In this regard, it is important to bear in mind the total context in which the physical destruction is carried out. (§590.)

As to the fact that the persons systematically killed at Srebrenica were 'only men of military age', the Trial Chamber emphasized that, while these men were being massacred, at the same time the rest of the Bosnian Muslim population was being forcibly transferred out of the area. In this respect it stressed that:

> The Bosnian Serb forces could not have failed to know, by the time they decided to kill all the men, that this selective destruction of the group would have a lasting impact upon the entire group. Their death precluded any effective attempt by the Bosnian Muslims to recapture the territory. Furthermore, the Bosnian Serb forces had to be aware of the catastrophic impact that the disappearance of two or three generations of men would have on

the survival of a traditionally patriarchal society, an impact the Chamber has previously described in detail. The Bosnian Serb forces knew, by the time they decided to kill all of the military aged men, that the combination of those killings with the forcible transfer of the women, children and elderly would inevitably result in the physical disappearance of the Bosnian Muslim population at Srebrenica. Intent by the Bosnian Serb forces to target the Bosnian Muslims of Srebrenica as a group is further evidenced by their destroying homes of Bosnian Muslims in Srebrenica and Potocari and the principal mosque in Srebrenica soon after the attack. Finally, there is a strong indication of the intent to destroy the group as such in the concealment of the bodies in mass graves, which were later dug up, the bodies mutilated and reburied in other mass graves located in even more remote areas, thereby preventing any decent burial in accord with religious and ethnic customs and causing terrible distress to the mourning survivors, many of whom have been unable to come to a closure until the death of their men is finally verified. The strategic location of the enclave, situated between two Serb territories, may explain why the Bosnian Serb forces did not limit themselves to expelling the Bosnian Muslim population. By killing all the military aged men, the Bosnian Serb forces effectively destroyed the community of the Bosnian Muslims in Srebrenica as such and eliminated all likelihood that it could ever re-establish itself on that territory. (§§595–7.)

The Chamber concluded that the intent to kill all the Bosnian Muslim men of military age in Srebrenica constituted an intent to destroy in part the Bosnian Muslim group within the meaning of Article 4 of the Genocide Convention and therefore must qualify as genocide.

Before making this ruling, the Trial Chamber had also discussed the question of the extent to which, while appraising whether or not genocide had been perpetrated in the case at issue, it could take into account evidence or facts relating to the cultural or social destruction of a group, as opposed to its physical or biological destruction. On this point it set out the following interesting remarks (which it then applied in the ruling just cited):

The Trial Chamber is aware that it must interpret the Convention with due regard for the principle of *nullum crimen sine lege.* It therefore recognises that, despite recent developments, customary international law limits the definition of genocide to those acts seeking the physical or biological destruction of all or part of the group. Hence, an enterprise attacking only the cultural or sociological characteristics of a human group in order to annihilate these elements which give to that group its own identity distinct from the rest of the community would not fall under the definition of genocide. The Trial Chamber however points out that where there is physical or biological destruction there are often simultaneous attacks on the cultural and religious property and symbols of the targeted group as well, attacks which may legitimately be considered as evidence of an intent to physically destroy the group. In this case, the Trial Chamber will thus take into account as evidence of intent to destroy the group the deliberate destruction of mosques and houses belonging to members of the group. (§580.)

5.4 GENOCIDE AND CRIMES AGAINST HUMANITY

As stated above, genocide was first recognized in international law as a subclass of the category of crimes against humanity. However, after the adoption of the Genocide Convention of 1948 and the gradual transformation of its main substantive provisions into customary international law, genocide became a category of crimes per se, with its own specific *actus reus* and *mens rea.*

True, both categories share at least three elements: (i) they encompass very serious offences that shock our sense of humanity in that they constitute attacks on the most fundamental aspects of human dignity; (ii) they do not constitute isolated events but are instead normally part of a larger context, either because they are large-scale and massive infringements of human dignity or because they are linked to a broader practice of misconduct; and (iii) although they need not be perpetrated by State officials or by officials of entities such as insurgents, they are usually carried out with the complicity, connivance, or at least the toleration or acquiescence of the authorities.

However, the objective and subjective elements of the two crimes differ in many respects (see also *supra*, 5.2). As for the objective element, the two crimes may undoubtedly overlap to some extent: for instance, killing members of an ethnic or religious group may as such fall under both categories; the same holds true for causing serious bodily or mental harm to members of a racial or religious group, or even for the other classes of protected group. However, crimes against humanity have a broader scope, for they may encompass acts that do not come within the purview of genocide (for instance, imprisonment and torture). By the same token, there may be acts of genocide that normally (at least under the Statutes of the ICTY, ICTR, and the ICC) are not held to fall within the other category of crime (for instance, killing detained military personnel belonging to a particular religious or racial group, by reason of their membership of that group). Thus, from the viewpoint of their objective elements, the two categories are normally 'reciprocally special', in that they form overlapping circles which nevertheless intersect only tangentially.

By contrast, from the perspective of the *mens rea* of both offences, the two categories do not overlap at all. In the case of crimes against humanity, international law requires the intent to commit the underlying offence plus knowledge of the widespread or systematic practice constituting the general context of the offence. For genocide, what is required is instead the special intent to destroy, in whole or in part, a particular group, in addition to the intent to commit the underlying offence. From this viewpoint, the two categories are therefore mutually exclusive. They form two circles that do not intersect. The only exception is the case where the underlying *actus reus* is the same, for instance, murder; in this case the intent to kill is required in both categories; nevertheless genocide remains an autonomous category, for it is only genocide that *also* requires the intent to destroy a group. Similarly, it is only for crimes against humanity that knowledge of the widespread or systematic practice is required. As for persecution, the intent of seriously discriminating against members of a particular group is shared by both crimes against humanity and genocide. For persecution-type crimes against humanity, however, it is sufficient to prove that the perpetrator intentionally carried out large-scale and severe deprivations of the fundamental rights of a particular group, whereas for genocide it is necessary to prove the intent to destroy a group, in whole or part. (It should be noted that in *Kayishema and Ruzindana* the majority of the ICTR Trial Chamber dismissed the charge of crime against humanity as already being covered and indeed 'completely absorbed' by genocide (§§577–9), Judge Khan dissenting.)

5.5 ARTICLE 6 OF THE ICC STATUTE

Article 6 reproduces word for word Article II of the Genocide Convention and the corresponding customary rule. In contrast, Article III of the Convention (and the corresponding customary rule) on responsibility for forms of participation in the crime other than perpetration, namely conspiracy, incitement, attempt, and complicity, have not been taken up in the provision on genocide, either because the notion has not been accepted by the Rome Diplomatic Conference (as was the case with conspiracy, a concept that has not found the support of all the civil law countries present at Rome), or because the relevant notion is laid down in general terms (i.e. in terms applicable to other crimes as well) in other provisions of the ICC Statute: this applies to incitement (at present envisaged in Article 25(3)(e)), attempt (which is provided for in Article 25(3)(f)), and complicity (which is contemplated in Article 25(3)(c) and (d)).

It follows that in at least one respect there is an inconsistency between customary international law and the Rome Statute. The former prohibits and makes punishable 'conspiracy to commit genocide'; that is, an inchoate crime consisting of the planning and organizing of genocide not necessarily followed by the perpetration of the crime, whereas Article 6 does not contain a similar prohibition.

It should be noted that in the process of drafting Article 6, it was suggested in the Working Group of the Preparatory Committee in February 1997 that 'the reference to "intent to destroy in whole or in part . . . a group as such" was understood to refer to the specific intention to destroy more than a small number of individuals who are members of a group'.[8] This suggestion was aptly assailed by two commentators, who noted that nothing in the Genocide Convention could justify such a restrictive interpretation and that in addition, international practice belied this interpretation, for 'successful counts or prosecutions of crimes against humanity, of which genocide is a species, have involved relatively small numbers of victims'.[9] It would seem that the customary international rule, as codified in Article 6, does not require that the victims of genocide be numerous. The only thing that can be clearly inferred from the rule is that genocide cannot be held to occur when there is only one victim. However, as

[8] UN Doc. A/AAC.249/1997/L.5 Annex I, p. 3, n. 1.

[9] L. Sadat Wexler and J. Paust, in 13(3) *Nouvelles Etudes Pénales* (1998), at 5.

long as the other requisite elements are present, the killing or commission of the other enumerated offences against more than one person may amount to genocide.

Finally, one should note a further view put forth with regard to the *mens rea* element of genocide. According to the proponent of this view, the ICC Statute 'appears to allow' that 'genocide may be committed with a lower level of *mens rea*' than the very high intent requirement mentioned above, for it 'contemplates [in Article 28, on command responsibility] liability of commanders for genocide committed by their subordinates even if they have no real knowledge of the crime'.[10] It may be objected to on the ground that this could be true only with regard to the case where the superior knows that genocide is about to be perpetrated, or is being committed, and deliberately refrains from forestalling the crime or stopping it. Indeed in this case the superior may be equated to a co-perpetrator or at least an aider and abettor (see *infra*, 10.4.2–4). Instead, one could not accuse a superior of genocide (as a co-perpetrator or an accomplice) when the superior fails to punish the subordinates who have engaged in genocide, or, although he has information that should enable him to conclude that genocide is being committed or may be committed, fails to act, in breach of his supervisory obligations (see Article 28(1)(a) and (2)(a)). In these cases the superior would be guilty of a different offence: intentional, reckless, or negligent breach of his supervisory duties. It follows that, with regard to such cases, it would not be correct to assert that he should be held responsible for genocide although with a subjective element lower than specific intent.

SELECT BIBLIOGRAPHY

THE GENOCIDE CONVENTION

R. Lemkin, 'Genocide as a Crime under International Law' AJIL (1947), 145–51; A. Finch, 'The Genocide Convention', 43 AJIL (1949), 732–8; J. Kunz, 'The UN Convention on Genocide', 43 AJIL (1949), 738–746; N. Robinson, *The Genocide Convention: A Commentary* (New York: Institute of Jewish Affairs, 1960); H. H. Jescheck, 'Genocide', in R. Bernhardt (ed.), *Encyclopedia of Public International Law*, vol. II (Amsterdam: North-Holland, 1995), 541–4; P. Akhavan, 'Enforcement of the Genocide Convention: A Challenge to Civilization,' 8 HHRJ (1995), 229–258; B. Van Schaack, 'The Crime of Political Genocide: Repairing the Genocide Convention's Blind Spot', 106 Yale LJ (1997), 2259–91.

CUSTOMARY INTERNATIONAL LAW

R. Lemkin, *Axis Rule in Occupied Europe* (Washington: Carnegie Endowment for International Peace, 1944), 79–95; L. Kuper, *The Prevention of Genocide* (New Haven and London: Yale University Press, 1985); M. N. Shaw, 'Genocide and International Law', in Y. Dinstein (ed.), *International Law at a Time of Perplexity* (*Essays in Honour of S. Rosenne*) (Dordrecht: Martinus Nijhoff, 1989), 797–820; A. Cassese, 'How Does the International Community React to Genocide?', in *Human Rights in a Changing World* (Cambridge: Polity Press, 1990), 71–87; J. Verhoeven, 'Le crime de génocide, originalité et ambiguité', 22 RBDI (1991), 5–26; R. Maison, 'Le crime de génocide dans les

[10] W. A. Schabas, in O. Triffterer (ed.), *Commentary*, at margin 4.

premiers jugements du Tribunal Pénal International pour le Rwanda', 103 RGDIP (1999), 129–145; W. A. Schabas, *Genocide in International Law, the Crime of Crimes* (Cambridge: Cambridge University Press, 2000).

THE ROME STATUTE

W. A. Schabas, in O. Triffterer (ed.), *Commentary on the Rome Statute*, 107–16; L. S. Sunga, 'La jurisdiccion "*ratione materiae*" de la Corte penal Internacional', in K. Ambos and O. J. Guerelo (eds), *Estatuto de Roma de la Corte Penal Internacional* (Bogota: Universidad Externado de Colombia, 1999) 242–6; K. Kittichaisaree, *International Criminal Law* (Oxford: Oxford University Press, 2001), 67–84; W. A. Schabas, *Genocide in International Law*, cit., at 89–98, 263–4, 335–44, 409–10, 414–15.

6

OTHER INTERNATIONAL CRIMES (AGGRESSION, TORTURE, AND TERRORISM)

6.1 INTRODUCTION

We will now discuss three classes of international crimes (aggression, torture, and terrorism) that share two main features. First, they are normally not regarded as being included in the so-called 'core crimes' (a category comprising the most heinous crimes: war crimes, crimes against humanity, and genocide). Secondly, at least at present they do not fall under the jurisdiction of any international criminal tribunal or court. It may prove useful briefly to dwell on this second distinguishing trait.

The reasons for the current exclusion of those three classes from international jurisdiction differ for each class. In the case of aggression, envisaged immediately after the Second World War as a crime over which two ad hoc tribunals were endowed with jurisdiction (the IMT and the IMTFE), the reason for the exclusion is that the offence is too politically charged to be defined in sufficiently clear and exhaustive criminal provisions and consequently entrusted to international independent judicial bodies for adjudication.

In the case of torture as a discrete international crime (see *infra*, 6.5–7), the fact that to date no international court or tribunal has been authorized to exercise its jurisdiction over such crime may probably be explained by noting that torture as a crime connected with armed conflicts (a war crime) or as large-scale or widespread criminal conduct (a crime against humanity) has been considered more in need of attention. In contrast, States feel that torture practised by State officials or with their connivance or complicity is a matter pertaining to their domestic domain, where international intrusions are not welcome, hence in principle falling under their own criminal jurisdiction. (It is common knowledge that despite the major merits of the 1984 Convention against Torture, State prosecutors and courts still are somewhat loath to prosecute and punish torturers allegedly committing offences abroad against foreigners.)

Finally, most States still feel that terrorism, being an offence that is imprecisely defined at the level of international criminal law, must be prosecuted at the national level, by individual or joint enforcement and judicial action.

Whatever the reasons for the present legal condition, the failure to extend international adjudication to these three classes of crimes is a matter of regret. Indeed, entrusting an international judicial body with the task of pronouncing upon aggression, torture as a crime per se, or international terrorism would offer at least two major advantages. First, it would significantly contribute, at a judicial level, to rein in impunity for these odious crimes. Secondly, it would ensure—more and better than any national court can do—full respect both for the principle of impartiality of courts and for the fundamental rights of the accused.

6.2 AGGRESSION: THE NOTION

Aggression by a State against another State in breach of international treaties (such as bilateral or multilateral treaties of alliance or the Covenant of the League of Nations, or the Paris Pact of 1928) was already prohibited by international law in interstate relations before the Second World War. Hence if a State engaged in aggression it committed an *international wrongful act* entailing State responsibility.

Aggression was first regarded as an international *crime* involving individual criminal liability in the London Agreement of 8 August 1945 establishing the IMT. Article 6(a) of the IMT Charter, annexed to the Agreement, provided as follows:

> The following acts, or any of them, are crimes coming within the jurisdiction of the Tribunal for which there shall be individual responsibility: (a) CRIMES AGAINST PEACE: namely planning, preparation, initiation or waging of a war of aggression, or a war in violation of international treaties, agreements or assurances, or participation in a Common Plan or Conspiracy for the accomplishment of any of the foregoing.

Thus, wars of aggression were only one of the subcategories of the broad category of 'crimes against peace'. The IMT dwelt at some length in its judgment on this category of crimes to prove that: (i) they had already been established before 1945; and (ii) consequently punishing the Nuremberg defendants for having committed these crimes did not fall foul of the *nullum crimen sine lege* principle. The IMT went so far as to define aggression as the 'supreme international crime' (at 186). Some defendants were found guilty on this count and sentenced either to death or to long terms of imprisonment. Subsequently the Tokyo International Military Tribunal found some defendants guilty of aggression. On 11 December 1946 the UN GA unanimously adopted resolution 95(I) by which it 'affirmed' the 'principles of international law recognized by the Charter of the Nuremberg Tribunal and the judgment of the Tribunal'. Thus, all the States that at that stage were members of the UN eventually approved both the definition of crimes against peace and its application by the IMTs. However, there was no follow-up to this specific matter in the subsequent years, whilst other crimes were spelled out in various conventions.

The problem with aggression was that the major Powers preferred to avoid defining this breach of the ban on force laid down in Article 2(4) of the UN Charter, so as to retain much leeway in the application of that provision both by each of them individually and by the Security Council (SC) collectively. The definition of aggression remained in abeyance, both with regard to aggression as a State delinquency entailing the international responsibility of the State and as an international crime involving criminal liability. Later the UN GA adopted a definition in resolution 3314 (XXIX) of 14 December 1974. However, it was deliberately incomplete, for Article 4 of the Definition provided that the definition was not exhaustive and left to the SC a broad area of discretion, by stating that it was free to characterize other acts as aggression under the Charter. Furthermore, the resolution did not specify that aggression could entail both State responsibility and individual criminal liability: in Article 5(2) of the definition it simply provided that war of aggression is a crime against international law, adding that it 'gives rise to international responsibility'. In addition, the definition propounded in the Draft Code of Crimes Against Peace and Security of Mankind, adopted by the ILC in 1996, is rather circular and disappointing. (Article 16 of the Draft Code provides that 'An individual, who, as leader or organizer, actively participates in or orders the planning, preparation, initiation or waging of aggression committed by a state, shall be responsible for a crime of aggression' (UN Doc. A/51/332).) The Statute of the ICC, while envisaging the crime of aggression in Article 5, stipulates that the Court shall exercise jurisdiction over such crime once a provision defining it is adopted through an amendment of the Statute.

Not surprisingly, since 1946 there have been no national or international trials for alleged crimes of aggression, although undisputedly in many instances States have engaged in acts of aggression, and in a few cases the SC has determined that such acts were committed by States. (The SC has defined as 'acts of aggression' certain actions or raids by South Africa and Israel; see, for example, resolution 573 of 4 October 1985, on Israeli attacks on PLO targets, and resolution 577 of 6 December 1985, on South Africa's attacks on Angola.) Furthermore, in the negotiations leading to the adoption in 1998 of the Statute of the ICC, no agreement was reached on the definition of aggression. Indeed, many African and Arab countries wanted to hold to the 1974 Definition, and even broaden it, while other States including Germany proposed solutions better tailored to suit the needs of criminal law. It would seem however that the main bone of contention was about the role to be reserved by the UN SC. (Were its determinations binding upon the Court? Could it thus stop the Court from prosecuting alleged cases of aggression? Or was the Court instead free to make its own findings, whatever the deliberations of the supreme UN body?) As stated above, in the event States agreed on Article 5(2) whereby the Court shall exercise jurisdiction over the crime of aggression only if and when an amendment to the Statute is adopted by the Assembly of States Parties with a view to both defining the crime and setting out the conditions under which the Court may exercise its jurisdiction.

It would however be fallacious to hold the view that, since no general agreement has been reached in the world community on an exhaustive definition of aggression, perpetrators of this crime may not be prosecuted and punished. True, as pointed out above, this is an area where States deliberately want to retain a broad margin of discretion. Nevertheless, at least some *traditional forms of aggression* are prohibited by customary international law, and are not authorized under the head of *self-defence* pursuant to Article 51 of the UN Charter (and the corresponding customary rule). These forms of aggression may therefore be held to provide the objective elements of the crime. These instances of aggression, constituting the core of the notion at issue, are basically those envisaged in terms in the 1974 Definition, and confirmed, at least in part, by the ICJ in 1986. In *Nicaragua*, in addressing the element of aggression defined in Article 3(g) of the Definition, whereby aggression includes the case where a State 'sends or is substantially involved in sending into another State armed bands with the task of engaging in armed acts against the latter State of such gravity that they would normally be seen as aggression', the Court held that:

> This description . . . may be taken to reflect customary international law. The Court sees no reason to deny that, in customary law, the prohibition of armed attacks may apply to the sending by a State of armed bands to the territory of another State, if such an operation, because of its scale and effects, would have been classified as an armed attack rather than as a mere frontier incident had it been carried out by regular armed forces. (§195.)

International practice, particularly as evinced by the aforementioned actions of the UN SC, the views set forth by States within the United Nations (in particular on the occasion of the adoption of the Definition), as well as the authoritative holding by the ICJ, seem to bear out the proposition that customary rules have evolved to the effect that at least some instances of aggression may be regarded as criminalized. For example, nobody would deny that the attack by Iraq on Kuwait in 1990 was not only a breach of Article 2(4) of the UN Charter (prohibiting the use or threat of force), not justified by self-defence, but also an international crime of aggression.

If the above remarks are correct, it would follow that the contrary view propounded by a US delegate in 2001 would be erroneous from the legal viewpoint.[1] In addition, arguably it is immaterial to the existence of the customary rules at issue, for it is an isolated statement not supported by similar views of other States.

[1] The views set forth by the US delegate to the Preparatory Commission for the establishment of an International Criminal Court are reported in 95 AJIL (2001), 400–1. The US representative of the US State Department noted that 'the [1974] Definition neither restated existing customary international law' nor generated such law, due to lack of subsequent practice and *opinio juris*. After noting that there was no '*opinio juris generalis*', the US representative pointed out that there was no practice: 'Obviously, there has been no concordant practice based on the [General Assembly resolution 3314 on the definition of aggression]. Just look at the records of the Security Council. And if anyone still had any doubts, the controversy about Resolution 3314 in our own discussions, has clearly demonstrated the absence of *opinio juris generalis*' (at 400).

6.3 OBJECTIVE AND SUBJECTIVE ELEMENTS OF AGGRESSION

Customary international law appears to consider as international crimes: the planning, or organizing, or preparing, or participating in the first use of armed force by a State against the territorial integrity and political independence of another State in contravention of the UN Charter, provided the acts of aggression concerned have large-scale and serious consequences.

In contrast, the following are not international crimes, although they may constitute international wrongful acts giving rise to State responsibility: (i) engaging in an armed conflict in violation of international treaties proscribing resort to armed violence, or (ii) participating in a conspiracy to wage aggressive war (that is, planning aggressive war without such planning being followed by action or at least an attempt). Indeed, it does not seem that the criminalization of these two classes of conduct, laid down in the London Agreement, has become part of customary law.

The category of aggression as an international crime comprises the following instances, substantially based on the 1974 Definition:

1. The invasion of or the attack by the armed forces of a State on the territory of another State, or any military occupation, however temporary, resulting from such invasion or attack, or any annexation by the use of force of the territory or part of the territory of another State.

2. Bombardment, or use of any weapon, by the armed forces of a State, against the territory of another State.

3. Blockade of the ports or coasts of a State by the armed forces of another State.

4. Attack by the armed forces of a State on the land, sea, or air forces, or marine and air fleets of another State.

5. The use of the armed forces of one State which are within the territory of another State with the agreement of the receiving State, in contravention of the conditions provided for in the agreement, or any extension of their presence in such territory beyond the termination of the agreement.

6. The action of a State in allowing its territory, which it has placed at the disposal of another State, to be used by that other State for perpetrating an act of aggression against a third State.

7. The sending by or on behalf of a State of armed bands, groups, irregulars, or mercenaries, which carry out acts of armed force against another State of such gravity as to amount to the acts listed above, or its substantial involvement therein.

Plainly, all these instances of the objective element of the crime relate to *traditional* forms of aggression. They are the only ones on which sufficient consent has evolved in the international community for their being criminalized. Conversely, there is still no agreement on possible new forms of aggression, that is, initiation of armed conflict against another State by new means or methods of warfare (for example, unleashing pre-emptive strikes by firing missiles or using nuclear weapons or other arms of mass destruction such as bacteriological or chemical weapons), or widespread or large-scale terrorist attacks by non-State organizations, or other forms of compulsion such as serious and massive economic coercion depriving a foreign State of its freedom of action or bringing about a change in its government.

This crime too requires *criminal intent* (*dolus*). It must be shown that the perpetrator intended to participate in aggression and was aware of the scope, significance, and consequences of the action taken or, at least, knowingly took the risk of bringing about the consequences of that action (*recklessness*). In *Krauch and others* (*IG Farben* case), a US Military Tribunal sitting at Nuremberg held that:

> If the defendants [senior staff or managers, of the German company I. G. Farben specializing in synthetic rubber, gasoline, nitrogen and light metals, as well as explosives], or any of them, are to be held guilty under either count one [planning, preparation, initiation, and waging of wars of aggression] or five [formulation and execution of a common plan or conspiracy to commit crimes against peace] or both on the ground that they participated in the planning, preparation, and initiation of wars of aggression or invasions, it must be shown that they were parties to the plan or conspiracy, or, knowing of the plan, furthered its purpose and objective by participating in the preparation for aggressive war. (At 1108.)

The Court concluded that none of the defendants were guilty of the crimes set forth in counts one and five (at 1128). In his Concurring Opinion Judge Hebert insisted on the need for knowledge and criminal intent for criminal liability for aggressive wars to arise. He stated:

> We are thus brought to the central issue of the charges insofar as the aggressive wars charges are concerned. Acts of substantial participation by certain defendants are established by overwhelming proof. The only real issue of fact is whether it was accompanied by the state of mind requisite in law to establish individual and personal guilt. Does the evidence in this case establish beyond reasonable doubt that the acts of the defendants in preparing Germany for war were done with knowledge of Hitler's aggressive aims and with the criminal purpose of furthering such aims? (At 1217.)

The Court concluded that the accused lacked the required *mens rea* (at 1306).[2]

It has been argued by Glaser[3] that aggression also requires a *special intent*, that is, the will to achieve territorial gains, or to obtain economic advantages, or to interfere with the internal affairs of the victim State. According to this distinguished criminal lawyer, not every armed attack in breach of the UN Charter may be regarded as an international crime. For instance, resort to force under the authority of the resolution of an international body or on humanitarian grounds but in contravention of the UN

[2] See also in *Göring and others*, the holding of the IMT concerning Schacht (at 307–10).

[3] S. Glaser, 'Quelques remarques sur la définition de l'agression en droit international pénal', in *Festschrift für Th. Rittler* (Aalen: Verlag Scientia, 1957), 388–93; idem., 'Culpabilité en droit international pénal', 99 HR 1960–I, 504–5.

Charter, or resort to self-defence in disregard of the conditions laid down in Article 51 of the UN Charter, would be illegal State conduct not amounting to aggression proper. By contrast, any time the Charter is breached with an illegal aim, namely the 'special intention' referred to above, we are faced with aggression proper.

It is submitted that this view, although at first sight convincing, might give rise to objections. Admittedly, the examples suggested by that author seem to amount to serious breaches of the ban on the use or threat of force, enshrined both in customary international law and in the UN Charter, without qualifying for the category of aggression. Nonetheless, it would seem that current international law proscribes engaging in aggression whatever the purpose or motivation of the aggressor. The rationale behind the sweeping prohibition of any armed attack not clearly in self-defence is that peace is such an overriding value that any breach of the peace involving an armed attack on another State not legally warranted by international law, constitutes both an international wrong and an international crime. To require a special intent would presuppose that aggression is only prohibited and thus only constitutes an international crime when, in addition to unlawfully attacking another State by military force, a State also pursues a special goal. In fact, it may happen that the aggressor State does pursue a particular goal when engaging in military action; this goal, however, does not acquire autonomous legal status; in other words, it does not rise to the level of a subjective legal ingredient of the crime. Were it otherwise, two problems would arise. First, who defines the class of goals that make up the special intent purportedly required for the crime? And what special instances would fall into this class? For instance, would the purpose of coercing the attacked State to stop committing atrocities against its own nationals qualify as the required intent for aggression? And what about the purpose of forestalling future use by the attacked State of weapons of mass destruction? Secondly, there would arise many problems that would be difficult to solve. For instance, an attack conducted by one State against another for inscrutable motives might escape the label of 'aggression', whereas a relatively less grave attack would be more culpable: for example, an attack which has a comprehensible, albeit illegal, economic motive (e.g. to gain access to water or to some other precious resource indispensable for the survival of a State's population), would be categorized as aggression because of the presence of the special intent.

Perhaps one could accept Glaser's suggestion, on condition however of applying it only to aggression as a crime, that is, as an offence involving criminal liability, and not as a State delinquency. This would of course presuppose the splitting of a unitary notion of aggression into two separate concepts, one valid for wrongful acts of States (where no special intent would be required, for the purpose of banning armed attacks in breach of Article 2.4 of the UN Charter as much as possible), the other for individuals' criminal offences (where instead the requisite subjective element of crime would include special intent). The possible merit of this distinction would perhaps lie in enabling courts to distinguish, for the purpose of establishing guilt or at least for sentencing purposes, between leaders planning or ordering aggression and those persons who merely carry out their plans or aid and abet aggression.

6.4 THE POSSIBLE IMPACT ON JUDICIAL FINDINGS OF THE APPRAISAL OF AGGRESSION BY INTERNATIONAL POLITICAL BODIES

In this area, involving both State responsibility and individual criminal liability, courts trying persons accused of aggression may legitimately take a judicial approach which differs from the political stand taken by international political bodies such as the UN SC or the GA. It follows that there may be cases where one of those bodies does not consider that it is faced with aggression, whilst a national or international court may take a contrary position and consequently find individuals criminally responsible for aggression. This consequence is quite understandable, in an area so politically charged. However, national or international courts should not be bound by any decision taken by a political body, whereas political bodies should duly take into consideration any judicial finding on the matter. One may well wonder whether a political body should be *bound* by the decisions of judicial bodies, at least by the decisions of an international court. Not to be bound would appear to show that the political body has chosen to *disregard* the decision of an international court, rather than that the political body and the judicial body simply have different spheres of competence.

It remains true that whenever the SC or the GA conclude that in a particular instance acts committed by a State amount to aggression, it could be easier for a national or international court to find that aggression was perpetrated and therefore to pronounce on the issue of whether the individuals involved are criminally liable.

6.5 TORTURE: GENERAL

Torture is not only prohibited when it is part of a widespread or systematic practice thus amounting to a crime against humanity. Torture is also proscribed when it is done as a single act, outside any large-scale practice. In this case, if torture is perpetrated in time of armed conflict, it is a war crime. It may also be a *discrete* crime under customary international law, whether committed in time of peace or in time of armed conflict. There is an important difference between these various categories.

In time of war or internal armed conflict a serviceman may incur criminal liability for a war crime if he engages in torture against an enemy military or an enemy civilian. Also a private individual not acting in an official capacity may perpetrate torture in time of war; in this case, to qualify as a *war crime*, it must be committed against (i) a member of the enemy belligerent army (or other lawful combatants), or (ii) a protected person who either has the nationality of the enemy or (particularly in the case of internal armed conflict) is under the control of the adversary. In these two classes of criminal conduct, to qualify as a war crime torture must be linked to the armed conflict. Thus for instance, acts of torture performed by a civilian against another civilian fall under the category of 'ordinary crimes' if committed outside the context of, and without any nexus with, the armed conflict (for example, torture practised by a civilian on a neighbour out of sadism, or on another civilian to take vengeance for a previous personal wrong). In such war crimes it is not therefore necessary that a State official be involved in the torture process, as was instead incorrectly held by the German Federal Court of Justice in *Sokolović*.[4]

Torture in time of internal or international armed conflict or in time of peace, to amount to a *crime against humanity*, needs among other things to be part of a widespread or systematic practice, as this is a general requirement of *all* crimes against humanity. Moreover, the accused must *know* that his acts of torture form part of this widespread or systematic practice. Private persons may commit torture; again, there is no need for the participation of a State official in the specific act of torture. It is, however, implicit in the very definition of this class of crimes that, in addition to the specific case of torture being prosecuted, numerous acts of torture are being or have been perpetrated without being punished by the authorities; in other words, there is, or has been, implicit approval or condonation by the authorities, or at least they have failed to take appropriate action to bring the culprits to book. To put it differently, there must be at least some sort of 'passive involvement' of the authorities. However, it is not required that a State official be involved in the torture process, as was instead incorrectly maintained in *Furundžija* (§162).

Things are different as regards torture as a discrete crime, i.e. not a crime against humanity nor a war crime. Torture as a discrete crime may be perpetrated either in time of peace or in time of armed conflict, as was rightly held in 2001 by the ICTY in *Kunarac and others* (§§488–97) with a slight departure from the previous judgments of the ICTR in *Akayesu* (§593) and the ICTY in *Furundžija* (§162). Under Article 1.1 of the UN Torture Convention of 1984, the 'pain or suffering' that is a necessary ingredient of torture must be inflicted 'by or at the instigation of or with the consent or acquiescence of a *public official or other person acting in an official capacity*'. The need for this sort of participation of a *de jure* or de facto State official stems from: (i) the fact that in this case torture is punishable under international rules even when it constitutes a single or sporadic episode; and (ii) the consequent necessity to distinguish between torture as a common or 'ordinary' crime (for example, torture of a woman by her husband, or of a young man by a sadist) and torture as an international crime covered by international rules on human rights.

It would seem that although they differ in many respects, the three categories of torture (as a war crime, as a crime against humanity, as a discrete crime) share one fundamental element: it is not exclusively required that the purpose of torture be the extraction of a confession or admission from the victim. Instead, the aim of torture as an international crime may be: (i) to obtain information or a confession; or (ii) to punish, intimidate, or humiliate a person; or (iii) to coerce the victim or a third

[4] At 16–19. The Court required, for a war crime to exist, that among other things torture be practised 'by a State organ or with State approval (*mit staatlicher Billigung*)' (at 16). The Court therefore expressed misgivings about the notion of torture laid down in Article 7(1)(f) of the ICC Statute (at 17–18).

person to do or omit something; or (iv) to discriminate, on any ground, against the victim or a third person (see among other cases *Furundžija* (§162), a case that however referred specifically to torture as a crime against humanity).

6.6 THE EMERGENCE OF A CUSTOMARY RULE ON TORTURE

The ban on torture perpetrated in the above circumstances has had a long evolution. Significant contributions to this process, at the norm-setting level, were made by an important Declaration passed by the UN GA (res. 3452(XXX) of 9 December 1975), by the increasing importance of the 1984 UN Convention on Torture, by general treaties on human rights and the judicial practice of the bodies responsible for their enforcement, by national case law (in particular cases such as *Pinochet*), and by the judgments of the ICTY in *Furundžija* (§146) and the European Court of Human Rights in *Aksoy* (§62) and *Selmouni* (§§96–105). Suffice it to mention that in *Filartiga* a US court held that 'the torturer has become, like the pirate or the slave trader before him, *hostis humani generis*, an enemy of all mankind' (at 980). And in 1998 in *Furundžjia* the ICTY, after mentioning the human rights treaties and the resolutions of international organizations prohibiting torture, stated that:

> the existence of this corpus of general and treaty rules proscribing torture shows that the international community, aware of the importance of outlawing this heinous phenomenon, has decided to suppress any manifestation of torture by operating both at the interstate level and at the level of individuals. No legal loopholes have been left. (§146.)

By now a *general rule* has evolved in the international community, (i) prohibiting individuals from perpetrating torture, regardless of whether it is committed on a large scale, and (ii) authorizing all States to prosecute and punish the alleged author of such acts, irrespective of where the acts were perpetrated and the nationality of the perpetrator or the victim.

6.7 OBJECTIVE AND SUBJECTIVE ELEMENTS OF TORTURE

As for the conduct prohibited, one may safely rely upon the definition of torture laid down in Article 1(1) of the 1984 UN Convention. As the ICTY held in *Delalić and others* (§§455–74), in *Furundžija* (§§257), and *Kunarac and others* (§§483–97), 'there is now general acceptance [in the world community] of the main elements contained' in that definition. The objective elements of torture may therefore be held to consist of: (i) 'any act by which severe pain or suffering, whether physical or mental, is . . . inflicted on a person'; (ii) 'such pain or suffering is inflicted by or at the instigation of or with the consent or acquiescence of a public official or other person acting in an official capacity'; and (iii) such pain or suffering does not arise 'only from' nor is it 'inherent in or incidental to lawful sanctions'.

The requirements for *mens rea* may be deduced from the very nature of torture, as set out in the definition just referred to. It should be noted that Article 1 of the 1984 Convention, which has to a large extent become part of customary law, provides that the infliction of pain or suffering must be 'intentional'. It appears, therefore, that criminal *intent* (*dolus*) is always required for torture to be an international crime. Other less stringent subjective criteria (recklessness, culpable negligence) are not sufficient (except where superior responsibility is at stake: see *infra*, 10.4.3).

6.8 TRANS-NATIONAL, STATE-SUPPORTED, OR STATE-SPONSORED TERRORISM

6.8.1 A CURRENT MISCONCEPTION: THE ALLEGED LACK OF A GENERALLY AGREED DEFINITION OF TERRORISM

For more than thirty years after the Second World War, States in the UN debated the question of punishing terrorism. However, they were seemingly unable to agree upon a definition of this crime. Third World countries staunchly clung to their view that this notion could not cover acts of violence perpetrated by so-called 'freedom fighters', i.e. individuals and groups struggling for their right to self-determination. Furthermore, developing countries vociferously insisted on the notion that no treaty could be adopted to ban terrorism unless at the same time the historical, economic, social, and political causes underlying resort to terrorism were studied in depth and thrashed out.[5]

As a result, both scholars and diplomats currently hold the view that States have never agreed upon a definition of terrorism. Hence, it would be impossible to criminalize this phenomenon as such. At present it would be possible to consider as criminal only single and specific instances of terrorism specifically prohibited by some treaties: hijacking of aircraft, terrorist acts against internationally protected persons including diplomatic agents, the taking of hostages, terrorist acts against the safety of maritime navigation, terrorist bombing, financing of terrorism, etc. This proposition amounts to saying that terrorism per se is not a discrete crime under customary international law.

To my mind, this view is not correct. A definition of terrorism does exist, and the phenomenon also amounts to a customary international law crime.

Let us see how an accepted definition has gradually emerged in the international community.[6] In fact a definition evolved after 1937 but developing countries in the

[5] See, among others, C. Greenwood, 'Terrorism and Humanitarian Law—The Debate over Additional Protocol I', in 19 *Israel Y. on Human Rights* (1989), 187–207; S. Oeter, 'Terrorism and "Wars of National Liberation" from a Law of War Perspective', 49 *Zeit. aus. Öff. Recht und Völkerrecht* (1989) 445–85; A. Cassese, *Terrorism, Politics and Law—The* Achille Lauro *Affair* (Cambridge: Polity Press, 1989), 1–16.

[6] On the question of whether and how terrorism is defined in international law, see in particular R. Baxter, 'A Skeptical Look at the Concept of Terrorism', 7 *Akron Law Rev.* (1974), 380 ff.; R. Mushkat, '"Technical" Impediments on the Way to a Universal Definition of International Terrorism', 20 *Indian J. of Int. Law* (1980),

United Nations (with the support of socialist States, whilst they existed) were loath to accept it without the addition of what they considered a *caveat* (but which could probably more accurately be defined as an *exception*): namely the exclusion from the definition of terrorism of the acts or transactions of national liberation movements or, more generally, 'freedom fighters'. The refusal of developed countries to accept this exception led to a stalemate, which has erroneously been termed as 'lack of definition'. What indeed was lacking was *agreement on the exception*. The general notion was not in question. To hold the contrary view would give rise to two objections, one based on logic, the other on existing legal rules. Logically, to say that, because there is no consensus on the exception, a general notion has not evolved would be a misconception. It is as if one were to say that, since in international criminal law it is doubtful whether murder may exceptionally be justified by duress, as a result one could not define murder. The second objection is based on the existence of international treaty provisions that explicitly prohibit terrorism, without adding any definition or qualification. For instance, one may mention Article 33(1) of the Fourth Geneva Convention of 1949 which provides that 'collective penalties and likewise all measures of intimidation or of terrorism are prohibited'. Similarly, Article 4(2)(d) of the Second Additional Protocol of 1977, on internal armed conflicts, prohibits 'acts of terrorism' 'at any time and in any place whatsoever'. One may also mention Article 4 of the Statute of the International Criminal Tribunal for Rwanda, which among other things adopts the Second Additional Protocol's criminalization (or rather, grants the Tribunal jurisdiction over) 'acts of terrorism' perpetrated in an internal armed conflict. Plainly, if all these treaties speak of 'terrorism' or 'acts of terrorists' without specifying what is covered by this notion, it means that the draftsmen had a fairly clear idea of what they were prohibiting. It is warranted to believe that they either deliberately or unwittingly were referring to a general notion underlying treaty provisions and laid down in customary rules. Furthermore, in 1999 a treaty was agreed upon in the UN GA that, in addition to prohibiting specific acts of terrorism, also added a definition of this phenomenon: this is the International Convention for the Suppression of the Financing of Terrorism (GA resolution 54/109 of 9 December 1999). In defining terrorism the Convention takes a twofold approach: first, in Article 2(a) it refers to the acts prohibited by nine treaties listed in the Annex (on hijacking, terrorist bombing, etc.); secondly, in Article 2(1)(b) it sets forth a sort of all-inclusive formula, that

448–71; W. R. Farrell, *The U.S. Government Response to Terrorism: In Search of an Effective Strategy* (Boulder, Col.: Westview Press, 1982) at 6; C. C. Joyner, 'Offshore Maritime Terrorism: International Implications and Legal response', 36 *Naval College Law Rev.* (1983), at 20; G. Levitt, 'Is "Terrorism" Worth Defining?' 13 *Ohio New Un. Law Rev.* (1986), at 97; J. F. Murphy, 'Defining International Terrorism: A Way Out of the Quagmire', in 19 *Israel Y. of Int. Law* (1989), 13–37; O. Schachter, 'The Extraterritorial Use of Force Against Terrorist Bases', 11 *Houston J. of Int. Law* (1989), at 309; K. Skubiszewski, 'Definition of Terrorism', 19 *Israel Y. of Int. Law* (1989), 39–53; G. Guillaume, 'Terrorisme et droit international', 215 *Hague Recueil* (1989-III), at 295–307; D. Kash, 'Abductions of Terrorists in International Airspace and on the High Seas', 8 *Florida J. of Int. Law* (1993) at 72; I. M. Porras, 'On Terrorism: Reflections on Violence and the Outlaw', *Utah Law Rev.* (1994) at 124; R. Higgins, 'The General International Law of Terrorism', in R. Higgins and M. Flory (eds), *Terrorism and International Law* (London and New York: Routledge, 1997), 14–19.

completes the previous 'definition by reference'; this provision stipulates that terrorism is:

Any . . . act intended to cause death or serious bodily injury to a civilian, or to any other person not taking an active part in the hostilities in a situation of armed conflict, when the purpose of such act, by its nature or context, is to intimidate a population, or to compel a government or an international organization to do or to abstain from doing an act.

The Supreme Court of Canada, in *Suresh*, held that the above definition 'catches the essence of what the world understands by "terrorism". Particular cases on the fringes of terrorist activity will inevitably provoke disagreement. Parliament is not prevented from adopting more details or different definitions of terrorism' (§98).[7] The Court nonetheless held the definition sufficiently 'certain to be workable, fair and constitutional' and therefore used it for interpreting the Canadian Immigration Act.

Finally, numerous national laws prohibit terrorism in terms.[8] Interestingly, they substantially converge in the definition of terrorism they set out.[9] Strikingly, even the 1998 Arab Convention for the Suppression of Terrorism defines terrorist acts along

[7] The Supreme Court stated (§93) that it shared the view of the Federal Court of Appeal in the same case that the term 'terrorism' is not inherently ambiguous 'even if the full meaning . . . must be determined on an incremental basis' (§69 of the appellate judgment).

[8] For a careful perusal of some of these laws, see J. F. Murphy, 'Defining International Terrorism: A Way Out of the Quagmire', cit., 22–9. In particular, for the text of US legislation, see H. S. Levie (ed.), *Terrorism—Documents of International and Local Control* (Dobbs Ferry, NY: Oceana, 1995), 317–68.

[9] For instance, the US Iran and Libya Sanctions Act of 1996 (Public Law 104-172, 5 August 1996, in H. S. Levie (ed.), *Terrorism, Documents of International and Local Control*, vol. 12 (Dobbs Ferry, NY: Oceana, 1997, at 487) provides that 'an act of international terrorism' means an act '(A) which is violent or dangerous to human life and that is a violation of the criminal laws of the United States or of any State or that would be a criminal violation if committed within the jurisdiction of the United States or any State; and (B) which appears to be intended (i) to intimidate or coerce a civilian population; (ii) to influence the policy of a government by intimidation or coercion; or (iii) to affect the conduct of a government by assassination or kidnapping.' See also the US Antiterrorism and Effective Death Penalty Act of 1996 (ibid., vol. 10, at 521–3).

In the UK the Terrorism Act 2000 provides in section 1 that 'terrorism'

(1) means the use or threat of action where—
   (a) the action falls within subsection (2),
   (b) the use or threat is designed to influence the government or to intimidate the public or a section of the public, and
   (c) the use or threat is made for the purpose of advancing a political, religious or ideological cause.
(2) Action falls within this subsection if it—
   (a) involves serious violence against a person,
   (b) involves serious damage to property,
   (c) endangers a person's life, other than that of the person committing the action,
   (d) creates a serious risk to the health or safety of the public or a section of the public, or
   (e) is designed to interfere with or seriously to disrupt an electronic system.

(**http://www.legislation.hmso.gov.uk/acts2000**)

See also paragraph 100.1(2) of the Schedule to the Australian Security Legislation Amendment (Terrorism) Bill 2002, as well as the Canadian Bill C–36 (Antiterrorism Act), section 2(2).

the same lines (although it then goes on to except from terrorism acts committed in struggles for the self-determination of peoples).[10]

Having pointed to the fallacious character of the current views about terrorism, I must add the following: the failure of States to agree upon an exception to the notion of terrorism impelled them to adopt a rather roundabout strategy for facing, and coming to grips with, this odious phenomenon. The majority of UN members preferred to draw up Conventions prohibiting individual sets of well-specified acts. In this way, the thorny question of hammering out a broad and generally acceptable definition plus exceptions, if any, was circumvented. The Conventions at issue deal with the hijacking of aircraft, crimes against internationally protected persons including diplomatic agents, the taking of hostages, unlawful acts against the safety of maritime navigation, terrorist bombing, and the financing of terrorism.[11] In addition, at the regional level, in 1971 the US and various Latin American countries plus Sri Lanka agreed upon a Convention for the prevention and punishment of acts of terrorism,[12] and a European Convention on the suppression of terrorism was adopted in 1977.[13]

The condemnation of terrorism did, however, increase over time. In addition, many States probably became convinced that the First Additional Protocol of 1977 provided an acceptable solution to the question of avoiding labelling 'freedom fighters' as terrorists. (The Protocol recognizes as combatants, and extends the protection of the laws of war to, those who 'are fighting against colonial domination and alien occupation and against racist regimes in the exercise of their right of self-determination' and Article 44(3) of the Protocol grants, under certain conditions, legal status as combatants, and prisoner of war status in case of capture, to fighters who are not members of the armed forces of a State and normally do not carry their arms openly.)[14]

[10] Article 1(2). Terrorism includes 'Any act or threat of violence, whatever its motives or purposes, that occurs in the advancement of an individual or collective criminal agenda and seeking to sow panic among people, causing fear by harming them, or placing their lives, liberty and security in danger, or seeking to cause damage to the environment or to public or private installations or property or occupying or seizing them, or seeking to jeopardize a national resource'.

[11] See the Conventions on the safety of civil aviation (the Tokyo Convention of 14 September 1963 on offences and certain other acts committed on board aircraft, the Hague Convention of 16 December 1970 for the suppression of unlawful seizure of aircraft, the Montreal Convention of 23 September 1971 for the suppression of unlawful acts against the safety of civil aviation); the UN Convention of 14 December 1973 on the prevention and punishment of crimes against internationally protected persons; the New York Convention of 17 December 1979 against the taking of hostages; the Montreal Protocol of 24 February 1988 for the suppression of unlawful acts of violence at airports serving international civil aviation, supplementary to the Montreal Convention of 1971; the Rome Convention of 10 March 1988 for the suppression of unlawful acts against the safety of maritime navigation, with a Protocol on the safety of fixed platforms located on the continental shelf; the UN Convention of 15 December 1997 for the suppression of terrorist bombings; and the UN Convention for the suppression of the financing of terrorism, of 1999.

[12] Convention to Prevent and Punish the Acts of Terrorism Taking the Form of Crimes Against Persons and Related Extortion that are of International Significance, of 2 February 1971, in D. J. Musch (ed.), *Terrorism—Documents of International and Local Control*, vol. 14 (Dobbs Ferry, NY: Oceana, 1997), at 523–8. The convention was signed by 22 Latin or Central American countries, plus the USA and Sri Lanka.

[13] See text in R. A. Friedlander (ed.), *Terrorism—Documents of International and Local Control*, vol. 2 (Dobbs Ferry, NY: Oceana, 1979) 565–9.

[14] See the writings cited in note 5 above.

Furthermore, the change in the general political climate in the world community following the downfall of socialist regimes, as well as the gradual demise of wars of national liberation, led to a change in attitude towards terrorism. For instance, General Assembly resolutions on terrorism adopted since 1991 have dropped the reference to the underlying causes of the terrorist phenomenon.

As a result, broad agreement gradually evolved on a general definition of terrorism that did not provide for any exception (in spite of the fact that, as pointed out above, in 1998 the League of Arab States adopted an Arab Convention for the Suppression of Terrorism that in Article 2(a) envisaged that exception). A resolution passed by consensus in the UN General Assembly (res. 49/60, adopted on 9 December 1994) reflects this agreement. In the annexed Declaration it contains a provision (para. 3) stating that:

> Criminal acts intended or calculated to provoke a state of terror in the general public, a group of persons or particular persons for political purposes are in any circumstance unjustifiable, whatever the considerations of a political, philosophical, ideological, racial, ethnic, religious or any other nature that may be invoked to justify them.[15]

This definition in substance takes up that laid down in Article 1(2) of the unratified 1937 Convention, whereby terrorism encompasses 'criminal acts directed against a State and intended or calculated to create a state of terror in the minds of particular persons, or a group of persons or the general public'.[16] In addition, the definition is not far from, and indeed to a large extent dovetails with, the notion of terrorism laid down in the aforementioned 1999 Convention on the financing of terrorism.

It is submitted in light of the above that there exists an acceptable and sufficiently clear definition of this crime, and in addition the crime is envisaged and banned by customary law, that is, it is no longer simply a treaty law crime.

Three main elements seem to be required for the crime of international terrorism: (i) the acts must constitute a criminal offence under most national legal systems (for example, assault, murder, kidnapping, hostage-taking, extortion, bombing, torture, arson, etc.); (ii) they must be aimed at spreading terror (that is, fear and intimidation) by means of violent action or the threat thereof directed against a State, the public, or particular groups of persons; (iii) they must be politically, religiously, or otherwise ideologically motivated, that is not motivated by the pursuit of private ends.

Let me add that, despite the gradually emerging consensus on an *unqualified*

[15] See also other resolutions adopted by the UN General Assembly, for instance res. 49/60 of 17 February 1995, res. 51/210, of 16 January 1997, res. 55/158 of 30 January 2001.

[16] In 1995 the Special Rapporteur of the UN International Law Commission on the Draft Code of Crimes Against the Peace and Security of Mankind, Mr Doudou Thiam, suggested the following definition for international terrorism imputable to State officials: 'Undertaking, organising, ordering, facilitating, financing, encouraging or tolerating acts of violence against another State directed at persons or property and of such nature as to create a state of terror [fear or dread] in the minds of public figures, groups of persons or the general public in order to compel the aforesaid State to grant advantages or to act in a specific way' (UN, Report of the ILC on the Work of its 47th Session (1995), GAOR, Suppl. no. 10, A/50/10 at 58, n. 45). However, any references to terrorism were subsequently dropped in the final Draft (see UN, Report of the ILC on the Work of its 48th Session (1996), GAOR, 51st Session, Suppl. no. 10 (A/51/10), 9–120.

definition of terrorism, in the recent drafting process of the ICC Statute States eventually decided not to include terrorism among the crimes under the Court's jurisdiction on a number of grounds. Chief among them was the alleged lack of an agreed definition of terrorism. (The other grounds were that: (i) the inclusion of the crime would have resulted in the politicizing of the Court, (ii) it was not sufficiently serious an offence to be within the Court's jurisdiction, and (iii) terrorism would be more effectively prosecuted at the national level, if need be by co-ordinated action of individual States.)

6.9 THE DIVERSE FORMS OF TERRORISM

6.9.1 THE MAIN FEATURES OF TERRORISM

Terrorism is a phenomenon that may take on diverse forms and manifestations. It has judiciously been said that it has a 'chameleon-like' character.[17] Hence it should not be surprising that it may fall under various categories of crimes, depending on the circumstances in which terrorist acts are perpetrated.[18]

Before considering each of these categories separately, the general features they all share may be outlined. One of the most striking hallmarks of terrorism is the 'depersonalization of the victim' (*dépersonnalisation de la victime*), to borrow an expression from the distinguished French criminal lawyer M. Delmas-Marty.[19] In the case of terrorism (as well as, albeit in a lesser striking manner, in genocide and in persecution as a crime against humanity) the perpetrator does not attack a specific victim, on account of a personal relationship or animosity, or of the victim possessing certain assets, or of his or her gender or age, or of his or her nationality, social position, etc. Here the perpetrator is 'blind', as it were, to the victim; it does not matter to him whether the victim is young or old, male or female, a fellow-countryman or a foreigner, wealthy or poor, etc. He attacks persons at random. What matters is that the victim be murdered, wounded, threatened, or otherwise coerced so that the political, religious, or ideological purpose of the perpetrator may be attained. In the eyes of the perpetrator, the victim is simply an anonymous and expendable tool for achieving his aim.

A further distinguishing trait is that, to amount to an international crime proper, terrorist acts must show a nexus with an *international* or *internal armed conflict* (that is, a military clash between two States or between two armed groups within one State), or they must acquire such a *magnitude* as to exhibit the hallmarks of a crime against

[17] A. Roberts, 'Can We Define Terrorism?', 14 *Oxford Today* (2002), at 18.

[18] See among others Y. Dinstein, 'Terrorism as an International Crime', 18 *Israel Y. on Human Rights* (1989), 55–73.

[19] See M. Delmas-Marty, 'Les crimes internationaux peuvent-ils contribuer au débat entre universalisme et relativisme des valeurs?' in Cassese and Delmas-Marty (eds), *Crimes internationaux*, at 67.

humanity, or they must involve State authorities and exhibit a *trans-national dimension*, that is, they do not remain confined to the territory of one State but massively spill over into and jeopardize the security of other States. This is among other things evidenced by provisions of international treaties that exclude from the treaties' application merely 'domestic' terrorism.[20]

Another general feature of terrorism is that it is criminal whether perpetrated by *individuals acting in a private capacity* (normally as members of a terrorist group or organization) or by *State officials*. In the latter case, of course, alongside individual criminal liability there may arise State responsibility: the State on whose behalf the agent engages in terrorist action may incur international responsibility for breaching the international customary norms and any applicable treaty rules that make it unlawful to organize, instigate, assist, finance, or participate in terrorist acts in territories of other States. In the former case States may be internationally responsible if they acquiesce in, tolerate, or encourage activities within their territory directed towards the commission of such acts abroad.[21]

Depending on the class of crimes to which the terrorist act may belong (war crimes, crimes against humanity, crimes of international terrorism), the victim protected by international law may vary. As we shall see, terrorist acts are prohibited as war crimes when directed against civilians or civilian objects; when they fall under the category of crimes against humanity, they are normally banned if they target civilians (although in my opinion this view, taken in the statutes of various international criminal tribunals, is at variance with customary law; see *supra*, 4.6.3); finally, when terrorist acts can be classified as international crimes of terrorism, they are prohibited whatever their target.

6.9.2 TERRORISM AS A WAR CRIME

As mentioned above, Article 33(1) of the Fourth Geneva Convention of 1949 prohibits acts of terrorism committed against civilians eligible for the status of 'protected persons', whether they are perpetrated by the armed forces of a belligerent against persons who find themselves in the belligerent's territory as internees, or in an occupied territory. As explained in the authoritative *Commentary* published by the ICRC, this prohibition is motivated by the need to forestall a common practice, that of belligerents resorting to 'intimidatory measures to terrorise the population' in the hope of preventing hostile acts.[22] The same acts are of course prohibited if committed by civilians fighting alongside one of the belligerents, or by civilians or organized armed groups fighting against an Occupying Power.

[20] See for instance Article 3 of the UN Convention on terrorist bombing, of 12 January 1998 ('this Convention shall not apply where the offence is committed within a single State, the alleged offender and the victims are nationals of that State, the alleged offender is found in the territory of that State and no other State has a basis under Article 8(1) or Article 6(2) of this Convention to exercise jurisdiction, except that the provisions of Articles 10 to 15 shall, as appropriate, apply in those cases'). For a similar provision see Article 3 of the Convention on financing of terrorism, of 20 January 2000.

[21] See among other things the various UN General Assembly resolutions cited in note 15 above.

[22] See ICRC, *Commentary, Fourth Geneva Convention* (Geneva: ICRC, 1958), at 225–6.

Similarly, acts of terrorism against civilians or persons that have ceased to take part in the conflict are prohibited in internal armed conflicts (see Article 4(2)(d) of the Second Additional Protocol of 1977), irrespective of the party to the conflict that resorts to terrorist methods.

In addition, under both the First and the Second Additional Protocol 'acts or threats of violence the primary purpose of which is to spread terror among the civilian population are prohibited' (Articles 51(2) and 13(2) respectively). These provisions to a large extent take up, extend the scope of, and codify a principle that had already been laid down, albeit exclusively with regard to aerial warfare, in Article 22 of the 1923 Hague Rules on Aerial Warfare. Pursuant to this provision, 'aerial bombardment for the purpose of terrorizing the civilian population, of destroying or damaging private property not of military character, or of injuring non-combatants is prohibited'.[23]

It is thus clear that, under international humanitarian law as laid down in treaties, terrorism is prohibited and criminalized so long as it is directed *against civilians.* The inference could be drawn that it is allowed against belligerents or, more generally, *combatants.* It is underlined in the ICRC Commentary to the Geneva Additional Protocols that the fact that some provisions prohibit acts of terrorism without specifying that such acts must be directed against civilians implies that terrorist acts which target *objects* (such as, for instance, civilian aerial installations) are also prohibited, and therefore criminalized.[24] However, the construction is warranted that also acts of terrorism against *combatants* are criminalized, although not as war crimes, but as discrete crimes of terrorism (see 6.9.4); think, for instance, of enemy civilians planting a bomb in an officers' mess, with the *specific intent* of spreading terror among the enemy combatants.

The *actus reus* is an attack or a threat of an attack on civilians (or civilian objects), or the adoption of other intimidatory measures designed to spread fear and anguish among civilians. The subjective element must be the intent to carry out unlawful acts or threats or violence against civilians. However, this *general intent* must always be accompanied by a *special criminal intent,* that is, to bring about terror (fear, anxiety) among civilians. It is apparent from the relevant provisions that the spreading of threat or fear among civilians must be the 'primary purpose' of the unlawful acts or threats of violence.

Interestingly, in a recent case (*Galić*) brought before the International Criminal Tribunal for the former Yugoslavia, the Prosecutor raised the issue of the criminal liability of the accused for unlawfully inflicting terror upon civilians as a war crime. The accused was a Bosnian Serb major-general who commanded the troops surrounding and besieging Sarajevo between September 1992 and August 1994. According to the Prosecutor he was responsible under the doctrine of command

[23] For the text of the Rules and their legal status in international law see A. Roberts and R. Guelff (eds), *Documents on The Laws of War,* 3rd edn (Oxford: Oxford University Press, 2000), 139–53.

[24] See ICRC, *Commentaire des Protocoles Additionnels* (Geneva: M. Nijhoff, 1986), at 1399 (§4538).

responsibility for the campaign of sniping and shelling of civilians in Sarajevo by Bosnian Serb troops.[25]

6.9.3 TERRORISM AS A CRIME AGAINST HUMANITY

Acts of terrorism may amount to crimes against humanity when they meet the special requirements of these crimes, that is, when: (i) they are part of a widespread or systematic attack on civilians; and (ii) the perpetrators are aware or cognizant of the fact that their criminal acts are part of a general or systematic pattern of conduct.

It would seem that, when it takes the form of crimes against humanity, terrorism may manifest itself as murder, extermination, torture, rape, persecution, or be encompassed by 'other inhumane acts'.

As under the Statutes of the ICTY, the ICTR, and the ICC, crimes against humanity may only be committed against civilians, terrorist acts perpetrated against servicemen or military installations would not fall under the jurisdiction of these Tribunals or the International Criminal Court. However, in my opinion customary international law on the matter has a broader scope than those provisions of treaty law (or of binding Security Council resolutions); it also encompasses acts targeting military people or military installations. Consequently, if this view were to be upheld, one could consider that also such terrorist acts as the crashing of a civilian aircraft into the Pentagon could amount to a crime against humanity (on the assumption that this act was part of a widespread or systematic practice of terrorism against US civilian or military personnel or installations).

6.9.4 TERRORISM AS A DISCRETE INTERNATIONAL CRIME

As I have pointed out above, not all terrorist acts amount to international crimes proper. Terrorist activities carried out within a State (say, attacks by ETA in Spain or the IRA in the UK, or by the Red Brigades in Italy) are criminal offences punishable under the law of the relevant State; other States, if bound by treaties with that State, may also be obliged to co-operate in searching for, prosecuting, and punishing the perpetrators of terrorist actions.[26]

[25] See the Indictment (Case no. IT-98-29-I) and the Prosecutor's Pre-Trial Brief, of 23 October 2001. In this brief the Prosecutor, after briefly referring to the 'sniping' and 'shelling' incidents (§§15–21), stated as follows:

> 'The principal objective of the campaign of sniping and shelling of civilians was to terrorize the civilian population. The intention to spread terror is evident, *inter alia*, from the widespread nature of civilian activities targeted, the manner in which the unlawful attacks were carried out, and the timing and the duration of the unlawful acts and threats of violence, which consisted of shelling and sniping. The nature of the civilian activities targeted demonstrates that the attacks were designed to strike at the heart, and be maximally disruptive, of civilian life. By attacking when civilians were most vulnerable, such as when seeking the necessities of life, visiting friends or relatives, engaging in burial rites or private prayer, or attending rare recreational events aimed precisely at countering the growing social malaise, the attacks were intended to break the nerve of the population and to achieve the breakdown of the social fabric.' (§§22–5.)

[26] See note 16 above and the treaty provisions mentioned there.

Terrorist acts amount to *international crimes* when, first, they are not limited in their effects to one State solely, but *transcend national boundaries* as far as the persons implicated, the means employed, and the violence involved are concerned; and, secondly, they are carried out with the support, the toleration, or the acquiescence of the State where the terrorist organization is located or of a foreign State. The element of *State promotion* or *State toleration*, or even *State acquiescence* due to inability to eradicate the terrorist organization, seems crucial for elevating the offence to the rank of international crime. This is so because it is at this stage that terrorism stops being a criminal activity against which States can fight by bilateral or multilateral co-operation, to become (and this is the third element) a phenomenon of concern for the *whole international community* and a threat to the peace.

On 12 September 2001 the UN Security Council, in its resolution 1368 (2001) on the terrorist attacks in New York and Washington, underscored this feature of terrorism, when it 'unequivocally' condemned 'in the strongest terms the horrifying terrorist attacks which took place on 11 September 2001 in New York, Washington (DC) and Pennsylvania' and stated that it regarded such acts, 'like any act of international terrorism, as a threat to international peace and security'. It would seem that terrorist acts, if they fulfil the above conditions and in addition, fourthly, are *very serious or large scale*, may be regarded as international crimes. To quote again that resolution of the Security Council, all States are called on 'to work together urgently to bring to justice the perpetrators, organizers and sponsors of these terrorist attacks . . . those responsible for aiding, supporting or harbouring the perpetrators, organizers and sponsors of these acts will be held accountable'. This recommendation was echoed by the General Assembly, in its resolution of 12 September 2001.

The general revulsion against this crime, as evinced by increasingly frequent and consistent statements and declarations of very many States as well as resolutions of international organizations, coupled with parallel acts and conduct of States fighting terrorism at various levels, arguably indicates that by now international terrorism, as defined above, is a crime proscribed by customary international law. Consequently any State is legally entitled to bring to trial the alleged authors of such acts of terrorism who happen to be on its territory.

The *actus reus* of the crime of terrorism has been substantially delineated above: (i) terrorist acts must constitute a criminal offence under most national legal systems (for example, assault, murder, kidnapping, hostage-taking, extortion, bombing, torture, arson, etc.); (ii) they must be aimed at spreading terror (that is, fear and intimidation) by means of threat or violent action among the public or particular groups of persons; (iii) they must be politically, ideologically, or religiously motivated, that is, not motivated by private ends.

It should be noted that the *victims* of terrorist acts may be both civilians and military personnel, or other public officials.

As for *mens rea*, State practice, national legislation, as well as the Conventions mentioned above, all point in the same direction. In addition to the subjective element required for the underlying offence (serious bodily harm, murder, kidnapping, arson, destruction of private or public property, etc.), there must be a *special intent*, that is, to spread terror among the population.

6.9.5 TREATY-BASED PROHIBITED CLASSES OF TERRORISM

In addition to the categories of crimes considered so far, one should also take into account those terrorist acts that are explicitly banned by the various treaties on terrorism mentioned above.[27]

Although in my opinion international crimes proper are those provided for in international customary law and which offend against universal values recognized in international legal rules, these specific acts of terrorism should also be characterized as international crimes proper. For the treaties at issue either restate customary rules or are indicative of, or have contributed to, the formation of customary rules; in other words, they have a legal value that goes beyond the strict 'treaty dimension'. What matters, however, more than any legal definition or classification of those crimes, is the manner in which they are repressed. What is striking in these treaties is that they aim at co-ordinating the prosecution and punishment of those terrorist offences by the contracting States. In other words, the primary purpose of those treaties is to achieve the prompt and effective punishment of terrorism by *national* authorities. Each contracting State is duty bound to co-operate in and lend assistance to the repression of terrorism, that is, the apprehension and prosecution or extradition of alleged perpetrators of terrorist acts. No international body is entrusted with the task of prosecuting and punishing those criminal offences.

6.9.6 CONCLUDING REMARKS

To sum up, it may be noted that international *substantive* rules on international crimes of terrorism are fairly satisfactory. In addition to covering most manifestations of terrorism, they regard as criminal all terrorist acts whether they emanate from private individuals or State officials. However, in spite of the apparent trend emerging in the United Nations towards universal and unqualified condemnation of terrorism, many developing States still cling to the old political doctrine whereby so-called 'freedom fighters' are entitled to avoid the stigma of terrorism on account of the political ends they pursue. This political stand has generated much confusion and spawned a tendency to hold the view that there still does not exist a generally accepted definition of terrorism. On the contrary, however, international rules do cover in sufficiently clear terms at least the most conspicuous and odious manifestations of this phenomenon.

Nonetheless, as usual, where international law fails is at the *enforcement* level. Even international treaties on specific classes of terrorism are relatively disappointing as far

[27] See on these treaties A. F. Panzera, *Attività terroristiche e diritto internazionale* (Naples: Jovene, 1978), 35–109; G. Guillaume, 'Terrorisme et droit international', 215 *Hague Recueil* (1989–III), cit., at 330–1, 338–71.

as repression is concerned, for in the event they do not impose upon contracting States a clear-cut obligation to apprehend, prosecute, and bring to justice alleged terrorists on their territory. In addition, neither national nor international courts have made effective use of the existing potential of international legal rules, subject to a few exceptions (such as Israeli or US courts[28] or Scottish courts in the *Lockerbie* case). In particular, it is a matter of regret that the ICC has not been granted jurisdiction over terrorist acts. Unfortunately many States still tend to tackle the question forcibly, that is by use of military violence, often preferring this response to that offered by criminal justice.

SELECT BIBLIOGRAPHY

AGGRESSION

S. Glueck, 'The Nuremberg Trial and Aggressive War', 59 HLR (1946), 396–456; S. Glaser, 'Quelques remarques sur la définition de l'agression en droit international pénal', in *Festschrift für Th. Rittler* (Aalen: Verlag Scientia, 1957), 383–99; S. Glaser, 'Définition de l'agression en droit international pénal', 35 *Revue de droit international et de droit comparé* (1958), 263–658; BVA. Röling, 'The question of defining aggression', in *Symbolae Verzijl* (The Hague, 1958), 314 ff.; S. Glaser, 'Culpabilité en droit international pénal', 99 HR 1960–I, 504–5; B. B. Ferencz, 'A Proposed Definition of Aggression: by Compromise and Consensus', 22 ICLQ (1973), 407–33; I. I. Lukashuk, 'International Illegality and Criminality of Aggression', in G. Ginsburgs and V. N. Kudriatsev (eds), *The Nuremberg Trial and International Law* (Dordrecht: Nijhoff, 1990), 121–40; A. Carpenter, 'The International Criminal Court and the Crime of Aggression', *Nordic J. of Int. Law*, 1995, 223 ff.; O. Triffterer, 'Prosecution of States for Crimes of State', RIDP (1996), 341–64; J. Hogan-Doran and B. T. van Ginkel, 'Aggression as a Crime under International Law and the Prosecution of Individuals by the Proposed International Criminal Court', NILR (1996), 321–51; A. Zimmermann, in O. Triffterer, *ICC Commentary*, cit., 102–6; M. Dumée, 'Le crime d'agression', in Ascensio, Decaux, Pellet (eds), *Droit international pénal*, 251–64.

TORTURE

Z. Haquani, 'La Convention des Nations Unies contre la torture', RGDIP (1986), 127–55; J. H. Burgers and H. Danelius, *The United Nations Convention against Torture* (Dordrecht: M. Nijhoff, 1988); A. Bouklesbaa, 'The Nature of the Obligations Incurred by States under Article 2 of the UN Convention Against Torture' 12 *Human Rights Q.* (1990), 53–93; H. Danelius, 'Article 5', in A. Eide and others (eds), *The Universal Declaration of Human Rights—A Commentary* (Oslo: Scandinavian University Press, 1992), 101–10; A. Cassese, 'Prohibition of Torture and Inhuman or Degrading Treatment or Punishment', in R. St. J. Macdonald, F. Matscher, H. Petzold (eds), *The European System for the Protection of*

[28] For US cases, see for example those reported in R. A. Friedlander (ed.), *Terrorism—Documents of International and Local Control*, cit., vol. 2, 227–317 and 369–429. For Israeli cases see, for example, 19 *Israel Y. on Human Rights* (1989), 371–97.

Human Rights (Dordrech: M. Nijhoff, 1993), 225–61; H. Danelius, 'Protection Against Torture in Europe and the World', ibid., 263–75; N. Rodley, *The Treatment of Prisoners under International Law*, 2nd edn (Oxford: Clarendon Press, 1999); E. Delaplace, 'La torture', in Ascensio, Decaux, Pellet, *Droit international pénal*, 369–76.

TERRORISM

J. Pradel, 'Les infractions du terrorisme. Un nouvel exemple de l'éclatement de la loi pénale. La loi du 9 septembre 1986', *Recueil Dalloz-Sirey, Chroniques*, 1987, p. 39 ff.; S. Williams, 'International Law and Terrorism: Age Old Problems, Different Targets', 26 CYIL (1989), 87–117; G. Guillaume, 'Terrorisme et droit international', 215 HR (1989–III), 287–416; J. F. Murphy, 'Defining International Terrorism: A Way Out of the Quagmire', 19 IYHR (1989), 13–37; K. Skubiszewski, 'Definition of Terrorism', ibid., 39–53; Y. Dinstein, 'Terrorism as an International Crime', ibid., 55–73; S. Sucharitkul, 'Terrorism as an International Crime: Questions of Responsibility and Complicity', ibid., 247–58; C. Bourguès-Habif, 'Le terrorisme international', in Ascensio, Decaux, Pellet, *Droit international pénal*, 457–66; P. Robinson, 'The Missing Crimes', in Cassese, Gaeta, Jones, *ICC Commentary*, vol. I, 497–526.

SECTION II

FUNDAMENTALS OF INTERNATIONAL CRIMINAL RESPONSIBILITY

7

GENERAL PRINCIPLES

7.1 PRELIMINARY REMARKS

In every legal order general principles are needed, which set out the overall orientation of the system, provide sweeping guidelines for the proper interpretation of the law whenever specific rules on legal construction prove insufficient or unhelpful, and also enable courts to fill the gaps of written or unwritten norms. International criminal law, being a branch of public international law, shares of course with any other sector of this body of law the general principles proper to it. However, given the unique features and the overarching purpose of this corpus of legal rules (see *supra*, 2.2), on many occasions those general principles may turn out to be of scant assistance. More useful and relevant appear to be the general principles proper to international criminal law, for they are more attuned to its specificities.

An international court has recently questioned reliance on such principles. In *Delalić and others* Trial Chamber III of the ICTY, after noting that these principles 'exist and are recognised in all the world's major criminal justice systems' stated that:

> [i]t is not certain to what extent they have been admitted as part of international legal practice, separate and apart from the existence of the national legal systems. This is essentially because of the different methods of criminalisation of conduct in national and international criminal justice systems. (§403.)

The Chamber then explained the difference between the two levels (national and international) as follows:

> Whereas the criminalisation process in a national criminal justice system depends upon legislation which dictates the time when conduct is prohibited and the content of such prohibition, the international criminal justice system attains the same objective through treaties and conventions, or after a customary practice of the unilateral enforcement of a prohibition by States. (§404.)

With respect, this explanation is not compelling. It would seem rather that the difference between national criminal laws and international criminal rules lies in the still rudimentary character of the latter. This body of law has not yet attained the degree of sophistication proper to national legal systems. It follows that the principles in question are not yet applicable at the international level in all their implications and ramifications. Whether or not this legal justification is more cogent that the one advanced by the Trial Chamber, one can however share at least the substance of the conclusions reached by the Chamber.[1]

It should be added that in international criminal law there exist principles that are not *specific* to this body of law, for the same principles can also be found in most State legal systems of the world. Nonetheless, as we shall see, often the unique features of the international legal order and the way law takes shape therein, condition the content and scope of some of those principles. One may therefore conclude that some of those principles ultimately bear scant resemblance to those of municipal legal systems, for they are uniquely shaped to suit the characteristic features of the world legal order.

7.2 THE PRINCIPLE OF INDIVIDUAL CRIMINAL RESPONSIBILITY

In international criminal law the general principle applies that no one may be held accountable for an act he has not performed, or in the commission of which he has not in some way participated, or for an omission that cannot be attributed to him.

The ICTY Appeals Chamber set this fundamental principle out most clearly in *Tadić (Appeal)*.[2] The principle in fact lays down *two notions*. First, nobody may be held accountable for criminal offences perpetrated *by other persons*. The rationale behind this proposition is that in modern criminal law the notion of collective responsibility is no longer acceptable. In other words, a national, ethnic, racial, or religious group to which a person may belong is not accountable for acts performed by a member of the group in his individual capacity. By the same token, a member of

[1] 'It could be postulated, therefore, that the principles of legality in international criminal law are different from their related national legal systems with respect to their application and standards. They appear to be distinctive, in the obvious objective of maintaining a balance between the preservation of justice and fairness towards the accused and taking into account the preservation of world order. To this end, the affected State or States must take into account the following factors, inter alia: the nature of international law; the absence of international legislative policies and standards; the ad hoc processes of technical drafting; and the basic assumption that international criminal law norms will be embodied into the national criminal law of the various States' (§405).

[2] Before ascertaining whether the Appellant could be found guilty under the notion of participation in a common criminal purpose, it stated that 'nobody may be held criminally responsible for acts or transactions in which he has not personally engaged or in some other way participated'. 'The basic assumption must be that in international law as much as in national systems, the foundation of criminal responsibility is the principle of personal culpability: nobody may be held criminally responsible for acts or transactions in which he has not personally engaged or in some other way participated (*nulla poena sine culpa*). In national legal systems this principle is laid down in Constitutions, in laws, or in judicial decisions. In international criminal law the principle is laid down, *inter alia*, in Article 7(1) of the Statute of the International Tribunal which states that: "A person who planned, instigated, ordered, committed . . . [a crime] . . . shall be *individually responsible* for the crime"' (emphasis added) (§186).

An ICTY Trial Chamber recently restated in *Kordić and Čerkez* that this is a general principle applicable at the international level (§364).

any such group is not criminally liable for acts contrary to law performed by leaders or other members of the group and to which he is extraneous. The principle of individual autonomy whereby the individual is normally endowed with free will and the independent capacity to choose his conduct is firmly rooted in modern criminal law, including international criminal law. Secondly, a person may only be held criminally liable if he is somehow *culpable* for any breach of criminal rules. In other words, he may only be deemed accountable if he entertains a frame of mind that involves, or expresses, or implies his mental participation in the offence, or his culpably negligent (or deliberate) omission to prevent or punish the commission of crimes by his subordinates. As a consequence, *objective* criminal liability is ruled out.

It follows from the first notion that among other things no one may be held answerable for acts or omissions of *organizations* to which he belongs, unless he bears personal responsibility for a particular act, conduct, or omission.

An exception was, however, provided for in Articles 9 and 10 of the Statute of the IMT at Nuremberg. Article 9, paragraph 1 stipulated that:

> At the trial of any individual member of any group or organization the Tribunal may declare (in connection with any act of which the individual may be convicted) that the group or organization of which the individual was a member was a criminal organization.

Under Article 10:

> In cases where a group or organization is declared criminal by the Tribunal, the competent national authority of any Signatory shall have the right to bring individuals to trial for membership therein before national, military, or occupation courts. In any such case the criminal nature of the group or organization is considered proved and shall not be questioned.

Thus, *mere membership in a criminal organization was regarded as criminal*, whether or not participation in that organization was voluntary. The idea behind the whole scheme for post-war trials for war crimes, first propounded by Colonel Murray C. Bernays in the US Pentagon in 1944, and eventually upheld by the Secretary of War Stimson, was that 'It will never be possible to catch and convict every Axis war criminal, or even any great number of them, under the old concepts and procedures'.[3] Given also that Anglo-American law to some extent upholds the notion of corporate criminal liability, it was suggested that it was for an international court to adjudicate and punish the crimes of the leaders and of the criminal organizations. Thereafter, every member of the Nazi Government and those organizations would be subject to arrest, trial, and punishment in the national courts of each State concerned. 'Proof of membership, without more, would establish guilt of participation in the mentioned conspiracy, and the individual would be punished in the discretion of the court.'[4] This scheme was confirmed by Control Council Law no. 10, of 20 December 1945, which

[3] See Memo by Colonel Bernays of 15 September 1944, in B. F. Smith, *The American Road to Nuremberg—The Documentary Record—1944–45* (Stanford, Cal.: Hoover Institution Press, 1982), at 35.

[4] Ibid., at 36.

provided in Article II(1)(d) that acts 'recognized as a crime' included 'membership in categories of a criminal group or organization declared criminal by the International Military Tribunal'.

In its judgment in *Göring and others* the IMT eventually labelled some organizations as criminal: the Leadership Corps of the Nazi Party; the Gestapo and the SD; the SS. However, the Tribunal discarded the doctrine of 'objective' or 'group responsibility' and brought back the provisions of the Statute to traditional concepts of criminal law. It made the following qualifying points (at 255–79).

First, it held that the labelling of a group or organization as criminal should not be based on 'arbitrary action' but on 'well-settled legal principles', chiefly the principle that 'criminal guilt is personal' and 'that mass punishments should be avoided'. In addition, 'the Tribunal should make such declaration of criminality so far as possible in a manner to insure that innocent persons will not be punished'.

Secondly, the Tribunal reduced the notion of 'criminal organization' to that of 'criminal conspiracy':

> A criminal organization is analogous to a criminal conspiracy in that the essence of both is cooperation for criminal purposes. There must be a group bound together and organized for a common purpose. The group must be formed or used in connection with the commission of crimes denounced by the Charter.

It followed that one 'should exclude persons who had no knowledge of the criminal purposes or acts of the organization and those who were drafted by the State for membership, unless they were personally implicated in the commission of acts declared criminal by Article 6 of the Charter as members of the organization'.

Thirdly, the Tribunal issued three 'recommendations' to other courts with regard to penalties to be inflicted on members of criminal organizations.[5]

Fourthly, the Tribunal, each time it termed an organization criminal, added a similar caveat: one could hold criminally liable only those members of the organization who had had '*knowledge* that it was being used for the commission' of international crimes, or were '*personally implicated*' in the commission of such crimes,[6] and in addition had not ceased to belong to the organization prior to 1 September 1939 (the start of the war of aggression by Germany).

[5] They were as follows: '1. That so far as possible throughout the four zones of occupation in Germany the classifications, sanctions and penalties be standardized. Uniformity of treatment so far as practical should be a basic principle . . . 2. [Control Council] Law no. 10 . . . leaves punishment entirely in the discretion of the trial court even to the extent of inflicting the death penalty. The De-Nazification Law of 5 March 1946, however, passed for Bavaria, Greater-Hesse, and Württemberg-Baden, provides definite sentences for punishment in each type of offense. The Tribunal recommends that in no case should imprisonment imposed under Law no. 10 upon any members of an organization or group declared by the Tribunal to be criminal exceed the punishment fixed by the De-Nazification Law. No person should be punished under both laws. 3. The Tribunal recommends to the Control Council that Law no. 10 be amended to prescribe limitations on the punishment which may be imposed for membership in a criminal group or organization so that such punishment shall not exceed the punishment prescribed by the De-Nazification Law' (at 267–7).

[6] Emphasis added. See ibid., at 262, 268, 273.

It would appear that subsequent courts complied. Consequently members of German organizations termed criminal by the IMT were not punished for the mere fact of belonging to one of them.

Furthermore, other Tribunals upheld the principle of personal responsibility laid down by the IMT in is judgment. Thus, in *Krupp and others*, where the 12 accused were officials of the Krupp industrial enterprises who occupied high positions in the political, financial, industrial, and economic life of Germany, a US Tribunal sitting at Nuremberg held that the defendants could be held criminally liable only if it could be proved that they had 'actually and personally' committed the offences charged.[7]

Another US Tribunal sitting at Nuremberg took a similar stand in *Flick and others* (at 1189), and then in *Krauch and others* (*I. G. Farben* trial, at 1108). In this latter case the 23 accused were all officials of I. G. Farben industrial enterprises, charged among other things with war crimes. The Tribunal took pains to emphasize that they did not bear collective responsibility but could only be found guilty of individual criminal liability.[8]

7.3 THE PRINCIPLE OF LEGALITY OF CRIMES (*NULLUM CRIMEN SINE LEGE*)

To fully grasp the significance and scope of this principle a few words of introduction are necessary.

National legal systems tend to embrace, and ground their criminal law on either the doctrine of *substantive justice* or that of *strict legality*. Under the former doctrine the legal order must primarily aim at prohibiting and punishing any conduct that is socially harmful or causes danger to society, whether or not that conduct has already been legally criminalized at the moment it is taken. The paramount interest is

[7] 'The mere fact without more that a defendant was a member of the Krupp Directorate or an official of the firm is not sufficient [for criminal liability to arise]'. It then cited a rule of the American *Corpus Juris Secundum* on corporate liability, whereby officers of a corporation, normally not criminally responsible for corporate acts performed by other officers or agents, are nevertheless liable if they actually and personally do the acts constituting the offence, or such acts are done by their direction or permission, so that an officer is liable 'where his scienter or authority is established, or where he is the actual present and efficient actor'. The Tribunal added that the same principles must apply in the case of war crimes (at 627–8).

[8] It noted the following: 'It is appropriate here to mention that the corporate defendant, Farben, is not before the bar of this Tribunal and cannot be subjected to criminal penalties in these proceedings. We have used the term Farben as descriptive of the instrumentality of cohesion in the name of which the enumerated acts of spoliation were committed. But corporations act through individuals and, under the conception of personal individual guilt to which previous reference has been made, the Prosecution, to discharge the burden imposed upon it in this case, must establish by competent proof beyond a reasonable doubt that an individual defendant was either a participant in the illegal act or that, being aware thereof, he authorized or approved it. Responsibility does not automatically attach to an act proved to be criminal merely by virtue of a defendant's membership in the *Vorstand* [administration board]. Conversely, one may not utilize the corporate structure to achieve an immunity from criminal responsibility for illegal acts which he directs, counsels, aids, orders, or abets. But the evidence must establish action of the character we have indicated, with knowledge of the essential elements of the crime' (at 1153).

defending society against any deviant behaviour likely to cause damage or jeopardize the social and legal system. Hence this doctrine favours society over the individual (*favor societatis*). Extreme and reprehensible applications of this doctrine can be found in the Soviet legal system (1918–58) or in the Nazi criminal law (1933–45). However, one can also find some variations of this doctrine in modern democratic Germany, where the principles of 'objective justice' (*materielle Gerechtigkeit*) have been upheld as a reaction to oppressive governments trampling upon fundamental human rights, and courts have had recourse to the celebrated 'Radbruch's formula'. Radbruch, the distinguished German professor of jurisprudence, formulated this 'formula' in 1946. In terms subsequently taken up in some German cases,[9] he pro-

[9] The German Federal Constitutional Court referred to that 'formula' in its judgment of 24 October 1996 in *Streletz and Kessler*. The question at issue was whether the accused, former senior officials of the former German Democratic Republic (GDR) charged with incitement to commit intentional homicide for their responsibility in ordering the shooting and killing by border guards of persons trying to flee from the GDR, could invoke as a ground of justification the fact that their actions were legal under the law applicable in the GDR at the material time, which did not make them liable to criminal prosecution. The defendants submitted that holding them criminally liable would run contrary to the ban on the retroactive application of criminal law and Article 103(2) of the German Constitution laying down the *nullum crimen* principle. The Court dismissed the defendants' submissions. It among other things noted that the prohibition on retroactive law derived its justification from the special trust reposed in criminal statutes enacted by a democratic legislature respecting fundamental rights. It then went on to state: 'This special basis of trust no longer obtains where the other State statutorily defines certain acts as serious criminal offences while excluding the possibility of punishment by allowing grounds of justification covering some of those acts and even by requiring and encouraging them notwithstanding the provisions of written law, *thus gravely breaching the human rights generally recognised by the international community.* By such means those vested with State power set up a system *so contrary to justice* that it can survive only for as long as the State authority which brought it into being actually remains in existence.

'In this wholly exceptional situation, the requirement of objective justice, which also embraces the need to respect the human rights recognised by the international community, makes it impossible for a court to accept such justifications . . .

'The Federal Republic has experienced similar conflicts when dealing with the crimes of National Socialism.

'In that connection, the Supreme Court of Justice for the British Zone, and later the Federal Court of Justice, ruled on the question whether an act might become punishable retroactively if a provision of written law was disregarded on account of a gross breach of higher-ranking legal principles. They took the view that *there could be provisions and instructions that had to be denied the status of law, notwithstanding their claim to constitute law, because they infringed legal principles which applied irrespective of whether they were recognised by the State*; whoever had behaved in accordance with such provisions remained punishable . . . The Federal Constitutional Court has so far had to deal with the problem of "statutory injustice" [*gesetzliches Unrecht*] only in spheres other than that of the criminal law. It has taken the view that *in cases where positive law is intolerably inconsistent with justice the principle of legal certainty may have to yield precedence to that of objective justice.* In that connection it has referred to the writings of Gustav Radbruch . . . and in particular to what has become known as Radbruch's formula . . . On that point it has repeatedly stressed that positive law should be disapplied only in absolutely exceptional cases and that a merely unjust piece of legislation, which is unacceptable on any enlightened view, may nevertheless, because it also remains inherently conducive to order, still acquire legal validity and thus create legal certainty . . . However, the period of National Socialist rule had shown that the legislature was capable of imposing gross "wrong" by statute . . . so that, where a statutory provision was intolerably inconsistent with justice, that provision should be disapplied from the outset . . .

'The Federal Court of Justice has since further developed its case-law when trying cases of so-called Government criminality [*Regierungskriminalität*] during the SED regime in the GDR . . . a court must disregard a justification if it purports to exonerate the intentional killing of persons who sought nothing more

pounded the notion that positive law must be regarded as contrary to justice and not applied where the inconsistency between statute law and justice is so intolerable that the former must give way to the latter. This 'formula' has been widely accepted in the legal literature.[10]

In contrast, the doctrine of strict legality postulates that a person may only be held criminally liable and punished if at the moment when he performed a certain act, the act was regarded as a criminal offence by the relevant legal order or, in other words, under the applicable law. Historically, this doctrine stems from the opposition of the baronial and knightly class to the arbitrary power of monarchs, and found expression in Article 39 of *Magna Charta libertatum* (Magna Carta) of 1215.[11] One must however wait for the principal thinkers of the Enlightenment to find its proper philosophical and political underpinning. Montesquieu and then the great American proclamations of 1774 and of the French revolution (1789) conceived of the doctrine as a way of restraining the power of the rulers and safeguarding the prerogatives of the legislature and the judiciary. As the German criminal lawyer Franz von Liszt later wrote, 'the *nullum crimen sine lege, nulla poena sine lege* principles are the bulwark of the citizen against the State's omnipotence; they protect the individual against the brutal force of the majority, against the Leviathan'.[12]

At present, most democratic civil law countries tend to uphold the doctrine of strict legality as an overarching principle. In civil law countries the doctrine is normally held to articulate four basic notions: (i) criminal offences may only be provided for in written law, namely legislation enacted by Parliament, and not in customary rules (less certain and definite than statutes) or secondary legislation (which emanates from the government and not from the parliamentary body expressing popular will); this principle is referred to by the maxim *nullum crimen sine lege scripta*; (ii) criminal legislation must abide by the principle of specificity, whereby rules criminalizing human conduct must be as specific and clear as possible, so as to guide the behaviour

than to cross the intra-German border unarmed and without endangering interests generally recognised as enjoying legal protection, because such a justification, which puts the prohibition on crossing the border above the right to life, must remain ineffective on account of a manifest and intolerable infringement of elementary precepts of justice and of human rights protected under international law. The infringement in question is so serious as to offend against the legal beliefs concerning the worth and dignity of human beings that are common to all peoples. *In such a case positive law has to give way to justice*' (emphasis added).

[10] See for instance the excellent book by G. Vassalli, *Formula di Radbruch e diritto penale* (Milan: Giuffré, 2001), in particular at 3–205, 279–319.

Of course, the notion propounded by Radbruch could simply be termed the Natural Justice view that an unjust law is no law and must be disregarded. As such, it might be susceptible to the criticism of positivists that it makes the law subjective, since the sense of justice varies from person to person.

[11] '*Nullus liber homo capiatur vel impresonetur aut dissaisiatur aut utlegatur aut exuletur aut aloquo modo destruatur nec super eum ibimus nec super eum mittemus nisi per legale judicium parium suorum vel per legem terrae*' (it is only through the legal judgment by his peers and on the strength of the law of the land that a freeman may be apprehended or imprisoned or disseised or outlawed or exiled or in any other manner destroyed, nor may we go upon him or send upon him).

[12] F. von Liszt, 'Die deterministischen Gegner der Zweckstrafe', 13 *Zeitschrift für das gesamte Strafrechtswissenschaft* (1893), at 357.

of citizens; this is expressed by the Latin tag *nullum crimen sine lege stricta*; (iii) criminal rules may not be retroactive, that is, a person may only be punished for behaviour that was considered criminal at the time the conduct was undertaken; therefore he may not be punished on the strength of a law passed subsequently; the maxim referred to in this case is *nullum crimen sine proevia lege*;[13] (iv) resort to analogy in applying criminal rules is prohibited.

Plainly, as stated above, the purpose of these principles is to safeguard citizens as far as possible against both the arbitrary power of government and possibly excessive judicial discretion. In short, the basic underpinning of this doctrine lies in the postulate of *favor rei* (in favour of the accused) (as opposed to *favor societatis* or in favour of society).

In contrast, in common law countries, where judge-made law prevails or is at least firmly embedded in the legal system, there is a tendency to adopt a qualified approach to these principles. For one thing, common law offences (as opposed to statutory offences) result from judge-made law and therefore may lack those requirements of rigidity, foreseeability, and certainty proper to written legislation. For another, common law offences are not strictly subject to the principle of non-retroactivity, as is shown by recent English cases contemplating new offences, or at any rate the extinguishing of traditional defences (see, for instance, *R.* v. *R.* (1992), which held that the fact of marriage was no longer a common law defence to a husband's rape of his wife).[14] However, the European Court of Human Rights has not regarded such cases as questionable or at any rate contrary to the fundamental provisions of the European Convention (see *SW and CR* v. *United Kingdom*, 1995).

Thus, the condition is not the same in every legal system. Let us now see which of the two aforementioned doctrines is applied in international law.

One could merely state that international law, being based on customary processes, is more akin to English law than to French, German, Argentinean, or Chinese law. This, however, is not sufficient. The main problem is that for a long period, and until recently, international law has applied the doctrine of *substantive justice* and it is only

[13] The German Federal Constitutionalal Court set out the principle in admirable terms in its aforementioned decision of 24 October 1996 in *Streletz and Kessler*. In illustrating the scope of Article 103(2) of the German Constitution, laying down the principle at issue, it stated the following: '(1.a) Article 103 §2 of the Basic Law protects against retroactive modification of the assessment of the wrongfulness of an act to the offender's detriment . . . Accordingly, it also requires that a statutory ground of justification which could be relied on at the time when an act was committed should continue to be applied even where, by the time criminal proceedings begin, it has been abolished. However, where justifications are concerned, in contrast to the definition of offences and penalties, the strict reservation of Parliament's law-making prerogative does not apply. In the sphere of the criminal law grounds of justification may also be derived from customary law or case-law'.

[14] It would seem that the English law used to be that a man could not rape his wife because, by agreeing to marry, she had implicitly consented to sexual intercourse for all time. This was obviously a somewhat mediaeval approach. The defence existed only as a matter of common law—it was not in any statute. The judge in *R.* v. *R.* rightly held that societal attitudes had changed and that it was no longer acceptable to hold that a husband could in law never be held guilty of raping his wife; hence he did not allow the old common law defence. In fairness, it was not the introduction of a *new offence*—rape had always been an offence. It was a question of disallowing a (retrograde) common law defence.

in recent years that it is gradually replacing it with the doctrine of *strict legality*, albeit with some important qualifications.

That international law has long applied the former doctrine is not to be attributed to a totalitarian or authoritarian streak in the international community. Rather, the rationale for that attitude was that States were not prepared to enter into treaties laying down criminal rules, nor had customary rules evolved covering this area. In practice, there only existed customary rules prohibiting and punishing war crimes, although in a rather rudimentary or unsophisticated manner (see *supra*, 2.2 and 3.1–3.4.1). Hence the need for the international community to rely upon the doctrine of substantive justice when new and extremely serious forms of criminality (crimes against peace, crimes against humanity) suddenly appeared on the international scene.

The IMT clearly enunciated this doctrine in *Göring and others*. From the outset the Tribunal had to face the powerful objections of German defence counsel that the Tribunal was not allowed to apply *ex post facto* law. These objections were grounded in the general principles of criminal law embedded in civil law countries, and also upheld in German law before and after the Nazi period. The French Judge H. Donnedieu de Vabres, coming from a country where the *nullum crimen* principle is deeply implanted, also showed himself to be extremely sensitive to the principle. As a consequence, when dealing with the crimes against peace of which the defendants stood accused, the Tribunal, before stating that in fact such crimes were already prohibited when they were perpetrated (at 219–23)—a finding that still seems highly questionable—noted that in any case it was not contrary to justice to punish those crimes even if the relevant conduct was not criminalized at the time of their commission:

> In the first place, it is to be observed that the maxim *nullum crimen sine lege* is not a limitation of sovereignty, but is in general a principle of justice. To assert that it is unjust to punish those who in defiance of treaties and assurances have attacked neighbouring states without warning is obviously untrue, for in such circumstances the attacker must know that he is doing wrong, and so far from it being unjust to punish him, it would be unjust if his wrong were allowed to go unpunished. (At 219.)

In other words, substantive justice punishes acts that harm society deeply and are regarded as abhorrent by all members of society, even if these acts were not prohibited as criminal when they were performed.

In his Dissenting Opinion in the Tokyo trial (*Araki and others*), Judge B. V. A. Röling spelled out the same principle, again with regard to crimes against peace. He noted that in national legal systems the *nullum crimen* principle 'is not a principle of justice but a rule of policy'; this rule was:

> valid only if expressly adopted, so as to protect citizens against arbitrariness of courts . . . as well as arbitrariness of legislators . . . the prohibition of *ex post facto* law is an expression of political wisdom, not necessarily applicable in present international relations. This maxim of liberty may, if circumstances necessitate it, be disregarded even by powers victorious in a war fought for freedom. (At 1059.)

Judge Röling then delineated two classes of criminal offences:

Crime in international law is applied to concepts with different meanings. Apart from those indicated above [war crimes], it can also indicate acts comparable to political crimes in domestic law, where the decisive element is the danger rather than the guilt, where the criminal is considered an enemy rather than a villain and where the punishment emphasizes the political measure rather than the judicial retribution. (At 1060.)

Judge Röling applied these concepts to crimes against peace and concluded that such crimes were to be punished because of the dangerous character of the individuals who committed them, hence on *security considerations*. In his view, however, given the novel nature of these crimes, it followed that persons found guilty of them could not be punished by a death sentence (ibid.).

As stated above, after the Second World War the doctrine of strict legality gradually replaced that of substantive justice (which had been upheld in a number of cases, among which one may cite *Peleus*).[15] *Two factors* brought about this change.

First, States agreed upon and ratified a number of important human rights treaties which laid down the *nullum crimen* principle, to be strictly complied with by *national* courts.[16] The same principle was also set out in such important treaties as the Third and Fourth Geneva Conventions of 1949, respectively on Prisoners of War and on Civilians.[17] The expansive force and striking influence of these treaties could not but impact on international criminal proceedings, leading to the acceptance of the notion that also in such proceedings the *nullum crimen* principle must be respected as a fundamental part of a set of basic human rights of individuals. In other words, the principle came to be seen from the viewpoint of the human rights of the accused, and no longer as essentially encapsulating policy guidelines dictating the penal strategy of States at the international level.

[15] In his summing up the Judge Advocate stated: 'You have heard a suggestion made that this Court has no right to adjudicate upon this case because it is said you cannot create an offence by a law which operates retrospectively so as to expose someone to punishment for acts which at the time he did them were not punishable as crimes. That is the substance of the Latin maxim [*nullum crimen sine lege, nulla poena sine lege*] that has been used so much in this Court. My advice to you is that the maxim and the principle [of legality] that it expresses has nothing whatever to do with this case. It has reference only to municipal or domestic law of a particular State, and you need not be embarrassed by it in your consideration of the problems that you have to deal with here' (at 132). It should be noted that the defendants had been accused of killing survivors of a sunken merchant vessel, the Greek steamship *Peleus*; they had raised the pleas of 'operational necessity' and superior orders. The British Judge Advocate in *Burgholz (No. 2)* took a clearer stand. After noting that the Allies had set up tribunals in Germany and Japan 'with the object of bringing to justice certain persons who have outraged the basic principles of decency and humanity', he pointed out: 'It may well be that no particular concrete law can be pointed to as having been broken, and you remember what Defence Counsel Dr. Meyer-Labastille said yesterday on the principle of "no punishment without pre-existing law." That principle I agree with but to this extent, that I do not regard it as limiting punishment of persons who have outraged human decency in their conduct' (at 79).

[16] See for instance Article 15 of the UN Covenant on Civil and Political Rights, Article 7 of the European Convention on Human Rights, or Article 9 of the American Convention on Human Rights.

[17] See Article 99(1) of the Third Convention and Article 67 of the Fourth Convention. See also Article 75(4)(c) of the First Additional Protocol of 1977.

The second factor is that gradually the network of international criminal law greatly expanded both through a number of international treaties criminalizing conduct of individuals (think of the 1948 Convention on Genocide, the 1949 Geneva Conventions, the 1984 Convention on Torture, and the various treaties on terrorism) and by dint of the accumulation of case law. In particular, this case law contributed to clarifying or specifying elements of crimes, defences, and other important segments of international criminal law. As a consequence, the principle of strict legality has been laid down first, albeit implicitly, in the two ad hoc Tribunals (ICTY and ICTR),[18] and then, explicitly, in the Statute of the ICC, which envisages it in terms in Article 22.

The conclusion is therefore warranted that nowadays this principle must be complied with also at the international level, albeit subject to a number of significant qualifications, which we shall presently consider.

7.4 ARTICULATIONS OF THE PRINCIPLE OF LEGALITY

7.4.1 THE PRINCIPLE OF SPECIFICITY

Under the principle of specificity, criminal rules must be as specific and detailed as possible, so as to clearly indicate to their addressees the conduct prohibited, namely, both the objective elements of the crime and the requisite *mens rea*. The principle is aimed at ensuring that all those who may fall under the prohibitions of the law know in advance which specific behaviour is allowed and which conduct is instead proscribed. They may thus foresee the consequences of their action and freely choose either to comply with, or instead breach, legal standards of behaviour. Clearly, the more accurate and specific the criminal rule, the greater is the protection accorded to the agent from arbitrary action of either enforcement officials or courts of law.

The principle is still far from being fully applicable in international law, which still includes many rules that are loose in their scope and purport. In this regard, suffice it to mention, as an extreme or most conspicuous instance, the provision first enshrined in the London Charter of 1945 and then restated in many international instruments (Control Council Law no. 10, the Statutes of the Tokyo Tribunal, the ICTY, and the ICTR), whereby crimes against humanity encompass 'other inhumane acts'. Similarly, the provisions of the four 1949 Geneva Conventions on grave breaches among other things enumerate, as 'grave breaches', 'torture or *inhuman treatment*'. In addition, many rules contain notions that are not defined at the 'legislative' level, such as 'rape', 'torture', 'persecution', 'enslavement', etc. Furthermore, most international rules

[18] See for instance Articles 1–8 of the ICTY Statute, as well as para. 29 of the UN Secretary-General Report to the Security Council for the establishment of the Tribunal (S/25704) ('It should be pointed out that, in assigning to the International Tribunal the task of prosecuting persons responsible for serious violations of international humanitarian law, the Security Council would not be creating or purporting to "legislate" that law. Rather, the International Tribunal would have the task of applying existing international humanitarian law').

proscribing conduct as criminal do not specify the *subjective* element of the crime. Nor are customary rules on defences crystal clear: they do not indicate the relevant excuses or justifications in unquestionable terms.

Given this legal indeterminacy, and the consequent legal uncertainty for the possible addressees of international criminal rules, the contribution of courts to defining law, not infrequent even in civil law systems, and quite normal in common law countries, becomes of crucial importance at the international level, as has already been pointed out above (2.4.7). Both national and international courts play an immensely important role in gradually defining notions, or spelling out the objective and subjective elements of crimes, or defining such general legal concepts as excuses, justifications, etc.

Thus, for instance, the District Court of Tel Aviv, in *Ternek* spelled out, by way of construction, the notion of 'other inhumane acts' in a manner that seems acceptable (at 540, and §7).[19] Similarly, in defining the concept of 'rape' a Trial Chamber of the ICTY in *Furundžija* had recourse to international law as well as general principles common to the major legal systems of the world, and general principles of law.[20]

One should not underestimate, however, another drawback of international criminal law: the lack of a central criminal court endowed with the power and authority to clarify for the whole international community the numerous hazy or unclear criminal rules. To put it differently: the contribution of courts to the gradual specification and precision of legal rules, emphasized above, suffers from the major shortcoming that such judicial refinement is 'decentralized' and fragmentary. In addition, when such

[19] The Court stated that: 'The defence counsel argue, secondly, that the words "other inhumane acts" which appear in the definition of "crimes against humanity" should be interpreted subject to the principle of *ejusdem generis*. That is, that an "other inhumane act" should be of the type of the specific action mentioned before it, in the same definition, which are "murder, extermination, enslavement, starvation and deportation" . . . We believe that there is truth in the defence counsel's second claim. The punishment determined in Article 1 of the [Israeli] Law [of 1950 on the Doing of Justice to Nazis and their Collaborators] for "crimes against humanity" is death (subject to extenuating circumstances pursuant to Article 11(b) of the Law), and it can be assumed that the legislator intended to inflict the most extreme punishment known to the penal code only for those inhumane actions which resemble in their type and severity "murder, extermination, enslavement, starvation and deportation of a civilian population". If we measure by this yardstick the actions proven against the defendant [beating with bare hand other detainees and making detainees kneel, in the Concentration camp of Auschwitz-Birkenau, where the defendant herself was an inmate, with the role of custodian of Block 7] we shall find that even if some of these actions could be considered inhumane from known aspects, they do not, under the circumstances, reach the severity of the actions which the legislator intended to include in the definition of "crimes against humanity" in Article 1 of the Law' (§7).

[20] It is worth citing the relevant passage, for that Trial Chamber proved alert to the principle of specificity. It stated the following: 'This Trial Chamber notes that no elements [for defining rape] other than those emphasised may be drawn from international treaty or customary law, nor is resort to general principles of international criminal law or to general principles of international law of any avail. The Trial Chamber therefore considers that, to arrive at an accurate definition of rape based on the criminal law principle of specificity (*Bestimmtheitgrundsatz*, also referred to by the maxim "*nullum crimen sine lege stricta*"), it is necessary to look for principles of criminal law common to the major legal systems of the world. These principles may be derived, with all due caution, from national laws' (§177).

process is effected by national courts, it suffers from the another flaw: each court tends to apply the general notions of criminal law proper to the legal system within which such court operates. Hence, the possibility frequently arises of a contradictory and 'cacophonic' interpretation or application of international criminal rules.

Fortunately, the draftsmen of the ICC Statute made a significant contribution, when they endeavoured to define as precisely as possible the various categories of crimes. (However, as the Statute is not intended to codify international customary law, one ought always to take it with a pinch of salt, for in some cases it may go beyond existing law.)

For the time being international criminal rules still make up a body of law in need of legal precision and some major refinement at the level of definitions and general principles. To take account of these features and at the same time safeguard the right of the accused, currently some notions play a role that is far greater than in most national systems: the defence of *mistake of law* (see *infra*, 13.4), the principle of *strict interpretation* (barring extensive or broad constructions of criminal rules; see *infra*, 7.4.3), the principle of *favor rei* (imposing that in case of doubt a rule should be interpreted in such a manner as to favour the accused; see *infra*, 7.4.4). These notions act as *countervailing factors*, aimed at compensating for the present flaws and lacunae of international criminal law.

7.4.2 THE PRINCIPLE OF NON-RETROACTIVITY

A. General

As stated above, a logical and necessary corollary of the doctrine of strict legality is that criminal rules may not cover acts or conduct undertaken prior to the adoption of such rules. Otherwise the executive power, or the judiciary, could arbitrarily punish persons for actions that were legally allowed when they were carried out. By contrast, the ineluctable corollary of the doctrine of substantive justice is that, for the purpose of defending society against new and unexpected forms of criminality, one may go so far as to prosecute and punish conduct that was legal when taken. These two approaches lead to contrary conclusions. The question is: which approach has been adopted in international law?

It seems indisputable that the London Agreement of 1945 provided for two categories of crime that were new: crimes against peace and crimes against humanity. The IMT did act upon the Charter provisions dealing with both categories. In so doing, it applied *ex post facto* law; in other words, it applied international law retroactively, as the defence counsel at Nuremberg rightly stressed.[21] The Tribunal gave two justifications for its application of the Charter provision relating to crimes against peace.

[21] See the Motion adopted by all defence counsel on 19 November 1945, in *Trial of the Major War Criminals Before the International Military Tribunal, Nuremberg 14 November 1945–1 October 1946* (Nuremberg, 1947), vol. I, at 168–9.

(In contrast it did not offer any justification relating to *ex post facto* application of the provisions on crimes against humanity. It is striking that the Tribunal did not consider it fitting to articulate its general view with regard to this class of offences. Probably this was also due to the fact that in their joint Motion of 19 November 1945, all defence counsel insisted on crimes against peace being contrary to the *nullum crimen sine lege* principle, whereas they passed over in silence crimes against humanity.)

First, the Tribunal stated that the Charter was 'the expression of international law existing at the time of its creation; and to that extent [it was] itself a contribution to international law' (at 218). This, however, was not the case so far as crimes against peace and crimes against humanity were concerned. Indeed, the reasoning developed by the IMT to prove that as early as 1939 aggression amounted to an international crime (in addition to being an international wrongful act) is unconvincing.

The second proposition of the Tribunal—again, only articulated with regard to 'crimes against peace' but also applicable to crimes against humanity—was that, as stated above, 'the maxim *nullum crimen sine lege* is not a limitation of sovereignty, but is in general a principle of justice' (at 219). This proposition is no doubt valid for grave atrocities and inhuman acts. In the case of newly established crimes, however, the courts would have been wise to refrain from meting out the harshest penalty, namely the death sentence, to defendants found guilty of these new crimes only.[22]

Nevertheless, many tribunals sitting in judgment over Germans in the aftermath of the Second World War,[23] as well as the German Supreme Court in the British Occupied Zone,[24] took up and endorsed the legal reasoning of the IMT, for all its deficiencies. This stand, while it had scant persuasive force with regard to the past, nonetheless contributed to the slow consolidation of the principle of non-retroactivity in international criminal law.

Subsequently, a general rule prohibiting the retroactive application of criminal law gradually evolved in the international community. This rule was laid down in numerous human rights treaties[25] and in some of the 1949 Geneva Conventions,[26] as well as the First Additional Protocol (Article 75(4)(c)), all relating of course to criminal trials held at the domestic or national level. The provisions of these treaties were not without faults. In particular, they all contained a reference to international law that

[22] As stated above, this view was forcefully defended by Röling, the Dutch member of the Tokyo International Tribunal, in his dissenting opinion appended to the Tokyo judgment (at 1048 ff.).

[23] See in particular the *Justice* case (at 974–85), *Einsatzgruppen* (at 458–9), *Flick and others* (at 1189), *Krauch and others* (*I. G. Farben* case) (at 1097–8, 1125), *Krupp* (at 1331), *High Command* (at 487), *Hostages* (at 1238–42).

[24] See the *Bl.* case (at 5), the *B. and A.* case (at 297), the *H.* case (at 232–3), the *N.* case (at 335), and *Angeklagter H.* (at 135).

[25] See such treaties as the 1950 European Convention on Human Rights (Article 7), the 1966 UN Covenant on Civil and Political Rights (Article 15), the Inter-American Convention on Human Rights (Article 9), and the African Charter of Human and Peoples' Rights (Article 7, para. 2).

[26] See for instance Article 99 of the Third Convention and Article 67 of the Fourth Convention.

was either devoid of any legal significance or questionable.[27] Nevertheless, gradually the view crystallized that international criminal proceedings should also be subject to the prohibition on retroactive application of criminal law. This was implicitly enshrined in the Statutes of the ICTY and the ICTR (see for instance §§29 and 34 of the UN Secretary-General's Report on the Statute of the ICTY), while it was laid down in terms in Article 22(1) of the Statute of the ICC.

Thus, the principle of non-retroactivity of criminal rules is *now* solidly embedded in international law. It follows that courts may only apply substantive criminal rules that existed at the time of commission of the alleged crime. This of course does not entail that courts are barred from refining and elaborating upon, by way of legal construction, *existing* rules. The ICTY Appeals Chamber clearly set out this notion in *Aleksovski* (*Appeal*). After commenting on the significance and legal purport of the *nullum crimen* principle, it added that this principle

> does not prevent a court, either at the national or international level, from determining an issue through a process of interpretation and clarification as to the elements of a particular crime; nor does it prevent a court from relying on previous decisions which reflect an interpretation as to the meaning to be ascribed to particular ingredients of a crime. (§127.)

B. Expansive adaptation of some legal ingredients of criminal rules to new social conditions

One should duly take account of the nature of international criminal law, to a large extent made up of customary rules that are often found, or spelled out, or given legal determinacy by courts. In short, that body of law to a large extent consists of judge-made law (with no doctrine of precedent). Consequently, one should reconcile the principle of non-retroactivity with these inherent characteristics of international criminal law. In this respect a landmark ruling of the European Court of Human Rights in *CR* v. *United Kingdom* may prove of great assistance. It is therefore appropriate briefly to summarize the case and the Court's holding.

In 1989 a British national went back to see his estranged wife, who had been living for some time with her parents, and attempted to have sexual intercourse with her against her will; he also assaulted her, squeezing her neck with both hands. He was charged with attempted rape and assault occasioning actual bodily harm, and convicted. Before the European Court he repeated the claim already advanced before British courts, that at the time when the facts occurred, marital rape was not prohibited in the UK. Indeed, at that time a British Statute only prohibited as rape sexual

[27] Take for instance Article 15(2) of the 1966 UN Covenant on Civil and Political Rights, whereby 'Nothing in this article shall prejudice the trial and punishment of any person for any act or omission which, at the time when it was committed, was criminal according to the general principles of law recognized by the community of nations'. Here, the reference to this category of 'general principles of law' is, to say the least, questionable, because in fact such principles of law do not contain any specific prohibition of crimes, which can only be found in *customary* international law. As pointed out above, those principles may only be drawn upon to fill gaps in treaty law or in customary rules (see *supra*, 2.4.5). Hence, the reference to those 'principles' would be legally meaningful only if it is taken to refer to 'general international law'.

intercourse with a woman who did not consent to it if such intercourse was 'unlawful' (see section 1(1) of the Sexual Offences (Amendment) Act 1976); hence the question turned on determining whether forced marital intercourse was 'unlawful'. Various English courts had ruled, until 1990, that a husband could not be convicted of raping his wife, for the status of marriage involved that the woman had given her consent to her husband having intercourse with her during the subsistence of the marriage and could not unilaterally withdraw such consent. In contrast, Scottish courts had first held that that view did not apply where the parties to a marriage were no longer cohabiting, and then ruled, in 1989, that the wife's *implied* consent was a legal fiction, the real question being whether as a matter of fact the wife consented to the acts complained of. The word 'unlawful' in the Act referred to above was deleted in 1994 by the Criminal Justice and Public Order Act. This being the legal situation in the UK, before the European Court the applicant argued that the British courts had gone beyond a reasonable interpretation of the existing law and indeed extended the definition of rape in such a way as to include facts that until then had not constituted a criminal offence.

Both the European Commission and the European Court held instead that the British courts had not breached Article 7(1) of the European Convention on Human Rights ('No one shall be held guilty of any criminal offence on account of any act or omission which did not constitute a criminal offence under national or international law at the time when it was committed'). The Commission noted, in its report (adopted by 14 votes to 3), that the applicant's wife had withdrawn from co-habitation and they were de facto separated and intended to seek a divorce; hence:

> there was a basis on which it could be anticipated that the courts could hold that the notional consent of the wife was no longer implied. In particular, given the recognition by contemporary society of women's equality of status with men in marriage and outside it and of their autonomy over their own bodies . . . this adaptation in the application of the offence of rape was reasonably foreseeable to an applicant with appropriate legal advice. (§60.)

The Commission consequently found that:

> the judgments of the domestic courts in the applicant's case did not go beyond legitimate adaptation of the ingredients of a criminal offence to reflect the social conditions of the time and . . . the applicant was not as a result convicted of conduct which did not constitute a criminal offence at the time it was committed. (§62.)

The Court, by a unanimous ruling, held in general that the European Convention could not be read 'as outlawing the gradual clarification of the rules of criminal liability through judicial interpretation from case to case, provided that the resulting development is consistent with the essence of the offence and could reasonably be foreseen' (§34). With regard to the specific case at issue, the Court noted that:

> There was no doubt under the law as it stood on 12 November 1989 that a husband who forcibly had sexual intercourse with his wife could, in various circumstances, be found guilty of rape. Moreover, there was an evident evolution, which was consistent with the very

essence of the offence, of the criminal law through judicial interpretation towards treating such conduct generally as within the scope of the offence of rape. This evolution had reached a stage where judicial recognition of the absence of immunity had become a reasonably foreseeable development of the law. The essentially debasing character of rape is so manifest that the result of the decisions of the Court of Appeal and the House of Lords—that the applicant could be convicted of attempted rape, irrespective of his relationship with the victim—cannot be said to be at variance with the object and purpose of Article 7 of the Convention, namely to ensure that no one should be subjected to arbitrary prosecution, conviction or punishment. . . . What is more, the abandonment of the unacceptable idea of a husband being immune against prosecution for rape of his wife was in conformity not only with a civilised concept of marriage but also, and above all, with the fundamental objectives of the Convention, the very essence of which is respect for human dignity and human freedom. (§§41–2.)[28]

In a subsequent case, *Cantoni* v. *France*, the Court restated the above principles. It insisted on the notion that, in order for criminal law (that is, a statutory provision or a judge-made rule) to be in keeping with the *nullum crimen* principle, it is necessary for the law to meet the requirements of accessibility and foreseeability. It added two important points. First, a criminal rule may be couched in vague terms. When this happens, there may exist 'grey areas at the fringe of the definition':

This penumbra of doubt in relation to borderline facts does not in itself make a provision incompatible with Article 7 [of the European Convention on Human Rights, laying down the *nullum crimen* principle], provided that it proves to be sufficiently clear in the large majority of cases. The role of adjudication vested in the courts is precisely to dissipate such interpretational doubts as remain, taking into account the changes in everyday practice. (§33.)

The second point related to the notion of foreseeability. The Court noted that the scope of this notion:

depends to a considerable degree on the content of the text in issue, the field it is designed to cover, and the number and status of those to whom it is addressed (see *Groppera Radio AG and others* v. *Switzerland*, §68). A law may still satisfy the requirement of foreseeability even if the person concerned has to take appropriate legal advice to assess, to a degree that is reasonable in the circumstances, the consequences which a given action may entail (see among other authorities, the *Tolstoy Miloslavsky* v. *the UK*, §37). This is particularly true in relation to persons carrying on a professional activity, who are used to having to proceed with a high degree of caution when pursuing their occupation. They can on this account be expected to take special care in assessing the risk that such activity entails. (§35.)[29]

It would seem that the following legal propositions could be inferred from the Court's reasoning. First, while *interpretation and clarification* of existing rules is

[28] See also *S.W.* v. *United Kingdom*, §§37–47.

[29] In the case at issue the applicant was the owner of a supermarket, convicted of unlawfully selling pharmaceutical products in breach of the Public Health Code. In his application he had contended that the definition of medicinal product contained in the relevant provision of that Code was very imprecise and left a wide discretion to the courts.

always admissible, adaptation is only compatible with legal principles subject to stringent requirements. Secondly, such requirements are that the *evolutive adaptation*, by courts of law, of criminal prohibitions, namely the extension of such legal ingredients of an offence as *actus reus* in order to cover conduct previously not clearly considered as criminal must: (i) be in keeping with the rules of criminal liability relating to the subject matter, more specifically with the rules defining 'the essence of the offence'; (ii) conform with, and indeed implement and actualize, fundamental principles of international criminal law or at least general principles of law; and (iii) be reasonably foreseeable by the addressees; in other words the extension, although formally speaking it turns out to be to the detriment of the accused, could have been reasonably anticipated by him, as consonant with general principles of criminal law. To put it differently, courts may not create a new criminal offence, with new legal ingredients (a new *actus reus* or a new *mens rea*). They can only adapt provisions envisaging criminal offences to changing social conditions as long as this adjustment (resulting in the broadening of *actus reus* or, possibly, in lowering the threshold of the subjective element, for instance, from intent to recklessness, or from recklessness to culpable negligence) is consonant with, or even required by, *general principles.*

This process, particularly if it proves to be to the detriment of the accused (which is normally the case) must presuppose the existence of a *broad* criminal prohibition (for instance, the prohibition of rape) and no clear-cut and explicit enumeration, in law, of the acts embraced by this definition. It is in the penumbra left by law around this definition that the adaptation may be carried out. Admittedly, the frontier between such adaptation process and the analogical process, which is instead banned (see below), is rather thin and porous. It falls to courts to proceed with great caution and determine on a case-by-case basis whether the adaptation under discussion is legally warranted and consonant with general principles, and in addition does not unduly prejudice the rights of the accused.

Perhaps an instance of the expansive interpretation of existing law can be seen in the judgment delivered by the ICTY Appeals Chamber in *Tadić* (*Interlocutory Appeal*), where the Appeals Chamber unanimously held that some customary rules of international law criminalized certain categories of conduct in *internal* armed conflict (see §§94–137).[30] It is well known that until that decision many commentators, States as

[30] Before pointing to practice and *opinio juris* supporting the view that some customary rules had evolved in the international community criminalizing conduct in internal armed conflict, the Appeals Chamber emphasized the rationale behind this evolution, as follows: 'A State-sovereignty-oriented approach has been gradually supplanted by a human-being-oriented approach. Gradually the maxim of Roman law *hominum causa omne jus constitutum est* (all law is created for the benefit of human beings) has gained a firm foothold in the international community as well. It follows that in the area of armed conflict the distinction between interstate wars and civil wars is losing its value as far as human beings are concerned. Why protect civilians from belligerent violence, or ban rape, torture or the wanton destruction of hospitals, churches, museums or private property, as well as proscribe weapons causing unnecessary suffering when two sovereign States are engaged in war, and yet refrain from enacting the same bans or providing the same protection when armed violence has erupted "only" within the territory of a sovereign State? If international law, while of course safeguarding the legitimate interests of States, must gradually turn to the protection of human beings, it is only natural that the aforementioned dichotomy should gradually lose its weight' (§97).

well as the ICRC, held the view that violations of the humanitarian law of internal armed conflict did not amount to war crimes proper, for such crimes could only be perpetrated within the context of an international armed conflict. The ICTY Appeals Chamber authoritatively held that the contrary was true and clearly identified a set of international customary rules prohibiting as criminal certain classes of conduct. Since then this view has been generally accepted.

Similarly, it would seem that, contrary to the submission made by defence counsel in *Hadzihasanović and others*,[31] an expansive interpretation (corroborated by a logical construction) should warrant the contention that persons may be held accountable under the notion of command responsibility even in *internal* armed conflicts. Two arguments support this proposition. First, generally speaking the notion is widely accepted in international humanitarian law that each army or military unit engaging in fighting either in an international or in an internal armed conflict must have a commander charged with holding discipline, ensuring compliance with the law, and executing the orders from above (with the consequence that whenever the commander culpably fails to ensure such compliance, he may be called to account). The notion at issue is crucial to the existence and enforcement of the whole body of international humanitarian law, because without a chain of command and a person in control of each military unit, anarchy and chaos would ensue and no one could ensure compliance with law and order. Secondly and with specific regard to the Statute of the ICTY, Article 7(3) of this Statute is couched in sweeping terms and clearly refers to the commission by subordinates of any crime falling under the jurisdiction of the Tribunal: any time such a crime has been perpetrated involving the responsibility of a superior, this superior may be held accountable for criminal omission (of course, if he is proved to have the requisite *mens rea*: see *infra*, 10.4.4). If this is so, it is sufficient to show that crimes perpetrated in internal armed conflicts fall under the Tribunal's jurisdiction, as held in 1995 in *Tadić* (*Interlocutory Appeal*), for inferring that as a consequence a superior's responsibility for failing to prevent or punish such crimes falls under the Tribunal's jurisdiction.

7.4.3 THE BAN ON ANALOGY

National courts (particularly in civil law countries) as well as international courts normally refrain from applying international criminal law by analogy, that is, they do not extend the scope and purport of a criminal rule to a matter that is unregulated by law (*analogia legis*). In national law the prohibition on the application of criminal rules by analogy (which was not provided for in the German Nazi State or in the Soviet Union, and was banned in China only in 1997, when a new Criminal Code was enacted) is rooted in the need to safeguard citizens and in particular to prevent their being punished for actions that were not considered illegal when they were

[31] See the Decision on Challenge to Jurisdiction issued by ICTY Trial Chamber II on 7 December 2001, at 3–4.

performed. By the same token, the prohibition is intended to restrict the so-called *arbitrium judicis*, that is, arbitrary judicial decisions.

The same principle applies in international law. There, the ban on analogy derives from the general prohibition of analogical application of *treaties*, stemming from the principle of respect for State sovereignty.[32] This principle imposes the requirement that a treaty between two States may not be applied by analogy to the relations between one of those States and a third one. However, in the specific field of international criminal law the prohibition of analogy has a different rationale: the need to protect individuals from arbitrary behaviour of States or courts, which is another side, or a direct consequence, of the exigency that no one be accused for an act that at the time of its commission was not a criminal offence. In other words, the primary rationale is to safeguard the rights of the accused as much as possible. To satisfy this requirement, analogy is prohibited with regard to both treaty and customary rules. Such rules (for instance, norms proscribing certain specific crimes against humanity) may not be applied by analogy to classes of acts that are unregulated by law.

Article 22(2) of the ICC Statute thus codifies existing customary law where it provides that 'The definition of a crime shall be strictly construed and shall not be extended by analogy. In case of ambiguity, the definition shall be interpreted in favour of the persons being investigated, prosecuted or convicted'. For example, one is not allowed to apply by analogy the rule prohibiting a specific weapon (such as blinding weapons) to a new weapon or, at any rate, to another weapon not prohibited. Nor may one apply by analogy a rule prohibiting a particular use of a specific weapon (for instance, the use of napalm and other incendiary weapons contrary to Protocol III to the 1980 UN Convention on Conventional Weapons) to another use of that weapon. Consequently, one is not allowed to criminalize the use of those weapons when their use was permitted.

As the aforementioned provision of the ICC Statute makes clear, a prohibition closely bound up with that of analogy is the ban on broad or *extensive interpretation* of international criminal rules, and the consequent duty for States, courts, and other relevant officials and individuals to resort to *strict interpretation.* This principle entails that one is not allowed to broaden surreptitiously, by way of interpretation, the content of criminal rules, so as to make them applicable to instances not specifically envisaged by the rules.

An example of strict construction can be found in some post-Second World War cases relating to the notion of crimes against humanity. In *Altstötter and others* a US Military Tribunal sitting at Nuremberg held that that notion, as laid down in Control Council Law no. 10,

> must be strictly construed to exclude isolated cases of atrocity or persecution whether committed by private individuals or by governmental authorities. As we construe it, that

[32] See D. Anzilotti, *Corso di diritto internazionale* (1928), 4th edn (Padua: Cedam, 1955), 105–10.

section [of the aforementioned Law] provides for the punishment of crimes committed against German nationals only where there is proof of conscious participation in systematic governmentally organized or approved procedures, amounting to atrocities and offences of that kind specified in the act and committed against populations or amounting to persecution on political, racial or religious grounds. (At 284–5.)

The finding was cited with approval in *Flick and others*, handed down by another US Military Tribunal sitting at Nuremberg (at 1216), where the Tribunal also held that under a strict interpretation of the same notion, crimes against humanity do not encompass offences against property, but only those against persons (at 1215).[33]

Three qualifications must however be set out restricting the ban on analogy.

First, international law only prohibits the so-called *analogia legis* (that is, the extension of a rule so as to cover a matter that is formally unregulated by law). It does not bar the regulation of a matter not covered by a specific provision or rule, by *resorting to general principles* of international criminal law, or to general principles of criminal justice, or to principles common to the major legal systems of the world.[34] National and international courts or tribunals have repeatedly affirmed that it is permissible to rely upon such principles for establishing whether an international rule covers a specific matter in dispute. To be sure, the question has always been framed as one of *interpretation*, rather than analogical application. Nevertheless, whatever the terminology employed, the fact remains that gaps or lacunae have been filled by resort to those principles. It should however be clear that drawing upon general principles should never be used to criminalize conduct that was previously not prohibited by a criminal rule. It may only serve to spell out and clarify, or give a clear legal contour to, prohibitions that have already been laid down in either customary law or treaties. In other words, this sort of 'analogical method' may only be used for the *interpretation* of existing rules, not for the creation of new classes of criminal conduct. To hold the contrary would mean to admit serious departures from the *nullum crimen* principle, contrary to the whole thrust of current international criminal law.

Secondly, in quite a few cases international rules themselves invite or request analogy, through the *ejusdem generis* canon of statutory construction (whereby when in a legal rule general words follow the enumeration of a particular class of persons or things, the general words must be construed as applying to persons or things of the same kind or class as those enumerated). For instance, the customary and treaty rules prohibiting and penalizing as crimes against humanity 'other inhumane acts', as well as the provisions of the 1949 Geneva Conventions criminalizing as 'grave breaches' of the Convention 'inhuman acts' in addition to torture, impose upon the interpreter the need to look at acts and conduct analogous in gravity to those prohibited. This indeed

[33] Subsequently the Dutch Special Court of Cassation took up in *Albrecht* (at 397–8) and in *Bellmer* (at 543) as well as in *Haass* (at 432) the same strict interpretation advanced in *Altstötter and others*.

[34] Resort to general principles of law recognized by civilized nations is termed by Anzilotti (op. cit., 106–7) *analogia juris*. It should be noted, however, that according to the celebrated international lawyer those general principles did not constitute an autonomous source of international law.

was the reasoning of the Tel Aviv District Court in *Ternek*.[35] The draftsmen of the ICC Statute took the same logical approach when they criminalized in Article 7(1)(k) 'other inhumane acts *of a similar character* intentionally causing great suffering, or serious injury to body or to mental or physical health' (emphasis added).

Thirdly, in some cases international law allows a logical approach that at first glance runs foul of the ban on analogy, but which is in fact permissible because it applies to general principles. An example will better explain this proposition. In the case of a new weapon that does not fall under any specific prohibition precisely because of its novel features, analogical extension of an existing *treaty* ban is not allowed, as pointed out above. Nevertheless, one is authorized to enquire whether the new weapon is at variance with the *general principle* proscribing weapons that are inherently indiscriminate or cause unnecessary suffering. For this purpose, one may justifiably look at those weapons that have been prohibited by treaty because they either are indiscriminate or cause superfluous sufferings. The object of this enquiry will not be the application of these treaty prohibitions by analogy, but rather a better ascertainment of whether the characteristics of the new weapon are such as to make them contrary to the general principle. It would seem that the District Court of Tokyo in *Shimoda and others* took precisely this approach.[36]

7.4.4 THE PRINCIPLE OF FAVOURING THE ACCUSED (*FAVOR REI*)

Another principle is closely intertwined with the ban on analogy, and is designed to invigorate it. This is the principle requiring, in the case of conflicting interpretations of a rule, the construction that favours the accused (*favor rei*): see also ICC Statute, Article 22(2). An ICTR Trial Chamber upheld this principle in *Akayesu* with regard to the interpretation of the word 'killing' in the Genocide Convention and the Statute of the ICTR.[37] An ICTY Trial Chamber reaffirmed the principle in *Krstić*. The question

[35] See *supra*, note 19.

[36] After noting that the use of an atomic bomb was 'believed to be contrary to the principle of international law prohibiting means of injuring the enemy which cause unnecessary suffering or are inhuman', the District Court of Tokyo noted that the bomb was a new weapon. It then pointed out that the employment of asphyxiating, poisonous, and other gases and bacteriological methods of warfare was prohibited, noting that it could 'safely be concluded that besides poisons, poisonous gases and bacteria, the use of means of injuring the enemy which cause injury at least as great as or greater than these prohibited materials is prohibited by international law'. The Court concluded that 'it is not too much to say that the sufferings brought about by the atomic bomb are greater than those caused by poisons and poisonous gases; indeed the act of dropping this bomb may be regarded as contrary to the fundamental principle of the law of war which prohibits the causing of unnecessary suffering' (at 1694–5).

[37] With regard to the word '*meurtre*' (in French) and 'killing' in English, contained in the phrase 'killing members of the group' (as a category of genocide), the Trial Chamber noted the following: 'The Trial Chamber is of the opinion that the term "killing" used in the English version is too general, since it could very well include both intentional and unintentional homicides, whereas the term "*meurtre*", used in the French version, is more precise. It is accepted that there is murder when death has been caused with the intention to do so, as provided for, incidentally, in the Penal Code of Rwanda, which stipulates in its Article 311 that "Homicide committed with intent to cause death shall be treated as murder". Given the presumption of innocence of the accused, and pursuant to the general principles of criminal law, the Chamber holds that the

was how to interpret the notion of 'extermination' as a crime against humanity. The Chamber pointed out that the ICC Statute provides that extermination may embrace acts 'calculated to bring about the destruction of *part* of the population', namely only a limited number of victims; it stressed that under customary law extermination generally involves a large number of victims. It went on to hold as follows:

The Trial Chamber notes that this definition [that is, that contained in the ICC Statute] was adopted after the time the offences in this case were committed. In accordance with the principle that where there is a plausible difference of interpretation or application, the position which most favours the accused should be adopted, the Chamber determines that, for the purpose of this case, the definition should be read as meaning the destruction of a numerically significant part of the population concerned. (§502.)

It should be noted that the principle of *favor rei* has also been conceived of as a standard governing the *appraisal of evidence*: in this case the principle is known as *in dubio pro reo* (in case of doubt, one should hold for the accused). For instance, in *Flick and others*, a US Military Tribunal sitting at Nuremberg held that it would be guided among other things by the standard whereby 'If from credible evidence two reasonable inferences may be drawn, one of guilt and the other of innocence, the latter must be taken' (at 1189).[38]

7.5 THE PRINCIPLE OF LEGALITY OF PENALTIES (*NULLA POENA SINE LEGE*)

It is common knowledge that in many States, particularly in those of civil law tradition, it is considered necessary to lay down in law a tariff relating to sentences for each crime, so as: (i) to ensure the uniform application of criminal law by all courts of the State, and (ii) to make the addressees cognizant of the possible punishment that may be meted out if they transgress a particular criminal provision.

This principle is not applicable at the international level, where these tariffs do not exist. Indeed States have not yet agreed upon a scale of penalties, due to widely differing views about the gravity of the various crimes, the seriousness of guilt for each criminal offence, and the consequent harshness of punishment. It follows that courts enjoy much greater judicial discretion in punishing persons found guilty of international crimes. However, some statutes of international tribunals set forth limitations on the absolute discretion of judges. Thus, for instance, Article 24(1) of the ICTY Statute provides, first, that penalties will be limited to imprisonment (thus ruling out the death sentence), and, secondly, that 'In determining the terms of imprisonment, the Trial Chambers shall have recourse to the general practice

version more favourable to the accused should be upheld and finds that Article 2(2)(a) of the Statute must be interpreted in accordance with the definition of murder given in the Penal Code of Rwanda, according to which "*meurtre*" (killing) is homicide committed with the intent to cause death' (§§500–1).

38 Another US Military Tribunal sitting at Nuremberg upheld the principle in *Krauch and others* (*I. G. Farben* case) (at 1108).

regarding prison sentences in the courts of the former Yugoslavia'. This last provision was applied in various cases, for instance in *Erdemović* and *Tadić* (*Sentencing judgment 1997*) (§§7–10), *Tadić* (*Sentencing judgment 1999*) (§§10–13), *Delalić and others* (§§1193–212), *Kupreškić and others* (§§839–47), although it was generally not held mandatory. Article 23 of the ICTR Statute is identical, except in referring of course to the general practice regarding prison sentences in the courts of Rwanda.

As for the Statute of the ICC, Article 23 provides that 'A person convicted by the Court may be punished only in accordance with this Statute' and Article 77 confines itself to envisaging imprisonment for a maximum of 30 years, while at the same time admitting life imprisonment 'when justified by the extreme gravity of the crime and the individual circumstances of the convicted person'. It thus implicitly rules out the death penalty, but does not establish a scale of sentences, nor does it suggest that the Court should take into account the scale of penalties of the relevant territorial or national State. The Court is thus left with a very broad margin of appreciation.

SELECT BIBLIOGRAPHY

GENERAL PRINCIPLES

General theory

H. H. Jescheck, *Lehrbuch*, 21–8, 126–60; G. Vassalli, 'Nullum crimen sine lege', XI *Novissimo Digesto* (1965), 493–506; Fletcher, *Basic concepts*, 3–92; F. Mantovani, 3–14, 42–100.

International criminal law

S. Glaser, 'Le principe de la légalité des délits et des peines et les procès de criminels de guerre', 28 RDPC (1947–8), 230–8; Jescheck, *Entwicklung*, 233–44; E. M. Wise, 'General Principles of Criminal Law', in L. Sadat Wexler and C. Bassiouni (eds), *Model Draft Statute for the ICC based on the Preparatory Committee's Text to the Diplomatic Conference, Rome, June 15–17 July 1997* (Association internationale de droit pénal, 1998) 39 ff.; P. Saland, 'International Criminal Law Principles' in R. S. Lee (ed.), *The International Criminal Court. The Making of the Rome Statute—Issues, Negotiations, Results* (The Hague, London, Boston: Kluwer, 1999), 189–216; K. Ambos, 'General Principles of Criminal Law in the Rome Statute', 10 *CLForum* (1999), 1–32; B. Broomhall, W. A. Schabas, R. P. Pangalangan, K. Ambos, R. S. Clark, W. J. Fenrick, D. K. Piragoff, A. Eser, O. Triffterer, in O. Triffterer, *Commentary*, 447–78; S. Lamb, in Cassese, Gaeta, and Jones, *ICC Commentary*, I, 733–66; A. Eser, ibid., 767–822; M. Catenacci, *'Legalità' e 'tipicità del reato' nello Statuto della Corte Penale Internazionale* (Teramo: Edigrafital, 2001); F. Mantovani, 'Sui principi generali del diritto internazionale penale', *Riv. It.* (forthcoming).

THE BAN ON ANALOGY

S. Glaser, 'Culpabilité en droit international pénal', 99 HR (1960–I), 574–8.

THE PRINCIPLE OF LEGALITY OF PENALTIES (*NULLA POENA SINE LEGE*)

W. A. Schabas, 'International Sentencing: From Leipzig (1923) to Arusha (1996)', in M. C. Bassiouni (ed.), *International Criminal Law*, 2nd edn, vol. 3 (Ardsley, NY: Transnational Publishers Inc., 1999), 171–93; W. A. Schabas, 'Perverse Effects of the *Nulla Poena* Principle: National Practice and the Ad Hoc Tribunals', 11 EJIL (2000), 521–39.

8

MENS REA

8.1 THE METHODOLOGICAL PROBLEM

As in national legal systems, conduct contrary to a substantive rule of international law is not sufficient for individual criminal responsibility to arise. A mental element is also required, in some way directed to or linked with the commission of the crime.

It is not easy to identify the various forms and shades of *mens rea* in international criminal law. Two problems arise there. First, substantive rules concerning crimes often do not specify the subjective element required for each specific offence. An exception may be found in the various substantive provisions of the ICC Statute: Articles 6 (on genocide), 7 (on crimes against humanity), and 8 (on war crimes), and the accompanying 'Elements of Crime' elaborated pursuant to Article 9. These provisions most of the time set out the subjective element required for each class of crime. However, in this respect the provisions of the Statute are hedged about with two major limitations. They are only designed to set out the categories of crimes over which the ICC may exercise jurisdiction; in other words they are not couched as provisions of a criminal code. Furthermore, they are not intended to codify, or restate, or contribute to the development of, customary international law. Their legal value is therefore limited (although of course they may gradually have a bearing on, and bring about a change in, existing law).

Secondly, there is no customary rule setting out a *general definition* of the various categories of *mens rea* (such as intent, recklessness, or negligence). In this respect the only exception is Article 30 of the ICC Statute, on 'mental element'.[1] However, it is

[1] Article 30 provides as follows:

'1. Unless otherwise provided, a person shall be criminally responsible and liable for punishment for a crime within the jurisdiction of the Court only if the material elements are committed with intent and knowledge.

'2. For the purposes of this article, a person has intent where:
In relation to conduct, that person means to engage in the conduct;
In relation to a consequence, that person means to cause that consequence or is aware that it will occur in the ordinary course of events.

'3. For the purposes of this article, "knowledge" means awareness that a circumstance exists or a consequence will occur in the ordinary course of events. "Know" and "knowingly" shall be construed accordingly.'

doubtful that it reflects customary international law. In addition, as we shall see, even at the level of treaty law, it is doubtful that it encompasses all the various possible subjective elements of international crimes.

This difficult condition is compounded by the fact that the case law tends not to be enlightening on this score. For it is State courts that have handed down the bulk of judicial decisions dealing with this matter, and each court has applied the general principles of criminal law proper to its legal system. For instance, depending on the legal system to which it belonged, each court has placed its own interpretation on the notion of intent, or fault, or negligence.

To tackle the first of the two problems outlined above, one should first identify all the international *substantive* provisions which themselves lay down, if only implicitly, the subjective element required for their violation to amount to an international crime. One ought also to draw upon the *case law* of such international tribunals as the ICTY and the ICTR, to the extent that they have pronounced on the matter.

To come to grips with the second problem, one must start from the assumption that here, as in other fields of international criminal law, what matters is to identify the possible existence of general rules of international law or principles common to the major legal systems of the world. To pinpoint such rules one may chiefly rely on: (i) the *case law* of courts, with special attention being paid to the judicial decisions of international tribunals, in particular the ICTY and the ICTR; and (ii) the existence of some *basic notions* common to all major legal systems of the world, as evidence of a convergence of these systems and confirmation that parallel principles have taken shape at the international level as well.

I shall briefly mention some instances of how each of the two problems may be solved. I shall then concentrate on the second of these problems, that is, the *general definitions* of the various *categories* of subjective element, which one may deduce from a perusal of international rules and the relevant case law.

8.1.1 SUBSTANTIVE RULES SETTING OUT THE MENTAL ELEMENT REQUIRED FOR THE CRIME

With regard to such substantive rules, one may recall, as major illustrations, a set of important treaty provisions. The first is Article 2 of the 1948 Genocide Convention (now an international customary rule), whereby genocide as an international crime requires that there be 'the intent to destroy, in whole or in part, a national, ethnical, racial or religious group, as such'. Similarly, Article 1 of the 1984 Convention on Torture prohibits torture when it is among other things 'intentionally inflicted'. Although the Convention belongs to a different body of law, namely human rights law, some elements of its definition of torture have been incorporated into international humanitarian law, as ICTY Trial Chambers held in *Delalić and others* (§§452–60), *Furundžija* (§§143–59), and *Kunarac and others* (§§465–97). Furthermore, Article 85, paragraphs 3 and 4, of the First Additional Protocol of 1977 makes punishable a host of violations of the Protocol so long as they are committed 'wilfully'. Plainly, all these provisions require intentional conduct, thereby automatically excluding any other subjective frame of mind such as recklessness, negligence, etc.

8.1.2 GENERAL NOTIONS OF *MENS REA* COMMON TO MOST LEGAL SYSTEMS OF THE WORLD

A survey of the attitude taken towards the definition of the major facets of *mens rea* by the major legal systems of the world makes it apparent that, in spite of broad differences in terminology, most legal systems tend to take the same basic approach to the specific regulation of each aspect of *mens rea*, and its implications. They tend to require one of the following frames of mind, for conduct to be considered criminally punishable (these are listed in decreasing order of criminal liability):

1. Intention, namely the will to bring about a certain result: I use a gun to shoot at a person because I want to kill him. This class of *mens rea* is normally called intent, *dol, Vorsatz, dolus.*

2. Awareness that undertaking a course of conduct carries with it an unjustifiable risk of producing harmful consequences. (I perceive the risk that using a certain weapon may entail killing hundreds of innocent civilians, and nevertheless ignore this risk.) This class is normally called recklessness, or *dol éventuel, Eventualvorsatz* (or *Eventualdolus*, or *bedingter Vorsatz*), *dolus eventualis.*

3. Failure to pay sufficient attention to or to comply with certain generally accepted standards of conduct thereby causing harm to another person when the actor believes that the harmful consequences of his action will not come about, thanks to the measures he has taken or is about to take. (For instance, an attendant at a mental hospital causes the death of a patient by releasing a flow of boiling water into the bath; one of two persons playing with a loaded gun points it at the other and pulls the trigger believing that it will not fire because neither bullet is opposite the barrel; however, as the gun is a revolver, it does fire, killing the other person.)[2] This class is normally referred to as advertent or culpable negligence, *négligence consciente, bewusste Fahrlässigkeit.*

4. Failure to respect generally accepted standards of conduct, without however being aware of the risk that such failure may bring about harmful effects; this class is normally termed inadvertent negligence, *négligence inconsciente, unbewusste Fahrlässigkeit.*

These are of course only general trends of national criminal law. The courts of some States often do not draw such a fine distinction between the aforementioned shades on the scale of criminal culpability.[3] Similarly, national laws or military

[2] See Ashworth, *Principles*, 303–4.

[3] For instance, in 1975 in *Robert Strong* the Court of Appeals of New York held that, from the point of view of the mental state of the defendant at the time the crime was committed, the essential distinction between the crime of 'manslaughter in the second degree' (that is, recklessly causing the death of a person, or

manuals may set out notions that do not fully fit in the above enumeration of forms of *mens rea.*[4]

Depending upon the category of crime and the degree of responsibility, international *customary* rules (resulting from *opinio juris seu necessitatis* and international practice, as evidenced by some treaty provisions, case law, and the convergence of the major legal systems of the world) envisage various modalities of the mental element.

8.2 GENERAL CATEGORIES OF *MENS REA*: INTENT

By intent (or intention: *dolus*) is meant *the will to bring about a certain result* (such as, for example, the death of a civilian). For instance: I want to kill a civilian. So I shoot him and he dies as a result of my act. I must answer for this crime. Or else, I think he is dead but in fact he has not died. He only dies later of exposure because he is left in the cold. It does not matter that my conduct did not kill him—I am guilty of murder because: (i) I intended him to die (*mens rea*); and (ii) he died as a result of my acts (because he would never have been lying exposed were it not for my acts). As a rule, my intent only has to be linked to a certain result (the death of the victim), not a certain result brought about by certain conduct.

International rules require intent for most international crimes, although, as we shall see, under certain circumstances other forms of *mens rea* are admissible for international individual liability to arise.

As an illustration of intent one may mention *Enigster.* The accused, a Jewish internee in a Nazi concentration camp having the rank of *Schieber* or group leader, had been charged with crimes against humanity, in particular grievous injuries, against his fellow inmates. In examining the alleged grievous attack on another

intentionally causing or aiding a person to commit suicide, or committing upon a female an abortion causing her death), and 'criminally negligent homicide' (that is, causing the death of a person with criminal negligence) is that in the former class of crime 'the actor perceives the risk but consciously disregards it' whereas in the latter the actor 'negligently fails to perceive the risk'. In the case at issue the accused, a leader of a Muslim sect with a sizeable following, purportedly exercising his powers of 'mind over matter' used to perform ceremonies such as walking though fire, performing surgical operations without anaesthesia, or stopping a follower's heartbeat and breathing while he plunged knives into his chest without any injury to the person. Although he had performed this last-mentioned ceremony countless times without once causing an injury, in the case brought before the court the follower had died as a result of the wounds. The jury found that the defendant was guilty of manslaughter in the second degree, as charged, without considering whether he could have been guilty of the lesser crime of criminally negligent homicide. The Court of Appeals held that in this case the jury could have found that the defendant 'failed to perceive the risk inherent in his actions . . . The defendant's conduct and claimed lack of perception, together with the belief of the victims and the defendant's followers, if accepted by the jury, would justify a verdict of criminally negligent homicide' rather than manslaughter in the second degree (568–9).

[4] Thus, for example, according to the Australian Defence Force Discipline Manual, 'A person can be said to have acted *recklessly* when he is aware that certain harmful consequences are likely to flow from a particular act but he performs the act despite the risk. A person acts *negligently* when he performs an act without consideration of the probably harmful consequences which will flow from it but where those harmful consequences would be foreseeable by a reasonable man' (§533).

inmate, named Schweizer, the District Court of Tel Aviv had to establish whether all the necessary elements were present; it therefore asked itself, among other things, whether the requisite intent also existed. It noted that in this respect no special testimony had been brought to the Court; it nonetheless had to determine whether the accused had that intent. The Court noted the following:

As to 'intent', it is a well known rule that any person in his right mind is held to intend the natural consequences of his actions. As it appears from the severe results of the blows struck by the defendant, the blows were landed with some significant force, and for this reason, and barring any proof that the defendant landed the blows other than from his own free will, it must be concluded of his mind, that he intended to cause Schweizer grievous damage.[5]

Premeditation, which is normally not required for criminal responsibility, occurs when the intent to engage in conduct contrary to an international substantive rule is formed before the conduct is actually embarked upon. As the Turin Military Tribunal pointed out in *Sävecke* in 1999 (at 14) and repeated in *Engel* in 2000 (at 13), premeditation necessarily requires two elements: one of a temporal nature, namely that some time must pass between the formation of the criminal intent and its being carried out; the other of a psychological nature, namely that the criminal intent must persist from the moment of its formation until the perpetration of the crime. In 1971 a US military judge took a similar stand in *Calley*, although less accurately spelled out, when he issued instructions to the Court Martial. He pointed out that premeditated murder (which under US law is a distinct category from, and not an aggravating circumstance for, unpremeditated murder) is a murder where the actor had 'a premeditated design to kill'; this expression means 'formation of a specific intent to kill and consideration of the act . . . or the acts intended to bring about death . . . prior to doing them. It is not necessary that the "premeditated design to kill" shall have been entertained for any particular or considerable length of time, but it must precede the killing'. In contrast, in the case of unpremeditated murder, only 'intent to kill' is required (whereas in the case of voluntary manslaughter the person entertains 'an intent to kill but kills in the heat of sudden passion caused by adequate provocation') (at 1708–10).

In some instances premeditation may coincide with, or overlap, *planning* the criminal action. However, while planning, as we shall see, has an autonomous scope and legal significance, premeditation has not. In international criminal law premeditation may only be material to sentencing, for it may amount to an aggravating circumstance.[6]

[5] The Court went on to say that 'In regard to this it must be remembered that the defendant denied the entire action and did not give any explanation that could have shown another intent or arouse doubts as to his evil intent. In addition, it is clear from the testimony that no Germans were present while the blows were being landed, and it was not proven, as mentioned above, that the defendant was bound by the orders of the Germans, to do the deed he did in general, and in the way he did it, in particular' (§14). See also *Götzfrid*, at 22–3, 62.

[6] In the two cases quoted above, the Turin Military Tribunal held that premeditation had been proved and consequently considered it an aggravating circumstance: see *Säveke*, at 14–15, and *Engel* at 13.

8.2.1 THE ROLE OF KNOWLEDGE WITHIN INTENT

'Knowledge' is not a notion familiar to civil law countries, where it is not regarded as an autonomous category of *mens rea*, being absorbed either by intent or by recklessness. In contrast, the notion as a distinct class of mental attitude in criminal behaviour is widespread in some common law countries, particularly the United States, where one may find a clear-cut definition in the Model Penal Code. There it is stated at section 2.02 that:

A person acts knowingly with respect to a material element of an offence when:

(i) if the element involves the nature of his conduct or the attendant circumstances, he is aware that his conduct is of that nature or that such circumstances exist; and

(ii) if the element involves a result of his conduct, he is aware that it is practically certain that his conduct will cause such a result.[7]

In such countries as the UK some distinguished commentators consider knowledge as having the same value and intensity as intent, with the difference that intent 'relates to the consequences specified in the definition of the crime' (for instance, death as a result of killing, in the case of voluntary murder), whereas knowledge 'relates to circumstances forming part of the definition of the crime'[8] (for instance, the circumstance that property belongs to another person, in the case of criminal damage to property).

In short, it would seem that in some common law countries, knowledge denotes two different forms of mental attitude, depending on the *contents of the substantive penal rule* at stake: (i) if the substantive penal rule prescribes the existence of a *particular fact or circumstance* for the crime to materialize, knowledge means awareness of the existence of this fact or circumstance; (ii) if instead the substantive criminal rule focuses on the *result of one's conduct*, then knowledge means (a) awareness that one's action is most likely to bring about that harmful result, and nevertheless (b) taking the high risk of causing that result. Plainly, category (i) is part of intent (which involves not only the will to accomplish a certain action and thereby attain a certain result, but also awareness of the factual circumstances implicated in the action). Category (ii) substantially coincides with recklessness, as defined below (see 8.3).

International rules, probably under the influence of US negotiators, uphold the notion under discussion, *in both versions.* Thus, for instance, Article 85(3)(e) of the First Additional Protocol of 1977 enumerates among the grave breaches of the Protocol (which must be 'committed wilfully' and cause 'death or serious injury to body or

[7] See *Model Penal Code and Commentaries (Official Draft and Revised Comments)*, Part I, vol. 1 (Philadelphia, Pa.: The American Law Institute, 1985), at 225–6.

The Model Penal Code then specifies that 'when knowledge of the existence of a particular fact is an element of an offence, such knowledge is established if a person is aware of a high probability of its existence, unless he actually believes that it does not exist' (at 227).

[8] See Ashworth, *Principles*, 191–7. In contrast, the notion is discussed only in passing by Smith and Hogan (see at 103 and 117).

health') 'making a person the object of attack in the knowledge that he is *hors de combat*'. Similarly, Article 7(1) of the ICC Statute provides that crimes against humanity comprise the various acts enumerated there, 'when committed as part of a widespread or systematic attack directed against any civilian population, with knowledge of the attack'. Here knowledge means awareness of the requisite circumstances, namely that the person is *hors de combat* or that there exists a pattern of attacks against civilians. Similarly, international rules on command responsibility require simple knowledge of circumstances, in the case of a commander who knows that his subordinates have committed crimes, and yet fails to take any action to repress those crimes. Here no other mental attitude is required in addition to awareness of the fact that troops under the control or authority of the commander have committed or are committing international crimes.

Other international rules focus instead on result, and hence substantially consider knowledge as amounting or equivalent to recklessness. Thus, Article 85(3)(b) of the First Additional Protocol considers as a grave breach 'launching an indiscriminate attack affecting the civilian population or civilian objects in the knowledge that such attack will cause excessive loss of life, injury to civilians or damage to civilian objects'. A fairly similar definition is laid down in Article 8(2)(b)(iv) of the ICC Statute.

The notion at issue has finally been consecrated in international law in Article 30(2) of the ICC Statute, where it is stipulated that knowledge 'means awareness that a circumstance exists or a consequence will occur in the ordinary course of events'. Thus, this provision upholds both versions of the notion.

For an example of knowledge as awareness of facts, hence as part of intent, one may mention that, for instance, to be held responsible for complicity in planning or waging an aggressive war, it must be proved either that an accused participated in the preparation or execution of these plans (and in this case the criminal intent may be inferred from such participation), or that the accused was *apprised* of the plans, in addition to taking some sort of action furthering their implementation. In *Göring and others*, in considering the charges of crimes against peace made against Schacht (President of the Reichsbank and Minister without Portfolio until 1943), the IMT noted that he was responsible for rearmament of Germany, but this as such was not a crime; for it to become a crime it must be shown that he carried out rearmament as part of the Nazi plans to wage aggressive wars; however, the Tribunal found that while organizing rearmament Schacht did not know of the Nazi aggressive plans; hence it acquitted him (at 307–10). A US Military Tribunal at Nuremberg took the same position and came to the same conclusion in *Krauch and others* (*I. G. Farben* case), where it also showed that the defendants' lack of knowledge of Hitler's aggressive plans proved that they lacked the requisite criminal intent (at 1115–17).

Another important instance where knowledge is required by international criminal rules is *aiding and abetting an international crime* (for example, a war crime such as killing a prisoner of war or an enemy civilian). Here criminal responsibility arises if the aider and abettor *knows* that his action will assist the commission of a specific crime by the principal. Various courts have taken this position.[9] As the ICTY Trial Chamber put it in *Furundžija*, the accomplice need not share the *mens rea* of the principal: 'mere knowledge that his actions assist the perpetrator in the commission of the crime is sufficient to constitute *mens rea* in aiding and abetting the crime' (§236). (In this case the accused interrogated the victim while she was being subjected to rape and serious sexual assaults by another person; the Trial Chamber found that the accused's presence and continued interrogation of the victim while she was being subjected to violence amounted to aiding and abetting the crime, for the accused provided assistance, encouragement, or moral support to the sexual offender and knew that these acts assisted the commission of the rape and sexual assault.)

As will be shown below (10.4.4), knowledge is also required in most cases of *command responsibility*. The issue was well put by the US Judge Advocate in his instructions to a US Court Martial in *Medina*:

> [A] commander is . . . responsible if he has *actual* knowledge that troops or other persons subject to his control are in the process of committing or are about to commit a war crime and he wrongfully fails to take the necessary and reasonable steps to insure compliance with the law of war. You will observe that these legal requirements placed upon a commander require actual knowledge plus a wrongful failure to act. Thus mere presence at the scene without knowledge will not suffice. That is, the commander-subordinate relationship alone will not allow an inference of knowledge. While it is not necessary that a commander actually see an atrocity being committed, it is essential that he know that his subordinates are in the process of committing atrocities or are about to commit atrocities. (At 1732.)

Finally, let it be emphasized that in international criminal law knowledge as awareness of circumstances *does not mean awareness of the legal appraisal* of those circumstances. It only denotes cognizance of the factual circumstances envisaged in a particular international rule. International law, like most national systems, does not require awareness of the illegality of an act for the act to be regarded as an international crime. As we shall see (13.4.1) it starts from the assumption that everybody must know the law; it therefore makes culpable even acts that were performed without the author being fully aware of their unlawfulness (as long as the required intent, recklessness, knowledge, etc. are there).[10] International law only takes into

[9] For instance, a US Military Tribunal sitting at Nuremberg, in *Einsatzgruppen* (at 568–73), two British courts respectively in *Schonfeld* (at 64) and *Zyklon B* (at 93), the German Supreme Court in the British Occupied Zone in the *Synagogue* case (at 229), a chamber of the ICTY in *Kupreškić and others*, and then the Appeals Chamber in *Tadić* (§229).

In *Veit Harlan* the Court of Assizes of Hamburg held in 1950 that in the case at issue there existed the requisite subjective element of the offence of complicity in a crime against humanity (persecution of the Jews), in that the accused, a film director who had produced a strong anti-Semitic film at the behest of Goebbels, 'knew the intention of Goebbels, namely to justify through the film, beyond the usual propaganda, the persecutory measures against Jews that had been taken and planned' (at 66), and in addition 'had taken into account the possible materializing of the [adverse] consequences of the film, such consequences having been described [in general terms] by the Supreme Court [in the British Occupied Zone]' (at 66).

[10] In *Burgholz (No. 2)*, the British Judge Advocate, in delineating to the Military Court the scope of *mens rea* in international crimes, stated: '[Y]ou might think it difficult to say that any man could have a guilty mind

account knowledge, or lack of knowledge, of the law when the defence of *mistake of law* can be regarded as admissible, for the law on a particular matter is uncertain or unclear (see below 13.4.2). In other words, international rules do not attach importance to the *subjective* mental attitude of the perpetrator with regard to law, unless this subjective attitude coincides with the *objective* condition of the law, namely its uncertainty.

To sum up, *in most cases* knowledge should not be considered as an autonomous criminal state of mind, but only as *a means of entertaining criminal intent* or *recklessness.*

Nonetheless, *in other instances* knowledge cannot be reduced to either of those categories, and it remains indispensable as a subjective element on its own. For example, with the *mens rea* required for crimes against humanity, the accused must know of the widespread or systematic attack against a civilian population. It is not that he *intends* the civilian population to be subject to the attack nor that he knows that there is a risk of them being subjected to an attack—both of which are beside the point. What one wants is simply to be sure that he knew of the attack. In these instances knowledge is a useful way of describing the *mens rea* and it is irreducible.

8.2.2 SPECIAL INTENT (*DOLUS SPECIALIS*)

International rules may require a special intent (*dolus specialis, dol aggravé*) for particular classes of crimes. There is such special intent when an international rule, in addition to requiring the intent to bring about a certain result by undertaking certain conduct (for example, death by killing), also requires that the agent pursue a *specific goal* that goes beyond the result of his conduct, with the consequence that attainment of such goal is not necessary for the crime to be consummated. (Examples include the goal of destroying the religious, racial, or ethnic group to which the victims of murder belong; or the purpose of spreading terror among civilians; clearly, the murder of dozens of Muslims or Jews may be termed genocide if the required special intent is present, regardless of whether the general purpose of destroying the group as such is achieved; the same holds true for terrorist attacks, which may amount to international crimes even if in fact the specific attacks do not achieve the purpose of terrorizing the population.)

This special intent is provided for in some categories of crimes against humanity, namely persecution. Here, in addition to the intent necessary for the commission of the underlying offence (murder, rape, serious bodily assault, expulsion from a village, an area or a country, etc.) a discriminatory intent is required, namely the will to

in respect of his conduct if he is not aware that his conduct is in breach of any law, or if there is no formalized law to fit his participatory conduct and to involve the breach thereof. But *Mens Rea* goes a little further than that. If a man ought to have known that he was doing wrong, then the law presumes a guilty mind, and the requirements of the doctrine of *Mens Rea* are fulfilled if you find the accused either knew that they were doing wrong or ought to have known: the fact that they may have had no conscious thought of wrongdoing will not protect them from conviction if a breach of law has been committed' (at 84–5).

discriminate against members of a particular national, ethnic, religious, racial, or other group. As an ICTY Trial Chamber put it in *Kupreškić and others* (§634), and another Trial Chamber restated it in *Kordić and Čerkez* (§§214 and 220), the acts of the accused must have been 'aimed at singling out and attacking certain individuals on discriminatory grounds', with the aim of 'removal of those persons from the society in which they live alongside the perpetrator, or eventually from humanity itself'. In *Blaškić*, another Trial Chamber worded that intent as follows: 'the specific intent to cause injury to a human being because he belongs to a particular community or group' (§235).

Similarly, international rules require a special intent for genocide: the agent must possess 'the intent to destroy, in whole or in part, a national, ethnical, racial or religious group'. Thus, it is not sufficient for the person to intend to kill, or cause serious bodily harm, or deliberately inflict on a group seriously adverse and discriminatory conditions of life, or forcibly transfer children from one group to another, etc. It also must be proved that he did all this with the (further and dominant) intention of destroying a group. For, as the German Federal Court of Justice (*Bundesgerichtshof*) stated in *Jorgić* on 30 April 1999, in the crime of genocide a single person is the object of an attack 'not as an individual but rather in his capacity as a member of a group whose social existence the perpetrator intends to destroy . . . the particular inhumanity that characterizes genocide as distinct from murder lies in that the perpetrator or perpetrators do not see the victim as a human being but only as a member of a persecuted group' (at 401).[11]

The rules on crimes of international terrorism require a special intent: that of spreading terror in the population by killing, hijacking, blowing up buildings, etc. (see *supra*, 6.9.4).

8.3 RECKLESSNESS

Recklessness (*dolus eventualis*) is a state of mind where *the person foresees that his action is likely to produce its prohibited consequences*, and nevertheless *takes the risk of so acting*. In this case the degree of culpability is less than in intent. While in the case of intent the actor pursues a certain result and knows that he will achieve it by his action, in the case of recklessness he only envisages that result as *possible* or *likely* and deliberately takes the risk; however, he does not necessarily desire the result.

A good definition of this notion—as set out in the criminal law of the State of New York—can be found in Rule 15.5(3) of the New York Penal Code, which defines recklessness as follows:

> A person acts recklessly with respect to a result or to a circumstance described by a statute defining an offence when he is aware of and consciously disregards a substantial and

[11] That a specific or special intent is required for genocide has also been stressed in *Akayesu* (§498), *Musema* (§§164–7), *Jelisić (Appeal)* (§§45–6).

unjustifiable risk that such result will occur or that such circumstance exists. The risk must be of such nature and degree that disregard thereof constitutes a gross deviation from the standard of conduct that a reasonable person would observe in the situation.

Instances of recklessness are clearly envisaged in some international rules. Thus, for instance the rule on superiors' responsibility provides that the superior is criminally liable for the crimes of his subordinates if 'he consciously disregarded information which clearly indicated' that his subordinates were about to commit, or were committing, international crimes (see *infra*, 10.4.4). In this case the superior is liable to punishment for having taken the risk, knowing that his subordinates were likely to commit or were committing crimes.

Furthermore, in the case of responsibility for crimes perpetrated by a multitude of persons pursuant to a common design (see *infra*, 9.4.2), as the Appeals Chamber of the ICTY held in *Tadić* (*Appeal*), what is required is that, under the circumstances of the case, (i) it was foreseeable that the crime might be perpetrated by one or other members of the group and (ii) the accused willingly took that risk (§§227–8).

The notion of recklessness was also applied in many cases brought before German courts after the Second World War. These courts, which administered criminal justice in Germany under Control Council Law no. 10, were seized with crimes against humanity committed by Germans against other Germans. Most cases concerned denunciations to the Gestapo, with all the ensuing inhuman consequences. In many of these cases German courts as well as the German Supreme Court in the British Occupied Zone held that, for the denunciation to amount to a crime against humanity, it was not necessary for the author of the denunciation to foresee and will all the nefarious consequences of his denunciation; it was sufficient that he be aware of the authoritarian and arbitrary system of Nazi violence then prevailing in Germany and of the consequent risk that the victim would be subjected to persecution and great suffering. In this connection the German Supreme Court employed the German equivalent of the notion of recklessness, namely *Eventualvorsatz* (or *bedingter Vorsatz*).

For instance, one may mention *K. and M.*, decided by the Offenburg Tribunal (*Landgericht*) on 4 June 1946. In January 1944, K., the principal accused, a member of the Nazi party, over a dinner with friends and acquaintances, had a discussion with Könninger, a soldier who was on home leave. Already tipsy, Könninger inveighed against the German leadership, noting among other things that the war was about to be lost. A few weeks later K. reported Könninger's tirade to various persons including some dignitaries attending a party meeting at a restaurant. As a result, the Gestapo arrested Könninger and brought him to trial. In July 1944 he was sentenced to death for defeatism and executed. Before the Offenburg court K. submitted that he had not intended to have the victim prosecuted and punished for his utterances. The court held, however, that when he reported his statements to the party meeting,

he must expect that his words would have adverse consequences for Könninger. The accused caused proceedings against Könninger to be instituted, witnesses to be heard, and the victim eventually to be sentenced. It is entirely credible that the accused K. did not intend all that. However, he was to expect that this would be the result of his talk at the restaurant. He must foresee this result. He tacitly approved it. There was therefore recklessness on his part. (At 67.)

The court found K. guilty of a crime against humanity (persecution on political grounds) under Article II(1)(c) of Control Council Law no. 10.[12]

K., decided on 27 July 1948 by the German Supreme Court in the British Occupied Zone, is also interesting. In February 1942 the accused, a member of the Waffen SS working at the headquarters of the Gestapo in D., had denounced at his headquarters a Jewish businessman (M.) because the latter had gone to the apartment of a non-Jew. The denunciation led to the Jew being taken into preventive custody for three weeks. The accused was found guilty of a crime against humanity. On appeal the Supreme Court confirmed the judgment. It held that under the relevant rules the accused had engaged in 'offensive conduct that was conscient and deliberate'; he must be aware that he was 'handing over the victim directly or indirectly to forces which [would], on account of the facts in the denunciation, treat him solely according to their purposes and ideas without being bound by considerations of justice or legal certainty'. According to the court the accused 'was aware that the denunciation could have entailed the most grave consequences for M., as the accused knew of the criminal and arbitrary manner in which the Gestapo abused its power at the time'. This mental element was sufficient: it was not required for the perpetrator to have acted with 'an inhumane cast of mind', nor was 'approval of the result' required (at 50–1).[13]

The Supreme Court in the British Occupied Zone also required recklessness in other cases not dealing with denunciations. For instance, in *L. and others* (judgment of 14 December 1948) the events had occurred on 5 May 1933. In a parade by SA

[12] A very similar case is *W.*, brought before the Tribunal of Waldshut (judgment of 16 February 1949, at 147).

[13] *R.* was heard by the Supreme Court in the British Occupied Zone, and decided on 27 July 1948. In March 1944, in Hamburg, the accused, a member of the Nazi party, had an argument with a soldier in uniform, who had insulted the political leaders while drunk. Later on he reported him to the police, and as a result the victim was arrested on the Eastern front, brought back to Germany in September 1944, charged with undermining military morale and brought to trial. He was sentenced first to five years' imprisonment and then a death sentence was sought, but not imposed due to the Russian occupation. The Court held that for the denunciation to be a crime against humanity, it was necessary that 'the offensive behaviour of the perpetrator be conscious and intentional (or at least the perpetrator took the risk), that it actually occurred and the perpetrator, through his act, willed that the victim be handed over to powers that did not obey the rule of law, or at least, that he took this possibility into account'. The Court insisted that the mental element of the crime was met if the perpetrator had intended 'to deliver the victim to the uncontrollable power machinery of the power and the State or at the very least he had taken the risk that he would be treated arbitrarily'. And the Court added that 'negligence' (*Fahrlässigkeit*) was not sufficient (at 47).

The Supreme Court took the same position in *O.* (judgment of 19 October 1948) (at 106–7), and in *Th.* (judgment on the same date), where it restated that, for the accused's denunciation of another person to the police to be characterized as a crime against humanity, it was necessary that a mental element be present, namely that she 'at least was cognizant of and took into account the possibility that the victim, as a consequence of her denunciation, would be treated in an arbitrary manner' (at 115–16). The same judgment was restated in another case of denunciation, *J. and R.* (judgment of 16 November 1948, at 170), *S.* (judgment of 8 March 1949, at 260–1), and *F.* (judgment of 2 May 1950, at 367).

(assault troopers) through the main streets of a small German town a prominent socialist senator and a Jewish inhabitant were publicly humiliated and subjected to inhuman treatment (they were led along in a pig cart, with demeaning inscriptions hung around their necks and were vilified in various ways). The defendants took part in the parade. The Court held that, as far as the involvement of three accused went, 'it was inconceivable' that they, who were old officials of the Nazi party, 'did not at least think it possible and consider that in the case at issue, through their participation, persons were being assaulted by a system of violence and injustice; more is not required for the mental element' (at 232). In contrast, in the case of another defendant, who had simply followed the procession among the onlookers and in civilian clothes, the Court held that he was not guilty because he 'had not participated in causing the offence nor had he at least entertained *dolus eventualis* in taking part in the causation of the offence (at 234).[14] It would thus seem that according to the Court at least some of the defendants took an unjustified risk of the victims being assaulted.

8.4 CULPABLE NEGLIGENCE

Generally speaking negligence entails that the person (i) acts in *disregard of certain elementary standards* with which any reasonable man should comply; and (ii) either does not *advert at all to the risk of harm* to another person involved in his conduct (simple negligence), or *is aware of that risk*, but is sure that it will not occur (gross

[14] Another significant case is *P. and others* (judgment of 7 December 1948). On the night after Germany's partial capitulation (5 May 1945) four young German marines had tried to escape from Denmark back to Germany. The next day they were caught by Danes and delivered to the German troops, who court-martialled and sentenced three of them to death for desertion; on the very day of the general capitulation of Germany, i.e. 10 May 1945, the three were executed. The German Supreme Court found that some of the participants in the trial before the Court Martial were guilty of complicity in a crime against humanity. According to the Supreme Court, the glaring discrepancy between the offence and the punishment proved that the execution of the three marines had constituted a clear manifestation of the Nazis' brutal and intimidatory justice, which denied the very essence of humanity in blind deference to the superior exigencies of the Nazi State; in this case as well there had taken place 'an intolerable degradation of the victims to mere means for the pursuit of a goal, hence the depersonalisation and reification of human beings'; consequently, by sentencing to death those marines, the members of the Court Martial had also injured humanity as a whole. As for the mental element of the crime, the Court held that intent (indisputably present in the case of the judges who had sentenced the marines to death and of the military commander who had confirmed the sentence and ordered the execution) was not necessarily required; recklessness, for instance in the case of the prosecutor, was sufficient: 'it is sufficient for the defendant concerned to have taken into account the possibility and have consented to the fact that his conduct would contribute to cause the resulting killing' (at 224).

In *Eschner*, the accused, an SS officer who had held an important position in the concentration camp of Gross-Rosen between 1941 and 1945, was accused, among other things, of having requested Kapo V., a criminal by profession, to 'get rid of' a camp inmate who had tried to escape; the inmate had probably died. The Würzburg Tribunal held that the accused knew the violent behaviour of the Kapo and 'approvingly took into account that the inmate might suffer death as a result of the intended ill-treatment. Thus he willed recklessly the death of a man contrary to law.' However, in view of the fact that the inmate's death was not certain, the court found the accused guilty of 'attempted murder' by recklessness (at 253).

negligence). Mere negligence is the least degree of culpability. Normally it is not sufficient for individual criminal liability to arise.

It would seem that, given the intrinsic nature of international crimes (which always amount to serious attacks on fundamental values) in international criminal law negligence operates as a standard of liability only when it reaches the threshold of *gross* or *culpable negligence* (*culpa gravis*). This occurs when the person: (i) is *expected or required to abide by certain standards of conduct or take certain specific precautions*, and in addition (ii) is aware of the risk of harm and nevertheless takes it, for *he believes that the risk will not materialize owing to the steps he has taken or will take.* (In contrast, in the case of recklessness the agent deliberately runs the risk regardless of any step he may have taken to forestall the ensuing harm; it follows that with culpable negligence there is a lesser degree of guilt than with recklessness.) However, given the aforementioned nature of international crimes, it would seem that the mental element just referred to only becomes relevant when, in addition, there exist some specific conditions relating to the objective elements of the crime, that is, the *values* attacked are fundamental and the *harm* caused is serious.[15]

That national legal systems may penalize a mental state that is less grave than the one criminalized at the international level should not be surprising. Given the consequences following from, and the stigma inherent in, international crimes, it is only natural that international criminal rules should be more exacting, with regard to subjective requirements of the offence, than some national criminal legislation.

Case law bears out the above international notion. *John G. Schultz*, a case brought before a US Court of Military Appeals in 1952, deserves mention. Schultz, driving a car, had struck and killed two Japanese pedestrians in 1950 in Japan, a country militarily occupied by the USA. The US Court stated the following:

> A careful perusal of the penal codes of most civilized nations leads us to the conclusion that homicide involving less than culpable negligence is not universally recognized as an offense. Even in those American jurisdictions—still relatively few in number—which have given statutory recognition to either negligent homicide or vehicular homicide, the degree of negligence required is often held to be 'culpable' or 'gross'—the same as that required for involuntary manslaughter. Imposing criminal liability for less than culpable negligence is a relatively new concept in criminal law and has not, as yet, been given universal acceptance by civilized nations.[16]

[15] This definition of culpable negligence is in some respects at variance with that upheld in some common law and civil law countries. For instance, under the New York Penal Code, Rule 1505(4): 'A person acts with criminal negligence with respect to a result or to a circumstance described by a statute defining an offence when he fails to perceive a substantial and unjustifiable risk that such result will occur or that such circumstance exists. The risk must be of such nature and degree that the failure to perceive it constitutes a gross deviation from the standard of care that a reasonable person would observe in the situation.' Clearly, this definition corresponds to what we termed above 'inadvertent negligence', or *culpa levis* (see *supra*, 8.1.2).

[16] 4 CMR (1952), 104, 115–16 (CMA Lexis 661). On this case see also *supra*, 3.3, note 8. A definition of negligence as a possible subjective element in international crimes can be found in the instructions given by the Judge Advocate to a Canadian Court Martial in *Major A.G. Seward*. The defendant had among other things been charged with negligently performing his military duty while in Somalia in 1993. The particulars of his

Gross negligence is clearly required by the customary rules on superiors' responsibility (see *infra* 10.4.3) whereby a superior is responsible for the crimes of his subordinates if he did not know but 'should have known' that they were about to commit, or were committing, or had committed crimes. In this case, the superior was required to become cognizant of, and verify, all the information necessary to monitor the activities and the conduct of his subordinates. If he disregards these standards of conduct, he acts with gross negligence and is consequently liable if all the other conditions are fulfilled (see *infra* 10.4.4).[17]

Culpable negligence has also been considered sufficient in other circumstances. A case where a court held negligence to be the mental element of the crime is *Stenger and Crusius*, decided in 1921 by the Leipzig Supreme Court. In the battle near Saarburg in Lorraine between the French and the German Army, on 21 August 1914 the accused Crusius, a captain of the German army, thought that Major-General Stenger had verbally ordered the killing of all French wounded. Acting under this erroneous assumption, he passed on this alleged order to his company. The Court held that:

> the act of will which in the further course of events caused the objectively illegal outcome . . . included an act of carelessness which ran contrary to his duty, and neglect of the consideration required in the situation at hand which was perfectly reasonable to expect from the accused. Had he applied the care required of him, he would not have failed to notice what many of his men realized immediately, namely that the indiscriminate killing of all wounded represented an outrageous and by no means justifiable war manoeuvre . . . Captain Crusius was certainly familiar with the provisions of the field operating procedures which require a written order as the basis for troop command by the higher troop leaders, as well as the drill manual which makes the written order a rule, especially concerning orders for brigades and higher. This circumstance is also not entirely without significance, particularly in view of the

negligence were stated to be that he 'by issuing an instruction to his subordinates that prisoners could be abused, [he] failed to properly exercise command over his subordinates, as it was his duty to do'. As a result of his instructions, some of his subordinates had beaten up and killed a Somali civilian. In instructing the Court Martial on the notion of negligence, the Judge Advocate stated: '[A]s a matter of law the alleged negligence must go beyond mere error in judgment. Mere error in judgment does not constitute negligence. The alleged negligence must be either accompanied by a lack of zeal in the performance of the military duty imposed, or it must amount to a measure of indifference or a want of care by Major Seward in the matter at hand, or to an intentional failure on his part to take appropriate precautionary measures' (at 1081). The Court Martial found the defendant guilty on this count. In commenting on this finding by the Court Martial, the Court Martial Appeal Court of Canada stated that the Court Martial 'must be taken to have concluded that the respondent did issue an "abuse" order and that his doing so was no mere error in judgment. He himself confirmed that he was taking a "calculated risk" in doing so and that nothing in his training or in Canadian doctrine would permit the use of that word during the giving of orders' (ibid.)

[17] Among the cases that may be cited to support the applicability of gross negligence in cases of superior responsibility, *Schmitt* stands out. This case, concerning the commander of a concentration camp in Breendonck, was brought before the Brussels Military Tribunal, which held in 1950 that 'although it is true that generally speaking jurisprudence does not consider that, in case of murder, simple lack of action or negligence are punishable, this however does no longer apply when a person's failure to act amounts to the non-fulfilment of a duty . . . in this case failure to take action amounts to material conduct sufficient for the realisation of criminal intent' (at 936–7).

personality of the accused who was described as a diligent, zealous and benevolent officer. In view of the accused's background and personality, he should have anticipated the illegal outcome which was easily demonstrated even if his mental and emotional states at the time were to be fully taken into consideration. (At 2567–8.)

The Court concluded that Crusius was guilty of causing 'death through culpable negligence' (*fahrlässige Tötung*) and sentenced him to two years' imprisonment.

Another court also took into account negligence, this time with regard to crimes against humanity: *Hinselmann and others*, decided by the British Court of Appeal in the British Zone of Control in Germany, in 1947. A Trial Court had convicted a group of German doctors and police officers of crimes against humanity, under Control Council Law no. 10 (Article I(c)). It had found that they were concerned with carrying out, in 1944–45, sterilization operations 'on a number of persons of gypsy blood, to prevent the increase of the race' (three doctors had performed the operations and two police officers had induced persons to sign consent to the operations by threats). Counsel for one of the doctors, Günther (a gynaecological specialist), argued that there was no evidence that he knew that the gypsies were being sterilized on account of their race; in counsel's view, the case against Günther could only be one of negligence; however, negligence was not sufficient to constitute an offence under Control Council Law no. 10, which required extremely gross negligence; hence, Günther, if he were to be convicted at all, could only be convicted under section 230 of the German Criminal Code.[18] The Prosecutor countered that Günther must have known the correct procedure in the case of sterilization, but made no enquiries, and saw no legal documents. In addition, in his view there was no difference 'in the degree of negligence required to constitute an offence under Section 230 and that required to constitute an offence under [Control Council] Law 10'.

The Court of Appeals found that the appellant's frame of mind amounted to negligence: a German law of 1933, as amended in 1935, made it clear that sterilization operations were illegal unless: (i) they were performed to avert a serious threat to the life and health of the person operated upon, and with the consent of that person, or (ii) they were carried out in pursuance of an order of the Eugenics Court. The Court of Appeals noted that in the case at issue neither of these conditions was fulfilled:

The operations were of so special a nature, and the limits within which they could be legally performed so narrow, that Günther was put upon his enquiry before he operated. His failure to make the necessary enquiry was negligence. Although 'negligence' as used by British lawyers [in English law there is negligence when the conduct of a person fails to measure up to an objective standard and the person ought to have foreseen the risk involved in his conduct[19]] and '*Fahrlässigkeit*' as used by German lawyers are not co-extensive terms [in German law there is negligence when a person, acting in breach of a duty of precaution

[18] Under this provision, 'Whoever through negligence causes bodily harm to another is punished by a pecuniary penalty or imprisonment up to three years' (see A. Schönke, *Strafgesetzbuch für das Deutche Reich—Kommentar*, 2nd edn (Munich and Berlin: Beck, 1944), at 484; and see 172–3 for the notion of negligence).

[19] See, for instance, Smith and Hogan, 90–6.

brings about a certain result he has not willed, and this result occurs either because the person is not cognizant of the breach of duty, or else is aware that the breach may occur, but trusts that the result will not materialize[20]], there was undoubtedly *Fahrlässigkeit* on Günther's part; and the sterilization of the persons operated upon was a bodily injury.

The crucial point was however whether negligence or *Fahrlässigkeit* could suffice for the requisite *mens rea* in the case of a crime against humanity. As mentioned above, counsel for the appellant had argued that negligence, if any, on the part of Günther was not serious enough to constitute an offence under Control Council Law no. 10; German law was therefore applicable; however, under this law, unless the rule under which a person was charged expressly stated that negligence was sufficient, the person could not be convicted of a criminal offence if the act constituting it was merely negligent and not intentional. The Court of Appeals dismissed this argument. It held:

> We do not accept the proposition that this is necessarily so [namely that negligence may not amount to the requisite subjective element unless this is explicitly provided for in the relevant law] where a charge under [Control Council] Law 10 is tried in a Control Commission Court; but, in the present case, there is no suggestion that the operations were cruelly performed, and the evidence was inadequate to establish a degree of negligence which could have amounted in any event to a Crime against Humanity.

The Court consequently set aside Günther's conviction under Control Council Law no. 10, substituted it with a finding that he was guilty of an offence under section 230 of the German Criminal Code, and reduced the sentence of two years' imprisonment to six months (58–60).

It may be clearly inferred from this finding that, for the Court of Appeals, crimes against humanity may result from negligence, provided however that negligence is gross.

Finally, it should be pointed out that there are also cases where culpable negligence has been so conceived of as to border on recklessness.[21]

[20] See, for instance, Jescheck, *Lehrbuch*, at 563.

[21] Thus in *Medina*, in 1971 a US military judge issued to the Court Martial instructions with regard to command responsibility arising in a case where the commander allegedly had actual knowledge that troops or other persons subject to his control were in the process of committing war crimes (killing of innocent civilians in the Vietnamese village of My Lai), and wrongfully failed to take the necessary and reasonable steps to ensure compliance with the laws of war. The military judge pointed out that the legal requirements of international law 'placed upon a commander require actual knowledge plus a wrongful failure to act'. He then stated that the omission to exercise control must constitute culpable negligence and then pointed out that 'culpable negligence is a degree of carelessness greater than simple negligence. For purposes of making the distinction between the two, you are advised that simple negligence is the absence of due care, that is an omission by a person who is under a duty to exercise due care, which exhibits a lack of that degree of care for the safety of others which a reasonable, prudent commander would have exercised under the same or similar circumstances. Culpable negligence, on the other hand, is a higher degree of negligent omission, one that is accompanied by a gross, reckless, deliberate, or wanton disregard for the foreseeable consequences to others of that omission; it is an omission showing a disregard of human safety. It is higher in magnitude than simple inadvertence, but falls short of intentional wrong. The essence of wanton or reckless conduct is intentional conduct by way of omission where there is a duty to act, which conduct involves a high degree of likelihood that substantial harm will result to others' (at 1732–4).

8.5 THE ICC STATUTE

As stated above, the ICC Statute contains the only international provision setting out a general definition of the subjective element of international crimes: Article 30. This provision envisages intent and knowledge as the only mental elements of those crimes (as set forth in Articles 6–8 of the ICC Statute). Article 30(1) provides that 'Unless otherwise provided, a person shall be criminally responsible and liable for punishment for a crime within the jurisdiction of the Court only if the material elements are committed with intent and knowledge'. Paragraph 2 then defines those two notions.[22]

Article 30 raises two problems. First, it does not envisage in terms recklessness and culpable negligence, although recklessness (*dolus eventualis*) may be held to be contemplated in the definition of intent laid down in paragraph 2. Secondly, it always requires *both* intent and knowledge, whereas there may be cases where only intent, as defined in the provision, is sufficient, and other cases where instead only knowledge (which, according to the definition given in the provision, may be regarded as equivalent to the US version of recklessness) would be sufficient (think of aiding and abetting, referred to *infra*, 9.4.3).

To solve the first problem one may focus on the initial proviso of the rule ('Unless otherwise provided'): whenever a provision of the Statute or a rule of international customary law requires a different mental element, this will be considered sufficient by the Court. For instance, Article 28(a)(i) provides for the responsibility of superiors where the 'military commander or person . . . owing to the circumstances at the time, should have known that the forces [under his effective command, control or authority] were committing or about to commit . . . crimes'. Plainly, this provision envisages culpable negligence (see *supra*, 8.4 as well as 10.4.4). This case would be covered by the proviso just referred to.

Nonetheless, when a specific substantive provision of the Statute does *not* specify the mental element required, one may deduce from Article 30 that one must take that substantive provision to require intent and knowledge. In this manner the Statute may eventually require a mental element *higher* than that set down in customary law. Indeed, differences may arise between customary international law and treaty law whenever a customary rule concerning a specific crime considers as a sufficient requirement for that crime a subjective element other than intent (for instance, culpable negligence).

As for the second problem (the use of the conjunctive 'and'), one ought to note that in international law the standard of construction applies that a purely grammatical construction must yield to a logical interpretation whenever this is dictated by the

[22] Para. 2 provides that: 'For the purposes of this article, a person has intent where (a) in relation to conduct, that person means to engage in the conduct; (b) in relation to a consequence, that person means to cause that consequence or is aware that it will occur in the ordinary course of events'.

Para. 3 provides that: 'For the purposes of this article, "knowledge" means awareness that a circumstance exists or a consequence will occur in the ordinary course of events. "Know" and "knowingly" shall be construed accordingly.'

principle of effectiveness (*ut res magis valeat quam pereat*) and is consonant with the object and purpose of the rule. It is therefore admissible to construe the word 'and' as also including the word 'or' when this is logically required. [23]

8.6 JUDICIAL DETERMINATION OF THE SUBJECTIVE ELEMENT

As in national law, in international criminal law a culpable state of mind is normally proved in court by circumstantial evidence. In other words, one may infer from the facts of the case whether or not the accused, when acting in a certain way, willed, or was aware, that his conduct would bring about a certain result. To put it differently, one may normally deduce from factual circumstances whether the action contrary to international criminal law was accompanied by a mental attitude denoting some degree of fault.

This is the position taken by national and international courts. For instance, one may mention the statement made by the Judge Advocate addressing a Canadian Military Court in *Johann Neitz*. The question at issue was whether the accused, who had shot at a member of the Royal Canadian Air Force who had been taken prisoner, wounding the prisoner without killing him, had intended to cause his death. The Judge Advocate put the issue to the Military Court as follows:

Intention is not capable of positive proof, and, accordingly, it is inferred from the overt acts. Evidence of concrete acts is frequently much better evidence than the evidence of an individual for, after all, an individual alone honestly knows what he is thinking. The Court cannot look into the mind to see what is going on there. The individual may protest vehemently what his intentions were, but such evidence is subject to human frailty and human perfidy. Accordingly, intention is presumed from the overt act. It is a simple application of the principle that actions speak louder than words, and, I add, often more truthfully. It is also a well-established maxim of law that a man is presumed to have intended the natural consequences of his acts. If one man deliberately strikes another over the head with an axe, the law presumes he intended to kill the other. Similarly so, if one man deliberately shoots a gun at another, an intent to kill will be presumed . . . If a man points a gun at another and deliberately fires, it is presumed that he intends to kill the other. However, this is a presumption of fact, but it may be rebutted.' (At 209.) (The Court found the accused had committed a war crime with intent to kill and sentenced him to life imprisonment.)

A court of Bosnia and Herzegovina took the same approach in *Tepež* with regard to intent,[24] while an ICTY Trial Chamber pointed out in *Delalić and others*, with regard

[23] An application of this rule of construction was made by the ICTY Trial Chamber I in *Tadić*, decision of 7 May 1997, §§712–13.

[24] In setting out the mental element of the crimes of torture and murder of civilians, the Sarajevo Cantonal Court stated that 'The accused perpetrated the crime deliberately; he was aware that together with others from Rajko Kuj's group he was taking part in torture, beatings and killing of prisoners. Since the accused repeated these actions many times, he definitely wished to do that and was aware that repeated beatings of prisoners with hard objects, fists and boots in vital parts of their bodies can certainly result in their death. By repeating these actions it is evident that the accused wanted these people killed' (at 7).

to the subjective element of command responsiblity, that it could be established 'by way of circumstantial evidence'.[25]

Interestingly, in *Jelisić* an ICTY Trial Chamber, in order to establish whether the accused had entertained the special intent required for genocide, examined various statements he had made to the effect that he wished to exterminate Muslims, for he hated them and wanted to kill them all (§§102–4). The Court concluded, however, that these utterances revealed a disturbed personality and consequently, for lack of the requisite special intent, the acts of the accused were not 'the physical expression of an affirmed resolve to destroy in whole or in part a group as such' (§107). Out of a concern for wasting the Tribunal's resources, the Appeals Chamber did not reverse the Trial Chamber's decision on this point, although it strongly disapproved of the Trial Chamber's verdict (*Jelisić* (*Appeal*), §§ 53–77).

SELECT BIBLIOGRAPHY

GENERAL THEORY

H. H. Jescheck, *Lehrbuch*, 232–321, 405–75; G. P. Fletcher, *Basic Concepts*, 11–129; H. L. A. Hart, 'Negligence, *Mens Rea* and Criminal Responsibility', in A. Guest (ed.), *Oxford Essays in Jurisprudence* (Oxford: Clarendon Press, 1961–8), 29–49; F. Mantovani, 293–371.

COMPARATIVE LAW

H. Donnedieu de Vabres, *Traité*, 74–87; J. Pradel, 251–70; Ashworth, *Principles*, 159–208; M. Delmas-Marty (ed.) *Corpus Juris* (Paris: Economica, 1997), 64–78; J. Vogel, 'Criminal Law General Part: Articles 9–17 Corpus Juris', in M. Delmas-Marty and J. A. E. Vervalle (eds), *The Implementation of the Corpus Juris in the Member States*, I (Antwerp, Groningen, Oxford: Intersentia, 2000) 249–304.

INTERNATIONAL CRIMINAL LAW

Jescheck, *Verantwortlichkeit*, 242–55; 374–85; S. Glaser, 'Culpabilité en droit international pénal', HR 99 (1960–I), 473–593; K. Ambos, *Der 'Allgemeine Teil'*, 652–67, 719–66; C. Elliott, 'The French Law of Intent and Its Influence on the Development of International Criminal Law', 11 *Crim. L. Forum* (2000), 35–46.

ICC STATUTE

D. K. Piragoff, in O. Triffterer (ed.), *Commentary*, 527–35; A. Eser, in Cassese, Gaeta, and Jones (eds), *ICC Commentary*, 767–822.

[25] The Trial Chamber pointed out that 'in the absence of direct evidence of the superior's knowledge of the offences committed by his subordinates, such knowledge cannot be presumed, but must be established by way of circumstantial evidence' (§386).

Again, with regard to 'knowledge' that the subordinates were committing or had committed crimes in the case of command responsibility, an ICTY Trial Chamber stated in *Kordić and Čerkez* that, 'Depending on the position of authority held by a superior, whether military or civilian, *de jure* or *de facto*, and his level of responsibility in the chain of command, the evidence required to demonstrate actual knowledge may be different. For instance, the actual knowledge of a military commander may be easier to prove considering the fact that he will presumably be part of an organized structure with established reporting and monitoring systems. In the case of *de facto* commanders of more informal military structure, or of civilian leaders holding *de facto* positions of authority, the standard of proof will be higher' (§428).

9

PERPETRATION AND OTHER MODALITIES OF CRIMINAL CONDUCT

9.1 GENERAL

As in any national legal system, also in international criminal law responsibility arises not only when a person materially commits a crime but also when he or she engages in other forms or modalities of criminal conduct. In the following paragraphs I shall set out these different modalities of participation.

Before I do so, it may however prove fitting briefly to discuss the position in national legal systems. They converge in holding that, where a crime involves more than one person, all performing the same act, all are equally liable as co-perpetrators, or principals. In contrast, national legal orders differ when it comes to the punishment of two or more persons participating in a crime, where these persons do not perform the same act but in one way or another contribute to the realization of a criminal design. Many systems (for instance those of the United States, France, Austria, Italy, Uruguay, Australia) do not provide for different categories of participants, and consequently do not attach different penalties to each of the classes (principals or accessories) under which a person may eventually fall. They provide that each participant, whatever his degree of participation, must be considered as a principal; consequently the same penalty may be meted out to each of them. As the California Penal Code provides at §31, all those 'concerned in the commission of a crime' including those who aid and abet the crime, are to be held liable as principals. Nonetheless, a distinction is often drawn between three categories of participation: perpetration, on the one side, and two categories of accomplice liability, on the other, namely instigation (*complicité par instigation*) and aiding and abetting (*complicité par aide et assistance*). This distinction is based on the difference in *actus reus* and *mens rea* for each class (see below). In spite of the difference in such objective and subjective elements, the law does not however attach to each of these categories *different consequences* as far as penalties are concerned; or, at least, under the general sentencing tariff no distinction is made. It is only provided that for accomplices or accessories extenuating circumstances may be taken into account if their participation in the offence is less serious than that of the principal or principals. In fact, for the purposes of sentencing, judges often draw a distinction between principals, instigators, and aiders and abettors.

In other national legal systems (for instance, Germany and Russia) the law draws instead a *normative* distinction between two categories, principals, and accomplices or accessories, and provides in terms that the persons falling under the latter category must be punished less severely. Thus, for instance, in German law, the scale of penalties for accomplices (at least in the case of aiders and abettors, *Gehilfe)* is less harsh than for the perpetrator (*Täter*).[1]

We will see that in international law neither treaties nor case law (as indicative of customary rules) make any legal distinction between the various categories, at least as far as the consequent penalties are concerned. This lack of distinction follows both from: (i) the absence of any agreed scale of penalties in international criminal law and from (ii) the general character of this body of law, that is, its still rudimentary nature and the ensuing lack of formalism (see *supra*, 2.2).

Consequently, the differentiation between the various classes of participation in crimes, which I shall set out below, is merely based on the intrinsic features of each modality of participation. It serves a *descriptive and classificatory purpose* only. It is devoid of any relevance as far as sentencing is concerned. It is for judges to decide in each case on the *degree of culpability* of a participant in an international crime and assign the penalty accordingly, whatever the modality of participation of the offender in the crime.

9.2 PERPETRATION

Whoever physically commits a crime, either alone or jointly with other persons, is criminally liable. For instance, the soldier who kills a war prisoner or an innocent civilian is liable to punishment for a war crime. Similarly, the serviceman who rapes an enemy civilian as part of a widespread or systematic sexual attack on civilians is accountable for a crime against humanity.

Perpetration is thus the physical carrying out of the prohibited conduct, accompanied by the requisite psychological element.[2]

[1] In two cases, the Extraordinary Court Martial established in the Ottoman Empire to try persons accused of participating in massacring Armenians in 1915 and plundering their possessions, applied the 'Imperial Penal Code for Officers', which drew a normative distinction between principals and accessories. The Court therefore made a point of distinguishing between the 'principal perpetrators' and the 'accessories', and assigning a different sentence to each category of defendant. In *Kemâl and Tevfik* it sentenced the principal perpetrator to death and the accessory to 15 years of hard labour (at 5–6); in *Bahâeddîn Şâkir* the majority of judges held that two defendants were accessories, while three dissenting judges held that they 'were equally guilty of having been principal co-perpetrators' (at 4 and 8).

[2] In some cases courts have minimized the role of perpetrators executing illegal orders. This for instance holds true for *Alfons Götzfrid*, which concerns mistreatment at the Majdanek camp. The Stuttgart Court (*Landgericht*) held in a decision of 20 May 1999 that 'According to established case-law (cf. Federal Supreme Court, Part 18, 87 et seq.), the offender or accomplice is defined as one whose thoughts and actions coincide

9.3 CO-PERPETRATION

Crimes are often committed by a *plurality of persons*. If all of them materially take part in the actual perpetration of the same crime and perform *the same act* (for instance, they are all members of an execution squad shooting innocent civilians), we can speak of co-perpetration. All participants in the crime partake of the same criminal conduct and the attendant *mens rea*.

9.4 PARTICIPATION IN A COMMON PURPOSE OR DESIGN

9.4.1 PARTICIPATION ENTAILING RESPONSIBILITY FOR ALL THE ACTS FLOWING FROM THE CRIMINAL PLAN

When the crime results from the *action of a multitude of persons*, it may happen that *not all participants perform the same act*. In the case of torture one person may order the crime, another may physically execute it, yet another may watch to check whether the victim discloses any significant information, a medical doctor may be in attendance to verify whether the measures for inflicting pain or suffering are likely to cause death so as to stop the torture just before the measures become lethal, another person may carry medicine, or food for the executioners, and so on. The question arises of whether all these participants are equally responsible for the same crime, torture. Similarly, in the case of deportation of civilians or prisoners of war to an extermination camp, a commander may issue the order, several officers may organize the transport, others may take care of food and drinking water, others may carry out surveillance over the inmates so as to prevent their escape, others may search the detainees for valuables or other things before deportation, and so on.

As in most national legal systems, also in international criminal law all participants in a common criminal action are equally responsible if they (i) participate in the action, *whatever their position and the extent of their contribution*, and in addition (ii)

with those of the author of the crime, who willingly gives in to incitement to political murder, silences his conscience and makes another person's criminal aims the basis of his own conviction and his own action or who sees to it that orders of that kind are ruthlessly carried out, or who in so doing otherwise displays consenting enthusiasm or who exploits State terror for his own purposes. Accordingly, the accused could only be shown to have an attitude denoting guilt if, over and above the activity he was instructed to carry out, he had performed some contributory act on his own initiative beyond the call of duty, shown particular enthusiasm, had acted with particular ruthlessness in the extermination operation or had shown a personal interest in the killings. These conditions cannot be shown to exist in the case of the accused. He was at the end of the chain of command, had no power of decision himself and no authority to act . . . Similarly, there is no evidence that the accused had any personal interest in the killings. He merely wanted to carry out the order which had been issued to him.'

intend to engage in the common criminal action. Therefore they are all to be treated as *principals*,[3] although of course the varying degree of culpability may be taken into account at the sentencing stage.[4]

It is important to add that the common plan or purpose need not be formally set out. As the ICTY Appeals Chamber rightly noted in *Tadić* (*Appeal*),

> there is no necessity for this plan, design or purpose to have been previously arranged or formulated. The common plan or purpose may materialize extemporaneously and be inferred from the fact that a plurality of persons acts in unison to put into effect a joint criminal enterprise. (§227.)

As in national legal systems, the rationale behind this legal regulation is clear: if all those who take part in a common criminal action are aware of the purpose and character of the criminal action and share the requisite criminal intent, they must perforce share criminal liability, whatever the role and position they may have played in the commission of the crime. This is the case because: (i) each of them is indispens-

[3] However, some courts of common law countries have taken the view that participants in a common criminal design may play the role of, and be regarded as, accessories. Thus, for instance, in *Einsatzgruppen*, with regard to common design, the Prosecutor T. Taylor, in his closing statement noted that 'the elementary principle must be borne in mind that neither under Control Council Law No. 10 nor under any known system of criminal law is guilt for murder confined to the man who pulls the trigger or buries the corpse. In line with recognized principles common to all civilized legal systems, paragraph 2 of Article II of Control Council Law No. 10 specifies a number of types of connection with crime which are sufficient to establish guilt. Thus, not only are principals guilty but also accessories, those who take a consenting part in the commission of crime or are connected with plans or enterprises involved in its commission, those who order or abet crime, and those who belong to an organization or group engaged in the commission of crime. These provisions embody no harsh or novel principles of criminal responsibility' (at 372).

[4] In this connection one may mention, by way of example, a decision of the Supreme Court of Bosnia and Herzegovina in *Tepež*, delivered on 1 October 1999: 'The appeal by the defence counsel argues that the contested judgment has not individualised the criminal responsibility of the accused and his personal involvement in actions characteristic of a war crime against the civilian population. For this crime to exist it is necessary to "commit murder, torture, inhumane acts, inflict severe suffering, physical and mental injuries on civilians, destroying their health and physical integrity". The disposition does not include these essential elements of this criminal act and therefore represents a major violation of the provisions of criminal procedure. This Court finds these allegations groundless.

'The appeal fails to note that the contested judgment states that the accused carried out these actions with three other named individuals (as well as others), which means that he perpetrated the crime for which he has been pronounced guilty in complicity with others. It further means that in cases of this kind where it is not possible to isolate individual actions and their consequences or to distinguish the degree to which each person was involved in their execution, it suffices that these actions complement each other and together form a single entity, which the accused [Tepe] wishes to achieve by being involved. Therefore it was neither possible nor necessary for the court of first instance to separate only the actions of the accused. It suffices that the accused participated in executing these actions, even if it had only been one or two actions of personal involvement in the beating of civilians. However, the court of first instance has established that the accused personally beat up many individuals on many occasions' (at 2).

One may also mention the decision of a Canadian court in *Moreno*: 'In reaching this conclusion, I am influenced by one commentator's view that the closer a person is involved in the decision-making process and the less he or she does to thwart the commission of inhumane acts, the more likely criminal responsibility will attach . . . of course, the further one is distanced from the decision makers, assuming that one is not a "principal", then it is less likely that the required degree of complicity necessary to attract criminal sanctions, or the application of the exclusion clause, will be met' (at 18). See also *Ramirez* (at 6–9).

able for the achievement of the final result, and on the other hand (ii) it would be difficult to distinguish between the degree of criminal liability, except for sentencing purposes.

One may find a particularly clear and significant *illustration* of this category of criminality in *Alfons Klein and others* (the *Hadamar* trial), heard by a US Military Commission sitting at Wiesbaden. It may prove fitting to dwell on this case at some length, because it best shows how the category of criminality at hand works.

The accused were seven Germans. Between July 1944 and April 1945, they killed over 400 Polish and Russian nationals, who had been obliged to work in Germany for the German war effort and were suffering from tuberculosis or pneumonia. Brought to Hadamar, in Germany, where there was a hospital or institution originally designed to care for the mentally unsound, but with no medical facilities to treat persons sick with tuberculosis or pneumonia, they were told that they would be given medication. In fact they were killed by injections of poisonous drugs; afterwards the relevant medical records and death certificates were falsified. It would seem that the primary purpose of these killings was to make space in hospitals for German war victims. The accused comprised Klein, the administrative head of the hospital, a local Nazi Party leader who made all the arrangements leading to the perpetration of the atrocities; Wahlmann, a physician specializing in mental diseases, the Institution's only doctor (he participated in the conferences designed to plan the murders, knew what was going on at the hospital, and acquiesced in it); three nurses, Ruoff, Willig, and Huber, who administered the poisonous drugs; Merkle, the institution's bookkeeper (who registered incoming patients for the purpose of recording dates and causes of death, actually falsifying these documents); and Blum, a doorman and telephone switchboard operator, who also served as caretaker of the cemetery, charged with burying the victims in mass graves (but he sometimes walked through the wards to inspect the victims before they were taken, dead, to his cellars a few hours later).

The charge for all of them was of 'violation of international law', namely, as the Prosecutor specified in his opening argument, breach of the laws of warfare (at 202). The specification stated that the seven accused 'acting jointly and in pursuance of a common intent' 'did . . . wilfully, deliberately and wrongfully aid, abet and participate in the killing of human beings of Polish and Russian nationality'. Thus, in addition to the notion of 'participation in killing based on common intent' also the notion of 'aiding and abetting' was used. However, in his Opening Argument the Prosecutor, when setting out the applicable law (there was no Judge Advocate), emphasized that all those who participate in a common criminal enterprise are equally guilty as 'co-principals' whatever the role played by each single participant. Referring to the case of murder committed by several persons, he pointed out that:

> Every single one of those who participated in any degree towards the accomplishment of that result [murder] is as much guilty of murder as the man who actually pulled the trigger . . . That is why under our [that is, US] Federal Law all distinctions between accomplices, between accessories before the fact and accessories after the fact, have been completely eliminated. Anyone who participates in the commission of any crime, whether formerly

called as an accessory or not, are now co-principals and have been so for several years. (At 203.)

Moving then to the case at bar, the Prosecutor in fact offered an eloquent illustration of the rationale behind the legal notion he was invoking:

At this Hadamar mill there was operated a production line of death. Not a single one of these accused could do all the things that were necessary in order to have the entire scheme of things in operation. For instance, the accused Klein, the administrative head, could not make the initial arrangements, receive those people, attend to undressing them, make arrangements for their death chamber, and at the same time go up there and use the needle that did the dirty work, and then also turn around and haul the bodies out and bury them, and falsify the records and the death certificates. No, when you do business on a wholesale production basis as they did at the Hadamar Institution, that murder factory, it means that you have to have several people doing different things of that illegal operation in order to produce the results, and you cannot draw a distinction between the man who may have initially conceived the idea of killing them and those who participated in the commission of those offences. Now, there is no question but that any person who participated in that matter, no matter to what extent, technically is guilty of the charge that has been brought . . . every single one of the accused has overtly and affirmatively participated in this entire network that brought about the illegal result. (At 205–7.)

The defence counsel did not dispute these concepts, but in their arguments preferred to rely upon the notions of necessity and superior orders, or argued that German law rather than US or international law should apply. The Court upheld the charge. The administrative head of the hospital and two nurses were sentenced to death; the physician (a 70-year-old man) to life imprisonment and hard labour; the book-keeper to 35 years and hard labour; the third nurse to 25 years and hard labour; the doorman and caretaker to 30 years and hard labour (at 247).

In international *case law* there are many other notable examples of this form of criminality. Some British and US courts, influenced by common law concepts, have utilized the notion of 'persons concerned' in, for instance, the killing of the victim, or the concept of 'common purpose' or 'common design'.[5] In contrast other courts, for instance Dutch, German, and Italian, holding to civil law terminology, have preferred

[5] See for instance *Josef Kramer and others* (the *Belsen* trial), at 638–40; *Heinz Heck and others* (the *Peleus* trial), at 122 as well as *Burgholz* (*No. 2*) at 82 and the *Loibl Pass* (*No. 1*) case, at 2. See also *Erich Killinger and others* (the *Dulag Luft* trial), at 224–5, 235. In the latter case the Prosecutor, in the absence of a Judge Advocate, submitted that each of the five accused 'was concerned, in his respective capacity on the staff of Dulag Luft, as a party to the ill-treatment of prisoners of war, and concerned with sufficient proximity to make him criminally responsible on the ordinary standards of criminal responsibility in English law, either by being an accessory before the fact, or a principal in the second degree, or a principal in the first degree, or an accessory after the fact'. He further submitted that the five accused 'were all there at times when that system was working, and . . . those incidents occurred in circumstances in which a reasonable man can only come to the firm judgment that each one of those five accused was criminally concerned in that ill-treatment borne out in the evidence before you' (at 235). However, the Court found that two of the accused were not guilty (at 236).

Falkenhorst also deserves to be mentioned. The Judge Advocate, addressing the third charge against the accused, General von Falkenhorst (that he, 'as Commander-in-Chief, with knowledge, with understanding and with the intention, was concerned in the killing of . . . fourteen British prisoners'), stated that '"Concerned in the killing" is a wide phrase, and we all agree it is not confined to the person who actually

to rely upon the notion of 'concurrence of persons in a crime'. As the cases brought before the former courts are more numerous, it may prove useful to dwell on some of these cases.

does the killing; I think we all agree that it could only apply to somebody who has some power or authority to influence the result, and the case for the Prosecution on this is very straightforward, that is nothing more nor less than they allege you should find that these people, who should have been treated, according to the Prosecution, as prisoners of war, were shot, or murdered as the Prosecution put it, because of the specific order to which I have already referred emanating from the Commander-in-chief which was binding on the forces of the Wehrmacht who carried out these executions' (at 231); the Court found the accused guilty and sentenced him to 'death by being shot' (at 240–1).

Wolfgang Zeuss and others (the *Natzweiler* trial) is also interesting. Four women working for the Resistance movement were arrested by the Gestapo in France, sent to a detention camp in Struthof/Natzweiler, taken to the crematorium, and executed by injection. The accused included the commandant as well as the head of the political department of the concentration camp, the camp doctor, a prisoner employed in the crematorium, a camp medical orderly, a clerk in the political department, the camp dentist, and some military staff. The Judge Advocate, discussing the charge against the accused, that is, that all of them were concerned in a killing, noted that that charge did not make it necessary 'that any person should actually be present'. 'None of the accused is actually charged with killing any of the women concerned. They are charged with being concerned in a killing, and you can be concerned in a killing without being actually present at the time when the killing takes place. If two or more men set out on a murder and one perhaps stands half a mile away from where the actual murder is committed, perhaps to keep guard, although he is not actually present when the murder is done, if he is taking part with the other man with the knowledge that the other man is going to do the killing, then he is just as guilty as the person who fires the shot or delivers the blow, or however the murder is committed. Although much evidence in this case has been directed towards establishing who was actually present in the crematorium, you have got to cast your vision further afield and consider whether, in spite of anybody not having been proved to be present, they may nevertheless still be concerned in the killing' (at 200–1). The Court found three defendants not guilty and sentenced the camp doctor to death and the others to various terms of imprisonment (at 218 and 222).

It is also worth mentioning *Sumida Haruzo and others* (the '*Double Tenth*' trial). This case is relevant in two respects: the possible criminal responsibility of interpreters, and that of members of special units.

The accused, a Japanese military unit, were charged with ill-treatment and torture of British prisoners of war in Singapore. Among the accused were some interpreters. The defence argued that they had simply acted as a medium of communication (at 245–9). 'The responsibility of an interpreter . . .—argue defence counsel—is a non-commissive responsibility. An interpreter has neither the right nor the authority to stop an act of torture' (at 249). The Prosecution submitted instead that they had in some way participated in ill-treatment by actually taking part in the beating or torture of the prisoners (at 255, 264–5). The Court sentenced the interpreters either to imprisonment or to death (at 280–1).

On the question of criminal liability of members of a military unit committing crimes, the Prosecutor noted that 'where a branch of [a] unit of the Kempei Tai [Japanese military police force; the Singapore branch was charged with preserving public peace and military policing] has been proved beyond reasonable doubt to have been participating in a war crime, then every man who is proved to have been a member of that particular unit during the relevant period may, *prima facie*, be held responsible for that war crime, even though no concrete criminal act has been brought home to him specifically as an individual. And I would go further than that, and suggest respectfully, that in a case such as this, where the very closest privity and connection has been proved to have existed between all members of the Singapore Kempei Tai, *which was charged as a unit with the prosecution of this specific No. 1 Work*, then the Court should consider very carefully whether the mere presence of a man with such a unit does not constitute *prima facie* evidence of his complicity, but goes much further and establishes a strong presumption of guilt. I do not go so far as to suggest a shifting of the burden of proof, which does, and always must, remain with the Prosecution . . . The *degree* of complicity on the part of any particular individual is, of course, a matter to which you, gentlemen, would have to direct your minds much later in apportioning any sentence which might be necessary; but in the determination of the question of guilt or innocence of a crime such as this—the result of a deliberate policy carried out by a whole unit—such a consideration is, in my submission, totally irrelevant' (at 259; see also 271–2). The Court acquitted six defendants and condemned the others to varying sentences (at 275–82).

In *Ponzano*, a case concerning the unlawful killing of four British prisoners of war by German troops, the Judge Advocate adopted the approach suggested by the Prosecutor, and stressed:

the requirement that an accused, before he can be found guilty, must have been concerned in the offence . . . [T]o be concerned in the commission of a criminal offence . . . does not only mean that you are the person who in fact inflicted the fatal injury and directly caused death, be it by shooting or by any other violent means; it also means an indirect degree of participation . . . [I]n other words, he must be the cog in the wheel of events leading up to the result which in fact occurred. He can further that object not only by giving orders for a criminal offence to be committed, but he can further that object by a variety of other means. (At 7.)

The Judge Advocate also underlined the necessity of knowledge on the part of the accused as to the intended purpose of the criminal enterprise.[6]

Courts also applied the notion of common purpose in cases where the crimes had allegedly been committed by members of military or administrative units running concentration camps; that is, by groups of persons acting pursuant to a concerted plan. In this respect one may mention such cases as *Dachau Concentration Camp*, brought before a US Tribunal under Control Council Law no. 10 (at 5, 14), *Nadler and others*, decided by a British Court of Appeal under Control Council Law no. 10 (at 132–4), *Auschwitz Concentration Camp*, decided by a German Court (at 882), as well as *Belsen*, decided by a British military court sitting in Germany (at 121). In these cases the accused held some position of authority within the hierarchy of the concentration camps. Normally, the accused were charged with having acted in pursuance of a common design to kill or mistreat prisoners and hence to commit war crimes.[7]

The accused, when found guilty, were regarded as co-principals in the various crimes of ill-treatment, because of their objective 'position of authority' within the concentration camp system and because they had 'the power to look after the inmates

[6] *Georg Otto Sandrock et al.* (also known as the *Almelo Trial*) can also be cited. Three Germans had killed a British prisoner of war; it was clear that they all had had the intention of killing the British soldier, although each of them played a different role. The British Court found all of them guilty of murder under the doctrine of 'common enterprise' (at 35, 40–1). In *Hölzer and others*, brought before a Canadian military court, in his summing up the Judge Advocate emphasized that the three accused (Germans who had killed a Canadian prisoner of war) knew that the purpose of taking the Canadian to a particular area was to kill him. The Judge Advocate spoke of a 'common enterprise' with regard to that murder (at 341, 347, 349). In *Jepsen and others* a British court had to pronounce upon the responsibility of Jepsen and others for the death of inmates of a concentration camp in transit to another concentration camp. The Prosecutor argued that '[I]f Jepsen was joining in this voluntary slaughter of eighty or so people, helping the others by doing his share of killing, the whole eighty odd deaths can be laid at his door and at the door of any single man who was in any way assisting in that act'. The Judge Advocate did not rebut the argument (at 241). In *Schonfeld* the Judge Advocate stated that: 'if several persons combine for an unlawful purpose or for a lawful purpose to be effected by unlawful means, and one of them in carrying out that purpose, kills a man, it is murder in all who are present . . . provided that the death was caused by a member of the party in the course of his endeavours to effect the common object of the assembly' (at 68).

[7] In his summing up in the *Belsen* case, the Judge Advocate took up the three requirements set out by the Prosecution as necessary to establish guilt in each case: (i) the existence of an organized system to ill-treat the detainees and commit the various crimes alleged; (ii) the accused's awareness of the nature of the system; and (iii) the fact that the accused in some way actively participated in enforcing the system, i.e., encouraged, aided, and abetted or in any case participated in the realization of the common criminal design (at 637–41).

and make their life satisfactory' but failed to do so. In these cases, as the ICTY Appeals Chamber pointed out in *Tadić (Appeal)*:

the required *actus reus* was the active participation in the enforcement of a system of repression, as it could be inferred from the position of authority and the specific functions held by each accused. The *mens rea* element comprised: (i) knowledge of the nature of the system and (ii) the intent to further the common concerted design to ill-treat inmates. It is important to note that, in these cases, the requisite intent could also be inferred from the position of authority held by the camp personnel. Indeed, it was scarcely necessary to prove intent where the individual's high rank or authority would have, in and of itself, indicated an awareness of the common design and an intent to participate therein. All those convicted were found guilty of the war crime of ill-treatment, although of course the penalty varied according to the degree of participation of each accused in the commission of the war crime. (§203.)

9.4.2 PARTICIPATION ENTAILING RESPONSIBILITY FOR THE FORESEEABLE CRIMES OF OTHER PARTICIPANTS

In other cases where a multitude of persons participates in the commission of a crime, it may happen that, although all participants share from the outset the common criminal design, *one or more perpetrators commit a crime that had not been (expressly or implicitly) agreed upon or envisaged at the beginning*, and therefore did not constitute part and parcel of the joint criminal enterprise. For instance, a group of soldiers, acting under superior orders, set out to detain, contrary to international law, a group of civilians; however, one of the servicemen, in the heat of military action, tortures or rapes one or more of those civilians. Are the other soldiers equally responsible for this additional crime, not envisaged in the joint criminal design?

The ICTY Appeals Chamber clarified this legal issue in *Tadić (Appeal)*. There it held that 'responsibility for a crime other than the one agreed upon in the common plan arises only if, under the circumstances of the case, (i) it was *foreseeable* that such a crime might be perpetrated by one or other members of the group and (ii) the accused *willingly took that risk*' (§228). The Appeals Chamber showed that this proposition was based on case law, had a solid underpinning in many national legal systems, and in addition was consonant with the general principles on criminal responsibility laid down both in the ICTY Statute and in customary international law (§§224–9).

In the case at issue the Appeals Chamber held that Tadić, the appellant, was 'an armed member of an armed group' that attacked a village in Bosnia and Herzegovina, during the armed conflict raging in the Prijedor region; he took an active part in the attack, rounding up and severely beating some members of the non-Serb population living there. The armed group, in pursuance of its violent action against non-Serbs, killed five of them. According to the Appeals Chamber the only possible inference was that Tadić 'had the intention to further the criminal purpose to rid the Prijedor region of the non-Serb population, by committing inhumane acts against them. That non-Serbs might be killed in the effecting of this common aim was, in the circumstances of the . . . case, foreseeable. The Appellant [Tadić] was aware that the actions of the group of which he was a member were likely to lead to such killings, but he nevertheless willingly took that risk'. The Chamber consequently found Tadić guilty of wilful killing as a grave breach as well as a war crime and a crime against humanity (§§230–7).[8]

9.4.3 AIDING AND ABETTING

A person may participate in a crime without sharing the criminal intent of the principal perpetrator, but simply by assisting him in the commission of the crime. In aiding and abetting the objective element is constituted by *practical assistance, encouragement, or moral support*, by the accessory to the principal (namely the author of the main crime); in addition, such assistance, support etc. *must have a substantial effect on the perpetration of the crime.* The subjective element resides in the accessory having *knowledge* that 'his actions assist the perpetrator in the commission of the crime'. (This, with convincing arguments, an ICTY Trial Chamber held in *Furundžija* (§§190–249); see also *Musema* (§126), *Aleksovski* (§63), *Kunarac and others* (§391).)

Thus, unlike the instances considered previously, aiding and abetting does not necessarily presuppose that the aider and abettor shares a common plan or purpose with the principal or his criminal intent or other form of *mens rea*; as stated by the ICTY Appeals Chamber in *Tadić*, 'the principal may not even know about the accomplice's contribution' (§229). What is required is that the person supporting or assisting in the crime be aware that his action furthers and helps the perpetrator or perpetrators in the commission of the crime.

Among the various cases where the notion was applied[9] *Akayesu* can be cited, not so much for outlining the legal contours of the notion (the Trial Chamber at one point stated that 'complicity' was to be defined in the light of the Rwandan Penal Code: §537), as for the legal findings on this matter. The Trial Chamber found that:

[8] The ICTY Appeals Chamber confirmed the decision in *Tadić* (*Appeal*) in *Aleksovski* (*Appeal*) (§§163–4). Also a Trial Chamber referred approvingly to that decision in *Kordić and Čerkez* (§§393–400).

[9] Such cases include *Schonfeld* and *Rohde*, both heard by British military courts (at 64 and 56 respectively), *Zyklon B*, also heard by a British court (at 93), *Einsatzgruppen*, brought before by a US Military Tribunal sitting at Nuremberg (at 569–85), *S. and others* (*Hechingen Deportation* case), brought before a German court in the French Occupied Zone (at 484–90). However, in most of these cases the notion of aiding and abetting was not clearly defined as distinct from that of 'participation in a common purpose'. Trial Chambers of the ICTR and the ICTY have made a better jurisprudential contribution to the outlining and enunciation of the concept in *Akayesu* (dealing with the notion of 'complicity in genocide': §§525–48), in *Tadić* (§§688–92), and in *Furundžija* (§§190–249).

One may also mention a Canadian case involving torture: in *Moreno* (decision of 14 September 1993) the Court held that 'Presence at the commission of an offence can be evidence of aiding and abetting if accompanied by other factors, such as prior knowledge of the principal offender's intention to commit the offence or attendance for the purpose of encouragement . . . While mere presence at the scene of a crime (torture) is not sufficient to invoke the exclusion clause [of the Refugee Convention], the act of keeping watch with a view to preventing the intended victim from escaping may well attract criminal liability' (at 16–17). See also *Ramirez* (at 5–9).

Akayesu, in his capacity as *bourgmestre* [mayor], was responsible for maintaining law and public order in the commune of Taba and . . . had the effective authority over the communal police. Moreover, as 'leader' of Taba commune, of which he was one of the most prominent figures, the inhabitants respected him and followed his orders. Akayesu himself admitted before the Chamber that he had the power to assemble the population and that they obeyed his instructions. It has also been proved that a very large number of Tutsi were killed in Taba between 7 April and the end of June 1994, while Akayesu was bourgmestre of the Commune. Knowing of such killings, he opposed them and attempted to prevent them only until 18 April 1994, after which date he not only stopped trying to maintain law and order in his commune, but was also present during the acts of violence and killings, and sometimes even gave orders himself for bodily or mental harm to be caused to certain Tutsi, and endorsed and even ordered the killing of several Tutsi . . . The Chamber holds that the fact that Akayesu, as a local authority, failed to oppose such killings and serious bodily or mental harm constituted a form of tacit encouragement, which was compounded by being present [during] such criminal acts. (§§704–5.)

The Chamber added that Akayesu was present during numerous incidents of rape and sexual violence against Tutsi women and, by his attitude and utterances, encouraged such acts, thus giving 'tacit encouragement' to the rapes being committed. The Court concluded that he was criminally responsible 'for having abetted in the preparation or execution of the killings of members of the Tutsi group and the infliction of serious bodily and mental harm on members of the said group' (§§706–7).

In *Furundžija* an ICTY Trial Chamber found that the accused, an officer of the Bosnian Croat armed forces, was present while the victim was being raped by another officer, and interrogated her. It held that in this way he had given assistance, encouragement, or moral support, having a substantial effect on the crime by the other officer, with the knowledge that these acts assisted the commission of the offence. The Trial Chamber therefore found the defendant guilty of aiding and abetting outrages upon personal dignity including rape (§§270–5).

9.5 INCITEMENT OR INSTIGATION AS A FORM OF PARTICIPATION IN INTERNATIONAL CRIMES

Incitement to commit a crime is some form of inducement, encouragement, or persuasion to perpetrate the crime. Incitement does not necessarily presuppose a hierarchical position. It simply means taking all those psychological or physical measures designed to prompt somebody else to commit a crime. It also requires the intent to have the crime perpetrated.

As held in *Blaškić*, 'both positive acts and omissions may constitute instigation' (§280). Furthermore, incitement is a crime only under certain conditions: (i) it must be *direct and explicit*; (ii) *commission of the crime* must follow it up. In other words, incitement is not punished per se, but only if it leads to the commission of a crime. As we shall see, international criminal law provides for an exception to this rule, in the case of genocide.

An ICTY Trial Chamber held in *Kordić and Čerkez* that:

although a causal relationship between the instigation and the physical perpetration of the crime needs to be demonstrated (i.e., that the contribution of the accused in fact had an effect on the commission of the crime), it is not necessary to prove that the crime would not have been perpetrated without the accused's involvement. (§387.)

The requisite subjective element may be set out as follows: (i) the person intended to induce the commission of the crime by another person, or in other words 'directly intended to provoke the commission of the crime' (*Kordić and Čerkez*, §387), or (ii) the person was at least aware of the likelihood that commission of the crime would be a consequence of his action; (iii) the person must possess the *mens rea* concerning the crime he is instigating.

In *Kurt Mayer*, tried by a Canadian Military Court sitting at Aurich in Germany, the accused, a Commander of the 25 SS Panzer Grenadier Regiment, was among other things charged with having incited and counselled troops under his command to deny quarter to Allied troops in 1943–4 in Belgium and France. The Judge Advocate stated:

The first charge is quite clear and I advise the Court that the particulars in that charge allege or constitute a war crime. As it is an offence to deny quarter to prisoners I think an officer may be convicted of a war crime if he incites and counsels troops under his command to deny quarter, whether or not prisoners were killed as a result thereof. It would seem to be common sense to say that not only those members of the enemy who unlawfully kill prisoners may be charged as war criminals, but also any superior military commander who incites and counsels his troops to commit such offences. (At 840.)[10]

9.6 INCHOATE CRIMES: GENERAL

Many legal systems punish not only consummated criminal offences (for instance, murder, theft, etc.), but also 'inchoate', that is preliminary or 'just begun' criminal wrongdoings. These are acts that: (i) are *preparatory* to prohibited offences, (ii) have not been completed, therefore *have not yet caused any harm*, and (iii) are *punished on their own*, that is, in spite of the fact that they have not led to a completed offence.

The rationale behind criminalization of such offences is clear: the legal system intends to protect society as far as possible. Therefore, in addition to punishing offences already perpetrated, it endeavours to prevent the commission of potential transgressions. It consequently intervenes with its prohibitions at an early stage, before crimes are completed, that is, at the stage of their preparation, so as to forestall the consummation of the harmful consequences of actual crimes.

However, within this general category, one ought to distinguish three subcategories:

1. Criminal conduct that is preparatory to crimes proper, and is punished per se, that is, even if it does not lead to the actual perpetration of the crime, but, when this

[10] Cases where incitement to commit war crimes was punished include *Falkenhorst* (at 23 and 29–30).

perpetration follows, it is no longer punishable per se, as it is 'absorbed' into the actual crime (although it may be taken into account as an aggravating circumstance). This subcategory includes planning and ordering.

2. Criminal conduct that is preparatory to a crime, but which by definition cannot be followed by the intended crime. This subcategory encompasses attempt, where, by definition, the subsequent offence is not consummated (because subjective or external circumstances prevent consummation).

3. Criminal conduct that is punished per se, whether or not it is followed by the consummation of a crime; where a crime does follow, this conduct, as well as the consummated crime is punished. This subcategory includes incitement to commit genocide and conspiracy to genocide.

In many national legal systems (particularly in common law countries) three categories of such crimes are envisaged: attempt, conspiracy, and incitement. In international law, while attempt is regarded as admissible as a *general class* of inchoate crimes, conspiracy and incitement are only prohibited as 'preliminary' (not consummated) offences when connected to the most serious crime, genocide. The very limited acceptance of conspiracy is probably due to the fact that this class of criminal offence is not accepted in most civil law countries; hence it has been considered admissible at the international level only with regard to the most heinous and dangerous crime. Indeed, genocide is a crime that by definition attacks individuals qua members of a group and with a view to destroying the group as such.

As for incitement, as we have seen above, in international criminal law it is prohibited only if it leads to the actual perpetration of the crime, that is, as a form of participation in a crime, probably because States and courts have felt that prohibiting incitement per se in connection with *any* international crime including war crimes and crimes against humanity would excessively broaden the range of criminal conduct, the more so because of the difficulty of clearly delineating the notion of incitement. Incitement as such has been exceptionally prohibited, subject however to some stringent conditions, in connection, again, with the most harmful and serious international crime, genocide.

As for planning and ordering, the rationale behind the tendency of international law to punish them as inchoate crimes lies primarily in this: the most serious and large-scale international crimes result from careful preparation and concerted action by many agents, or are the result of instructions and directives issued by military or political leaders. In consequence, international criminal rules aim to prevent or at least circumscribe such conduct by stigmatizing it as criminal and making it penally punishable.

9.7 PLANNING

Planning consists of devising, agreeing upon with others, preparing, and arranging for the commission of a crime. Think, for instance, of planning an air attack on civilians or the use of such prohibited arms as chemical or bacteriological weapons, or the indiscriminate killing of civilians as part of a widespread or systematic attack on civilians. As an ICTR Trial Chamber held in *Akayesu* (§480) and ICTY Trial Chambers in *Blaškić* (§279), and in *Kordić and Čerkez* (§386) planning implies that 'one or several persons contemplate designing the commission of a crime at both the preparatory and executory phases'.

As far as international crimes are concerned, given the nature and features of such crimes, it is often the higher military or civilian authorities that carry out the planning of such crimes.

Whoever takes part in the planning of an international crime is liable to punishment for the relevant crime, whatever his rank in the hierarchy and the level of his participation. (Of course, the rank and role may be germane to punishment; it is evident that the higher the status of the planner and the intensity of his participation in the planning, the harsher should be his penalty.) The subjective element required is the intent to carry out the criminal conduct.

A difficult question is whether planning an international crime is punishable per se, regardless of whether or not it leads to the actual commission of the crime planned, or instead is only punishable if planning is followed up by perpetration of the crime. Trial Chambers of the ICTR opted for the latter solution in *Akayesu* (§475), *Rutaganda* (§34), and *Musema* (§115). They grounded this conclusion on the works of the International Law Commission and on the interpretation of the relevant rule of the ICTR Statute (Article 6(1)) laying down the principle of individual criminal responsibility, which 'implies that the planning or the preparation of a crime actually must lead to its commission' (*Musema*, §115).

It may be noted that prosecuting someone for planning, where the planning is not put into effect, comes close to prosecuting *conspiracy* (although with conspiracy there must be an agreement of two or more persons, whereas planning may be carried out by one person alone, and if done by more persons, no agreement is required). The ICTY and ICTR Statutes allow conspiracy for genocide, but not for crimes against humanity and war crimes. (This was also the position of the IMT at Nuremberg: conspiracy to commit crimes against peace was held admissible whereas conspiracy to commit crimes against humanity and war crimes were not.)

An ICTY Trial Chamber, ruling in *Kordić and Čerkez*, propounded a contrary view. It held that 'an accused may be held criminally responsible for planning alone' (§386). The reason for this conclusion is that 'planning constitutes a discrete form of responsibility under Article 7(1) of the Statute'. The Trial Chamber set forth, however, two caveats: first, 'a person found to have committed a crime will not be found responsible for planning the same crime'; secondly, 'an accused will only be held responsible for planning, instigating or ordering a crime if he directly or indirectly intended that the crime be committed' (§386).

Although there is no consistent case law on this matter, it would seem that the gravity of international crimes (or at least of the most serious among them) may warrant the conclusion that planning the commission of one or more of such crimes is punishable per se even if the crime is not actually perpetrated. The rationale is that international criminal law aims not only to punish persons found guilty of crimes, but also to prevent persons from engaging in serious criminal conduct. Consequently, in case of doubt criminal rules must be interpreted as being also designed as far as possible to prevent offences. It is warranted to infer that planning an international crime is also punishable per se as a distinct form of criminal liability, subject to a set of conditions that can be derived from the general system of international criminal law:

1. Only the planning of serious or large-scale international crimes constitutes a discrete offence: for instance, the planning of massive war crimes (such as the extermination of a large number of prisoners of war, or the large-scale deportation of civilians to extermination camps), or of crimes against humanity, or genocide. Since the rules on planning do not specify the legal ingredients of this crime, it seems warranted to maintain that, for international crimes of lesser gravity (for instance, ill-treatment of one prisoner of war, the taking by members of the Occupying Power of private property belonging to civilians), those rules must be construed in such a way as to favour the accused (*favor rei*). Consequently the mere planning of those crimes of lesser gravity may be held not to constitute a crime per se.

2. If planning is followed up by execution of the crime, planning is no longer punishable as a crime distinct from that resulting from its execution (in this respect planning is different from, hence may not be equated to, such 'inchoate crimes' as conspiracy to commit genocide and incitement to genocide, to be discussed below). As for the requisite *mens rea*, it is necessary for the author to intend that the planned crime be committed, or else he must be aware of the risk that the planned crime would be perpetrated by him or by someone else (recklessness or *dolus eventualis*).

9.8 ORDERING

Ordering presupposes that whoever issues the order is *de jure* or de facto *superior* (within a military or civilian hierarchy) to the one who executes it. However, as a Trial Chamber of the ICTY rightly held in *Kordić and Čerkez* (§388), 'no formal superior-subordinate relationship is required for a finding of "ordering" so long as it is demonstrated that the accused possessed the authority to order'. This proposition, albeit not supported by any legal reason in the judgment, is warranted because international criminal law is not a formalistic body of law geared to legal technicalities but aims at proscribing and punishing crimes whatever the modalities of their commission.

As ICTY Trial Chambers rightly held in *Blaškić* (§281) and *Kordić and Čerkez* (§388), there is no need for the order to be given in writing or in any particular form. In addition, the existence of an order may be proved through circumstantial evidence.

It would seem that it is not necessary for the order to be executed. An officer or any other higher authority issuing a criminal order may be found guilty even if the order is not carried out by the subordinates, if the superior intended the order to be executed and knew that the order was illegal, or else the order was manifestly illegal. Thus, in *General Jacob H. Smith*, in 1902 a US Court Martial held that General Smith was guilty of ordering that no quarter should be given to the enemy in the Philippines, even though in fact his troops did not comply with this order (at 799–813). In many other cases courts have convicted officers for issuing criminal orders, even if they were not executed.[11]

If the internationally unlawful order is executed, the person issuing the order is criminally liable qua co-perpetrator of the crime carried out by the subordinate.

Also for this category of criminality the requisite mental element is the *intent* to have the crime committed,[12] at least, as long as the order is specific, that is, instructs to perform a specific crime. However, when the order is generic, recklessness or even gross negligence may be considered sufficient.[13]

9.9 ATTEMPT

Attempt as a distinct criminal offence occurs whenever a person intending to commit a crime tries to carry it out without, however, the normal outcome of his action

[11] See, for instance, *High Command* (at 118–23), *The Hostages Trial* (at 118–23), *Kurt Mayer* (at 98 and 108), *Falkenhorst* (at 18, 23, 29–30), *Hans Wickmann* (at 133). In *Tzofan and others* v. *IDF Advocate and others* (*Yehuda Meir* case), Judge D. Levin (concurring) held that 'the higher the rank of the commanding officer and the more comprehensive and more decisive his authority, the greater the responsibility incumbent upon him to examine and determine the justification and legality of the order' (at 745).

It should be noted that ordering is sometimes treated as a species of instigation, for instance ordering that no quarter be given may be regarded as the same thing as inciting troops to commit war crimes.

[12] In *Jung and Schumacher*, decided by a Canadian Military Court sitting at Aurich in Germany, the Judge Advocate, in discussing the position of the defendant Jung, who had ordered the other defendant to shoot and kill a Canadian war prisoner, noted the following: 'The Court may find that the accused uttered the words or some words to do harm to the prisoner, but it must be found that he uttered them with the expectation and intention that they should be acted upon by someone who heard them, including Schumacher. In this event he would have either incited, counselled or procured the acts to have been done, and so be concerned [in the crime]. Now, if you find that the accused Jung handed the prisoner over to Schumacher, knowing or expecting he would be killed, then again he would be concerned [in the killing of the Canadian POW]' (at 219–20).

[13] In one case a Canadian Court Martial held that the defendant was guilty of *negligence* for issuing unlawful orders (he had instructed his subordinates that prisoners 'could be abused'): see *Major A.G. Seward* (at 1079–81); on this case see also above, note 16 in Chapter 8.

Interestingly, the defendant was acquitted on another count, namely of having caused bodily harm to the Somali civilians beaten up, tortured, and killed by his subordinates. The Court Martial Appeal Court of Canada noted in this regard that by this acquittal the defendant 'must be taken to have been found neither to have intended nor to have been capable or reasonably foreseeing that any of his subordinates would mistreat unto death any Somalian [sic] prisoner' (at 1082).

coming about. One should distinguish between two different possibilities: (i) the perpetrator takes the initial steps but is then *stopped by others*, or (ii) on account of circumstances independent of his will, his action does not produce the effects of his intention. In other words, he *performs all the necessary acts without, however, the intended result following*. An example of the first category is when a soldier starts to beat a prisoner of war savagely with the intention of killing him, and is only prevented from so doing by others who drag him off his intended victim. An example of the second category is when a soldier shoots at a prisoner of war, intending to execute him, but the intended victim is not fatally wounded and subsequently manages to escape.

Although in the case of attempt the intended harm is not caused to the victim, international law nevertheless makes attempt punishable, in order to prevent breaches of international rules as far as possible. Thus, this offence is punished in various national laws on war crimes,[14] or is regarded as a distinct offence in national case law on the same crimes.[15] Recently, customary law on the matter has been codified in Article 25(3)(f) of the ICC Statute, whereby a person is criminally responsible if he 'attempts to commit [a crime under the Court's jurisdiction] by taking action that commences its execution by means of a substantial step, but the crime does not occur because of circumstances independent of the person's intentions'.

Clearly, what is required for the attempt to be punishable, is: (i) conduct consisting of a *significant commencement of the criminal action* (to hold to the example given above, it is not sufficient for the guard to take the prisoner out of his cell and possibly even shout at, or abuse, him; it is necessary for the guard to start beating him savagely); (ii) the *clear intention to commit a crime*; (iii) *failure of that intention to take effect owing to external circumstances.*

This last ingredient of the objective element may also occur when the victim of the attempted crime is already dead (unless, of course, the agent *knew* that the victim was dead). In *Charles W. Keenan* the accused had been ordered by his superior to 'finish off' a civilian woman at whom the superior had already shot. A US Court of Military Appeal held that in the case at issue attempted murder was to be ruled out only because the subordinate knew that she was no longer alive when he fired at her (at 114).[16] To support its ruling the Court cited an important case, unrelated to war crimes, where the same Court had extensively dealt with the notion at issue: *Rodger D. Thomas*, a case of attempted rape, which had offered the Court the opportunity to

[14] See, for instance, the laws cited in UN *Law Reports*, vol. XV, at 89 (Norway, Yugoslavia, the Netherlands).

[15] See the cases reported in UN *Law Reports*, vol. VI, 120, as well as in UN *Law Reports*, vol. VII, at 73.

[16] The Court stated that 'so far as attempted murder is concerned, military law "has tended toward the advanced and modern position" that holds one accountable for conduct which would constitute a crime if the facts were as he believed them to be (see *United States* v. *Thomas* 13 USCMA 278, 286, 32 CMR 278). Here the accused expressly testified that he believed the woman was dead; and the board of review specifically refused to find that she was still alive when the accused fired at her. Moore and Eakins also testified that they believed the victim was dead before the accused fired. The board of review could, therefore, reasonably conclude that the accused knew he was firing at a corpse. This conclusion necessarily absolves him of attempted murder' (at 113).

discuss the requisite ingredients of the offence, with a reasoning that is along the same lines as the notion propounded above for international criminal law (at 287–92).[17]

The ICC Statute codifies international customary laws in another respect as well. Article 25(3)(f) duly takes account of the cessation of the attempter's criminal intention and leaves his initial steps unpunished:

However, a person who abandons the effort to commit the crime or otherwise prevents the completion of the crime shall not be liable for punishment under this Statute for the attempt to commit that crime if that person completely and voluntarily gave up the criminal purpose.

Thus, to continue with the aforementioned example, if the guard, after beating the prisoner for a while, suddenly decides not to carry through his initial purpose and takes the prisoner back to his cell, he is not guilty of attempted murder (although he may well be guilty of other crimes). Similarly, if an officer gives an order to shoot and kill a group of innocent civilians and then, just before the order is carried out, changes his mind and orders that their lives be spared, he is not considered criminally liable for murder (although he may be guilty of inhuman treatment or even torture, if he intended to carry out a mock execution).

As for the *mens rea* required for attempt, it may be noted that in common law systems, what is required is normally the *intention* to carry out the offence (recklessness is not enough). This makes it difficult to prosecute, because the question always arises: if the accused wanted, for example to kill his victim, then why did he not do so? (This is why the only cases where prosecutions are successful are where: (i) the would-be perpetrator is dragged off his victim, or (ii) the would-be perpetrator leaves his victim for dead.) It would seem that also in international criminal law the subjective element required is intent.

9.10 CONSPIRACY TO COMMIT GENOCIDE

It is common knowledge that conspiracy is a form of criminality punished in common law systems but either unknown to, or accepted to a very limited extent by, civil law countries. Conspiracy is a group offence, consisting of the *agreement of two or more persons to commit a crime.* It is punished *even if the crime is never perpetrated.* In addition, if the crime is carried out, the perpetrators are held *liable both for conspiracy and for the substantive crime* they commit. The *mens rea* element of conspiracy required for each and every participant is twofold: (i) *knowledge* of the facts or circumstances making up the crime the group intend to commit; (ii) *intent* to carry out the conspiracy and thereby perpetrate the substantive offence. Plainly, the basic rationale behind the prohibition of this crime is the need to prevent offences,

[17] The Court held that the elements of the offence of attempted rape were: '(i) an overt act; (2) specific intent, (3) more than mere preparation, (4) tending to effect the commission of the offense, and (5) failure to effect its commission' (at 286).

especially when they involve several persons and are thus more dangerous to the community.

As noted above, in international law no customary rule has evolved on conspiracy on account of the lack of support from civil law countries for this category of crime. (In civil law systems, entering into agreement to commit a crime is not punishable per se, unless it leads to the perpetration of the crime; only exceptionally, and for such categories of serious offences as those aimed at undermining State security or at setting up associations or organizations systematically bent on criminal conduct in various areas, is conspiracy as such prohibited.)

The only international rules on conspiracy can be found in the London Agreement of 1945. In Article 6 it made punishable persons 'participating in a Common Plan or Conspiracy for the accomplishment' of any crime against peace and in addition made 'leaders, organizers, instigators or accomplices participating in the formulation or execution of a Common Plan or Conspiracy to commit any of the foregoing crimes [that is, crimes against peace, war crimes, and crimes against humanity] responsible for all acts performed by any persons in execution of such plan'. This provision laid down *ex post facto* law. However, as it referred to conspiracy to commit a crime against peace, it punished persons who had conspired to wage the war *that had just ended.* In addition, to the extent that it referred to other crimes, it also made conspiracy punishable for acts already accomplished. In other words, in the end conspiracy was held to be punishable to the extent that any plan or agreement to commit an international crime *had been actually carried out.* (Strikingly, Control Council Law no. 10 only referred to conspiracy to commit crimes against peace: see Article 2(1)(a).) Nevertheless, generally speaking, both the IMT at Nuremberg and the Military Tribunals sitting at Nuremberg took a restrictive view of conspiracy (see in particular *Göring and others* (at 224–6) and *Alstötter and others* (at 289–90). In the former case the influence of the French Judge Donnedieu de Vabres, and his insistence on the novel nature of conspiracy in international law, were indisputably decisive.[18]

Another international provision on the matter is Article 3(b) of the 1948 Genocide Convention, which, on the grounds and motivations set out above, makes 'conspiracy to commit genocide' punishable. It would seem that, like most other substantive provisions of the Convention, it has turned into customary law. Among other things it has been taken up in the Statutes of both the ICTY and the ICTR (but, strikingly, not in Article 6 of the ICC Statute, which consequently differs in this respect from international customary law).

In *Musema* an ICTR Trial Chamber held that conspiracy to commit genocide 'is to be defined as an agreement between two or more persons to commit the crime of genocide' (§191); as for *mens rea*, it 'rests on the concerted intent to commit genocide,

[18] Donnedieu de Vabres, *Procès*, 528–42. He among other things held the view that in the event Article 6 (in fine), of the Nuremberg Charter upheld the French notion of '*complicité*' (at 541). He also emphasized that, with regard to crimes against peace, the IMT ultimately avoided holding that there was a general conspiracy (at 541–2).

that is, to destroy, in whole or in part, a national, ethnical, racial or religious group, as such. Thus . . . the requisite intent for the crime of conspiracy to commit genocide is *ipso facto* the intent required for the crime of genocide, that is the *dolus specialis* of genocide' (§192).

The Chamber also emphasized that the crime of conspiracy to commit genocide is punishable even if it fails to lead to its result, that is, even if genocide is not perpetrated (§194).

9.11 INCITEMENT TO GENOCIDE

International law requires that incitement to genocide be not only *direct* but also *public.* At the same time incitement is punishable even if it is not followed by the commission of genocide.

In *Akayesu* a Trial Chamber of the ICTR held that direct and public incitement to commit genocide:

> must be defined for the purposes of interpreting Article 2(3)(c) [of the ICTR Statute], as directly provoking the perpetrator(s) to commit genocide, whether through speeches, shouting or threats uttered in public places or at public gatherings, or through the sale or dissemination, offer for sale or display of written material or printed matter in public places or at public gatherings, or through the public display of placards or posters, or through any other means of audiovisual communication. (§559.)

As for the subjective element of the crime, it held that:

> [it] lies in the intent to directly prompt or provoke another to commit genocide. It implies a desire on the part of the perpetrator to create by his actions a particular state of mind necessary to commit such a crime in the minds of the person(s) he is so engaging. That is to say that the person who is inciting to commit genocide must have himself the specific intent to commit genocide, namely, to destroy, in whole or in part, a national, ethnical, racial or religious group, as such. (§560.)

In the case at issue the Trial Chamber concluded that the accused was indeed guilty of the offence under discussion (§§672–5).

Another relevant case is *Ruggiu*, the journalist of 'Radio Mille Collines' accused by the ICTR's Prosecutor of 'direct and public incitement to commit genocide and crimes against humanity (persecution)'. He pleaded guilty. ICTR Trial Chamber I found that:

> when examining the acts of persecution which have been admitted by the accused, it is possible to discern a common element. Those acts were direct and public radio broadcasts all aimed at singling out and attacking the Tutsi ethnic group and Belgians on discriminatory grounds, by depriving them of the fundamental rights to life, liberty and basic humanity enjoyed by members of wider society. The deprivation of these rights can be said to have as its aim the death and removal of those persons from the society in which they live alongside the perpetrators, or eventually even from humanity itself. (§22.)

SELECT BIBLIOGRAPHY

GENERAL THEORY

Jescheck, *Lehrbuch*, 641–739; Fletcher, *Basic Concepts*, 188–205; Mantovani, 525–78.

INTERNATIONAL CRIMINAL LAW

Jescheck, *Verantwortlichkeit*, 268–76; K. Ambos, *Der 'Allgemeine Teil'*, 502–624.

THE ICC STATUTE

K. Ambos, in O. Triffterer (ed.), *Commentary*, 475–92; A. Eser, in Cassese, Gaeta, and Jones, *ICC Commentary*, 767–822.

INCHOATE CRIMES

General

R. A. Duff, *Criminal Attempts* (Oxford: Oxford University Press, 1996); Fletcher, *Basic Concepts*, 171–87; Ashworth, *Principles*, 460–89.

International criminal law

K. Ambos, in O. Triffterer, *Commentary*, 475–92.

10

CRIMINAL LIABILITY FOR OMISSIONS

10.1 GENERAL

International criminal liability may arise not only as a result of a positive act or conduct (killing an enemy civilian, unlawfully destroying works of art, etc.) but also from an omission, that is, failure to take action. Omission is only criminalized when the law imposed a clear obligation to act and the person wilfully or recklessly failed to do what was legally required.

It took a long time for a general rule on this matter to evolve in international criminal law. The reason for this state of affairs is clear. The first body of substantive rules restraining conduct in war, namely traditional international humanitarian law, tended to prohibit action; in other words, it imposed on combatants the obligation *not to engage* in conduct contrary to some international standards (killing civilians, raping women, shelling hospitals, etc.). By the same token it refrained, as a rule, from imposing *positive obligations* to do *something*. The purpose of this body of law was to ensure respect for a modicum of legal standards by belligerents. Law largely respected the autonomy of States, leaving them free to pursue their ends and purposes in war, and only banned and criminalized glaring breaches of the most fundamental standards of behaviour. The law did not go so far as also to require that belligerents should take some kind of positive action to protect civilians and other victims of warfare. International law-makers did not deem it expedient to restrict States' conduct by establishing obligations requiring States to do a particular thing under some specific circumstances.

Progress was made after the Second World War, when an 'interventionist' attitude in international humanitarian law, intended to broaden the protection of war victims, gradually replaced the previous liberal, individualistic, 'laissez-faire approach', substantially geared to freedom of States subject to some exceptional prohibitions. As we shall soon see, many provisions of the 1949 Geneva Conventions clearly laid down the duty to do something and considered failure so to act as criminal. However, it was only in 1977 that the draftsmen of the First Additional Protocol to the Geneva Conventions laid down the principle in Article 86(1), where they stipulated that:

The High Contracting Parties and the Parties to the conflict shall repress grave breaches, and take measures necessary to suppress all other breaches of the Conventions or of this Protocol which result *from a failure to act under a duty to do so.* (Emphasis added.)

Formally speaking this provision is only addressed to States (and national liberation movements, in the case of wars of national liberation). Nevertheless one could deduce from it legal implications at the level of criminal law. It may therefore seem warranted to hold that it also crystallized a general principle on criminal liability for omission.

As we shall see below, after the Second World War one particular class of responsibility by omission, that is, superiors' responsibility, has taken on distinct features and evolved as a discrete and important form of this category.

10.2 RULES IMPOSING THE POSITIVE OBLIGATION TO ACT

As pointed out above, it was in 1949 that many provisions were adopted laying down positive obligations.

Some provisions of the Geneva Conventions lay down *unconditional* (in other terms, unqualified) positive obligations. This for instance holds true for Article 16(4) of the First Geneva Convention (on the wounded and sick armed forces in the field), which contains positive prescriptions concerning the preparation, and transmission by one belligerent to the other, of death certificates or lists of the dead. It also holds true for Article 17 of the same Convention, which provides for the burial or cremation of the dead.[1] Other provisions lay down positive obligations that are however very sweeping and therefore leave to Contracting States a fairly *broad margin of appreciation.* This applies for instance to Article 14(2) of the Third Geneva Convention (on prisoners of war), concerning the duty to protect prisoners of war against acts of violence or intimidation; Article 15 of the same Convention, on maintenance free of charge for prisoners of war; and Article 29 of the same Convention, on the duty to take all sanitary measures necessary to ensure the cleanliness and hygiene of detention camps. Similarly, Article 36 of the First Additional Protocol obliges States studying, developing, acquiring, or adopting new weapons to ascertain whether these weapons are prohibited by international law. Articles 76 and 77 of the same Protocol protect

[1] Similar provisions may be found in Articles 19 and 20 of the Second Geneva Convention (on the wounded, sick, and shipwrecked at sea); as well as in Article 32(5) of the First Geneva Convention (on the treatment of neutral personnel lending assistance to a belligerent and falling into the hands of the adversary belligerent); in Articles 69–77 of the Third Geneva Convention (on prisoners of war), relating to relations of prisoners of war with the external world; Article 118 of the same Convention, concerning release and repatriation of prisoners of war at the close of hostilities (violation of this provision amounting to a grave breach, pursuant to Article 85(4)(b) of the First Additional Protocol); Article 121 of the same Convention, concerning the duty to establish an official inquiry into the death or serious injury of prisoners of war; Article 122 of the same Convention, providing for the establishment, by each belligerent, of an information bureau concerning prisoners of war.

respectively women and children against various forms of assault by imposing on States broad positive obligations. Articles 82 and 83 of the same Protocol similarly lay down positive obligations concerning respectively the provision and availability of legal advisers, and dissemination of the Conventions and Protocol.

As stated before, some provisions contain *qualified* obligations. For instance, Article 12(5) of the First Geneva Convention provides that a party to the conflict compelled to abandon wounded or sick to the enemy must leave with them a part of its medical personnel as well as material, 'as far as military considerations permit'. Similarly, Article 12(2, in fine) of the Second Geneva Convention provides that enemy wounded, sick, or shipwrecked 'shall not be *wilfully* left without medical assistance and care, nor shall conditions exposing them to contagion or infection be created' (emphasis added). Article 60 of the Third Geneva Convention imposes on the Detaining Power the duty to grant all prisoners of war a monthly advance of pay, and specifies the amount of advance each class of prisoner must obtain (depending on their rank); however the provisions go on to state that this amount may be modified by special agreement between the parties to the conflict, or by the Detaining Power, subject to some conditions. Articles 55 and 56 of the Fourth Geneva Convention (on civilians), relating respectively to provision of food and medical supplies and hygiene and public health, are qualified by the proviso 'to the fullest extent of the means available' to the Occupying Power. Similarly, Article 69(1) of the First Additional Protocol imposes upon the Occupying Power the obligation to provide to the civilian population means for satisfying its basic need, 'to the fullest possible extent of the means available' to that Power. Article 70 of the same Protocol provides for relief actions in favour of the civilian population in occupied territories 'subject to the agreement of the Parties concerned in such relief actions'.

It should be noted that serious violations of many of the above positive obligations (for instance those enjoining to protect women and children from assault), as well as others laid down in other provisions, amount to a war crime. Of course, it is necessary for the conditions set forth in the decision of the ICTY Appeals Chamber in *Tadić* (*Interlocutory Appeal*) (§§94–5), determining which violations may be regarded as war crimes, to be met. However, in some instances, specified in the relevant provisions, a serious violation may amount to a 'grave breach', with the attendant consequences with regard to the mandatory character of judicial repression at the national level (see *infra*, 15.5.1(A)).[2]

[2] See for instance *Sumida Haruzo and others* (at 228–9, 278, and 280–2) for the breach of the duty to provide food and care to detained civilians as a war crime. In *Gozawa Sadaichi and others* it was held that the lack of food and medical supplies, as well as the existence of bad conditions for prisoners of war, amounted to a crime of which the detaining authorities were guilty (at 200–1, 210–11, 222–3, and 227–31). See also *Schmitt* (decision of the Antwerp Court Martial, at 751–2, and the subsequent decision of the *Cour militaire de Bruxelles*, at 752, nt. 89*bis*) as well as *Köppelmann Ernst* (decision of the Brabant Court Martial, at 753–4, and of the Belgian Court of Cassation, at 185–6). In both cases the courts dealt with the positive obligations of the commanders of detention camps for prisoners of war.

10.3 *MENS REA*

As in the case of crimes consisting of positive conduct, criminal omission also may only be punished if accompanied by a certain subjective frame of mind. As in those cases, this mental element may vary, depending on the requirements of international rules. Normally *intent* is required. However, in some cases the relevant rules or provisions of international criminal law may require a less demanding subjective element, that is *recklessness* or *culpable negligence*, for criminal liability to arise.[3]

10.4 THE RESPONSIBILITY OF SUPERIORS

10.4.1 THE HISTORICAL EMERGENCE OF THE NOTION

Although it was adumbrated in 1919, after the First World War,[4] it was in the aftermath of the Second World War that there evolved in international law the notion of criminal responsibility of superiors for failure to prevent or punish crimes perpetrated by their subordinates. Some national laws set out the notion tersely,[5] and it was then enunciated and spelled out, with regard to *military* commanders, in a leading if controversial case, *Yamashita* (1946). This is a case where the principle was affirmed, based, as two dissenting judges of the US Supreme Court rightly noted, on a highly questionable interpretation of existing rules of international humanitarian law, as well as a wrong application of the principles to the case at bar, in addition to total disregard for the required mental element for the crime. A few words on the case are necessary.

[3] A case where it would seem that a British court considered culpable negligence sufficient is *Heinrich Gerike and others* (the *Velpke Baby Home* trial). The defendants were charged with war crimes for violating Article 46 (on respect for family honour and life by the Occupant) of the 1907 Hague Rules, for leaving without food and care the children of Polish female workers compulsorily separated from their parents and brought to a home for infants in Velpke; as a result of lack of care many children had died. The Prosecutor, Major Draper (a Judge Advocate being absent) argued that the staff in charge of the children 'were so grossly and criminally negligent that they did in fact cause the death of something over 80 children in six months' (at 326). He then noted that one of the questions arising in the case was whether 'that neglect [was] more than something that was gross and reckless, or was . . . wilful disregard of consequences to such an extent that the party or parties responsible are deemed to have intended the natural and probable consequences of their act, namely, that death would result' (at 326). He then pointed out that 'In either event it is the contention of the Prosecution that they are within the charge which is laid before this Court, namely, that the accused are concerned between the relevant dates in the killing by wilful neglect of a number of children, Polish nationals' (ibid.). He then cited Archbold on gross negligence and recklessness (at 336–7), noting that his propositions were 'in point in this case' (at 337). The Court found two defendants not guilty (neither of them had been entrusted with the care of the children; one had consistently disapproved of the running of the Home and consequently decided to keep aloof, the other had tried unsuccessfully to have the Home removed); it sentenced the remaining four either to death by hanging or to imprisonment (at 339–43).

[4] See the proposals of the 1919 International Commission on the Responsibility of the Authors of the War and on Enforcement of Penalties, in 14 AJIL (1920), at 121.

[5] See the French Law of 1944 and the Chinese Law of 1946 quoted in UN *Law Reports*, vol. IV, at 87–8.

The Japanese general Yamashita had been Commanding General of the Japanese Army in the Philippines between 1943 and 1945. His soldiers had massacred a large part of the civilian population of Batangas Province and inflicted acts of violence, cruelty, and murder upon the civilian population and prisoners of war, as well as wholesale pillage and wanton destruction of religious monuments in the occupied territory. The US authorities accused the General, before a US Military Commission, of breaching his duty as an army commander to control the operations of his troops 'by permitting them to commit' extensive and widespread atrocities. The majority of the US Supreme Court held that commanders had a duty to take such appropriate measures as are within their power to control the troops under their command for the prevention of violations of the laws of warfare. It derived this duty from a number of provisions of such laws: Articles 1 and 43 of the Regulations annexed to the Fourth Hague Convention of 1907 (under the former, combatants, to be recognized as legitimate belligerents, must 'be commanded by a person responsible for his subordinates'; pursuant to the latter, the commander of a force occupying enemy territory 'shall take all the measures in his power to restore, and ensure, as far as possible, public order and safety, while respecting, unless absolutely prevented, the laws in force in the country'); Article 19 of the Tenth Hague Convention of 1907, relating to bombardment by naval vessel and providing that commanders-in-chief of the belligerent vessels 'must see that the above Articles are properly carried out'; Article 26 of the 1929 Geneva Convention on the wounded and sick, which made it the duty 'of the commanders-in-chief of the belligerent armies to provide for the detail of execution of the foregoing Articles [of the Convention] as well as for unforeseen cases'. The Court's majority held that these provisions made it clear that the accused had:

an affirmative duty to take such measures as were within his power and appropriate in the circumstances to protect prisoners of war and the civilian population. This duty of a commanding officer has heretofore been recognized, and its breach penalized by our own military tribunals. (At 13.)

However, two judges, Murphy and Rutledge, forcefully (and rightly) disagreed and set forth their views in important Dissenting Opinions. They noted among other things that the Court's majority had not shown that Yamashita had 'knowledge' of the gross breaches perpetrated by his troops (at 31, 36, 48–9, 50) or had any 'direct connection with the atrocities' (at 36), or could be found guilty of 'a negligent failure . . . to discover' the atrocities (at 49) or in other words, had 'personal culpability' (at 36–79).[6]

At present international criminality increasingly tends to be planned, organized,

[6] Justices Murphy and Rutledge did not only dissent on the application of the law to the facts by the Commission—they also objected to the whole notion of command responsibility as a matter of law. Justice Murphy stated: 'The recorded annals of warfare and the established principles of international law afford not the slightest precedent for such a charge. This indictment in effect permitted the military commission to make the crime whatever it willed dependent on its biased view as to the petitioner's duties and his disregard thereof, a practice reminiscent of that pursued in less respected nations in recent years' (327 US, at 28).

ordered, or condoned or tolerated by superior authorities. In other words, a clear trend is emerging in the world community towards commission of crimes either by high-level military or political leaders or by low-level officials or military personnel, who however perpetrate crimes because superior authorities (be they military or civilian) do not prevent, or they tolerate or at any rate fail to repress them. Hence, the issue of superior responsibility has gradually acquired enormous importance in international criminal law. Indeed, the views set out in *Yamashita* were taken up in a string of cases heard by US courts or tribunals after the Second World War.[7] Most cases related to the responsibility by omission of *military* commanders; other cases, however, extended this form of responsibility to *civilian or political* authorities.[8] These cases contributed considerably to the formation of a customary rule on the matter, as an ICTY Trial Chamber rightly emphasized in *Delalić and others* (§343). At present, the notion is firmly embedded in international humanitarian law (see Article 87 of the First Additional Protocol) as well as in the Statutes of the ICTY, ICTR, and the ICC. It covers superior responsibility for *any* international crime committed by subordinates, that is not only war crimes but also crimes against humanity, genocide, etc.

This class of responsibility is different from the others considered so far, in that it is responsibility *by omission*: the person is criminally liable not for an act he has performed, but for failure to perform an act required by international law. In other words, he is responsible for the breach of an international *obligation* incumbent upon any commander or superior authority, to prevent or suppress crimes by subordinates.[9]

[7] See in particular *Soemu Toyoda* (at 5005–6), *Takashi Sakai* (at 1–7), *Karl Brand and others* (at 207–12), *Wilhelm List and others* (at 1230, 1303), and *Wilhelm von Leeb and others* (at 512).

[8] For this latter category of cases see in particular, the *Tokyo* trial, heard by the Tokyo International Tribunal (vol. 20, at 791, 816, 831), *Flick and others*, brought before a US Military Tribunal sitting at Nuremberg (at 1202–12), *Röchling and others*, heard by a French court in the French Occupation Zone in Germany (at 1061, or 377–8), and *Delalić and others* (§§ 370, 377–8).

[9] According to the ICTY Appeals Chamber in *Delalić and others* (*Appeal*) (§240) there is no duty, incumbent upon military or civilian authorities, to ascertain that their subordinates are not committing crimes. This proposition is questionable, in light of the abundant case law on the matter as well as some clear treaty provisions and provisions of important Military Manuals. With regard to international rules, it may suffice to mention Article 87 of the First Additional Protocol of 1977, on 'Duty of commanders'. The obligation in question is clearly set out in many national Military Manuals, for instance, those of Switzerland, *Règlement* (1987), Article 196 ('Les commandants doivent informer la troupe de ses obligations aux termes des Conventions. Ils sont responsables du fait que leurs troupes respectent les Conventions et de punir d'éventuelles infractions'); Russia's Military Manual (1990), Part VII, §§*a* and *b* (commanders of all grades must 'call to account persons who committed violations of the rules of international humanitarian law defined by Articles 85–87 of the First Additional Protocol'); Germany, Military Manual (1992), ch. 1, no. 138; New Zealand, Military Manual (1992), ch. 16, s. 2, §1603–2 ('It is incumbent upon a commanding officer to ensure that the forces under his command behave in a manner consistent with the laws and customs of war . . . and it is part of his responsibility to ensure that the troops under his command are aware of their obligations'); Australia, Defence Force Manual (1994), §1304 ('Military commanders of all Services and at all levels bear responsibility for ensuring that forces under their control comply with the Law of Armed Conflict'); Benin, Military Manual (1995), ch. V ('Chaque chef militaire est responsable du respect du droit de la guerre dans sa sphère de commandement . . . il est particulièrement responsable de l'instruction du droit de la guerre afin de communiquer à sa troupe un comportement conforme au droit'); Canada, Law of Armed Conflict Manual

10.4.2 CRIMINAL CATEGORIES INTO WHICH THE GENERAL NOTION MAY BE SUBDIVIDED

Normally international rules tend to lump together various classes of superior responsibility, without drawing any distinction. This for instance holds true both for Articles 7(3) and 6(3) of the Statutes of the ICTY and ICTR respectively and for Article 28 of the ICC Statute. These provisions are essentially of a descriptive nature, in that they indicate the prohibited conduct by enumerating the various forms this conduct may take. They do not, however, differentiate between these categories, nor do they attach any legal relevance to conduct falling under one particular category rather than another.

Nonetheless, it would seem both logically appropriate and relevant for practical purposes of sentencing to draw a distinction between different classes. It is not sound and warranted, for instance, to hold that a commander who failed to punish subordinates who had perpetrated acts of genocide, is responsible for genocide, if only as an accomplice. Plainly, in this case the requisite conduct and subjective element are neatly distinct, and different from those required for the perpetrators of genocide, or for persons aiding and abetting genocide. A superior official may be accused of and be held responsible for genocide or another international crime only if it is proved that he knew that crimes were about to be, or were being, perpetrated, and deliberately failed to stop or forestall that commission. In other words, only when the superior in some way knows of the crime and willingly fails to prevent its commission, may he be deemed to participate in the crime as a co-perpetrator or accomplice.

This approach, which seems logically and theoretically more correct and also more consonant with general principles of justice (because of its consequences at the level of sentencing) is reflected in the excellent German Bill on the Code of Crimes Against International Law, submitted to Parliament in 2002. The Bill distinguishes three categories:

1. Responsibility of military commanders and other superiors (section 4), envisaging the case where the superior knows that an offence is about to be or is being committed by his subordinates and willingly fails to stop the crime; in this case the offender 'shall be punished in the same way as a perpetrator of the offence committed by [the] subordinate'; in other words, he is legally treated as a co-perpetrator (but in

(1999), at 15–1 and 16–1 ('Commanders have responsibility to ensure that forces under their command are aware of their responsibilities'); and France, Manual on the Law of Armed Conflict (2001), Introduction, at 14, para. 7 ('Le commandement . . . doit s'assurer que les membres des forces armées connaissent leurs droits et appliquent les obligations qui en sont le parallèle. Il est à ce titre responsable de leur instruction').

As for case law, one may recall, in addition to *Yamashita* (see *supra*, 10.4.1), the instructions a Judge Advocate issued to a US Court Martial in *Medina*; he stated: 'In relation to the question pertaining to the supervisory responsibility of a Company Commander, I advise you that as a general principle of military law and custom a military superior in command is responsible and required, in the performance of his command duties, to make certain the proper performance by his subordinates of their duties as assigned by him. In other words, after taking action and issuing an order, a commander must remain alert and make timely adjustments as required by a changing situation' (at 1732).

the Commentary it is specified that he may also be classified as a mere accomplice (*blosse Beihilfe*, at 40).

In this case there is a clear nexus of causality between the superior's omission and the crime.

2. Responsibility of a commander or a superior who 'intentionally or negligently omits properly to supervise a subordinate', where 'the imminent commission' of the offence 'was discernible to the commander and he or she could have prevented it' (section 13); in this case, as is clarified in the Commentary (at 83), one envisages the hypothesis where the superior does not know that the subordinate is about to commit or is committing a crime, but negligently or deliberately breaches his duty of supervision, and does not impede the perpetration of crimes that he could foresee and avoid. In these cases the offence imputable to the superior is arguably different from that perpetrated by the subordinate, in that it merely consists of the deliberate or negligent dereliction of supervisory duties (the German law envisages a sentence up to a maximum of five years in the case of intentional violation and three years when the violation is due to negligence). However a different view is also admissible. One could contend that failure by the superior to exercise his duty of supervision has a causal link with the crime, in that by breaching his supervisory duty he has in some way contributed to bringing about the offence. In other words, the superior's conduct may be considered as serious as that of the subordinate; the former could therefore be punished by a sentence similar to that of the subordinate.

3. Liability for omission to report a crime, when the superior knows that a crime has been perpetrated and fails 'immediately to draw the attention of the agency responsible for the investigation or prosecution' of the crime (section 14); in this case the superior is liable to be punished for the specific crime of failure to report. Again, his offence is different from that of his subordinates: he is responsible if he is cognizant of the crimes of his subordinates and either deliberately or negligently fails to report them to the appropriate authorities for punishment or prosecution. The superior's conduct may not be regarded as causing, or contributing to cause, the criminal offence.

The German law envisages imprisonment for a maximum of five years for this offence.

10.4.3 GENERAL CONDITIONS OF SUPERIOR RESPONSIBILITY

We shall follow here the same approach as that taken in the German law, and accordingly distinguish between three major categories of responsibility.[10] Before so doing, it

[10] The various categories are instead merged in *Toyoda*. The Tribunal stated the following: 'The Tribunal considers the essential elements of command responsibility for atrocities of any commander to be: 1. That offenses, commonly recognized as atrocities, were committed by troops of his command; 2. The ordering of such atrocities. In the absence of proof beyond a reasonable doubt of the issuance of orders, then the essential elements of command responsibility are: 1. As before, that atrocities were actually committed; 2. Notice of the

may however be helpful to set out the general conditions required for all three categories.

Superior authorities, whether military or civilian, bear responsibility for crimes committed by their subordinates in the following *cumulative* conditions:

1. They exercise *effective command, control, or authority over the perpetrators.* It is not necessary for there to be a formal hierarchical structure; de facto positions of authority or control may suffice. As an ICTY Trial Chamber rightly held in *Delalić and others* (§§377–8), individuals in positions of authority, whether within civilian or military structures, may incur criminal responsibility under the doctrine of command responsibility on the basis of their de facto or *de jure* position as superiors. The mere absence of formal legal authority to control the actions of subordinates should therefore not be understood to preclude the imposition of such responsibility.[11]

Control must be effective. Thus in the *Ministries* case a US Military Tribunal sitting at Nuremberg held that the mere appearance of an official's name on a distribution list attached to an official document could only provide evidence that it was intended that he be provided with the relevant information, and not that 'those whose names appear on such distribution lists have responsibility for, or power and right of decision with respect to the subject-matter of such document' (at 693).[12] In *Kordić and Čerkez* an ICTY Trial Chamber provided some important examples.[13] And in

commission thereof. This notice may be either: a. Actual, as in the case of an accused who sees their commission or who is informed thereof shortly thereafter; b. Constructive. That is the commission of such a great number of offenses within his command that a reasonable man could come to no other conclusion than that the accused must have known of the offenses or of the existence of an understood and acknowledged routine for their commission. 3. Power of command. That is, the accused must be proved to have had actual authority over the offenders to issue orders to them not to commit illegal acts, and to punish offenders. 4. Failure to take such appropriate measures as are within his power to control the troops under his command and to prevent acts which are violations of the laws of war. 5. Failure to punish offenders. In the simplest language it may be said that this Tribunal believes the principle of command responsibility to be that, if this accused knew, or should by the exercise of ordinary diligence have learned, of the commission by his subordinates, immediate or otherwise, of the atrocities proved beyond a shadow of a doubt before this Tribunal or of the existence of a routine which would countenance such, and, by his failure to take any action to punish the perpetrators, permitted the atrocities to continue, he has failed in his performance of his duty as a commander and must be punished' (at 5005–6).

[11] The ICTY Appeals Chamber confirmed this finding in *Delalić and others (Appeal)* (§§197–8). Another ICTY Trial Chamber subsequently cited the finding with approval in *Kordić and Čerkez* (§§405–7).

[12] See, e.g., *Delalić and others*, §354–78; *Delalić and others (Appeal)*, §§192–5; *Blaskić*, §§295–303; *Kordić and Čerkez*, §§405–17).

[13] It thus stated that: 'For instance, a government official who knows that civilians are used to perform forced labour or as human shields will be held liable only if it is demonstrated that he has effective control over the persons who are subjecting the civilians to such treatment. A showing that the official merely was generally an influential person will not be sufficient. In contrast, a government official specifically in charge of the treatment of prisoners used for forced labour or as human shields, as well as a military commander in command of formations which are holding the prisoners, may be held liable on the basis of superior responsibility because of the existence of a chain of command' (§415).

In addition, with reference to civilian authorities, the same Trial Chamber stated in the same case: 'Evidence that an accused is perceived as having a high public profile, manifested through public appearances and

Cappellini and others the Milan Court of Cassation held that a superior who in fact had been deprived of his authority although he still was formally vested with his position could not be held responsible for crimes perpetrated by his subordinates unbeknownst to him or even in breach of his orders, for lack of the required intent (at 86–7).

It is interesting to note that in *Kordić and Čerkez*, the Trial Chamber found that one of the accused, Kordić, a civilian leader and politician having 'tremendous influence' and playing an important role in military matters, nevertheless did not possess the authority to prevent the crimes that were being committed or to punish the perpetrators. It therefore acquitted the accused of charges involving command responsibility, while nonetheless convicting him of various offences on the basis of perpetration under Article 7(1) of the Statute (§§838–41).

2. The superior *knew*, or *had information which should have enabled him to conclude in the circumstances at the time that crimes were being committed or had been committed*, or owing to the circumstances prevailing at the time, *should have known*, and consciously disregarded information indicating that his subordinates were going to commit (or were about to commit, or were committing, or had committed), international crimes.

3. He *failed to take the action necessary* to prevent or repress the crimes, thereby breaching his duty to prevent or suppress crimes by his subordinates.

It is clear from the above that command responsibility, or responsibility by omission of superior authorities, *is not a form of strict or objective liability*, that is, liability for offences for which one may be convicted without any need to prove any form or modality of *mens rea*.[14] Even for this category of crimes a mental element is required, as we shall soon see.

10.4.4 THE SUBJECTIVE ELEMENT OF THE CRIME AND THE VARIOUS CLASSES OF OMISSION

The objective element of the crime is apparent from what has just been set out. As for the subjective element, it would seem that intent is not required.[15]

statements, and thus as exercising some authority, may be relevant to the overall assessment of his actual authority although not sufficient in itself to establish it, without evidence of the accused's overall behaviour towards subordinates and his duties. Similarly, the participation of an accused in high-profile international negotiations would not be necessary in itself to demonstrate superior authority. While in the case of military commanders, the evidence of external observers such as international monitoring or humanitarian personnel may be relied upon, in the case of civilian leaders evidence of perceived authority may not be sufficient, as it may be indicative of mere powers of influence in the absence of a subordinate structure' (§424).

[14] Recently ICTY Trial Chambers rightly took this view in *Delalić and others*, §239, and in *Kordić and Čerkez*, §369.

[15] In *Baba Masao*, the Judge Advocate summed up the law for the Australian Military Court trying the case: 'In order to succeed [in proving charges of command responsibility] the prosecution must prove . . . that war crimes were committed as a result of the accused's [Commanding General of the Japanese Army in

One should distinguish various situations:

1. The superior knows that crimes are about to be or are being committed by his subordinates and nonetheless takes no action. Here international rules, which consider that the superior *in some way takes part in the crime of his subordinates*, require, for culpability, (i) *knowledge*, that is awareness that the crimes are being or are about to be committed;[16] and (ii) *intent*, that is the will not to act,[17] or at least *recklessness*, that is awareness that failure to prevent the action of subordinates risks bringing about certain harmful consequences (commission of the crimes), and nevertheless ignoring this risk.[18]

2. The superior has information which should enable him to conclude in the circumstances at the time that crimes are being or will be committed, and fails to act, in breach of his supervisory duties. According to *Delalić and others*, this is the case when the commander or the superior authority 'had in his possession information of a nature, which at least, would put him on notice of the risk of such offences [by his subordinates] by indicating the need for additional investigation in order to ascertain whether such crimes were committed or were about to be committed by his subordinates' (§383).

Here either *recklessness* or *gross or culpable negligence* (*culpa gravis*) may be held sufficient. The latter state of mind, as pointed out above (8.4), may be found when: (i) the commander is required to abide by certain standards of conduct or take certain

Borneo] failure to discharge his duties as a commander, either by deliberately failing in his duties or by culpably or wilfully disregarding them, not caring whether this resulted in the commission of a war crime or not' (at 207).

16 In *Maltauro and others* the Court of Assize of Milan held in 1952 that the head of police, being cognizant of the massacre that was about to be carried out by partisans, failed to prevent it. He was therefore held responsible as a co-perpetrator of the massacre (at 176–7). The massacre took place in a prison where numerous fascists, previously arrested by partisans on 28 April 1945 (the day when Schio, the small town in northern Italy, had been liberated), were being held.

See also *Sumida Haruzo and others* (at 260–1).

17 See for instance *Cappellini and others* (at 86–7), *Leoni* (Milan Court of Cassation, decision of 31 July 1945, at 128), *Bonini* (Court of Cassation, decision of 3 March 1948, at 1137–8), *Tabellini* (Rome Military Tribunal, decision of 6 August 1945, at 394–8). This last case is particularly interesting: the defendant was a colonel of the *Carabinieri*, accused of having allowed, in October 1943, at the request of the German occupying forces, the disarming and transfer of the *Carabinieri* stationed in Rome to Northern Italy; they had been subsequently deported to Germany and detained in concentration camps. The Court found that the defendant was not guilty of failure to prevent the commission of a crime. He was not aware of the real reasons for the transfer and believed that it was done in the exercise of the Occupant's power to transfer civil servants and police forces; according to the Court 'he lacked the requisite intent, because he carried out the execution of the order believing that such order was not inconsistent with his duties and those of the police forces to which he belonged, pursuant to international law' (at 398).

18 In *Notomi Sueo and others* a Temporary Court Martial in the Netherlands East Indies, in dealing with the responsibility of the commander of a prisoner of war camp in Celebes, held in 1947 that: 'Even though a particular act had been neither ordered nor condoned by a superior, who might even [have] been unaware of it, he must nevertheless be held responsible for the outrages of those under his command, on the ground that as a Commander he was bound to prevent their occurrence, the more so as he could reasonably foresee that they would be committed' (at 209).

specific precautions; and in addition (ii) he is aware of the risk of harm and nevertheless takes it, for he believes that the risk will not materialize owing to the steps he has taken or will take.[19]

3. The superior should have known that crimes were being or had been committed. Here again *gross or culpable negligence* (*culpa gravis*) is sufficient.[20]

4. The superior knows that crimes have been committed and fails to repress them by punishing the culprits. Here, *knowledge* and *intent or culpable negligence* would seem to be required for criminal liability.

As stated above, one ought of course to distinguish between the *mens rea* required for the crimes perpetrated by the subordinates (normally: intent, as in the case of killing of civilians, rape, use of unlawful weapons, torture, etc.) and that required for the superior. That law should admit for the superior a less culpable mental element as sufficient for his liability to arise (for instance, gross negligence instead of the intent required for the subordinates), is justified by his hierarchical position, the obligation attendant upon this position to control the subordinates and ensure that they comply with the law of international armed conflict, and the consequent need to make him accountable for the conduct of his subordinates.

SELECT BIBLIOGRAPHY

P. Speyer, 'Les crimes de guerre par omission', 30 *Revue de droit pénal et de criminologie* (1949–50), 903–43; W. Parks, 'Command Responsibility for War Crimes', 62 MLR (1973), 1–25; W. G. Eckhardt, 'Command Criminal Responsibility: A Plea for a Workable Standard', 97 MLR (1982), 1–25; W. Burnett, 'Command Responsibility of Israeli Military Commanders for the Pogrom at Shatila and Sabra', 107 MLR (1985), 71–189; W. J. Fenrick, in O. Triffterer, *Commentary*, 515–22.

19 In *Sumida Haruzo and others* the Prosecutor stated that, 'with respect to the torture inflicted by the members of his unit [on the prisoners], this may be attributed to his [of Sumida Haruzo] neglect in exercising sufficient supervision, and he may, as a result, be condemned on a charge arising out of responsibility for supervision, which is entirely different from being condemned on criminal responsibility' (at 235).

20 In this connection it may be useful to quote *Röchling and others* (where a French court stated that 'lack of knowledge . . . can only be the result of criminal negligence', at 1106), *Soemu Toyoda* (where a US Military Commission held that the accused 'should have known, by use of reasonable diligence the perpetration of atrocities by his troops' (at 5006)), as well as *Medina* (cited above). A Canadian Court Martial relied upon the notion of negligence in *Sergeant Boland*. The defendant had failed to prevent two subordinates from torturing and beating to death a Somali civilian taken prisoner (at 1075–8).

11

MULTIPLICITY OF OFFENCES

11.1 GENERAL

As in national law, also in international criminal law there may be instances of multiple offences (for instance, rape followed by murder of the same victim), or of offences that simultaneously affect numerous victims (for example, killing of numerous civilians), or of offences consisting of the simultaneous breach of many rules (this for instance occurs when by the same act a military officer breaches the rule prohibiting the use of certain weapons and that banning the killing of innocent civilians). It is therefore appropriate to try to distinguish and categorize all these instances, both for theoretical purposes (that is, in order logically to characterize and classify the various cases that may occur) and for practical purposes (which relate to two levels: when the prosecution prefers its charges and when courts sentence the convicted person; see *infra*, 11.2 and 11.4).

At the national level, these questions have primarily been discussed and explored in civil law countries, where the legal literature has reached considerable theoretical results. In common law countries the matter has been left to courts, which have gradually developed a set of criteria for at least the most important distinctions.

Based on the jurisprudential and scholarly contributions of national law and international case law, a few distinctions will be set out below.

11.2 DIFFERENTIATING CLASSES OF MULTIPLE OFFENCES

When a person, by a set of closely linked but separate actions, perpetrates several crimes against various victims, his conduct may be easily classified. Take for instance the case of a soldier in charge of a detention camp, who in a brief time-span beats up a prisoner of war, rapes another, then takes part in an execution squad charged with shooting a third prisoner of war allegedly responsible for war crimes (but not regularly tried and sentenced). Clearly, in this case the soldier is accountable for breaches of different rules of international law, against different persons. No particular problem arises with regard to the charging of the offender and his sentencing by a court: he will be accused of a set of different war crimes (ill-treatment, rape, unlawful killing of prisoners of war); if found guilty, he will be sentenced for each of these crimes.

A person may instead breach the same rule against various persons: for instance, a soldier in a spray of gunfire murders ten innocent civilians in a combat area. In this case only one rule is breached, that prohibiting the unlawful killing of civilians, but the offence is committed against several victims.

The legal literature has termed these two sets of cases a '*real concurrence of offences*'. As an ICTY Trial Chamber stated in *Kupreškić and others*, we are faced here with 'an accumulation of separate acts, each violative of a different provision' (§678c). These cases do not pose any major problem of charging: the accused will be charged with three different war crimes, in the first case, and with a war crime against several persons (or, more accurately, with as many war crimes in the form of murder, as there are victims), in the second.

Matters become complicated in other instances. Think for example of the case where a person, by a *single* act or transaction, simultaneously violates several rules. These cases are defined as an '*ideal concurrence of offences*'. Here again one ought to distinguish between various categories of breaches.

First, it may happen that the same act violates one rule in some respects and another rule in other respects, the two rules covering different matters. In such cases the same criminal conduct simultaneously breaches two different rules and amounts to two different crimes. For example, a serviceman, by using such a weapon as a flame-thrower, burns out a civilian building in occupied territory housing some innocent civilians, thus causing their death; here the soldier by the same act becomes responsible for both murder of civilians and arson. Or, to mention the example suggested by an ICTY Trial Chamber in *Kupreškić and others*, take the case of 'the shelling of a religious group of enemy civilians by means of prohibited weapons (e.g. chemical weapons) in an international armed conflict, with the intent to destroy in whole or in part the group to which those civilians belong'. Here this 'single act contains an element particular to . . . genocide to the extent that it intends to destroy a religious group, while the element particular to Article 3 [of the ICTY Statute] (on war crimes) lies in the use of unlawful weapons' (§679a). Clearly, when faced with these cases the prosecution must charge the defendant with two different crimes. Similarly, if it is satisfied that the accused is guilty of the breach of both rules, the court ought to sentence him for both breaches (although, it would seem, the sentences should run concurrently).

Another problem may arise when we are faced with a single conduct or transaction that successively breaches two different rules and may thus amount in theory to two offences, *one lesser than the other*. For instance, a soldier seriously wounds an enemy prisoner of war, thereby causing his death: we are here faced with the crimes of grievous bodily harm and murder. Or a soldier sexually harasses a civilian woman and then rapes her; we have here sexual assault and rape. Or a serviceman pillages private property in occupied territory, but in appropriating goods belonging to enemy civilians, faced with their resistance, uses force against them; we have here theft and robbery. In these cases the common law doctrine of the 'lesser included offence' and the civil law 'principle of consumption' coincide. Under both doctrines the more serious offence *prevails over and absorbs, as it were, the other*. Hence, the charge and conviction may be only for the more serious offence.

Thirdly, it may happen that an act or transaction simultaneously breaches *various rules covering the same subject matter*. For instance, depending upon the specific circumstances, the rape of a civilian woman by a soldier may be classified as a war crime, or a crime against humanity, or even as an act of genocide. On the basis of which principles or criteria should one decide which of the three classes referred to a specific rape falls? The answer to this query is important not only for courts, but also for prosecutors, when they decide how to charge a person suspected of international crimes.

One may deduce the criteria for settling these last issues from the principles of criminal law common to the major legal systems of the world as well as international case law.

One test or criterion seems to commend itself. It is known in common law countries as the *Blockburger* test (based on a famous decision by the US Supreme Court delivered in 1932 in *Blockburger* (at 304) and confirmed by the US Supreme Court in *Rutledge* (1996) (at 297) and in civil law countries as 'the principle of reciprocal speciality'. As the ICTY Appeals Chamber pithily put it in *Delalić and others* (*Appeal*):

> multiple criminal convictions entered under different statutory provisions but based on the same conduct are permissible only if each statutory provision involved has a materially distinct element not contained in the other. An element is materially distinct from another if it requires proof of a fact not required by the other. (§339.)[1]

In short, it must be established if each of the two or more provisions that appear at first sight to be breached requires an element that the other does not. *Three eventualities* may occur.

First, the offence may meet the requirements prescribed by one of the rules but not those demanded by the other. If this is the case, the offence is only covered by that rule. For instance, as stated in *Kupreškić and others* (§708), murder could be charged both as a crime against humanity and as a form of persecution qua crime against humanity. The rule on murder as a crime against humanity sets forth two requirements: that murder be the wilful taking of life of innocent civilians, and that it be part of a widespread or systematic practice. The rule on persecution requires that the act be performed with a discriminatory intent, and in addition within a widespread or systematic practice. Thus, each of the two rules enunciates a requirement that the other does not provide for. Hence, if a specific murder meets the requirements of the rule on murder as a crime against humanity but lacks the persecutory intent, then it may only amount to a breach of such a rule. In these cases the prosecution should charge the accused with the commission of one crime only. However, as a precaution, in case it then does not succeed in proving in court the specific requirement or legal

[1] See also *Jelisić* (*Appeal*), §82.

ingredient, the prosecution may deem it expedient to also charge the crime, either *alternatively*, as suggested in *Kupreškić and others* (§727) or *cumulatively*, as held in *Delalić and others* (*Appeal*) (§400).

In this last-mentioned case the Appeals Chamber ruled as follows:

> Cumulative charging is to be allowed in light of the fact that, prior to the presentation of all of the evidence, it is not possible to determine to a certainty which of the charges brought against an accused will be proved. The Trial Chamber is better poised, after the parties' presentation of the evidence, to evaluate which of the charges may be retained, based upon the sufficiency of the evidence. In addition, cumulative charging constitutes the usual practice of both this Tribunal and the ICTR. (§400.)

Judges Hunt and Bennouna, in their Separate and Dissenting Opinion, concurred with the majority on this point (§12). They offered, however, a more convincing reasoning:

> As a practical matter, it is not reasonable to expect the Prosecution to select between charges until all of the evidence has been presented. It is not possible to know with precision, prior to that time, which offences among those charged the evidence will prove, particularly in relation to the proof of differing jurisdictional pre-requisites . . . Further, . . . the offences in the Statute do not refer to specific categories of well-defined acts, but to broad groups of offences, the elements of which are not always clearly defined and which may remain to be clarified in the Tribunal's jurisprudence. The fundamental consideration raised by this issue is that it is necessary to avoid any prejudice being caused to an accused by being penalised more than once in relation to the same conduct. In general, there is no prejudice to an accused in permitting cumulative *charging* and in determining the issues arising from accumulation of offences after all of the evidence has been presented . . . [However] there may be specific examples of obviously duplicative cumulative charging, where there is no reason in the particular circumstances that the Prosecution needs to see how the evidence turns out before selecting the most relevant charge. In those circumstances it may be oppressive to allow cumulative charging. (§12 and n. 14.)

It may instead happen that, although, as in the case just mentioned, each of two rules sets out different requirements, the offence in fact meets all the requirements of both rules. In this case, the crime will amount to an offence under both rules. For instance, the rule on murder of civilians as a crime against humanity requires an element (the act must be part of a widespread or systematic practice) that the rule on murder of civilians as a war crime does not require. This last rule, in its turn, requires an element (that the murder be connected with an international or an internal armed conflict) that the other rule does not require (at least under customary international law). Hence, if the murder has been perpetrated within an internal armed conflict as part of a systematic practice, the offence may be regarded as both a war crime and a crime against humanity.[2]

[2] However, things may be different if, as under the ICTY Statute, the requirement of being linked to an armed conflict is common to all the crimes falling under the Tribunal's jurisdiction, with the exception of genocide. In that case, a murder committed in an armed conflict as part of a widespread or systematic practice may only be considered as a crime against humanity.

It would seem that in these cases the prosecution should charge *cumulatively*, that is, under both heads; similarly, if found guilty of both crimes, the accused should be sentenced for both (but the two sentences should be served concurrently).

A third eventuality may occur. It may be that two rules cover the same crime, but *one* of them requires an *additional* element or legal ingredient not provided for in the other rule. It may then happen that a specific offence meets that requirement but also is squarely covered by the other rule (which does not require a special element or requirement). In this case the offence falls within the ambit of both rules. For instance, under the ICTY Statute, murder in an armed conflict may be classified as a war crime, but if it is part of a widespread or systematic practice, it may amount to a crime against humanity. The murder of a civilian by a soldier, perpetrated within the context of a widespread practice, is in theory covered by both provisions, that on war crimes (Article 3), and that on crimes against humanity (Article 5).

Which of the two rules should one apply in this last eventuality? The *principle of speciality* ought to be relied upon, as an ICTY Trial Chamber held in *Kupreškić and others* (§683) and the ICTY Appeals Chamber authoritatively confirmed in *Delalić and others (Appeal)* (§340). On the strength of this principle one may conclude that the rule providing for the special requirement should prevail: in the case just referred to, the rule on crimes against humanity should take precedence. Hence, the offence would only amount to a crime against humanity. As was stated in *Kupreškić and others* (§684),

> the rationale behind the principle of speciality is that if an action is legally regulated both by a general provision and by a specific one, the latter prevails as most appropriate, being more specifically directed towards that action. Particularly in case of discrepancy between the two provisions, it would be logical to assume that the law-making body intended to give pride of place to the provision governing the action more directly and in greater detail.

In these cases the prosecution should charge the accused with violation of the special rule. However, as a precaution, in case it is unable to provide convincing evidence of the special requirement prescribed by that rule, it may also charge the accused with violation of the other rule. This charge ought to be put forward *in the alternative*, as suggested in *Kupreškić and others* (§727) or, according to the Appeals Chamber in *Delalić and others (Appeal)* (§400), may be preferred *cumulatively*.[3]

[3] For instances of judicial consideration of the possible overlap of international crimes, see *Delalić and others (Appeal)*, where the ICTY Appeals Chamber discussed among other things the relations between murder as a war crime and as a grave breach of the Geneva Conventions (§423), between 'willfully causing great suffering or serious injury to body or health' as a grave breach, and 'cruel treatment' as a war crime (§424) and between torture as a grave breach and as a war crime (§425). In *Jelisić (Appeal)* the ICTY Appeals Chamber discussed the relations between murder as a war crime and as a crime against humanity as well as between cruel treatment as a war crime and 'inhumane acts' as a crime against humanity. It held that each of the relevant provisions of the ICTY Statute required an element not demanded by the other (war crimes, under Article 3 of the ICTY Statute, requires 'a close link between the acts of the accused and the armed conflict'; according to the Court, this element was not required by Article 5 of the Statute, on crimes against humanity; in contrast, Article 5, on crimes against humanity, requires 'proof that the act occurred as part of a widespread or systematic attack against a civilian population, an element not required by Article 3' (§82). A

11.3 THE TEST BASED ON PROTECTED VALUES

In *Kupreškić and others* an ICTY Trial Chamber held that together with the test discussed so far (the *Blockburger* test and the 'principle of reciprocal speciality', as well as the principles of 'speciality' and that of 'consumption'), one should also use another test, based on the *values* that each of the various rules at stake intend to protect. As the Trial Chamber put it, 'Under this test, if an act or transaction is simultaneously in breach of two criminal provisions protecting different values, it may be held that that act or transaction infringes both criminal provisions' (§694). According to the Trial Chamber this test should be used in conjunction with, or in support of, the other tests (§§693–5). In contrast, the Appeals Chamber in *Delalić and others* (*Appeal*) (§§412–13 and, more generally, §§400–26) as well as in *Jelisić* (*Appeal*) (§§82–3) held, albeit implicitly, that this test is not necessary.

The test indubitably attaches importance to the concerns and interests that international criminal provisions intend to take into account when prohibiting criminal conduct. It is substantially grounded upon the notion that the international community establishes a sort of hierarchy among the various values it intends to protect by its criminal proscriptions. Admittedly it is difficult always to pinpoint with certainty the specific values each international criminal rule intends to safeguard. Perhaps the better solution is to use, as a rule, the other tests referred to above and then fall back on that based on the nature and scope of protected values in the event of those tests leading to uncertain results. In those cases consideration of the protected values might perhaps prove of some assistance.

11.4 THE IMPACT OF MULTIPLICITY OF CRIMES ON SENTENCING

Of course, when a court satisfies itself that the accused is guilty on several heads for the same conduct, it should impose a sentence that reflects the whole of the culpable conduct. It would seem that the principles governing this matter were appropriately set out by the ICTY Appeals Chamber in *Delalić and others* (*Appeal*), where the court stated that:

> the overarching goal in sentencing must be to ensure that the final or aggregate sentence reflects the totality of the criminal conduct and overall culpability of the offender. This can be achieved through either the imposition of one sentence in respect of all offences, or several sentences ordered to run concurrently, consecutively, or both. The decision as to how this should be achieved lies within the discretion of the Trial Chamber. (§430.)

Trial Chamber upheld this view in *Kvočka and others* (§219). It is submitted, with respect, that this interpretation of the ICTY Statute is wrong, for under *both* provisions a close link with an internal or international armed conflict is required.

This approach has however been rejected in the ICC Statute, Article 78(3) of which provides that when a person has been convicted of more than one crime, the Court shall pronounce a sentence for each crime and a joint sentence specifying the total period of imprisonment. This implies that a specific penalty should be attached to each offence, and the Court cannot impose a single term of imprisonment for a variety of offences.

SELECT BIBLIOGRAPHY

F. E. Horack, 'The Multiple Consequences of a Single Criminal Act', 21 *Minnesota Law Rev.* (1937), 805ff.; C. F. Stuckenberg, 'Multiplicity of Offences: Concursus Delictorum', in H. Fischer, C. Kress, and S. R. Lüder (eds), *International and National Prosecution of Crimes Under International Law*, 559–604.

12

CIRCUMSTANCES EXCLUDING CRIMINAL LIABILITY: JUSTIFICATIONS AND EXCUSES

12.1 THE DISTINCTION BETWEEN JUSTIFICATIONS AND EXCUSES

It is widely accepted in most national criminal systems, particularly in civil law countries, that it is necessary to draw a distinction between two categories of defences: justifications and excuses.

According to many criminal lawyers, when the law provides for a justification, an action that would per se be considered contrary to law is regarded instead as lawful and thus does not amount to a crime. For an example of justifiable homicide, one may mention the US Manual for Courts Martial (1951), para. 197(b):

> A homicide committed in the proper performance of a legal duty is justifiable. Thus executing a person pursuant to a legal sentence of death, killing in suppression of a mutiny or riot, killing to prevent the escape of a prisoner if no other reasonably apparent means are adequate, killing an enemy in battle, and killing to prevent the commission of an offence attempted for force or surprise such as burglary, robbery, or aggravated arson, are cases of justifiable homicide.

Society, and the legal system it has created, positively wants a person to do the otherwise illegal act, in that (i) the act, though criminal, is the lesser of two evils (for instance, when one kills in lawful self-defence, the death of the attacker is regarded as a lesser evil than that of the person unlawfully attacked), or (ii), in the case of execution of a sentence of imprisonment or of the death penalty the taking of liberty or life is a measure positively required by law. Take also the case of lawful belligerent reprisals (for example, the use of prohibited weapons). The commander ordering the reprisals as well as those carrying them out do not act contrary to law, although the weapons used are prohibited by principles or rules of international law. Resort to those weapons is warranted by the need to stop gross breaches of international law by the adversary, or to respond to those breaches with a view to preventing their recurrence. In these and other similar cases, society and the legal order make a positive appraisal of what would otherwise be misconduct. Society and law want the person so to behave, because in weighing up two conflicting values (the need not to use prohibited weapons and the necessity to impose on the enemy belligerent compliance with law) they give pride of place to one of them, although this entails the exceptional infringement of the legal rules designed to satisfy the other need. The person acting under a justification intends to attain the result caused by his action and is aware that by undertaking the conduct he will bring about that result (for instance, he intends to cause the death or wounding of enemy combatants through the use of prohibited weapons). However, society and the legal order do not consider this intent as culpable *mens rea*, that is as intent to murder, for they see that action and the attendant mental element as legally justified.

By contrast, in the case of excuses, an action contrary to a norm is regarded as *unlawful*, but the wrongdoer is *not punished.* Here the positive appraisal by society and law of the conduct covered by an excuse is *less strong* than that relating to conduct covered by a justification. In other words, the value judgment enshrined in law is not so favourable as to consider the conduct as lawful. Rather, conduct is regarded as unlawful, but the law considers that nevertheless the agent should not be punished. This is because society and law, while disapproving of that behaviour, intend to take account of special circumstances. Furthermore, in the case of excuses the required subjective element of the crime is lacking. Think, for instance, of the following case: a captain acts under a mistake of fact, in that he orders the shooting of a number of civilians in occupied territory who, he had been told, had committed war crimes and had been duly court-martialled, whereas in fact they either had not committed the crimes or had not been duly tried, as required by international humanitarian law. In this case the agent believes himself to be engaged in conduct (lawful execution of war criminals) different from that prohibited by the criminal rule (the execution of enemy civilians not duly tried and sentenced). The *actus reus* cannot be called into doubt, whereas *mens rea* is lacking. True, he intended to order the killing of the civilians and was aware that by his order he would bring about their death. However, he did not intend to act contrary to international prescriptions and therefore lacked the requisite *culpable* mental element. In short, he intended to bring about the *death* of those civilians, not their *murder.*

Society and the law-making bodies choose between a justification and an excuse on the basis of an *appraisal* of the various *values* at stake. It follows that in international law one has to look to international customary and treaty rules for the appropriate legal characterization of each defence (see however *infra*, 12.2).

Generally speaking, the characterization of a defence as a justification or as an excuse entails various practical consequences from the point of view of substantive law. In particular, three consequences should be pointed out:

1. In the case of an excuse, any *aider and abettor or accomplice* would be responsible for the excused crime (if, of course, none of them was also entitled to invoke

an excuse). In contrast, in the case of justification there would of course be no aider, abettor, or accomplice, for the simple reason that the conduct is not unlawful.

2. In the case of excuse, any *action in self-defence* by the victim of the excused criminal conduct would be allowed, provided of course it was in compliance with the requirements of self-defence. Self-defence is permissible because the criminal conduct to which the actor acting in self-defence intends to react, although excused by the relevant legal system, nevertheless remains per se contrary to law. Instead, in the case of conduct covered by a ground of justification, self-defence by the 'victim' of that conduct is not warranted, because the action at issue must be regarded as lawful from the outset (whereas self-defence is only admissible to repel *unlawful* violence by another subject).

3. In the case of excuse, the person who has committed the crime may be liable to *pay compensation* for any damage resulting from his misconduct. By contrast, if the behaviour is covered by a justification, no such obligation arises, for the action is not considered illegal.

12.2 CUSTOMARY INTERNATIONAL LAW: GENERAL

International criminal law envisages both justifications and excuses, although it is not yet clear whether it draws a legal distinction between these two categories.

Among defences that one may logically classify as justifications, one may mention the following: (i) *lawful punishment* of enemy civilians or combatants guilty of war crimes or other international crimes such as crimes against humanity (e.g. the execution, after conviction and sentencing by a duly constituted Court Martial, of civilians who had engaged in prohibited attacks on the belligerents, amounting to war crimes or other international crimes); (ii) *lawful belligerent reprisals* (as stated before, they may include the use of prohibited weapons as a response to a serious violation of international humanitarian law by the adversary, for instance, the killing of prisoners of war or the intentional shelling of civilians); (iii) *self-defence* (see *infra*). Perhaps consent (*volenti non fit iniuria*) may also be regarded as a justification, provided the acts consented to do not amount to unlawful attacks on the life, body, or dignity of human beings (with regard to such attacks, consent would be inadmissible as a justification, because the life, body, and dignity of human beings are protected by international norms having the rank of *jus cogens*, and are therefore not derogable by either States or individuals). As an instance of consent as admissible justification, one could perhaps think of the (albeit far-fetched) case of a State consenting to the destruction, by the enemy belligerent, of a church likely to be used as a military depot by rebels siding with the State.

Far more numerous are the classes of defences that may be defined as excuses from the point of view of legal logic: mental disease, state of intoxication, mistake of fact, mistake of law, duress, physical compulsion.[1] It is doubtful whether *force majeure* is admissible (the existence of an irresistible force or an unforeseen external event beyond the control of a belligerent which makes it absolutely and materially impossible for the belligerent to comply with a rule of humanitarian law: for instance, non-compliance with some rules on the treatment of prisoners of war on account of an earthquake, or of a famine not caused by the belligerent); this excuse, if admissible, should however be strictly construed to avoid abuse by combatants. In contrast, it is certain that under customary international criminal law neither superior order nor immunity for acting as a State official (the so-called 'act of State doctrine') may ever amount to an excuse.

Whether or not a legal distinction between the two categories is drawn by customary international law, it is indisputable that until now, *no practical distinction has been made between them*, similar to that upheld in national legal systems, particularly in civil law countries. For generally, international prosecutors and courts or, in the case of national proceedings, prosecutors and courts of common law countries, confine themselves to respectively requesting the culpability of the accused, or satisfying themselves either that he is culpable or that he may rightly plead a defence. They seldom go so far as to claim or order that the accused, if found not guilty on account of an excuse, should also pay compensation. Similarly, it would seem that to date there have not been cases where self-defence has been invoked as a response to another person's criminal conduct which, although by itself contrary to international humanitarian law, was nevertheless not punishable in that it was covered by an excuse. Nor have there been cases where aiders and abettors have assisted the author of a crime, and a court found that he was excused, whereas they were not covered by the same or another excuse.

12.3 SELF-DEFENCE

A person may plead the justification of self-defence whenever he commits an international crime in order to prevent, or put an end to, a crime by another person against the agent or another person. Self-defence is lawful provided it fulfils the following requirements: (i) the action in self-defence is taken *in response to an imminent or actual unlawful attack* on the life of the person or of another person; (ii) there is *no other way of preventing or stopping the offence*; (iii) the unlawful conduct of the other *has not been caused by the person acting in self-defence*; (iv) the conduct in self-defence is *proportionate* to the offence to which the person reacts.

As examples of self-defence one may mention the killing by a prison guard of an enemy prisoner of war who was about to murder the guard; the wounding of an

[1] According to the British Manual of Military Law, 'no criminal responsibility is incurred by a person for such acts as he is physically compelled, against his will and in spite of his resistance, to perform'; 'thus, if A by force takes the hand of B in which is a weapon, and therewith kills C, A is guilty (of murder), but B is excused' (§628).

enemy serviceman by a civilian woman in the hands of the enemy occupant, for the purpose of preventing or halting torture or rape.

In *Kordić and Čerkez* a Trial Chamber of the ICTY held that self-defence as a ground for excluding criminal responsibility is one of the defences that 'form part of the general principles of criminal law which the International Tribunal must take into account in deciding the cases before it' (§449).[2]

Plainly this defence must not be confused with self-defence under public international law. The latter relates to conduct by States or State-like entities, whereas the former concerns actions by individuals against other individuals. This confusion is often made. For instance, in *Kordić and Čerkez* defence counsel argued that the Bosnian Croats engaging in armed action under the authority of the two accused were acting in self-defence, to react to a policy of aggression by Muslim forces (§448). The ICTY Trial Chamber rightly rejected the argument, noting that 'military operations in self-defence do not provide a justification for serious violations of international humanitarian law' (§452).

In a number of cases courts discussed this justification, even if often they did not uphold it on the facts.[3]

[2] It went on to note that the 'principle of self-defence' enshrined in Article 31(1)(c) of the Statute of the ICC 'reflects provisions found in most national criminal codes and may be regarded as constituting a rule of customary international law' (§451).

[3] That self-defence may validly be put forward was held in *obiter dicta* by a US Tribunal sitting at Nuremberg in *Alfried Felix Alwyn Krupp and others*. Also the Judge Advocate in the trial of *Willi Tessmann and others* by a British Military Court sitting at Hamburg accepted that self-defence could be pleaded subject to certain strict conditions (177). In the former case the US Tribunal in *obiter dicta*, after noting that 'self-defence excuses the repulse of a wrong', insisted on the mental attitude of the person invoking the defence; it emphasized that 'the mere fact that . . . a danger was present is not sufficient. There must be an actual *bona fide* belief in danger by the particular individual' (148).

The plea also failed in *Yamamoto Chusaburo*, brought before a British Military Court sitting in Kuala Lumpur. A Japanese sergeant, charged with a war crime for killing a Malayan civilian who was stealing rice from a military store, claimed among other things that he had acted in self-defence: after arresting the civilian, he had been surrounded by a hostile crowd; fearing a grave danger to life and property, the more so because he was in pitch darkness, he had lost control of himself and in a rage killed the civilian with a bayonet. The Prosecutor rebutted that there was evidence that the act had not been committed in defence of property or person while the civilian was in the process of looting; it had been committed after the civilian had been taken from his house into custody (76–9).

Similarly, in *Frank C. Schultz*, heard in 1969 by a US Court of Military Appeals, the plea, while implicitly admitted in theory, failed on the facts. Schultz, a US marine, was a member of a four-man patrol commonly referred to as a hunter-killer team designed to ambush and kill Viet Cong. He killed an innocent Vietnamese farmer in a Vietnamese village. Before the Appellate Court he pleaded that he believed that the individual killed was a member of the Viet Cong, or that he was in communication with the enemy and was signalling the enemy and attempting to lead the appellant and his patrol into an ambush; he claimed that he did 'what he was instructed to do and what he felt he had to do to survive'. The Court rejected the defence, noting that 'The testimony of the accused shows his actions to be intentional. Thus removed is the possibility that death of the victim resulted from accident or misadventure . . . Moreover, self-defence is unavailable for it is a plea of necessity not available, normally speaking, to one who is an aggressor' (136–8). It is worth noting that in this case the Court relied upon another case, not dealing with a war crime, namely *Carl D. O'Neal*, where the same Court had ruled that 'a person cannot provoke an incident, and then excuse himself from responsibility for injury inflicted by him upon another in the course thereof, on the ground of self-defence . . . A plea of self-defence is a plea of necessity . . . It is generally not available to one who engages with another in mutual combat' (193).

The plea was successful in *Erich Weiss and Wilhelm Mundo*, before a US Military Court in Ludwigsburg. An American airman who in May 1944 had safely parachuted from his military aircraft over Germany was captured and turned over to two policemen; when, during an air raid, a crowd gathered around them demanding that the prisoner be killed, he suddenly moved his right hand in his pocket; the two policemen fired at him and he was instantly killed. The two defendants pleaded that they had felt threatened by the prisoner's movement of his hand in his pocket and had fired in self-defence. The US Court upheld the plea (149–50).

12.4 EXCUSES: TWO MAIN CATEGORIES

Let us now move on to excuses. Within this category of circumstances precluding criminal liability one ought to distinguish between two classes.

The first is those instances where, on account of his (transient or permanent) psychological conditions (insanity or intoxication), the person is not possessed of individual autonomy, that is, is not endowed with the capacity and free will to decide upon his conduct. It is because of this incapacity to freely choose his actions or omissions that the person lacks *mens rea* and cannot therefore be regarded as culpable if he engages in a criminal offence. For such cases it is held in some national legal systems that the person is 'criminally not imputable'.

A second class of excuses embraces instances where the person may not be held culpable because, although he is fully possessed of his individual autonomy and may in theory freely choose a course of action, he nonetheless lacks a criminal frame of mind. This may be because (i) he intends to bring about conduct (for instance, execution of enemy war criminals duly tried and sentenced) that is different from that which actually occurs and is prohibited by the criminal rule (execution of civilians without a proper trial), because he is *under a non-culpable misapprehension* about the facts or about the applicable rules. Or else, (ii) although he is aware of the consequences of his conduct (for instance, killing of a prisoner of war), he does not will those consequences but is *obliged by another person* to carry out the prohibited act through an unavoidable and serious threat to his life or limb.

12.5 EXCUSES BASED ON LACK OF INDIVIDUAL AUTONOMY

12.5.1 INSANITY OR MENTAL DISORDER

Insanity, or serious mental disorder, or mental incapacitation, or mental disease, may be urged as an excuse whenever this state of mind entails that the person is deprived of the mental capability necessary for deciding whether an act is right or wrong. The plea may be urged when at the time of commission of the crime the accused was unaware of what he was doing and hence of forming a rational judgment about his conduct. As a consequence, the accused lacks the requisite *mens rea* and may not be held responsible for his behaviour (see Article 31(1) (a) of the ICC Statute).

A case that supports the availability of this defence in international humanitarian law is *Stenger and Crusius*, decided by the Leipzig Supreme Court in 1921. The German Captain Crusius, commander of a German Company, had been accused of passing on to his subordinates, in the battle of 26 August 1914 against the French troops in the forest near Sainte Barbe (Alsace), an order from Major General Stenger not to take prisoners of war, or in other words to kill all captured enemy soldiers. The Supreme Court of Leipzig found that he had misunderstood that order, and hence wrongly ordered the killing of prisoners of war. The Court also found, on the basis of the testimony of various witnesses and expert witnesses, that the accused had undergone 'a complete mental and psychological collapse, that is a state of utter mental confusion, . . . induced by a psychopathic disposition and by the particular disturbance' of the battles of the previous days, . . . which would unequivocally preclude responsibility pursuant to criminal law' (at 2571–2).[4] The Court therefore acquitted Crusius on that count (2568–72).

In contrast, in the same case the German Supreme Court of Leipzig rejected the plea with respect to another episode. Captain Crusius had been accused of transmitting unlawful orders of Major General Stenger to his subordinates, on 21 August 1914. The Court found that in fact he had misunderstood the superior orders; when he passed them on to his subordinates, he was in 'extreme agitation and psychological suffering'; however, his mental state was not such as to preclude his 'free determination of will' (at 2567). Crusius was therefore found guilty on that count.

Similarly, the plea was rejected in other cases, for instance in *Kotälla*, by a Special Criminal Court of Amsterdam[5] as well as in *Frank C. Schultz*, a case heard before a US Court of Military Appeal.[6]

[4] The Court admitted that this mental state only emerged gradually in the afternoon: 'at around the time when the accused, distraught, with a bright red face and swollen eyes, came running out of the forest, screaming and rushing towards Dr. Döhner [another German serviceman, who testified in court], grabbing his arm, desperately uttering calls, and leaving the overall impression of a maniac . . . this state did not occur suddenly and abruptly but rather gradually worsened after having developed from an already existing nervous condition induced by a psychopathic disposition and by the particular disturbance' of the battles of the previous days. The Court found that when the supposed superior order was passed on to his subordinates 'the accused was suffering from a mental disorder rendering him incapable of forming a rational intention' (at 2572). After suffering from 'so-called diminished responsibility' (*verminderte Zurechnungsfähigkeit*, ibid.), he then found himself in a state of mind 'precluding responsibility'.

[5] The Court rejected the plea of mental disorder invoked by the accused (who had been charged with war crimes and crimes against humanity). It held that it had established, 'on the basis of its own observations at the hearing and further information presented . . . at the hearing, that the accused [did] not suffer from such a limited development of his mental faculties or mental disorder which could result in the offences committed by him not being attributed to him or being attributed to him to a lesser extent' (at 6). See also the decision delivered in the same case by the Dutch Special Court of Cassation on 5 December 1949 (at 13).

[6] The defence had raised the issue of insanity. The appellant had been accused and then convicted of premeditated murder, for having killed an innocent Vietnamese civilian. The Court rejected the plea of insanity. After noting that the testimony of two psychiatrists, one for the government, the other for the defence, showed that the accused had suffered from probable mental impairment, the Court referred to two previous cases unrelated to war crimes, *Michael F. Kunak* (354–66) and *Vadis Storey* (426–30), and approvingly

National laws and courts have upheld the notion that, in addition to insanity, there may exist other forms of abnormality of mind that may have a bearing on, and diminish, responsibility. In some States (in particular common law countries, notably Great Britain) the plea, if successful, entails *reducing the gravity of the offence* with which a defendant pleading the defence might be charged (for instance, reducing murder to manslaughter, whenever there is a mandatory sentence for murder, namely death or life imprisonment). In other States (chiefly civil law countries), if the plea is successful, the accused *qualifies for mitigation of sentence.*

National cases can be found where courts, when adjudicating war crimes, applied national law. For instance, in *Calley*, a case brought in 1971 before a US Court artial, the accused had been charged with premeditated murder in violation of Article 118 of the Uniform Code of Military Justice (the charge was of killing a number of Vietnamese civilians in the village of My Lai (4) in South Vietnam). The defence raised among other things the issue of mental capacity. In his instructions to the Court, the Judge Advocate stated the following:

> The law recognizes that an accused may be sane and yet, because of some underlying mental impairment or condition, be mentally incapable of entertaining a premeditated design. You should therefore consider, in connection with all other relevant facts and circumstances, all evidence tending to show that Lt. Calley may have been suffering from a mental impairment or condition of such consequence and degree that it deprived him of the ability to entertain the premeditated design to kill required in the offence of premeditated murder. The burden of proof is upon the government to establish the guilt of Lt. Calley beyond a reasonable doubt. Unless, in light of all the evidence, you are satisfied beyond a reasonable doubt that Lt. Calley, on 16 March 1968, in the village of My Lai (4), at the time of each of the alleged offences, was mentally capable of entertaining, and did in fact entertain, the premeditated design to kill required by law, you must find him not guilty of each premeditated murder offence for which you do not find premeditated design. You may, however, find Lt. Calley guilty of any of the lesser offences in issue [unpremeditated murder or voluntary manslaughter], provided you are convinced beyond a reasonable doubt as to the elements of the lesser offence to which you reach a guilty finding, bearing in mind all these instructions. (At 1716.)

The US Army Court of Military Review took the same stand in its judgment of 16 February 1973 on the same case.[7]

cited their holding whereby 'More than partial mental impairment must be shown in order to raise the issue. There must be evidence from which a court-martial can conclude that an accused's mental condition was of such consequences and degree as to deprive him of the ability to entertain the particular state of mind required for the commission of the offence charged' (138). See also *Sergeant W.* (decision of the Military Court, at 2).

[7] The two defence psychiatrists had asserted that the accused was acting automatically and did not have capacity to premeditate because he was effectively without ability to reflect upon alternative courses of action and choose from them; he did not have the mental capacity to 'contrive' the deaths of the villagers. The Court noted however that both psychiatrists agreed that Calley had 'capacity to perceive and predict, the two functions essential to the pertinent *mens rea.* Appellant knew he was armed and what his weapon would do. He had the same knowledge about his subordinates and their arms. He knew that if one aimed his weapon at a villager and fired, the villager would die. Knowing this, he ordered his subordinates to "waste" the villagers

A Special Court in Amsterdam took a different approach, typical of civil law countries, in *Gerbsch*. Between 1944 and 1945 the accused was a guard at a penal camp in Zoeschen, Germany and there he ill-treated many detainees, in particular Dutchmen and other persons transferred from the Netherlands. The Court found him guilty of a crime against humanity, but took into account as a mitigating circumstance the fact that his 'mental faculties were defective and undeveloped' when the crime was committed as well as at the time of trial (at 492).

Some international cases must also be mentioned. In *Delalić and others* an ICTY Trial Chamber, based on national legislation, admitted that there might be an impairment of mind affecting criminal liability.[8] The Appeals Chamber convincingly clarified the matter in the same case (*Delalić and others, Appeal*):

The Appeals Chamber recognises that the rationale for the partial defence provided for the offence of murder by the English *Homicide Act* 1957 is inapplicable to proceedings before the Tribunal. There are no mandatory sentences. Nor is there any appropriate lesser offence available under the Tribunal's Statute for which the sentence would be lower and which could be substituted for any of the offences it has to try. The Appeals Chamber accepts that the relevant general principle of law upon which, in effect, both the common law and the civil law systems have acted is that the defendant's diminished mental responsibility is relevant to the sentence to be imposed and is not a defence leading to an acquittal in the true sense. This is the appropriate general legal principle representing the international law to be applied in the Tribunal. Rule 67(A)(ii)(b) [of the ICTY Rules of Procedure and Evidence] must therefore be interpreted as referring to diminished mental responsibility where it is to be raised by the defendant as a matter in mitigation of sentence. As a defendant bears the onus of establishing matters in mitigation of sentence, where he relies upon diminished mental responsibility in mitigation, he must establish that condition on the balance of probabilities—that more probably than not such a condition existed at the relevant time.' (§590.)[9]

It would seem that, in any case, uncontrollable fits of temper may not be considered as falling under this category of possible excuses. At the most, and under strict

at the trail and ditch, to use his own terminology; and fire upon the villagers himself. These bare facts evidence intent to kill, consciously formed and carried out'. The Court concluded (at 1178–9) that Calley had acted with premeditation.

[8] It held that 'the accused must be suffering from an abnormality of mind which has substantially impaired his mental responsibility for his acts or omissions. The abnormality of mind must have arisen from a condition of arrested or retarded development of the mind, or inherent causes induced by disease or injury. These categories clearly demonstrate that the evidence is restricted to those which can be supported by medical evidence. Consequently killings motivated by emotions, such as those of jealousy, rage or hate, appear to be excluded' (§1166).

However, as in that case the defence was rejected (the Chamber found that the accused suffered from a personality disorder which did not entail his inability to control his physical acts on account of abnormality of mind), the Court did not specify the legal consequences of the plea of diminished responsibility (ibid., §1186). In particular, it did not specify whether the plea, if successful, entailed reducing the gravity of the offence with which a defendant pleading the defence might be charged, or instead qualified for mitigation of sentence.

[9] The matter was raised again in mitigation of sentence in *Todorović (sentencing judgment)*, but the Trial Chamber dismissed the claim that the accused was suffering from a personality disorder during the relevant period, namely when he committed the crimes (§§93–5).

conditions, it might prove appropriate to take them into account, if need be, as extenuating circumstances.[10]

12.5.2 INTOXICATION

Being in an intoxicated state as a result of taking alcohol, drugs, or other intoxicants may amount to an excuse only under very strict conditions: (1) the intoxication is so serious as to negate *mens rea*, (that is, it alters the agent's mental state to such a point that he is not in a position to be aware of his actions and to appraise the unlawfulness of his conduct); (2) in the case of voluntary intoxication, the person has not become voluntarily intoxicated knowing the risk that, as a result of his state, he was likely to engage in criminal action (see Article 31(1)(b) of the ICC Statute).

As an example of an acceptable excuse, the case can be mentioned of a soldier to whom a medical doctor or a nurse administers powerful sedatives or pain-killers, which seriously alter his mental state; as a result he kills or wounds a prisoner of war or an enemy civilian, or rapes a civilian.

There are a few cases on this matter. In *Yamamoto Chusaburo* a British Military Court sitting at Kuala Lampur rejected a plea of drunkenness. The accused, a sergeant of the Japanese Army, had been charged with a war crime for killing a civilian who had stolen rice from the army store. He pleaded among other things that he had acted under the influence of alcohol. According to the summary of the UN War Crime Commission, the Prosecutor said that:

> drunkenness in itself was not an excuse for crime, but where intention was of the essence of the offence, drunkenness might justify a court in awarding a lesser punishment than the offence would otherwise have deserved or it might reduce the offence to one of a less serious character. In such a case the man must be in such a state of drunkenness as to make him incapable of formulating any intention to commit the offence, and such a state would clearly affect the degree of killing of which the Court would find the accused guilty. (At 78.)

In *Kvočka and others*, one of the accused, Zigić, had beaten up and brutalized inmates in some detention camps, abusing and humiliating his victims; the defence argued that he had been intoxicated during many of the 'incidents' (§§616 and 680); at

[10] In *Erhard Milch* one of the judges serving on a US Military Tribunal sitting at Nuremberg, Judge Phillips, in his concurring opinion implicitly conceded that uncontrollable temper might be taken into account, although he did not specify for what legal purposes. Nonetheless, in the case at issue he rejected a defence claim that the accused (Field-Marshal in the German *Luftwaffe*, Aircraft Master General, Member of the Central Planning Board and State Secretary in the Air Ministry), who had been charged with war crimes and crimes against humanity involving deportations of civilian populations, forced labour and illegal experiments, had made violent statements due to uncontrollable temper, overwork, and head injuries. The judge noted that:

'If but only a few of such remarks could be attributed to the defendant, his protestations might be given some credence; but when statements such as appear in the documents have been persistently made over a long period of time, at many places and under such varying conditions, the only logical conclusion that can be reached is that they reflect the true and considered attitude of the defendant toward the Nazi foreign labour policy and its victims and are not mere aberrations brought on by fits of uncontrollable anger' (47).

the sentencing stage the Trial Chamber rejected the claim that intoxication was a mitigating factor, and found instead that it was an aggravating factor. However, as the Prosecutor had not previously raised the matter, the Chamber declined to treat intoxication as a factor germane to sentencing in the case at issue (§748).

12.5.3 MINORS

In many national legal systems it is normally considered that persons under a certain age do not possess full individual autonomy and therefore may not freely decide how to act: a child is regarded as *doli incapax*, that is, unable to entertain criminal intent. Consequently, children are normally considered exempt from criminal responsibility if they engage in criminal conduct. At present in some countries the threshold has been lowered. For instance, in Britain, children aged ten and above may be held accountable in some respects and liable to conviction. Trials for children are normally held before special courts.

In international criminal law no customary rule has emerged on this matter. However, a provision on the issue can be found in the ICC Statute: under Article 26, 'The Court shall have no jurisdiction over any person who was under the age of 18 at the time of the alleged commission of a crime.' Plainly, this provision is couched in terms referring to the Court's jurisdiction, and not as a substantive rule of criminal law whereby minors may not be held criminally responsible. It follows that, under that provision, it would be lawful for a contracting State to bring to trial before its national courts persons under eighteen (say, of fifteen) for allegedly committing war crimes, if this is allowed under the relevant national legislation.

The aforementioned provision may appear to be somewhat at variance with another provision of the same Statute, Article 8(2)(e)(vii), whereby 'conscripting or enlisting children under the age of fifteen years into armed forces or groups or using them to participate actively in hostilities' may amount to a war crime. It follows that a State, a national liberation movement, or insurgents may lawfully enlist children of sixteen or seventeen—but if these children engage in criminal conduct, they are not amenable to judicial process before the ICC (although of course they could be brought to trial before national courts, assuming such courts have jurisdiction over them).

12.6 THE ICC STATUTE

Article 31(1)(c) of the ICC Statute envisages self-defence as a ground excluding responsibility, in the following terms:

> [A person shall not be criminally responsible if, at the time of that person's conduct . . .] the person acts reasonably to defend himself or herself or another person or, in the case of war crimes, property which is essential to the survival of the person or another person or property which is essential for accomplishing a military mission, against an imminent and

unlawful use of force in a manner proportionate to the degree of danger to the person or the other person or property protected. The fact that the person was involved in a defensive operation conducted by forces shall not in itself constitute a ground for excluding criminal responsibility under this subparagraph.

In its essence, to a large extent Article 31 codifies a rule of customary international law, as the ICTY Trial Chamber rightly emphasized in *Kordić and Čerkez* (§451). However, the provision also contains a clause that is extraneous to customary international law and in a way surreptitiously introduces, through a criminal provision, a new substantive rule into international humanitarian law. I am referring to the clause whereby the defence applies to cases where one intends to defend property 'which is essential for accomplishing a military mission'. It would appear that customary law does not cover this eventuality, nor is there any rule in international humanitarian law to prohibit attacks against property which is essential for accomplishing a military mission.

Article 31(1)(a) and (b) deals with mental disease and intoxication in terms that may be held to restate or codify customary international law.

SELECT BIBLIOGRAPHY

GENERAL THEORY

H. H. Jescheck, *Lehrbuch*, 321–404, 475–509; H. Donnedieu de Vabres, *Traité*, 192–248; A. Eser, 'Justification and Excuse' 24 AJCL (1976), 621–37; J. Hall, 'Comment on Justification and Excuse', 24 AJCL (1976), 638–45; G. Arzt, 'Ignorance or Mistake of Law' 24 AJCL (1976), 646–79; J. Hall, 'Comment on Error Juris', 24 AJCL (1976), 680–8; Fletcher, *Rethinking*, 759–875; P. H. Robinson, 'Criminal Law Defenses: a Systematic Analysis', 82 CLR (1982), 199–291; G. Williams, 'The theory of Excuses', *Crim LR*, (1982), 732–42; K. Greenewalt, 'The Perplexing Borders of Justification and Excuse', 84 CLR (1984), 1897–1927; G. P. Fletcher, 'The Right and the Reasonable', 98 HLR (1985), 949–54; J. C. Smith, *Justification and Excuse in the Criminal Law* (London: Stevens, 1989); D. N. Husak, 'The Serial View of Criminal Law Defences', 3 *CLForum* (1992), 369–400; P. H. Robinson, 'The Bomb Thief and the Theory of Justification Defences', 8 *CLForum* (1997), 387–409; G. P. Fletcher, *General Concepts*, 130–70; F. Mantovani, 249–92, 374–402, 686–713.

INTERNATIONAL CRIMINAL LAW

S. Glaser, 'Culpabilité en droit international pénal', 99 HR (1960–I), 512–25; A. L. Dienstag, 'Fedorenko v. United States: War Crimes, the Defence of Duress, and American Nationality Law, 82 CLR (1982), 120–83; A. Eser, '"Defences" in War Crimes Trials', 24 IYHR (1994), 201–22; Y. Dinstein, 'Defences', in McDonald and Swaak-Goldman (eds), 367–88; K. Ambos, *Der 'Allgemeine Teil'*, 325–30, 767–832.

ICC Statute

A. Eser, in Cassese, Gaeta, and Jones (eds), *ICC Commentary*, I, 889–948.

13

OTHER EXCUSES: SUPERIOR ORDER, NECESSITY, DURESS, AND MISTAKE

In the preceding chapter we have discussed, among other things, those classes of excuses where the lack of *mens rea* derives from the agent lacking individual autonomy and consequently being not 'imputable'. We will now consider other categories of excuses—that is, those where the absence of the requisite subjective element derives from *external circumstances.*

On this score, the first question to be discussed is whether one of the most invoked excuses in national and international criminal trials, that is, superior orders, may be legally considered, under international criminal law, as a circumstance precluding criminal liability.

13.1 SUPERIOR ORDERS: MAY THEY BE PLEADED AS A DEFENCE?

13.1.1 NOTION

The basic assumption of the whole question of superior orders is that a subordinate may be faced with two conflicting obligations: that deriving from international law (which would impose not to execute an unlawful order), and that stemming from the specific order issued to him (and which enjoins to perform an act contrary to international rules). In the dilemma between (i) respect for military hierarchy and the consequent principle *respondeat superior* (only the superior should be held accountable) and (ii) the morally exacting demand that whoever seriously deviates from fundamental standards of conduct should be held responsible for his action even at the risk of jeopardizing military discipline, international law eventually opts for the second option. As international instruments (in particular the Statutes of ad hoc International Tribunals, as well as Control Council Law no. 10) and national and international case law clearly show, a customary rule has evolved in international law whereby an international crime by a subordinate may not be excused by the plea that he acted upon superior orders. Wherever the conduct amounts to a serious violation of international humanitarian law or international criminal law, and whatever the category of crime may be (a war crime, a crime against humanity, or another crime such as torture) the perpetrator must be held accountable. However, the fact that he acted following superior orders may be urged in mitigation of punishment.

The regulation just outlined applies to orders of both *military* and *civilian* authorities, and whatever the rank of the superior authority, provided (i) the subordinate is under a legal obligation to obey (otherwise he would not face a clash of obligations), and (ii) the authority issuing the order wields formal or substantial control over that subordinate.

13.1.2 THE INTERNATIONAL AND NATIONAL LAW TESTS

The question of superior orders is often framed in different terms: both national legislation and national judgments frequently state that, whenever a subordinate executes a superior order that is contrary to international rules, he is responsible when the order is *manifestly unlawful.* In this respect one can mention national legislation.[1] Some national Military Manuals also take the same stand.[2] There is abundant case law on this matter, starting with a case decided by the Austrian Supreme Military Tribunal on 30 March 1915 (case of the *Russian prisoner of war J.K.*, at 20).

This legal regulation of the matter may appear to be somewhat inconsistent with the definition of superior order set out above. However, as a commentator has conclusively demonstrated,[3] this seeming contradiction does not exist. National

[1] For example, the French Penal Code (Article 122–4) of 1994, the Spanish Military Criminal Code of 1985 (article 21), the Criminal Code of Sweden (1999) (Chapter 24, Section 8), the Israeli law and Israeli Defence Forces' internal regulations, the Peruvian Code of Military Justice (Article 19, para. 7).

[2] See, for instance, the US Field Manual of 1956 (§509), the Canadian Manual for Courts Martial (1999, at 16–5) and the US Manual for Courts Martial (2002 edn), Rule 916(d).

[3] Gaeta, 'The Defence of Superior Orders: the Statute of the International Criminal Court v. Customary International Law' 10 EJIL (1999), at 172–91. Various courts have taken this stand. For instance, in SIPO-*Brussels* the Brussels Court Martial clearly stated in 1951 that whenever the execution of an order involves a war crime, the order may not amount to a defence and the subordinate is punishable. As the Court pointed out, 'the execution of such orders, particularly the gruesome slaughter [of Resistance fighters, by members of the SIPO—*SicherheitPolizei*] at Gangelt, should be considered as a flagrant breach of the laws and customs of war and the laws of humanity and should be punished as such' (at 1522).

See also *Hass and Priebke* (*Appeal*) (decision of 15 April 1998). Discussing the acts of German military in Rome in 1943, and the claim of the defendants that they had executed civilians as a reprisal and upon superior order, the Court noted that Article 40 of the Italian Military Penal Code in Time of Peace was applicable, whereby an order must be executed unless it is manifestly illegal. The Court went on to state that 'Article 8 of the Statute establishing the Nuremberg Tribunal had not derogated from that provision; indeed, by laying down that a superior order could not excuse an order, [Article 8] simply took away from the judge the task of verifying the concrete manifest illegality of the order and was based on the presumption that such illegality existed whenever the offence ordered and executed amounted to a war crime or at any rate to a crime subject to the jurisdiction of the Tribunal. This standard of appraisal was patently grounded on the very essence of war crimes: these crimes are envisaged for the purpose of protecting fundamental values endowed with absolute character and valid for the whole of mankind; hence they are laid down regardless of any particular viewpoint, are clear in their essence and intend to criminalize highly condemnable conduct' (at 52–3).

military manuals and laws approach the issue in the manner just outlined because they intend to cover *any violation of military law*, whether or not it amounts to an international crime. International rules, instead, only regulate *the more limited question* of international *crimes*, and take it for granted that any such crime is manifestly unlawful, with the consequence that a subordinate executing an order to commit the crime is no less responsible than his superior. The only exception is where the law on a particular matter is obscure or highly controversial, in which case the defence of mistake of law may be raised.

In practice, two different approaches are taken in case law in determining whether or not the plea at issue may be upheld. International courts and tribunals, applying the customary rule outlined above, as well as the provisions of their statutes restating that rule, simply satisfy themselves that: (i) the act at issue amounted to a war crime or any other international crime over which the court or tribunal has jurisdiction; (ii) the order was given by a superior authority and, if so, the subordinate carried it out.

In contrast, national courts, relying upon the test of 'manifestly unlawful orders', take a different approach. They ask themselves whether: (i) the order concerned the performance of an act that was undisputedly unlawful, for it constituted an international crime; and (ii) the person executing the order knew or should have known the order to be manifestly unlawful.

The best illustration of how a national court proceeds under this text may be found in the instructions issued by the Judge Advocate to a US Court Martial in *Calley*. The Judge Advocate first spelled out the test. He noted that

> The acts of a subordinate done in compliance with an unlawful order given him by his superiors are excused and impose no criminal liability upon him unless the superior's order is one which a man of ordinary sense and understanding would, under the circumstances, know to be unlawful, or if the order in question is actually known to the accused to be unlawful.

The Judge Advocate then instructed the Court as follows:

> [U]nless you find beyond a reasonable doubt that he [Calley] was not acting under orders directing him in substance and effect to kill unresisting occupants of My Lai (4), you must determine whether Lt. Calley actually knew those orders to be unlawful. Knowledge on the part of any accused, like any other fact in issue, may be proved by circumstantial evidence, that is by evidence of facts from which it may justifiably be inferred that Lt. Calley had knowledge of the unlawfulness of the order which he has testified he followed. In determining whether or not Lt. Calley had knowledge of the unlawfulness of any order found by you to have been given, you may consider all relevant facts and circumstances, including Lt. Calley's rank, educational background, OCS schooling, other training while in the Army, including Basic Training, and his training in Hawaii and Vietnam, his experience on prior operations involving contact with hostile and friendly Vietnamese, his age, and any other evidence tending to prove or disprove that on 16 March 1968, Lt. Calley knew the order was unlawful. If you find beyond reasonable doubt, on the basis of the evidence, that Lt. Calley actually knew the order under which he asserts he operated was unlawful, the fact that the order was given operates as no defence.

> Unless you find beyond reasonable doubt that the accused acted with actual knowledge that the order was unlawful, you must proceed to determine whether, under the circumstances, a man of ordinary sense and understanding would have known the order was unlawful. Your deliberations on this question do not focus solely on Lt. Calley and the manner in which he perceived the legality of the order found to have been given him. The standard is that of a man of ordinary sense and understanding under the circumstances.
>
> Think back to the events of 15 and 16 March 1968. Consider all the information which you find to have been given Lt. Calley at the company briefing, at the platoon leaders' briefing, and during his conversation with Captain Medina before lift-off. Consider the gunship 'prep' and any artillery he may have observed. Consider all the evidence which you find indicated what he could have heard and observed as he entered and made his way through the village to the point where you find him to have first acted causing the deaths of occupants, if you find him to have so acted. Consider the situation which you find facing him at that point. Then determine, in light of all the surrounding circumstances, whether the order, which to reach this point you will have found him to be operating in accordance with, is one which a man of ordinary sense and understanding would know to be unlawful. Apply this to each charged act which you have found Lt. Calley to have committed. Unless you are satisfied from the evidence, beyond reasonable doubt, that a man of ordinary sense and understanding would have known the order to be unlawful, you must acquit Lt. Calley for committing acts done in accordance with the order. (1723–4.)

It is clear from this and other cases that the application of the national law test is more cumbersome and, what is more important, leaves more discretionary power to the judicial body. In contrast, the international test is straightforward and easy to apply.

Nonetheless, we shall see that, in practice, both tests have led to the same results. Indeed, the national law test has mostly been applied in cases where the act performed was in blatant breach of universally recognized rules of international law. In those instances where instead the plea of superior order has been upheld by national courts under the national law test, either the courts erred, or the relevant international rules were absolutely unclear and probably international courts and tribunals would also have reached the same conclusion.

13.1.3 CASE LAW REJECTING THE PLEA OF SUPERIOR ORDER

National courts and international courts or tribunals have dismissed this plea in numerous cases, in particular in cases concerning the killing or ill-treatment of: (i) defenceless shipwrecked persons;[4] (ii) innocent civilians in occupied territory;[5]

[4] See, for instance, *Llandovery Castle* (at 2580–6); *Peleus* (at 128–9).

[5] See for instance *Schintlholzer and others* (Military Tribunal of Verona, 21 February 1989, unpublished, p. 44 of the typescript); *Josef Kramer and others* (the *Belsen* trial), at 631–2; *Heinrich Gerike and others* (the *Velpke Baby Home* trial), at 338; *Sipo-Brussels* case (at 3–10); *Götzfrid* (at 62–6).

(iii) prisoners of war;[6] (iv) non-combatants detained in the combat area;[7] and also in cases concerning (v) the taking of illegitimate reprisals against civilians;[8] or (vi) unlawfully punishing civilians who are acting on behalf of, or collaborating with, the enemy;[9] or (vii) refusing quarter.[10]

13.1.4 CASE LAW UPHOLDING THE PLEA

In a few cases courts have upheld the plea because, in their view, either the order was lawful,[11] or the accused lacked the requisite *mens rea* due to: (i) absence of freedom of judgment; or (ii) mental disorder; or (iii) mistake of law. In other cases courts found it necessary first to appraise whether a generic order was lawful, and then to determine

[6] See for instance *Gozawa Sadaichi and others* (at 225, 229, 231), *Sumida Haruzo and others* (at 232, 240–1, 258), *Strauch and others* (at 562–3).

[7] See for instance *Lages* (at 2), *Zühlke* (at 133–4), *Rauter* (at 157–9), *Zimmermann* (at 30–1), *Bellmer* (at 543), *Thomas L. Kinder* (at 770–4), *Walter Griffen* (at 587–91), *Frank C. Schultz* (at 137), *Charles W. Keenan* (at 114–19), *Michael A. Schwarz* (at 859–61), *William L. Calley* (US Army Court of Military Review, at 1180–2; US Court of Military Appeals, at 541–5), *Sergeant W.* (Brussels War Council, at 3, and Military Court, at 2), *Sablić and others* (at 120–1), *M. and G.* (at 989–90), *Major Shmuel Malinki and others* (at 88–132).

See also a case where, in an *obiter dictum*, the Court held that the plea was not applicable in a civil war (*Nwaoga*, at 3).

[8] See *Wagener and others* (Rome Military Tribunal, at 52–3; High Military Tribunal, at 746), *Neubacher Fritz* (at 39–41).

[9] See for instance *Wolfgang Zeuss and others* (at 206–7, 216).

[10] See for instance *Nikolaus von Falkenhorst* (at 226–7, 237).

[11] See for instance *Neumann*. Upon the orders of a superior officer, the accused had taken part in an attack on prisoners of war who had refused to work, and had in addition 'belaboured a prisoner with his fists and feet'. The German Supreme Court at Leipzig held that the accused could not be held responsible for these events, for there could be no doubt as to the legality of the order ('*Wie die Dinge liegen, wird auch sich nicht in Zweifel ziehen lassen, dass der Befehl rechtmässig war*', at 2554). The Court went on to state that 'Unless there is to be irreparable damage to military discipline, even in a body of prisoners, disorderly tendencies have to be nipped in the bud relentlessly and they have to be stamped out by all the means at the disposal of the commanding officer and if necessary even by the use of arms. It is of course understood that the use of force (*Gewaltanwendung*) in any particular case must not be greater than is necessary to compel obedience. It has not been established that there was any excessive use of force here. The accused has been charged with having continued to belabour [the Scottish prisoner of war] Florence when he was lying on the ground and after the resistance of the prisoners generally had already been overcome. For this, however, no adequate proof has been forthcoming' (at 2553–4; at 699 for the English translation). It is notable that in the same case the Court also ruled out the defence being available to the accused with regard to other instances where he had ill-treated prisoners of war using what the Court held to be excessive force, not justified by the order (ibid. at 2554–6 and 699–704, for the English translation).

In *von Falkenhausen* the Brussels Court Martial (*Conseil de guerre*) held that the superior orders concerning the execution of reprisals against the population could amount to an admissible plea to the extent that the reprisals were necessary to ensure the security of the Occupant; indeed according to the Court at the time these reprisals were carried out, under international law such reprisals could not be regarded as a 'flagrant violation of the laws of warfare' (at 868–70).

whether the execution of the order by the subordinate was in keeping with international legal standards.[12]

We shall discuss here only the cases where according to the courts the defendant lacked the requisite subjective element (*mens rea*).

1. Lack of *mens rea* due to purported absence of freedom of judgment

In *Kappler and others* (1948) the Rome Military Tribunal dealt with the unlawful reprisals ordered by Hitler for the murder in Via Rasella, Rome, of 32 members of an SS unit. The SS Lieutenant Colonel Kappler, besides carrying out those orders, decided to kill ten more Italians because meanwhile another SS had died as a result of the bombing. In addition, he had five more Italians killed by mistake: a total of 335 persons. The Court held that the reprisals were unlawful, and Kappler was guilty of ordering the shooting of ten persons plus the additional five people. However, it found that he was not guilty for the killing of 320 persons ordered by Hitler. It held that:

The mental habit of prompt obedience that the accused had developed working in an organization based on very strict discipline, the fact that orders with the same content had been previously executed in the various areas of military operation, the fact that an order from the Head of State and Supreme Commander of the armed forces, owing to the great moral force inherent in it, cannot but diminish, especially in a serviceman, that freedom of judgment which is necessary for an accurate appraisal, all these are elements which lead this Court to believe that it may not be held with certainty that Kappler was aware and willed to obey an unlawful order.' (At 30.[13] The Supreme Military Tribunal upheld the judgment by a decision of 25 October 1952, at 97–118.)

[12] One may mention *V. J. F. G.* (*Korad Khalid* v. *Paracommando soldier*), brought in 1995 before a Belgian Military Court. In 1993 a member of the Belgian military troops in Somalia had wounded a Somali child who was trying to enter the safety area, through barbed wire fencing guarded by the accused. The Court found that the order 'to defend and prevent anyone from penetrating into the cantonment of various Belgian military units' was lawful (at 1064–6). It then considered how the defendant had carried it out. It noted that 'on observing the child creep through the concertina and thus arrive in the immediate vicinity of the bunker, he [the defendant] first gave the necessary verbal warning in both Somali and English . . . he then fired two warning shots into the ground about 50 cm away from the child, who still showed no reaction, . . . he finally decided to fire an aimed shot . . . at non-vital organs, viz. the legs . . . the procedure followed by the accused was the only possible one to fulfil his defensive duties . . . he was physically incapable of catching the intruder (in view of the special position of the bunker, which was accessible only from the rear along an aperture in the cantonment wall) . . . and [in addition] it was unrealistic to call upon other reserve facilities, e.g. the picket; [furthermore] in view of the possible imminent attack, the reaction had to be prompt and this reaction was also commensurate; . . . all being considered, there was no other action suitable in the circumstances which could be taken to prevent further penetration . . . [and] the force used was unmistakably proportional to the nature and extent of the threat' (at 1066–7).

A similar case is *D. A. Maria Pierre* (*Osman Somow* v. *Paracommando Soldier*). A Belgian Military Court held that the order was lawful and that, in accidentally causing the death of a Somali civilian, the Belgian soldier on guard duty who had executed the order was not responsible for he had not failed 'to exercise foresight and care' when firing a warning shot which by ricochet had fatally wounded the Somali (at 1069–71).

[13] The Court applied the same reasoning to the four other accused, who had executed Kappler's order, and found them not guilty (at 51).

The Court's reasoning is highly questionable and, indeed, was 'reversed' in subsequent judgments of Italian courts.[14] If one were to share this approach, in all cases where a superior gives an unlawful order the subordinate would be relieved of responsibility. Indeed, one could easily prove that the superior authorities' widespread practice of issuing unlawful orders, together with the great clout of such authorities, bring about a frame of mind whereby the subordinate forfeits his awareness and will, and hence lacks the requisite mental element for the commission of the crime.

2. Lack of *mens rea* due to alleged mental disorder

There are also other instances where, according to some national courts, the execution of unlawful superior orders, while not constituting per se a valid defence, may bring about such a state of mind in the subordinate, that in the end he lacks any autonomous will as well as the intent necessary for his criminal responsibility to arise. In such cases courts have found that the accused found himself in such state of confusion that he was unable to entertain the mental attitude required for *mens rea.*

A case in point is *Caroelli and others* decided by the Italian Court of Cassation on 10 May 1947. In northern Italy, in the area under the control of the Republic set up in 1943–5 by Italian fascists with the support and under the control of Germans (the so-called *Repubblica Sociale Italiana*), the provincial representative of the government (*prefetto*) had ordered the head of *Guardia Nazionale Repubblicana* (GNR), Mr Caroelli, to execute ten partisans by way of reprisal following the killing of a National Guard officer. The reprisal, in addition to being unlawful, was absolutely arbitrary (the *prefetto* had been informed by one of his subordinates that the killing of the officer was due more to jealousy than to political motives, and at any rate the police were about to ferret out the perpetrator). The case was brought before the Court of Assize of Padua which acquitted Caroelli, his deputy, and another officer, on the strength of Article 51, last paragraph, of the Italian Criminal Code, whereby 'whoever executes an unlawful order is not punishable, whenever the law does not allow him to scrutinize the lawfulness of the order'. On appeal from the Prosecutor, the Court of Cassation held that reliance upon that provision was wrong, because the order was patently unlawful and arbitrary, and the subordinates were not bound to carry it out, pursuant to Article 40 of the Military Criminal Code applicable in Time of War. Nevertheless, the three accused were acquitted, because they 'lacked freedom of will, in the conduct ordered by their superior'. The Court emphasized that, when the order was given, Caroelli tried to oppose it 'in two agitated talks' with the *prefetto* and, when he left the *prefetto*'s office, he had 'a cadaverous appearance' and 'could hardly stand on his feet'. According to the Court this showed that the order brought about in Caroelli a state of 'psychic confusion that was also accompanied by clear physical manifestations' and this 'confusion was transmitted to his aides'. According to the Court,

14 See in particular *Hass and Priebke (Appeal)*, 15 April 1998, at 52–4.

when the manifestation of will contrary to the criminal action ordered by the superior is such as to cause clear physical troubles and a psychic confusion that nullifies the subordinate's freedom of decision, clouding a clear vision of hierarchical relations, evidently there does not exist that integrity of awareness and will required for making up a generic criminal intent, and even more the specific criminal intent necessary for the crime at issue. (At 2.)

The above reasoning does not comport with the relevant rules and principles of international law. In any event, assuming that the legal grounds set out by the court were correct, it remains that in this and similar cases the excuse the defender might validly raise is not superior order, but that of *mental disorder* (see *supra* 12.5.1). In addition, in all such cases, it would of course be necessary for the courts to be extremely cautious in establishing the facts and the credibility of witnesses, lest the plea of superior orders should become a general pretext for negating criminal responsibility.

3. Lack of *mens rea* due to uncertainty of law

In addition to some cases I will cite below (13.4.3)—that is *Wagener and others* and *Thomas L. Kinder*—it is worth mentioning a significant case, brought before a US Military Tribunal sitting at Nuremberg. In *Wilhelm von Leeb and others* (*High Command* case), the Tribunal discussed the question of whether the field commanders under trial, by obeying an order issued by their superior authorities to use prisoners of war for the construction of fortifications, had complied with an unlawful order and were therefore guilty. The Tribunal rightly held that the order was not patently illegal because the law on the matter was unclear; consequently the accused were not responsible under this count. It is worth quoting the Tribunal's reasoning:

One serious question that confronts us arises as to the use of prisoners of war for the construction of fortifications. It is pointed out that the Hague Convention [of 1907] specifically prohibited the use of prisoners of war for any work in connection with the operation of war, whereas the later Geneva Convention [of 1929] provided that there shall be no *direct* connection with the operations of war. This situation is further complicated by the fact that when the proposal was made to definitely specify the exclusion of the building of fortifications, objection was made before the [Geneva] conference to that limitation, and such definite exclusion of the use of prisoners was not adopted. There is also much evidence in this case to the effect that Russia used German prisoners of war for such purposes. It is no defence in the view of this Tribunal to assert that international crimes were committed by an adversary, but as evidence given to the interpretation of what constituted accepted use of prisoners of war under international law, such evidence is pertinent. At any rate, it appears that the illegality of such use was by no means clear. The use of prisoners of war in the construction of fortifications is a charge directed against the field commanders on trial here. This Tribunal is of the opinion that in view of the uncertainty of international law as to this matter, orders providing for such use from superior authorities, not involving the use of prisoners of war in dangerous areas, were not criminal upon their face, but a matter which a field commander had the right to assume was properly determined by the legal authorities upon higher levels. (At 534; see also 535.)[15]

Arguably, in this and other similar cases, the defence that can be validly raised is not that of superior order but of *mistake of law.*

13.1.5 WHETHER UNLAWFUL ORDERS MAY RELIEVE OF RESPONSIBILITY IF GIVEN ON THE BATTLEFIELD

In some cases courts have denied in the case at bar that the execution of an unlawful order could amount to a defence, while conceding in *obiter dicta* that, however, this might have been the case had the order been given in the heat of the battle, when the subordinate had no time for reflection.

Thus, in *Kotälla*, in its judgment of 14 December 1948, an Amsterdam Special Criminal Court rejected the claim of the accused, an SS commander of the security staff in the police-run transit camp at Amersfoort, that he had acted under superior orders, when ill-treating, torturing, and murdering inmates in the period 1942–45. The Court held that:

according to a universal sense of justice, orders to carry out acts—which, as has been proven in this case, bear the stamp of inhumanity and unlawfulness—do not simply absolve a subordinate of responsibility under criminal law and the latter remains personally responsible. . . . This is all the more compelling in this case where the issue in question does not under any circumstance concern the kind of orders that are given in action and on the battlefield, which in themselves must be obeyed immediately, but, rather, acts of lengthy duration on numerous occasions during which the accused could have given more sincere signs of his own goodwill and a sense of responsibility.

Similarly, in *US* v. *Calley* (judgment of 21 December 1973), the Court of Military Appeals held, *per* Judge Quinn, that:

In the stress of combat, a member of the armed forces cannot reasonably be expected to make a refined legal judgment and be held criminally responsible if he guesses wrong on a question as to which there may be considerable disagreement. (At 543–4.)

Admittedly, it is more difficult for a subordinate to make up his mind and refuse to obey an illegal order in the midst of battle. Nonetheless, even under those

[15] Another case in point is *E. van E.*, decided after the Second World War by a Dutch Special Court of Cassation. In April 1945 a Dutch unit of resistance fighters in occupied Netherlands, recognized by Royal decree as members of the Dutch armed forces, shot and killed four members of the Dutch Nazis (NSB) they had captured. The order to kill them, given by the commander B., was executed by van E. with two other members of the unit. The Court found that 'given the circumstances in which the order was given, the accused was entitled to assume in good faith that his commanding officer was authorized to give that order for the liquidation of the prisoners, and that this order was within the scope of his subordination'. The Court therefore found van E. not criminally liable and acquitted him (in *NederJ.*, 1952, 514–16). To better grasp the purport of this decision, it must be recalled that in the case against the commander, B., the same Court held that he was not guilty for ordering to shoot and kill the prisoners, because the law was unclear and he committed a pardonable error of law (see above).

extraordinary circumstances he is required to appraise the legality or illegality of the order, provided the legal regulation of the matter is universally accepted and clear beyond doubt. Various US Courts Martial rightly recognized this principle. In this connection *Calley*, as well as two cases related to another episode, *Schwarz* and *Green*, stand out.

In the first case, a US Court Martial convicted Calley of the 'premeditated murder' of twenty-two infants, children, women, and old men in the village of My Lai in South Vietnam on 16 March 1968. First Lieutenant Calley, a platoon leader, claimed that he had acted upon orders from Captain Medina, given before the occupation of the village and as soon as the village was invaded. Medina allegedly ordered the killing of every living thing—men, women, children, and animals—adding that under no circumstances were they to leave any Vietnamese behind them as they passed through the villages en route to their final objective. Whether or not this order was truly given (Medina always denied having issued it), the Court Martial held that the deliberate killing of unarmed persons offering no resistance and under the control of armed forces was patently illegal. It thus took the view that even in the heat of battle, manifestly illegal orders must not be executed and, if complied with, may not be used in defence.[16] The Court of Military Appeals took the same stand (at 538–46).[17]

In short, the particular circumstances under which the order is given and executed should no doubt be taken into account, not however for the purpose of relieving the subordinate of his responsibility, but as a possible extenuating circumstance.[18]

[16] See the *Instructions* from the military judge to the Court Martial, March 1971 (at 1720–4).

[17] See also *Schwarz* and *Green*. In 1970 a five-man US Marines patrol in South Vietnam had been sent out, overnight, to search out, locate, and kill Viet Cong. In a small hamlet called Son Thang they came across sixteen civilians, women and children, in three huts, and killed all of them upon order of the team leader. The plea entered by two members of the team, to have acted upon orders and under conditions of extreme tension and stress for fear of ambushes, was rejected. In the first case (*Schwarz*), the Navy Court of Military Review held that 'the accused could not have honestly and reasonably believed that Herrod's [the team leader] order to kill the apparently unarmed women and children was legal . . . The record . . . before us shows beyond any doubt that Herrod's orders to kill the unarmed women and children were patently illegal and were recognized as being so by members of the patrol including private Schwarz' (at 860, 863). The same view was taken in *Green* (see NCMR 70–3811, 19 May 1971).

[18] In the war crime case of *Major Shmuel Malinki and others*, an Israeli court, in applying Paragraph 19(B) of the Israeli Criminal Law, drew a distinction between 'sudden and unexpected orders' and 'other orders'. It stated that 'A soldier . . . is educated and trained to use his weapon in two types of activities—independently and in a group framework. In a group framework he is trained to act most mechanically with general reliance on the commander's order, without hesitation. He is trained to act quickly and immediately, as automatically as possible, in order to fulfil his task in the framework suitably. In training and in the daily routine the soldier is educated towards battle activity, where there is no time for deliberation, no place for independent thoughts on the part of the private who forms part of a unit, where the results of the battle and the fate of the soldier and his comrades might depend on his unquestioned obedience to his commander's orders and his speed in operating his weapon before the enemy. The modern and sophisticated weapon of our era adds and obliges educating the soldier in speed and maximum automatism in its use . . . The soldier who operates within a framework and obeys a sudden and unexpected order to fire from his commander, will in general be relieved of criminal responsibility for the results in taking a man's life through his actions, since the necessary training of the soldier to respond immediately and almost automatically to orders of this kind deprives him of the possibility that he consider the circumstances under which the order was given and forces him to rely on the commander regarding the reason for using his weapon' (at 134–5).

13.1.6 THE ICC STATUTE

It follows from the above that Article 33(3) of the ICC Statute (whereby 'orders to commit genocide or crimes against humanity are manifestly unlawful')[19] is at odds with customary international law, since it does not include, in this category of manifestly unlawful orders, those concerning *war crimes*. This inconsistency is all the more striking because, while one could consider that traditional international law was not crystal clear about the list of prohibited war crimes, at present the ICC Statute enumerates in detail the various classes of such crimes. In addition, the 'Elements of Crime' specify the various subjective and objective ingredients of each individual class of crimes. Hence, at present any serviceman is expected and required to *know* whether the act he is about to commit falls under the category of war crimes and must be aware of whether or not the execution of a superior order involves the commission of such a crime. This is all the more true because the ICC Statute implicitly provides in its preamble that it intends to address 'the most serious crimes of concern to the international community as a whole'.

Furthermore, under the ICC Statute approach, if in a particular case the Prosecutor in his indictment characterizes the same offence as both a war crime and a crime against humanity (cumulative charges are allowed, under existing case law: see 11.2), it might happen that the defence of superior orders could be urged and relied upon with respect to the offence as a crime against humanity, whereas it would not automatically hold should the same offence be classified as a war crime. This result would hardly prove consistent with the object and purpose of the Statute and its intent 'to put an end to impunity for the perpetrators' of 'the most serious crimes'.

The inconsistency between customary and treaty law should arguably prompt the interpreters, and in particular the Court, to construe Article 33 strictly, so as to make it as consonant as possible with customary international law. In other words, when dealing with serious violations of international humanitarian law perpetrated on superior orders, the Court should begin from the assumption that an order to engage in such violations is by definition 'manifestly unlawful', unless one is faced with the exceptional or rare occurrence that the substantive law on the matter (that is, a particular provision of the ICC Statute) is unclear and the agent may usefully plead the defence of mistake of law (see *infra*, 13.4).

[19] Article 33 provides as follows:

'1. The fact that a crime within the jurisdiction of the Court has been committed by a person pursuant to an order of a Government or of a superior, whether military or civilian, shall not relieve that person of criminal responsibility unless:
  (a) The person was under a legal obligation to obey orders of the Government or the superior in question;
  (b) The person did not know that the order was unlawful; and
  (c) The order was not manifestly unlawful.

'2. For the purposes of this article, orders to commit genocide or crimes against humanity are manifestly unlawful.'

13.2 NECESSITY AND DURESS

13.2.1 NOTION

Necessity or duress may be urged as a defence when a person, *acting under a threat of severe and irreparable harm to his life or limb, or to life and limb of a third person*, perpetrates an international crime. The person under threat, although he breaches an international rule and consequently commits an international crime, is not punishable.

Duress is often termed 'necessity', both in national legislation and in cases relating to war crimes and crimes against humanity. However, there are some important differences between these two categories of defences:

1. Necessity designates threats to life and limb emanating from *objective circumstances.* As pointed out in the British Manual of Military Law, necessity proper covers situations *other than* those where one is faced with threats or compulsion of a third party. Necessity denotes, for instance, the condition where a person 'in extremity of hunger kills [another person] to eat him' (§630, no. 1).

2. In the case of necessity the agent intends to cause an unlawful harmful effect; to put it differently, he does entertain the *criminal intent* required by the criminal rule (he is not only aware that by his action he causes the death of another person but he indeed wills that death, because achieving this result is the only means for him to avert a serious imminent threat to his life); for instance, he wills the death of the other shipwrecked person who is attempting to climb into the small boat capable of carrying only one person; nevertheless, the law considers that he must be excused by not being punished. In contrast, duress to a large extent negatives the subjective element of the person under coercion (he does not will the death of the prisoner of war he is constrained to kill); the criminal intent of the person causing duress in a way substitutes for his *mens rea*; hence, with duress, unlike necessity, a third person, that is, the person threatening the agent, is held criminally responsible for the harm caused by the person acting under duress (for instance, a lieutenant is responsible for the death of an innocent civilian he has constrained a soldier to kill).

The requirements prescribed by international rules for each of these two defences are however the same. The relevant case law (see below) is almost unanimous in requiring *four strict conditions* for duress and necessity to be upheld as a defence, namely:

(1) the act charged is done under an immediate threat of severe and irreparable harm to life or limb;

(2) there is no adequate means of averting such evil;

(3) the crime committed is not disproportionate to the evil threatened (the contrary would, for example, occur in case of killing in order to avert a sexual assault). In other words, to be proportionate, the crime committed under duress or necessity must, on balance, be the lesser of two evils or an evil as serious as the one to be averted;

(4) the situation leading to duress or necessity must not have been voluntarily brought about by the person coerced.

13.2.2 NECESSITY

As stated above, generally speaking, necessity is a broader heading than duress. It designates *threats to life and limb emanating from objective circumstances* and not from another person.

Although, according to the British Manual, necessity may not constitute a defence,[20] it would seem that instead international law admits this defence,[21] although under strict conditions.[22]

The law on necessity was clearly set out in *Krauch and others* (*I. G. Farben* case, at 1174–9). The defendants had claimed that the utilization of slave labour in I. G. Farben plants was the necessary result of compulsory production quotas imposed upon them by the government as well as the obligatory governmental measures requiring them to use slave labour to achieve such production. The US Military Tribunal sitting at Nuremberg summed up the conditions under which necessity is admissible as follows:

From a consideration of the IMT, *Flick* and *Roechling* judgments, we deduce that an order of a superior officer or a law or governmental decree will not justify the defence of necessity unless, in its operation, it is of a character to deprive the one to whom it is directed of a moral choice as to his course of action. It follows that the defence of necessity is not available where the party seeking to invoke it was, himself, responsible for the existence or execution of such order or decree, or where his participation went beyond the requirements thereof, or was the result of his own initiative. (At 1179.)

An interesting case concerning necessity is *Stanislaus Bednarek*, brought before the Austrian Supreme Military Tribunal (judgment of 9 September 1916). The accused, a Russian subject, while being on territory under Russian control, had reported to the Russian police that three German soldiers were in hiding; as a result they had been arrested; later on, captured by the Austrian army, the Russian had been accused of treason and sentenced on 11 October 1915 by an Austrian military court. On appeal, the Supreme Military Tribunal found that he was not guilty. The General Military Prosecutor, in submissions of 26 July 1916, had noted that the accused, being subject to Russian law, was obliged to report the three German soldiers to the police, pursuant to §164 of the 'New Russian Criminal Law' of 22 March 1903; he had therefore acted under 'irresistible coercion' (at 4). The Supreme Military Tribunal upheld this submission and found that the accused had found himself in a condition akin to 'state of necessity' (*notstandähnliche Lage*); there therefore existed a 'circumstance excluding culpability', namely 'irresistible coercion' (at 2).

20 'Compulsion arising from hunger or from immediate danger to a person's life or property will not excuse the commission of a war crime, although such compulsion may be considered in mitigation of punishment' (§ 630).

21 The law on necessity (and duress, treated on the same footing) is summarized in vol. XV of the UN *Law Reports*, at 174. For the relevant case law see, in particular, *Ohlendorf and others* (*Einsatzgruppen* case), at 471 and 480–1; the *High Command* case, at 509; the *Trial of Gustav Alfred Jepsen and others* (*Jepsen* case), at 357; the *Fullriede* case, at 549; *Eichmann (Appeal)* at 318; *Götzfrid*, at 68–70; *Zühlke* (134–5); *Finta*, at 837.

22 For these criteria see *Erdemović*, Dissenting Opinion of Judge Cassese, §§14–16.

Another case where the defence of necessity was upheld is *Flick and others*. The question was whether some defendants (Steinbrinck, Burkart, Kaletsch, and Terberger), managers of various companies belonging to the 'Flick Konzern' were guilty of having employed conscripted foreign workers, concentration camp inmates, or prisoners of war allocated to them through the slave-labour programme of the German Government. The defendants claimed that they had done so 'under the circumstances of compulsion under which such employment came about'. The US Military Tribunal upheld the plea. It noted that the defendants lived 'in a reign of terror'. 'The Reich, through its hordes of enforcement officials and secret police, was always "present", ready to go into instant action and to mete out savage and immediate punishment against anyone doing anything that could be construed as obstructing or hindering the carrying out of governmental regulations or decrees.' The Tribunal therefore found that the defendants had acted 'under clear and present danger' and acquitted them (at 1199–202). In contrast, the Tribunal rejected the plea of necessity urged by two other defendants (Flick and Weiss), for they had taken steps not initiated in governmental circles but in the plant management; they therefore had acted not as a result of compulsion or fear 'but admittedly for the purpose of keeping the plant as near capacity production as possible' (at 1202).

Necessity was also accepted as a defence in *Veit Harlan*. In 1950 the Court of Assizes (*Schwurgericht*) of Hamburg found that the accused, the film director who in 1940, at the request and instigation of Goebbels, and under his constant control, had directed the infamous film *Jud Süss* (The Jew Süss) had indisputably perpetrated a crime against humanity pursuant to Control Council Law no. 10: both the objective and subjective elements of such a crime were present (at 65–8). Indeed, by making the film, which had been viewed by 16 million Germans (at 9), he had significantly contributed to the persecution of Jews. Nevertheless he was not guilty, for he had acted under necessity (*Notstand*). The Court showed that the accused director had produced the film on the direct orders of Goebbels. The accused could not have refused to obey such orders, for such a refusal 'since the beginning of the war would have been regarded as refusal to execute a military order', and would have been punishable 'with the most severe penalties and even the death sentence'. Hence, according to the Court, 'the possibility of an open refusal was a priori ruled out' (at 69). In addition, the Court noted that:

> a great number of distinguished persons enjoying wide consideration were removed from their influential positions, taken to concentration camps, pushed to commit suicide or executed, on many occasions without even the outward appearance of legal process. All these facts make it clear that Goebbels, like the other nazi leaders, did not shy away from any violent action in order to put into effect his purposes and intentions. (At 69–70.)

The Court went on to show that the production of propaganda films had become of crucial importance to Goebbels' policy of anti-Semitic persecution, and for that purpose he closely monitored and kept an eye on the production of the film at issue. The Court concluded that, considering all these circumstances, it was not to be ruled out that, in case of an open or 'hidden' refusal, there could arise a 'danger for the body and life' of the film director (at 70). The Court then examined if the accused could have avoided executing Goebbels' order to produce the film by, for example, pretending to be taken ill, or escaping abroad, and concluded that none of these means would have profited him (at 71–84). In sum, the accused had executed Goebbels' order 'under threat of danger to body and life' and was therefore not culpable.[23]

13.2.3 UNAVAILABILITY OF NECESSITY TO MEMBERS OF SPECIAL UNITS BENT ON DISREGARDING LAW

It is worth emphasizing the fourth requirement mentioned above, in order to highlight its particular relevance to war-like situations. According to case law, which is consonant with general principles of international criminal law, necessity cannot excuse from criminal responsibility a person who *freely and knowingly* chooses to become a member of a unit, organisation, or group institutionally intent upon actions contrary to international humanitarian law.[24] In other words, if a person has voluntarily

[23] When appraising these cases, one should always consider them against their historical background. As far as German cases relating to the Second World War are concerned, one should be mindful of the fact that, according to academic research (carried out among other things by perusing the investigative or judicial documentation available at Ludwigsburg), in almost no cases where subordinates refused to carry out illegal orders did the superior authorities take punitive measures. See in particular H. Jäger, *Verbrechen unter totalitärer Herrschaft—Studien zur nationalsozialistichen Gewaltkriminalität* (Frankfurt: Suhrkamp, 1982), 83–160; D. Goldhagen, 'The "Cowardly" Executioner: On Disobedience in the SS', 19 *Patterns of Prejudice* (1985), 19–32; D. H. Kitterman, 'Those Who Said "No!": Germans Who Refused to Execute Civilians during World War II', in 11 *German Studies Review* (1988), 241–54. See also A. Rückerl, *The Investigation of Nazi Crimes 1945–1978—A Documentation* (Heidelberg, Karlsruhe: C. F. Müller, 1979), at 80–4. It is apparent from these studies that most cases of refusal to obey unlawful orders did not result in any negative consequence for the subordinate but in some cases refusal resulted in lack of promotion or demotion. It would seem that there were no cases where, following a refusal, the subordinate suffered loss of life or limb (see Jäger, op. cit., 158–60; Kitterman, op. cit., 251–2).

[24] In addition to *Einsatzgruppen* (at 91) and *Erhard Milch* (at 40), both decided by US courts sitting at Nürnberg, some cases brought after the Second World War before German courts are particularly significant in this respect, for those courts also acted on the strength of Control Council Law no. 10. Thus, in *T. and K.*, a case decided by the German Supreme Court in the British Zone, the two accused had been members of the National-Socialist party, one being Colonel (*Standartenführer*) of the SA, the other a committee member of the NSDAP (Nazi party). They had participated in attacks on synagogues on 10 Nov. 1938 (*Kristallnacht*) and in arson. They claimed that they acted upon superior orders and in addition under duress (*Notstand*). The Court dismissed the claim, pointing out that: 'As an old member of the [National-Socialist] Party T. knew the programme and the fighting methods of NSDAP. If he nevertheless made himself available as official Standartenführer, he had to count from the start that he would be ordered to commit such crimes. Nor, in this condition of necessity for which he himself was to blame, could he have benefited from a possible misapprehension of the circumstances that could have misled him as to the condition of necessity or compulsion' (at 200–1). See also the decision of 17 Feb. 1949 of the *Oberlandesgericht* of Freiburg im Breisgau in the *Gestapo informer* case, at 200–3 as well as the decision of 5 Sept. 1950 by the German Supreme Court in the British Occupied Zone in *H. and others* (at 129–30).

A number of cases brought before the Italian Court of Cassation can also be mentioned: see, e.g., the decision of 24 Sept. 1945 in *Spadini* (at 354), the decision of 10 May 1947 in *Toller* (at 920), the decision of 24 Feb. 1950 in *Fumi* (at 380). The same position was taken by the Court of Appeal of Versailles in *Touvier* (decision of 2 June 1993, at 341).

joined a military or paramilitary unit whose main purpose is to engage in criminal action, he is not allowed to plead in defence to the crimes perpetrated in that capacity that he acted under threat to his life or limb. Indeed, when he chose to acquire membership in that unit he knew or should have known that its primary purpose was to perpetrate criminal offences and consequently any member refusing to join in those offences would be under strong pressure or irresistible threats.[25]

13.2.4 DURESS AND SUPERIOR ORDER

In the case law, duress is commonly raised in conjunction with superior orders. However there is no necessary connection between the two. Superior orders may be issued without being accompanied by *any* threats to life or limb. In these circumstances, if the superior order involves the commission of an international crime (or, under the different heading referred to above, is manifestly illegal under international law), the subordinate is under a duty to refuse to obey the order. If, following such a refusal, the order is reiterated under a threat to life or limb, then the defence of duress may be raised, and the superior orders lose any legal relevance. Equally, duress may be raised independently of superior orders, for example, where the threat issues from a fellow serviceman, or even a subordinate. In evaluating the factual circumstances that may be relevant to duress, according to a trend discernible in the case law there may arise the need to distinguish between the various ranks of the military or civilian hierarchy. Clearly, the lower the rank of the recipient of an order accompanied by duress, the less likely it is that he enjoyed any real moral choice.

13.2.5 MAY DURESS BE A DEFENCE TO KILLING?

In some cases under the influence of English criminal law, courts have set forth the proposition that for crimes involving killing duress cannot be admitted as a defence, but may only be urged in mitigation. That this defence is not available if the offence charged is murder is a principle that goes back to Blackstone[26] (who however only adumbrated it) and was eloquently justified by the English criminal lawyer J. F. Stephen in 1883.[27] In short, this principle is grounded on the notion that human life is such a

[25] Interestingly, in the *Sipo–Brussels* case the Brussels Court Martial took into account voluntary participation in a criminal organization, not from the viewpoint of duress, but with regard to the relevance of superior orders. In restating a decision in previous cases, it held that 'superior orders cannot be considered to provide extenuating circumstances, at least in the case where the accused has voluntarily and consciously joined such an organization [i.e., a criminal organization such as the Gestapo or the SD]' (at 1519). On superior orders given within a 'criminal organization' see also *Sch. O.* at 306–7.

[26] *Commentaries*, Book IV, at 30.

[27] J. F. Stephen, *History of the Criminal Law of England* (1883), ii (New York: B. Franklin, 1964), at 107–9. He wrote among other things the following: 'It is of course a misfortune for a man that he be placed between two fires but it would be a much greater misfortune for society at large if criminals confer immunity upon their agents by threatening them with death or violence if they refuse to execute their commands. If immunity could be so secured a wide door would be open to collusion and encouragement would be given to malefactors secret or otherwise . . . these reasons lead me to think that compulsion by threats ought in no case whatever be admitted as an excuse for crime though it may and ought to operate in mitigation of punishment in most, though not all, cases' (at 108–9).

sacred asset that its taking may never be justified, not even when a person is under a very serious threat to his own life. For the sake of safeguarding the value of human life, English law therefore prefers to consider guilty a person acting under duress, although it then attenuates the harshness of this approach by considering duress a mitigating circumstance and consequently meting out a very lenient sentence, as occurred in the celebrated case of *Dudley* v. *Stephens* (also called the *Mignonette* case),[28] where the court also set out the basic rationale for this attitude.[29] This balancing of values has been called 'moralistic' and 'hypocritical'[30] and assailed for absurdly requiring men to act as heroes ('To require a person to die so that another (though innocent) man may be saved will be to invoke in him a standard of heroism that can hardly be expected', has written a distinguished Nigerian criminal lawyer).[31] In case of killing, a choice between the two possible options (duress as a defence or as an extenuating circumstance) may of course only be based on policy considerations.

Let us consider how courts had dealt with this delicate matter when pronouncing upon *international* crimes, and whether a correct solution can be reached by way of interpretation of existing law.

An important case is *Hölzer and others*, decided on 6 April 1946 by a Canadian Military Court sitting at Aurich, Germany, and applying Canadian law. In March 1945 three Canadian airmen abandoned their disabled aircraft near Opladen, in Germany, and were captured by German soldiers. One of the Canadians, who was wounded, was subsequently killed by the three German accused. The accused raised the defence of

28 Three seamen and a cabin boy of seventeen or eighteen had been cast away in a storm on the high seas, and compelled to put into an open boat that soon went drifting on the ocean; after eighteen days, being without food and water, two of the seamen, namely Dudley and Stephens, decided to kill the boy and eat him, while the third dissented; one of the two then killed the boy, and they, with the third seaman, fed on his flesh for four days. On the fourth day a passing vessel picked up the boat, and the men were rescued, still alive but 'in the lowest state of prostration'. They were carried to a British port and committed for trial. The Court held that the defendants were guilty of murder and sentenced them to death. However, the Crown afterwards commuted the sentence to six months' imprisonment (at 608).

29 The Court among other things stated that 'Though law and morality are not the same, and many things may be immoral which are not necessarily illegal, yet the absolute divorce of law from morality would be of fatal consequence; and such divorce would follow if the temptation to murder in this case were to be held by law an absolute defence of it. It is not so. To preserve one's life is generally speaking a duty, but it may be the plainest and the highest duty to sacrifice it . . . The duty, in case of shipwreck, of a captain to his crew, of the crew to the passengers, of soldiers to women and children . . .; these duties impose on men the moral necessity, not of the preservation, but of the sacrifice of their lives for others, from which in no country, least of all, it is to be hoped, in England, will men ever shrink, as indeed they have not shrunk. It is not correct, therefore, to say that there is any absolute or unqualified necessity to preserve one's life' (at 607).

30 See for instance H. L. Packer, *The Limits of Criminal Sanction* (Stanford, CA.: Stanford University Press, 1968), at 118.

31 K. S. Chkkol, *The Law of Crimes in Nigeria* (Zaria: Kola, 1989), at 152. And see more generally the sharp reflections set out at 150–8. This author also notes the following: 'True, the notion of sacrifice of one's own life has in fact some religious foundations when it is remembered that according to Christian theology it was the sacrifice made by Jesus of his own life that has redeemed mankind so that as the Bible tells us "whoever believeth in him shall not perish but have everlasting life". However, no matter how grandiose the notions of sacrifice or heroism may sound it must be realized that an average man or woman can hardly be expected to be overwhelmed by them when faced with the threat of death' (at 152).

superior orders, as well as that of duress, claiming that they had been compelled at gunpoint by Lieutenant Schaefer (not among the accused) to kill the wounded airman. Hölzer's defence counsel insisted on this plea of duress, both in his Opening Address and in his Closing Address. He relied generally on international law, but on the issue of duress he quoted German law and in particular Articles 52 and 54 of the German Criminal Code. Also the defence counsel for the other two accused insisted on this plea. The plea was however assailed by the prosecutor in his Closing Address: citing English law he excluded duress as a defence in the case of the taking of innocent lives. In stating the law to the members of the court, the Judge Advocate took the same position as the prosecutor and he too relied on English law. The court sentenced both Hölzer and another accused (Weigel) to death, while it sentenced the third accused (Ossenbach) to 15 years' imprisonment (vol. 1, at 289–99, 304, 312, 315, 338, 345–6; vol. II, 1–4).

In sum, in this case the prosecutor and the Judge Advocate clearly upheld—unquestionably by way of *ratio decidendi*—the traditional common law position. However, the weight of this decision is belittled by the fact that in his summing up the Judge Advocate explicitly stated that the court should apply the Canadian War Crimes Regulations and Canadian law, *not* international law.

The majority of the ICTY Appeals Chamber took a similar stand in *Erdemović*, in its judgment of 7 October 1997 (Judges A. Cassese and Sir Ninian Stephen dissenting).[32]

Other cases support instead the proposition that duress may be a defence even where the underlying offence involves the killing of innocents. *Ohlendorf and others* (*Einsatzgruppen* case), decided by the United States Military Tribunal II sitting at Nürnberg, deserves to be mentioned (56–9, 61–82, 462–3, 471–2, 480–1). Indeed, this Tribunal acted under Control Council Law no. 10, and therefore its decisions are more indicative of international law than the ones by national courts acting under national legislation.

The defence counsel for Ohlendorf, the lead defendant, submitted in his opening statement that the question of duress (or necessity, as he termed it) was to be looked at on the basis of three legal systems: United States law (as the law of the State administering justice in the case at issue), German law (as the law of the defendant), and Soviet law (as the law of the place where the alleged crimes had been committed). He

[32] In July 1995 the accused, a member of a Bosnian Serb military unit, had participated in the shooting and killing of many unarmed Bosnian Muslims as a member of an execution squad. Before the ICTY he pleaded guilty and claimed that he had refused to shoot at the civilians, because he felt sorry for them, but his commander had told him 'If you are sorry for them, stand up, line up with them and we will kill you too'.

The Appeals Chamber's majority held that 'duress does not afford a complete defence to a soldier charged with crimes against humanity and/or a war crime involving the killing of innocent human beings' (§19). The same majority consequently held that in such cases duress could only be used in mitigation of punishment.

The view propounded in *Hölzer and others* and taken up in *Erdemović* by the majority of the ICTY Appeals Chamber had already been upheld in the provisions of two military manuals. One is the British Military Manual, para. 629 of which provides: 'No criminal responsibility is incurred by a person for an act performed by him under an immediate and well-grounded fear for his own life, provided that the act does not involve the taking of innocent life. Otherwise threats afford no defence to a person accused of a war crime but may be considered in mitigation of sentence'. The other is the United States Manual for Courts Martial, of 1984, whereby duress is a defence 'to any offence except killing an innocent person'.

then expounded the position under the three legal systems and concluded that necessity was applicable. The Military Tribunal, in dealing with the plea of duress, cited both Soviet law and German law, and held that duress could be urged as a defence even in cases of unlawful killing, provided certain requirements were met. It is worth quoting the most important passage of the judgment:

> [I]t is stated that in military law even if the subordinate realizes that the act he is called upon to perform is a crime, he may not refuse its execution without incurring serious consequences, and that this, therefore, constitutes duress. Let it be said at once that there is no law which requires that an innocent man must forfeit his life or suffer serious harm in order to avoid committing a crime which he condemns. The threat, however, must be imminent, real and inevitable. No court will punish a man who, with a loaded pistol at his head, is compelled to pull a lethal lever. Nor need the peril be that imminent in order to escape punishment. But were any of the defendants coerced into killing Jews under the threat to be killed themselves if they failed in their homicidal mission? The test to be applied is whether the subordinate acted under coercion or whether he himself approved of the principle involved in the order. (At 480.)

In the event, the defence of duress was rejected and all the accused but one were convicted.

Other cases, and in particular *Gustav Alfred Jepsen and others*, may be cited in support of the proposition that duress may excuse the taking of human life.[33]

[33] *Gustav Alfred Jepsen and others* related to the killing of six internees by Jepsen, a Dane who worked as a guard in a German concentration camp. In April 1945, as the Allied troops were approaching, the German authorities ordered that the internees be transferred to another camp, those who were fit on foot, those who were ill by train. Jepsen was one of the guards escorting the train. During the transfer there were various air raids and a large number of internees died, many of illnesses or starvation. At one point it was ordered that 52 internees still alive should be shot 'to avoid typhus'. Jepsen participated in the shooting by killing six internees. Although in his deposition made under oath he had not mentioned duress, during the trial proceedings, and then before sentencing, he claimed that the German *Obermaat* Engelmann who had given the order to kill all the internees, had compelled him at gunpoint to participate in shooting the internees. His defence counsel pleaded among other things the state of necessity (*Notstand*) as provided for in Section 54 of the German Criminal Code. The Judge Advocate, in his summing up, stated that duress could be invoked in the case, provided the requisite conditions were met. The court found Jepsen guilty but, as the Judge Advocate put it, since there was 'an element of doubt as to whether or not [he] acted under some degree of compulsion', he was sentenced to life imprisonment rather than to death (at 222–4, 233–51, 357–9, 363).

Also some judgments of German and Italian courts are particularly important (they are quoted in Judge Cassese's Dissenting Opinion in *Erdemović*). In many of them the plea of duress was not upheld across the board, as it were, but only with regard to some of the defendants, while it was rejected with respect to other defendants, i.e., it was applied with discrimination. It must be noted that almost all of these cases concern execution squads or execution groups and duress was upheld with regard to minor executants, whereas it was ruled out with respect to those who had issued orders or to senior officials who, following orders from the highest authorities, had in their turn ordered the execution of innocent persons.

Finally, one should mention other cases, where the court conceded the possibility of raising duress as a defence to a charge of killing innocent people, although the defence failed *on the facts*. See for instance *Llandovery Castle* by the German Supreme Court of Leipzig, *Kotälla* by a Dutch court, *Eichmann* by an Israeli court, *Müller and others* brought first before the Belgian Military Court of Brussels and then the Belgian Court of Cassation, *Touvier* and *Papon*, by French courts, *Priebke*, by an Italian court, *Retzlaff and others* by a Soviet court, as well as a string of German cases and a case recently dealt with by a Military Court of Belgrade. For references to these cases see Judge Cassese's Dissenting Opinion, §§31–4.

In spite of this contradictory case law, it would seem that, generally speaking, the customary rule of international law on duress does not exclude the applicability of this defence to war crimes and crimes against humanity whose underlying offence is murder or unlawful killing. However, as the right to life is the most fundamental human right, the rule demands that the general requirements for duress be applied particularly strictly in the case of killing of innocent persons. The following propositions would seem to commend themselves.

First, it is extremely difficult to meet the requirements for duress where the offence involves killing of innocent human beings. Indeed, courts have rarely allowed the defence to succeed in those cases even where they have in principle admitted the applicability of this defence. But for the two cases cited above, plus some Italian and German decisions,[34] which stand out as exceptional, the only cases where national courts have upheld the plea in relation to violations of international humanitarian law relate to offences other than killing. This bears out the strong reluctance of national courts to make duress available for offences involving killing. The reason for this restrictive approach no doubt has its roots in the fundamental importance of human life to law and society. As the Court of Assize of Arnsberg (Germany) rightly pointed out in *Wetzling and others* (at 623), the right to life is one of the most fundamental and precious human rights, and *any legal system* is keen to safeguard it at the utmost. It follows that any legal excusing of attacks on this right must be very strictly construed and only exceptionally admitted.

Secondly, it is relevant to examine whether a crime would have been committed *in any case* by a person other than the one acting under duress, in which case duress seems admissible as a defence. In fact, where the accused has been charged with *participation* in a collective killing which would have proceeded irrespective of whether the accused was a participant, the defence has in principle been *allowed.* Thus the case law seems to make an exception for those instances where—on the facts—it is highly probable, if not certain, that if the person acting under duress had refused to commit the crime, the crime would in any event have been carried out by persons other than the accused. The best example is where an execution squad has been assembled to kill the victims, and the accused participates, in some form, in the execution squad, either as an active member or as an organizer, albeit only under the threat of death. In this case, if an individual member of the execution squad first *refuses to obey* but has then to comply with the order as a result of duress, he may be excused: indeed, whether or not he is killed or instead takes part in the execution, the civilians, prisoners of war, etc., *would be shot anyway.* Were he to comply with his legal duty not to shoot innocent persons, he would forfeit his life *for no benefit to anyone and no effect whatsoever* apart from setting a heroic example for mankind (which the law cannot demand him to set). His sacrifice of his own life would be to no avail.

[34] For detailed references to these cases see Judge Cassese's Separate and Dissenting Opinion in *Erdemović (appeal)*, §§35–9.

13.2.6 THE ICC STATUTE

Article 31(1)(d) rightly lumps necessity and duress together as grounds for excluding criminal responsibility. They are defined as follows:

The conduct which is alleged to constitute a crime within the jurisdiction of the Court has been caused by duress resulting from the threat of imminent death or of continuing or imminent serious bodily harm against that person or another person, and the person acts necessarily and reasonably to avoid this threat, provided that the person does not intend to cause a greater harm than the one sought to be avoided. Such a threat may either be (i) made by another person; or (ii) constituted by other circumstances beyond that person's control.

It would seem that to a very large extent this provision codifies customary international law as interpreted above, in that, among other things, it *does not exclude in principle* the plea of duress in the event of a person under duress killing another person.

13.3 MISTAKE OF FACT

13.3.1 GENERAL

This excuse, as a defence to a criminal charge, may be invoked when, although there is *actus reus*, that is conduct contrary to international criminal law, the requisite *mens rea* is lacking because *the person mistakenly was of the honest and reasonable belief that there existed factual circumstances making the conduct lawful* (see Article 32(1) of the ICC Statute).[35]

The erroneous belief must thus be honest and reasonable: the mistake about factual circumstances must be based on reasonable grounds or in other words not be specious or far-fetched. More specifically, the mistake must not result from negligence. This proposition is grounded on the general spirit of international criminal law, directed to ban as much as possible behaviour contrary to international rules protecting human values, as well as the general principle of interpretation whereby rules setting forth exceptions to general prohibitions must be strictly construed.

The proposition is consonant with the general approach to the issue of mistake of fact taken in most national legal systems (for instance, in France and the UK). It is also supported by case law on international crimes. The plea was urged by the defence, and acted upon by the court in *Michael A. Schwarz*, a case brought before a US Court Martial (judgment of 21 June 1970, at 171–83). The accused, a member of a five-man night patrol called 'killer team', had gone out on 19 February 1970 to search out, locate, and kill enemy Viet Cong in South Vietnam. They had soon entered a small hamlet, Son Thang, where there were three huts, occupied by civilian women and

[35] 'A mistake of fact shall be a ground for excluding criminal responsibility only if it negates the mental element required by the crime.'

children. The team killed 16 civilians. When they had surrounded the first hut, four women had come out and lined up on the patio in front of it. The accused had gone inside the empty hut to search it out. While inside he had heard the team leader yell outside 'Shoot them, shoot them all, kill them'. He had jumped up and run out, and participated in killing the four women. His defence counsel argued that Schwarz had mistakenly believed that they were under attack because the people standing on the patio were performing hostile acts. In his instruction to the jury the Military Judge illustrated the scope of mistake of fact; he told the jury that if they found that the accused mistakenly, but reasonably, believed that he was returning fire, and shot the victims only by accident, they must acquit. The Military Judge stated the following:

> The court is advised that if the accused was of the honest belief that he and his team-mates were being attacked by enemy forces he cannot be found guilty of any offence charged or the lesser included offences thereto. Such belief no matter how unreasonable will exonerate the accused. In determining whether the accused was of the belief that enemy forces were attacking him and his team-mates you should consider the accused's age, education, military training, and combat experience together with all the other evidence bearing upon this issue. The burden is upon the prosecution to establish the accused's guilt of each offence charged by legal and competent evidence beyond a reasonable doubt. The accused committed no crime unless he knew that the enemy forces were not attacking him. (Reported in *Michael A. Schwarz, Appeal*, at 862–3.)

The Court Martial, while finding the accused guilty of the murder of the other twelve civilians, found him not guilty of the four homicides at the first hut, accepting that he had been inside when the firing had begun. On appeal, defence counsel argued that the aforementioned instructions unduly restricted the members of the court, for they limited the defence to the case where the accused believed that he was under enemy attack, without extending it to the case where he believed that the 'killer team' was attacking the enemy. The Court of Military Review rejected the argument, ruling that:

> In the setting of this case we are certain that the instructions conveyed to the court the direction that the accused must be acquitted unless they found beyond a reasonable doubt that he did not honestly believe that he was in immediate contact with the enemy either offensively or defensively. (At 862–3.)

A US Court Martial rejected the plea of mistake of fact in *William L. Calley*. Lieutenant Calley, accused of summarily killing a number of defenceless civilians detained by US troops in a Vietnamese village, claimed among other things that he genuinely thought that the villagers had no right to live because they were enemy, and thus was devoid of the requisite *mens rea*, namely 'malice' because he was not conscious of the criminal quality of his acts. The US Army Court of Military Review dismissed the argument as follows:

> To the extent this state of mind reflects a mistake of fact, the governing principle is: to be exculpatory, the mistaken belief must be of such a nature that the conduct would have been lawful had the facts actually been as they were believed to be . . . An enemy in custody may not be executed summarily. (At 1180.)

13.3.2 MISTAKE OF FACT AND SUPERIOR ORDER

Mistake of fact may in particular be used in defence when executing an unlawful order, where the accused may prove that *he was not aware that the order was unlawful in point of fact.*

In many cases the accused raised this defence claiming that he had executed enemy persons because he had reasonably believed that the victims had been properly tried and sentenced to death, whereas it had then turned out that this was not the case. In a number of cases courts admitted the defence, while however finding that it was untenable on the facts.

In the *Almelo* case, in March 1945, four German members of a special security detachment had arrested a British pilot in the Dutch village of Almelo. The pilot, after bailing out of a burning Lancaster, was hiding in a Dutch house in civilian clothes, together with a Dutch civilian, who was hiding from the Germans to avoid compulsory labour service in Germany. The German officer in charge of the detachment (not on trial) had told the four accused that the British officer had been sentenced to death and was to be executed, together with the Dutchman. The two were then shot dead. Defence counsel argued that, so far as the accused knew, it was quite possible that the two victims were in fact liable to be shot. The Judge Advocate stated that if the Court found that the accused honestly believed, or that *a reasonable man might have believed*, that the British officer had been tried according to the law, and that they were carrying out a lawful execution, they must acquit the accused. The Court found however that the accused were guilty (at 41 and 45).[36]

The Norwegian Supreme Court upheld the defence in *Hans*, quashing a contrary decision of the Court of Appeal. The accused, an officer of the German Security Police, had been charged with executing without trial Norwegian nationals during the belligerent occupation of Norway by Germany. He had claimed that the execution took place on the orders of his superior, who had acted pursuant to a secret decree

[36] In *Stalag Luft III*, tried by a British Court Martial in 1947, the accused were charged with killing some fifty British officers who had escaped in March 1944 from a German internment camp (Stalag Luft III). Some of the accused pleaded that they had shot the British officers upon superior orders and without knowing that they were prisoners of war on the run, in the belief that they were liable to punishment and were to be lawfully executed. Thus, in the case of the accused Jacobs, he claimed that he had been told that the British officers were 'parachute sabotage agents' who had been sentenced to death but had then escaped and killed two German officials during the break-out. The Judge Advocate admitted that this defence was based on mistake of fact and regarded it as admissible if the facts alleged by the accused were proved (at 15–16). In the case of the accused Preiss, his plea, regarded as admissible by the Judge Advocate, was that 'he thought this was a legal execution and . . . he did not know for certain that Cochran [the British prisoner he shot dead] was actually an escaped prisoner-of-war' (at 23). Similarly, in the case of the accused Schulz, according to the Judge Advocate his defence was that 'he really believed that this was a legal shooting which was being carried out in secret for some special purpose and that it was the shooting of two spies, although he knew they might have been officers, on the orders of some high authority' (at 27).

The Italian High Military Tribunal in *Wagener and others* admitted that this defence may be invoked and found valid on its merits; it held that 'a military, notwithstanding the manifest criminal nature of an order, may be relieved of responsibility when he makes a culpable mistake of fact' (in the case at issue the Tribunal found however that the defence was not available to the accused) (at 763–4). See also *Buck and others* (at 39–44).

issued by Hitler in June or July 1944 abolishing German tribunals in occupied territories and vesting in the German secret police the authority to carry out executions for offences considered to be of a political character. The Court of Appeal of Eidsivating (Norway) found the accused guilty, for he had not taken steps to establish the legality of the execution orders. However, on appeal the Supreme Court of Norway quashed the decision, among other things because 'it was not sufficient to support a conviction for wilful murder that the accused *ought to have known* the circumstances which made his act unlawful' (at 306) and in addition the decision of the Court of Appeal 'did not disclose sufficiently clearly whether the accused had been aware of the unlawfulness of his acts, a fact which the Court seemed to have taken for granted' (at 306).[37]

In many cases German courts upheld the defence under discussion. For instance, in a case brought before a German court after the Second World War, *Wülfing and K.*, the two accused were respectively an officer and a sergeant of the German army, serving on the army's Special Services (*Truppensonderdienst*). They were accused of a crime against humanity: on 13 April 1945, while the American troops were approaching the German town where they were stationed, they had killed a German civilian opposed to national socialism, whom they considered guilty of instigation to desertion. Wülfing, the officer, had ordered the other accused (K.) and a non-commissioned officer to execute the German civilian; the officer then finished him off with his pistol. In a decision of 4 August 1947 the District Court of Hagen, acting by virtue of Control Council Law no. 10, found that the offence, 'murder' (*Mord*), was a crime against humanity and therefore sentenced Wülfing to life imprisonment (at 613–21). In contrast it found that K., who in any case might have been held responsible for 'intentional killing' (*Totschlag*) only, was in fact not guilty because he had acted under mistake: he had believed that he was participating in the execution of a death sentence passed by a regular court (the Court held in addition that he had acted under duress (*Notstand*) for he had feared that, if he did not carry out the order to shoot, he himself would be killed by the officer who was standing by, pistol in his hand) (at 618–20).

Similarly, in a decision of 12 December 1950, the German Federal Court of Justice (*Bundesgerichtshof*) upheld this excuse in the *Polish prisoner of war* case. On 10 October 1940 the accused, the commander of a detachment of border guards also entrusted with assignments by the Gestapo, on the orders of the Gestapo officer superior to him had commanded the execution squad that had carried out a death sentence by hanging of K., a Polish prisoner of war. The Court of Assize (*Schwurgericht*) of Flensburg acquitted the accused. It found that he lacked the intent or negligence required for the charge of 'intentional killing'. The Federal Court of Justice dismissed the Prosecutor's appeal and upheld the acquittal. It noted that it was not necessary to establish whether or not awareness of the unlawful character of his action

[37] Interestingly, in another case, *Flesch*, both the Court of Appeal of Frostating (Norway) and the Supreme Court of Norway convicted an officer of the German Security Police because he knew that the executed persons (Norwegian nationals and Russian prisoners of war) had not been sentenced to death by a court (at 307).

was part of the *mens rea*, and more specifically was part of the intent required for the crime. What mattered was:

whether the lack of awareness of unlawfulness was based on a mistake of fact or on a non-criminal mistake of law (*ausserstrafrechtliches Rechtsirrtum*). Indeed, in its case law the Imperial Supreme Court (*Reichsgericht*) had treated non-criminal mistakes of law in the same manner as it did mistakes of fact, that is, it denied intent if it were established that the perpetrator, as a result of a non-criminal mistake of law, was not aware of the unlawfulness of his act. (At 234.)

According to the Federal Court, this proposition applied to the case at issue. The Court noted that:

at the time of the offence the accused knew that offices of the Gestapo imposed and executed penalties against nationals of eastern peoples. At the time of the offence he also assumed that K. had been sentenced to death in this manner. As the Court of assize explicitly stated, 'the accused had no doubt that the judgment had been issued by the competent and appropriate authority in accordance with properly conducted proceedings and was legally binding and final'. The accused had based his conviction on a telex he had received in October 1944 from the Regional office (*Gau*) of the Gestapo. The telex was signed by the head of the office, a senior governmental official (*Regierungsrat*) and stated more or less that the Polish K. had been sentenced to death for a violation of the 'Order for the Protection of Law Enforcement Agents' and that the main office of the Reich Security Service had ordered that the execution should take place in the district where the offence had been committed. Such an Order did not in fact exist; but that is immaterial. The crucial fact is that the accused . . . had believed in some type of 'judgment' based on legal requirements (even if not rendered by a regular court). Furthermore, he knew that fully qualified lawyers were employed at the higher office of the Gestapo. In a prior conversation in the Gestapo office it had been explicitly pointed out that the conviction of foreigners by the Gestapo occurred with the participation of fully qualified lawyers in something akin to 'Chamber of Judges'. (At 234.)[38]

[38] The Federal Court also dismissed the Prosecution's ground of appeal against the lower court's finding that the accused had not acted 'negligently in either a factual or legal sense' in his assumption that the Pole had been legally sentenced to death and that the task of executing the sentence, entrusted upon him, was lawful. The Federal Court concluded that the accused was not guilty, because he lacked either intent (*Vorsatz*) or negligence (*Fahrlässigkeit*). It stated that the international law question of whether or not the legal Regulations issued by the Nazi authorities (on the punishment of Polish war prisoners by Gestapo officers, outside of any regular trial proceedings) were valid, could be left undecided. In any case, at least at the time of the offence, the legal issue was still dubious, as was held by a United States Military Tribunal at Nuremberg in the *Wilhelm von Leeb and others* case (see *Law Reports of Trials of War Criminals* 1949, vol. 12, at 86, where a contrary conclusion is reached). Rather, what really mattered was to establish whether the accused, 'based on his personal circumstances, could and should have recognized the possible legal invalidity' of those Regulations.

The Court of Assize had answered this question in the negative, after admitting the illegality of those Regulations. It had pointed out that at the time of the offence one could not expect that the accused, 'based on his personal circumstances' 'could recognize that possibly those Regulations were contrary to international law and consequently the death sentence issued by the Gestapo, of whose execution he had been charged, was legally invalid'. This was all the more true because the accused, based on the record of police interrogation of the Pole, 'was convinced and could be convinced that the Pole had attacked the Police Superintendent Sch. and seized him by the neck, thereby committing a criminal offence punishable by death. Although the

13.4 MISTAKE OF LAW

13.4.1 GENERAL

Like most national legal systems, international law does not consider ignorance of law as a ground for excluding criminal responsibility. Article 32(1) first sentence of the ICC Statute ('A mistake of law as to whether a particular type of conduct is a crime within the jurisdiction of the court shall not be a ground for excluding criminal responsibility') may be held to codify existing customary law.

The rationale behind the principle *ignorantia legis non excusat* (ignoring the law may not amount to a justification for the commission of a crime) is self-evident: everybody living in a State is bound to know the law; were one allowed to successfully plead that he committed a crime because he ignored that that conduct was prohibited, the road would be open to general non-compliance with the law. The foundations of society would be undermined. In addition, (i) if ignorance of law were admitted as a defence, the applicability of international criminal law would differ from person to person, depending on their degree of knowledge of law; (ii) the admission of such a defence would eventually constitute an incentive for persons to break the law, by simply proving that in fact they were not aware of the existence of a legal ban.

Nevertheless, there may be cases where a mistake of law may become relevant as an excuse. This defence may be invoked when one may prove that the offender, because of his ignorance of a legal element, did not possess the requisite mental element, that is intent, or recklessness, or knowledge, or culpable negligence. Also in this respect Article 32(2) of the ICC Statute may be regarded as codifying customary international law (it provides that 'A mistake of law may . . . be a ground for excluding criminal responsibility if it negates the mental element required for such a crime').

It is submitted that mistake of law may be pleaded as a valid excuse not when the offender was unaware of the unlawfulness of his conduct, but when: (i) he *had no knowledge of an essential element of law* referred to in the international prohibition of a certain conduct; (ii) this lack of knowledge *did not result from negligence*; (iii) consequently the person, when he took a certain action, *did not possess the requisite mens rea*.

accused may have been a particularly capable, knowledgeable and experienced official within the group of criminal investigators to which he had belonged for 24 years, nevertheless, according to the legally incontrovertible evidence presented to the Court of assize, he did not have the knowledge necessary for appraising these legal issues of public law and international law. There are no indications that, at the time of the offence, the accused had any reason to mistrust the academically trained head of the Gestapo office. Moreover, the accused had learned from experience prior to the offence that the administration of criminal justice against Poles had passed from the hands of the judiciary to the offices of the Gestapo and that, according to his observations, generally Public Prosecutors and ordinary courts had not opposed this development' (at 234–5). See also *Schzeiner Z.*, at 712–5.

13.4.2 LIMITATIONS OF THE PRINCIPLE *IGNORANTIA LEGIS NON EXCUSAT*

The principle at issue is predicated on a fundamental assumption: that the law is a body of rules which are fairly deep-rooted (in that the rules are consonant with the fundamental moral, or religious, values obtaining in society), and in addition are accessible and clear. Indeed, in those areas of international humanitarian law or criminal law where the rules are *clear, incontrovertible, and universally recognized*, one is barred from invoking the plea (or, if one puts forward the defence, the court must dismiss it out of hand).

Many cases support this proposition.[39] However, legal certainty and clarity are not commonly found in international criminal law. As was pointed out above (2.2), this body of law has grown gradually, in a somewhat haphazard manner, and largely consists of customary, that is, unwritten rules. Often some of these rules of customary nature are loose or ambiguous. In the case of treaty rules, frequently they are not couched in clear and exhaustive terms. In addition, State agents normally tend to behave in accordance with their own national law, ignoring the legal commands deriving from international law. National law implementing international rules may contain gaps, or be unclear or refrain from explicitly referring to international rules on points not covered by it. Case law has undoubtedly elucidated many obscure points, but is still far from clarifying all the main areas of that body of law. And it is indeed true what the Judge Advocate said in his summing up in *Peleus*, that is that

[39] In *Jung and Schumacher*, a case brought before a Canadian Military Court sitting at Aurich in Germany, the Judge Advocate, after discussing the legal position of the two defendants (one had ordered the other to execute a Canadian prisoner of war), noted: 'Both Jung and Schumacher have admitted that they knew the killing of a prisoner to be wrong. If I am wrong in this, the Court will correct me since they find the facts. In any event, ignorance of the law is no excuse' (at 221).

Similarly, in *Buhler*, the accused (Secretary of State and Deputy Governor General of that part of Poland occupied by German armed forces and known as the Government-General), charged with war crimes and crimes against humanity, had pleaded ignorance of international law; the Polish Supreme National Tribunal sitting in Cracow rejected the plea on the grounds that as a doctor of laws the accused must have possessed sufficient knowledge of the rights and duties of an Occupying Power and of the general principles of criminal law common to all civilized countries (at 682). In *Enkelstrohth* a Dutch Special Court at Arnhem held that the accused, a German police officer, must know that the shooting without previous trial even of a spy caught red-handed was contrary to the Hague Regulations, the more so because several German Ordinances promulgated in occupied Netherlands had enacted precise rules for the trial of saboteurs; according to the court the shooting in question was so clearly at variance with international law that even a police officer of inferior rank must have known that it was unlawful (at 685–6).

Similarly, in *William L. Calley* a US Court of Military Review held that the accused could not rely upon the defence of mistake of law for he had willingly summarily executed enemy civilians in custody. The Court stated the following:

'Mere absence of a sense of criminality is . . . not mitigating, for any contrary view would be an excrescent exception to the fundamental rule that ignorance of the very law violated is no defence to violating it. The maxim *ignorantia legis neminem excusat* applies to offences in which intent is an element . . . "It matters not whether appellant realized his conduct was unlawful. He knew exactly what he was doing; and what he did was a violation . . . [of a nature which had to be shown to be knowing and wilful]. He intended to do what he did, and that is sufficient' (*United States* v. *Gris*, at 864) (at 1180).

'no sailor and no soldier can carry with him a library of international law'.[40] As a *countervailing factor to these flaws of international criminal law*, courts therefore tend to attach to mistake of law *a greater weight than the one most national legal systems attribute to the same excuse.*

This point was well made in 1921 by the German Supreme Court in *Llandovery Castle.* After noting that the law of nations prohibits the killing of enemies counter to the conditions and limitations imposed by such law, the Court added:

The fact that his deed is a violation of international law must be well known to the doer, apart from acts of carelessness, in which negligent ignorance (*fahrlässige Unkentniss*) is a sufficient excuse. In examining the question of the existence of this knowledge, the ambiguity of many of the rules of international law as well as the actual circumstances of the case must be borne in mind, because in war time decisions of great importance have frequently to be made on very insufficient material. (At 2585.)

However, the Court went on to add that these considerations did not apply to the case at issue, because the relevant rule of international law (on the duty not to attack shipwrecked persons) was 'simple and universally known' (at 2585).

A generally balanced approach to the delicate legal issue can be found in the Dutch jurisprudence. Some cases need in particular to be mentioned. In *Wintgen* the Special Court of Cassation upheld the defence. The accused, a member of the German Security Police in occupied Netherlands, acting under orders set fire to a number of houses near Amsterdam as a reprisal for acts of sabotage perpetrated by unknown persons on a nearby railway line. The Court held that his action amounted to a war crime, for it was contrary to Article 50 of the Hague Regulations of 1907: 'No general penalty, pecuniary or otherwise, shall be inflicted upon the population on account of the acts of individuals for which they can not be regarded as jointly and severally responsible'. Nevertheless, the accused could not be punished, for he was not aware that his conduct constituted a war crime. According to the court, the force of the plea of mistake of law depended on the intellectual status and military position of the individual concerned and on the nature of the acts committed. The accused held a very subordinate rank in the Security Police and the destruction of property was generally held to be morally a less grave offence than, for example, the killing of innocent civilians or prisoners of war (at 484–6).

In *B.*, a case brought before a Dutch Court Martial, the Court again upheld the

40 Addressing the question of superior orders, he stated the following: 'It is quite obvious that no sailor and no soldier can carry with him a library of International law, or have immediate access to a professor in that subject who can tell him whether or not a particular command is a lawful one' (at 129). With specific regard to the case at bar (alleged killing of shipwrecked persons), the Judge Advocate note that 'If this were a case which involved the careful consideration of questions of International Law as to whether or not the command to fire at helpless survivors struggling in the water was lawful, you might well think it would not be fair to hold any of the subordinates accused in this case responsible for what they are alleged to have done; but it was not fairly obvious to you that if in fact the carrying out of Eck's command involved the killing of these helpless survivors, it was not a lawful command, and that it must have been obvious to the most rudimentary intelligence that it was not a lawful command, and that those who did that shooting are not to be excused for doing it upon the ground of superior orders?' (at 129).

defence. The accused B. was commander of a unit of the Dutch Resistance movement which had been granted the status of armed forces as part of the Royal Dutch Army, by a Dutch royal decree of 1944. In April 1945 the unit joined with a detachment of French parachutists who had landed in the Netherlands. Shortly thereafter the group took prisoner four Dutch Nazis, members of the NSB, in civilian clothes; they regarded those Dutch Nazis as *franc-tireurs* and traitors. One of them escaped. As Germans had surrounded the group, there was a danger that with the help of the escaped prisoner, the Germans would attack them. Under these circumstances the presence of the prisoners (meanwhile the group had captured other Dutch Nazis and released others) presented a serious danger to the unit. B. consulted with the French commander, who did not instruct him to kill the prisoners. However, 'he did gather from his behaviour, and also from that of the other French parachutists who were present, consisting of pointing to their Sten guns and drawing their hands across their throats, that, in his position, they would have proceeded to liquidate [the prisoners].' B. then ordered v. E. to kill the prisoners with the assistance of other members of the unit. When the case was brought before a Dutch Field Court Martial in 1950, the Prosecuting Officer, in his statement, argued that the conduct of the accused was unlawful. However, with regard to the accused's defence that he was mistaken as to the unlawfulness of the offence, he stated that:

> This is not in itself sufficient to relieve him of responsibility; for that the error must also have been pardonable. Only if there was no intent and no negligence as to the unlawfulness, is the accused not liable criminally.

In conclusion he asked the Court to find the accused guilty of being an accomplice to manslaughter and to sentence him to six months' imprisonment. The Court Martial agreed with the Prosecuting Officer that the action by B. was unlawful, for the prisoners' legal status was 'even inferior to that of *franc-tireurs*' but they could not be shot and killed immediately after being caught. However, the Court noted, the views among the Dutch unit were that the shooting and killing of the Dutch prisoners was not unlawful. This conclusion resulted from the instructions issued to those units. In addition, it was 'general knowledge that the broadcasts of Radio Orange from England were intended to give the impression that members of the N.S.B. were to be regarded as traitors and that it was unnecessary to show them any consideration, nor would they be shown any'. Consequently, according to the Court, 'the accused believed that he was entitled to act as he did and [his] intent was not therefore directed at the unlawfulness of his actions'. He 'had to take his decision without being able to consult a superior, he was placed in a position for which he was not trained and in circumstances in which it was practically impossible quietly to consider the relative merits of the various interests'. The Court concluded that the accused was 'mistaken as to the unlawfulness of his actions', hence was 'not criminally liable' and must be acquitted (at 516–25).[41]

[41] Another Dutch case where the court upheld the defence of excusable mistake of law is *Arlt*, decided on 7 November 1949 by the Special Court of Cassation. The accused, a German judge, had been charged with a war

In principle, and as can be inferred from these cases, a court should take into account various factors: (i) whether the international rule allegedly breached is universally admitted and recognized or is instead obscure or controversial; (ii) the intellectual status including the education, training, etc. of the person relying upon this defence; (iii) his position within the military hierarchy (clearly, a commander is expected and required to know the laws of war and more generally, international prohibitions, while a subordinate, particularly if he ranks very low, may not be required to possess such knowledge); (iv) the importance of the value protected by the rules allegedly breached (normally such values as life and dignity of a human being are universally protected, even under national criminal law, and one may therefore be more demanding with regard to such values).[42]

crime for having sentenced to death a Dutchman who had participated in a strike. The Court held that the establishment by the civil administration of the German Occupying Power of a summary Court Martial (*Polizeistandgericht*) was contrary to international law. Nevertheless, it stated that:

> With regard to the question of what penalty the accused deserves—perhaps even to the question of whether he deserves at all punishment on the ground of excusable error in law—the judgment should take into account the manner in which he, within the established framework, has discharged his judicial functions. (At 2.)

In contrast, in *Zimmermann* the same Court held that the defence under discussion was not available to the accused. Zimmermann, during the German occupation of the Netherlands, was a German official attached to the Dutch Provincial Labour Office of Meppel; in this capacity he was responsible for the deportation of many Dutch workers to Germany for forced labour there. His reliance, in the appeal to the Court, on 'his alleged ignorance of the criminal nature of the German deportation of Dutch men to slave labour to Germany' was of no avail. The Court stressed that 'similar practices applied by Germany on a much smaller scale in the First World War in Belgium and Northern France gave rise to general outrage and even prompted attempts at intervention on the part of neutral countries . . .; such responsible German officials as the then Head of the Political Department and Representative of the Foreign Office [*Auswärtiges Amt*] in Belgium, von der Laneken, and the then Governor-General, von Bissing, opposed this measure as a violation of international law or as a dangerous error . . . [hence] it must be regarded as a matter of general knowledge that public opinion condemned these practices' (at 30–2).

42 Other examples of cases where the excuse in question might be raised can be mentioned. For instance, the Occupying Power, while it normally may appropriate the produce of public immovable property (land and buildings) belonging to the occupied State, under Article 56 of the Hague Regulations may not appropriate (i) the produce of those immovable assets belonging to the occupied State that have been set aside for religious purpose, for the maintenance of charitable or educational institutions or for the benefit of art and science, or (ii) the produce of the immovable property belonging to municipalities. Hence, if it can be proved that the officer of an Occupying Power selling the produce of foreign immovable property *bona fide* ignored that a certain immovable of the enemy State had been set aside for educational purposes, or that it belonged to a municipality, and mistakenly believed that it instead belonged to the enemy State, this mistake of law might be relied upon as an excuse if it can also be proved that, as a consequence of that ignorance the officer lacked the requisite criminal intent.

Similarly, under the Third Geneva Convention of 1949 prisoners of war may only be punished for offences against the law in force in the armed forces of the Detaining Power after a trial has been conducted before a court offering all the essential guarantees of justice. If the officer of the Detaining Power charged with enforcing the penalties meted out by courts of that Power ignores that in particular cases the international prescriptions on the proper conduct of trials against prisoners of war have not been complied with, he may raise his ignorance as a defence provided he can prove that as a result of his mistake of law he did not have the requisite *mens rea* when executing the penalty.

Another example may be taken from *Hinrichsen*, brought before the Dutch Special Court of Cassation in 1950. Article 53(2) of the Hague Regulations of 1907 provides that the Occupant may seize 'all the appliances . . . adapted . . . for the transport of persons or things, even if they belong to private individuals', but then must 'restore' them and 'fix compensation' when peace is made. In the spring of 1945 Hinrichsen,

13.4.3 MISTAKE OF LAW AND SUPERIOR ORDER

A subordinate executing an unlawful order is relieved of criminal responsibility if he can prove his ignorance of law, under the conditions set out above with regard to this defence. Clearly, if the rules of international law on a particular matter, instead of being universally and clearly established, are confused and controversial, the subordinate may not be aware that the order he has to carry out is contrary to international humanitarian law or to international criminal law. This mistake of law may be such as to negate *mens rea*. If that is the case, the subordinate is not criminally liable, not however because the order is lawful, but simply because the law on the matter is not straightforward and universally recognized, and the subordinate is not required to settle controversial legal issues when deciding whether or not to execute an order. This is the approach taken by most courts (for some exceptions where in contrast the plea was upheld, see *supra*, 13.1.4(3)).

In *Wagener and others* in 1950 the Italian High Military Tribunal upheld the plea in theory but rejected it *in casu*. According to defence counsel, General Wagener, when obeying the order to take reprisals against Italian internees in territory occupied by Germany, had erred, not however about criminal law, but about international law (as far as the lawfulness of reprisals was concerned) and constitutional and international law (with regard to the power to issue military proclamations). The Court, while implicitly conceding the admissibility of the defence, rejected it in the case at bar, noting first, that the violation of the laws of warfare entailed criminal punishment and, second, that

> a military may not invoke as a defence ignorance of the duties inherent in his military status. The commander of a big unit in time of war may not ignore international obligations deriving from the laws of war, the more so when these obligations coincide with the principles, prevailing in any law, directed to safeguard the life and limb of individuals. (At 763.)

Other cases worth mentioning are *Grumpelt* (*Scuttled U-Boats* case)[43] and *Thomas*

a member of the German Frontier Customs Guard seized in occupied Netherlands two privately-owned motorcycles without payment or receipt. After the war he pleaded before a Dutch Criminal Court that his action was not at variance with international law. The Special Court of Cassation held on the contrary that his action was contrary to Article 53(2), for the accused did not provide the means for later verification of the seizure. It added however that in determining the penalty it was appropriate to take into consideration the fact that, unlike the case of requisition under Article 52 of the Regulations, giving a receipt was not expressly prescribed for seizure of means of transport; consequently, the punishment must not be severe (at 486–7). This is clearly a case where international law is not absolutely clear and unambiguous and therefore invocation of the defence at issue might be regarded as admissible.

[43] In this case Grumpelt, an officer in the German Navy, had scuttled two German U-boats after the belligerents had signed the terms of surrender, providing among other things that all German vessels would be handed over to the British Command on 5 May 1945. A few hours after the signature of the Instrument of Surrender but before the cessation of hostilities, the German Naval Command had issued a coded order that all U-boats must be scuttled. A few hours later the same Command issued another order countermanding the first. The accused claimed that (i) he had received the first order but not the second, and (ii) when he had decided to scuttle the two submarines he was not apprised of the terms of surrender; had he known them, he would have been able to refrain from obeying the first order. He thus implied that he lacked *mens rea*, for, ignoring the terms of surrender, he honestly believed that the (first) order was legal. The Judge Advocate put

L. Kinder, heard by a US Court Martial in 1954. In the latter case the defendant, a US airman serving in a US airbase in Korea situated south of the actual battle line, and assigned to the air police section to perform guard duty at a bomb dump, had been accused of killing a detained Korean civilian, who had been apprehended near the base, and whose legal status was uncertain. In addition to invoking superior orders, the defence counsel also urged in defence to the murder charge a mistake of law on the part of the accused as to (i) the legality of the order of the superior officer, and as to (ii) whether or not the airman was required to obey all orders without exception of a superior officer. The US Air Force Board of Review, on appeal from the General Court Martial, admitted the plea in principle, but dismissed it on the facts. It first cited paragraph 154*a*(4) of the 1951 Manual for Courts Martial, whereby:

As a general rule, ignorance of law . . . is not an excuse for a criminal act. However, if a special state of mind on the part of the accused, such as specific intent, constitutes an essential element of the offence charged, an honest and reasonable mistake of law, including an honest and reasonable mistake as to the legal effects of known facts, may be shown for the purpose of indicating the absence of such a state of mind. (At 775.)

The Court then went on to say that 'As the offence of murder charged in the instant case involves a specific intent to kill, "mistake of law" is in principle an applicable defence to negative the unlawfulness of the element of the specific intent to kill.' Turning to the case at issue, the Court pointed out the following:

However, viewing the defence of mistake of law as based on a claim in the instant case that the accused was mistaken in law as to the legality of the order of the superior officer, the defence fails for a prerequisite of such defence is that the mistake of law was an honest and reasonable one and as pointed out in the preceding paragraph the evidence not only does not raise a reasonable doubt as to whether or not the accused possessed an honest and reasonable belief that the order was legal, but justifies the inference that the accused was aware of the illegality of the order. Viewing the defence of mistake of law as based on a claim that the accused mistakenly believed the law to be that a soldier must without exception obey every order of a superior officer, we must also reject the defence for not [only] is such a view unreasonable, but is so absurd as to render unbelievable an honest belief by the accused that he entertained such an opinion of the law. The absurdity of such a belief can be illustrated by innumerable examples such as a superior officer's orders to commit rape, to steal for him, for the subordinate to cut off his own head, etc. Accordingly, under the circumstances of the instant case, we find no merit to a defence based on the principle of mistake of law. (At 775–6.)

As is clear from this case law, courts only admit mistake of law as a defence to the

the question to the Military Court as follows: 'Are you satisfied that the man's state of mind at the time in question was this: "I honestly believed I had an order: I did not know anything about any surrender; it was not for me to inquire why the higher command should be scuttling submarines; I honestly, conscientiously and genuinely believed I had been given a lawful command to scuttle these submarines and I have carried out that command and I cannot be held responsible"? Gentlemen, that is a matter for you to consider (at 70). The Court found the accused guilty of the charge of committing a war crime.

execution of an illegal superior order when it may be proved that the subordinate acted under the *honest and reasonable belief* that the law allowed the execution of that superior order. It follows that this defence is not admissible when the law on the matter is clear or should be known to any serviceman engaged in armed conflict (or, more generally, to any person of average intelligence and education).

SELECT BIBLIOGRAPHY

SUPERIOR ORDERS

H. H. Jescheck, *Verantwortlichkeit*, 255–61; N. C. H. Dunbar, 'Some Aspects of the Problem of Superior Orders', in 63 *Juridical Review* (1951), 234–61; S. Glaser, 'L'Ordre hiérarchique en droit international pénal', 33 RDPC (1953), 283–330; G. Hoffmann, *Strafrechtliche Verantwortung im Völkerrecht—Zum gegenwärtigen Stand des völkerrechtlichen Strafrechts* (Frankfurt, Berlin: Metzner Verlag, 1962) 129–33; Y. Dinstein, *The Defence of 'Obedience to Superior Order' in International Law* (Leiden: A. W. Sijthoff, 1965); H. S. Levie, 'The Rise and Fall of an Internationally Codified Denial of the Defense of Superior Orders', 30 RDMDG (1990), 185–209; M. J. Osiel, 'Obeying Orders: Atrocity, Military Discipline, and the Law of War', 86 *California Law Review* (1998), 939–1129; P. Gaeta, 'The Defence of Superior Orders: the Statute of the International Criminal Court v. Customary International Law', 10 EJIL (1999), 172–91; A. Zimmermann, in Cassese, Gaeta, and Jones (eds), *ICC Commentary*, vol. I, 957–74.

NECESSITY

S. Glaser, 'Quelques remarques sur l'état de nécessité en droit international', 33 RDPC (1952–3), 283–330.

DURESS

S. Glaser, 'Quelques remarques sur l'état de nécessité en droit international', 33 RDPC (1952–3), 283–330; A. Reed, 'Duress and Provocation as Excuses to Murder: Salutary Lesson from Recent Anglo-American Jurisprudence', 6 *Journal of Transnational Law and Policy* (1996), 51–92; A. Paphiti, 'Duress as Defence to War Crimes Charges', 38 RDMDG (1999), 249–88; M. Shahabuddeen, 'Duress in International Humanitarian Law', in C. A. Armas Barea *et al.* (eds), *Liber Amicorum 'In Memoriam' of Judge José Maria Ruda* (London, Boston, The Hague: Kluwer, 2000), 563–74; K. Ambos, in Cassese, Gaeta, and Jones, *ICC Commentary*, vol. I, 1003–48.

MISTAKE OF FACT

V. L. Oliver, 'Ignorance or Mistake of Fact as a Defence in Military Law', *The JAG Journal* (January 1957), 13–16; A. Eser, in Cassese, Gaeta, and Jones, *ICC Commentary*, vol. I, 889–948.

14

IMMUNITIES

14.1 GENERAL: VARIOUS CLASSES OF IMMUNITIES

One of the possible obstacles to international prosecution for international crimes may be constituted by rules intended to protect the person accused and grant him immunity from prosecution.

The following immunities may in principle come into play and be relied upon.

1. Those accruing under *customary international law*, on the strength of the so-called Act of State doctrine, to all State agents acting in their official capacity (so-called *functional immunities*). In principle, an individual acting on behalf of a sovereign State may not be called to account for any violations of international law he may have committed while acting in an official function. Only the State may be held responsible at the international level.

2. Those granted by *international customary or treaty rules* to some categories of individuals on account of their functions (*personal immunities*) and intended to protect both their private and their public life, or in other words to render them inviolable while in office. Such individuals comprise Heads of State, senior members of cabinet, diplomatic agents, high-ranking agents of international organizations. They enjoy these immunities so as to be able to discharge their official mission free from any impairment or interference. These immunities end with the cessation of the agent's official duties.

3. Those provided for in *national* legislation and normally granted to the Head of State, members of cabinet, and parliamentarians. They normally cover the acts of the individuals concerned and involve exemption from jurisdiction. In addition, often they also include immunity from prosecution for ordinary crimes having no link with the function and committed either before or during the exercise of the functions. However, such immunity terminates as soon as the functions come to an end, although normally the individual remains immune from jurisdiction for any official act performed during the discharge of his functions.

The rationale behind these national immunities is grounded on the principle of separation of powers and in particular the need to protect State organs (say, the Head of State) from interference by other State organs (say, courts) that could jeopardize their independence or political action.

These immunities normally apply to ordinary crimes. Do they also apply to international crimes? To answer this question one must of course establish whether there are international customary or treaty rules that cover this matter.

14.2 FUNCTIONAL AND PERSONAL IMMUNITIES PROVIDED FOR IN INTERNATIONAL CUSTOMARY LAW

Let us now return to and dwell upon an issue that is of great importance for our purposes: the distinction between two categories of immunities laid down in international law, that is, functional (or *ratione materiae* or organic) immunities and personal (or *ratione personae*) immunities. One ought always to distinguish between these two categories of, among other things, exemptions from foreign jurisdiction.

As pointed out above, the first category is grounded on the notion that States must respect other States' internal organization and may not therefore interfere with the structure of foreign States or the allegiance a State official may owe to his own State. Hence no State agent is accountable to other States for acts undertaken in an official capacity and which therefore must be attributed to the State. The second category is predicated on the notion that any activity of a Head of State or government, or diplomatic agent[1] or senior member of cabinet, must be immune from foreign jurisdiction. This is to avoid foreign States either infringing sovereign prerogatives of States or interfering with the official functions of a foreign State agent under the pretext of dealing with an exclusively private act (*ne impediatur legatio*). This distinction is made in the legal literature,[2] and is based on State practice. With regard to the

[1] However, as is well known, international rules provide for exceptions to immunities of diplomatic agents for private acts (see Article 31(1) of the Vienna Convention on Diplomatic Relations of 18 April 1961).

[2] See, e.g., G. Morelli, *Nozioni di diritto internazionale* (Padua: Cedam, 1943, 7th edn, 1967), at 215–16; P. Niboyet, 'Immunité de juridiction et incompétence d'attribution', 39 RCDIP (1950), 139; H. Kelsen, *Principles of International Law* (New York: Rinehart & Co., 1952), at 236–7 (according to Kelsen, 'the principle that no state has jurisdiction over another state excludes individual—civil or criminal—responsibility for acts of state'); G. Dahm, *Völkerrecht*, I (Stuttgart: W. Kohlhammer Verlag, 1958), at 225, 237, 303–5, 338–9 (for Dahm also the immunity of State organs for officials' acts is a consequence of State immunity); G. Sperduti, *Lezioni di diritto internazionale* (Milan: Giuffré, 1958), 117–21; M. Giuliano, 'Les relations et immunités diplomatiques', 100 HR (1960–II), 166–80 (only with reference to the functions of diplomatic agents); H. F. van Panhuys, 'In the Borderland between the Act of State Doctrine and Questions of Jurisdictional Immunities', 13 ICLQ (1964), 1205–8; F. Seyersted, 'Jurisdiction over Organs and Officials of States, the Holy See and Intergovernmental Organizations', 14 ICLQ (1965), 31–82 and 493–527, at 33–43; Y. Dinstein, 'Diplomatic Immunity from Jurisdiction *ratione materiae*', 15 ICLQ (1966), 76–89; M. Bothe, 'Die strafrechtliche Immunität fremder Staatsorgane', in 31 *Zeit. Ausl. Öff. Recht Völk* (1971), 246; M. Akehurst, 'Jurisdiction in International Law', 46 BYIL (1972–3), 240–4; A. Verdross and B. Simma, *Universelles Völkerrecht*, 3rd edn (Berlin: Duncker and Humblot, 1984), 773–4 (para. 1177); R. Jennings and A. Watts (eds), *Oppenheim's International Law*, 9th edn, vol. I (London: Longman, 1992), 346; I. Brownlie, *Principles of Public International Law*, 5th edn (Oxford: Clarendon Press, 1998), 361–2; P. De Sena, *Diritto internazionale e immunità funzionale degli organi statali* (Milan: Giuffrè, 1996), 109–250; P. Malanczuk, *Akehurst's Modern Introduction to International Law*, 7th edn (London and New York: Routledge, 1997), 122; A. Cassese, *International Law* (Oxford: Oxford University Press, 2001), 93–6; S. Zappalà, 'Do Heads of States in Office Enjoy Immunity

first class of immunities, suffice it to refer to the famous *McLeod* incident and the *Rainbow Warrior* case[3] as well as some recent judicial decisions: one may mention the judgment rendered by the Supreme Court of Israel in *Eichmann* (at 308–9), that handed down by the German Supreme Court (*Bundesgerichtshof*) in *Scotland Yard*,[4] and the judgment delivered by the ICTY Appeals Chamber in *Blaškić* (*subpoena*) (at §§38 and 41).[5]

The distinction is relevant, for the *first class of immunity*: (i) relates to substantive law, that is, it is a substantive defence (although the State agent is not exonerated from compliance with either international law or the substantive law of the foreign country, if he breaches national or international law, this violation is not legally imputable to him but to his State;[6] (ii) covers official acts of any *de jure* or de facto State agent; (iii) does not cease at the end of the discharge of official functions by the State agent (the reason being that the act is legally attributed to the State, hence any legal liability for it may only be incurred by the State); (iv) is *erga omnes*, that is, may be invoked towards any other State. In contrast, the *second class of immunities*: (i) relates to procedural law, that is, it renders the State official immune from civil or criminal jurisdiction (it is a procedural defence); (ii) covers official or private acts carried out by the State agent while in office, as well as private or official acts performed prior to taking office; in other words, assures total inviolability; (iii) is intended to protect only *some categories* of State officials, namely diplomatic agents, Heads of State, heads of government, foreign ministers (under the doctrine set out by the International Court of Justice in its judgment in the *Case Concerning the Arrest Warrant of 11 April 2000*, at §§51–5) and possibly even other senior members of cabinet; (iv) comes to an end after cessation of the official functions of the State agent; (v) may not be *erga omnes* (in the case of diplomatic agents it is only applicable with regard to acts performed as between the receiving and the sending State, plus third States through whose territory the diplomat may pass while proceeding to take up, or to return to, his post, or when returning to his own country: so-called *jus transitus innoxii*).

from Jurisdiction for International Crimes? The *Ghaddafi* Case before the French *Cour de Cassation*', 12 EJIL (2001), 595; P. Gaeta, 'Official Capacity and Immunities', in Cassese, Gaeta, and Jones (eds), *ICC Commentary*, vol. I, 975–1002.

[3] For the *McLeod* case, see *British and Foreign Papers*, vol. 29, at 1139, as well as Jennings, 'The *Caroline* and *McLeod* Cases', 32 AJIL (1938), 92–9; see also the decision of 1841 of the New York Supreme Court in *People* v. *McLeod*, at 270–99. For the *Rainbow Warrior* case, see *UN Reports of International Arbitral Awards*, XIX, at 213. See also the *Governor Collot* case, in J. B. Moore, *A Digest of International Law*, vol. II (Washington: Government Printing House, 1906), at 23.

[4] See the judgment of 26 September 1978, in 32 *Neue Juristische Wochenschrift* (1979), 1101–2 (the Director of Scotland Yard was not amenable to German civil jurisdiction for he had acted as a State agent).

[5] For other cases see in particular Bothe, *supra* n. 2, at 248–53.

[6] Nevertheless, it would seem that if the State official acting abroad has breached *criminal* rules of the foreign State, he *may* incur criminal liability and be liable under foreign criminal jurisdiction (at least, this is what happened both in *McLeod* and in the *Rainbow Warrior* case). Be that as it may, it seems certain however that the State official in question will not in any case be asked to pay for any damage his act may have caused. The State for which he acted remains internationally responsible for that act and will have to bear all the legal consequences of such responsibility.

The above distinction permits us to realize that the two classes of immunity *coexist* and somewhat *overlap* as long as a State official who may also invoke personal or diplomatic immunities is in office. While he is discharging his official functions, he always enjoys personal immunity.[7] In addition, he enjoys functional immunity, subject to one *exception* that we shall see shortly, namely in the case of perpetration of international crimes. Nonetheless, the personal immunity prevails even in the case of the alleged commission of international crimes, with the consequence that the State official may be prosecuted for such crimes only after leaving office.

14.3 THE CUSTOMARY RULE LIFTING FUNCTIONAL IMMUNITIES IN THE CASE OF INTERNATIONAL CRIMES

The traditional rule whereby senior State officials may not be held accountable for acts performed in the discharge of their official duties was significantly undermined after the Second World War, when international treaties and judicial decisions upheld the principle that this 'shield' no longer protects those senior State officials accused of war crimes, crimes against peace, or crimes against humanity. More recently, this principle has been extended to torture and other international crimes.

It seems indisputable that by now an international general rule has evolved on the matter. Initially this rule only applied to war crimes and covered any member of the military of belligerent States, whatever their rank and position. When the major provisions of the London Agreement of 8 August 1945 (setting forth the Statute of the IMT) gradually turned into customary law, Article 7 ('The official position of defendants, whether as Heads of State or responsible officials in Government departments, shall not be considered as freeing them from responsibility or mitigating punishment') also has come to acquire the status of a customary international rule.

National case law proves the existence of such a customary rule. Many cases where State military officials were brought to trial demonstrate that State agents accused of *war crimes*, *crimes against humanity*, or *genocide* may not invoke before national courts their official capacity as a valid defence. Even if we leave aside cases where tribunals adjudicated on the strength of international treaties or Control Council Law no. 10, cases that were therefore decided on the strength of written provisions, mention may be made of a string of significant decisions.[8] Admittedly, in most of these cases the accused did not challenge the court's jurisdiction on the ground that he had acted as a State official. The fact remains however that the courts did pronounce on

[7] For a recent departure from this rule, see the 2002 decision of the European Union concerning the freezing of Mugabe's private assets, mentioned *infra* (23.2).

[8] One may recall, for instance, *Eichmann* in Israel (at 277–342), *Barbie* in France (see the various judgments in 78 ILR, 125 ff., and 100 ILR 331 ff.), *Kappler* (193–9), and *Priebke* in Italy (959 ff.), *Rauter* (526–48), *Albrecht* (747–51), and *Bouterse* in the Netherlands (see the decision of 20 November 2000 of the Amsterdam Court of Appeal on-line, at **www.icj.org/objectives/decision.html**), *Kesserling* (9 ff.) before a British Military

acts performed by those officials in the exercise of their functions. The accuseds' failure to raise the 'defence' of acting on behalf of their State shows that they were aware that such defence would have been of no avail. In addition, in some cases the defendant did plead that he had acted in his official capacity and hence was immune from prosecution. This for example happened in *Eichmann*, where the accused raised the question of 'Act of State'. Although the Court used that terminology, which could be misleading, in essence it took the right approach to the question at issue[9] and explicitly held that State agents acting in their official capacity may not be immune from criminal liability if they commit international crimes (at 309–12).

It can also be conceded that most of the cases under discussion deal with *military* officers. However, it would be untenable to infer from that that the customary rule only applies to such persons. It would indeed be odd that a customary rule should have evolved only with regard to members of the military and not for all State agents who commit international crimes.

Besides, it is notable that the Supreme Court of Israel in *Eichmann* (at 311) and more recently various Trial Chambers of the ICTY have held that the provisions of, respectively, Article 7 of the Charter of the IMT at Nuremberg and Article 7(2) of the Statute of the ICTY (both of which relate to *any person* accused of one of the crimes provided for in the respective Statutes) 'reflect a rule of customary international law'.[10] Furthermore, Lords Millet and Phillips of Worth Matravers in the House of Lords' decision of 24 March 1999 in *Pinochet* took the view, with regard to any senior State agent, that functional immunity cannot excuse international crimes.[11]

Court sitting in Venice and *von Lewinski* (called *von Manstein*) before a British Military Court in Hamburg (523–4), *Pinochet* in the UK (see *infra*, note 8), *Yamashita* in the USA (1599 ff.), *Buhler* before the Supreme National Tribunal of Poland (682), *Pinochet* and *Scilingo* in Spain (respectively at 4–8 and 2–8), *Miguel Cavallo* in Mexico (see the decision of 12 January 2001 delivered by the Judge Jesus Guadalupe Luna and authorizing the extradition of Ricardo Miguel Cavallo to Spain, text (in Spanish) on-line in **www.derechos.org/nizkor/arg/espana/mex.html**).

[9] The Court rightly pointed out that 'The theory of "Act of State" means that the act performed by a person as an organ of the State—whether he was Head of the State or a responsible official acting on the Government's orders—must be regarded as an act of the State alone. It follows that only the latter bears responsibility therefore, and it also follows that another State has no right to punish the person who committed the act, save with the consent of the State whose mission he performed. Were it not so, the first State would be interfering in the internal affairs of the second, which is contrary to the conception of the equality of States based on their sovereignty' (at 308–9).

Thus, clearly, the Court did not approach the 'Act of State' doctrine as a conflict-of-laws concept, namely as a doctrine relating to the power of a State to adjudicate on acts performed by a foreign State in the latter's territory. As is well known, under this reading of the doctrine, as propounded among others by the *US Restatement Third*, 'Courts in the United States will generally refrain from examining the validity of a taking by a foreign state of property within its own territory, or from sitting in judgment on other acts of a governmental character done by a foreign state within its own territory and applicable there' (I, at 366–7).

[10] See *Karadžić and others* (§24), *Furundžija* (§140), and *Slobodan Milošević* (*decision on preliminary motions*) (§28).

[11] See at 171–9 (Lord Millet) and 186–90 (Lord Phillips of Worth Matravers). Instead, according to Lord Hope (at 152), Pinochet lost his immunity *ratione materiae* only because of Chile's ratification of the Torture Convention. In other words, for him the unavailability of functional immunity did not derive from customary law; it stemmed from treaty law.

The ICTY Appeals Chamber had already set out this legal proposition in *Blaškić* (*subpoena*) (§41).

In addition, important national Military Manuals, for instance those issued in 1956 in the United States and in 1958 in the United Kingdom, expressly provide that the fact that a person who has committed an international crime was acting as a government official (and not only as a serviceman) does not constitute an available defence.[12]

One should also recall that on 11 December 1946 the UN General Assembly unanimously adopted Resolution 95, whereby it 'affirmed' 'the principles recognized by the Charter of the Nuremberg Tribunal and the judgment of the Tribunal'. These principles include Principle III as formulated in 1950 by the UN International Law Commission.[13] All of these principles, Israel's Supreme Court noted in *Eichmann*, 'have become part of the law of nations and must be regarded as having been rooted in it also in the past' (at 311).

It also seems significant that, at least with regard to one of the crimes at issue, genocide, the International Court of Justice implicitly admitted that under *customary* law official status does not relieve responsibility. In its Advisory Opinion on *Reservations to the Convention on Genocide*, the Court held that 'the principles underlying the Convention are principles which are recognized by civilized nations as binding on States, even without any conventional obligation' (at 24). Among these principles one cannot but include the principle underlying Article IV, whereby 'Persons committing genocide . . . shall be punished, whether they are constitutionally responsible rules, public officials or private individuals'. It is notable that the UN Secretary-General took the same view of the customary status of the Genocide Convention (or, more accurately, of the substantive principles it lays down), a view that was endorsed implicitly by the UN Security Council,[14] and explicitly by a Trial Chamber of the ICTR in *Akayesu* (§495) and of the ICTY in *Krstić* (§541).

12 See the US Department of the Army Field Manual, *The Law of Land Warfare* (July 1956). At para. 498 it states that: 'Any person, whether a member of the armed forces or a civilian, who commits an act which constitutes a crime under international law is responsible therefore and liable to punishment. Such offenses in connection with war comprise: *a.* Crimes against peace; *b.* Crimes against humanity; *c.* War crimes. Although this manual recognizes the criminal responsibility of individuals for those offenses which may comprise any of the foregoing types of crimes, members of the armed forces will normally be concerned only with those offenses constituting "war crimes".' At para. 510 it is stated that: 'The fact of a person who committed an act which constitutes a war crime acted as the head of a state or as a responsible government official does not relieve him from responsibility for his act'.

See also the British manual, *The Law of War on Land* (1958), at para. 632 ('Heads of States and their ministers enjoy no immunity from prosecution and punishment for war crimes. Their liability is governed by the same principles as those governing the responsibility of State officials except that the defence of superior orders is never open to Heads of States and is rarely open to ministers').

13 Principle II provides as follows: 'The fact that a person who committed an act which constitutes a crime under international law acted as Head of State or responsible Government official does not relieve him from responsibility under international law'. See YILC (1950–II), 192.

14 See Report of the Secretary-General Pursuant to Para. 2 of Security Council Resolution 808 (1993), UN Doc. S/25704, at para. 45.

A further element supporting the existence of a customary rule having a general purport can be found in the pleadings made by the two States (the Congo and Belgium) that were in dispute before the International Court of Justice in the aforementioned *Case Concerning the Arrest Warrant of 11 April 2000.* In its *Mémoire* of 15 May 2001, the Congo explicitly admitted the existence of a principle of international criminal law, whereby the official status of a State agent cannot exonerate him from individual responsibility for crimes committed while in office; the Congo also added that on this point there was no disagreement with Belgium.[15]

Arguably, while each of these elements of practice, on its own, cannot be regarded as indicative of the crystallization of customary rule, taken together they may be deemed to evidence the formation of such a rule (a rule, it should be added, on whose existence legal commentators seem to agree, although admittedly without producing compelling evidence concerning State or judicial practice,[16] and which the *Institut de droit international* has recently restated, at least with regard to Heads of State or government).[17]

Let me emphasize that the logic behind this rule, which was forcefully set out as early as 1945 by Justice Robert H. Jackson in his Report to the US President on the works for the prosecution of major German war criminals,[18] is in line with present-day trends in international law. Today, more so than in the past, it is State officials, and

[15] *Mémoire,* at 39, para. 60 ('*La R.D.C. ne conteste pas qu'est un principe de droit international pénal, notamment forgé par les jurisprudences de Nuremberg et de Tokyo, la règle suivant laquelle la qualité officielle de l'accusé au moment des faits ne peut pas constituer une cause d'exonération de sa responsabilité pénale ou un motif de réduction de sa peine lorsqu'il est jugé, que ce soit par une juridiction interne ou une juridiction internationale. Sur ce point, aucune divergence existe avec l'Etat belge.*')

[16] See, e.g., S. Glaser, 'L'Acte d'Etat et le problème de la responsabilité individuelle', *Revue de droit pénal et de criminologie* (1950), 1 ff.; S. Glaser, *Introduction*, 71–6; G. Hoffmann, *Strafrechtliche Verantwortung im Völkerrecht—Zum gegenwärtigen Stand des völkerrechtlichen Strafrechts* (Frankfurt, Berlin: Metzner Verlag, 1962), 133–9 (only with regard to war crimes); M. Bothe, *supra* n. 2, 254–7; M. Akehurst, *supra*, n. 2, 241; Y. Dinstein, 'International Criminal Law', 5 IYHR (1975), 82–3; P. De Sena, *supra* n. 2, 139–87; P. Malanczuk, *supra* n. 2, 122; A. Bianchi, 'Immunity versus Human Rights: The *Pinochet* Case', 10 EJIL (1999), 269–70.

[17] See the Resolution on 'Immunities from Jurisdiction and Execution of Heads of State and of Governments in International Law' adopted at the Session of Vancouver (August 2001). At Article 13(2) it is stated that, although a former Head of State (or government) enjoys immunity in respect of acts performed in the exercise of official functions and related to the exercise thereof, he or she nevertheless may be prosecuted and tried 'when the acts alleged constitute a crime under international law'.

[18] In his Report to the US President of 6 June 1945, Justice R. H. Jackson (who had been appointed by President Roosevelt as 'Chief Counsel for the United States in prosecuting the principal Axis War Criminals') illustrated as follows the first draft of Article 7 of the London Agreement (whereby 'The official position of defendants, whether as Heads of State or responsible officials in Government departments, shall not be considered as freeing them from responsibility or mitigating punishment'), contained in a US memorandum presented at San Francisco on 30 April 1945: 'Nor should such a defence be recognized as the obsolete doctrine that a head of state is immune from legal liability. There is more than a suspicion that this idea is a relic of the doctrine of the divine right of kings. It is, in any event, inconsistent with the position we take toward our own officials, who are frequently brought to court at the suit of citizens who allege their rights to have been invaded. We do not accept the paradox that legal responsibility should be the least where power is the greatest. We stand on the principle of responsible government declared some three centuries ago to King James by Lord Justice Coke, who proclaimed that even a King is still "under God and the law"' (in *International Conference on Military Trials*, 47).

in particular senior officials, that commit international crimes. Most of the time they do not perpetrate crimes directly. They order, plan, instigate, organize, aid and abet or culpably tolerate or acquiesce, or willingly or negligently fail to prevent or punish international crimes. This is why 'superior responsibility' has acquired, since *Yamashita* (1946), such importance. To allow these State agents to go scot-free only because they acted in an official capacity, except in the few cases where an international criminal tribunal has been established or an international treaty is applicable, would mean to bow to and indeed strengthen traditional concerns of the international community (chiefly, respect for State sovereignty).

The rationale behind the forfeiture of a right to immunity by State officials who have perpetrated international crimes is simple: in the present international community respect for human rights and the demand that justice be done whenever human rights have been seriously and massively put in jeopardy, override the traditional principle of respect for State sovereignty. The new thrust towards protection of human dignity has shattered the shield that traditionally protected State agents acting in their official capacity.

14.4 INTERNATIONAL PERSONAL IMMUNITIES

The problem of international personal immunities arises with regard to State officials accused of international crimes when they are abroad: may they be arrested and brought to trial for the alleged crimes? (As we shall see, the problem can be differently framed and solved when the State official is in his own country; the question then arises of whether national courts are empowered to take proceedings against him.)

It would seem that the conflict between international rules granting personal immunities and the customary rules proscribing international crimes may be settled as indicated by the International Court of Justice in its judgment in the *Case Concerning the Arrest Warrant of 11 April 2000* (§§51–7). The Court logically inferred from the rationale behind the rules on personal immunities of senior State officials, such as Heads of State or government (or diplomatic agents), that such immunities must perforce prevent any prejudice to the 'effective performance' of their functions. They therefore bar any possible interference with the official activity of such officials. It follows that an incumbent senior State agent is immune from jurisdiction, even when he is on a private visit or acts in a private capacity while holding office. Clearly, not only the arrest and prosecution of such a State agent while on a private visit abroad, but also the mere issuing of an arrest warrant, may seriously hamper or jeopardize the conduct of international affairs of the State for which that person acts.

In sum, even when accused of international crimes, the State agent entitled to personal immunities is inviolable and immune from prosecution on the strength of the international rules on such *personal* immunities. This proposition is supported by some case law (for instance, *Pinochet*[19] in the UK and *Fidel Castro*[20] in Spain, which relate respectively to a former and an incumbent Head of State).

If the allegations about international crimes committed by foreign State officials are known before they enter a foreign territory, and the territorial State wishes to avoid conflicts with its judicial authorities or at any rate having contacts with individuals accused of serious crimes, it may ask the foreign State official to refrain from entering the territory; if that official is already on the territory, the State may declare him *persona non grata* and request him to leave forthwith.

Of course, it may be that an international treaty on specific international crimes implicitly or expressly prescribes that personal immunities may not relieve officials of responsibility for the international crimes they envisage. Many treaty rules do impose obligations upon contracting States that, although couched in general terms, could be interpreted to this effect. In this respect one may mention the Genocide Convention of 1948 (Article IV), the 1984 Convention on Torture (see in particular Article 4), as well as a number of treaties on terrorism. To these treaties one should add the Statutes of the ICTY and ICTR. Both contain a provision (respectively, Articles 7(2) and 6(2)), whereby 'The official position of any accused person, whether as Head of State or Government or as responsible Government official, shall not relieve such person of criminal responsibility nor mitigate punishment'. The strictness of this provision can be construed to the effect that the provision rules out the possibility of invoking personal immunities as a legal ground for not being prosecuted or tried.[21] However, the only treaty that explicitly excludes the right to invoke or rely upon personal immunities is the Statute of the ICC (Article 27(2)).

The same interpretation could be advanced with regard to the 1984 Convention on

[19] See, e.g., the speech of Lord Browne-Wilkinson, in *R.* v. *Bow Street Stipendiary Magistrate and others, ex parte Pinochet Ugarte*, judgment of 24 March 1999, at 112–15. See also the speeches of Lord Hope of Craighead, at 145–52, Lord Saville of Newdigate, at 169–70, Lord Millet, at 171–91, and Lord Phillips of Worth Matravers, at 181–90.

[20] See Order (*auto*) of 4 March 1999 (no. 1999/2723). The *Audiencia Nacional* held that the Spanish Court could not exercise its criminal jurisdiction, as provided for in Article 23 of the Law on the Judicial Power, for the crimes attributed to Fidel Castro. He was an incumbent Head of State, and therefore the provisions of Article 23 could not be applied to him because they were not applicable to Heads of State, ambassadors, etc. in office, who thus enjoyed immunity from prosecution on the strength of international rules to which Article 21(2) of the same Law referred (this provision envisages an exception to the exercise of Spanish jurisdiction in the case of 'immunity from jurisdiction or execution provided for in rules of public international law'). See Legal Grounds nos 1–4. The Court also stated that its legal finding was not inconsistent with its ruling in *Pinochet*, because Pinochet was a former Head of State, and hence no longer enjoyed immunity from jurisdiction (see Legal Ground no. 5). For the (Spanish) text of the order, see the CD-Rom, EL DERECHO, 2002, Criminal case law.

[21] Therefore, it would seem that one ought to reject as unfounded the claim made by the Serbian authorities of the FRY that some of the co-accused of Mr Slobodan Milošević, in particular the former foreign minister of the FRY and incumbent president of Serbia, Mr M. Milutinović, could not be arrested and handed over to the ICTY because they enjoyed immunities under the national or federal Constitution. Assuming this were correct under national law, the rules of the ICTY Statute would prevail, because those rules were enacted by the Security Council under Chapter VII of the UN Charter, and therefore override contrary treaties, customary rules, and also national legislation pursuant to Article 103 of the UN Charter.

Torture, Articles 1–4 of which are so strict as to warrant such interpretation. However, there is still resistance to this trend. For example, in March 2000 the US State Department allowed a Peruvian alleged torturer to go free on the ground that he enjoyed personal (that is, diplomatic) immunity. This case is indicative of the reluctance of States to embrace a new and forward-looking approach to international crime, preferring instead to cling to old values such as respect for State sovereignty and its corollary of the immunity of State officials or diplomatic immunity.[22]

All this applies to *incumbent* senior State officials. As soon as the State agent leaves office, he may no longer enjoy personal immunities and, in addition, he becomes liable to prosecution for any international crime he may have perpetrated while in office (or before taking office). This is rendered possible by the aforementioned customary international rule on international crimes that has evolved in the international community. The rule provides that, in case of perpetration by a State official of such international crimes as genocide, crimes against humanity, war crimes, torture, and serious crimes of international, State-sponsored terrorism, such acts, in addition to being imputed to the State of which the individual acts as an agent, also involve the criminal liability of the individual. In other words, for such crimes there may coexist State responsibility and individual criminal liability.

14.5 NATIONAL PERSONAL IMMUNITIES

The question of whether a national court is authorized to start proceedings against a national accused of international crimes, who happens to be a senior State official enjoying immunities under national law (for instance, the Head of State, a member of cabinet, a member of parliament) must be looked at from the viewpoint of international and national law.

Customary international law, it would seem, does not contain any rule imposing upon a State the obligation to disregard national legislation on immunities. However,

[22] In the above example, Major Tomas Ricardo Anderson Kohatsu, a retired official of Peru's notorious Army Intelligence Service, was alleged by the US State Department to have perpetrated 'horrendous crimes' in 1997. In early March 2000 the Peruvian authorities sent him to the USA to appear before a hearing of the Inter-American Commission on Human Rights in Washington. When he was about to leave the USA to return to Peru, FBI agents detained him, pursuant to the 1984 UN Convention Against Torture, duly ratified by the USA. However, a few hours later he was released following a decision by the Under-Secretary of State, Thomas Pickering. According to Pickering, Anderson was entitled to diplomatic immunity because he held a G-2 visa, granted to accredited members of the staff of the Peruvian Mission to the Organization of American States. Consequently, he could not be arrested or prosecuted (on-line: at **www.windos\temp\center for constitutional rights.htm**).

It was pointed out by M. Ratner, a leading lawyer of the US Center for Constitutional Rights, that Anderson had not in fact been accredited to the Peruvian Mission. More importantly, it would seem that the 1984 Convention on Torture does not permit exemption for diplomatic immunity. In any case, it was for the US *courts* to determine the matter. As Ratner pointed out, in the case of Anderson, unlike Pinochet, 'despite serious doubts as to Anderson's claimed immunity, the decision to allow him to return to Peru was made by the State Department and not the courts' (see ibid., at 2, para. 3).

treaty rules may impose the obligation to punish the authors of international crimes. If this is the case, any national legislation granting immunity would be in conflict with the treaty obligation.

National law may contain general rules granting immunity from prosecution for any crime, including international crimes. It very much depends on each particular national system. However, after the entry into force of the ICC Statute, those States that are gradually ratifying such Statute are no longer able to rely upon any possible national legislation on immunities. The national implementation of the ICC Statute requires that States change their legislation (including their constitutional provisions, if any) on immunities, removing any such immunities for the international crimes that fall under the jurisdiction of the Court.

SELECT BIBLIOGRAPHY

P. M. Dupuy, 'Crimes et immunités', 100 RGDIP (1999), 289–96; S. Zappalà, 'Do Heads of State Enjoy Immunity from Jurisdiction for International Crimes? The Ghadafi case before the French *Cour de Cassation*', 12 EJIL (2001), 595–612; M. Delmas-Marty, 'La responsabilité pénale en échec (prescription, amnistie, immunités)', in A. Cassese and M. Delmas-Marty (eds), *Juridictions nationales*, 613–52; P. Gaeta, 'Les règles internationales sur les critères de compétence des juges nationaux', in A. Cassese and M. Delmas-Marty, *Crimes internationaux*, 191–213; M. Frulli, 'Le droit international et les obstacles à la mise en œuvre de la responsabilité pénale pour crimes internationaux', ibid., 215–53.

PART III

PROSECUTION AND PUNISHMENT BY NATIONAL COURTS

15

LEGAL GROUNDS OF JURISDICTION

15.1 INTRODUCTION

To bring the alleged authors of international crimes to book, States need to have not only laws, statutes, or some sort of judge-made legal regulation punishing those crimes, but also legal provisions authorizing courts to prosecute and punish the alleged perpetrators. These legal provisions normally empower State courts to take proceedings if the offence, its alleged author, or its victim have some sort of link with the State. Indeed, traditionally, States bring alleged perpetrators of international crimes to trial before their courts on the basis of one of three principles: *territoriality* (the offence has been perpetrated on the State's territory), *passive nationality* (the victim is a national of the prosecuting State), or *active nationality* (the perpetrator is a national of the prosecuting State). In contrast, the principle of *protection of national interests* whereby courts possess jurisdiction over crimes committed abroad by nationals or foreigners when the crimes jeopardize or imperil the State's national interests (for instance, counterfeiting the national currency, planning attacks on the State's security, etc.) is normally not used with respect to international crimes proper, on obvious grounds (States still tend to consider these crimes as not directly relevant to, or affecting, their national interests whenever a national or territorial link is lacking).

Recently the *universality principle* has emerged, whereby any State is empowered to bring to justice alleged authors of international crimes (in some cases, subject to their being present on the territory of the prosecuting State).

15.2 THE PRINCIPLE OF TERRITORIALITY

The basic principle is that a crime committed in a State's territory is justiciable in that State. In the celebrated *Lotus* case, the Permanent Court of International Justice stated in 1927 that 'in all systems of law the principle of the territorial character of criminal law is fundamental', although it also added that 'the territoriality of criminal law . . . is not an absolute principle of international law and by no means coincides with territorial sovereignty' (at 20). The Canadian Supreme Court held in *United States* v. *Burns* that 'individuals who choose to leave Canada leave behind Canadian law and procedures and must generally accept the local law, procedures and punishments which the foreign state applies to its own residents' (§72). Similarly a US court stated in *Rivard* v. *United States*, that '[a]ll the nations of the world recognize the principle that a man who outside of a country wilfully puts in motion a force to take effect in it is answerable at the place where the evil is done' (at 887).

The latter legal proposition is a corollary of the principle of territoriality: *even where a crime is committed outside the territory*, if its *effects* will be felt *in* the territory, then it is amenable to the State's jurisdiction (for example, if, standing outside the territory, I shoot a pistol which kills someone in the territory; or if I manufacture drugs outside the territory and then smuggle them into the territory of the State. In both cases, I can be judged in the State where the effects of the crimes were felt, even though I committed the prohibited acts outside the territory).

The principle is grounded on ideological and political reasons: the need to affirm territorial sovereignty, which evolved in the age of reason and was linked to the consolidation of modern States. This need led States to replace the previous principle of 'personality of laws' (everybody is governed by his national law, wherever he resides) with that of territoriality (what matters is the law of the place where an act is performed).

Montesquieu, Voltaire, Rousseau, and Beccaria insisted on the importance of territoriality in criminal law. The French Revolution confirmed it in the decree of 3–7 September 1792 ('foreigners charged with offences in their homeland may only be tried under the laws of their own country and by their own judges'; consequently, 'no foreigner will be retained on the galleys of France for crimes committed outside French territory'). In 1764 Beccaria, more than any other, developed the theory of territoriality. In his opinion, the adoption of this principle was warranted on two grounds. First of all, as State laws vary, one should only be punished in the place where one has infringed the law. Secondly, it is only just that a crime, which constitutes a violation of the social contract, be punished in the place where the contract was breached.[1]

The principle has numerous advantages. First, the *locus delicti commissi* (the place where the offence has allegedly been committed) is usually the place where it is easiest to collect evidence. It is therefore considered the *forum conveniens*, or the appropriate place of trial, as was restated in *Eichmann* (at 302–3). Secondly, it normally is the place where the rights of the accused are best safeguarded, for—if he is not a foreigner

[1] In his *Crimes and Punishments*, Beccaria wrote that 'There are those who think, that an act of cruelty committed, for example, at Constantinople, may be punished at Paris; for this abstracted reason, that he who offends humanity, should have enemies in all mankind, and be the object of universal execration; as if the judges were to be the knights errant of human nature in general, rather than guardians of particular conventions between men. The place of punishment can certainly be no other, than that where the crime was committed; for the necessity of punishing an individual for the general good subsists there, and there only.' C. Beccaria, *An Essay on Crimes and Punishments*, translated from the Italian, 4th edn (London: F. Newberry, 1775), repr. (Brooklyn Village: Branden Press Inc., 1983), at 64. (For the original text, which differs slightly, see C. Beccaria, *Dei delitti e delle pene*, edited by F. Venturi (Turin: G. Einaudi, 1965), at 71–2.)

fleetingly residing there—he is expected to know the law of the territory, hence he is likely to know the criminal law in force there as well as his rights as a defendant in a criminal trial. In addition, unless he is a non-resident foreigner, he knows and speaks the language in which the trial unfolds. Thirdly—and this applies in particular to international crimes, whose gravity may have serious repercussions on the society within which the crime has been committed—if the prosecution and punishment occur on the territory where the crime was perpetrated, it is more likely for the cathartic process of criminal trials to have effect: the victims and their families relive their tragedies, the whole society becomes aware of what has happened and is thus put in a position of better coming to terms with, hence of psychologically overcoming, past crimes. Moreover, the judges, jury, and advocates, being members of the community where the crimes took place, are aware of local feelings about the crimes and conscious of the press and public's close scrutiny of their administration of justice; they are thus broadly accountable to the community for the manner in which they dispense justice. Finally, by administering justice over crimes perpetrated in the territory, the territorial State affirms its authority over attacks on peace and security within its bounds; by the same token it helps to deter the commission of future offences.[2]

However, in the case of international crimes, there may be a major obstacle to the territoriality principle: these crimes are often committed by State officials or with their complicity or acquiescence: for example, war crimes committed by servicemen, or torture perpetrated by police officers, or genocide carried out with the tacit approval of State authorities. It follows that State judicial authorities may be reluctant to prosecute State agents or to institute proceedings against private individuals that might eventually involve State organs.

Whenever the territoriality principle is applicable, two problems may arise. First, what should be meant by 'territory' subject to the sovereignty of a State? Here one must turn to the international rules delimiting State territory, with the consequence that offences perpetrated in a State's territorial waters or on its ships or aircraft on the high seas are considered committed on the territory of that State. Similarly, territory comprises space under the control or 'under the jurisdiction' of a State, such as for example territory occupied following an international armed conflict. By contrast, crimes perpetrated in a State's embassy abroad are not carried out on national territory but abroad (hence the contrary view of the Spanish *Audiencia nacional* in the case of the *Guatemalans* (at 130), whereby crimes committed in the Spanish embassy in Guatemala were regarded as perpetrated in Spain, was wrong).

[2] In *Sawonjuk* the British Court of Appeal (Criminal Division) stated that: 'The criminal jurisdiction of the English courts is, generally speaking, territorial. Until enactment of the War Crimes Act 1991 [under which, proceedings may be brought in the UK "against a person in the United Kingdom irrespective of his nationality at the time of the alleged offence" for war crimes committed during the Second World War "in a place which at the time was part of Germany or under German occupation"] the appellant could not be tried here for an offence of murder or manslaughter committed in Byelorussia since he has never been a British subject and the exception made by Section 9 of the Offences against the Person Act 1861 to the ordinary rule of territoriality was confined to offences of murder or manslaughter committed outside the United Kingdom by British subjects (at 4).

The second problem relates to the determination of the *locus commissi delicti* in the case of complex crimes: when the crime is planned in a country and committed in another country, or the crime is committed in a country but takes its effects in another, which is the territory where trial proceedings may be instituted? The tendency of national legal systems is to give priority to the place of commission or to the place where the effects of the crime materialize. Many States have jurisdiction if *one of the elements of the offence* is committed in the State's territory even if other elements occur abroad. It would seem that there are no international rules on this issue, nor may one infer from national legal systems a uniform regulation of the matter.

Problems specific to international criminal law may arise when the alleged perpetrator of a crime is a State official enjoying immunity from prosecution under national legislation (for instance, the Head of State, the head or a senior member of the government, or a member of parliament). Clearly, if this is the case, national courts are barred from instituting criminal proceedings against the accused, because the latter enjoys personal immunity (*ratione personae*). It may also be that the alleged perpetrator, whatever his official status, is covered by an amnesty law. In this case, again, the national authorities of the State where the amnesty was granted may be precluded from taking judicial action. By contrast, a foreign court, assuming it has jurisdiction over the crime, may consider that it does not have to recognize the amnesty, particularly if this law turns out to be in conflict with international rules of *jus cogens*, that is peremptory norms of international law.[3] Thus, whereas national jurisdiction based on the territoriality principle may sometimes fail, other grounds of jurisdiction invoked by foreign courts may prove workable and lead to the prosecution of the alleged culprit.

Among the international treaties providing for grounds of jurisdiction over international crimes, the Convention on Genocide of 1948 should be mentioned. In Article VI it stipulates that persons accused of genocide must be brought to trial before the competent courts of the State where the act has been performed (or before an International Criminal Court, if and when it is established and assuming it has jurisdiction over the crimes in question). This rule, however, has never been applied, except in Rwanda, where national courts prosecuted alleged authors of acts of genocide committed in 1994 alongside the international prosecutions brought before the ICTR. This was only possible due to the rare circumstance that the victims of the genocide, the Tutsi, had seized power in Rwanda (the Tutsi-led party having in 1994 deposed the Hutu-led government that planned and waged the genocide), and were therefore strongly intent on bringing prosecutions for genocide, not least since the fact of the genocide legitimized the minority Tutsis' hold on power.

[3] In England courts are under no obligation to recognize an amnesty granted by another State, irrespective of whether the alleged violation breaches peremptory norms. Since an amnesty is not a judgment, the principle of *autrefois acquit/autrefois convict*—the English equivalent of the *non bis in idem* principle—does not apply. This arose in *Pinochet*—he had been granted an amnesty—but the English courts considered that irrelevant.

15.3 THE PRINCIPLE OF ACTIVE NATIONALITY

Normally the principle of active nationality is implemented in one of two forms. In some States, courts have jurisdiction over certain criminal offences committed by their nationals abroad. This is so, whether or not those offences are criminal under the law of the territorial State, that is, the State in which the conduct constituting the offences under the law of the State of nationality were committed. In this case the underlying motivation is the will of a State that its nationals comply with its law, whether at home or abroad, regardless of what is provided for in the foreign State when the crime is committed. In other countries jurisdiction over crimes committed by nationals abroad is subordinated to the crime being punishable under the law of the territorial State as well (this, for instance, holds true for Egypt). In this case the essential rationale behind the principle is the desire—or constitutional prohibition in many cases—of the State of nationality not to extradite its nationals to the State where the crime has been perpetrated. Hence the law of the State of active nationality must provide for the possibility of trying the accused in that State, so that he does not escape justice altogether. Indeed, it is striking that countries such as the UK, which have no constitutional or other prohibition on the extradition of their nationals, normally do not provide for active nationality as a basis for jurisdiction.[4]

All this holds true, generally speaking, for criminal offences. As for international crimes, States that uphold this ground of jurisdiction do so in order to bow to international dictates, that is to make international law effective by complying with its commands. Thus, they normally do not require that the offence be also punishable by the territorial State, as it is sufficient for the offence to be regarded as an international crime by international rules (be they customary or treaty provisions).

This principle is normally upheld with regard to war crimes, as well as such crimes as torture. Many States, particularly under the pressure arising from the conclusion of treaties setting out international crimes, have passed legislation providing for jurisdiction based on nationality. For instance, in the UK, as a result of the International Criminal Court Act 2001, designed to implement the Statute of the ICC, courts possess jurisdiction over all crimes envisaged in the Court's Statute and committed by British nationals either at home or abroad. The active nationality principle is also laid down in a number of international treaties, which include the 1984 Convention against Torture (Article 5(1)) and various treaties against terrorism.[5]

4 Nonetheless, as stated above, the courts in England and Wales have jurisdiction over murder and manslaughter committed abroad on the basis of the active nationality principle. See Offences against the Person Act 1861, s. 9. The same is true of High Treason under the Treason Act 1351. These exceptions can be explained on the basis of the gravity of the crimes in question.

5 See for instance the 1973 Convention on internationally protected persons (Article 6(1)(b)), the 1979 Convention on the taking of hostages (Article 6(2)(e)), the 1980 Convention on the protection of nuclear material (Article 8(1)(b)), the 1988 Convention and Protocol on the security of maritime navigation (Article 6(1)(c)), the 1994 Convention on the Safety of UN and Associated Personnel (Article 10(1)(b)), the 1998

A problem that may arise where jurisdiction is exercised on the basis of the active nationality principle concerns the moment at which the alleged perpetrator must possess the nationality of the prosecuting State: is it when the crime is perpetrated, or when criminal proceedings are instituted? It would seem that most States tend to accept that the nationality may be possessed at either moment, thus broadening the jurisdiction of the State and better ensuring the punishment of international crimes. Other States (for instance, Egypt) require instead that the person be a national of the State at the time of commission of the crime.

One may also notice a tendency of States to broaden this ground by including residents (this applies for instance to the UK with regard to war crimes committed during the Second World War as well as the crimes envisaged in the Statute of the ICC; to Brazil with regard to genocide) or stateless persons residing on the territory of the prosecuting State (this for instance applies to Italy and the Russian Federation).

Some States have passed legislation concerning crimes perpetrated during the Second World War, for the purpose of punishing persons who, whatever their nationality at the time of commission of crimes, have subsequently acquired their nationality, possibly with the hope of sheltering behind their newly acquired nationality.[6]

15.4 THE PRINCIPLE OF PASSIVE NATIONALITY

By virtue of the principle of passive nationality States may exercise jurisdiction over crimes committed abroad against their own nationals. Plainly, the principle is grounded both on: (i) the *need to protect nationals living or residing abroad* and (ii) a substantial *mistrust* in the exercise of jurisdiction by the foreign territorial State.

Normally States invoking this ground of jurisdiction also provide that, whenever the accused is abroad, a 'double incrimination' is required for prosecuting a crime, namely that the offence be considered as such both in the territorial State and in the State of the victim. 'Double criminality' is usually considered a procedural requirement of extradition: to extradite from State X to State Y, the crimes in question must be a crime in both States. Normally, where passive nationality is exercised, the State will have to seek extradition of the perpetrator as he will be abroad. Of course, that is not always the case. If the perpetrator, for example a Chilean accused of murdering a Spaniard, is in the State exercising jurisdiction, e.g. Spain, then Spain will be able to

Convention on terrorist bombing (Article 6(1)(c)), the 1999 Convention on the financing of terrorism (Article 7(1)(c)). See also the 2000 Convention Against Transnational Organized Crime (Article 15(2)(b)).

6 Thus, §§1091 and 2342 of the US Code so provide with regard to genocide and war crimes. In the UK a law was passed in 1991 (the War Crimes Act) whereby proceedings may be brought for war crimes committed during the Second World War against persons who, whatever their nationality at the time of the alleged offence, are British citizens or residents as from 8 March 1990. (This cut-off date was chosen to prevent persons evading the Act by changing their nationality or residence.) Other States such as Australia and Canada have passed similar laws.

proceed against him without going through extradition proceedings and therefore without having to worry about 'double criminality'.

Outside extradition law the requirement at issue is intended to avoid prosecuting a person for an act that is not considered a criminal offence by the State where it has been performed; in other words, the rationale for this requirement may be found in the general principle of legality (*nullum crimen sine lege*) which is common to all national legal systems, in addition to being a general principle of international criminal law (see 7.3). However, as far as international crimes are concerned, this requirement is replaced by the requirement that the offence be considered as an international crime by international law, whatever the content of the legal regulation in the territorial State. In this connection, the decision of the Supreme Court of Argentina delivered in *Priebke* on 2 November 1995, concerning the extradition to Italy of a German national who had subsequently acquired Argentinian nationality, is pertinent: the Court explicitly held that as the offence of which the defendant stood accused, namely a war crime, was internationally regarded as an international crime, this sufficed for the purpose of the double incrimination principle.[7]

There has been frequent resort to this ground of jurisdiction to prosecute war crimes, particularly after the cessation of hostilities and by the victor State against the vanquished (former) enemies. (Notable departures based on the active nationality principle are the trials instituted in 1902 by US Courts Martial against American servicemen who had fought in the Philippines, the Leipzig trials against Germans, imposed upon Germany by the Allies, and the various trials before US Courts Martial for crimes committed in Vietnam.)

More recently courts have relied upon this jurisdictional ground with regard to crimes against humanity and torture. Significant in this respect are some cases tried *in absentia*: *Astiz*, a case brought before French courts (an Argentinian officer had tortured two French nuns in Argentina), as well as some cases brought before Italian courts against Argentinian officers for crimes allegedly perpetrated against Italians (or Argentinians also having Italian nationality) in Argentina.[8] Furthermore, this ground of jurisdiction has been laid down in national legislation with regard to terrorism, for instance in the United States (see §§2331 and 2332 of the Federal Criminal Code), in France (Articles 113–17 of the Criminal Code), and in Belgium. It is also stipulated in a number of international conventions against terrorism[9] and in the 1984 Convention against Torture (Article 5(1)).

Resort to the passive nationality principle is, however, particularly incongruous in the case of international crimes such as for instance those against humanity, and torture. By definition, these are crimes that injure humanity, that is, our sense of

[7] Fallos CSJN 318:2148, opinion of Judges Nazareno and O'Connor, §77; opinion of Judge Bossert, §91.

[8] See for instance *Suárez Masón and others*, at 8–15.

[9] For example, the 1973 Convention on internationally protected persons, the 1979 Convention on hostage-taking, the 1988 Convention and Protocol on maritime safety, the 1994 Convention on the protection of UN agents, the 1997 Convention on terrorist attacks, the 1999 Convention on the financing of terrorism, and the 2000 Convention on transnational organized crime.

humanity, in other words our concept of respect for any human being, *regardless* of the nationality of the victims. As a consequence, their prosecution should not be based on the national link between the victim and the prosecuting State. This is indeed a narrow and nationalistic standard for bringing alleged criminals to justice, based on the interest of a State to prosecute those who have allegedly attacked one of its nationals. The prosecution of those crimes should instead reflect a universal concern for their punishment; it should consequently be based on such legal grounds as territoriality, universality, or active nationality.

It follows that, as far as such crimes as those against humanity, torture, and genocide are concerned, the passive nationality principle should only be relied upon as a *fall-back*, whenever no other State (neither the territorial State, nor the State of which the alleged criminal is a national, nor other States acting upon the universality principle) is willing or able to administer international criminal justice. Perhaps this is the reason why in international conventions such as that on torture this ground of jurisdiction, unlike those just mentioned, is envisaged not as an obligation of contracting States but simply as an *authorization* to prosecute (see Article 5(1)(c) of the 1984 Convention against torture).

Conversely, the ground of jurisdiction under discussion may prove appropriate for such offences as war crimes or terrorism as a discrete offence, where the need to protect national interests and concerns acquires greater relevance.

15.5 THE UNIVERSALITY PRINCIPLE

Under the principle of universality any State is empowered to bring to trial persons accused of international crimes, regardless of the place of commission of the crime, or the nationality of the author or of the victim.

The principle was first proclaimed in customary international law in the seventeenth century, with regard to piracy. Any State was authorized to arrest and bring to justice persons suspected of engaging in piracy, whatever their nationality and the place of commission of the crime. The rationale behind this exceptional authorization to States to depart from the classic principles of territoriality or nationality was the need to fight jointly against a form of criminality that affected all States. Universal jurisdiction was therefore based on a *joint concern of all States*. Each State knew that by bringing to justice suspected pirates it was acting to protect at the same time its own interests and those of other States.

Subsequently the same jurisdictional ground was included in the 1949 Geneva Conventions on war victims, the 1984 Convention against Torture, and a string of international treaties on terrorism. The rationale for universal jurisdiction in these cases differed, however, from that invoked for piracy. States were not empowered to exercise jurisdiction for the purpose of protecting a joint interest. They were authorized to prosecute and punish, on behalf of the whole international community, persons responsible for a special class of war crimes (grave breaches of the 1949 Geneva

Conventions), torture or terrorism, with a view to safeguarding *universal* values. For instance, contracting States were authorized by the 1984 Convention to bring to justice persons who had engaged in torture abroad, in particular in their own country against their countrymen. The purpose was not to prevent those persons from equally perpetrating torture against nationals of the prosecuting State (in which case one would have been faced with the protection of a joint interest). The purpose was rather that of not leaving the crime of torture unpunished, were the territorial State to refrain from putting the alleged torturer in the dock. Contracting States were thus authorized to act as 'universal' guardians against attacks on human dignity taking the form of torture.

In short, the crimes over which such jurisdiction may be exercised are of such a gravity and magnitude that they warrant their universal prosecution and repression, as the Supreme Court of Israel eloquently held in *Eichmann* as long ago as 1962. (Subsequently the Spanish Constitutional Court, in a judgment of 10 February 1997,[10] and the Spanish national criminal court (*Audiencia nacional*) in an order of 4 November 1998[11] set out this view.) Thus, any State is authorized to substitute itself for the natural judicial forum, namely the territorial or national State, should neither of them bring proceedings against the alleged author of an international crime.

Under the strong influence and pressure of these international rules, States have begun to lay down the principle of universal jurisdiction in their national legislation: in this connection mention may be made of Spain and Belgium, as well as Germany and Austria.

15.5.1 TWO DIFFERENT VERSIONS OF UNIVERSALITY

The universality principle has been upheld in two different versions, both predicated on the notion that the judge asserting universal jurisdiction so acts in order to substitute for the defaulting territorial or national State: the narrow notion (conditional universal jurisdiction) and the broad notion (absolute universal durisdiction).

A. The narrow notion (conditional universal jurisdiction)

According to the more widespread version, the narrow notion, only the State where the accused is in custody may prosecute him or her (the so-called *forum deprehensionis*,

[10] See the Judgment of 10 February 1997, in the *Panamanian Ship* case, at 6, Legal Ground no. 3A. The Court held that the Spanish legislator had intended 'to attribute universal scope to the Spanish jurisdiction over those specific crimes [mentioned in Article 23 of the 1985 Law on Judicial Power], on account both of the gravity of these crimes and the need for international protection'.

[11] Order (*auto*) of 4 November 1998, in *don Adolfo Francisco (Scilingo)*, at 3, Legal Ground no. 2. The Court held that it was contrary to the spirit of the Genocide Convention to interpret Article 6 of this Convention (which provides that the accused may be tried either by a territorially competent court or by an international court) to the effect that such provision would limit the jurisdiction of States. This interpretation would run counter to the fact that genocide is 'regarded as a crime of extreme gravity in the whole world and affects directly the international community, indeed all humanity, as is intended by the same Convention'.

or jurisdiction of the place where the accused is apprehended). Thus, the presence of the accused on the territory is a *condition for the existence of jurisdiction.*

This class of jurisdiction is accepted, at the level of customary international law, with regard to piracy.[12] At the level of treaty law it has been upheld with regard to *grave breaches* of the 1949 Geneva Conventions and the First Additional Protocol of 1977, *torture* (under Article 7 of the 1984 Torture Convention), as well as *terrorism* (see the various UN-sponsored treaties on this matter).[13] These treaties, however, do not confine themselves to granting the power to prosecute and try the accused. They also *oblige* States to do so, or alternatively to extradite the defendant to a State concerned (the principle of *aut prosequi aut dedere*).

This version of the universality principle is also applied in the national legislation of some States, such as Austria, Germany, and Switzerland.[14] In France, courts have applied Article 2 of the law of 2 January 1995 implementing the Statute of the ICTY to the effect that, for the application of the relevant provision of the Geneva Conventions on grave breaches, it was required that the offender be on French territory.[15]

B. The broad notion of universality (absolute universal jurisdiction)

Under a different version of the universality principle, a State may prosecute persons accused of international crimes regardless of their *nationality*, the place of commission of the crime, the nationality of the victim, and even of *whether or not the accused is in custody or at any rate present in the forum State.* However, as many legal systems do not permit trials *in absentia*, the presence of the accused on the territory is then a condition for the initiation of trial proceedings. Clearly, this conception of universality allows national authorities to commence criminal investigations of persons suspected

[12] See A. Cassese, 'When may Senior State Officials be Tried for International Crimes? Some comments on the *Congo* v. *Belgium* Case,' 13 EJIL (2002), at 857–8.

[13] See for instance Article 7 of the Hague Convention for the suppression of unlawful seizure of aircraft of 1970; Article 7 of the Montreal Convention on the suppression of unlawful acts against the safety of civil aviation (sabotage), of 1971; Article 8 of the 1979 Convention against the taking of hostages; Article 7 of the 1988 Convention for the suppression of unlawful acts against the safety of maritime navigation.

[14] Article 65.1.2 of the Austrian Penal Code provides that Austrian criminal law may apply in respect of offences committed abroad, so long as the acts are also punishable in the place where they were performed, and provided that the offender, if a foreigner, is in Austria and may not be extradited to another State (see to this effect *Cvjetković*, at 5–6). In Germany, Article 6.9 of the Penal Code provides that German criminal law shall apply to offences committed by non-nationals abroad if such offences are made punishable by an international treaty binding upon Germany. Article 7(2).2 of the same Penal Code allows for prosecution of foreigners apprehended in Germany for crimes perpetrated abroad, if they are not extradited (either because a request for extradition was never made, or was refused, or because extradition is not feasible). Articles 108 and 109 of the Swiss Military Penal Code provide for universal jurisdiction over violations of international humanitarian law and the laws and customs of war. Article 6 *bis* of the Swiss Criminal Code makes the Code applicable to crimes committed abroad, (i) whenever Switzerland is obliged to pursue such crimes under an international treaty, and provided that (ii) the act is also punishable in the State where it was committed, and (iii) the perpetrator is in Switzerland and is not extradited. See the *G.* case, at 7 and *Niyonteze*, at 35–41.

[15] See *Javor and others* Cass. Crim. 26 March 1996, in *Bull.* No. 132 at 380–3. See also *Munyeshyaka*, where the French Court of Cassation rightly reversed (at 6–7) a decision of the Nîmes Court of Appeal denying French jurisdiction in spite of the presence of the accused in France (1085–9).

of serious international crimes, and gather evidence about these alleged crimes, as soon as such authorities are seized with information concerning an alleged criminal offence. They may thus exercise criminal jurisdiction over such persons, without requiring that the person first be present, even temporarily, in the country. As stressed above, such exercise of jurisdiction is premised on the failure of the territorial or national State to take proceedings, and should therefore not be activated whenever one of those States initiates proceedings. (In this connection, it may be interesting to recall that in Spain, a ruling (*auto*) by the *Audiencia nacional* dated 13 December 2000 in the case of the *Guatemalan Generals* rejected a claim to the exercise of universal jurisdiction by Spanish courts on the basis that the complaints against the accused persons (Guatemalan Generals) could be investigated and tried in Guatemala (at 145). Thus the *Audiencia* interpreted Spanish law to the effect that Spanish jurisdiction is subsidiary, and can only be exercised in case of failure by a State to try serious crimes.)[16]

This principle is laid down in such national legislation as that of Spain and Belgium.[17] It is notable that Regulation no. 2000/15 of the United Nations Transitional Administration in East Timor (UNTAET) also applies this principle in Articles 2.1 and 2.2 with regard to such crimes as genocide, war crimes, crimes against humanity, and torture.

One might also construe Article 7.5 of the Italian Criminal Code (whereby Italian nationals or foreigners who commit abroad any crime 'for which either special legislative provisions or international treaties establish that Italian criminal law shall apply, may be punished under Italian law') to the effect that alleged authors of international crimes may be prosecuted even if they do not find themselves on Italian territory,

[16] The subsidiary nature of universality may also follow from international rules. Interestingly, in its decision of 5 November 1998 in *Pinochet*, the Spanish *Audiencia nacional* held that universal jurisdiction may have to yield to territorial jurisdiction whenever this is imposed by an international treaty. It stated that, because of the prevalence in Spanish law of treaties over national legislation, Article 6 of the Genocide Convention of 1948 (whereby persons accused of genocide must be tried by courts of the territorial State or by an 'international penal tribunal') entails that in Spain the exercise of other grounds of jurisdiction (including universality) is '*subsidiary* in nature', 'so that courts of a State should refrain from exercising jurisdiction over acts of genocide that are being tried by courts of the State where they occurred, or by an international criminal court' (at 3, second legal ground; emphasis added).

[17] In Spain, Article 23 of the 1985 Law on Judicial Power provides that Spanish courts have jurisdiction over crimes committed outside Spain when such crimes constitute genocide, terrorism, or other crimes which Spain is obliged to prosecute under international treaties. However, in Spain trials by default or *in absentia* are not allowed.

In Belgium, under a Law of 16 June 1993 Belgian courts have jurisdiction over grave breaches of the 1949 Geneva Conventions and 1977 Protocols, no matter where such offences are committed, by whom or against whom they are committed, and whether or not the offender is on Belgian territory. A law of 3 February 1999 added genocide and crimes against humanity to the international crimes over which Belgian courts possess universal jurisdiction. See the order of the Brussels Investigating Judge in *Pinochet* (at 281–8), as well as the *Rwandan* case (where however the accused was already in custody in Belgium), at 2–3.

It should however be noted that in a decision of 6 March 2002 in *Sharon and others* the *Chambre des mises en accusation* of the Brussels Court of Appeal held that Belgian legislation must be construed to the effect that it provides only for *conditional* universal jurisdiction (at 7–20).

provided that: (i) the crimes are envisaged in international treaties ratified by Italy and (ii) under these treaties Italian courts may exercise jurisdiction.[18]

Furthermore, the relevant Spanish case law is worthy of mention. (In addition to a judgment of the Constitutional Court,[19] the decisions of the *Audiencia nacional* in *Pinochet*,[20] *Scilingo*,[21] and *Fidel Castro*[22] should be recalled.) In addition, under the

[18] Recently some national judges attempted to place a broad interpretation on the notion of universal jurisdiction laid down in the Geneva Conventions and the First Additional Protocol of 1977. A French investigating judge unsuccessfully made this attempt on 9 May 1994 (Order of the *Juge d'instruction*, in *Javor and others*). (He intended to institute proceedings against Bosnian Serbs who were alleged to have committed grave breaches of the Geneva Conventions and who found themselves on the territory of Bosnia and Herzegovina.)

See the cases discussed in R. Maison, 'Les premiers cas d'application des dispositions pénales des Conventions de Genève par les juridictions internes', 6 EJIL (1995), 260 ff.

[19] See the judgment of 10 February 1997 (no. 1997/56) in the *Panamanian ship* case. The ship of the accused (flying Panama's flag) had been chased and seized on the high seas for drug trafficking; the accused had been prosecuted before Spanish courts for one of the crimes over which the Law of 1985 granted universal jurisdiction to those courts. In its lengthy decision, the Constitutional Court took the opportunity to state in an *obiter dictum* that Article 23, para. 4 of the 1985 Law, granting universal jurisdiction, was in keeping with the Constitution: the Spanish legislator had 'conferred a universal scope (*un alcance universal*) on the Spanish jurisdiction over those crimes, corresponding to their gravity and to the need for international protection' (Legal Ground no. 3A). Spanish text on CD-Rom of Spanish legislation and case law: EL DERECHO, 2002, Constitutional decisions.

[20] See, in particular, the Order (*auto*) of 5 November 1998 (no. 1998/22605). In this order the Spanish National High Court (*Audiencia nacional*) confirmed that national courts have jurisdiction over genocide and terrorism committed in Chile (see Legal Grounds nos 3 and 4; as for torture, where the Court held that Spanish jurisdiction was based on Article 23(4)(g), on the strength of the 1984 Torture Convention, see Legal Ground no. 7). It should be noted that the Court concluded that 'Spain has jurisdiction to judge the acts (*conocer de los hechos*), based on the principle of universal prosecution of certain crimes . . . enshrined in our domestic law. It also has a legitimate interest (*interés legítimo*) in exercising that jurisdiction as more than fifty Spaniards were killed or made to disappear in Chile, victims of the repression reported in the orders' (Legal Ground no. 9). In other words, as is apparent from both the words reported and the entire text of the decision, Spanish jurisdiction was not grounded on passive nationality; the presence of Spaniards among the victims of the alleged crimes only amounted to a 'legitimate interest' of Spain in the exercise of universal jurisdiction. This order was confirmed by the decision of the *Audiencia nacional* of 24 September 1999 (no. 1999/28720). There, the Court reiterated that the Spanish Court had jurisdiction over the crimes attributed to Pinochet, namely genocide, terrorism, and torture (Legal Grounds nos 1 and 10–12), and also stated that Pinochet could not invoke the immunities pertaining to Heads of State, for he no longer held this status (Legal Ground no. 3). For the (Spanish) text of the order and the subsequent decision, see the Spanish case law on CD-Rom, EL DERECHO, 2002, Criminal jurisprudence, as well as on-line: **www.derechos.org/nizkor/espana.**

[21] See the Order (*auto*) of 4 November 1998 (no. 1998/22604), very similar in its tenor to that of 5 November referred to *supra*.

[22] See Order (*auto*) of 4 March 1999 (no. 1999/2723). The *Audiencia nacional* held that the Spanish Court could not exercise its criminal jurisdiction, as provided for in Article 23 of the Law on the Judicial Power, for the crimes attributed to Fidel Castro. He was an incumbent head of state, and therefore the provisions of Article 23 could not be applied to him because they were not applicable to heads of state, ambassadors, etc. in office, who thus enjoyed immunity from prosecution on the strength of international rules to which Article 21(2) of the same Law referred (this provision envisages an exception to the exercise of Spanish jurisdiction in the case of 'immunity from jurisdiction or execution provided for in rules of public international law'). See Legal Grounds nos 1–4. The Court also stated that its legal finding was not inconsistent with its ruling in *Pinochet*, because Pinochet was a former head of state, and hence no longer enjoyed immunity from jurisdiction (see Legal Ground no. 5). For the (Spanish) text of the order, see the CD-Rom, EL DERECHO, 2002, Criminal case law.

interpretation of the German Penal Code propounded by the German Supreme Court (*Bundesgerichtshof*) in a judgment of 21 February 2001 in *Sokolović*, the same principle should also apply in Germany, at least whenever the obligation to prosecute is provided for in an international treaty binding upon Germany.[23] One should also mention that in the course of the drafting of the Statute of the International Criminal Court, Germany forcefully expressed the view that international customary law at present authorizes universal jurisdiction over major international crimes.[24] In line with this view, Article 1 of the bill on international criminal law proposed by the German government and now pending before the German *Bundesrat* (Senate), namely the *Entwurf eines Gesetzes zur Einführung des Völkerstrafgesetzbuches*, provides that German law applies to all criminal offences against international law envisaged in the law (namely genocide, crimes against humanity, war crimes), even when the criminal conduct occurs abroad and does not show any link with Germany.[25]

What are the merits and the flaws of asserting absolute universal jurisdiction? This is a matter that deserves some consideration.

No one will fail to understand the generous ideal underpinning this system. Nonetheless, in my opinion various reasons militate against such absolute universal jurisdiction, at least if resorted to with regard to political or military leaders.[26]

First of all, the existence in some States of national laws granting absolute universal jurisdiction may prompt victims of atrocities to engage in so-called forum-shopping.

[23] The Court noted that in its decision of 29 November 1999, the Court of Appeal (*Oberlandsgericht Düsseldorf*), following the traditional German case law, had held that a factual link was required by law (*legitimierender Anknüpfungspunkt*) for a German court to exercise jurisdiction over crimes committed abroad by foreigners. (In the case at issue the offender was a Bosnian Serb accused of complicity in genocide perpetrated in Bosnia.) The Court of Appeal had found this link in the fact that the accused had lived and worked in Germany from 1969 to 1989 and had thereafter regularly returned to Germany to collect his pension and also to seek work. After recalling these findings by the Court of Appeal, the Supreme Court added: 'The Court however inclines, in any case under Article 6 para 9 of the German Criminal Code, not to hold as necessary these additional factual links that would warrant the exercise of jurisdiction . . . Indeed, when, by virtue of an obligation laid down in an international treaty, Germany prosecutes and punishes under German law an offence committed by a foreigner abroad, it is difficult to speak of an infringement of the principle of non-intervention' (judgment of 21 February 2001, 3 StR 372/00, still unreported, at pp. 19–20 of the typescript).

[24] In a document submitted in 1998 to the Preparatory Committee drafting the Statute, Germany stated the following: 'Under current international law, all States may exercise universal criminal jurisdiction concerning acts of genocide, crimes against humanity and war crimes, regardless of the nationality of the offender, the nationality of the victims, and the place where the crime was committed. This means that, in a given case of genocide, crime against humanity or war crimes, each and every state can exercise its own national criminal jurisdiction, regardless of whether the custodial State, territorial State or any other State has consented to the exercise of such jurisdiction beforehand. This is confirmed by extensive practice' (UN Doc. A/AC.249/1998/DP.2, 23 March 1998).

[25] 'Dieses Gesetz gilt für alle in ihm bezeichneten Straftaten gegen das Völkerrecht, für die in ihm bezeichneten Verbrechen auch dann, wenn die Tat im Ausland begangen wurde und keinen Bezug zum Inland aufweist' (see Bundesrat, *Drucksache 29/02*, 18 January 2002, *Gesetzentwurf der Bundesregierung*, at 3; German text on-line at **www.bmj.bund.de/images/10185.pdf**). See the precisions made in the Commentary, at 29).

[26] See also the critical remarks by J. Verhoeven, 'Vers un ordre répressif universel? Quelques observations', 55 AFDI (1999), 62–3.

In other words, it may attract such victims and induce them to file complaints against alleged perpetrators.[27]

Secondly, if the accused never enters the country where the court is located, or is not extradited to that country, a situation that appears most likely, the judge will end up investigating hundreds of complaints about which he can do nothing.

Thirdly, a judge who decides to go ahead with the trial regardless of the absence of the accused, conducting proceedings *in absentia*, is likely to be criticized for violating the fundamental rights of the accused. Moreover, the absence of the accused, normally linked to the fact that the State of nationality refuses to extradite, could worsen the problem of establishing the facts because neither the accused nor the State in question will co-operate in the search for evidence.

Fourthly, the power of national judges to issue arrest warrants against foreign State officials may lend itself to abuse if the power is not exercised with caution and is not predicated on two basic conditions: that (i) compelling evidence is available against the accused, and (ii) the person charged with international crimes does not enjoy, or no longer enjoys, personal immunities (this holds true for Heads of State, prime ministers, some senior members of cabinet, and diplomatic agents). Whenever the necessary prudence is not used, the exercise of universal jurisdiction may easily lead to international disputes. This for instance happened in the aforementioned case of the Congolese former foreign minister against whom a Belgian investigating judge had issued an arrest warrant. The Congo filed an application with the International Court of Justice, claiming that the arrest warrant ran counter to the principle of sovereign equality of States and the rules on diplomatic immunity attached to such a State official (see *infra*, 15.6). Thus, a case pertaining to the criminal responsibility of individuals became the subject of an interstate dispute. In other words, the case was moved from an inter-individual level to that of State-to-State relations. This is contrary to the very logic of international criminal justice.

A further possible criticism is that, if all countries put a system modelled on Belgian (or Spanish) law into practice, the risk of inconsistent rulings would be great and no one would know how to establish priorities between competing courts.

Finally, given the number of diplomatically and politically high-profile cases which would be brought before the courts, the judge would eventually become entangled in roles normally played by the political authorities,[28] with consequent danger of infringing the sound principle of separation of powers.[29]

[27] On this issue see in particular J. F. Flauss, 'Droit des immunités et protection internationale des droits de l'homme', *Revue suisse de droit international et de droit européen* (2000), at 304.

[28] Take the *Pinochet* case: it would seem difficult to prove that Pinochet committed *genocide* in Chile, whereas it would seem that he can be accused of gross violations of human rights including torture; the fact that he was accused of genocide in Spain shows the sort of charges that can be put together, primarily for the purpose of taking into account the Spanish legislation (which provides for universal jurisdiction in the absence of a treaty only for genocide and terrorism).

Arguably these political matters should be left to politicians, legislatures, etc., and not brought before judges.

[29] It is, however, a fact that US courts have for many years asserted universal jurisdiction by default,

Should one conclude that unqualified universal jurisdiction should always be discarded? In fact, there are cases where it may prove fitting: when adopted for international crimes perpetrated by *minor defendants*. Often the person accused of international crimes does not hold a high position in government. Universal jurisdiction may be envisaged for cases involving *low-ranking* military officers or other junior State agents, or even *civilians*, culpable of alleged crimes such as torture, war crimes, crimes against humanity, and so on. With regard to such persons, one is at a loss to see why, if the national or territorial State fails to take proceedings, another State should not be entitled to prosecute and try them in the interests of the whole international community. With regard to these persons, the initiation of criminal proceedings in their absence, the gathering of evidence, and the issue of an arrest warrant would have the advantage of making their subsequent arrest and trial possible. Normally these persons are not well known, and their travels abroad do not make news, unlike those of foreign ministers or Heads of State or military leaders. Hence the only way of bringing them to trial is to issue arrest warrants so that at some stage they are apprehended and handed over to the competent State.

However, let us not be unmindful of the pitfalls of the universality principle. In essence, the search for and collection of evidence may prove extremely difficult, for most of the evidence may be found in the State where the crimes were committed, and the national authorities may not be forthcoming and co-operative, especially if the crimes were committed on behalf of or at the behest of those authorities. Admittedly, the same drawback also occurs with regard to the passive nationality principle: the State of nationality of the alleged perpetrator of the offence is often reluctant to hand over the relevant evidence to the State of nationality of the victim (whereas when the active nationality principle is resorted to the reverse is true, because the State of the victim is normally all too glad to co-operate in the prosecution of the perpetrator). It would seem however, that in the case of universal jurisdiction the danger or likelihood of lack of judicial co-operation by the foreign State is much greater. States tend to dislike the exercise of extraterritorial jurisdiction when even the link constituted by the presence in the forum State of the perpetrator or the victim is lacking. Hence, whenever faced with such a situation, they tend not to co-operate.

admittedly in *civil* proceedings, over serious violations of international law perpetrated by foreigners abroad (see the Alien Tort Claims Statute and the *Filartiga-Peña Irala* case. See, e.g., L. F. Damrosch, 'Enforcing International Law through Non-Forcible Measures', 269 *HR* (1997), 161–7). Although civil jurisdiction is less intrusive than criminal jurisdiction, when it is exercised over foreigners who possess official status (for instance, high-ranking State officials), it nevertheless amounts to interference with the internal organization of foreign States. Whether or not this trend of US courts is objectionable as a matter of policy, or on legal grounds, it is a fact that it has not been challenged, or in other words has been acquiesced in, by other States. This implicit acceptance through non-contestation would seem to evidence the generally shared legal conviction that, where there are serious and blatant breaches of universal values, national courts are authorized to take action, subject to fulfilment of some fundamental requirements, such as ensuring a fair trial. (Admittedly there is a conspicuous difference between civil and criminal suits: in civil suits only money is at stake whereas in a criminal trial, the accused may be deprived of his liberty for a long time. So States may be prepared to tolerate civil suits of this nature, but shrink from allowing criminal trials.)

15.6 OBJECTIONS TO UNIVERSALITY

The notion of universality has been subjected to two criticisms. The first is that State courts would interfere in the internal affairs of another State, in violation of a fundamental principle of international relations. For example, Chile put forward this argument in a memorandum to the UK on the possible extradition of General Pinochet to Spain.

It is clear that here we are witnessing a confrontation between two different conceptions of the international community. The first is an archaic conception, under which non-interference in the internal affairs of other States constitutes an essential pillar of international relations. The second is a modern view, based on the need to further universal values; it implies that national judges are authorized to circumvent, if not remove, the shield of sovereignty.

A Spanish court, the *Audiencia nacional*, in two recent cases (*don Alfonso Francisco* (*Scilingo*) (at Legal ground no. 10) and *don Augusto* (*Pinochet*) (at Legal ground no. 9)) as well as the German Federal High Court (in the *Sokolović* case) (at 20), have already rejected this objection, without however giving reasons. It would nevertheless appear that they considered that courts, when they stand in, under either international law or national legislation, for a defaulting foreign State and hand down decisions relating to crimes committed by foreigners against foreigners abroad, protect fundamental values recognized by the whole international community.

A second objection is that national courts would hinder international diplomatic relations, whenever the suspect or the accused is a State agent in office, all the more so when he is a high representative such as a Head of State or government, a foreign affairs minister, etc. In this connection, the case of *Fidel Castro*[31] is relevant, for in that case a Spanish court propounded a balanced and legally apposite solution to this intricate matter. The case dealt with charges laid against an incumbent Head of State, Fidel Castro; the Spanish court ruled that, as long as he was in office, Fidel Castro could not be prosecuted in Spain, not even for international crimes envisaged under the Spanish law of 1985.

The same objection against the exercise of universal jurisdiction was raised by the Congo against Belgium before the International Court of Justice, in the *Case*

[31] See Order (*auto*) of 4 March 1999 (no. 1999/2723). The *Audiencia nacional* held that the Spanish Court could not exercise its criminal jurisdiction, as provided for in Article 23 of the Law on the Judicial Power, over the crimes attributed to Fidel Castro. Since Castro was an incumbent Head of State, the provisions of Article 23 could not be applied to him. This was because they were not applicable to Heads of State, ambassadors, etc. in office, who thus enjoyed immunity from prosecution on the strength of international rules to which Article 21(2) of the same Law referred. (This provision envisages an exception to the exercise of Spanish jurisdiction in the case of 'immunity from jurisdiction or execution provided for in rules of public international law'.) See Legal Grounds nos 1–4. The Court also stated that its legal finding was not inconsistent with its ruling in *Pinochet*, because Pinochet was a *former* Head of State, and hence no longer enjoyed immunity from jurisdiction (see Legal Ground no. 5). For the (Spanish) text of the order, see the CD-Rom, EL DERECHO, 2002, Criminal case law.

Concerning the Arrest Warrant of 11 April 2000. A Belgian investigating judge, at the Brussels Tribunal de Première Instance, had issued an international arrest warrant against the foreign minister of the Democratic Republic of Congo for grave breaches of the Geneva Conventions and crimes against humanity. The crimes of which the Congolese minister was accused, following complaints by Congolese and Belgian nationals, had allegedly been committed on Congolese territory against Congolese nationals. The accused was not on Belgian territory when the arrest warrant was issued: thus Belgium was not even the *forum deprehensionis*.[32] In its judgment of 14 February 2002, the Court made an important contribution to a clarification of the law of (what one ought correctly to term) *personal* immunities (including inviolability) of foreign ministers. This is an area where State practice and case law are lacking. To reach its legal findings, the Court did not, therefore, have to establish the possible content of customary law. Rather, it logically inferred from the rationale behind the rules on personal immunities of senior State officials, such as Heads of State or government (or diplomatic agents), that such immunities must perforce prevent any prejudice to the 'effective performance' of their functions. They therefore bar any possible interference with the official activity of foreign ministers. It follows that an incumbent foreign minister is immune from jurisdiction, even when on a private visit or when acting in a private capacity while holding office. Clearly, not only the arrest and prosecution of a foreign minister while on a private visit abroad, but also the mere issuance of an arrest warrant, may seriously hamper or jeopardize the conduct of international affairs of the State for which that person acts as a foreign minister.

15.7 IS THE EXERCISE OF UNIVERSAL JURISDICTION ALLOWED BY CUSTOMARY INTERNATIONAL LAW?

It would appear that the first case in which a person accused of crimes against humanity was tried in a State with which he had no formal links was *Eichmann* (although it could be argued that most of the surviving victims, and the relatives of victims, of Eichmann's offences were in Israel). It is extremely significant that no State concerned protested against that trial: neither the two German States nor the countries on whose territory the acts of genocide planned or organized by Eichmann had been perpetrated, nor the States of which the victims of genocide were nationals. Thus, States did not challenge the principle enunciated in 1962 by the Supreme Court of Israel whereby 'the peculiarly universal character of these crimes [against humanity] vests in every State the authority to try and punish anyone who participated in their commission' (at 287). The Court concluded as follows:

[32] See the relevant documents submitted by the parties in the case brought before the ICJ by Congo versus Belgium in *Case Concerning the Arrest Warrant of 11 April 2000*. (Those documents are summarized in the oral pleadings: see the verbatim records of the Court's sittings of 21 and 23 November 2000, www.icj-cij.org.)

Not only do all the crimes attributed to the appellant bear an international character, but their harmful and murderous effects were so embracing and widespread as to shake the international community to its very foundations. The State of Israel therefore was entitled, pursuant to the principle of universality of jurisdiction and in the capacity of a guardian of international law and an agent for its enforcement, to try the appellant. (At 304.)

This proposition was taken up by US courts in *Yunis* (at 903) and in two decisions in *Demjanuk* (at 27–43 and 23–7) and, in *Pinochet*, by Lords Browne-Wilkinson and Millet. Lord Browne-Wilkinson stated that 'the *jus cogens* nature of the international crime of torture justifies States in taking universal jurisdiction over torture wherever committed' (837–8). Lord Millet stated that 'crimes prohibited by international law attract universal jurisdiction under customary international law if two criteria are satisfied. First, they must be contrary to a peremptory norm of international law so as to infringe *jus cogens.* Secondly, they must be so serious and on such a scale that they can justly be regarded as an attack on the international legal order' (at 911–12). These propositions were taken up and restated by an Argentinian judge in *Simon Julio, Del Cerro Juan Antonio* (at 55–6).

As we shall see, some States have, at least recently, passed legislation applying the universality principle, and their courts have begun to apply this principle. The acceptance by States of the exercise of 'universal' jurisdiction by Israel, as well as the most recent practice of some States, and the authoritative opinions of some judges of the International Court of Justice in the aforementioned *Case Concerning the Arrest Warrant of 11 April 2000*[33] would seem to be in line with the *Lotus* principle (whereby

[33] In their Joint Separate Opinion, Judges Higgins, Kooijmans, and Buergenthal set out a series of conditions for the exercise of absolute universal jurisdiction. These conditions are as follows: (i) the State intending to prosecute a person must first 'offer to the national state of the prospective accused person the opportunity itself to act upon the charges concerned'; (ii) the charges may only be laid by a prosecutor or investigating judge who is fully independent of the government; (iii) the prosecution must be initiated at the request of the persons concerned, for instance at the behest of the victims or their relatives; (iv) criminal jurisdiction is exercised over offences that are regarded by the international community as the most heinous crimes; (v) jurisdiction is not exercised as long as the prospective accused is a foreign minister (Head of State, or diplomatic agent) in office; after he leaves office, it may be exercised over 'private acts' (see paras 59–60 and 79–85).

Some of the conditions may however give rise to objection. For instance, one fails to see why, in the first of the five conditions set out by the three judges, it is required that 'the national state of the prospective accused' be 'offered' the opportunity to act upon the charges. Why should one leave aside the territorial State (normally the *forum conveniens*) or the State of which the victim is a national? In addition, why should one envisage that the State exercising universal jurisdiction 'offer' to another State the chance to prosecute the suspect? To make such an offer would involve shifting the whole matter from the judiciary to foreign ministries and might imply making a bilateral agreement. It would be easier to require that the court intending to exercise jurisdiction should first establish whether courts of the territorial or national State have (deliberately) failed to prosecute the suspect at issue; only then should a court proceed to assert universal jurisdiction.

It is submitted that also the fifth condition should be couched differently, to take account of the existence of the customary rule referred to in the text above, and which is intended to remove functional immunity in the case of international crimes.

States are authorized to prosecute extraterritorial offences provided that by so doing they do not breach a prohibitive rule of international law).[34]

15.8 TRENDS IN THE EXERCISE OF NATIONAL CRIMINAL JURISDICTION

15.8.1 THE PROSECUTION AND PUNISHMENT OF WAR CRIMES

The merits and shortcomings of the penal repression of international crimes may be best assessed if considered in the light of the fundamental distinction drawn by Röling, with regard to war crimes, between 'individual' and 'system' criminality.[35] The former encompasses war crimes committed by combatants on their own initiative and for 'selfish' reasons (rape, looting, murder, and so on). The latter refers to war crimes perpetrated on a large scale, chiefly to advance the war effort or for ideological reasons, at the request or at least with the encouragement or toleration of the government authorities (killing civilians to spread terror, refusing quarter, using prohibited weapons, engaging in torture of captured enemies to obtain information, and so on). It also refers to other classes of international crimes, the perpetration of which by single individuals presupposes the complicity, participation, toleration, or acquiescence of State authorities, or which is even effected by State agents themselves. I am referring to crimes against humanity, genocide, or egregious forms of terrorism.

[34] On 2 August 1928 a collision occurred between the French mail steamer *Lotus* and the Turkish collier *Boz-Court* on the high seas off Mitylene. The *Boz-Court*, which was cut in two, sank, and eight Turkish nationals who were on board perished. The French steamer, after having done everything possible to succour the shipwrecked persons, continued on its course to Constantinople. There the French officer who was at the time of the collision officer of the watch on board the *Lotus* was arrested and brought to trial (under the passive nationality principle), together with the Turkish captain of the *Boz-Court*, on a charge of manslaughter. The French Government brought the case before the Permanent Court of International Law, claiming that the institution of criminal proceedings against the French national was inconsistent with the principles of international law, and contending in particular that the Turkish courts, in order to have jurisdiction, would have to point to some title of jurisdiction recognized by international law in favour of Turkey. No such title existed, according to France: in its view international law did not allow a State to take proceedings with regard to offences committed by foreigners abroad, simply by reason of the nationality of the victim (the principle of passive nationality); in the case at issue the offence would have to be regarded as having been committed on board the French vessel, and therefore subject to the French exclusive jurisdiction. The Court dismissed the French claim and held, albeit by the President's casting vote, in favour of Turkey (at 32). It first set out the principle whereby 'Far from laying down a general prohibition to the effect that States may not extend the application of their laws and the jurisdiction of their courts to persons, property and acts outside their territory, it [international law] leaves them in this respect a wide measure of discretion which is only limited in certain cases by prohibitive rules; as regards other cases, every State remains free to adopt the principles which it regards as best and most suitable' (at 19). The Court then asked itself whether under international law there was a principle which would have prohibited Turkey, in the circumstances of the case at issue, form prosecuting the French officer (at 21) and answered in the negative (22–31).

[35] B. V. A. Röling, 'The Significance of the Laws of War', in A. Cassese (ed.), *Current Problems of International Law* (Milan: Giuffré, 1975), at 137–9.

Normally 'individual criminality' is repressed by the culprit's national authorities. (Army commanders do not like this sort of misbehaviour, for it is bad for the morale of the troops and makes for a hostile enemy population.) By contrast, 'system criminality' as a rule is only repressed by international tribunals or by the courts of the adversary. There are, of course, exceptions, such as some cases of war crimes committed by US armed forces in the Philippines in 1900–1, the crimes against the Armenians repressed, in a few instances, by courts of the Ottoman Empire in 1919–20, or, in more recent times, the *Calley* case, 'a typical example of system criminality', in which the prosecution of Calley was urged upon the US authorities by American and foreign public opinion (but, revealingly, Calley received a very light sentence, which he served under house arrest, and was then pardoned by President Nixon; this seems to bear out that his acts were part of 'system criminality' as they were to a large extent tolerated or condoned by the US government).

By and large, repression of 'individual criminality' is a more frequent occurrence than that of 'system criminality', for the simple reason that the latter involves an appraisal and condemnation of a whole system of government, of misbehaviour involving the highest authorities of a country.

Apart from this distinction, one may however note that, in the case of *war crimes*, in time of war belligerents endeavour as far as possible to refrain from trying enemy combatants for fear of retaliation. Once the war is over, victor States tend to prosecute and punish crimes committed by the enemy forces against nationals of those victor States (on the passive nationality principle), whereas the contrary is not true. (There are however exceptions, such as the aforementioned criminal proceedings instituted in 1902 before US Courts Martial for crimes committed by American troops in the Philippines). Victor States often pass legislation granting amnesty to their own armed forces with regard to any war crime they may have perpetrated. After the First World War, once it proved impossible to set up an international tribunal for the punishment of German authors of war crimes, Germany was obliged to punish German military people accused by the Allies of war crimes. The Leipzig Supreme Court took upon itself the task of so doing, in 1921. In some cases Allied courts brought to trial Germans accused of war crimes, but no such court prosecuted and tried nationals of the Allies. Similarly, after the Second World War, in addition to establishing the two ad hoc International Tribunals (for the principal German and Japanese war criminals), the Allies passed Control Council Laws authorizing (in fact, obliging) German courts to try Germans. Various Allied courts also tried Germans. In Italy courts tried Germans and Italians who had collaborated with them, whereas partisans were granted amnesty. (Subsequently the amnesty was extended to Fascists and collaborators.) Similarly, in France in 1944 a law was passed granting amnesty to the French members of the Resistance, whereas trials were authorized for both the enemy and the French who had collaborated with Germans.

Recently war crimes have been tried under special national legislation, such as that enacted in the UK, Canada, or Australia, relating to a specific set of crimes, namely those committed by Nazis during the Second World War (see, for instance, the

Sawoniuk case, brought before British courts:[36] the accused, a Polish-Byelorussian resident of the UK, was convicted of murder of unknown Jewish women in a village of Byelorussia occupied by the Germans; at 506–9).

It must be added that, strikingly, for about forty years the innovative and forward-looking repressive system instituted by the 1949 Geneva Conventions concerning the universal jurisdiction of any State party over grave breaches of the Conventions has remained unapplied. Only after the establishment of the ICTY and the ICTR have States commenced to resort to it. Thus, German, Danish, and Swiss courts have made use of universal jurisdiction by prosecuting and trying persons who allegedly perpetrated grave breaches in the former Yugoslavia.[37]

These cases, however, still constitute exceptions. As a rule States have confined themselves to taking criminal proceedings based on the more *traditional* grounds of jurisdiction. In practice they have instituted proceedings only against alleged authors of crimes committed on their *territory* or against their nationals (or persons living on their territory and having acquired their nationality).

It should be added that many States still tend to claim *exclusive* jurisdiction over their nationals when they commit war crimes at home or abroad. Thus for instance, in the USA the territoriality principle is widely accepted for criminal offences.[38] However, when it comes to prosecuting US military personnel, the USA refuses to accept foreign jurisdiction, either by entering into agreements with foreign States to the effect that the national jurisdiction of the accused prevails (this also applies to NATO agreements) or by refraining from participating in such international treaties as the Statute of the ICC.

15.8.2 THE PROSECUTION AND PUNISHMENT OF OTHER INTERNATIONAL CRIMES

As far as crimes against humanity and genocide are concerned, once trials of such crimes committed during the Second World War were over, in practice no or very little use has been made of the relevant international rules. In relatively recent times French courts tried Germans or French collaborators accused of having committed crimes against humanity during the Second World War (see the *Barbie*, *Papon*, and *Touvier* cases). In contrast, they have declined to exercise criminal jurisdiction over crimes against humanity committed by the French in Indochina in 1952–4, on legalistic grounds (chiefly a wrong interpretation of a resolution of the UN General

36 [2000] *Crim. LR*, at 506–9.

37 See the *Djajić* and *Jorgić* cases in Germany, the *Sarić* case in Denmark, *Javor* and *Munyeshayka* in France, and the *G.* case in Switzerland.

38 In *Yapp* v. *Reno* and in *Extradition of Charles Philip Smith*, US courts pointed out that 'When an American citizen commits a crime in a foreign country, he cannot complain if required to submit to such modes of trial and to such punishment as the laws of that country prescribe for its own people, unless a different mode be provided by treaty stipulations between that country and the United States' (at 1565 and 965).

Assembly and of the French law that referred to it: see the *Boudarel* case). Genocide has been brought before Israeli courts in *Eichmann* (based on the principle of universal jurisdiction, which however *in fact* largely coincided with that of passive nationality). German courts have pronounced upon genocide in a few cases, all relating to crimes committed by Serbs in the former Yugoslavia (see *Djajić*, *Jorgić*, and *Sokolović*, already referred to above). Courts in Rwanda are now trying alleged perpetrators of genocide.[39]

Torture as a discrete crime has been the subject of important proceedings in *Pinochet*, based on various grounds of jurisdiction (that of the custodial State, for British courts; the principle of universality in conjunction with that of passive nationality, for Spanish courts). However, for all its theoretical and principled significance, this case has not led to a proper trial, not even in Chile. (See the decision of the Court of Appeal of Santiago of 5 June 2000 in *Pinochet*.)

15.8.3 CONCLUDING REMARKS

In sum, national courts are still loath to bring to justice persons accused of international crimes. The fact that very often such crimes are perpetrated by State agents, or with their support, tolerance, or acquiescence, accounts for the hesitation or reluctance of courts to bring to book nationals accused of such crimes. Furthermore, when it is foreigners who allegedly perpetrate those crimes, the fear of meddling in the domestic affairs of other States holds national courts back. Generally speaking, these courts are still dominated by nationalistic, short-term interests. They are still far from realizing community concerns. Few national judges share the sense that it is necessary to vindicate and judicially to enforce respect for fundamental values, wherever they may have been breached.

SELECT BIBLIOGRAPHY

GENERAL

R. Wolfrum, 'The Decentralized Prosecution of International Offences Through National Courts', in Y. Dinstein and M. Tabory (eds), *War Crimes in International Law* (The Hague, Boston, London: Kluwer, 1996), 233–49; J. I. Charney, 'International Criminal Law and the Role of Domestic Courts', 95 AJIL (2001), 120–4.

LEGAL GROUNDS OF JURISDICTION

H. Donnedieu de Vabres, *Les principes modernes du droit pénal international* (Paris: Sirey, 1928), 1–170; J. L. Brierly, 'The Nature of War Crimes Jurisdiction' (1944) in J. L. Brierly, *The Basis of Obligation in International Law and Other Papers* (Oxford: Clarendon Press, 1958), 297–305; F. A.

[39] Some courts have dealt with genocide only tangentially. See for instance *Hipperson and others*, at 587–9, *Mugesera*, at 529–33, and *Niyonteze*, decision of 26 May 2000, at 28–32.

Mann, 'The Doctrine of Jurisdiction in International Law', 111 HR (1964–I), 82–95; C. Lombois, *Droit pénal international*, 2nd edn (Paris: Dalloz, 1979), 302–419; A. Huet and R. Koering-Joulin, *Droit pénal international*, 2nd edn (Paris: Presses Universitaires de France, 2001), 193–223.

THE PRINCIPLE OF TERRITORIALITY

G. E. Langemeijer, 'Le principe de territorialité', in *Le droit Pénal International—Recueil d'études en hommage à J. M. van Bemmelen* (Leiden: E. J. Brill, 1965), 17–37.

THE UNIVERSALITY PRINCIPLE

K. Mikliszanskli, 'Le système de l'universalité du droit de punir et le droit pénal subsidiaire', 1 *Revue de science criminelle et droit pénal comparé* (1936), 331–41; H. Donnedieu de Vabres, 'Le système de répression universelle, 18 *Revue de droit international privé* (1922–3), 533–64; H. Donnedieu de Vabres, 'De la piraterie au génocide—Les nouvelles modalités de la répression universelle', *Mélanges Ripert* (Paris: L.G.D.J, 1950), I, 226ff.; G. Guillaume, 'La compétence universelle. Formes anciennes et nouvelles', *Mélanges Levasseur* (Paris: Litec, 1992), 23–37; K. Randall, 'Universal Jurisdiction under International Law', *Texas Law Review*, 66 (1988), 786–91; B. Stern, 'A propos de la compétence universelle', *Liber Amicorum Judge Mohammed Bedjaoui* (The Hague, London, Boston: Kluwer, 1999), 735–53; J. Verhoeven, 'Vers un ordre répressif universel? Quelques observations', 55 AFDI (1999), 62–3; G. de la Pradelle, 'La compétence universelle', in Ascensio, Decaux, and Pellet (eds), *Droit international pénal*, 905–18; M. Henzelin, *Le principe de l'universalité en droit pénal international* (Basle, Geneva, Munich: Helbing and Lictenhahn, 2000); L. Reydams, 'Universal Criminal Jurisdiction: the Belgian State of Affairs', 11 *CLForum* (2000), 183–216; A. Hays Butler, 'The Doctrine of Universal Jurisdiction: A Review of the Literature', 11 *CLForum* (2000), 353–73; H. A. Kissinger, 'The Pitfalls of Universal Jurisdiction', 80 *Foreign Affairs* (2001), 86–92; J. R. W. D. Jones, 'Immunity and "Double Criminality": General Augusto Pinochet before the House of Lords', in S. Yee and W. Tieya (eds), *International Law in the Post-Cold War World* (London and New York: Routledge, 2001), 254–67; D. Vandermeersch, 'La compétence universelle', in A. Cassese and M. Delmas-Marty (eds), *Juridictions nationales*, 589–611.

TRENDS IN THE PROSECUTION OF INTERNATIONAL CRIMES:

(1) GENERAL

I. A. Lediakh, 'The Application of the Nuremberg Principles by Other Military Tribunals and National Courts', in G. Ginsburgs and V. N. Kudriavtsev (eds) *The Nuremberg Trial and International Law* (Dordrecht, Boston, London: Nijhoff, 1990), 263–83. R. Wedgwood, 'National Courts and the Prosecution of War Crimes' in Kirk McDonald and Swaak-Goldman (eds), *Substantive and Procedural Aspects*, I, 391–415.

(2) PROSECUTION OF CRIMES IN GERMANY

H. Meyrowitz, *La répression par les tribunaux allemands des crimes contre l'humanité et de l'appartenance à une organisation criminelle, en application de la loi no. 10 du Conseil de contrôle allié* (Paris: LGDJ, 1960); R. Henkys, *Die Nationalsozialistischen Gewaltverbrechen. Geschichte und Gericht* (Stuttgart: Kreuz Verlag, 1964); A. Rückerl (ed.), *NS-Prozesse nach 25 Jahren Strafverfolgung: Möglichkeiten—Grenzen—Ergebnisse* (Heidelberg-Karlsruhe: C. F. Müller Verlag, 1971); A. Rückerl, *The Investigation of Nazi Crimes 1945–1978—A Documentation*

(Heidelberg, Karlsruhe: C. F. Müller Verlag, 1979); A. Rückerl, *NS—Verbrechen vor Gericht. Versuch einer Vergangenheitsbewältigung* (Heidelberg-Karlsruhe: C. F. Müller Verlag, 1982); D. H. Kitterman, 'Those Who Said "No!": Germans Who Refused to Execute Civilians during World War II', 11 *German Studies Review* (1988), 241–54; H. Ostendorf, 'Die—widersprüchlichen—Auswirkungen der Nürnberger Prozesse auf die westdeutsche Justiz' in G. Hankel, G. Stuby (eds), *Strafgerichte gegen Menschheitsverbrechen* (Hamburg: Hamburger Edition, 1995), 73–97; K. Ambos, S. Wirth, 'Genocide and War Crimes in the Former Yugoslavia Before German Criminal Courts', in H. Fischer, C. Kress, S. R. Lüder (eds), *International and National Prosecution of Crimes Under International Law—Current Developments* (Berlin: Berlin Verlag Arno Spitz, 2000), 769–97.

(3) PROSECUTION OF CRIMES IN FRANCE

E. Schwinge, 'Angehörige der ehemaligen deutschen Wehrmacht und der SS vor französischen Militärgerichten', 2 *Monatsschrift für deutsches Recht* (1949), 650–4; A. Eiselé, 'Réflexions sur les procès de criminels de guerre en France' in 31 *Revue de droit pénal et de criminologie* (1950–1), 305–17; H. H. Jescheck, 'Zum Oradour-Prozess', 8 *Juristenzeitung* (1953) 156–7; J. P. Maunoir, *La répression des crimes de guerre devant les tribunaux français et alliés* (Geneva: Editions Médecine et hygiène, 1956).

(4) PROSECUTION OF CRIMES IN ITALY

G. Vassalli, G. Sabatini, *Il collaborazionismo e l'amnistia politica nella giurisprudenza della Corte di Cassazione* (Rome: Edizioni "La Giustizia penale", 1947) G. Schreiber, *Deutsche Kriegsverbrechen in Italien* (Munich: O. Beck, 1996); R. Ricci, 'Processo alle stragi naziste? Il caso ligure. I fascicoli occultati e le illegittime archiviazioni', in 7 *Storia e Memoria* (1998), 119–64; F. Focardi, 'La questione della punizione dei criminali di guerra in Italia dopo la fine del Secondo Conflitto Mondiale' in 80 *Quellen und Forschungen aus Italienischen Archiven und Bibliotheken*, 2000, 543–624; P. Gaeta, 'War Crimes Before Italian Criminal Courts: New Trends' in H. Fischer, C. Kress, S. R. Lüder (eds), *International and National Prosecution of Crimes Under International Law* cit., 751–68.

(5) PROSECUTION OF CRIMES BY BRITISH COURTS

R. J. Pritchard, 'The Gift of Clemency following British War Crimes Trials in the Far East, 1946–1948' 8 *CLForum* (1996), 15–50.

(6) PROSECUTION OF CRIMES IN BELGIUM

L. Reydams, 'Prosecuting Crimes Under International Law on the Basis of Universal Jurisdiction: The Experience of Belgium', in H. Fischer, C. Kress, S. R. Lüder (eds), *International and National Prosecution of Crimes Under International Law—Current Developments* (Berlin: Berlin Verlag Arno Spitz, 2000), 799–816; D. Vandermeersch, 'Droit belge', in Cassese and Delmas-Marty (eds), *Juridictions nationales*, 69–119.

(7) PROSECUTION OF CRIMES IN THE USA

T. Taylor, *Nuremberg and Vietnam: an American Tragedy* (Chicago: Quadrangle Books, 1970); N. G. Cooper, 'My Lai and Military Justice—To What Effect?' in 59 *Mil. Law Review* (1973), 93–127; J. F. Addicott, 'The lessons of My Lai', 31 RDMDG (1992), 75–107; G. D. Solis, *Son Thang—An American War Crime* (Annapolis, Maryland: Naval Institute Press, 1997).

16

THE IMPACT OF INTERNATIONAL LAW ON NATIONAL LEGISLATION

16.1 ARE THERE INTERNATIONAL CUSTOMARY RULES OBLIGING STATES TO PROSECUTE INTERNATIONAL CRIMES?

We have seen so far that States tend to lay down in their legislation a limited range of legal grounds of criminal jurisdiction. We have also mentioned a number of treaties providing for grounds of jurisdiction over international crimes. We should now ask ourselves whether there are international customary rules empowering or mandating States to exercise jurisdiction over war crimes, crimes against humanity, genocide, aggression, torture, and terrorism.

State practice shows that there are no international *customary* rules endowed with *a general scope* (that is, concerning all international crimes) that oblige States to exercise jurisdiction on any of the grounds considered so far. Nor are there international rules imposing on States the obligation to act upon a specific ground of jurisdiction, when they decide to bring to justice alleged perpetrators of international crimes. The choice of such grounds is left to each State.

In this respect, it seems significant that the Paris Court of Appeal, in its decision of 20 October 2000 in *Qadafi*, cited the preamble of the Rome Statute of the ICC (whereby 'it is a duty of every State to exercise its criminal jurisdiction over those responsible for international crimes') as evidence of the alleged obligation to prosecute authors of international crimes, incumbent upon any contracting party as a result of 'the intent of the international community to prosecute the most serious facts, even though perpetrated by heads of State in the exercise of their functions, whenever they amount to international crimes, contrary to the demands of universal conscience'. In that case, the Court had duly stressed that it had jurisdiction because the alleged crimes had been committed by foreigners abroad against *French* nationals (later, however, the Court of Cassation overruled that decision, although on different grounds: decision of 20 October 2000, at 4–5). One could perhaps infer from the court's decision that in its view the international customary rule it postulated makes it mandatory for States to exercise jurisdiction on any of the grounds laid down in national law. This interpretation seems to be borne out by the fact that the Rome Statute refers in terms to the 'duty' of every State to exercise criminal jurisdiction, hence it clearly implies that this ought to be done by each State on the strength of its own legal grounds of jurisdiction.

As for a possible emerging customary rule imposing an international obligation to prosecute and try alleged terrorists, or alternatively to hand them over to the States concerned, an admittedly not compelling piece of evidence is constituted by paragraph 5(b) of the GA Declaration of 1994 referred to above (see 6.8.1), that 'urges' States to, among other things, 'ensure the apprehension and prosecution or extradition of perpetrators of terrorist acts, in accordance with the relevant provisions of their national law'.

Besides there being no customary rule with a general content, no general international principle can be found that might be relied upon to indicate that an obligation to prosecute international crimes has crystallized in the international community.

Nonetheless, one could argue that in those areas where *treaties* provide for such an obligation, a corresponding customary rule may have emerged or be in the process of evolving. Clearly, as soon as it may be proved that customary rules have formed, they will reinforce for all the contracting parties the obligations to the same effect laid down in the aforementioned Conventions. They will impose on States not parties to any of those Conventions, or parties to only some of them, a significant obligation, with a correlative legal entitlement for all other States to demand compliance with that obligation. This applies to the obligation to search for, bring to trial, or extradite alleged authors of grave breaches, imposed by the four 1949 Geneva Conventions In its judgment of 1986 in *Nicaragua* (§220), the International Court of Justice appositely held that Article 1 common to the four Geneva Convention, whereby any contracting State must 'respect and ensure respect' for the Convention obligations 'in all circumstances' had turned into a general principle of humanitarian law binding upon contracting and non-contracting States alike. In its Advisory Opinion on *Legality of the Threat or Use of Nuclear Weapons* (§79), the International Court of Justice rightly held in 1996 that the fundamental principles of the Geneva Conventions have turned into customary international law. No doubt among these principles one should include those underlying the repressive penal system provided for in the Conventions. If this is so, it follows that there now exists a *customary obligation specifically concerning grave breaches*: it is the obligation to search for, and bring to trial (or extradite) the alleged perpetrators of grave breaches of those Conventions, who happen to be on the territory of the prosecuting State.

In addition, it cannot be denied that at least with regard to the most odious international crimes such as genocide and crimes against humanity, there exists a general obligation of international *co-operation* for their prevention and punishment.

This general obligation, clearly referred to with regard to genocide by the ICJ in 1951 in *Genocide* (at 23) and restated in 1996 in *Application of the Convention on the Prevention and Punishment of the Crime of Genocide* (at §31) may among other things entail for States the general duty to set up appropriate judicial mechanisms or procedures for the universal repression of those crimes.

16.2 ARE THERE CUSTOMARY RULES AUTHORIZING STATES TO PROSECUTE INTERNATIONAL CRIMES?

Under the general principle enunciated in 1927 by the PCIJ in *Lotus*, States are free to exercise their criminal jurisdiction over acts performed outside their territory, whenever no specific international limitations (provided for either in treaties or in customary rules) restrict such freedom. As stressed above (15.7) the Court held that:

> Far from laying down a general prohibition to the effect that States may not extend the application of their laws and the jurisdiction of their courts to persons, property and acts outside their territory, it [international law] leaves them in this respect a wide measure of discretion which is only limited in certain cases by prohibitive rules; as regards other cases, every State remains free to adopt the principles which it regards as best and most suitable. (At 19.)

As stated above, with regard to universal jurisdiction (see 15.7), one fails to discern any customary or treaty limitation on the power of States to try and punish crimes against humanity and other crimes perpetrated at home or abroad either by nationals or by foreigners, except of course for the limitations deriving from international rules on personal immunities, referred to above (14.4; see also 15.6).

16.3 THE LIMITED IMPACT OF INTERNATIONAL LAW ON NATIONAL COURTS

16.3.1 THE RELEVANCE OF INTERNATIONAL CUSTOMARY LAW

Normally national courts do not undertake proceedings for international crimes only on the basis of international *customary* law, that is, if a crime is only provided for in that body of law. They instead tend to require either a national *statute* defining the crime and granting national courts jurisdiction over it, or, if a treaty has been ratified on the matter by the State, the passing of *implementing legislation* enabling courts to fully apply the relevant treaty provisions.

That courts decline to prosecute and punish individuals charged with crimes only envisaged in customary international law is evidenced among other things by

Niyonteze, where in 2000 a Swiss Appellate Military Tribunal held that it could not apply the rules on genocide, because Switzerland had not yet ratified the Genocide Convention of 1948, nor, on account of a provision of the Military Penal Code (Article 108(2)), could it apply the Convention's provisions declaratory of customary law to *internal* armed conflicts (at 30–2).[1]

Similarly, in a judgment of 6 November 1995 in *Reporters sans frontières* v. *Mille Collines* (at 48–51), the Paris Court of Appeal held that it lacked jurisdiction over genocide, grave breaches of the four 1949 Geneva Conventions, crimes against humanity, and torture allegedly committed abroad by foreigners against foreigners. As far as 'genocide, war crimes and crimes against humanity' were concerned, the Court held that it had no jurisdiction because:

> in the absence of provisions of domestic law international custom cannot have the effect of extending the extraterritorial jurisdiction of the French courts. In that respect, only the provisions of international treaties are applicable under the national legal system, provided they have been duly approved or ratified by France and, on account of their contents, the provisions of such treaties produce a direct effect.

As for grave breaches of the Geneva Conventions, the Court held that French courts lacked jurisdiction because no implementing legislation had been passed. Finally, with regard to torture, French courts did possess jurisdiction on account of the adoption by French authorities of legislation implementing the 1984 UN Convention on Torture. However, in the case at issue the petitioners had not shown that they had suffered direct damage from the alleged crimes.

Furthermore, in two 1999 cases (*Nulyarimma* v. *Thompson* and *Buzzacott* v. *Hill*), the Federal Court of Australia dismissed claims of members of the aboriginal community that conduct engaged in by certain senior State officials was contributing to the destruction of the aboriginal people as an ethnic or racial group, thus amounting to genocide. The legal ground for the dismissal was that, although genocide was prohibited by an international peremptory norm as well as by the 1948 Genocide Convention, and although a statute had been enacted approving ratification of that Convention, the Australian courts lacked jurisdiction over genocide because no legislation had been passed providing for the trial within Australia of persons accused of genocide (at 20–68. One of the three judges, Merkel, disagreed, contending that a legislative act creating genocide as an offence and granting jurisdiction to courts was not necessary for the court to exercise jurisdiction over genocide; however, he also held that the claims should be dismissed, on other legal grounds).

16.3.2 THE IMPLEMENTATION OF INTERNATIONAL TREATIES

The existence of treaties designed among other things to oblige States to prosecute and punish the alleged authors of some categories of international crimes (genocide,

[1] In its judgment of 27 April 2001 the *Tribunal Militaire de Cassation* did not overrule the Court's decision on this point (at 6–9).

grave breaches of the Geneva Conventions and the First Protocol, torture, terrorism) has had a considerable bearing on State legislation and national courts.

A reservation must however be entered. States have found many means of evading international obligations.

First, many States have *failed to pass legislation to implement* duly ratified international treaties.

For instance, Egypt, while it has ratified many international treaties on international crimes, has then refrained from enacting the necessary implementing legislation, particularly with regard to genocide and the 1949 Geneva Conventions. In China, only the Geneva Conventions of 1949 and the Convention on Torture of 1984 have been translated into national legislation. By contrast, no such legislation exists with regard to the crimes of genocide, crimes against humanity, aggression, or terrorism. In Morocco, neither the four 1949 Geneva Conventions nor the 1948 Convention on Genocide have ever been published in the *Bulletin officiel* (it is as a result of such publication that international treaties take effect in the national legal system). In Brazil, the 1949 Geneva Conventions were ratified in 1957, but no implementing legislation has yet been passed. In Italy, no detailed legislation implementing the 1949 Geneva Conventions has ever been passed. (A legislative 'order' imposing compliance with the Conventions was enacted, but no legislation has been passed rendering non-self-executing provisions of the Conventions susceptible to application.) Furthermore, the 1984 Convention on Torture was duly ratified and implementing legislation was passed, but no legislative provision has been enacted on the definition of torture (which is not provided for as a distinct crime in the Italian Criminal Code). Similarly, such States as Morocco, Tunisia, Jordan, and Kuwait have not enacted legislation defining torture, whereas Algeria has passed a definition that the UN Committee against Torture held incomplete.[2]

This phenomenon is all the more serious because many national courts are not prepared to exercise jurisdiction if *express national legislation* to this effect is lacking. Often they require that the legislation implementing international treaties include not only rules on the criminalization of certain acts (that is legislation providing that certain acts amount to crimes), but also provisions expressly granting jurisdiction to courts over those offences. If such legislation is lacking, courts refuse to take proceedings. As in many States (for instance, Brazil, Egypt, Morocco, and other Islamic countries) no legislation has been passed to adopt the universality principle at least with reference to the ratified international treaties providing for this ground of jurisdiction, such jurisdiction may not be exercised.

Secondly, some States have *entered reservations* upon ratification of some treaties. Thus on ratifying the Convention on Genocide, Morocco stated that only Moroccan courts were competent to deal with genocide in Morocco, and any international court could adjudicate cases of genocide only if Morocco expressly consented thereto. A similar reservation was entered by Algeria.

[2] CAT, 8 November 1996, UN Doc. A/52/44, §74.

Thirdly, some States have passed implementing legislation that in fact *restricts or narrows the scope of grounds of jurisdiction* laid down in international treaties. A case in point is the US legislation implementing the four 1949 Geneva Conventions. After defining the crimes over which US courts will have jurisdiction as a result of such implementation, that is war crimes including grave breaches of the Geneva Conventions as well as violations of common Article 3, the US legislation sets forth the grounds on which US courts may assert jurisdiction over these crimes, as follows:

(a) Offense. Whoever, whether inside or outside the United States, commits a war crime, in any of the circumstances described in subsection (b), shall be fined under this title or imprisoned for life or any term of years, or both, and if death results of the victim, shall be subject to the penalty of death.
(b) Circumstances. The circumstances referred to in subsection (a) are that the person committing such war crime or the victim of such war crime is a member of the Armed Forces of the United States or a national of the United States.

Thus, while the Geneva Conventions lay down the universality principle, this principle is *replace*d in the USA, in blatant breach of the Conventions, by the traditional principles of active and passive personality.

Fourthly, national courts have developed in their judicial practice a *restrictive tendency* to limit as much as possible the impact of international rules on the exercise of jurisdiction by national courts over international crimes.

For instance, in France, courts have held that the 1949 Geneva Conventions could not be applied without the necessary implementing legislation. In addition, their provisions on universal jurisdiction 'are too general in character for them directly to create rules on extraterritorial jurisdiction in criminal matters, for such rules must be laid down with legal precision'.[3]

Another case in which a State has refused to apply international provisions of international treaties is the decision delivered in Senegal on 20 March 2001 in *Hissène Habré*. The Supreme Court refused to apply Article 6 of the 1984 Convention on Torture (which imposes on every State party on whose territory an alleged torturer is present a duty to institute criminal proceedings against him). This Convention had been ratified by Senegal on 16 June 1986 and published in the *Journal officiel* on 9 August 1986, thus becoming part of Senegalese legislation pursuant to Article 79 of the Constitution. When proceedings were initiated against the former Chadian dictator Habré, then residing in Senegal, for torture allegedly sponsored when he led his country, the Supreme Court, to which the case had been brought, held that Article 4

[3] See for instance the decision of 24 November 1994 of the Paris Court of Appeal in *Javor and others* (at 9), as well as the decision handed down on 6 November 1995 by the same Paris Court of Appeal in *Reporters sans frontières* v. *Mille Collines* (at 49).

One could also mention that in Italy the Bologna Court of Appeal held in 1963 in *Kröger* that, genocide being a political offence, a German national accused of genocide could not be extradited to the Federal Republic of Germany, the more so because the Genocide Convention, although ratified by Italy, had not yet been implemented in the Italian legal system, although a general 'legislative implementing Act' had already been passed by Parliament (at 318–21).

of the Convention (obliging every State party to 'ensure that all acts of torture are offences under its criminal law') had not been fully implemented in Senegal. The Senegalese legal system had been made to comply with the Convention by providing in Article 295–1 of the Criminal Code (passed by law no. 96 of 28 August 1996) that torture was a crime. Nevertheless, Article 669 of the Code of Criminal Procedure had not been changed. (Under this provision any foreigner who has committed a crime abroad against State security or counterfeited the national seal may be prosecuted in Senegal if arrested in Senegal or extradited to that country.) Hence, according to the Court, 'no provision of criminal procedure confers universal jurisdiction on Senegalese courts for the prosecution and judgment of persons who happen to be on the territory of Senegal and are allegedly perpetrators or accomplices of acts coming within the purview of the law of 28 August 1996 designed to implement Article 4 of the Convention, if such acts have been performed by foreigners abroad' (at 7). This reasoning could appear specious, for arguably the ground of jurisdiction provided for in Article 6 of the Convention (the principle of *forum deprehensionis*) did not need to be translated into an express provision of national legislation to become operational.[4]

In addition, one cannot fail to mention the holding of the Amsterdam Court of Appeal in 1995 in *Pinochet*. Although the Chilean leader was staying in Amsterdam, the Prosecutor refused to apply the 1984 Convention on Torture, ratified by the Netherlands, arguing among other things that Dutch courts did not have jurisdiction. On appeal by the complainants, the Court held that it was 'evident that prosecution of Pinochet by the Dutch Public Prosecutions Department would encounter so many legal and practical problems that the Public Prosecutor was perfectly within his rights to decide not to prosecute' (at 365).

Nevertheless, it should be stressed that in some States, courts, in interpreting international treaties, have adopted an *expansive approach* that has resulted in a broadening of their jurisdiction over international crimes.

Thus, for instance, in the Netherlands the question had arisen in *Bouterse* of whether a Surinamese political activist, allegedly involved in the killing of a number of political opponents in 1982, could be brought to trial for torture under the universality principle laid down in the 1984 Convention on Torture, implemented in the Netherlands in 1989. The Amsterdam Court of Appeals held in a decision of 20 November 2000 that the exercise by a Dutch court of universality of jurisdiction with regard to facts that occurred in 1982, that is before the 1984 Convention came into existence, was not contrary to the principle of legality. Following the opinion of an expert in public international law, the Court held that the Torture Convention was of a declaratory nature, merely restating the customary international prohibition of torture. Consequently the prosecution in 2000 of acts of torture was not contrary to

[4] At the most the court could have agued that it was Article 5(2) of the Convention that had not been implemented. (Under this provision, 'Each State Party shall likewise take such measures as may be necessary to establish its jurisdiction over such offences in cases where the alleged offender is present in any territory under its jurisdiction and it does not extradite him pursuant to Article 8 to any of the States mentioned in paragraph 1 of this Article'.)

Article 15 of the UN Covenant on Civil and Political Rights, which allowed the trial and punishment of acts that at the time they were performed were criminal according to the general principles of law recognized by the community of nations. According to the Court, the Dutch Torture Convention Implementation Act of 1989 could be applied 'retrospectively' to cover conduct such as assault and murder that was illegal under Dutch law before 1989 but did not constitute the criminal offence of torture. Thus, the Court concluded that: (i) it was sufficient for the acts to be punishable at the moment of their commission under international rules; the incriminating rules in the Netherlands could be derived from these international rules, together with the provisions of the Dutch implementing legislation, to be applied 'retrospectively'; (ii) universality of jurisdiction could be exercised on the strength of the general criminal law of the Netherlands (which authorized such jurisdiction in connection with an international treaty obligation) and in light of the 1984 Convention. The Court had stressed, however, in its previous decision of 3 March 2000, that 'at least one of the victims [of the alleged crimes] and possibly more had Dutch nationality' and 'the complainants, who are relatives of two of the victims', lived in the Netherlands; it also stressed the 'close historic ties [of the Netherlands] with Surinam. (§4.2). The second decision was however reversed by the Supreme Court (*Hoge Raad*) through a judgment of 18 September 2001.[5]

Similarly, Dutch courts have placed a liberal interpretation on Dutch legislative provisions on jurisdiction over war crimes.[6]

In Spain, the *Audiencia nacional* in an order of 5 November 1998 in *Adolfo Scilingo* placed a broad interpretation on Article 6 of the Convention on Genocide (which limits *mandatory* jurisdiction over this crime to territorial courts and envisages a future international criminal court), by stating that 'if the contracting States have not envisaged the universal repression of this crime, this does not prevent the establishment by a contracting party of universal jurisdiction over this crime, which has such scope in the world and directly affects the international community and indeed the whole of humanity' (Legal Ground no. 5).

[5] The Court of Cassation dismissed the interpretation advanced by the Court of Appeal (at §7.6) and in addition held that universal jurisdiction could only be exercised by Dutch courts if the defendant was in the Netherlands, in keeping with the Convention on Torture (at §8.5). On this decision see J. K. Kleffner, 'Droit néerlandais', in Cassese and Delmas-Marty (eds), *Juridictions nationales*, at 224–5, 241.

[6] Thus in the *Knezević* case, first the District Court (Military Division) of Arnhem and then the Supreme Court held that Dutch courts may exercise universal jurisdiction over war crimes committed in an internal armed conflict in 1992 in the former Yugoslavia. The District Court, after interpreting Article 3(1) of the 1952 Wartime Criminal Law Act as applying the universality principle to war crimes, added that 'any other view would not result in the complete fulfilment of the treaty obligations by which the Netherlands is bound, including the obligations of the Geneva Conventions. According to the text and history of these Conventions, they are based expressly on the universality principle. The question whether this view also applies—in brief—to war crimes committed during a civil war must, in the view of the court sitting in chambers, be answered in the affirmative. There is nothing in the text of the Act or in the parliamentary history to show that any other view should apply, and the Wartime Criminal Law Act expressly provides that war includes civil war' (§§8–9). The Supreme Court (*Hoge Raad*), in its decision of 11 November 1997, confirmed this view (at 463).

16.4 INTERNATIONAL RULES IMPOSING RESPECT FOR FUNDAMENTAL SAFEGUARDS IN NATIONAL TRIALS

There exist many international customary and treaty rules which impose upon States the obligation to respect a core of procedural standards, when national courts prosecute and try persons accused of international crimes, regardless of the specific legal ground of jurisdiction on which the courts assert their jurisdiction.

There are principally two sets of rules. Some belong to the corpus of rules on human rights, and are essentially treaty provisions, which therefore only bind contracting States. Chief among them are the provisions of Articles 15 and 16 of the UN Covenant on Civil and Political Rights, the former relating to the safeguards of a fair trial, the latter imposing respect for the *nullum crimen* principle. Similar rules can be found in the 1950 European Convention on Human Rights (Articles 6 and 7), the 1969 American Convention on Human Rights (Articles 8 and 9), and the 1981 African Charter on Human and Peoples' Rights (Article 7). Contracting States must always comply with these provisions for any criminal trial, whether concerning an 'ordinary' crime or an international crime. However, they may be derogated from, under certain strict conditions, 'in time of public emergency which threatens the life of the nation'.

The other set of rules comprises customary and treaty rules on international humanitarian law, relating to situations of armed conflict. These rules allow the trial of prisoners of war or civilians for crimes committed during armed hostilities, on condition however that the detaining authorities respect some basic safeguards laid down in these rules.

It should be stressed that *traditionally* international rules simply required that States, before punishing a person for a war crime, should hold a trial. For instance, Rule 449 of the 1912 British Military Manual provided that 'charges of war crimes may be dealt with by military courts or by such courts as the belligerent concerned may determine. In every case, however, there must be a trial before punishment, and the utmost care must be taken to confine the punishment to the actual offender'. Subsequently, treaty rules were agreed upon (through the 1929 Geneva Convention on prisoners of war) that obliged States parties to respect some basic principles, for instance the principle whereby sentence can be pronounced against a prisoner of war only by the same courts and according to the same procedure used for members of the armed forces of the detaining Power. However, in the United States both the President and subsequently the Supreme Court took a different view. In 1942 the President set up Military Commissions to try enemy combatants. These Commissions were authorized among other things to depart from the standard rules of evidence (for instance, admitting affidavits produced by the Prosecutor without the defence being able to exercise the right of confrontation of witnesses and cross-examination and other means to establish the credibility of the deponents or affiants; using hearsay and opinion evidence tendered by the prosecution). In addition they did not give the accused reasonable opportunity for preparing their defence, could hold proceedings *in camera*, did not provide for the right of the accused to appoint a defence counsel of his choice, and did not provide for a right of appeal. Various cases were brought before the US Supreme Court: the appellants had applied for leave to file a petition for writs of *habeas corpus* and a petition for *certiorari* to review an order of other authorities denying the applications: *Ex parte Quirin* (1942), *Yamashita* (1946), *Homma* (1946) and *Hirota* v. *MacArthur* (1948). In all these cases the petition was rejected, and the Court's majority held that the establishment and functioning of the Military Commission was in conformity with both the US Constitution and international law. However, in the second and third cases, Judges Murphy and Rutledge appended powerful dissenting opinions, showing in a very persuasive way that the view taken by the majority was wrong (see in particular *Yamashita*, at 23–38 and at 38–78).

At present the rules obliging States to conduct in time of armed conflict trial proceedings consistent with the fundamental principles of fair trial (or due process) are laid down in Articles 5, 82–8 and 99–108 of the Third Geneva Convention of 1949 on Prisoners of War and Articles 65–78 of the Fourth Geneva Convention of 1949 on the Protection of Civilians.[7]

On 13 November 2001, President G. W. Bush issued a Military Order authorizing the establishment of Military Commissions charged with trying foreign terrorists. These persons were to be tried 'for violations of the laws of war and other applicable laws' (section 1(e)). The Order also provided that is was not 'practicable' for these Military Commissions to apply 'the principles of law and the rules of evidence generally recognized in the trial of criminal cases in the United States district courts' (section 1(f)). It is clear from the Order that secret (that is, not public) trials could be held, that the accused might not be permitted to choose his defence counsel, and that no appeal is provided for, not even where the death penalty is imposed, although the US President is entitled to grant reprieves or pardons. A number of American commentators have argued that the Order is not in keeping with the US Constitution. Whether or not this is true, it seems indisputable that the Order is not consonant with the aforementioned provisions of the 1949 Geneva Conventions (in the event of the basic assumption underlying the Order being well founded, that is that the foreign terrorists coming within the purview of the Order have or had acted within the framework of an international armed conflict, as 'unlawful combatants'). If instead it is contended that the acts of terrorism envisaged in the Order were committed in time of peace, the Order would not be in keeping with Article 14 of the UN Covenant on Civil and Political Rights, ratified by the USA, as long as the US Government would not submit to the other contracting States, through the intermediary of the UN Secretary-General, a report on its intent to derogate from that provision, pursuant to Article 4 of the Covenant.

[7] Article 5(2) provides that 'Should any doubt arise as to whether person, having committed a belligerent act and having fallen into the hands of the enemy, belong to any of the categories enumerated in Article 4 [the category of lawful combatants], such persons shall enjoy the protection of the present Convention until such time as their status has been determined by a competent tribunal'.

SELECT BIBLIOGRAPHY

H. Fischer, C. Kress, and S. R. Lüder (eds), *International and National Prosecution of Crimes under International Law—Current Developments* (Berlin: Berlin Verlag, 2001); Cassese and Delmas-Marty (eds), *Juridictions nationales*; P. Gaeta, 'Les règles internationals sur les critères de compétence des juges nationaux', in Cassese and Delmas-Marty (eds), *Crimes internationaux*, 191–213.

17

LEGAL IMPEDIMENTS TO THE EXERCISE OF NATIONAL JURISDICTION

Many obstacles in national legislation may hamper or put in jeopardy the institution of criminal proceedings for international crimes. The principal ones are: (i) laws granting amnesty for broad categories of crimes; (ii) national statutes of limitation; (iii) the prohibition of double jeopardy (the principle of *ne bis idem*), whereby a person may not be brought to trial twice for the same offence; (iv) national laws on immunity from prosecution of Heads of State, members of government or parliamentarians.

17.1 AMNESTY

Many States have passed legislation granting amnesty, with regard to specific episodes in the States' histories, for war crimes or crimes against humanity, or for broad categories of crimes that include the two classes just referred to. They have thus cancelled the crimes. After the enactment of such laws, conduct that was previously criminal is no longer such, with the consequence that: (i) prosecutors forfeit the right or power to initiate investigations or criminal proceedings; and (ii) any sentence passed for the crime is obliterated.

After the Second World War, States such as France and Italy granted amnesty to those nationals who had fought against the Germans. (Later on the Italian authorities passed an amnesty law for fascists and collaborators as well.) On 18 June 1966, when the Algerian war was over, the French Parliament passed a law granting amnesty for all crimes committed in that conflict as well as in Indochina. Chile and Argentina passed laws providing for amnesty for all crimes committed during the post-Allende period, in the former case, and the military dictatorship, in the latter. Other countries such as Peru and Uruguay also enacted similar laws covering gross violations of human rights comprising torture or crimes against humanity.

The rationale behind amnesty is that in the aftermath of periods of turmoil and deep rift, such as those following armed conflict, civil strife, or revolution, it is best to heal social wounds by forgetting past misdeeds, hence by obliterating all the criminal offences that may have been perpetrated by any side. It is believed that in this way one may more expeditiously bring about cessation of hatred and animosity, thereby attaining national reconciliation. However, in some recent instances the incumbent military and political leaders themselves passed amnesty laws, in view of an expected change in government and for the clear purpose of exempting themselves from future prosecution.

On the practical side, it is doubtful that amnesty laws may heal open wounds. Particularly when very serious crimes have been committed involving members of ethnic, religious, or political groups and eventually pitting one group against another, moral and psychological wounds may fester if attempts are made to sweep past horrors under the carpet. Resentment and hate are temporarily suppressed; sooner or later, however, they resurface and spawn even greater violence and crimes.

The choice between forgetting and justice must in any event be left to policy-makers and legislators. From a legal viewpoint, one may nevertheless note that international rules often oblige States to refrain from granting amnesty for international crimes. Here we should distinguish between treaty rules and customary rules.

In many instances international bodies or national courts have considered amnesty laws incompatible with treaty provisions on human rights, in particular with those provisions which require the granting of a right to judicial remedies for any violations of human rights. This is the opinion that the UN Human Rights Committee set out in 1994 in its General Comment no. 20 as well as its 'views' in *Laureano Atachahua* v. *Peru*, and in its comments on the reports of Peru and Haiti. The Committee took the same position in *Rodríguez* v. *Uruguay* with regard to torture.[1]

The Inter-American Commission shared this view in its reports on El Salvador,[2] Uruguay,[3] Argentina,[4] Chile,[5] and Colombia.[6]

One may also recall that the Inter-American Court of Human Rights recently held in the *Barrios Altos* case (*Chumbipuma Aguirre and others* v. *Peru*) that the granting of amnesty to the alleged authors of such gross violations of human rights as torture, summary executions, and forced disappearances was contrary to the non-derogable rights laid down in the body of international law on human rights and in particular to some provisions of the American Convention on Human Rights; it consequently held that two laws passed by Peru to grant such amnesty were 'devoid of legal effects' and

1 In its 'views' in that case, the UN Human Rights Committee stated that amnesties for gross violations of human rights 'are incompatible with the obligations of the State Party under the Covenant'. The Committee noted 'with deep concern that the adoption of this Law [a Uruguayan law of 1986, called the Limitations Act or Law of Expiry] effectively excludes in a number of cases the possibility of investigation into past human rights abuses and thereby prevents the State Party from discharging its responsibility to provide effective remedies to the victims of those abuses. Moreover, the Committee is concerned that, in adopting this law, the State Party has contributed to an atmosphere of impunity which may undermine the democratic order and give rise to further grave human rights violations' (§12).

2 Report no. 26/92, IACHR Annual Report, 1992–3 (at **www.oas.org**).

3 Report no. 29/92, IACHR Annual Report, 1992–3 (ibid.).

4 Report no. 24/92, IACHR, Annual Report, 1992–3 (ibid.).

5 Report no. 25/98, IACHR Annual Report, 1997 (ibid.).

6 Third Report on Colombia, Chapter IV, §345, IACHR 1999 (ibid.).

the Peruvian authorities were obliged to initiate criminal proceedings against the alleged authors of those crimes (§§41–4, and 51(3–5)).

Finally, a Spanish judge refused to take into account an amnesty law as being contrary to international law in *Fortunato Galtieri* (order of 25 March 1997, at 7–9).[7]

It should be added that, as one commentator has noted,[8] some international treaties (for instance, the Convention on Genocide of 1948 and the four Geneva Conventions of 1949) impose upon State parties the obligation to prosecute and punish the alleged authors of crimes prohibited by such treaties. To pass and apply amnesty laws to alleged authors of any such crime would run counter to those treaty obligations.

Let us now ask ourselves whether there has evolved any rule of customary international law prohibiting amnesty for international crimes.

Against the existence of such a rule one could note that States have made agreements explicitly providing for amnesty for a set of offences including such offences as war crimes, torture, or crimes against humanity. It may suffice to cite here the Evian Agreements of 1962 between France and Algeria.[9] Mention may also be made of a legally binding Community act, the Framework decision of the Council of the European Union of 10 December 2001 (Article 5 of which envisages amnesty as one of the legal grounds on which a State may refuse the execution of arrest warrants, without making any exception for the international crimes referred to in the enumeration of Article 2). All these treaties and other acts have as their underpinning the principle of respect for State sovereignty, and its implication that the power to decide who may be exempted from criminal punishment belongs to the sovereign prerogatives of each State.

To support instead the gradual evolution of a customary prohibition of amnesty for the crimes under discussion, one may mention other elements of State practice. On 7 July 1999 the Special Representative of the UN Secretary-General attached a disclaimer to the Peace Agreement between the Government of Sierra Leone and the Revolutionary United Front of Sierra Leone,[10] which provided for amnesty in Article 9. Under this disclaimer:

[7] The Chilean Supreme Court first held that amnesty laws were admissible and applicable (see *Osvaldo Romo Mena*, decision of 26 October 1995, at 3–5), then, in a decision of 9 September in the same case, held the contrary view (at 2–6).

[8] P. Gaeta, 'Les règles internationales sur les critères de compétence des juges nationaux', in Cassese and Delmas-Marty (eds), *Crimes internationaux*, 197–209.

[9] See also the 1977 Second Protocol Additional to the Geneva Conventions of 1949. In Article 6(5) it provides that at the end of hostilities the authorities in power must endeavour to grant amnesty 'to persons who have participated in the armed conflict'. The idea is that those who have simply fought, *and not necessarily committed any crimes*, against the government—or for the government in a conflict where the government lost—should not be prosecuted for murder, treason, etc. or any of the offences under national law with which a person who fought against the government, and perhaps killed government soldiers in combat, could be charged. Article 6(5) exists to promote national reconciliation by having those 'offences' forgiven. It must also be noted that, when the Protocol was drafted (between 1974 and 1977), the idea that serious violations of international rules on internal armed conflict could be classified as war crimes, had not yet been adopted.

[10] See UN Doc. S/1999/777.

The United Nations interprets that the amnesty and pardon in Article 9 of the Agreement shall not apply to international crimes of genocide, crimes against humanity, war crimes, and other serious violations of international humanitarian law.

In its turn, Article 10 of the Statute of the Special Court for Sierra Leone provides that an amnesty granted for the crimes falling under the Court's jurisdiction 'shall not be a bar to prosecution'. Interestingly, the same language may be found in Article 40 of the Cambodian Bill of 2000 on the Establishment of Extraordinary Chambers in the Courts of Cambodia for the Prosecution of Crimes Committed during the Period of Democratic Kampuchea. Furthermore, in 2000, France revised its Constitution to implement the Statute of the ICC, after the Constitutional Council had held in 1999, in *Constitutionality of the ICC Statute* (§34), that the principle of complementarity laid down in the ICC Statute entailed that France might have to arrest and hand over to the Court for trial a person benefiting from amnesty in France, and this consequence was contrary to the French Constitution, in particular to the principle laid down in Article 34 whereby it is the prerogative of the French Parliament to decide on amnesty. Thus, in the event France bowed to the principle that laws on amnesty may not be relied upon for crimes falling under the Court's jurisdiction.

These innovative manifestations of international practice find their rationale in the notion that, as international crimes constitute attacks on *universal* values, no *single* State should arrogate to itself the right to decide to cancel such crimes, or to set aside their legal consequences. These manifestations therefore reflect the concept that the requirement to dispense justice should trump the need to respect State sovereignty. However, they are not yet so widespread as to warrant the contention that a customary rule has crystallized, the more so because, as stated above (16.1) no customary rule having a general purport has yet emerged imposing upon States the obligation to prosecute and punish the alleged authors of any international crime. Indeed, if such a rule could be held to have taken shape, one could infer from it that granting amnesty would conflict with such a rule.

Perhaps the current status of international practice, in particular its inconsistency combined with the more and more widespread *opinio juris* in the international community that international crimes should be punished, could be conceptualized as follows. There is not yet any general obligation for States to refrain from enacting amnesty laws on these crimes. Consequently, if a State passes any such law, it does not breach a customary rule. Nonetheless, if the courts of another State having in custody persons accused of international crimes decide to prosecute them although in their national State they would benefit from an amnesty law, such courts would not thereby act contrary to general international law, in particular to the principle of respect for the sovereignty of other States. One might add that, in light of the current trends of the international community, one may find much merit in the distinction suggested, at least for minor defendants, by a distinguished judge and commentator,[11] between

11 D. Vandermeersch, 'Droit belge', in Cassese and Delmas-Marty (eds), *Juridictions nationales*, at 108. See also J. Dugard, in Cassese, Gaeta, John, *ICC Commentary*, at 695–8.

amnesties granted as a result of a process of national reconciliation, and blanket amnesties. The legal entitlement of foreign States not to take into account an amnesty passed by the national State of the alleged perpetrator should apply to the second category. Instead, if the amnesty results from a specific individual decision of a court or a Truth and Reconciliation Commission, the exigencies of justice could be held to be fulfilled, and foreign courts should refrain from adjudicating those crimes. It should be added that whenever general rules prohibiting specific international crimes come to acquire the nature of peremptory norms (*jus cogens*), they may be construed as imposing among other things the obligation not to cancel by legislative or executive fiat the crimes they proscribe. At any rate, this is the view an ICTY Trial Chamber spelled out in *Furundžija*, with regard to torture as a war crime (§155). An Argentinian judge took a similar view in *Simon Julio, Del Cerrro Juan Antonio* (at 43–64, 103–4). Also the Spanish *Audiencia nacional* held amnesty laws concerning international crimes to be contrary to *jus cogens* in *Scilingo* (at 7, Legal Ground 8) and *Pinochet* (at 7–8, Legal Ground 8).

17.2 STATUTES OF LIMITATION

Many States lay down rules providing that after the elapse of a certain number of years (normally, 10 or 20) *no prosecution may any longer be initiated* with regard to some major categories of crimes such as murder, robbery, etc. Some States also add provisions whereby, if *a final sentence* pronounced for a crime has not been served after a certain number of years, it is no longer applicable. (For instance, in France, under Article 7 of the Code of Criminal Procedure, the right to prosecute a crime is forfeited within 10 years of the perpetration of the crime, whereas, pursuant to Article 132–2 of the Criminal Code, a penalty is no longer applicable 20 years after the issuance of a final sentence; similar provisions may be found in the codes of such European countries as Austria, Germany, Switzerland, Portugal, and Denmark.)

The rationale behind this legislation is that the passage of time renders the collection of evidence very difficult (in that witnesses are no longer available, material evidence may have disappeared or got lost, etc.). In addition, it is felt that it is better for society to forget, the more so because, once many years have gone by, the victims or their relatives may have become reconciled to past crimes. Another ground warranting statutes of limitation is often found in the fact that as a result of the failure of prosecuting officers to search for evidence or find the alleged culprit, the deterrent effect of criminalization dwindles and eventually comes to naught; consequently, leaving open the possibility for prosecution no longer proves appropriate.

In many States the general provisions on the statute of limitation also apply to at least some classes of international crimes. For instance, in Spain, pursuant to Article 113 of the Criminal Code, after 20 years no prosecution is admissible for crimes involving *reclusion mayor* (imprisonment of 26 to 30 years), whereas the statutory period is of 15 years for crimes entailing *reclusion menor* (imprisonment of 12 to 20 years). In Italy, the 20-year statute of limitation also applies to such international crimes as war crimes, crimes against humanity, and genocide as long as they do not entail a sentence of life imprisonment. (When such sentence is applicable, no statute of limitation applies.) A similar rule applies in Germany, where murder is not considered subject to statutes of limitation. In Japan, under the general rule laid down in Article 250 of the Code of Criminal Procedure, if a crime involves the death penalty, the period of statutory limitation is 50 years, whereas it runs to 10 years if the crime involves life imprisonment, or to 7 years if the penalty is imprisonment for more than 10 years.

In other countries there are instead special rules for international crimes. For instance, in Colombia the statute of limitation for torture, genocide, and forced disappearances is 30 years; in Spain, 20 years for torture and terrorism. In France, the statute of limitation for terrorism is 20 years (if the offence amounts to a misdemeanour or *délit*) and 30 years if it amounts to a serious offence (*crime*). Furthermore, a distinction is made between war crimes and crimes against humanity: for the former the statute of limitation is that provided for in general criminal rules (20 years); for the latter, a law of 26 December 1964 provides that there may be no statute of limitation. In common law countries, where there is no general rule on statutory limitation but there may be specific rules concerning specific crimes, no statutory limitation is provided for such serious offences as international crimes.

To date a few international treaties have been concluded on this matter: for instance, the UN Convention on the Non-Applicability of Statutory Limitations to War Crimes and Crimes against Humanity, of 26 November 1968, and the European Convention of 25 January 1974, on the same subject. Only a relatively small number of States have, however, ratified such treaties. The ICC Statute provides in Article 29 that 'The crimes within the jurisdiction of the Court shall not be subject to any statute of limitation'.

As already stated above with regard to amnesties, whenever international treaties, or such customary rules as those on grave breaches of the Geneva Conventions, impose upon States the obligation to take proceedings against the alleged authors of the international crimes they envisage, the establishment or application of a statute of limitation may prove contrary to such treaties or rules.

Could one contend that the aforementioned treaty rules either reflect, or have gradually turned into, customary rules? Much depends on the legal weight one attributes to various elements of international practice.

In this regard, one should first of all recall a few recent regulations of the matter. Interestingly, the Cambodian Bill of 2000 on the Establishment of Extraordinary Chambers in the Courts of Cambodia for the Prosecution of the Crimes committed During the Period of Democratic Kampuchea provides in Articles 4 and 5 that there shall be no statute of limitation for genocide and crimes against humanity, whereas in Article 3 it extends for an additional period of 20 years the statute of limitation set forth in the 1956 Penal Code for homicide, torture, and religious persecution. Similarly, section 17 of Regulation no. 2000/15 adopted by the UN Transitional Administration in East Timor, on the Establishment of Panels with Exclusive

Jurisdiction over Serious Criminal Offences, provides that genocide, war crimes, crimes against humanity, and torture 'shall not be subject to any statute of limitation' whereas the other crimes under the panels' jurisdiction (murder and sexual offences) 'shall be subject to applicable law'.

In addition, some national and international courts have ruled out the applicability of statutes of limitation for international crimes. It is worth noting that, in the aforementioned *Barrios Altos* case, the Inter-American Court of Human Rights held that the establishment of a statute of limitations for egregious violations of fundamental human rights was contrary to the non-derogable norms making up the international rules on human rights (§41). An Argentinean federal judge took the same view on 6 March 2001 in *Simon, Julio, Del Cerro, Juan Antonio* (at 78–84). A Mexican federal judge propounded this same view in a decision on the extradition of an Argentinean officer to Spain (*Ricardo Miguel Cavallo* case).[12] In France the Court of Cassation held in 1985 that the inapplicability of statutes of limitation to crimes against humanity, laid down in French law, derives from principles recognized by all civilized nations.[13] In Italy, in 1997, the Rome Military Tribunal noted in *Hass and Priebke* that the inapplicability of statutes of limitation to war crimes was asserted to derive from a general principle of international law (at 49). In a significant *obiter*, a Trial Chamber of the ICTY held in *Furundžija* that, as a result of international rules on torture being of a peremptory nature, no statute of limitation may apply to that crime (at §157).

Apart from referring to practice, the following arguments also support the existence of an international customary rule. The application of statutes of limitation to the most serious international crimes proves contrary to the very nature of international rules prohibiting such crimes. These are so abhorrent that their authors must be punished, even after the lapse of much time. Such punishment not only has a retributive effect, but also serves to deter potential perpetrators as far as possible from engaging in similar actions. Furthermore, the universal dimension of those crimes (that is, the fact that they affect the whole international community and not only the community of the State on whose territory they have been perpetrated) entails that it would be incongruous to take into account the statute of limitation of one particular State (for instance the territorial State or the national State of the victim or the perpetrator). In addition, as rightly pointed out by a distinguished criminal lawyer,[14] in the case of international crimes the reasons militating for, or underpinning resort to, statutes of limitation no longer hold good. In particular: if the victims or their relatives do not set in motion criminal proceedings, normally this failure is not due to negligence or lack of interest; initiating such proceedings may indeed prove 'psycho-

[12] It is notable that in this case the judge had held that the accused could only be extradited for the charges of genocide and terrorism, as that of torture was covered by the statute of limitation in Argentinean law. However, the Argentinean Minister of Foreign Affairs, to whom it fell to take the final decision, subsequently held that Cavallo could also be extradited for torture, because this crime could not be covered by any statute of limitation (at 58–9).

[13] 20 Dec. 1985, D. 1986, p. 500, JCP 1986, I, 322.

[14] M. Delmas-Marty, 'La responsabilité pénale en échec (prescription, amnistie, immunités)' in A. Cassese and M. Delmas-Marty (eds), *Juridictions nationales*, 617–18.

logically painful, or politically dangerous, or legally impossible'; as for the national authorities' failure to prosecute, it may be due to political motivations which the passage of time may sooner or later efface.

Nevertheless, the proposition that a customary rule has evolved on this matter could be objected to by noting that in some States only some categories of international crimes are the subject of statutory limitations. For instance, in France, as stated above, a law of 26 December 1964, restated in Article 213–5 of the Criminal Code in 1994, removes any statutory limitation for crimes against humanity alone (with the consequence that in *Barbie* and *Touvier*, French courts went to great lengths to prove that the crimes with which the defendants were charged were crimes against humanity and not war crimes, hence not subject to normal statutory limitations). It would seem that no State has ever protested against that law, nor has it been assailed in international fora as being contrary to internationally accepted legal standards.

It would therefore seem that the better view is that *no customary rule endowed with a far-reaching content has yet evolved on this matter*. In other words, no rule has come into being prohibiting the application of statutes of limitations to all international crimes. It appears to be a sounder view that specific customary rules render statutes of limitation inapplicable with regard to some crimes: genocide, crimes against humanity, torture.

Whether or not the above arguments about the customary rule on the matter are held sound, in any case State parties to the ICC Statute are barred from invoking any statute of limitations in proceedings before the Court (see Article 29).

17.3 THE PROHIBITION OF DOUBLE JEOPARDY (*NE BIS IN IDEM*)

Under the principle of double jeopardy a court may not institute proceedings against a person for a crime that has already been the object of criminal proceedings in the same State (internal *ne bis in idem* principle) or in another State, or in an international court (*ne bis in idem* principle applying to relations between States, or a State and an international court), and for which the person has already been convicted or acquitted.

While the 'internal' *ne bis in idem* principle may be held to be prescribed by a customary rule of international law, the legal status of the 'international' equivalent principle is still controversial It is not clear whether this principle has turned into customary international law. Italian courts have held the view that it has not (see for instance the *Zennaro* case (at 301–2), where the Italian Constitutional Court took this view in 1976). Similarly, in 1987 the Italian delegate to the UN maintained in the discussion on the Draft Code of Offences against Peace and Security of Mankind that it was difficult to consider the principle as 'a full-fledged principle of customary international law applicable to criminal judgments of foreign States' and found the reasons for this conclusion in:

that, outside some bilateral or limited multilateral circles of states, there is not sufficient trust in the administration of justice by other States, especially when offences with political aspects are concerned. States are concerned that a person having committed a heinous crime against peace and security of mankind might find protection from prosecution in the rest of the world in an acquittal or mild sentence given in a given State for reasons of political sympathy.[15]

It is warranted to hold that a customary rule, concerning all crimes generally, has not yet crystallized. Even in Europe, where, due to the multiplicity of treaties on the execution of foreign judgments, there is an increasing tendency to apply the *ne bis in idem* principle in the relations between national courts of different States, quite a few States tend to hold the view that they are not bound to consider themselves foreclosed from again trying crimes on which foreign courts have already pronounced, when these crimes have been committed *on their own territory*. It is significant that Article 55 of the Schengen Convention of 19 June 1990 authorizes a contracting State to declare that it is not bound by Article 54 (on *ne bis in idem*) when the facts envisaged in the foreign judgment have taken place in whole or in part on its territory, except if, in the latter case, the facts have occurred in part on the territory of the State where the judgment has been rendered. Plainly, this claim to the exercise of territorial jurisdiction is based on the notion of sovereignty and, more specifically, on the claim of States that they are entitled to prosecute and punish crimes committed on their territory, because such crimes have troubled the social order and infringed values upheld in the local community.

However, a customary rule is arguably evolving, *at least with regard to international crimes*. Indeed the rationale behind the claim of States to exercise territorial jurisdiction, referred to above, does not hold true for international crimes. Such crimes breach values that transcend individual States and their communities; they affect and involve all States. Hence, any State is entitled to prosecute and punish them. It follows that, as long as the court of the State where those crimes are tried conforms to some fundamental principles on fair trial and acts independently, impartially, and with all due diligence, other States, including the State where the crime has been committed, as well as international courts, must refrain from sitting in judgment on the same offence.

This conclusion is borne out by a number of resolutions and treaties which concern however not 'horizontal' relations (such as those between States) but 'vertical' relations, that is, relations between national and international courts. On this score one should mention Article 10 of the ICTY Statute and Article 9 of the ICTR Statute, as well as Article 20 of the ICC Statute. It would seem that the first two of these texts, having being adopted by the UN Security Council and endorsed by the UN General Assembly, carry much weight as expressions of *opinio juris* of most States. Similarly, the Statute of the ICC has been adopted by 120 States; although it is only binding upon contracting States, it nonetheless reflects the legal views of all those States,

[15] See IYIL (1988–92), at 196–7.

except of course for those that opposed the Statute, voting against or abstaining. The other States, by voting for the Statute, expressed the view that they did not consider that it was fundamentally wrong, although of course, by this mere vote, they did not undertake any obligation—qua treaty obligation—before ratification. One should also note, with respect to interstate relations, the 1990 Convention of Schengen (Article 54; see, however, Article 55) and the 1987 European Convention on the *Ne Bis in Idem* Principle.

It is submitted that the purport of this principle is reflected in the relevant provisions of the Statutes of international criminal courts, just referred to. No person may be tried twice for the same crime, by national or international courts (whether the first trial was conducted before a national or an international court). However, this principle does not apply when in the first trial: (i) the person was prosecuted and punished for the same fact or conduct, but the crime was characterized as an 'ordinary crime' (e.g. murder) instead of an international crime (e.g. genocide) with a view to deliberately avoiding the stigma and implications of international crimes; or (ii) the court did not fully comply with the fundamental safeguards of a fair trial, or did not act independently or impartially; or (iii) the court in fact conducted a sham trial, for the purpose of shielding the accused from international criminal responsibility; or (iv) the prosecution or the court did not act with the diligence required by international standards.

17.4 IMMUNITIES

The matter of immunities is discussed in Chapter 14. The reader is therefore referred to what is stated there.

It may suffice to emphasize here that courts may be barred from exercising their jurisdiction by national provisions granting immunity from prosecution to national State agents (Head of State, members of government, parliamentarians). Or they may be precluded from trying foreigners who enjoy immunity under their own national legislation. Or else they may be foreclosed by international rules affording immunities to foreign dignitaries (Heads of State, diplomatic or consular agents, etc.) who either are discharging their functions on the territory or are in transit there, on their way to or from the country where they are fulfilling their mission.

The question arises, however, of whether at least some of these immunities must be set aside on the strength of international law. This problem is particularly acute with regard to national courts. (We have seen above that the Statutes of international criminal tribunals and courts contain provisions designed to deprive accused persons of immunities provided for in either international or national law.)

National courts are obliged by international rules to set aside any *functional* immunity the accused may invoke, any time he is charged with an international crime. In contrast, if he pleads personal immunities (for instance diplomatic immunities), courts are bound to respect them, hence to refrain from initiating prosecution, whether or not the accused is on an official mission on the territory of the courts or in transit (see above 14.4).

SELECT BIBLIOGRAPHY

AMNESTY

N. Roht-Arriaza (ed.), *Impunity on Human Rights in International Law and Practice* (New York, Oxford: Oxford University Press, 1995); A. Gitti, 'Impunity under National Law and Accountability under International Human Rights Law: Has the Time of A Duty to Prosecute Come?', 9 IYIL (1999), 64–85; M. Starita, 'Amnesty for Crimes Against Humanity: Coordinating the State and Individual Responsibility for Gross Violations of Human Rights', 9 IYIL (1999), 86–109; M. Delmas-Marty, 'La responsabilité pénale en echec (prescription, amnistie, immunités)', in Cassese and Delmas-Marty (eds), *Juridictions nationales*, 613–52.

STATUTES OF LIMITATION

J. B. Herzog, 'Etudes des lois concernant la prescription des crimes contre l'humanité', 20 RSCDPC (1965), 337–71; G. Levasseur, 'Les crimes contre l'humanité et le problème de leur prescription', *Journal du droit international* (1966), 259–84; C. Lombois, 'Crimes contre l'humanité, crimes de guerre', RSCDPC (1987), 937–42; P. Mertens, 'L'imprescriptibilité des crimes contre l'humanité dans les travaux du Conseil de l'Europe et dans la Convention de l'ONU', in *Le procès de Nuremberg, conséquences et actualisation* (Brussels: Ed. Bruylant, 1988); J. Pradel, *Droit international comparé*, 481–3, 655–6; G. P. Fletcher, *Basic Concepts*, 10–14; P. Poncela, 'L'imprescriptibilité', in Ascensio, Decaux, and Pellet (eds), *Droit international pénal*, 887–95; M. Delmas-Marty, 'La responsabilité pénale en échec (prescription, amnistie, immunités)', cit., 617–26; M. Frulli, 'Le droit international: II Les obstacles à la mise en œuvre de la responsabilité pénales pour crimes internationaux', in Cassese and Delmas-Marty (eds), *Crimes internationaux*, 215–53.

THE PROHIBITION OF DOUBLE JEOPARDY (*NE BIS IN IDEM*)

A. Huet and R. Koering-Joulin, *Droit Pénal International* (Paris: Thémis, PUF, 2001), 229–36; C. van den Wyngaert and G. Stessens, 'The International *Non Bis In Idem* Principle: Resolving Some of the Unanswered Questions', 48 ICLQ (1999), 779–804.

IMMUNITIES

M. Ruffert, 'Pinochet Follow Up: The End of Sovereign Immunity?', 48 NILR (2001), 171–95; S. Zappalà, 'Do Heads of States in Office Enjoy Immunity from Jurisdiction for International Crimes? The Ghaddafi Case before the French *Cour de Cassation*', 12 EJIL (2001), 595–612.

PART IV

PROSECUTION AND PUNISHMENT BY INTERNATIONAL COURTS

SECTION I

GENERAL

18

THE ESTABLISHMENT OF INTERNATIONAL CRIMINAL TRIBUNALS

The idea of setting up an international criminal court to bring to justice individuals, including leading State officials, allegedly responsible for serious international crimes goes back to the aftermath of the First World War. The attainment of that goal has been slow and painstaking. The process toward the eventual adoption of a Statute for a permanent International Criminal Court can be conceptualized in terms of various distinct phases: (i) abortive early attempts (1919–45); (ii) criminal prosecutions in the aftermath of the Second World War: the Nuremberg and Tokyo Tribunals (1945–47); (iii) elaboration by the ILC of the Statute of a permanent Court; (iv) the post-Cold War 'new world order': the development of the two ad hoc Tribunals (1993–94); (v) the drafting of the ICC Statute (1994–98).

18.1 ABORTIVE EARLY ATTEMPTS (1919–1945)

The period immediately following the First World War is notable for numerous attempts to establish a variety of international criminal institutions, all of which ended in failure. For instance, in 1919 the 'Commission on the Responsibility of the Authors of the War and on Enforcement of Penalties' proposed the establishment of a 'high tribunal composed of judges drawn from many nations'.[1] In the same year the victors had agreed upon a few provisions of the peace treaty with Germany, signed at Versailles, which provided for the punishment of the leading figures responsible for war crimes committed during the war and went so far as to lay down in Article 227 the responsibility of the German Emperor (Wilhelm II) for 'the supreme offence against international morality and the sanctity of treaties'. The same provision envisaged the establishment of 'a special tribunal', composed of five judges (to be appointed by the USA, Great Britain, France, Italy, and Japan) and charged with trying the Emperor. The Allies were clearly motivated by their outrage at the atrocities

[1] See the Report of the Commission, in 14 AJIL (1920), at 116. As for the objections of the US delegates, see ibid., 129, 139 ff.

perpetrated by the vanquished Powers, in particular Germany, and wished to set an example. Since the accused would have been judged by their erstwhile opponents, this would throw doubt on the fairness of the proceedings and the impartiality of the tribunal. However, the Netherlands, where the German Emperor had taken refuge, refused to extradite him, chiefly because the crimes of which he was accused were not contemplated in the Dutch Constitution.[2] In addition, the aforementioned provisions of the Versailles Treaty were harshly criticized by some eminent publicists, among them the Italian leading jurist and politician V. E. Orlando.[3]

As for the trials of German military personnel alleged to have committed war crimes, no international court was set up, nor were they tried by courts of the Allies, as had been envisaged in Articles 228–30 of the Versailles Treaty. Eventually, out of the 895 Germans accused (who comprised various generals and admirals including the Chief of Staff of the Army, General E. Ludendorff, General Paul von Hindenburg, later Chief of Staff of the Army, as well as the former Chancellor Bethmann-Hollweg), the Allies selected only 45 cases for prosecution.[4] Ultimately 12 minor indictees were brought to trial in 1921, and before a German court, the 'Imperial Court of Justice' (*Reichsgericht*, sitting at Leipzig). Six of the 12 indictees were acquitted. Thus, the attempts to establish some sort of international criminal justice ended in failure. (However some of the judgments delivered by the Leipzig Court set significant precedents, chiefly because of the high legal quality of those judgments. Similarly, although the attempts to bring to justice the 'Young Turks' responsible for the Armenian genocide of 1915 were generally failures, courts in Istanbul brought some accused to trial: see in particular *Kemâl and Tevfik* (at 1–7) and *Bahâeddîn Şâkiz* (at 1–8)).

In 1920, the 'Advisory Committee of Jurists', summoned to prepare the project for the Permanent Court of International Justice, proposed that the 'High Court of International Justice' to be established should also 'be competent to try crimes constituting a breach of international public order or against the universal law of nations, referred

2 On the non-implementation of Article 227, see, *inter alia*, A. Merignhac and E. Lemonon, *Le Droit des gens et la guerre de 1914–1918*, II (Paris: Pedone, 1921), 580 ff.

The Dutch diplomatic note of 21 January 1920 to the Allies stated that 'Or, ni les lois constituantes du Royaume qui sont basées sur des principes de droit universellement reconnus, ni une respectable tradition séculaire qui a fait de ce pays de tout temps une terre de refuge pour les vaincus des conflits internationaux, ne permettent au Gouvernement des Pays-Bas de déférer au désir des Puissances en retirant à l'ex-empereur le bénéfice de ces lois et cette tradition' (see the text of the Dutch diplomatic notes in A. Mérignhac, 'De la responsabilité pénale des actes criminels commis au cours de la guerre 1914–1918' in 47 *Revue de droit international et de législation comparée* (1920), 37–45. According to a distinguished author, B. Swart, 'Arrest and Surrender' in Cassese, Gaeta, and Jones (eds), *ICC Commentary*, II, at 1643, 'Given the fact that the former Article 4 of the Dutch Constitution permitted extradition on the basis of a treaty only, that the acts alleged did not constitute criminal offences according to Dutch law or to extradition treaties concluded with the Allied and Associated Powers, and that the Constitution did not permit the conclusion of an extradition treaty for the surrender of one person only, it is hard to see that the Dutch government could have reacted in a different way'.

3 V. E. Orlando, 'Il processo del Kaiser' (1937), reprinted in *Scritti varii di diritto pubblico e scienza politica* (Milan: Giuffrè, 1940), 97 ff.

4 See C. Mullins, *The Leipzig Trials—An Account of the War Criminals' Trials and a Study of German Mentality* (London: Witherby, 1921), at 27.

to it by the Assembly or by the Council of the League of Nations'.[5] However, a few months later the Assembly of the League of Nations rejected out of hand the proposal as being 'premature'.[6] Thereafter, draft statutes of an international criminal court were adopted by non-governmental organizations such as the Inter-Parliamentary Union, in 1925,[7] and by scholarly bodies such as the International Law Association, in 1926.[8] None of these drafts, however, led to anything concrete.[9]

Such early attempts were laudable for their far-sighted recognition of the need for an international organ of criminal jurisdiction. Nevertheless, these initiatives could not bear fruit in a period which placed an exceptionally high premium upon considerations of national sovereignty. Although new values had emerged which transcended narrow nationalistic concerns (such as the gradual elaboration of principles seeking to limit the methods of warfare, or the protection of workers through the establishment of the International Labour Organization, or the protection of minorities through the numerous treaties entered into after the First World War), State sovereignty was nevertheless still very much the bedrock of the international community. The practical import of this was that no feasible mechanism could be brought into being enabling a State official—let alone a Head of State—accused of war crimes or other outrages to be tried. It is no coincidence that the first provision criminalizing international action was Article 227 of the Versailles Treaty, which provided for the criminal liability of the most important and representative among State officials, a Head of State, and that that provision remained a dead letter and indeed caused an uproar in the international community.

18.2 CRIMINAL PROSECUTION IN THE AFTERMATH OF THE SECOND WORLD WAR: THE NUREMBERG AND TOKYO TRIBUNALS (1945–1947)

It was nevertheless this scenario (an international community dominated by State sovereignty) that led to the successful establishment, in the immediate post-war period, of the Nuremberg and Tokyo Tribunals. These Tribunals were a response to the overwhelming horrors of the Nazi genocide in Europe and the Japanese crimes perpetrated during the wartime occupation of large parts of many South East Asian nations (for instance, the so-called rape of Nanking, biological experiments in

[5] See the text of the Second Resolution adopted by the Advisory Committee in Lord Phillimore, 'An International Criminal Court and the Resolutions of the Committee of Jurists', 3 BYBIL (1922–3), 80.

[6] Ibid., at 84.

[7] See the text of the draft in B. Ferencz (ed.), *An International Criminal Court—A Step Toward World Peace—A Documentary History and Analysis*, vol. I (London, Rome, New York: Oceana, 1980), 244 ff.

[8] Text reproduced in Ferencz, ibid., at 252 ff.

[9] A Convention for the creation of an International Criminal Court to try terrorist offences was also adopted on 16 November 1937 by the League of Nations, but never entered into force. See generally V. V. Pella, 'Towards an International Criminal Court', 44 AJIL (1950), 37–68.

Manchuria, the fall of Singapore and the loss of life there, and other crimes). It took the full extent of the atrocities committed during the war to demonstrate the pernicious consequences that could follow from the pursuit of extreme notions of State sovereignty and to jolt the international community out of its complacency. The widespread conviction gradually emerged that never again could tyranny and the attendant disregard for human dignity be allowed to go unchecked and unpunished.

It is worthwhile to consider what, in particular, induced the Allies to hold trials of the Germans and their collaborators after the Second World War and what, more recently, has persuaded governments to hold similar trials for war crimes and crimes against humanity.

After the defeat of Germany, the British led by Churchill stated that it was enough to arrest and hang those primarily responsible for determining and applying Nazi policy, without wasting time on legal procedures; minor criminals, they suggested, could be tried by specially created tribunals.[10] However, neither President F. D. Roosevelt, nor Henry Stimson, the US Defense Secretary, agreed; nor, indeed, did Stalin. In the end, they prevailed, and the International Military Tribunal was set up in Nuremberg to try the 'great Nazi criminals', while lesser Allied tribunals in the four occupied zones of Germany were to deal with minor criminals. The Americans advanced various arguments to support their view, later accepted by the other Allies.

First, how could a defeated enemy be condemned without due process of law? To hang them without trial would mean to do away with one of the mainstays of democracy: no one can be considered guilty until his crimes have been proved in a fair trial. To relinquish such a fundamental principle would have put the Allies on a par with the Nazis who had ridden roughshod over so many principles of justice and civilization, when they had held mock trials, or punished those allegedly guilty without even the benefit of judicial process.

Secondly, those who set up the Nuremberg Tribunal felt that the dramatic rehearsal of Nazi crimes—and of racism and totalitarianism—would make a deep impression on world opinion. Thus, the trial was designed to render great historical phenomena plainly visible, and was conceived of as a means of demythologizing the Nazi State by exposing their hideous crimes for all humanity to see.

The third reason was a desire on the part of the Allied powers to act for posterity. The crimes committed by the Third Reich and its Nazi officials were so appalling that some visible record had to be left. A trial held on a grand scale would allow the Tribunal to assemble a massive archive useful not only in court, but also to historians and to the generations to come. The trial was therefore seen as a method of compiling a dossier of historical documents that might otherwise vanish; it would also serve as a lesson in history for future generations.

In addition, for the Americans there was a particular motivation behind the establishment of an international tribunal. It was eloquently set forth by Justice

[10] See F. Smith (ed.), *The American Road to Nuremberg: the Documentary Record, 1944–1945* (Stanford, Cal.: Hoover Institution Press, 1982), 31–3, 155–7.

Robert H. Jackson (the special representative of the US President to the London Conference and later the US Chief Prosecutor at Nuremberg) in a Memorandum he submitted on 30 June 1945, together with a Redraft of the US proposals for the new International Tribunal, to the representatives of the UK, France, and the Soviet Union participating in the London Conference on military trials. He wrote the following:

> The Unites States . . . has conceived of this case as a broad one. It must be borne in mind that Russian, French, English and other European peoples are familiar with the Hitlerite atrocities and oppressions at first-hand. Our country, three thousand miles away, has known of them chiefly through the press and radio and through the accusations of those who have suffered rather than through immediate experience. German atrocities in the last war were charged. The public of my country was disillusioned because most of these charges were never authenticated by trial and conviction. If there is to be continuing support in the United States for international measures to prevent the regrowth of Nazism, it is necessary now to authenticate, by methods which the American people will regard as of the highest accuracy, the whole history of this Nazi movement, including its extermination of minorities, its aggressions against neighbors, its treachery and its barbarism.[11]

A further rationale for the Nuremberg trial was the collective character of the Nazi crimes. The massacre of civilians and prisoners of war, the persecution of Jews, gypsies, and political opponents were not only large-scale phenomena but, in addition, indicative of a policy pursued assiduously by the highest echelons of the Nazis and applied by the whole military and bureaucratic apparatus. The crimes commissioned by the directives of the Nazi leaders belonged to 'collective or system criminality': such was their nature that it would have been impossible to punish them by using the courts of the State to which the perpetrators belonged. In consequence, and as mentioned above, only an adversary (together with neutral States, as had been suggested)[12] could have made sure that justice was done, upon winning the war.

In the summer of 1945, the nations that were victorious in the Second World War (the 'Big Four': the United Kingdom, France, the United States, and the Soviet Union) convened the London Conference to decide by what means the world was to punish the high-ranking Nazi war criminals. The resultant Nuremberg Charter established the IMT to prosecute individuals for 'crimes against peace', 'war crimes', and 'crimes against humanity'. The IMT met from 14 November 1945 to 1 October 1946. In addition, in occupied Germany, the four major Allies, pursuant to Control Council Law no. 10, prosecuted through their own courts sitting in Germany, in their respective zones of occupation, the same crimes committed by lower-ranking defendants.

[11] International Conference on Military Trials, at 126.

[12] See for instance C. C. Hyde, 'Punishment of War Criminals', *Proceedings of the American Society of International Law, Thirty-Seventh Annual Meeting, 1943* (1943), 43–4.

On 26 July 1945, two weeks before the conclusion of the London Conference, the 'Big Four' issued the Potsdam Declaration announcing, to the surprise of many, their intention to prosecute leading Japanese officials for these same crimes.[13] Subsequently, on 19 January 1946, General Douglas MacArthur, Supreme Commander for the Allied Powers in Japan, approved, in the form of an executive order, the Tokyo Charter, setting forth the constitution, jurisdiction, and functions of the International Military Tribunal for the Far East (IMTFE). Like the Nuremberg Charter, the Tokyo Charter, which was issued on 26 April 1946, included the newly articulated crimes against peace and humanity.[14]

By and large, the Tokyo Charter was modelled on the Nuremberg Charter. However, there were some differences between the two texts and the way they regulated the structure of the Tribunals and the charges that could be brought against the defendants.[15] It is also notable that the bench comprised persons from newly independent countries, such as India and the Philippines.

The Tokyo Trial (which commenced on 3 May 1946, and lasted for approximately two and a half years) was the source of much controversy both during and after the event. Some have claimed that the trial was either a vehicle for America's revenge for the treacherous attack on Pearl Harbor, or a means of assuaging American national guilt over the use of atomic weapons in Japan. Others, defence counsel at the trial included, attacked the trial's legitimacy on legal grounds.[16]

Whereas the post-First World War experience showed the extent to which international justice can be compromised for the sake of political expedience, the post-Second World War experience revealed, conversely, how effective 'international' justice could be when there is political will to support it as well as the necessary resources. These sets of experiences were nevertheless one-sided, as everybody knows. They imposed 'victors' justice' over the defeated. The major drawback of the two 'international' Tribunals was that they were composed of judges (respectively 4, and 11) appointed by each of the victor Powers; the prosecutors too were appointed by each of those Powers and acted under the instructions of each appointing State (but at Tokyo there was a chief prosecutor, or 'Chief of Counsel' as he was called, namely the American Joseph B. Keenan, and 10 associate prosecutors). Thus, the view must be shared that the two Tribunals were not independent international courts proper, but judicial bodies acting as organs common to the appointing States. The Nuremberg IMT admitted this legal reality when it stated that:

[13] Some of the Allies in the Pacific Theatre prosecuted the Japanese for 'war crimes' under their respective military laws: see, *inter alia*, R. John Pritchard, 'War Crimes Trials in the Far East,' in R. Bowring and P. Kornick (eds), *Cambridge Encyclopedia of Japan* (Cambridge: Cambridge University Press, 1993), 107.

[14] The Charter had been drafted by the Americans only, essentially by Joseph B. Keenan, Chief Prosecutor at the Tokyo Trial, and the other Allies were only consulted after it was issued: B. V. A. Röling and A. Cassese, *The Tokyo Trial and Beyond* (Cambridge: Polity Press, 1993), 2.

[15] For a summary of the principal differences see ibid., 2–3.

[16] For instance, the legal categories of the crimes against peace and humanity have been criticized as *ex post facto* legislation on the part of the London Conference, in that these crimes did not exist in international law prior to 1945 (ibid., 3–5).

> The making of the Charter [of the IMT] was the exercise of the sovereign legislative power by the countries to which the German Reich unconditionally surrendered; and the undoubted right of these countries to legislate for the occupied territories has been recognised by the civilised world . . . The Signatory Powers created this Tribunal, defined the law it was to administer, and made regulations for the proper conduct of the Trial. In doing so, they have done together what any one of them might have done singly; for it is not to be doubted that any nation has the right thus to set up special courts to administer law. (At 218.)

However, the IMTs were important in many respects. First, they broke the 'monopoly' over criminal jurisdiction concerning such international crimes as war crimes, until that moment firmly held by States. For the first time non-national, or multi-national, institutions were established for the purpose of prosecuting and punishing crimes having an international dimension and scope. Secondly, new offences were envisaged in the London Agreement and made punishable: crimes against humanity and crimes against peace. Whether or not this was done in breach of the principle of *nullum crimen sine lege*, it is a fact that since 1945 those crimes gradually became the subject of international customary law prohibitions. Thirdly, the statutes and the case law of the IMT and the IMTFE and the various tribunals set up by the Allies in the aftermath of the Second World War contributed to the development of new legal norms and standards of responsibility which advanced the international rule of law, for example the elimination of the defence of 'obedience to superior orders', and the accountability of Heads of State. Finally, a symbolic significance emerged from these experiences in terms of their moral legacy, which was drawn on by those seeking a permanent, effective, and politically uncompromised system of international criminal justice.[17]

18.3 THE WORK OF THE ILC (1950–1954) FOR THE ELABORATION OF THE STATUTE OF AN INTERNATIONAL CRIMINAL COURT

In order to build on the positive dimensions of the establishment of the IMT and IMTFE, and perhaps stung by the inevitable association of these Tribunals with 'victor's justice', the United Nations system in the late 1940s commenced its quest to establish more permanent and impartial mechanisms for dispensing international criminal justice. (The 1948 Convention on Genocide confined itself to envisaging in Article VI the future establishment of an 'international penal tribunal'.)

The efforts of the United Nations to establish a permanent criminal tribunal can be traced along two separate tracks: codification of international crimes and the elaboration of a draft statute for the establishment of an international court.

Pursuant to a request by the General Assembly on 21 November 1947 (res. 177/II),

[17] M. Lippman, 'Nuremberg: Forty-Five Years Later', 7 *Conn. J. Int. L.* (1991), 1.

the International Law Commission (ILC) commenced the formulation of the principles recognized in the Charter of the Nuremberg Tribunal, to prepare a draft code of offences against the peace and security of mankind. Concurrently, the task of formulating a draft statute for the establishment of an international criminal court was assigned to another special rapporteur, who submitted his first report to the ILC in March 1950.[18]

The 1940s and 1950s were characterized by much work by a variety of international bodies on tasks that, while designed to be complementary and interlocking, were nevertheless poorly co-ordinated. The ILC special committee charged with preparing a draft statute for an international criminal court produced a text in 1951 that was revised in 1953.[19] However, neither the early discussions in the Commission, nor the provisions of Article VI of the 1948 Genocide Convention referring to a (future) 'international penal tribunal' were translated into reality. The 1953 Draft Statute of the Court was shelved because the definition of aggression, which had been entrusted to another body, was not completed. That result was expected since there were differing bodies working separately at different venues (Geneva and New York), and producing different texts at different times. It was, therefore, easy for the General Assembly to put off discussion of each text successively because the one or the other was not then ready. The lack of synchronization was not entirely fortuitous; it was the result of a political will to delay the establishment of an international criminal court due to the fact that the world was then sharply divided and frequently at risk of war.[20]

The overriding explanation for the failure of the substantial work of this period to come to fruition can thus be found in the political stagnation caused by the Cold War and the impeded functioning of UN due to the fact that its member States were subsumed into two rival and antagonistic political blocs.

18.4 THE POST-COLD WAR 'NEW WORLD ORDER' AND THE DEVELOPMENT OF AD HOC TRIBUNALS (1993–1994)

18.4.1 GENERAL

Various factors led to the establishment of international criminal tribunals in the early 1990s.

The end of the Cold War proved to be of crucial importance. It had significant effects. For one thing, the animosity that had dominated international relations for

[18] *Report of the International Law Commission on the Question of International Criminal Jurisdiction*, UNGAOR, 5th Sess., UN Doc. A/CN.4/15 (1950).

[19] *Report of the Committee on International Criminal Jurisdiction*, UNGAOR, 7th Sess., Supp. No. 12 at 21, UN Doc. A/26645 (1954).

[20] M. C. Bassiouni, *The Statute of the International Criminal Court: A Documentary History* (Ardsley, NY: Transnational Publishers, 1998), 13–15.

almost half a century dissipated. In its wake, a new spirit of relative optimism emerged, stimulated by the following factors: (i) a clear reduction in the distrust and mutual suspicion that had frustrated friendly relations and co-operation between the Western and the Eastern bloc; (ii) the successor States to the USSR (the Russian Federation and the other members of the Confederation of Independent States) came to accept and respect some basic principles of international law; (iii) as a result there emerged unprecedented agreement in the UN Security Council (SC) and increasing convergence in the views of the five permanent members, with the consequence that this institution became able to fulfil its functions more effectively.

Another effect of the end of the Cold War was no less important. Despite the problems of that bleak period, during the Cold War era the two power blocs had managed to guarantee a modicum of international order, in that each of the Superpowers had acted as a sort of policeman and guarantor in its respective sphere of influence. The collapse of this model of international relations ushered in a wave of negative consequences. It entailed a fragmentation of the international community and intense disorder which, coupled with rising nationalism and fundamentalism, resulted in a spiralling of mostly internal armed conflicts, with much bloodshed and cruelty. The ensuing implosion of previously multi-ethnic societies led to gross violations of international humanitarian law on a scale comparable to those committed during the Second World War.

Another crucial factor contributing to an enlarged need for international criminal justice was the increasing importance of the human rights doctrine, which soon became a sort of 'secular' religion. This doctrine's emphasis on the need to respect human dignity and consequently to punish all those who seriously attack such dignity begot the quest for, or at least gave a robust impulse to, international criminal justice.

This period can be characterized by the development of institutions empowered to prosecute and punish serious violations of international humanitarian law and can be subdivided into two distinct stages. The first is comprised by the establishment, by the UN Security Council, of the two ad hoc tribunals for the former Yugoslavia and Rwanda and the second by the eventual adoption, through the multilateral treaty-making process, of the Statute for a permanent International Criminal Court.

18.4.2 THE ESTABLISHMENT OF THE TWO AD HOC TRIBUNALS FOR YUGOSLAVIA AND RWANDA

The conflicts which erupted in, amongst other places, the former Yugoslavia and Rwanda served to rekindle the sense of outrage felt at the closing stage of the Second World War.[21] Thus, the UN Security Council set up ad hoc Tribunals pursuant to its

[21] See for example the letters to A. Cassese of Lawrence Eagleburger of 8 May 1996 ('the United States could no longer remain silent on the issue of war crimes . . . [A]cts against humanity could not and would not be ignored') and Elie Wiesel of 28 June 1996 ('not to prosecute the criminals would amount to condoning their crimes. In extreme situations, speaking out is a moral obligation') reprinted in *The Path to the Hague: Selected Documents on the Origins of the ICTY* (UN: ICTY, 1996), at 89 and 91 respectively.

power to decide on measures necessary to maintain or restore international peace and security: in 1993 the International Criminal Tribunal for the former Yugoslavia (ICTY), and in 1994 the International Criminal Tribunal for Rwanda (ICTR). The former was empowered to exercise jurisdiction over grave breaches of the Geneva Conventions, violations of the laws and customs of war, genocide, and crimes against humanity allegedly perpetrated in the former Yugoslavia since 1 January 1991. The latter was called upon to adjudicate genocide, crimes against humanity, and violations of Article 3 common to the Geneva Conventions and of the Second Additional Protocol, allegedly perpetrated in Rwanda (or in 'the territory of neighbouring States in respect of serious violations of international humanitarian law committed by Rwandan citizens') between 1 January and 31 December 1994.

The response of the international community to the conflict in Yugoslavia had been tardy and conflicting, due to impotence at the military and political levels. The establishment of a Tribunal was thus seized upon during the conflict not only as a belated face-saving measure but also in the pious hope that it would serve as a deterrent to further crimes.[22] As the UN Security Council itself noted, the ICTY was established in the belief that an international tribunal would 'contribute to ensuring that such violations are halted and effectively redressed'.[23]

In terms of the ICTY's establishment, the idea that an international court should be set up to try those responsible for war crimes and crimes against humanity committed in the former Yugoslavia was spontaneously mooted in various quarters: in the European Community, notably at the instigation of Germany and France, and in the United States. The proposal for the establishment of the ad hoc Tribunals was preceded by a number of UN statements proclaiming the principle that the authors of grave breaches of the Geneva Conventions and other crimes were 'individually responsible' and would be called to account.[24]

22 See in this regard the letter of Lawrence Eagleburger of 8 May 1996 to A. Cassese: 'There can be—and are—arguments about the wisdom of external armed intervention in the tragedy that is Bosnia . . . Of far greater precedential significance is the UN's decision to try accused war criminals before an International Tribunal especially created for that purpose . . . [T]hese trials will serve to put potential future war criminals on notice that the international community will not tolerate crimes against humanity' (ibid.).

23 See in this regard UNSC Resolution 827 of 25 May 1993.

24 This resulted in a call, from various parties, for an international Tribunal to this effect to be set up. For instance, the concept was propounded in spring 1992 by Robert Badinter, a former Justice Minister of France, at the time acting as President of the 'Arbitration Commission for the Former Yugoslavia'. At the London Conference on the Former Yugoslavia of 26 August 1992, the German Foreign Minister Dr Klaus Kinkel proposed the establishment of a criminal court; his proposal was taken up by the French Foreign Minister, Mr Roland Dumas and became part of the final Decision of the London Conference. The idea was revamped by Dr Kinkel on 23 September 1992 before the UN General Assembly (see UN Doc. A./47/PV.8, p. 61). A suggestion to the same effect was also made by Elie Wiesel, in December 1992, to US Secretary of State Lawrence Eagleburger. The latter also forcefully promoted the idea of bringing to trial all war criminals in a statement to the Geneva International Conference on the Former Yugoslavia on 16 December 1992. This suggestion was restated by the French Foreign Minister, Roland Dumas, who proposed the creation of a permanent criminal court in a Declaration of 6 October 1992, made on the occasion of the adoption of Resolution 780 by the UN Security Council, and preceded by a similar statement by the French Permanent representative to the UN in the Security Council (*The Path to the Hague*, cit., at 11).

Rather than being products of the multilateral treaty-making process, both the ICTY and the ICTR were established by resolutions of the UN Security Council.[25]

The Security Council established the ICTY in its Resolution 827 of 25 May 1993.[26] A striking feature of this Resolution was that the Security Council determined that the situation in the former Yugoslavia, and in particular in Bosnia and Herzegovina—where there were 'reports of mass killings, massive, organised and systematic detention and rape of women and . . . the practice of "ethnic cleansing"'—constituted a threat to international peace and security under Chapter VII of the UN Charter.[27]

The setting up of the ICTY has given rise to many objections.[28] In brief, the principal criticisms were that: (i) the Tribunal was established to make up for the impotence of diplomacy and politics, and revealed the inability of both the Great Powers and the UN Security Council to find a swift and proper solution to the conflict in the former Yugoslavia; the Tribunal was therefore conceived of as a sort of 'fig leaf'; (ii) by establishing the Tribunal the Security Council exceeded its powers under the Charter, adopting an act that was patently *ultra vires*; (iii) by the same token, by creating a criminal court dealing only with crimes allegedly committed in a particular country, instead of granting to the new court jurisdiction over crimes committed everywhere in the world, the Security Council had opted for 'selective justice'; and (iv) the Tribunal was clearly based on an anti-Serbian bias. It has also been argued that

25 Security Council Resolution 780 (1992) had established a Commission of Experts to investigate and report on evidence of grave breaches of the 1949 Geneva Conventions and other violations of international humanitarian law in the former Yugoslavia. The Security Council decision to establish the ICTY was taken after the findings of this Commission of Experts. See UN Doc. S/25221, Annex I, para. 9.

26 The resolution was adopted following consideration of the Secretary-General's Report (S/25704, 3 May 1993), submitted pursuant to Security Council Resolution 808. The Secretary-General's Report proposed a Statute for the ICTY, which was unanimously adopted without amendment.

In terms of the drafting of the Statute of the ICTY, it appears that the first draft was prepared by a group of three rapporteurs appointed by the Conference on Security and Cooperation in Europe (CSCE). In a letter of 24 November 1992 the British Government, then holding the Presidency of the European Union, proposed 'to draft a convention establishing an *ad hoc* tribunal to deal with war crimes and crimes against humanity committed in the former Yugoslavia'. The Ministers of Foreign Affairs of the CSCE, meeting in the CSCE Council, responded favourably on 15 December 1992. The three rapporteurs then produced a draft on 9 February 1993. On 16 January 1993 the French Foreign Minister, Roland Dumas, appointed a Commission of Experts with the task of drafting a statute of an ad hoc international tribunal. Various drafts were subsequently submitted by a number of States and international bodies to the UN Secretary-General and used by him in his drafting of the Statute of the ICTY after the Security Council, at the proposal of France, adopted on 22 February 1993 Resolution 808 (1993), by which it decided to establish an international Tribunal (*The Path to the Hague*, cit., at 13).

27 In operative paragraph 2 of Resolution 827 of 25 May 1993, the Security Council decided 'to establish an international tribunal for the sole purpose of prosecuting persons responsible for serious violations of international humanitarian law committed in the territory of the former Yugoslavia between 1 January 1991 and a date to be determined by the Security Council upon the restoration of peace and to this end to adopt the Statute of the International Tribunal annexed to the above-mentioned [Secretary-General's] report'. The Security Council amended the ICTY Statute by resolution 1166 (1998) on 13 May 1998 to add a third Trial Chamber and three new judges. Likewise, the Statute of the ICTR was amended by the Security Council in its Resolution 1165 of 30 April 1998 to provide for a third Trial Chamber.

28 See in particular G. Robertson, *Crimes against Humanity—The Struggle for Global Justice* (London: Penguin, 2000), 300 ff.

(v) there was no complete separation at the Tribunal of the prosecutorial function from the judicial one (the prosecutors and judges working in the same building and being serviced by the same administration, the Registry).

The first criticism is right. However, half a loaf is better than pie in the sky. As long as an international criminal court endowed with universal jurisdiction was lacking, the establishment of ad hoc Tribunals proved salutary.

The Tribunal's Appeals Chamber in *Tadić* (*Interlocutory Appeal*) proved the second criticism to be wrong (see §§9–40).

With regard to the objection that the Tribunal is administering justice in a biased manner, by bringing to trial mostly Serbs (and in addition failing to prosecute NATO servicemen or leaders for the 1999 attacks on Serbia), one should note that a distinction ought to be made between the Prosecutor and the Bench. The Prosecutor enjoys sweeping powers and among other things decides whom to prosecute. Judges are on the receiving end and cannot interfere with specific choices made by the Prosecutor. In addition, it is highly questionable whether the various Prosecutors who have held that prestigious position so far have had any anti-Serbian bias: they have always claimed that their prosecutorial objectives were based simply on the availability of evidence.

As for the criticism that the Prosecution and the Bench are housed in the same building, it may be countered that this, however, does not mean that the two organs are mutually dependent. In fact, with the exception of the Tribunal's President, who is also vested with important non-judicial functions, judges are not allowed to enter the floors where the prosecutors' offices are located, and vice versa. What matters is that the two bodies are independent, as is proved among other things by the fact that the only *ex parte* proceedings in which defence counsel do not take part, those for the confirmation of indictments, are videotaped and kept in the Tribunal's archives, so as to ensure that everything takes place in a proper and dignified manner. In addition, judges have severely reprimanded the Prosecutor's Office for failing to respect the rights of the accused.[29]

[29] See for instance the order of Trial Chamber I of 29 April 1998 in *Blaškić* (*Decision on the Defence Motion for Sanctions for the Prosecutor's Repeated Violations of Rule 68*), at 3–6, as well as *Furundžija* (*Formal Complaint to the Chief Prosecutor*) of 5 June 1998, unreported, quoted in *Furundžija*, decision of 10 December 1998, at §15.

Another criticism advanced by Robertson (op. cit.) relates to the role played by the Tribunal's President in the initial stages of the Tribunal's existence. He claims that in 1996 the President meddled in prosecutorial policy by suggesting that not the small fry but rather the alleged major culprits should be prosecuted. In fact this 'meddling' occurred not at the hands of the President but at the hands of all the judges: in a plenary administrative meeting they called into question the approach taken until then by the Prosecutor and aimed essentially at targeting low-level culprits; the judges stated that in their view the mission of the ICTY, as laid down in its Statute, was to prosecute and punish those persons who bore major responsibility for the most appalling crimes perpetrated in the former Yugoslavia. Accordingly, they adopted a statement, to which the Prosecutor eventually subscribed, and which was later made public. Arguably this step was not contrary to judicial ethics or judicial propriety. One should not gloss over the huge differences between international and national criminal courts. The latter are part of a complex State machinery called upon to perform the functions set out by Parliament, each court in its own district, and may avail themselves of State enforcement agencies to execute their judicial orders. By contrast, international courts perform unique functions, having to deal with a potentially huge range of criminal offences; they lack autonomous enforcement agencies, but must

The International Criminal Tribunal for Rwanda (ICTR) was established in like fashion to the ICTY in response to the civil war and genocide in Rwanda and the ensuing horrific loss of life and bloodshed. While many of the factors mentioned above with regard to the former Yugoslavia were also motivations for the establishment of the ICTR, the overwhelming magnitude of the crimes committed there and the fact that they assuredly amounted to genocide lent particular urgency to the establishment of the ICTR. Sensitive to criticism that the establishment of the ICTY represented yet another illustration of the disproportionate attention paid to the problems of Europe *vis-à-vis* the developing world, the international community was also anxious to establish a Tribunal for Rwanda so as to assuage its conscience and shield itself from accusations of double standards. An additional feature leading up to the establishment of the ICTR was that, in the early stages at least, the proposal to establish an international Tribunal was an initiative of the new Rwandan government. As they set about their task of post-war reconstruction, the new government had initially felt that one means of attracting international blessing for the new regime would be through a national process of self-examination and judicial condemnation of the worst abuses that had occurred during the civil war.[30]

The Security Council adopted the Statute and judicial mechanism for the Rwanda Tribunal by Security Council Resolution 955 of 8 November 1994, after having noted a number of reports on the situation in Rwanda which indicated that 'genocide and other systematic, widespread and flagrant violations of international

rely on State co-operation. If the organ charged with setting in motion prosecution and punishment fails to act in conformity with the general goals laid down in the court's statute, and the competent international bodies (the UN Security Council, the General Assembly, or the Secretary-General) cannot intervene lest this be perceived as undue political pressure on the Prosecutor, then the judges as a whole are the only body that can try to reorient the prosecutorial action so as to keep it within the Statute's objectives.

More generally, it should be noted that the Tribunal's President, unlike his counterparts in the domestic courts, is granted, by the Tribunal's Statute, a non-judicial role. Under Article 33 of the Statute he is to report annually to the two major political bodies of the UN: the Security Council and the General Assembly. Furthermore, as borne out in practice, he may need to contact senior members of cabinet in the relevant States to persuade them to co-operate with the Tribunal. In addition, he may have to address international bodies dealing with the problems of the former Yugoslavia, to urge them to take action in support of the Tribunal. Most importantly, the Tribunal's President may have to call upon the Security Council to take the necessary measures for impelling those States that fail to comply with their obligation to co-operate with the Tribunal to fulfil that obligation. Thus, the Tribunal's President is vested with supervisory and 'diplomatic' functions not normally accruing to judicial bodies.

For an indirect answer to further criticisms by Mr Robertson see ICTY *Yearbook 1996*, at 261–4.

[30] In July 1994, the Security Council passed Resolution 935, using the precedent of the former Yugoslavia as a model, to establish a commission of experts to investigate violations committed during the Rwandan civil war (see SC Res. 935, UNSCOR, 49th Sess., 3400th mtg 1, UN Doc. S/RES/935 (1994)). The Rwandan commission lasted only four months, which was not long enough for it to perform its task effectively. On 1 October 1994, the Rwandan commission submitted its preliminary report to the Secretary-General, and submitted a final report on 9 December 1994 (see *Preliminary Report of the Independent Commission of Experts Established in accordance with Security Council Resolution 935* (1994), UNSCOR, UN Doc. S/1994/1125 (1994); *Final Report of the Commission of Experts Established pursuant to Security Council Resolution 935* (1994) and Annex, UNSCOR, UN Doc. S/1994/1405 (1994).

humanitarian law' had been committed in Rwanda, and having determined that 'this situation continues to constitute a threat to international peace and security'.[31]

Even though the Statutes for the ICTY and the ICTR differ, the Tribunals share a common Prosecutor and a common Appellate Chamber. This may appear to be a curious formula for separate ad hoc Tribunals; but it demonstrates the need for ensuring some uniformity in administering international criminal justice.

After the decision to create the Rwanda Tribunal, which took much time and effort to establish and function, the Security Council arguably reached a point of 'tribunal fatigue'.[32] Indeed, the logistics of setting up the ad hoc Tribunals for the former Yugoslavia and for Rwanda had strained the capabilities and resources of the UN and consumed the Security Council's time. The Security Council found itself frequently seized with issues and problems concerning these Tribunals and their administration, and as a result became less inclined to establish other similar organs. Furthermore, it did not consider that other international conflicts deserved the establishment of an ad hoc Tribunal. After 1994, at least for some time, the Security Council simply did not see fit to take the same approach with regard to situations that were meanwhile arising in the world. Subsequently, the Council did consider the situations in, among other places, Sierra Leone, Cambodia, and East Timor as being suitable for the establishment of ad hoc international courts. In the case of Sierra Leone, it actively dealt with the matter and eventually, in October 2000, at its request the Secretary-General drafted the statute of a Special Tribunal;[33] in the case of Cambodia the Secretary-General discussed at length the establishment, by the Cambodian Parliament, of a Cambodian special tribunal dealing with crimes committed in the past by the Khmer Rouge, and composed partly by Cambodian judges, partly by international judges (see below).

18.5 THE DRAFTING AND ADOPTION OF THE STATUTE OF THE ICC (1994–1998)

18.5.1 GENERAL

It was only in 1989, once the Cold War had drawn to a close, that the General Assembly once again requested the ILC 'to address the question of establishing an international

[31] Article 1 of the Statute of the ICTR thus declared that the ICTR 'shall have the power to prosecute persons responsible for serious violations of international humanitarian law committed in the territory of Rwanda and Rwandan citizens responsible for such violations committed in the territory of neighbouring States, between 1 January 1994 and 31 December 1994, in accordance with the provisions of the present Statute'.

[32] A term aptly coined by David Scheffer, then Senior Counsel and Advisor to the US Permanent Representative to the UN; cited in M. C. Bassiouni, *The Statute of the International Criminal Court: A Documentary History*, cit., 10, n. 50.

[33] See UN Doc. S/2000/915. See also SC Res. 1315 (2000). For an overview, see M. Frulli, 'The Special Court for Sierra Leone: Some Preliminary Comments', 11 EJIL (2000), 857–69.

criminal court'.[34] The question of an international criminal court came back on to the United Nations' agenda by an unexpected route in 1989 after a hiatus of 36 years, following a suggestion in the General Assembly by Trinidad and Tobago that a specialized international criminal court be established to deal with the problem of drug trafficking. In response to the General Assembly's mandate arising out of the 1989 special session on drugs, the ILC in 1990 completed a report which was submitted to the 45th session of the General Assembly. Though that report was not limited to the drug trafficking question it was, nonetheless, favourably received by the General Assembly, which encouraged the ILC to continue its work. The ILC produced a comprehensive text in 1993, which was modified in 1994.[35]

The judicial institution envisaged in the 1994 ILC Draft to a very great extent took account of the concerns of States and in particular of major Powers. Among the salient features of the ICC delineated in the Draft, the following should be emphasized: (i) the Court had 'automatic jurisdiction' (that is, jurisdiction following from the mere fact of ratifying the Statute) only over genocide; for other crimes such as war crimes and crimes against humanity the Court could exercise its jurisdiction only if such jurisdiction had been accepted by the custodial State, the territorial State, as well as any other States seeking jurisdiction over the accused (Article 21); (ii) only States parties or the Security Council could initiate proceedings (Articles 23 and 25); the Prosecutor had no such power; (iii) the Security Council had extensive powers with regard to prosecution of cases relating to situations falling under Chapter VII of the UN Charter (threat to the peace, breach of the peace, or act of aggression); under Article 23(3), in these cases a prosecution could not be commenced except in accordance with a decision of the Security Council.

18.5.2 THE PREPARATORY COMMITTEE (1995–1998) AND THE ROME DIPLOMATIC CONFERENCE OF 1998

Although the two ad hoc Tribunals were limited both temporally and geographically to the conflicts in the former Yugoslavia and Rwanda respectively, their overall successes provided a final spur to the emergence of the ICC, an organ of global jurisdictional reach and thus potentially able to respond to violations occurring anywhere.

34 UN General Assembly Resolution 44/39 of 4 December 1989. In addition, a proposal to establish a criminal court dealing with international crimes such as aggression and war crimes did appear to be revived again in August 1990, in response to the Iraqi invasion of Kuwait and to hostage-taking of foreigners and atrocities allegedly committed in Kuwait (see various dispatches cited in *The Path to the Hague*, op. cit., at 7, 9, 11). However, it is unclear to what extent it was envisaged that the court would have a truly international character (see *The Times*, 26 September 1990, 'Echo of Nuremberg Trials in Iraq'). In any case, these steps did not lead to any proposal at the international level, although moves towards the establishment of an international tribunal to prosecute and punish war crimes committed by Iraqi forces in Kuwait seems once more to be gaining momentum. (See in this regard A. Cassese, 'On Current Trends towards Criminal Prosecution and Punishment of Breaches of International Humanitarian Law', 9 EJIL (1998), 8–9.)

35 *Report of the International Law Commission*, 46th Sess., 2 May–22 July 1994, UN GAOR, 49th Sess., Supp. No. 10, UN Doc. A/49/10 (1994).

Furthermore, much jurisprudence had accumulated regarding the interpretation of the offences punishable in terms of the new Statute. Those seeking a permanent, effective, and politically uncompromised system of international criminal justice drew upon all these factors.

The General Assembly established in 1996[36] a Preparatory Committee on the Establishment of an International Criminal Court (PrepCom). This Committee held various meetings, and submitted to the Diplomatic Conference at Rome (15 June–17 July 1998) a Draft Statute and Draft Final Act consisting of 116 articles contained in 173 pages of text with some 1,300 words in square brackets, representing multiple options either to entire provisions or to some words contained in certain provisions.

Both in the works of the PrepCom and in the Rome negotiations, three major groupings of States emerged.

The first was the group of so-called Like-Minded States, which included countries from all regions of the world and was to a large extent led by Canada and Australia. This group favoured a fairly strong Court with broad and 'automatic jurisdiction', the establishment of an independent prosecutor empowered to initiate proceedings, and a sweeping definition of war crimes embracing crimes committed in internal armed conflicts.

A second group comprised the permanent members of the Security Council (P-5) minus however the UK (which during the preparatory negotiations joined the Like-Minded States) and France (which also joined the Like-Minded States in Rome). The three remaining permanent members, and in particular the USA, were opposed to 'automatic jurisdiction' and to granting to the prosecutor the power to initiate proceedings. By the same token they were eager to assign extensive tasks to the Security Council. This body was to be empowered both to refer matters to the Court and to prevent cases from being brought to the Court. In addition, these States were opposed both to envisaging aggression among the crimes subject to the Court's jurisdiction, and to including any reference to the use of nuclear weapons among the violations of humanitarian law over which the Court was to exercise jurisdiction.

The third grouping embraced members of the non-aligned-movement (NAM). They insisted on envisaging aggression among the crimes provided for in the Statute; some of them (Barbados, Dominica, Jamaica, and Trinidad and Tobago) pressed for the inclusion of drug trafficking, whereas others (India, Sri Lanka, Algeria, and Turkey) supported providing for terrorism. They strongly opposed the assignment of any role to the Security Council and opposed any jurisdiction over war crimes committed in internal armed conflicts. In contrast, they insisted on the inclusion of the death sentence among the possible penalties.

A group of distinguished diplomats, and in particular the Canadian Philippe

[36] The 1994 ILC report on the Draft Statute for an International Criminal Court was submitted to the 49th session of the General Assembly, which resolved to consider it at its 50th Session, but first it set up an ad hoc committee to discuss the proposal. This committee, referred to as the 1995 Ad Hoc Committee for the Establishment of an International Criminal Court, met inter-sessionally for two sessions of two weeks each from April to August 1995 (ibid.).

Kirsch, who chaired the Committee of the Whole (where the major points of the draft Statute were substantially negotiated) must be credited with having been able skilfully to devise and suggest a number of compromise formulas that in the event permitted the Conference to adopt the Statute by 120 votes to 7 (USA, Libya, Israel, Iraq, China, Syria, Sudan) with 20 abstentions.

18.6 THE ESTABLISHMENT OF SO-CALLED INTERNATIONALIZED OR MIXED CRIMINAL COURTS OR TRIBUNALS

In recent years, faced with emergency situations involving the commission of large-scale atrocities, States have preferred to resort neither to national nor to international criminal courts, but rather to establish courts that are mixed in their composition, and the statutes and rules of which combine aspects of international law and municipal law. Such courts have been set up for Sierra Leone, East Timor, and Kosovo; an attempt is being made to establish them for Cambodia as well.[37]

It is fitting first to set out a *definition* of 'mixed' or, as they are often termed, 'internationalized' courts and tribunals. This notion will be used here as encompassing judicial bodies that have *a mixed composition*, consisting of both international judges and of judges having the nationality of the State where trials are held. There may be two versions of these courts and tribunals. First, they may be organs of the relevant State, being part of its judiciary. This applies to the proposed Cambodian Extraordinary Chambers (if they are ever established), as well as the courts in Kosovo and the 'Special Panels for Serious Crimes' in East Timor. Alternatively, the courts may be international in nature: they may be set up under an international agreement and not be part of the national judiciary. This holds true for the Special Court for Sierra Leone (the Statute of which was adopted on 16 January 2002, after an agreement was entered into by the UN and Sierra Leone).

A multitude of historical and practical reasons combine to warrant the establishment of courts that are neither national nor international, but mixed.

First, as a result of *an emergency situation* (armed conflict, civil strife, strong religious and ethnic tension), serious and widespread crimes are committed. When

[37] In Cambodia, after years of pressure by the international community, and after a UN Commission had proposed the establishment of an international criminal tribunal, Cambodian authorities have opted for the creation of special Cambodian courts with mixed composition. On 2 January 2001 Cambodia's Parliament (the National Assembly) passed a Law on the Establishment of Extraordinary Chambers in the Courts of Cambodia for the Prosecution of Crimes Committed during the Period of Democratic Kampuchea. In East Timor the UN provisional administration (UN Transitional Administration in East Timor, or UNTAET) adopted Regulation 2000/11 in 2000 setting up mixed panels within the District Court of Dili and Regulation 2000/15 established Panels with exclusive jurisdiction over 'serious criminal offences'. In Sierra Leone, after the drafting of a Statute of a Special Court in 2000, on 16 January 2001 the UN and the Sierra Leone Government signed an agreement establishing a mixed court, accompanied by a Statute. In Kosovo the UN provisional administration (UNMIK or UN Interim Administration in Kosovo) passed a Regulation on the appointment of international judges to serve on Kosovar courts; these judges were appointed in January 2000.

the emergency situation is over, it is considered that an appropriate reaction to those crimes should not lie in granting amnesty and forgetting about them, or in putting in place truth and reconciliation commissions designed to foster national reconciliation processes (and to avoid overburdening the local judiciary under reconstruction or reform). Rather, it is felt that bringing to trial those responsible for serious crimes may help in the post-conflict peace-building process and may also serve to deter the future commission of large-scale offences.

Secondly, as a result of the emergency situation a *breakdown of the judicial system* may have come about. This may have been caused by civil war (as in East Timor and Sierra Leone), possibly followed by an international conflict (as in Kosovo). Alternatively, even if a very long time has elapsed since the crimes were perpetrated, and a stable government has taken root, as a result of a series of historical factors the judiciary may not be capable of administering justice in an unbiased and even-handed manner: this is what has happened in Cambodia, where the presence in the government of persons who allegedly are closely linked to the perpetrators of genocide, together with the lack of a really independent judiciary, might lead to unfair trials. It may also happen that the population prevents or hampers the conduct of fair trials. In Kosovo, the ethnic biases of Kosovo Albanians and Serbs rendered the presence of international judges indispensable for administering justice.[38]

Thirdly, it is however considered that the judicial response *must not lie in the establishment of an international tribunal.* This option is normally ruled out because of the combination of two factors: (i) lack of political will of the relevant organs of the international organization that should set up the international tribunal, for the country or the situation at issue are regarded as either inconsequential in geo-political terms, or likely to spawn further friction and thus to embroil the international organization in a never-ending conflict; and (ii) lack of will of major Powers to fund the international tribunal.

Fourthly, those in charge of finding a solution feel that *using the national judiciary* under some sort of international scrutiny, or even control, may prove *advantageous and useful in many respects*:

1. It assuages the nationalistic demands of local authorities, loath to hand over to international bodies an essential prerogative of sovereign Powers, the administration of justice.

2. It involves, in rendering justice, persons (the local prosecutors and judges) familiar with the mentality, language, habits, and so on of the accused.

[38] As the UN Secretary-General pointed out in his Report of 6 June 2000, 'Despite the appointment of more than 400 judges, prosecutors and lay judges [of whom 46 were non-ethnic Kosovo Albanians, 7 of whom Kosovo Serbs] and the increased capacity of the courts, the unwillingness of witnesses to testify and the ethnic bias and risk of intimidation of some judicial personnel have hampered the administration of justice' (see S/2000/538, §57). The detainees of the Mitrovica detention centre who had gone on a hunger strike in protest over the length of their pre-trial detention, stopped the strike only when the UN Special Representative promised that he would ensure that a Kosovo Serb or an international judge would preside over their cases, in addition to Kosovo Albanian judges (ibid., §59).

3. By holding trials in the territory where the crimes have been perpetrated, it exposes the local population to past atrocities, with the twofold advantage of making everybody cognizant of those atrocities, including those who sided with the perpetrators, and bringing about a cathartic process in the victims or their relatives, through public stigmatization of the culprits and just retribution; thus, exposure of past misdeeds to the local population contributes to the process of gradual reconciliation.

4. It may expedite prosecution and trials without compromising respect for international standards and international law in general.

5. It may produce a significant spill-over effect, in that it may contribute to gradually promoting the democratic legal training of local members of the prosecution and the judiciary.

18.6.1 THE MAIN PRACTICAL PROBLEMS THAT MAY ARISE

Nevertheless, one should not underestimate the practical problems and difficulties that may arise in mixed or hybrid, international-national courts.

The first problem is to ensure that the national and international component of the prosecution work in close, constructive, and constant agreement.[39]

Another, no less serious problem may be to ensure the smooth co-operation of the national and international component of the bench. There may be differences in mentality, language, experience, and legal philosophy.[40]

[39] This may not prove easy, because the local prosecutors may either tend to be over-zealous, when the accused belong to an ethnic or religious group to which they are hostile, or instead to engage in dilatory tactics, or even to create obstacles to prosecution, when the accused belong to their own group.

Article 20 of the Cambodian Draft Law provides that in case of disagreement between the two prosecutors (one national, the other international) the matter is referred to a Pre-Trial Chamber of five judges, two international and three national, deciding by an affirmative vote of at least four judges; if there is no majority, for a decision, 'the prosecution shall proceed'. The same procedure applies to possible disagreements between the two investigating judges (see Article 23). At least in some respects this solution appears to be fairly sensible, for in the last analysis it ensures that a prosecution will be instituted. However, as has been pointed out, it is indeed unusual and contrary to the principled distinction between prosecution and bench, for a panel of judges to settle disputes between co-prosecutors concerning prosecutorial strategy at trial.

[40] Particularly where international members of the Tribunal are the majority (as is the case in Sierra Leone and East Timor), they may be perceived by the local judges as intrusive and overwhelming, with the consequence that the local judges may seek to obstruct or otherwise hamper the process of administering justice. On the other hand, the action of the international component may be thwarted by the attitude of the local judges. Probably the main reasons that the internationalized courts operating in Kosovo have been assailed for their alleged flaws in ensuring fair trials, and full respect for the rights of the defence, are linked to this problem. The matter is further complicated where, as in the case of Cambodia, the relevant law provides that the majority belongs to national judges (three to two), but a decision may only be taken if four judges are infavour. This entails that if two national judges are not agreeable, no decision is made, and the court becomes deadlocked.

Things may become even worse, for under Article 46 of the Cambodian law, in cases of last resort Cambodians may be appointed to take the place of foreign judges (and prosecutors); hence, in case of adeadlock and the subsequent withdrawal of the international judges, judicial action may continue with all-Cambodian staff. It follows that ultimately the national component may gradually push the international component to withdraw, so as to take complete control of the judicial process.

Two other practical problems may prove crucial: funding and security. Making *financial resources* available is a sine qua non for a court to function.[41]

As for *security*, it is obvious that the dangers following from the hatred, resentment, and social conflict festering in those countries may pose a serious risk to those working in the judicial process.

SELECT BIBLIOGRAPHY

THE FIRST AD HOC TRIBUNALS

H. L. Stimson, 'The Nuremberg Trial: Landmark in Law', 25 *Foreign Affairs* (1947), 179–89; H. Kelsen, 'Will the Judgment in the Nuremberg Trial Constitute a Precedent in International Law?', 1 *International Law Quarterly* (1947), 153–9; A. S. Comyns Carr, 'The Judgment of the International Military Tribunal for the Far East', 34 *The Grotius Society—Problems of Public and Private International Law* (1949), 141–51; G. Ireland, 'Uncommon Law in Martial Tokyo', *The Yearbook of World Affairs* (1950), 54–104; J. A. Appleman, *Military Tribunals and International Crimes* (Indianapolis: Bobbs-Merrill Co., 1954), 257–64; H. H. Jescheck, 'Die Entwicklung des Völkerstrafrechts nach Nürnberg', 72 *Schweizerische Zeitschrift für Strafrecht* (1957), 15–48; B. F. Smith, *The American Road to Nuremberg—The Documentary Record, 1944–1945* (Stanford, Cal.: Hoover Institution Press, 1982); T. Taylor, *Nuremberg and Vietnam: An American Tragedy* (Chicago: Triangle Books, 1970); B. V. A. Röling, 'The Nuremberg and the Tokyo Trials in Retrospect' in Bassiouni and Nanda (eds), *A Treatise*, I, 590–608; R. H. Minear, *Victors' Justice—The Tokyo War Crimes Trial* (Princeton, NJ: Princeton University Press, 1973); T. Taylor, *The Anatomy of the Nuremberg Trial—A Personal Memoir* (London: Bloomsbury, 1993); B. V. A. Röling, *The Tokyo Trial and Beyond*, ed. A. Cassese (Cambridge: Polity Press, 1993); B. Simma, 'The Impact of Nuremberg and Tokyo: Attempts at a Comparison', in N. Ando (ed.), *Japan and International Law—Past, Present and Future* (The Hague, London, Boston: Kluwer, 1999), 59–84; T. Maga, *Judgment at Tokyo* (Lexington, Kentucky: University Press of Kentucky, 2001).

For some early German reactions to Nuremberg, see H. Kraus, *Gerichtstag in Nürnberg* (Hamburg: Gesetz und Recht Verlag, 1947); O. Kranzbühler, *Rückblick auf Nürnberg* (Hamburg: Zeitverlag E. Schmidt & Co., 1949).

AD HOC TRIBUNALS ESTABLISHED IN THE 1990S

A. Pellet, 'Le tribunal criminel international pour l'ex Jugoslavie: poudre aux yeux ou avancée decisive?', 98 RGDIP (1994), 7–87; D. Shraga and R. Zacklin, 'The International Criminal Tribunal for the former Yugoslavia', 5 EJIL (1994), 360–80; A. Cassese, 'The

[41] Indeed, the principal reason that the Special Court for Sierra Leone has not yet become operational is lack of funds. Money is needed not only to pay salaries to prosecutors and judges, but also to fund interpretation and translation from and to English and French, one of these two languages being the vehicular means of the international component. For instance, in his Report of 16 January 2001 on East Timor, the UN Secretary-General pointed out that a shortage of skilled translators had hampered efforts at all judicial levels (see S/2001/42, §23). In his Report of 18 October 2001 the Secretary-General noted that the lack of resources, including interpreters, had led to delayed hearings and unduly prolonged detention of suspects (see S/2001/983, §20). Money is also needed to provide those authorities with books and documents. (For instance, in Kosovo, the destruction of among other things law libraries has resulted in a dearth of relevant legal texts.)

International Criminal Tribunal for the Former Yugoslavia', *Studi in ricordo di Antonio Filippo Panzera*, vol. I (Bari: Cacucci Editore, 1995), 235–46; G. Hankel and G. Stuby (eds), *Strafgerichte gegen Menschheitsverbrechen—Zum Völkerstrafrecht 50 Jahre nach den Nürnberger Prozessen*, (Hamburg: Hamburger Edition, 1995); P. Akhavan, 'The International Criminal Tribunal for Rwanda', in F. Lattanzi and E. Sciso (eds), *Dai tribunali penali internazionali ad hoc ad una Corte permanente: atti del Convegno, Roma 15–16 dicembre* (Naples: Editoriale scientifica, 1996), 191–203; M. C. Bassiouni and P. Manikas, *The Law of the Criminal Tribunal for the Former Yugoslavia* (Ardsley, New York: Transnational Publishers, 1996); M. P. Scharf, *Balkan Justice—the Story behind the First International War Crimes since Nuremberg*, (Durham, NC: Carolina Academic Press, 1997); V. Morris and M. P. Scharf, *The International Criminal Tribunal for Rwanda* (Ardsley, New York: Transnational Publishers, 1998); P. Hazan, *La justice face à la guerre—De Nuremberg à La Haye*, (Paris: Stock, 2000); G. J. Bass, *Stay the Hand of Vengeance—The Politics of War Crimes Tribunals* (Princeton and Oxford: Princeton University Press, 2000); J. R. W. D. Jones, *The Practice of the International Criminal Tribunals for the former Yugoslavia and Rwanda* (Ardsley, New York: Transnational Publishers, 2000).

THE PREPARATORY CONFERENCE (1995–8) AND THE ROME DIPLOMATIC CONFERENCE OF 1998

C. K. Hall, 'The Third and Fourth Session of the UN Preparatory Committee on the Establishment of an International Criminal Court', 92 AJIL (1998), 124–33; P. Kirsch and J. T. Holmes, 'The Rome Conference on an International Criminal Court: the Negotiating Process', 93 AJIL (1999), 2–12; D. Scheffer, 'The United States and the International Criminal Court', 93 AJIL (1999), 12–22; R. Wedgewood, 'The International Criminal Court: an American View', 10 EJIL (1999), 93–107; P. Kirsch and D. Robinson, 'Reaching Agreement at the Rome Conference', in Cassese, Gaeta, and Jones (eds), *ICC Commentary*, I, 67–92.

THE ICC

H. Fujita, 'Establishment of the International Criminal Court—Historic Significance of the Rome Statute', 42 AJIL (1999), 32–61; A. Cassese, 'The Statute if the International Criminal Court: Some Preliminary Reflections', 10 EJIL (1999), 144–71; O. Triffterer (ed.), *Commentary on the Rome Statute of the International Criminal Court* (Baden-Baden: Nomos Verlag, 1999); R. S. Lee (ed.), *The International Criminal Court and the Making of the Rome Statute: Issues, Negotiations, Results* (The Hague: Kluwer, 1999); H. Fischer, C. Kress, and S. R. Lüder (eds), *International and National Prosecution of Crimes Under International Law* (Berlin: Berlin Verlag, 2001) 21–445.

THE ESTABLISHMENT OF SO-CALLED INTERNATIONALIZED CRIMINAL COURTS OR TRIBUNALS

M. Frulli, 'The Special Court for Sierra Leone: Some Preliminary Comments', 11 EJIL (2000) 857–69; H. Strohmeyer, 'Collapse and Reconstruction of a Judicial System: the United Nations Missions in Kosovo and East Timor', 95 AJIL (2001), 46–63; S. Linton, 'Cambodia, East Timor and Sierra Leone: Experiments in International Justice', 12 *Criminal Law Forum* (2001), 185–246; H. Strohmeyer, 'Making Multilateral Interventions Work: the UN and the Creation of Transitional Justice Systems in Kosovo and East Timor', 25 *Fletcher Forum of World Affairs Journal* (2001), 107–24.

19

INTERNATIONAL VERSUS NATIONAL JURISDICTION

19.1 PRIMACY AND COMPLEMENTARITY

The establishment of international criminal courts and tribunals has posed the tricky problem of how to co-ordinate their action with that of national courts: whenever both classes of courts are empowered to pronounce on the same crimes, which should take precedence, and under what conditions? Obviously, the problem does not arise in the area where those courts do not have *concurrent jurisdiction*, that is, with regard to crimes that fall under the exclusive jurisdiction of national courts (for example, piracy, serious instances of international terrorism falling short of crimes against humanity or of war crimes, large-scale drug trafficking, etc.). The problem only arises when one or more States may assert their criminal jurisdiction over a specific crime on such legal grounds as territoriality, active or passive nationality, or universality (see above 15.2–5), and at the same time an international tribunal is empowered to adjudicate the same crime by virtue of its Statute.

There are no *general* international rules determinative of this matter, just as there are no international customary rules designed to resolve the question of concurrent jurisdiction of two or more States, by giving pride of place to one legal ground of national jurisdiction (say, territoriality) over another such ground (say, passive nationality). Luckily, while not even treaty rules have settled the possible conflict between States asserting jurisdiction over the same person accused of the same crime, in the case of conflict between national and international criminal courts the conflict has been resolved by *treaty* rules or otherwise *binding resolutions*. In short, in the case of the ICTY and the ICTR, primacy has been given to the international tribunals, whereas in the case of the ICC national courts take precedence over the Court. Let us now dwell at some length on this matter, to consider both the legal implications and the underlying political motivations.

19.2 THE PRIMACY OF THE ICTY AND THE ICTR

The Statutes of these two Tribunals, respectively at Articles 9 and 8, provide that each international Tribunal shall have concurrent jurisdiction with national courts to prosecute persons for serious violations of international humanitarian law, but add under paragraph 2 that the Tribunal 'shall have primacy over national courts':

At any stage of the procedure, the International Tribunal may formally request national courts to defer to the competence of the International Tribunal in accordance with the present Statute and the Rules of Procedure and Evidence [RPE] of the International Tribunal.

The reasons for proclaiming the Tribunals' primacy were clear. In the case of the former Yugoslavia, the ongoing armed conflict among the successor States and the deep-seated animosity between the various ethnic and religious groups made it unlikely that national courts would be willing or able to conduct fair trials. It was considered that the authorities would have hesitated to bring their own people (Muslims, Croats, and Serbs) to book, whereas, had they initiated proceedings against their adversaries, probably such proceedings would have been highly biased. As for other States, the experience built up until that time showed that they shied away from bringing to trial alleged perpetrators of crimes committed elsewhere. Hence the need was felt to affirm the overriding authority of the international Tribunal. Similar considerations held true for Rwanda, where in addition the national judicial system had collapsed and consequently seemed unable to render justice.

However, the Statutes do not specify on what conditions and how primacy is to be exercised. In his Report to the Security Council elaborating upon the draft Statute of the ICTY, the UN Secretary-General simply stated that 'The details of how the primacy will be asserted shall be set out in the rules of procedure and evidence of the International Tribunal' (§65). The judges of the ICTY skilfully and wisely drew up a set of rules on primacy, which were subsequently taken up by the judges of the ICTR. These rules do not lay down the absolute primacy of the Tribunal; rather, they provide that the concurrent jurisdiction of the Tribunal and national courts may lead to the prevalence of national courts, and even that the Tribunal may divest itself of a case when it considers that the case may more appropriately be tried by a national court (Rule 11 *bis* of the ICTY RPE). Thus, judges worked out a mechanism whereby a case could be referred back to national courts whenever they deemed it appropriate. However, the Rules provide that at the request of the Prosecutor the Tribunal may assert its primacy in three cases:

1. When a national prosecutor investigates an international crime or a national court conducts criminal proceedings with regard to the crime not as an international crime, but as 'ordinary crime' (for instance, genocide is being investigated or tried as 'multiple murder', or serious ill-treatment of prisoners of war is handled as 'assault' and not as a war crime). In this case the classification of the offence as an ordinary crime presupposes a deliberate (or unconscious) proclivity to *misrepresent* the very

nature, hence to *belittle the seriousness*, of international crimes. In other words, the national court shows that, either intentionally or unwittingly, it is not cognizant of both the international dimension and the gravity of the criminal offence.

2. When a national court proves to be *unreliable*: this happens where it is proved, under Rule 9(ii) of the ICTY RPE, that there is 'a lack of impartiality or independence', or 'the investigations or proceedings are designed to shield the accused from international criminal responsibility', or else 'the case is not diligently prosecuted'. Clearly, in all these instances national authorities may not be trusted because they are intent on 'protecting' the accused or else take a persecutory attitude to him.

3. When, although the relevant national court appears to be reliable and able to conduct a fair trial, nonetheless the case is *closely related, or may be relevant, to other cases* being tried by the International Tribunal. Under Rule 9(iii), 'what is in issue is closely related to, or otherwise involves, significant factual or legal questions which may have implications for investigations or prosecutions before the Tribunal'. Plainly, these cases are of such overriding significance, or general import, or wide ramifications, that it appears appropriate for them to be brought before an international court rather than be adjudicated by a national court.[1]

By and large, the scheme adopted by the judges of the ICTY (and of the ICTR) seems wisely to reconcile (i) the need not to overload international institutions with relatively minor cases, leaving these cases to national courts, as well as (ii) the demands of State sovereignty, with (iii) the requirement that international courts should *replace* national institutions when these prove unreliable or unfair, and in addition should deal with *major international crimes* of relevance to the international community as a whole.

So far the two Tribunals have seldom relied upon their primacy. (See, for instance, the *Tadić* case, as far as the ICTY is concerned: on 8 November 1994 the ICTY made a request for deferral to the Federal Republic of Germany, whose authorities were investigating Tadić's alleged crimes; Germany immediately complied with the request and surrendered the accused to the Tribunal: see *Tadić, Decision on deferral to the competence of Tribunal*.[2] See also the order of 4 October 2002 in *Republic of Macedonia*

[1] Interestingly the first two exceptions are also exceptions for *non bis in idem*, and therefore can be justified by reference to the Statute's provisions on *non bis in idem*. (There is a clear parallel between conditions for exercising primacy and *non bis* in the sense that what justifies the court retrying an accused are surely also grounds for taking over the proceedings before they have reached their conclusion.) Instead, case (3) is somewhat unusual and dubious in that it has no basis in the Statute. Moreover it will nearly always apply—any national war crimes prosecution in the former Yugoslavia is bound to have implications for the ICTY's proceedings. This may therefore seem to be too all-encompassing.

[2] In that case the defence challenged the Tribunal's jurisdiction, arguing that its 'primacy' found no basis in international law because the national courts of Bosnia and Herzegovina or, alternatively, of the entity known as the Bosnian Serb Republic (known today as Republika Srpska) had primary jurisdiction to try the accused. The Trial Chamber dismissed the argument, noting, first, that in any case 'the two States most closely affected by the indictment against the accused', namely Bosnia and Herzegovina (where the accused had allegedly committed his crimes) and Germany (where he resided at the time of his arrest), had 'unconditionally accepted the jurisdiction of the International Tribunal and the accused cannot claim the rights that have

(*Prosecutor's Request for Deferral and Motion for Order to the Former Yugoslav Republic of Macedonia*), §6–53).

In recent times, the two ad hoc Tribunals have even emphasized the importance of national courts dealing with the crimes falling under the Tribunals' jurisdiction. There seem to be two grounds behind this new trend. First, national courts of the States concerned (those of the successors to the former Yugoslavia, and those of Rwanda) are now better structured, more efficient, and less prone to bias. Secondly, the workload of the international Tribunals is increasing and it therefore proves appropriate for national courts gradually to share the burden and even start to take over the job from the Tribunals.

19.3 THE COMPLEMENTARITY OF THE ICC

Unlike the ICTY and the ICTR, the ICC is based on the principle of complementarity whereby the Court is subsidiary or complementary to national courts: these courts enjoy *priority* in the exercise of jurisdiction except under special circumstances, when the ICC is entitled to take over and assert its jurisdiction. There are two underlying reasons for this approach.

First, States saw a practical ground: they considered it inappropriate for the Court to be flooded with cases from all over the world. The Court, having a limited number of judges and limited financial resources and infrastructure, would be unable to cope with a broad range of cases. It is healthy, it was thought, to leave the vast majority of cases concerning international crimes to national courts, which may properly exercise their jurisdiction based on a link with the case (territoriality, nationality) or even on universality. Among other things, these national courts may have more means available to collect the necessary evidence and to lay their hands on the accused.

Secondly, there was perhaps a principled motivation, namely the intent to respect State sovereignty as much as possible.

been specifically waived by the States concerned. To allow the accused to do so would be to allow him to select the forum of his choice, contrary to the principles relating to coercive criminal jurisdiction' (§41). Secondly, the crimes which the Tribunal was called upon to try were not 'of a purely domestic nature. They are really crimes which are universal in nature, well recognized in international law as serious breaches of international humanitarian law, and transcending the interests of any one State . . . in such circumstances, the sovereign rights of States cannot and should not take precedence over the right of the international community to act appropriately as they [the crimes] affect the whole of mankind and shock the conscience of all nations of the world. There can therefore be no objection to an international tribunal properly constituted trying these crimes on behalf of the international community' (§42). The Appeals Chamber upheld these conclusions. It noted among other things that 'when an international tribunal such as the present one is created, it *must* be endowed with primacy over national courts. Otherwise, human nature being what it is, there would be a perennial danger of international crimes being characterized as 'ordinary crimes' . . . or proceedings being 'designed to shield the accused', or cases not being diligently prosecuted . . . If not effectively countered by the principle of primacy, any one of those stratagems might be used to defeat the very purpose of the creation of an international criminal jurisdiction, to the benefit of the very people whom it has been designed to prosecute' (*Tadić, Interlocutory appeal*, §58).

Complementarity is laid down in paragraph 10 of the Preamble as well as in Article 1 of the Statute (whereby the ICC 'shall be complementary to national criminal jurisdictions') and is spelled out in Articles 15, 17, 18, and 19. In short, the Court is *barred from exercising its jurisdiction* over a crime whenever a national court asserts its jurisdiction over the same crime and (i) under its national law the State has jurisdiction; (ii) the case is being duly investigated or prosecuted by its authorities or these authorities have decided, in a proper manner, not to prosecute the person concerned; and (iii) the case is not of sufficient gravity to justify action by the Court (*ex* Article 17). In addition, the Court (iv) may not prosecute and try a person who has already been convicted of or acquitted for the same crimes, if the trial was fair and proper (Articles 17(c) and 20).

The Court is instead authorized to exercise its jurisdiction over a crime even if a case concerning the crime is pending before national authorities, and thus to override national criminal jurisdiction, whenever: (i) the State is unable or unwilling genuinely to carry out the investigation or prosecution, or its decision not to prosecute the person concerned has resulted from its unwillingness or inability genuinely to prosecute that person; and (ii) the case is of sufficient gravity to justify the exercise of the Court's jurisdiction.

The question of course arises of what is meant by 'unwillingness' or 'inability' of a State to prosecute or try a person accused or suspected of international crimes. These two notions are spelled out in Article 17(2) and (3). A State may be considered as '*unwilling*' when: (i) in fact the national authorities have undertaken proceedings for the purpose of shielding the person concerned from criminal responsibility; or (ii) there has been an 'unjustified delay' in the proceedings showing that in fact the authorities do not intend to bring the person concerned to justice; or (iii) the proceedings are not being conducted independently or impartially or in any case in a manner showing the intent to bring the person to justice. A State is '*unable*' when, chiefly on account of a total or partial collapse of its judicial system, it is not in a position: (i) to detain the accused or to have him surrendered by the authorities or bodies that hold him in custody, or (ii) to collect the necessary evidence, or (iii) to carry out criminal proceedings. One should also add cases where the national court is unable to try a person not because of a collapse or malfunctioning of the judicial system, but on account of legislative impediments, such as an amnesty law, or a statute of limitations, making it impossible for the national judge to commence proceedings against the suspect or the accused.

Complementarity applies not only with regard to the States parties to the ICC Statute but also with respect to States not parties (see Article 18(1)). Thus, for instance, if the national of a State not party (A) has committed an international crime on the territory of a State party (B) and then escapes to another State not party (C), and this State asserts its jurisdiction on the ground that the crime is provided for in an international treaty and the suspect is present on its territory (the *forum deprehensionis* principle) or on the ground of universality, the ICC may not exercise jurisdiction if it is proved that State C is willing and able to conduct a proper and fair trial.

Complementarity applies whatever the trigger mechanism of the Court's proceedings, that is, both when the case (i) has been brought to the Court by a State party (Articles 13(a) and 14), or (ii) has been initiated by the Prosecutor *motu proprio*, and the Prosecutor has been authorized by the Pre-Trial Chamber to commence a criminal investigation (Articles 13(c) and 15), and when (iii) it is the UN Security Council that has referred to the Court a 'situation in which one or more of... [the] crimes [falling under the Court's jurisdiction] appears to have been committed' (Articles 13(b) and 52(c)).

The ICC system of complementarity, globally considered, shows that the Court must generally defer to national courts, except when these courts are not in a position to do justice in a proper and fair way, and in addition the case is of sufficient gravity to warrant the Court's stepping in. Although one should of course wait until the system begins to operate in practice, at present the appraisal of complementarity is largely positive.[3] Its chief merits lie both in its substantial respect for national courts, and in the indirect but powerful incentive to their becoming more operational and effective, inherent in the power of the ICC to substitute for national judges, whenever they are not in a position to dispense justice or they deliberately fail to do so (see however what will be pointed out in 19.4).

19.4 THE NUREMBERG SCHEME VERSUS THE ICC SCHEME

It may useful to ask ourselves about the proper role to assign to an international criminal court. It would seem that two major models or schemes have so far been worked out.

One is that adopted in Nuremberg. This scheme was first drawn up in 1944 by an American officer (Lieutenant Colonel Murray C. Bernays, chief of the Special Projects Office of the Personnel Branch at the US War Department), was then refined by other staff, subsequently upheld by the US Secretary of War Henry L. Stimson[4] and finally accepted by the other three Great Powers in London in 1945. Under this scheme an international court was entrusted with the task of dealing with the major leaders accused of international crimes, whereas national courts were called upon to handle the criminal offences of minor culprits (after the Second World War, German courts were requested to adjudicate upon crimes committed

[3] One should also note that the ICC Statute provides for a monitoring mechanism enabling the ICC to be kept abreast of developments in national investigations and prosecutions, whenever the ICC defers to national courts. Pursuant to Article 18(5), 'When the Prosecutor has deferred an investigation in accordance with para 2, the Prosecutor may request that the State concerned periodically inform the Prosecutor of the progress of its investigations and any subsequent prosecutions. States Parties shall respond to such requests without undue delay.'

[4] See the documents published in B. F. Smith, *The American Road to Nuremberg—The Documentary Record, 1944–1945* (Stanford, Ca. Hoover Institution Press: 1982), 33–130.

by Germans against other Germans, while national courts of the Allies pronounced upon crimes committed by Germans against foreign nationals). Interestingly, the two ad hoc International Criminal Tribunals set up for the former Yugoslavia and Rwanda respectively, were based, as pointed out above (19.2) on the principle of their primacy over national courts because initially they were intended as a substitute for the national courts of States deemed unable or unwilling to dispense justice. Nonetheless, from the outset the ICTR concentrated on military and civilian leaders, leaving to Rwandan courts the task of trying minor offenders. The ICTY, whose first Prosecutor did not envisage at the prosecutorial level a distinction between major and minor offenders, is now gradually moving towards the Nuremberg scheme, in that it is increasingly asking national courts of the States concerned to try lesser accused, so that it may better concentrate on the trials of major defendants[5].

A different division of labour is provided for in the Statute of the ICC. As emphasized above (19.3), all crimes may be brought before national courts, whatever the magnitude of the crime or the status, rank, or importance of the accused. The ICC steps in only when such courts prove unable or unwilling to do justice, and provided the case 'is of sufficient gravity' to justify action by the Court (ex Article 17(1)(d) of the Court's Statute).

It would seem that the Nuremberg model still has much merit. It is logical and consistent for very serious international crimes allegedly perpetrated by leaders to be adjudicated by an international court offering all the advantages that will be outlined *infra* (see 22.22 and 23.5). Trials held in the country where the crime has been committed or where the victims or their relatives live, may arouse animosity and conflict and, by the same token, it may turn out to be difficult for judges to remain impartial. In particular, when crimes are very serious and large scale (think, for example, of grave instances of genocide or crimes against humanity) and where such crimes cannot but have been committed either by the central authorities or with their (tacit or explicit) approval, it will be difficult for a national court to prosecute the alleged planner or perpetrators, unless there is a change in government, in which case, there may be a risk of 'witch hunting' or of using the criminal courts for settling political accounts, a situation which cannot contribute to the fair and impartial administration

[5] See among other things the recently amended Rule 11 *bis* of the RPE. Under this provision, concerning 'Referral of the Indictment to Another Court':

(A) If an indictment has been confirmed, irrespective of whether or not the accused is in the custody of the Tribunal, the President may appoint a Trial Chamber for the purpose of referring a case to the authorities of a State (i) in whose territory the crime was committed; or (ii) in which the accused was arrested, so that those authorities should forthwith refer the case to the appropriate court for trial within that State.

(B) The Trial Chamber may order such referral *proprio motu* or at the request of the Prosecutor, after having given to the Prosecutor and, where applicable, the accused, the opportunity to be heard.

(C) In determining whether to refer the case in accordance with paragraph (A), the Trial Chamber shall, in accordance with Security Council Presidential Statement S/PRST/2002/21, consider the gravity of the crimes charged and the level of responsibility of the accused.

of justice. Hence, international courts are by definition better suited to pronounce upon large scale and very grave crimes allegedly perpetrated by political or military leaders. For such cases the rule of complementarity laid down in the Statute of Rome may appear to be questionable. However, since the draftsmen of the Statute have opted for that model, one can only hope that the Court will interpret and apply the relevant rules of the Statute in such a way as to assert the Court's jurisdiction whenever cases in that category are brought before the Court.

Perhaps a better path for the future might lie in both enhancing the role of international courts for major cases of criminality, and, with regard to other cases, in combining the action of those courts with that not only of national courts but also of other bodies charged with 'restorative justice', such as truth and reconciliation commissions.

19.5 THE NEED FOR INTERNATIONAL CRIMINAL COURTS AND TRIBUNALS TO RELY UPON STATE CO-OPERATION

For international criminal tribunals, State co-operation is crucial to the effectiveness of judicial process. Only other bodies or entities, that is, national authorities or international organizations, can enforce the decisions, orders, and requests of such criminal tribunals. Unlike domestic criminal courts, international tribunals have no enforcement agencies at their disposal: without the intermediary of national authorities, they cannot seize evidentiary material, compel witnesses to give testimony, search the scenes where crimes have allegedly been committed, or execute arrest warrants. For all these purposes, international courts must turn to State authorities and request them to take action to assist the courts' officers and investigators. Without the help of these authorities, international courts cannot operate. Admittedly, this holds true for all international institutions, which need the support of States to be able to operate. However international criminal courts are much more in need of such support, and more urgently, because their action has a direct impact on individuals living on the territory of sovereign States and subject to their jurisdiction. Trials must be expeditious; evidence must be collected before it becomes stale; the court must be able to summon witnesses to testify at short notice.

19.6 MODELS OF CO-OPERATION

In deciding upon how to regulate the co-operation of States with an international criminal court, the framers of the Statute of international criminal tribunals may choose between two possible models, namely, as the ICTY Appeals Chamber put it in *Blaškić (subpoena)* (§§47 and 54), the 'horizontal' and the 'vertical' model.

Under the former model the relations between States and the international court are shaped on the pattern of interstate judicial co-operation in criminal matters. As aptly stated by a distinguished criminal lawyer,[6] *interstate judicial co-operation and assistance* shows the following hallmarks: (i) it has a consensual basis, being grounded on treaty relations; (ii) treaties normally require that the offence for which extradition is requested be considered such in both the requesting and the requested State; (iii) often treaties provide for exceptions to extradition, relating to certain offences (for example, political or fiscal offences) or to some categories of persons (for instance, nationals of the requested State), or for some sentences (for instance, extradition is often excluded when the requesting State may impose the death penalty); (iv) extradition may be refused also when the requested State can assert its jurisdiction over the offence; (v) judicial assistance or co-operation may normally be refused on grounds of security, public order, overriding national interests, etc.; (vi) as a rule the collection of evidence, search, and other investigatory actions requested by a State may not be undertaken by the authorities of that State, but only by those of the requested State, through the system of 'letters rogatory'; normally a foreign country may not enter into direct contact with individuals subject to the sovereignty of the requested State.

If this model is applied to international courts, it follows that the court has no superior authority over States except for the legal power to adjudicate crimes perpetrated by individuals subject to State sovereignty. Otherwise, the international court cannot in any way force States to lend their co-operation, let alone exercise coercive powers within the territory of sovereign States.

The second model could be termed 'vertical' or 'supra-State'. It departs from the traditional setting of State-to-State judicial co-operation, where by definition all co-operating States are on an equal footing. This more progressive model presupposes that the international judicial body is vested with sweeping powers not only *vis-à-vis* individuals subject to the sovereign authority of States, but also towards States themselves. Under this model the international court is empowered to issue binding orders to States and, in case of non-compliance, may set in motion enforcement mechanisms. What is no less important, the international court is given the final say on evidentiary matters: States are not allowed to withhold evidence on grounds of self-defined national interests or to refuse to execute arrest warrants or other courts' orders. In short, the international court is endowed with an authority over States that markedly differentiates it from other international institutions.

[6] See B. Swart, 'International Cooperation and Judicial Assistance—General Problems', in Cassese, Gaeta, and Jones, *ICC Commentary*, II, 1590–2. The present author relies heavily on the excellent paper by Swart (1592–1605).

19.7 CO-OPERATION OF STATES UNDER THE ICTY AND ICTR SCHEME

The ICTY and the ICTR incarnate the coercive 'supra-State' model, both because they have the Chapter VII authority of the Security Council behind them, and on account of the practice developed by judges. Indeed, the law of the ad hoc international tribunals as it concerns State co-operation is largely judge-made. Article 29 of the ICTY Statute, and the corresponding Article 28 of the ICTR Statute, simply provide in a general way that 'States shall co-operate with the International Tribunal' and 'shall comply without undue delay with any request for assistance or an order issued by a Trial Chamber'. However, the specific practice relating to arrest warrants and orders for transfer of an accused, requests for assistance, the question of the persons or entities to whom *subpoenas* may be addressed, that of the breadth and specificity of the 'sanctions' against non-co-operative States, and many related questions, were left to the judges to define. This happened in due course in the *Blaškić* (*subpoena*) case. A Trial Chamber had issued *subpoenas* to Croatia and one of its senior ministers. On appeal the Appeals Chamber overturned the decision, confining *subpoenas* to individuals acting in a private capacity, while allowing binding *orders* to be directed to States.

It is apparent from the provisions of the Statute of the ICTY as developed and spelled out by the judges in the aforementioned case that the relations between the ICTY (and the ICTR) and States are shaped as follows: (i) the Statutes of the Tribunals impose upon States an obligation to co-operate; this obligation is at the same time sweeping (for it embraces any matter where the Tribunal may need the co-operation of a State), and strict (for it is assisted by the sanctioning powers of the Security Council in case of non-compliance by a State); (ii) it follows from that obligation that States are not allowed to rely upon such traditional clauses for refusing co-operation or extradition as 'double criminality', political offence, nationality of the person requested for surrender, etc.; (iii) the Tribunal is endowed with broad and binding powers, for it can issue binding orders to States (for the handing over of evidence, arrest of suspects, etc.), or *subpoenas* to individuals acting in a private capacity; (iv) although States may invoke national security concerns as a ground for refusing the transmission of documents and other evidence, this is subject to strict limitations, and the Tribunal may have the final say on the matter (see *Blaškić* (*subpoena*), §§61–9); (v) the collection of evidence may be carried out by the authorities of the relevant State, but the Tribunal's Prosecutor is authorized to undertake investigations and gather evidence directly (that is, without going through the official channels) on the territory of the States of the former Yugoslavia, as well as on the territory of those States which have passed implementing legislation authorizing such Tribunal's activity (see *Blaškić* (*subpoena*), §§53–4); (vi) in case of non-compliance by a State with the obligation to co-operate stemming from the Statutes, the Tribunals may make a judicial finding of failure to co-operate, and the President is then authorized to submit it to the Security Council. This organ, according to *Blaškić* (*subpoena*), §§36–7, is then legally bound by that finding, that is, it may not contest that that particular State has indeed failed to co-operate, as found by the Tribunal (the Security Council is however free to take, or not to take, sanctions); if it is an individual who fails to co-operate, the Tribunal may hold him in contempt and initiate contempt proceedings, even *in absentia* (*Blaškić* (*subpoena*), §§57–60).

19.8 CO-OPERATION OF STATES UNDER THE ICC SCHEME

In contrast to the ICTY and ICTR, which are creatures of the Security Council moulded into their present shape in large part by the judges, States have had the opportunity, in drawing up the ICC Statute (an international treaty that States may or may not ratify, given its consensual nature), to express themselves, in no uncertain terms, about how they wish international justice to work, and they have adopted a mostly *State-oriented* approach, which however, as has been rightly been pointed out, may be held to be 'a mixture of the "horizontal" and the "vertical" [model]'.[7]

A few points are relevant in this regard. First, the Statute does lay down in Article 86 a general obligation to co-operate. However, this obligation essentially serves as a general statement that is specified and spelled out in a number of specific provisions; as has been stated, in the ICC Statute 'the choice has been made to list the specific obligations of the States parties exhaustively and to indicate their scope and contents as precisely as possible'.[8] Plainly, this specific enumeration is intended to restrict as much as possible the judicial power of interpretation of the duty to co-operate, and by the same token to lay down extensive 'legislative' safeguards for States.

Secondly, the ICC Statute does not specify whether the taking of evidence, execution of summonses and warrants, etc. is to be undertaken by officials of the Prosecutor with the assistance, when needed, of State authorities, or whether instead it will be for State enforcement or judicial authorities to execute those acts at the request of the Prosecutor. Judging from the insistence in the Statute on the need to comply with the requirements of *national* legislation, however, the conclusion seems warranted that the framers of the Statute intended the latter. It would seem that this conclusion is borne out by the implementing legislation so far adopted by some of the States parties.[9]

Thirdly, both the principle of complementarity (with the ensuing power of the States concerned to decide whether they intend to exercise their jurisdiction over a crime) and

[7] B. Swart, cit., at 1594.

[8] Ibid., at 1595.

[9] See for instance the Canadian Crimes Against Humanity and War Crimes Act 2000, the Norwegian Act on Implementation of the Rome Statute of 15 June 2001, the Swiss Federal Law on Cooperation with the ICC of 22 June 2001, the French Law on the same matter of 26 February 2002. See however Article 2(1) of Part II of the United Kingdom International Criminal Court Act 2001 (C.17) whereby the British Secretary of State transmits any ICC request for arrest or surrender to 'the appropriate judicial officer', without exercising any scrutiny (see also Article 5(5) and (8)).

the general right of States to challenge the Court's jurisdiction may create obstacles to, or slow down or even hamper, States' co-operation and the Court's jurisdiction.

Fourthly, the possible surrender of persons to the Court is subject to a condition typical of interstate judicial co-operation: the principle of speciality, laid down in Article 101(1), whereby:

A person surrendered to the Court under this Statute shall not be proceeded against, punished or detained for any conduct committed prior to surrender, other than the conduct or course of conduct which forms the basis of the crimes for which that person has been surrendered.

Fifthly, in case of competing requests for surrender or extradition, i.e. a request for arrest and surrender of a person, emanating from the Court, and a request for extradition from a State not party, the request from the Court does not automatically prevail. Under Article 90(6) and (7), a State party may decide between compliance with the request from the Court and compliance with the request from a non-party State with which the State party is bound by an extradition treaty. This seems odd, for one would have thought that the obligations stemming from the Rome Statute should have taken precedence over those flowing from other treaties. Arguably, this priority would follow both from the primacy of a Statute establishing a *universal* criminal court over bilateral treaties (or multilateral treaties binding on a group of States) and from the very purpose of the Statute, to administer international justice in the interest of peace. It seems instead that the Statute, faced with the dilemma of international justice versus national justice, has left the option to the relevant States.

Furthermore, as regards the protection of national security information, the Statute substantially caters to State concerns by creating a national security exception to requests for assistance. Article 93(4) provides that 'a State Party may deny a request for assistance, in whole or in part, only if the request concerns the production of any documents or disclosure of evidence which relates to its national security'. Admittedly, Article 72, to which this provision refers, does envisage a complex mechanism designed to induce a State invoking national security concerns to disclose as much as possible of the information it wishes to withhold. This mechanism is largely based on the *Blaškić* (*subpoena*) decision of the ICTY Appeals Chamber. However, the various stages of this mechanism are turned in the Statute into formal modalities that will be cumbersome and time-consuming.[10] In addition, in *Blaškić* (*subpoena*) the emphasis

[10] Indeed, Article 72 ('Protection of national security information') establishes a three-step procedure when a State—or individual—invokes national security. Article 72 is triggered when a State is of the opinion that 'disclosure of information [requested by the Court or Prosecutor] would prejudice its national security interests'. First, co-operative means are employed to reach an amicable settlement, e.g. modification of the request, a determination by the Court of the relevance of the information sought or agreement of conditions under which the assistance could be provided. Secondly, if co-operative means fail, and the State decides against disclosure, it must notify the Court or Prosecutor of the specific reasons for its decision, unless a specific description of the reasons would itself necessarily result in such prejudice to the State's national security interests. The Court may then hold further consultations on the matter, if need be *ex parte* and/or in camera. The third step in the event that the State is found not to be complying with its obligations is for the Court to refer the matter to the Assembly of States Parties or, if the Security Council originally referred the matter to the Court, to the Security Council.

was on the obligation of States to disclose information; only in exceptional circumstances were States allowed to resort to special steps for the purpose of shielding that information from undue disclosure to entities other than the Court. In Article 72 emphasis is instead laid on the right of States to deny the Court's request for assistance.

Finally, in the event of failure of States to co-operate, Article 87(7) provides for the means substantially enunciated by the ICTY in the Appeals Chamber decision in *Blaškić* (*subpoena*), namely, 'the Court may make a finding to that effect and refer the matter to the Assembly of States Parties or, where the Security Council referred the matter to the Court, to the Security Council'. However, the ICC could arguably have gone further and articulated the consequences of a Court's finding of non-co-operation by a State. The Statute could have specified that the Assembly of States Parties might agree upon countermeasures, or authorize contracting States to adopt such countermeasures, or, in the event of disagreement, that each contracting State might take such countermeasures. In addition, it would have been appropriate to provide for the possibility of the Security Council's stepping in and adopting sanctions even in cases where the matter had not been previously referred by this body to the Court: one fails to see why the Security Council should not act upon Chapter VII if a State refuses to co-operate and such refusal amounts to a threat to the peace, even in cases previously referred to the Court by a State or initiated by the Prosecutor *proprio motu*. Of course, the ICC Statute does not *exclude* this possibility, but it also would have been a good idea expressly to include it.

19.9 THE QUESTION OF SURRENDER OF NATIONALS

The constitution or the laws of many civil law countries lay down the principle that nationals may not be extradited for prosecution abroad. The principle can be found, for example, in the Constitutions of Brazil (1988, revised in 1996; Article 50), the German Federal Republic (1949, Article 16(2), now amended to allow the handing over of Germans to the ICC and other members of the European Union), the Federal Republic of Yugoslavia (1992, Article 17–3), Poland (1997, Article 55–1), Slovenia (1991, revised in 2000, Article 47). The principle finds legislative recognition in France, in Article 3 of the Law of 10 March 1927, as well as in most bilateral treaties concerning mutual judicial assistance.

This rule is clearly the remnant of a bygone era when States intended to protect their nationals as much as possible against any foreign interference. It is a typical expression of the Westphalian international community of sovereign States that distrust one another and lack any common values of universal scope and purport. In today's international community, where respect for human rights counts among the universal values that all States are required to abide by, this rule has become a relic of the past. Provided that the rights of the accused are safeguarded and the trial is fair and expeditious, why should a State have the right to refuse the extradition of one of its nationals to another State on the territory of which the individual has committed a crime? The outdated nature of this legal tradition has come to light in the course of the work of the international criminal tribunals. Often, when the Prosecutor in The Hague requests a State to hand over a national accused of international crimes, the State takes refuge behind a constitutional provision forbidding extradition. This refusal is all the more absurd, in such cases, because it leads to the effective impunity of the persons in question, by protecting them against criminal prosecution for very serious crimes which transgress universal values.

The reaction of international tribunals has been twofold. First of all, such tribunals have held that, by virtue of a well-established principle of international law, States may not invoke their national legislation, even of constitutional rank, to evade an international obligation.[11] This objection is, of course, traditional. The other is, however, innovative. It posits that, at the very most, the constitutional rules in question only apply to relations between sovereign States, and not to relations between a State and an international court. The former relations are based on the principle of formal equality, whereas the latter are hierarchical in nature. Thus, while one may speak of *extradition* of the accused from one State to another, it is more appropriate to speak of *transfer* of the accused from a State to an international criminal tribunal.[12] Furthermore, given that the rights of the accused are fully respected before international judicial bodies, the protection of the national State no longer makes any sense. International judges have thus introduced a new legal concept, dissociated from obsolete principles, where the vision of the international community propounded by Immanuel Kant prevails over that extolled by Hobbes.

SELECT BIBLIOGRAPHY

GENERAL

C. Markees, 'The Difference in Concept between Civil and Common Law Countries as to Judicial Assistance and Cooperation in Criminal Matters', in Bassiouni and Nanda (eds), *A Treatise*, II, 171–88; P. B. Heymann, 'Two Models of National Attitudes toward International Cooperation in Law Enforcement', 31 HILJ (1990), 99–107; P. Wilkitzki, 'Development of Rules of International Criminal Procedure and Harmonization through Cooperation in Penal Matters', 17 *Nouvelles Etudes pénales* (1998), 450 ff.; B. Swart, 'International Cooperation and Judicial Assistance—General problems', in Cassese, Gaeta, and Jones, *ICC Commentary*, II, 1589–1605.

ICTY, ICTR, AND ICC

C. Warbrick and D. McGoldrick, 'Cooperation with the International Criminal Tribunal for Yugoslavia', 45 ICLQ (1996), 947–54; D. Sarooshi, 'The Powers of the United Nations Criminal Tribunals', 2 *Max-Planck*

[11] For this argument see, although on different matters, the Order of the ICTY President in *Blaškić* (3 April 1996, §7), the annual report for 1996 of the ICTY President to the General Assembly (A/51/292, 16 August 1996), at §182, as well as *Milošević* (*decision on preliminary motions*) (§47).

[12] The argument is for example set forth in the ICTY President's report to the UN General Assembly on the activities of the Tribunal during 1977 (UN Doc. A/RES/52/375, 18 September 1997, §§186–9; also in *ICTY Yearbook 1997*, at 145).

Yearbook of United Nations Law (1998) 141–67; G. Sluiter, 'Obtaining Evidence for the International Criminal Tribunal for the Former Yugoslavia: An Overview and Assessment of Domestic Implementing Legislation', 45 NYIL (1998), 87–113; B. Swart and G. Sluiter, 'The International Criminal Court and International Criminal Cooperation', in H. A. M. von Hebel, J. C. Lammers, and J. Schukking (eds), *Reflections on the International Criminal Court: Essays in Honour of Adriaan Bos* (The Hague, London, Boston: Kluwer, 1999), 92 ff.; C. Kress and F. Lattanzi (eds), *The Rome Statute and Domestic Legal Orders*, I, *Genezal Aspects and Constitutional Issues* (Baden-Baden: Nomos, 2000); M. Buteau and G. Oosthuizen, 'When the Statute and Rules are Silent: The Inherent Powers of the Tribunal' in R. May and others (eds), *Essays on ICTY Procedure and Evidence in Honour of G. Kirk McDonald* (The Hague, London, Boston: Kluwer, 2001), 65–81; A. Ciampi, 'The Obligation to Cooperate' in Cassese, Gaeta, and Jones, *ICC Commentary*, II, 1607–38; B. Swart, 'Arrest and Surrender', ibid., 1639–1703; A. Ciampi, 'Other Forms of Cooperation', ibid., 1705–47; G. Sluiter, *International Criminal Adjudication and the Collection of Evidence: Obligation of States* (Antwerp, Oxford, New York: Intersentia, 2002).

SECTION II

INTERNATIONAL CRIMINAL TRIALS

20

THE ADOPTION OF THE FUNDAMENTAL FEATURES OF THE ADVERSARIAL SYSTEM AT THE INTERNATIONAL LEVEL

20.1 THE ADVERSARIAL VERSUS THE INQUISITORIAL SYSTEM: GENERAL

It is well known that most national legal systems based on civil law tend to apply the inquisitorial system, while in common law countries the adversarial model is preferred.[1] It should be pointed out at the outset that these two models do not make up a rigid dichotomy: they do not constitute watertight categories. In fact neither model can ever be found in its 'pure' form anywhere, because in practice historical circumstances, local traditions, and the influence of the other model have led to an adaptation of each system, to take account of requirements specific to each country. Thus, the models at issue must be taken to be some sort of 'abstract intellectual constructs'

[1] It is common knowledge that there are differences in terminology, some authors speaking of 'adversarial' others of 'accusatorial' systems for common law countries. See the views of such distinguished authors as M. R. Damaška (*The Faces of Justice and State Authority—A Comparative Approach to the Legal Process* (New Haven and London: Yale University Press, 1986), at 3–6, 69, 88, 97–8) and W. R. LaFave, J. H. Israel, and N. King (*Criminal Procedure*, 3rd edn (St Paul, Minn.: Hornbook, 2000), at 30–3). According to the latter commentators: 'The key to an adversary system is the division of responsibilities between the decision-maker and the parties. An adversary system of adjudication vests decision-making authority, both as to law and fact, in a neutral decision-maker who is to render a decision in light of the materials presented by the adversary parties . . . The adversary model gives to the parties the responsibility of investigating the facts, interviewing possible witnesses, consulting possible experts, and determining what will or will not be told . . . The judge and jury are then to adjudicate impartially the issues presented by the opposing presentations' (at 31); 'The American criminal justice process is designed to be accusatorial as well as adversarial. The concepts of adversarial adjudication and accusatorial procedure complement each other, but are not virtual equivalents. The adversarial element assigns to the participants the responsibility for developing the legal and factual issues of the case, while the accusatorial element allocates burdens as between the parties with respect to the adjudication of guilt. An accusatorial procedure requires the government to bear the burden of establishing the guilt of the accused, as opposed to requiring the accused to bear the burden of establishing his innocence' (at 33).

similar to the 'ideal types' propounded by Max Weber (who used this notion for such categories as feudalism, ascetism, mysticism, etc.).[2]

According to anthropologists, the *adversarial system* was the first substitute for private vengeance. Social groups agreed that the wronged person must no longer use force to do justice by himself. He (as well as, later on, his relatives or members of his clan or group) could instead accuse the alleged culprit. An arbiter, referee, or judge was selected to hear the evidence. Each party (the accuser and the accused) autonomously searched for and collected all the available evidence, respectively to support the charges, and to rebut them to prove the innocence of the accused. The judge simply acted as a referee in the contest between the parties. The proceedings were public and oral. One reason for this was that most participants were illiterate. The trial normally took place before the popular assembly or at any rate in a public place. Thus, under this system the initiation of criminal action was left to the aggrieved party; no public official had the right to institute proceedings. This system can be found in the Greek polis as well as in Rome, in the Republican period. Later on some typical features of the inquisitorial model were incorporated: notably, public officials (the prosecutor) replaced the private accuser. In addition, the new notion of popular justice led to the establishment of juries. At present, the model can be found, in various forms, in many countries including England, the USA, Canada, Australia, New Zealand, and some African countries, as well as in Ireland and (since 1988) in Italy.

The *inquisitorial model* emerged in ancient Rome, at the time of the Empire, and was in full bloom in the Middle Ages, at least from the thirteenth century, when the kings and princes gradually adopted the system used by the Catholic Church as its standard method for investigating and prosecuting offences against clergymen and, later on, persons accused of heresy. Under this model, investigations were conducted in secret by an official, who questioned the suspect or accused, the victim, and any witness, recorded in writing their statements and then decided on the guilt or innocence of the person; thus, the same person investigated the offence and adjudicated it. In at least some respects it was a more advanced step than the adversarial system on the path towards criminal justice. It was based on the notion that justice was not a private business but must be administered by State officials, whose principal task was to collect evidence to establish whether the accused was guilty. Initially inquisitorial proceedings were secret and written, for they were run by cultured officials and based on evidence collected by the investigating judge. At a later stage it was provided that the investigating judge should make his own pronouncement on the charges and later submit the file to a court. At present, after the introduction of many improvements

[2] See for instance M. Weber, 'Religious Rejections of the World and Their Directions' (1915), in H. H. Gerth and C. Wright Mills (eds), *From Max Weber—Essays in Sociology* (London: Routledge & Kegan Paul, 1970), 323 ff. ('Such constructions make it possible to determine the typological locus of a historical phenomenon. They enable us to see if, in particular traits or in their total character, the phenomena approximate one of our constructions: to determine the degree of approximation of the historical phenomenon to the theoretically constructed type. To this extent, the construction is merely a technical aid which facilitates a more lucid arrangement and terminology' (at 324).)

borrowed from the adversarial system, including emphasis on the rights of the accused, the system prevails in such countries as France, Germany, Spain, all Latin American countries, French-speaking African countries, China, Japan, and so on.

20.2 HOW THE TWO MODELS WORK: A COMPARISON

I shall now try succinctly to set out the main traits distinguishing the two models.

20.2.1 INITIATION OF INVESTIGATION, PROSECUTION, AND TRIAL PROCEEDINGS

As stated above, in countries that adopted the adversarial system initially private citizens (normally the victim or his relatives) set in motion trial proceedings. Gradually, however, the centralized organs, or at any rate public officials, that is the police, were entrusted with the task of investigating criminal offences. Trial proceedings may be initiated by the prosecutor, who normally enjoys discretion (for instance, in England and Wales), that is, may choose the cases he considers worthy of being tried in court. Once proceedings are started, the victim or other private citizens do not play any role (except as possible witnesses).

In inquisitorial systems, investigations are set in motion either by the police (normally a special branch of enforcement officials, called '*police judiciaire*' and subordinate to the prosecutor) or by the victim (who reports to the police), or autonomously by the public prosecutor as soon as he becomes cognizant of the possible commission of a criminal offence. In such countries as Germany (previously) and Italy, the prosecutor is duty bound to begin investigations immediately on receipt of a *notitia criminis*, that is, as soon as he is aware of the possible commission of a criminal offence. If after investigating he considers that there are sufficient elements for prosecuting, he is legally bound to prosecute; in other words he does not enjoy any discretion (such discretion does, however, exist in other countries, for instance in France and Belgium). In some countries, for instance in France, proceedings may be started by the victim or even by private organizations (trade unions, associations, etc.) if they claim to have been prejudiced by the alleged criminal offence and undertake the so-called '*constitution de partie civile*', by which they claim compensation from a criminal court.

20.2.2 HOW EVIDENCE IS GATHERED

In the adversarial model each party (prosecution and defence) gathers the evidence autonomously on its own behalf, although often the prosecution is also under the obligation to look for exculpatory evidence. In general, each party must disclose its evidence to the other party before the hearings. More specifically, the prosecutor must hand over the evidence to the defence before the case for the prosecution starts, while, at the end of the case for the prosecution and prior to presenting its case for the accused, the defence may be under an obligation to disclose the evidence it has gathered.

In the inquisitorial system, after the prosecutor has initiated proceedings against a suspect and collected the evidence indicating that he may have committed an offence, an investigating judge (*juge d'instruction*), acting in the interest of the whole community as an 'organ of justice', gathers the evidence for both the prosecution and the defence. He may then either dismiss the charge and close the case or, if he considers that there are reasons for believing that a prima facie case has been made out and the case is 'ripe' for trial, he may turn over to the court and the parties the case file (*dossier de la cause*) containing the results of pre-trial investigations and the evidence collected.

The scheme hinging on the investigating judge was introduced by Napoleon in France in the code of criminal procedure adopted in 1808. As many authors have noted, the principal drawback of this scheme is that the investigating judge tends to use his extensive powers (including that of seizing evidence, ordering searches, or the arrest of suspects), and this may lead to abuses. Indeed, that judge may be inclined to put pressure on a suspect by deciding to detain him in police custody for the purpose of questioning. The investigating judge was therefore abolished in some civil law countries such as Germany (in 1974) and Italy, while a major reform of the procedural system was undertaken in 1988.

20.2.3 COMPOSITION OF THE COURT

In the adversarial model hearings are normally presided over by a judge, with the guilty or not guilty verdict being decided by a *jury* consisting of people elected, or chosen, or at least selected from the general public. The notion of popular justice, going back to ancient Greece, was revamped in England in the late Middle Ages, when people living in the place where the alleged offence had been committed would be asked to answer under oath whether the person was guilty or innocent (the underlying idea being that the neighbours, knowing the accused, would be in a better position to appraise his guilt or innocence). Gradually there began a process of selecting those people so as to make up a jury proper. The jury later came to be predicated on the notion that judgment should not be arbitrarily passed by the king or by the special courts set up by him, but by the accused person's 'peers' or equals. Article 39 of Magna Carta (1215) proclaimed a set of fundamental rights for 'freemen' (that is, for members of the aristocracy and the middle classes and for them only, as opposed to the monarch and members of the lower classes) including the right of every 'freeman' to stand trial for criminal offences 'by the lawful judgment of his *peers* and by the law of the land'.[3] The thinkers of the Age of Reason and the French Revolution, admiring the jury system existing in England, imported it into France and bolstered the notion by appealing to 'people's justice'. However, the appalling abuses of the

[3] 'Nullus *liber homo* capiatur vel impresonetur aut dissaisiatur aut utlegatur aut exuletur aut aloquo modo destruator nec super eum ibimus nec super eum mittemus *nisi per legal judicium parium suorum* vel per legem terrae' (emphasis added). In the English translation: 'No freeman shall be arrested, or detained in prison, or deprived of his freehold, or outlawed, or banished, or in any way molested; and we will not set forth against him nor send against him, unless by the lawful judgment of his peers and by the law of the land'.

French revolutionary courts led to the abandonment of this system on continental Europe (except for such countries as Belgium) and its replacement by the system of '*cour d'assises*' (see below).

In contrast, in the inquisitorial model, no *jury proper* exists. Normally the court is composed of professional judges (one, or three, or five, depending on the degree of jurisdiction). For some particularly serious offences, Assize Courts may be competent and they are made up of both lay judges and professional judges. For instance, in France, under Article 231 ff. of the Code of Criminal Procedure, Assize Courts (*Cour d'assises*) have jurisdiction over '*crimes*' or serious criminal offences (as opposed to *délits* or misdemeanours); they are composed of three professional judges (including the presiding judge) and a 'jury' of nine persons, chosen by lot. They pronounce upon both the facts and the law, on guilt or innocence and, in case of conviction, on the sentence; any decision against the accused must be taken by a minimum of eight votes to four. In many civil law systems, decisions taken by such courts are reasoned (they are drafted by the presiding judge or any of the professional judges serving on the court along with the lay judges). A similar system applies, for instance, in Italy, where Assize Courts have jurisdiction over serious crimes, as provided for in Article 5 of the Code of Criminal Procedure. They are made up of two professional judges (one of them as a presiding judge) and a jury composed of six persons (Article 3(1) of the law no. 287 of 10 April 1951).

20.2.4 TRIAL PROCEEDINGS

In the adversarial system when hearings commence, no file is submitted to the court. The *oral nature* of proceedings, in general, prevails.[4] The documents collected by the parties are tendered to the court after commencement of trial and only admitted into evidence after being introduced by a relevant witness. The same applies to testimonial evidence; the statements, if any, made prior to trial proceedings by a witness usually have no probative value unless they are scrutinized in oral testimony given in open court, and admitted into evidence.

Under the inquisitorial model the trial phase is based on the principle that *written proceedings* prevail; the evidence collected by the investigating judge is submitted in court for scrutiny by both parties and the judges. Any piece of information, document, or exhibit that is in the case file constitutes 'evidence' before being submitted to the court in oral proceedings. In practice witnesses testifying in court are very often asked simply whether they confirm the testimony they gave to the investigating judge.

20.2.5 GUILTY PLEA

In the adversarial system at the beginning of trial proceedings the court asks the defendant whether he pleads guilty or not guilty. If the defendant pleads guilty, there

[4] In England and in the USA there are provisions, quite commonly used, for introducing written statements into evidence without the witness being called. See section 9 of the British Criminal Justice Act 1967.

are no further trial proceedings and sentencing proceedings ensue, designed to establish the appropriate sentence. The 'guilty plea' procedure is sometimes the result of 'plea-bargaining' between the prosecution and defence counsel (or the accused).[5] The main merit of such procedure is to arrive at a sentence acceptable to both parties, and, what is even more important, to avoid trial proceedings proper. In this way in most common law countries up to 10–20 per cent of criminal cases are resolved through plea-bargaining, thus significantly reducing the workload of courts.[6] In England only some 1 or 2 per cent of all cases are finally disposed of by jury trial, the routine method being summary trial in the magistrates' courts (which normally simply record the guilty plea entered by the accused and the sentence inflicted).[7] In consequence, in common law countries proceedings are divided into two stages: *finding of guilt* (and, as already emphasized, this is a matter on which the jury decides); and *sentencing*, in case of a guilty plea or guilty verdict handed down by the jury (the sentence is passed by the judge).

This system does not exist in civil law countries, where trials are initiated even when the accused admits to being guilty. However, in these cases trials are relatively short. In addition, in inquisitorial systems the screening of cases, and the consequent reduction in the number of cases brought to trial, is carried out by the investigating judge: it is for the judge to select the cases where the charges are such as to make a prima facie case against the accused, and those which instead must be shelved, for the evidence is flimsy or inconsistent.

Whereas in common law systems trial proceedings are divided into two stages (the jury is the trier of fact while the judge decides on the sentence), in civil law systems trial proceedings are unified, as it were: the proceedings for pronouncing on the guilt or innocence of the defendant are, should he be convicted, combined with those on sentencing.

[5] It would seem that in the UK the majority of guilty pleas are not the result of plea-bargaining. Rather, what usually happens is that the accused realizes that the evidence against him is overwhelming and there is no point fighting it. Or he just wants to get the whole thing over with. There is usually 'credit' for a guilty plea, i.e. it is taken into account in mitigation, but that is not the same thing as plea-bargaining. Plea-bargaining most commonly occurs, in the USA, with drug offences. An accused is found with a drug. He can plead guilty to possession and the prosecution will drop the charge of possession with intent to supply (which is much more serious). But if the accused does not plead guilty to possession, the prosecution will go ahead with charges of both possession and possession with intent to supply. That is the 'bargain'—dropping one (serious) charge *in exchange for* a guilty plea on the other (less serious) charge.

[6] See, for the United Kingdom, the details provided by A. Ashworth, *The Criminal Process—An Evaluative Study*, 2nd edn (Oxford: Oxford University Press, 1998), 268–84.

Of course summary trial in the magistrates' courts is still a trial, though, and only occurs where there has been a 'not guilty' plea. Most cases are dealt with in the magistrates' courts, but there may be a trial or a guilty plea. The accused do not have a right to jury trial for minor (summary) offences and so there are many trials before either a lay bench (three laymen) or a professional magistrate (formerly known as a stipendiary judge, now known as a District Judge), while jury trial is reserved for the more serious offences (hence there are fewer of them).

[7] See J. R. Spencer, 'Introduction', in M. Delmas-Marty and J. R. Spencer (eds), *European Criminal Procedures* (Cambridge: Cambridge University Press, 2002), at 18.

20.2.6 THE POSITION OF THE ACCUSED

Traditionally in the adversarial model *trials in absentia* are prohibited. It is permitted for the defendant not to be in court only when by his behaviour he disrupts the hearings or if he escapes after the beginning of trial. The logic behind this principled position is clear: as trial proceedings consist of a contest between two parties (the prosecutor and the defendant), if one of them is missing no trial proper may start. In addition, as it falls to each party to gather the evidence, respectively supporting the charges and exculpating the accused, if the latter is absent, no one can play that crucial role in his stead.

The defendant may be held in custody (on remand) or *free on bail* (there is a 'right to bail', that is, a presumption or expectation of bail, but bail is easily refused for a repeat offender who has a history of failing to surrender to custody). That a defendant is free is substantially justified by the fact that in this position he is in a better position to prepare his defence and also on basic grounds of presumption of innocence and the right to liberty. However, if at the end of trial the accused is found guilty and sentenced to imprisonment, and an appeal is lodged, the convicted person often remains in jail pending the appellate proceedings (the right to bail is forfeited upon conviction).

While in court, the accused may only be heard (and examined and cross-examined) if he decides to appear as a witness on his own behalf, but then he is required to take an oath or make a solemn declaration that he will tell the truth. He enjoys the fundamental right to silence (in other words the right not to incriminate himself). In addition, no negative inference may be drawn by the court from his choosing to remain silent and not give evidence: since he is entitled to a presumption of innocence, there is no requirement that the accused contribute to the discovery of the truth, this task exclusively falling to the prosecution.[8]

In contrast, in many civil law systems, *trials in absentia are admissible*, that is the defendant may be tried even if he has never appeared in court and is on the run or in hiding. (This holds true for such countries as France, Belgium, Greece, the Netherlands, most Latin American countries, and China; among the exceptions are Spain and Germany.) The reason why this class of trials is not quintessentially regarded as inadmissible (as is the case in common law countries) is that the investigating judge gathers evidence not only for the prosecution but also for the defence. Hence, when trial proceedings begin, the court has exculpatory evidence available, and is therefore in a position to evaluate both the evidence against and that in favour of the accused.

[8] However, in 1964 a law passed in the UK, the Criminal Justice and Public Order Act, authorized trial courts to draw adverse inferences against defendants who, in some well-defined conditions, fail to give evidence. Equally the 5th Amendment to the US Constitution does not prevent adverse inferences being drawn from an accused's silence or failure to testify.

Furthermore, in *John Murray* v. *UK* the European Court of Human Rights held that the drawing of inferences from the refusal of an indictee, when arrested, to give an account of his presence in a certain place could not be regarded as 'unfair or unreasonable in the circumstances' (§54).

In addition, in most civil law systems it is considered that the public interest of the community in adjudicating alleged criminal offences should prevail over the right of the accused to be present in court, at least whenever the accused voluntarily tries to evade justice. (Nonetheless, we will see *infra* 21.5 that in most civil law countries trials *in absentia* are only admissible if a set of safeguards are respected, as repeatedly stated by the European Court of Human Rights.)

In inquisitorial systems the defendant is put *in jail*, either when the gravity of the crime automatically entails pre-trial imprisonment, or when pre-trial incarceration proves necessary because of the danger that the accused may interfere with the evidence, or may try to escape or engage again in criminal conduct. However, even in inquisitiorial systems the principle applies that pre-trial detention must not be the general rule. Therefore release (often on bail) is provided for. In any case, if at the end of trial the accused is convicted and enters an appeal (or an appeal is lodged by the Prosecutor), he may be released on bail, unless he must be kept in custody by law, but then only within certain time-limits.

When the defendant appears in court, he may be questioned, without taking an oath, by the presiding judge (or by any other member of the court, often with the explicit or tacit consent of the presiding judge), or by the parties, on any issue relevant to the trial.

20.2.7 THE POSITION OF VICTIMS

In the adversarial system victims may bring a private prosecution, but if the prosecutor decides to take up the case and commence investigations and subsequently bring proceedings, they no longer play a role. Victims only appear in court as witnesses. If they want to claim compensation, they must institute civil proceedings separately, after the criminal trial.

In contrast, as pointed out above, in the inquisitorial system victims may institute proceedings or take part in the criminal proceedings initiated by the prosecution, through the so-called *constitution de partie civile* (application to join criminal proceedings as a civil petitioner) aimed at claiming compensation. They may call evidence, question witnesses, and set out their legal views as to the guilt of the accused. Thus, in contrast with the adversarial system, criminal and civil proceedings are not separate but may be merged.

20.2.8 THE ROLE OF THE COURT

Under the adversarial scheme the judge, faced with a jury entitled to establish whether the accused is guilty or innocent, tends to play a rather passive role, as a sort of umpire or referee between two contending parties. When trial proceedings begin, the judge does not know the results of the investigations conducted by the prosecution: he only knows the charges preferred against the defendant, the facts as concisely set out in the indictment and the law the prosecution intend to invoke, as indicated in the indictment. The judge becomes cognizant of the facts of the case only through presentation of evidence in court (the same applies to the jury, which before the beginning of trial is totally unaware of the evidentiary material available to the prosecution and only comes to know it through its production in court). The principal role of the judge is to conduct the hearings, uphold or reject objections by a party to submissions of the other party, grant or dismiss motions by the parties. As stated by A. Orie, 'It is logical in a common-law system, where the jury is entirely dependent on the evidence presented to it at trial, that the trial judge be called by the parties to intervene whenever necessary in order to prevent the information on which the jury will base its verdict being polluted by improper elements.'[9] At the end of the proceedings and before the jury retires for deliberation, the judge then sums up the relevant facts (in the UK, but not in the USA), and (in trials in many countries including England and Wales) the applicable law as well as possible defences. The jury will then decide on the guilt or innocence of the accused.

Generally speaking, the court is not required actively to seek the truth but simply to decide whether the evidence produced in court by the prosecution is sufficient to substantiate its charges and prove beyond a reasonable doubt that the defendant is guilty.

In the inquisitorial model the court plays instead an active role in seeking the truth. When trial proceedings begin, the court is already cognizant of the facts of the case and the law invoked by the parties: the court acquires this knowledge by reading the case file (*dossier de la cause*) which contains the evidence collected by the investigating judge both for the prosecution and for the accused. In particular the presiding judge is a dominating figure in the conduct of proceedings. He may question both the witnesses and the accused (and the parties may question the witnesses). In particular, the presiding judge questions the accused from the outset and tends to ask him questions on many occasions, each time an important witness gives evidence in court. Thus a continuing dialogue between the presiding judge and the defendant unfolds during the trial. The role of witnesses is less important than in common law countries: as pointed out above, often they are simply asked to confirm or deny in court the statements made to the investigating judge. In addition, the court may call evidence *proprio motu*.

The different philosophy behind the two systems can perhaps be summed up as follows: in the inquisitorial system the court aims at actively discovering the truth; the defendant contributes to this discovery by answering questions in court; in an adversarial system, instead, the defendant, through his defence counsel, plays in some respects a greater role in contributing, as much as the prosecution, to the establishment of the truth, for the whole trial hinges on a contest between the parties.

[9] A. Orie, 'Adversarial v. Inquisitorial Approach in International Criminal Proceedings Prior to the Establishment of the ICC and in the Proceedings before the ICC', in Cassese, Gaeta, and Jones, *ICC Commentary*, at 1427.

20.2.9 RULES ON ADMISSION AND EVALUATION OF EVIDENCE

In the adversarial system there exist strict and detailed rules of evidence. In particular, hearsay evidence is inadmissible (subject to a string of exceptions that in some common law countries run to 40). The rationale behind the setting out of such rules is that the evaluation of the evidence produced in court falls to the jury, that is a group of laymen who normally are not familiar with legal technicalities and therefore do not know what weight to give to each piece of evidence. There also are strict rules for the order in which evidence is presented in court. Normally the prosecution starts, making its case, and of course the defence may cross-examine prosecution witnesses; once the prosecution case is closed, the defence may take over; at the end the prosecution may sometimes present evidence in rebuttal, if any, and then the defence may present evidence in rejoinder, if any. Closing statements by the prosecution and then the defence bring the trial proceedings to an end.

The test for establishing guilt is that the accused must be found guilty of the offences charged 'beyond a reasonable doubt'.

In the inquisitorial system, rules of evidence are normally flexible and general, for it is professional judges who apply them (even in assize courts, the presence of two or three such judges makes it possible to dispense with strict and extremely detailed rules of evidence). Ultimately, what matters is that the court forms its 'intimate conviction' as to the guilt or innocence of the defendant.

Also the order of presentation of evidence is different from that in common law countries. In the inquisitorial system no distinction is made between the prosecution and the defence case with regard to the order in which the evidence is presented in court: in any case the evidence is that contained in the case file submitted by the investigating judge.

A. Orie has aptly summed up the difference between the two models as follows:

> In the common law model, the law of evidence mainly functions as a mechanism at trial, keeping the parties on the right path in their presentation of evidence and preventing the jury from getting acquainted with anything that might be improper to consider in reaching a verdict. In civil-law systems the law of evidence mainly serves as a normative instrument for the judge while evaluating the content of the dossier and what has been adduced at trial.[10]

20.2.10 APPELLATE PROCEEDINGS

In the adversarial system, resort to appeal proceedings is quite restricted. These proceedings do not entail a retrial. The appellate court consists of professional judges, without any jury. Normally appellate judges pronounce on issues of law (for instance, wrong instructions given by the trial judge to the jury). Facts may not be again the subject of proceedings, unless the appellant claims that facts have been so grossly

10 Op. cit., at 1428.

misrepresented by the judge in his instructions to the jury as to result in a miscarriage of justice.

As we shall see (22.12), the range of appellate proceedings is restricted in many ways. The rationale behind this approach is twofold. First, there is a fundamentally ideological reason. As explained by J. Spencer, 'In England, the jury was introduced as a substitute for the judgment of God pronounced through the ordeal, and like the judgment of God it was not open to challenge on the ground that it had given an answer that was wrong'.[11] It was thought that it would be improper and illogical to ask an 'appellate' jury to pass judgment again on guilt or innocence (unless, on account of gross errors of law the Court of Appeal remits a case to the trial court for a new trial). In other words, the verdict of the jury at the trial level is final, unless it is invalidated by serious mistakes made by the judge in his instructions to the jury. Hence, there is no jury in the appeal court. The second reason is economic: reducing the number of cases that are appealed alleviates the burden of appeal courts.

In the inquisitorial system appellate proceedings may instead entail a sort of *retrial*, in that the same evidence may be scrutinized a second time and legal arguments reheard. In short, appellate proceedings consist of a full rehearing of the case. Furthermore, it is fairly easy for both the prosecution and the defence to appeal against conviction or sentence, and the prosecution may also appeal against acquittal. According to a leading authority, M. R. Damaška, the reason behind this civil law approach is twofold.[12] First, prosecution is conceived of as an ongoing process, while in common law countries there is a tendency to see it as a one-off event. Secondly, members of the judiciary (often both prosecutors and judges) are professionals working in a hierarchical system; it is therefore taken for granted that higher courts should normally re-do what has allegedly been done badly by inferior courts.

20.2.11 THE MAIN FEATURES OF EACH MODEL

The gist of the adversarial model is that it is based on two primary considerations: (i) to leave the establishment of judicial truth to a contest between *the parties*, to be essentially settled by a group of laymen representing the defendant's 'peers'; and (ii) to protect the rights of the accused as much as possible by laying down a set of strict procedural safeguards that act as the ultimate bulwark against a judiciary prone to abuses, or a potentially tyrannical executive. The essence of the inquisitorial model lies, on the other hand, in the strong emphasis on *public interest* in prosecuting and punishing all those who offend against societal values enshrined in criminal rules. Consequently public institutions such as the prosecutors and investigating judges play a significant role in administering justice, whilst lesser emphasis is placed on the role and the rights of the accused.

[11] Spencer, op. cit., at 28. See also p. 7.

[12] M. R. Damaška, *The Faces of Justice and State Authority—A Comparative Approach to the Legal Process*, cit., 48–50; Idem, 'Models of Criminal Procedure', 51 *Zbornik, Collected Papers of Zagreb Law School* (2001), 495–6.

Finally, it should be reiterated that those characteristics of the two models, referred to above, are only intended to point to trends, for often individual countries incorporate elements of the system prevailing in other legal systems, so that one never finds in one country a 'pure' system, but most of the time adversarial systems with some inquisitorial features or inquisitorial systems with some adversarial traits. Moreover, the two systems seem to be converging in many ways.

20.3 THE TRANSPOSITION OF THE ADVERSARIAL MODEL ON TO THE INTERNATIONAL LEGAL LEVEL

In international proceedings the adversarial system has basically prevailed, but without a jury. This system has been predominant since 1945, when the procedure for the IMT was being discussed in London. The US and UK delegates managed to make common law notions prevail, in spite of some resistance from the Soviet delegate. (No major objections were raised by the French representatives, who however expressed misgivings.) Subsequently the same system was easily taken up at Tokyo. (The Tribunal's Charter was drafted by Americans, primarily the Chief Prosecutor J. B. Keenan; it was promulgated as an executive decree of General D. MacArthur; it is said that US allies were only consulted after the Charter had been issued.)

It is useful briefly to trace the birth of the modern procedural model for international trials, to show how in the event the adversarial system has prevailed.

20.3.1 THE CHOICE OF THE ADVERSARIAL MODEL FOR THE NUREMBERG IMT AND THE MINOR QUALIFICATIONS INTRODUCED

When the four Powers (the USA, the UK, the Soviet Union, and France) met in London on 26 June 1945 to try to agree upon the establishment of an international tribunal on war crimes and other serious international offences, there was, in the words of the protagonist of that conference, Justice Robert H. Jackson, 'no treaty, precedent, or custom' determining 'by what method justice should be done'.[13] In addition, to quote Jackson again,

> The four nations whose delegates sat down at London to reconcile their conflicting views represented the maximum divergence in legal concepts and traditions likely to be found among occidental nations.[14]

Fortunately, the US delegates had already discussed at length the various problems and had gone to London with a draft, which they submitted on 14 June 1945 to the other delegations and which soon became the basis for discussion and the major

[13] International Conference on Military Trials, at v.
[14] Ibid.

reference point. This draft, which was a revised text of a draft presented by the USA at the San Francisco Conference on 30 April 1945, was not detailed on matters of procedure, but clearly assumed as the obvious model for the IMT the *adversarial* system, in that it provided for the power of prosecutors to collect the evidence and prefer charges, and for the Tribunal to hear the evidence. No investigating judge was envisaged, nor was there provision made for the court to receive evidence directly from the prosecution (see Articles 16–18).[15] In the meeting of 26 June 1945, Jackson illustrated the US draft and among other things emphasized the significance of the adversarial system proposed, founded on 'a complete separation' of the function of prosecution from 'the function of hearing charges', insisting that it reflected a 'very deep-seated part' of American legal philosophy. He then explained to the other participants how the American system worked. Thereafter the French and the Soviet delegates illustrated their systems, based on the inquisitorial model[16] and insisted that at least a major feature of this model should be upheld, that is, the prosecution should turn over the indictment with the relevant evidence not only to the defence but also to the court,[17] a proposal that the British and American delegates resisted, noting that the court should only 'sit as a referee', as the American delegate put it.[18]

After this first exchange of views, all the parties agreed on two points: first, it was necessary to depart from the procedural system followed in each of the four countries and *find a new system*, enshrining if possible the best features of all national systems; secondly, this international procedural scheme must be so conceived as to enable the conduct of a *speedy trial.*

Nonetheless, it is a fact, later acknowledged by Jackson, that 'a fundamental cleavage, which persisted throughout the negotiations' was caused by the difference between the adversarial and the inquisitorial models.[19]

Before examining the position of the two civil law countries attending the London Conference (France and the Soviet Union), let us ask ourselves whether the acceptance of the inquisitorial model would have been possible.

Were this model to have been adopted, it would have been necessary to appoint an investigating judge to whom the Prosecutors designated by each of the four victor countries would have handed over the evidence they had collected against the accused. This judge would then have gathered further evidence supporting the charges as well as evidence directed to prove the innocence of the defendants. After that, the judge would have passed on the case file to the Bench, for initiation of trial proceedings. This system would have been workable only on condition that that judge was not a national of any of the four countries, to avoid one of them having both a member of the Bench and the investigating judge. Would the four Powers have been prepared to appoint a national of another allied country or even of a

15 Ibid., at 58–9.
16 Ibid., at 77–80.
17 Ibid., at 81.
18 Ibid., at 82.
19 Ibid., at vi.

neutral country (for instance, a Swiss, or a Swede) to that position? This is doubtful, given the enormous powers with which the investigating judge would have to be endowed (powers involving the issuing of orders for searches, seizure, arrest of suspects, etc. to the military forces occupying Germany). The Big Four were eager to keep control of the proceedings from the outset, and would therefore never have granted such sweeping powers to a wholly independent person belonging to another country. (It should be remembered that the four Chief Prosecutors at Nuremberg were not independent, but acted on behalf of their respective States.) Equally, the possible appointment of a panel of investigating judges would have posed many problems, except in the event of their being nationals of the four Big Powers (an option that in any case was never envisaged by any of the four delegations in London).

Thus, the solution, whereby the Prosecutors appointed by each of the four Powers would collect evidence against the accused through the military forces of each of them occupying Germany, appeared to be the best suited to the historical, political, and military circumstances, besides being the one most familiar and acceptable to two of the four Powers.

Nonetheless the French delegation pressed, to some extent, for the inquisitorial model. In order, among other things, to set forth this model and try to outline the reasons behind the French and more generally continental Europe's views, the French delegation submitted a memorandum containing 'observations of the American draft', where they among other things suggested *two possible options* for the phase following the gathering of evidence by the prosecution.

The first option was as follows: the Prosecuting Officers, having prepared a case, would have to submit a bill of accusation as well as all the evidence both to the Tribunal and to defence counsel; after that, 'one of the judges is appointed as *rapporteur* and entrusted with the study of the case and the subsequent presentation of a report before the Court'. Before the opening of the trial defence counsel, having studied the file, would be in a position 'to lodge observations with the Court'; as a consequence, this 'method' would not be 'prejudicial to the impartiality of the Court'. According to the French delegation this proposal had two major advantages. First, 'the Court are acquainted with the case before the trial and the trial is mainly devoted to clearing up certain matters on which discussion appears to be necessary'. Secondly, the solution 'naturally offers the advantage of a speedy procedure'. The French delegation nevertheless acknowledged that against that system the argument could be raised 'that the Court must sit, with absolute impartiality, on the day of the trial'. This proposition seems to indicate that the French probably feared that for the Court to have available at the beginning of trial a 'case file' containing the prosecution's evidence alone, might be regarded as 'contaminating' the Court. More plausibly, the French were also aware of how lopsided their proposal was. Indeed, the Judge *rapporteur* was not an investigating judge, separate and independent of the court, gathering and sifting through evidence both for the prosecution and the defence. According to the French proposal, the Judge *rapporteur* would have examined only the evidence produced by the prosecution, together with any 'observations' lodged by the defence. Hence, his report or file to the court would have not reflected an impartial and dispassionate consideration of the evidence produced by both parties.

The other option suggested by the French was substantially based on the American proposal; in the words of the French memorandum:

> The preparation of the case is concluded by the framing of a bill of accusation, which would be the only document transmitted to the Court, which would receive no other documentary evidence until the day of the trial and would only become acquainted with the case at the time of the trial itself.

According to the French, if this second option were chosen, the Court would 'hear the proceedings dispassionately'.[20]

When the French proposal was discussed, the French delegate insisted that their main preoccupation was 'to insure a speedy punishment, whatever forms we use', whereas they did not insist on the adoption of the French model, which was, he said, merely the object of a recommendation.[21] Justice Jackson praised 'the spirit of the French memorandum'.[22] The Soviet delegate went further; he noted that the American and English system would cause 'unnecessary delay'. Insisting on the need for expeditious trials, he clearly opted for the French model, although he used words that were not unacceptable to the others. (In substance, he pointed out that one did not need 'to create a sort of fiction that the judge is a disinterested person who has no legal knowledge of what has happened before'.)[23] The Soviet insistence on the inquisitorial model, however, aroused deep misgivings in Justice Jackson.[24]

To try to overcome the split between the two groups of delegations, the British representative then proposed, as a compromise, what he termed 'an adaptation' of the French proposal. According to this compromise formula, the court should be fully informed of the prosecution's case; to this end, the prosecutor should transmit both to the defence and to the court, the indictment and all the evidence (or, in the case of the court, at least 'a full summary of the evidence').[25] No mention was made of the need for the court also to receive all the evidence from the defence, once the prosecution case was closed, so as to enable the court to become equally well

[20] International Conference on Military Trials, at 90–1.

[21] Ibid., at 104. [22] Ibid. [23] Ibid., at 105.

[24] While aware of the drawbacks of the American model ('which, as suggested by the Soviet delegates, leads to great delay and sometimes miscarriage by delay', he said), he nonetheless noted that the issues under discussion were 'matters of procedure so deeply ingrained in the thought of the American people that some of the theories of procedure mentioned here could not be supported by us . . . each of us has the problem of making the results here acceptable in the sight of his people, and we shall have to consider procedure in that light' (ibid., at 113).

[25] International Conference on Military Trials, at 113–14.

acquainted with the evidence produced by the defence, before its examination and cross-examination in court.[26]

A protracted discussion ensued,[27] during which the parties seemed often to speak at cross-purposes or at any rate not to be able to understand one another.[28] The bone of contention was twofold: (i) whether the prosecution was to hand over to the Court all the evidence gathered, or only some official documents, and (ii) whether, in the event of the documents being disclosed to the Court, the evidence was nonetheless to be called in court.

It was the British delegate (who, before the British elections of that year, was Sir David Maxwell Fyfe), who broke the deadlock. First he mentioned that in the UK the system was admitted whereby the judge trying a case could know the evidence beforehand.[29] Then, after various interventions of Justice Jackson, he put forward a compromise:

It seems to me there are two points and I think we are agreed, but we ought to make them quite clear. On the one hand, Mr Justice Jackson accepts that in this case the indictment will be accompanied by all possible documents such as treaties, public reports of atrocities,

[26] Clearly, in upholding in this watered-down manner the French proposal, an attempt was being made mechanically to transpose on to the international plane an element of the inquisitorial model, that whereby the court receives, prior to trial, a file with all the evidence; however, in this case, absent an investigating judge, the file submitted to court would only contain evidentiary material for the prosecution.

In any event, the Soviet delegate again insisted on the inquisitorial model and at least on the forwarding of the evidence to the court (International Conference on Military Trials, at 114–17). Under his proposal, in addition to the procedure being lopsided, the court must not hear all the evidence, as is instead required under the adversarial system, but only the evidence *selected* by the court, on which of course the defence could put in its observations, objections, or challenges.

[27] The British delegate asked the US delegation to revise the draft incorporating as much as it could of what had been put forward in the discussion (ibid., 118), but the new revised US draft did not uphold the system proposed (see Article 11, ibid., at 123). Obviously, there broke out another heated if polite argument between the USA and the Soviet delegation (ibid., at 153–5). Thereafter a document was circulated showing the different texts for the whole Statute proposed by the American and Soviet delegations. This revealed clearly, the difference on the issue we are discussing (ibid., 173–6). After that a new draft was circulated, which at first sight seemed to uphold the American position in one provision (Article 16(a): 'A copy of the indictment and of all the documents lodged with the indictment . . . shall be furnished to the defendant at a reasonable time before the trial'), and the Soviet view in another (Article 15(d): 'among the tasks of the Chief Prosecutors was that of the lodgement of the indictment and the accompanying documents with the Tribunal'). Thus, the word 'evidence', previously contained in both the American draft (which excluded the passing of any evidence could be passed on to the Court before trial) and the Soviet draft (which took the contrary position) was dropped, and the neutral and anodyne word 'documents' was used. This was a fairly skilful diplomatic solution for sweeping the thorny problem under the carpet, but its results could not but be ambiguous.

As was to be expected, the discussion was reopened at a later stage, and each party (the Soviet delegation supported by the French and the US delegation) insisted on its position (ibid., at 267).

[28] Ibid., at 267–8, 270.

[29] Ibid., at 270. After the French delegate's intervention, he stated: 'Along the same lines, in our system—I do not know whether this is the same in the United States—we have a preliminary hearing before a magistrate, and at that hearing the prosecution call all their witnesses and put in all their documents. It is obvious that the court, the judge who is going to try the case, knows what the case will be, knows the evidence, and sees the documents, and so do the defendants. But, if the defendant pleads 'not guilty', the whole of that evidence has to be heard again by the court, and you can supplement it by calling further witnesses'.

and the like—that this will be passed to the Tribunal. That is what the Americans are conceding toward the compromise of the system. On the other hand the French delegation agree that at the trial all evidence will be called, but, as suggested, in paragraph 24, the prosecution can put in additional documents if any have come to hand or seem desirable at that time. It seems to me that with these two compromises we have married the two systems.[30]

It would appear that, in substance, the provision was adopted as a sort of sop designed to assuage the misgivings of the French and Soviet delegates. It is difficult to know whether even this minor concession remained a dead letter, or the court was handed, with the indictment, also some official documents. What seems to be sure—from the proceedings of the trial,[31] as well as from accounts of distinguished persons who took part in the Nuremberg proceedings or closely watched them on the spot[32]—is that the evidentiary material was not handed over to the court prior to trial, but was submitted in court during the hearings in the first three months of trial. It was in this manner that the case file (or dossier) was gradually compiled for both the court and the defence.

Plainly, *in the event the adversarial system prevailed.* In retrospect, one should conclude that this was a sensible and wise move, in light of, in particular, the contradictory proposals put forward by the French and Soviet delegations, which on the whole were not such as to meet the requirements of a fair trial, and were not suitable for duly protecting the rights of the accused.

Nevertheless, these two delegations won, as it were, in other areas: (i) the *power of the court to play an active role*, in particular by calling witnesses and questioning witnesses and the accused;[33] (ii) the right of the accused to *make an unsworn statement*

[30] Ibid., at 271. The British then circulated a draft that substantially took up the compromise they had suggested (ibid., at 311 and 354), and then stated that it was only a question of 'perfecting' the drafting (ibid., at 326). The relevant provision upholding the Soviet-French proposal, as narrowed down by the British, became Article 14(d) of the Statute.

It should be noted that the British draft, which eventually became the Statute of the IMT, retained the neutral word 'documents' in both provisions (15(d)) and 16(a)), but added in the second provision, relating to the material that the prosecution must turn over to the defence, the word 'all', so as to emphasize that the material to be submitted to the court was more limited than that to be passed on to the defence with the indictment.

[31] See Trial of the Major War Criminals, II, 18–20 (preliminary hearing of 15 November 1945), and 26–30 (preliminary hearing of 17 November 1945).

[32] See in particular J. Descheemaeker, *Le Tribunal militaire international des grands criminels de guerre* (Paris: Pedone, 1947), 48–9; T. Taylor, *The Anatomy of the Nuremberg Trials—A Personal Memoir* (London: Bloomsbury, 1993), 174–7, 197, 203.

[33] The power of the court to ask questions of the accused and the witnesses was insisted upon by the Soviet delegate, with French support, and, in spite of the misgivings of Justice Jackson (International Conference on Military Trials, at 257, 262–4), found no opposition in the British delegate, who noted that after all the court was 'a complete master of the situation' (ibid., at 263). The matter was settled fairly easily, in light of the generally shared intent to conduct the future trial as expeditiously and effectively as possible, and also on account of the equally shared feeling that it was necessary to avoid any dilatory or obstructive tactics by the defence.

at the end of trial;[34] and (iii) the *rules of evidence*.[35] In addition, on the question (iv) whether the court should have the power to *try the accused in absentia*, one of the two delegations in question had the merit of clarifying, and giving final shape to, the initial tentative American proposal to this effect,[36] so that such power was eventually laid down in the Statute, in Article 12.

In sum, one may share the final assessment given by Justice Jackson of both the thrust of the split that emerged in London between legal philosophies and traditions, and the final felicitous amalgamation of these philosophies and traditions.

34 The two delegations from common law countries accepted that the accused, in addition to giving evidence on their own behalf under oath, be entitled to make a final statement, without taking any oath, although this system is well known to Continental Europe but unknown in the USA and the UK.

35 Also with regard to evidentiary requirements, the USA and the UK easily accepted the idea that rules of evidence should be simplified, the more so because there was no jury and the common law rules of evidence constituted, as Jackson put it, 'a complex and artificial science to the minds of Continental lawyers, whose trials usually are conducted before judges and do not accord the jury the high place it occupies in our system' (ibid., at xi).

36 A provision of the initial US draft tackled the issue without taking any definite position; nevertheless, the US draft did not rule out trials *in absentia*. It was worded as follows: 'The Tribunal shall determine to what extent proceedings against defendants may be taken without their presence' (ibid., at 25). Plainly, this remarkable departure from the US traditional opposition to trial *in absentia* was due to the extreme gravity of the crimes committed and the exceptional circumstances the negotiators were facing. The provision was restated in the subsequent drafts (ibid., at 58, 123 (with a slight change), 179, 183). Subsequently, a draft was proposed by the Soviet delegation, whereby 'The Tribunal shall have the right to take proceedings against persons charged with the crimes, set out in Article 2 of this Agreement, in the absence of the defendant, if the defendant should be hiding or if the Tribunal should for other reasons find it necessary to conduct the hearing in the absence of the defendant' (ibid., at 183).

The British delegation decided to incorporate and improve upon this Soviet draft, and proposed a new text (ibid., at 206 and 353) that, subject to minor drafting changes, eventually became the final Article 12 of the Statute.

At Nuremberg, discussing the defence motion that proceedings should be suspended against the accused Krupp von Bohlen und Halbach (because of his incapacity to stand trial) and whether otherwise he would be tried *in absentia*, the US Prosecutor Jackson noted that, 'Of course, trial *in absentia* has great disadvantages. It would not comply with the constitutional standard for citizens of the United States in prosecutions conducted in our country. It presents grave difficulties to counsel under the circumstances of this case. Yet, in framing the Charter, we had to take into account that all manner of avoidances of trial would be in the interests of the defendants, and therefore, the Charter authorized trial *in absentia* when in the interests of justice, leaving this broad generality as the only guide to the Court's discretion.' (Trial of the Major War Criminals, vol. II, at 5.) He went on to say that 'the Court should not overlook the fact that of all the defendants at this Bar, Krupp is unquestionably in the best position, from the point of view of resources and assistance, to be defended. The sources of evidence are not secret. The great Krupp organization is the source of most of the evidence that we have against him and would be the source of any justification. When all has been said that can be said, trial *in absentia* still remains a difficult and an unsatisfactory method of trial, but the question is whether it is so unsatisfactory that the interests of these nations in arraigning before your Bar the armament and munitions industry through its most eminent and persistent representative should be defeated' (at 6). In setting out the court's decision on the matter, to the effect that proceedings should be postponed for the accused, the Tribunal's President (Lord Justice Lawrence) stated that: 'It is the decision of the Tribunal that upon the facts presented the interests of justice do not require that Gustav Krupp von Bohlen be tried *in absentia*. The Charter of the Tribunal envisages a fair trial, in which the Chief Prosecutors may present the evidence in support of an indictment and the defendants may present such defense as they may believe themselves to have. Where nature rather than flight or contumacy has rendered such a trial impossible, it is not in accordance with justice that the case should proceed in the absence of a defendant' (ibid., at 21).

According to Jackson the difference lay in that under the Soviet practice 'a judicial inquiry is carried on chiefly by the court and not by the parties', whereas under the 'Anglo-American theory of a criminal trial', which 'the Soviet jurist rejects and stigmatises as the "contest theory"', *trial proceedings hinged on the parties.* As Jackson put it, 'The Soviets rely on the diligence of the tribunal rather than on the zeal and self-interest of adversaries to develop the facts'.[37] In addition, in essence the Continental approach was more geared to the *protection of the interests of society*; it consequently tended to emphasize the need for an *expeditious* hearing of the various issues, as well as the necessity to prevent attempts at unreasonable delays and eliminate all questions considered irrelevant by the court. The Anglo-American approach was instead bent on enhancing the *rights of the accused* and more generally on ensuring respect for the fundamentals of 'due process'. Jackson considered, and one can to a large extent share his views, that the final upshot of the debate *substantially amalgamated* the major features of both systems[38] (although, one may note, it eventually proved to be somewhat lopsided, leaning more towards the common law system).

What needs to be stressed again is that in 1945 it would have been impossible or absurd to take up the inquisitorial model and provide for an investigating judge charged with gathering evidence for both the prosecution and defence. Hence, all in all, opting for the adversarial system was a felicitous move.

20.3.2 THE TOKYO INTERNATIONAL TRIBUNAL (IMTFE)

As pointed out above, unlike the Statute of the IMT, the Charter of the IMTFE was not negotiated between the Allies, but drafted by the Americans, chiefly J. B. Keenan, subsequently US Chief Prosecutor at the trial. It was then issued as an executive decree of US General D. MacArthur. In essence, the Charter reproduced the substance of the Statute of the IMT; the procedure was very similar to that which unfolded in Nuremberg.

It would seem that the application of the adversarial system proved unfair to the defence, because all the documents and materials likely to be used in evidence before the court were in the hands of the prosecution, and defence counsel were not allowed to inspect the prosecution's files. The relative unfairness of the procedure was compounded by the authoritarian conduct of business by the President, the Australian Judge Webb, who in addition to sometimes treating some witnesses in a derogatory manner, did not allow his fellow judges to question the witnesses directly.

Some judges expressed misgivings about the conduct of trial. The Indian judge, Pal, in his lengthy Dissenting Opinion, criticized the inconsistency of procedural decisions taken by the majority (at 629–56). The French judge, Bernard, in his Dissenting

[37] International Conference on Military Trials, at vi. [38] Ibid. at x–xi.

Opinion, also assailed the Tribunal's procedure, arguing that the rights of the defendants had not been safeguarded.[39]

It should be added that the Dutch judge Röling also voiced criticisms of the manner in which the trial was conducted, not however in his Dissenting Opinion, but in scholarly writings.[40]

20.3.3 THE ACCEPTANCE OF THE ADVERSARIAL MODEL IN 1993–1994 AND IN 1998

The two ad hoc Tribunals established by the UN Security Council in 1993 (the ICTY) and in 1994 (the ICTR) also embodied the essentials of the adversarial system, probably because of: (i) the intellectual and psychological appeal of the Nuremberg and Tokyo model; and (ii) the prevailing influence, among the draftsmen, of persons with a common law background. In addition, it was perhaps felt that (iii) the adversarial system better safeguarded the rights of the accused.

The Statute of the ICTY laid down the fundamental features of the adversarial system, in that it entrusted the Prosecutor with the conduct of investigations and the submission of indictments. After the possible confirmation of the indictment by a review judge, trial proceedings could commence. The Statute thus discarded the model based on an investigating judge responsible for gathering evidence on behalf of both parties. However, it stopped there, without further setting out the details of the procedural system. It fell to the judges to decide, when drafting the Rules of Procedure and Evidence (RPE), how to fashion the system.

In their first text of the Rules, the judges in essence adopted a system very close to the US Memorandum circulated among judges by the US Department of Justice and containing proposal for draft Rules. Thus, the court was conceived of as a sort of referee, which could become cognizant of the material supporting the indictment or of the evidence produced by the defence only after commencement of trial proceedings, and subject to the production of such evidentiary material in court. Nevertheless, the Court was granted extensive powers in matters of evidence, on the Nuremberg model (Rules 89, on general provisions, and 94, on judicial notice). In addition it was empowered to order either party to produce additional evidence and

39 He stated: 'The Defendants, in spite of the fact that the charges concerned crimes of the most serious nature, proof of which [involved] the greatest difficulties, were directly indicted before the Tribunal and without being given an opportunity to endeavour to obtain and assemble elements for the defense by means of a preliminary inquest conducted equally in favour of the Prosecution as of the Defence by a magistrate independent of them both and in the course of which they would have been [sic] benefited by the assistance of the defence counsel. The actual consequences of this violation of principle have been, in my opinion, particularly serious at the present case' (at 494). The French judge also criticized the fact that, the Tribunal having no power of review of the action taken by the Prosecutors, the prosecution had not been exercised 'in an equal and sufficiently justified manner regarding all justiciable' (sic). In particular, the judge regretted that the Emperor of Japan had not been indicted. In his view, the Emperor's 'absence from the trial, while making one wonder whether, if his case is measured by a different standard, international justice would merit to be exercised, was certainly detrimental to the defense of the Accused' (at 494).

40 See, for instance B. V. A. Röling and A. Cassese, *The Tokyo Trial and Beyond*, cit., at 50–5.

summon witnesses (Rule 98). It also was provided that when appellate proceedings were instituted additional evidence could be submitted by the appellant (Rule 115). These were significant ameliorations of the adversarial system, essentially derived from the inquisitorial model. In short, the Court would be vested with fairly extensive powers, so as to be in control of the proceedings.

However, it became clear fairly soon that, to expedite proceedings which, being grounded on the adversarial model, were rather lengthy, it was necessary to depart from the system whereby the court acts as a referee and has no knowledge of the case before commencement of trial, and even during trial only becomes cognizant of the evidence offered by the parties.

It was in 1997 that a Trial Chamber first took a step in this direction in *Dokmanović* (following a *Scheduling Order* in *Mrkšić and others*). In an Order of 28 November 1998 the Trial Chamber decided that the Prosecutor must deliver to it witnesses' statements taken from witnesses the Prosecutor intended to call for trial and any other material on which it intended to rely at trial; in addition the prosecution must file a pre-trial brief clarifying the allegations in the indictment, setting out the details of the case and identifying the points in issue; it was also ordered to deliver, to both the Trial Chamber and the defence, at least one week prior to commencement of trial, a copy of the proposed opening statement. Similar and parallel obligations were imposed on the defence. As it was breaking new ground, the Trial Chamber took two precautionary measures. First, it promoted, and was given in a status conference summoned by a scheduling order of 20 November 1997, the agreement of the parties to the procedural measures it envisaged. Secondly, it set out the reasons explaining both the rationale behind this departure from a strict view of the adversarial system and the limits of such departure.[41]

This precedent was followed in other cases and then led to the adoption of a string of new Rules of Procedure and Evidence designed to enable the court to know the case file in advance of commencement of trial and thus better to control and conduct proceedings: in particular, Rule 65 *ter*, on the Pre-trial judge, Rule 73 *bis*, on Pre-trial conferences, and 73 *ter*, on Pre-defence conferences.

It would seem that the same approach was taken in the drafting of the ICC Statute. In essence, the draftsmen opted for the adversarial model, but introduced some significant qualifications, thanks primarily to the strong diplomatic efforts of the French delegation. Thus, for instance the role of victims was greatly enhanced (see *infra*, 20.4).

[41] As for the first point, the Trial Chamber stated that it considered that it would benefit from having access to the documentation requested, because such access would have promoted 'better comprehension of the issues and more effective management of the trial'. In addition, the rationale behind the Rule then applicable, that is Rule 15(C) whereby the judge reviewing an indictment was disqualified from sitting on the case, did not prevent the Trial Chamber from examining material supporting the indictment. This was because, as the European Court of Human Rights had held in *Hauschildt*, 'suspicion and a formal finding of guilt are not to be treated as being the same . . . the mere fact that a . . . Judge has also made pre-trial decisions in the case . . . cannot be held as in itself justifying fears as to his impartiality' (at 2). As for the limits within which the court intended to consider the material it was to receive, the Trial Chamber pointed out that it would not regard that material 'as evidence . . . unless and until submitted in the course of the trial' (ibid.).

20.4 THE PRINCIPAL ELEMENTS OF THE INQUISITORIAL MODEL INCORPORATED INTO INTERNATIONAL PROCEDURE

In spite of the basic incorporation of the adversarial system into international proceedings, in the procedure before the ICTY, the ICTR, and the ICC some elements of the inquisitorial system have been added so as to reduce some of the major disadvantages of the other system.

First of all, while in the system of the ICTY and the ICTR the Prosecutor must collect evidence against the accused but is legally obliged to hand over to the defence any exculpatory evidence so found, under Article 54(1)(a) of the ICC Statute he is entrusted with 'establishing the truth'. For this purpose he must investigate both 'incriminating' and 'exonerating' circumstances 'equally'. As has been rightly emphasized,[42] the Prosecutor has thus been conceived of truly as an '*organ of justice*'. It is also notable that in the ICC system the Pre-Trial Chamber plays a major role in scrutinizing and monitoring the action of the Prosecutor, in particular for the purpose of safeguarding both respect for the rights of the suspect or accused and correct conduct of business by the Prosecutor. In many respects this Chamber plays the role that, in some civil law systems which largely borrow from the common law tradition, is entrusted to a judge, who however is not the 'investigating judge' of civil law systems. This is a judge deprived of the power to conduct investigations and to order, among other things, the detention of suspects. He only acts as a judicial guarantee of full respect for law by the prosecuting authorities and for the issuing of any order requested by those authorities, which may entail curtailment of the rights of the suspect or other persons. (One may think for instance of the institution of the '*giudice delle indagini preliminari*' or 'the judge supervising preliminary investigations' in the Italian system.)

Furthermore, in the ICTY and ICTR system (and perhaps also in the future ICC system) before the beginning of trial the prosecution (later on the defence) hands over to the judges a *file* with the essentials about the case (a pre-trial brief addressing the legal and factual issues, admissions by the parties, a statement of matters which are not in dispute, a statement of contested matters of fact and law, and the list of witnesses the prosecution or the defence intends to call, with a summary of the facts on which each witness will testify). Thus, the judges are in possession of a case file (dossier) enabling them to better control the case.

In addition the court may *call evidence* and summon witnesses *proprio motu.*[43]

By and large, *the court is in control of the proceedings*, or at any rate may exercise

[42] See S. Zappalà, *Human Rights in International Criminal Proceedings* (Oxford: Oxford University Press, 2003), at 29–45.

[43] See for instance the ICTY decision in *Stakić* (*Decision summonsing Mr. Baltić proprio motu to appear as a witness*), at 2–3.

powers that are not always granted to courts in most common law systems (sometimes not even in civil law countries).

The two stages of determination of guilt and sentencing have been *merged* (except of course when at the outset the accused enters a guilty plea).

Rules of evidence tend to be very *flexible*; furthermore, affidavits are admissible, albeit to a limited extent (see *infra*, 22.7).

While awaiting trial and during trial the indictee is normally *in detention* (after his arrest, for security reasons or on political grounds the State hosting the Tribunal as well as other States are often reluctant to detain him or to ensure his presence at trial). However, there is an increasing tendency to free the indictee on bail, provided guarantees are given by the relevant State authorities that he will not be allowed to escape. Articles 58 and 60 of the ICC Statute are based on the principle of 'no deprivation of liberty unless necessary on certain grounds'.

In the *appellate proceedings* additional evidence may be heard when this is deemed to be in the interest of justice (see 22.12–14).

In addition, while in proceedings before the ICTY and the ICTR *victims* do not play any autonomous role, as they may only appear in court as witnesses if called by one of the parties (normally the prosecution) or the Court itself, in the Statute of the ICC they have been given several roles: although they are not entitled as of right to address Chambers, if admitted to do so they may submit briefs, attend the hearings and examine or cross-examine witnesses. However, the legal institution typical of civil law countries, namely the '*constitution de partie civile*' (application to join criminal proceedings as a civil petitioner), has not been fully upheld, not even before the ICC.

20.5 TOWARDS A 'MIXED' PROCEDURAL MODEL

In sum, over the years there has been a gradual incorporation of significant features of the inquisitorial model into the procedural system of the ICTY and ICTR, which initially was largely based on the adversarial scheme. The need to speed up proceedings has been the primary rationale for this gradual change. Subsequently, when the Statute of the ICC was being elaborated, the draftsmen took these developments into account. In addition, they inserted into the Court procedural scheme further elements of the inquisitorial model, that is, a larger role for victims, expanded functions for the Prosecutor (who is called upon to act as an organ of justice, and consequently is charged with gathering evidence on behalf of both parties—the prosecution and the defence), and a crucial role for the Pre-Trial Chamber, entrusted with the task of scrutinizing the activity of the Prosecutor.

This significant progress towards a procedural scheme still largely adversarial but enshrining important features of the other model is likely to need further honing with the passage of time and increased experience. Nonetheless it already seems capable of meeting the essential demands of international trials, that is, fairness and expeditiousness.

SELECT BIBLIOGRAPHY

GENERAL: THE ADVERSARIAL VERSUS THE INQUISITORIAL MODEL

V. Manzini, *Trattato di dinitto processuale penale italiano*, 6th edn., I (Turin: UTET, 1967), 31–67; A. Goldstein, 'Reflections on Two Models: Inquisitorial Themes in American Criminal Procedure', 26 *Stanford Law Review* (1974), 1009–19; M. R. Damaška, 'Evidentiary Barriers to Conviction and Two Models of Criminal Procedure: a Comparative Study', 121 *University of Pennsylvania Law Review* (1973/1983), 506–89; M. R. Damaška, *The Faces of Justice and State Authority—A Comparative Approach to the Legal Process* (New Haven and London: Yale University Press, 1986); G. Di Marino, 'L'implantation et les remises en cause des dogmes accusatoire et inquisitoire', 68 *Revue internationale de droit pénal* (1997), 17–30; J. Pradel, 'Inquisitoire-Accusatoire: une redoutable complexité', *ibid.*, 213–29.

THE CHOICE OF THE ACCUSATORIAL MODEL FOR THE NUREMBERG IMT AND THE MINOR QUALIFICATIONS INTRODUCED

International Conference on Military Trials, 1945; D. Irving, *Nuremberg: The Last Battle* (London: Focal Point, 1996), 116–17; E. J. Wallach, 'The Procedural and Evidentiary Rules of the Post-World War II War Crimes Trials: Did they Provide an Outline for International Legal Procedure?', 37 *Columbia Journal of Transnational Law* (1999), 851–83; S. Zappalà, *Human Rights in International Criminal Proceedings* (Oxford: Oxford University Press, 2003) at 1–194.

THE TOKYO INTERNATIONAL TRIBUNAL (IMTFE)

R. H. Minear, *Victors' Justice—The Tokyo War Crimes Trial* (Princeton, NJ: Princeton University Press, 1973), 74–124; B. V. A. Röling, *The Tokyo Trial and Beyond* (ed. A. Cassese) (Cambridge: Polity Press, 1993) 50–5.

THE ACCEPTANCE OF THE ADVERSARIAL MODEL IN 1993–1994 AND IN 1998

G. Champy, 'Inquisitoire—Accusatoire devant les juridictions pénales internationales', 68 *Revue internationale de droit pénal* (1997), 149–93; P. Robinson, 'Ensuring Fair and Expeditious Trials at the International Criminal Tribunal for the Former Yugoslavia', 11 EJIL (2000), 569–89; M. Findlay, 'Synthesis in Trial Procedure? The Experience of International Criminal Tribunals', 50 ICLQ (2001), 26–52; S. Zappalà, *International Criminal Trials and Respect for Human Rights*, cit; A. Orie, 'Accusatorial v. Inquisitorial Approach in International Criminal Proceedings', in Cassese, Gaeta, and Jones, *ICC Commentary*, II, 1439–95; C. Jorda and J. de Hemptinne, 'The Status and Role of the Victim', ibid., 1387–419.

21

THE GENERAL PRINCIPLES GOVERNING INTERNATIONAL CRIMINAL TRIALS

21.1 THE NATURE AND ROLE OF THE PRINCIPLES

By way of introduction it should be emphasized that there do not yet exist international general rules on international criminal proceedings. Each international court (the ICTY, the ICTR, and the ICC) has its own Rules of Procedure and Evidence (RPE). Probably, with the gradual winding down of the judicial activity of the ICTY and ICTR and the contemporaneous consolidation of the ICC, the rules of procedure of this Court may become generally accepted by States and then turn into general international rules. This is, however, a process that is likely to take a number of years.

Nonetheless, one may set out some general principles governing international trials. They may be extracted by way of generalization both from the Statutes of the current Tribunals and the ICC and their Rules of Procedure and Evidence, and the Charters of the two previous ad hoc Tribunals (the IMT and the IMTFE), as well as from judicial practice. In other words they may be drawn from a perusal of the relevant rules governing proceedings before international criminal tribunals, as well as existing case law and the general principles of law on the criminal process. These principles, which also give rise to basic human rights of the defendant (as well as, whenever appropriate, of the victims and the witnesses), are as follows: (i) the presumption of innocence (that is, the right of accused persons to be presumed innocent until proved guilty); (ii) the right of the accused to an independent and impartial court; (iii) the principle of a fair and expeditious trial; (iv) the principle whereby the accused must be present during trial (that is, the prohibition of trial *in absentia*). Such principles also reflect fundamental standards on human rights laid down in such international treaties as the 1950 European Convention on Human Rights, the 1966 UN Covenant on Civil and Political Rights, the 1969 American Convention on Human Rights and the 1981 African Convention on Human and Peoples' Rights, as well as the general principles on criminal law upheld in most countries of the world.

The principles under discussion may play a crucial role. They dictate the manner in which criminal proceedings must unfold, and by the same token confer fundamental rights that their beneficiaries may invoke and vindicate before the court, if need be by appealing decisions infringing such rights. The principles may also serve as a useful tool for the proper construction of procedural rules and regulations, whenever the latter are not clear or lend themselves to conflicting interpretations.

21.2 THE PRESUMPTION OF INNOCENCE

All major national legal systems proclaim the principle that an accused is presumed innocent until proved guilty. The provisions of the Statutes of the ICTY (Article 21(3), the ICTR (Article 20(3)), and the ICC (Article 66) also clearly set out the principle.

It is generally agreed that the presumption of innocence specifically entails that: (i) the person charged with a crime must be treated, within and outside criminal proceedings, as being innocent until proved guilty; (ii) the burden of proof, that the accused is guilty of the crimes with which he is charged, is on the Prosecutor; the defendant may limit himself to rebutting the evidence produced by the Prosecutor, but does not have to prove his innocence; (iii) in order to find the accused guilty of the crimes charged, the court must be convinced of his guilt according to a certain standard of proof, which in civil law countries normally is '*l'intime conviction du juge*' (the judge's innermost conviction) whereas in common law countries it is 'finding the accused guilty beyond a reasonable doubt'.

As for the *treatment of the accused* as presumed innocent, three major issues arise. First, as rightly stressed by commentators, there is the question of when a person should enjoy the presumption of innocence: from the moment he is formally charged with crimes, thereby becoming accused, or from the moment he becomes a suspect and may therefore be investigated and questioned before being formally charged? The text of the relevant provisions supports the former construction, for such provisions tend to link the presumption under discussion to the status of 'accused'. However, as has been sensibly noted,[1] the presumption must also apply during pre-trial investigations and should be considered even stronger with regard to a person against whom 'not even a prima facie case has been confirmed'.[2] It follows among other things that 'the investigating authorities must also investigate in favour of the suspect in order to exclude any reasonable doubt from their suspicion'.[3]

Another issue that constitutes a sore point in international criminal proceedings is the media coverage of the detention and trial of the accused. Faced with such horrendous offences as war crimes, crimes against humanity, and genocide, the media tend to take it for granted that persons accused of such crimes by a prosecutor are guilty, and even to portray them as 'monsters' or 'butchers'. At the national level, State

1 See C. J. M. Safferling *Towards an International Criminal Procedure* (Oxford: Oxford University Press, 2001), at 67–75, Zappalà op. cit., 84–5.

2 Zappalà, at 84.

3 Safferling, at 73.

authorities, especially in common law countries (where the media are often prohibited from publishing any evidence or specific information against the accused in advance of trial, and the media or photographers are frequently denied access to the courtroom during trial proceedings), courts may resort to safeguards against such intrusions. In any case the accused is offered the right to sue the media for libel. In contrast, no such remedy is available in international proceedings. Ultimately, the question is one of self-restraint on the part of the prosecutor and the media. However some sort of remedy should be devised against the excessive 'presence' of the media and their trampling underfoot of the presumption of innocence.

Thirdly, it is interesting to stress the main consequences of the applicability of the presumption of innocence to trial proceedings. If the accused refuses to enter a plea of guilty or not guilty, the Trial Chamber must enter a not guilty plea, precisely because of that presumption. Furthermore, the accused has the right not to incriminate himself and, more generally, to remain silent (the same right applies to suspects). As has been noted, the provisions covering this matter 'substantially aim at protecting the right of the accused [or the suspect] to refuse to answer questions, because he or she is presumed innocent and, hence, has no duty to contribute to the proceeding'.[4] It would seem that another consequence is that the accused has no obligation to give evidence in court, and in addition, no adverse consequence may be drawn from his decision not to testify on his own behalf.

With regard to the *burden of proof*, it is clear that it is for the Prosecutor to prove that the accused is guilty. If the Prosecuter does not produce convincing evidence to this effect, the charges are dismissed.[5] The charges may be thrown out even before the end of the trial, namely at the end of the prosecution case, either at the request of the defence or by the court acting *proprio motu* (indeed in *Jelisić* an ICTY Trial Chamber, based on Rule 98 *bis*, at the end of the Prosecutor's case acquitted the accused of some of the charges, namely those concerning genocide (see §§16–17), although this decision was much criticized on appeal).[6] Furthermore, as provided in Article 67(1)(i) of the ICC Statute, no reversal of the burden of proof is admissible. This provision, it is submitted, enshrines or codifies a general principle. It follows that, for instance, the reversal of the burden of proof provided for in Rule 92 of the ICTY Rules of Procedure and Evidence ('a confession by the accused given during questioning by the Prosecutor shall . . . be presumed to have been free and voluntary unless the contrary is proved') is perhaps of doubtful legality.[7]

One of the consequences of the principle under discussion is that the defendant has the right to a finding of guilt or innocence on *all* the charges preferred against him by

[4] Zappalà, at 90.

[5] In *Wolfgang Zeuss and others* (the *Natzweiler* trial) in his summing up the Judge Advocate insisted on the point that 'the onus of proving the charge which is made against these accused rests upon the Prosecution, and they have to satisfy you beyond reasonable doubt of the guilt of any of the accused before such accused can be convicted' (at 199).

[6] See *Jelisić* (*Appeal*), §§30–77.

[7] Zappalà, at 94.

the prosecution, unless they are cumulative. In particular, the defendant is entitled to have the charges against him considered by the Court if they are framed as *alternative* charges. Clearly, were the court to leave in abeyance the question of whether or not one of the charges was well founded, this would be prejudicial and unfair to the accused. For such a stand would imply that some charges would remain undetermined, thus leaving open the question of whether the defendant was guilty or innocent on those charges. Consequently, that position would run counter to the presumption of innocence. A British Court of Appeal set out these notions in *Paul Hermann* (on multiple charges, some of them preferred as alternative)[8] and in *Felix Schwittkowski* (on alternative charges).[9]

[8] The defendant, a Gestapo official, was accused of having been concerned in the shooting of a large number of Jews in Poland. Sixteen charges were made against him. The first (murder of a Jew) was framed under Control Council Law no. 10 as a crime against humanity; the same killing was charged as murder under the German Criminal Code; the third charge (killing a German woman) was again charged as a crime against humanity and, in charge no. 4, as a murder under German criminal law. The same held true for the other charges, concerning the killing of other Jews, and all presented as alternatives. At the request of the prosecution, and with the consent of the defence, the Court commenced by trying the first two charges. The defendant was found guilty on the first charge, and the Court made no finding on the alternative charge. The Court then proceeded to try the third and fourth charges, convicting the accused on the third charge, again without making any finding on the alternative fourth charge. The prosecution did not wish to proceed with the other charges; although the defence objected, asking that they should be tried, they were left on the file; the defendant was sentenced to death. On appeal the defence counsel stated that he had not been aware that the trial would come to an end after dealing with the four charges only. He wished the other charges to be dealt with. The defence was that the accused 'was the victim of a conspiracy, and this could not be fully brought out in the charges which were dealt with' (at 164). He therefore asked that the case be remitted to the High Court. The prosecutor argued that the first and third charges 'were complete in themselves and could properly be tried separately. Conviction on either of these would justify the sentence imposed, and it was unnecessary for the Prosecution to proceed further' (at 164). He added that, if however the Court felt 'that there is any possibility of there having been any injustice to the Appellant' he would not resist an order for some or all of the charges to be tried. The Court of Appeal held that the trial judge had been right in pronouncing on only two charges: 'After the convictions on the 1st and the 3rd charges it would have been unnecessary and almost inhumane to have gone on with a long string of capital charges; the Defence had no right to demand that the Prosecution should have gone on further' (at 164). In the Court's view, the defence counsel should have made a complete defence in respect of each of the 16 charges. The Court however added: 'On the other hand, the Court is sensible to the difficulties in which the Defence was placed, and we feel that, if there is any likelihood of a miscarriage having occurred, we will do what we can to cure it, whether or not there was any technical mistake on the part of the Defence . . . we feel that it would be more satisfactory if the Defence were allowed to have some of the other charges tried, as has been requested' (at 166). The Court therefore adjourned the appeal *sine die* and remitted the case to the trial judge.

[9] The appellant had stabbed a Norwegian officer in a café in Flensburg. He had been charged with assaulting a member of the Allied Forces in Germany contrary to a Military Government Ordinance, and on an alternative charge with causing dangerous bodily injury, contrary to the German Criminal Code. The trial judge found that the accused did not know that the man he had stabbed was a Norwegian officer, and convicted him on the second charge, adding, 'We do not think that if charges are framed as alternatives there should be conviction under both'; he consequently pointed out that there would be no verdict on the first charge, 'but it will of course remain on the Record' (at 20–2). The Court of Appeal held instead that, 'In a case where there are alternative charges, if a Court finds the necessary facts proved which would justify a conviction on each of the alternative charge (*sic*), we consider that it is a proper course to convict on one charge, but to record no formal finding in respect of the other; should an Appellate Court subsequently find it necessary to quash the conviction on the one charge, it would then be open to that Court, in a case where all the necessary elements constituting the alternative offence have been clearly stated by the Trial Court to have been

Finally, the judgments of international courts must provide the legal reasons for the court's findings. Hence, these courts must set out the grounds on which they have appraised the available evidence in such a manner as to reach the conclusion that the accused is guilty beyond reasonable doubt of the crimes charged. The setting out of the court's reasoning constitutes an important safeguard for the rights of the accused; it enables him to appeal against any conviction he may consider to be based on an erroneous evaluation of the evidence leading to a miscarriage of justice. Indeed, in *Kupreškić and others* (*Appeal*), the ICTY Appeals Chamber found that the appraisal of the evidence by the Trial Chamber had been so fallacious as to generate a miscarriage of justice (§§21–76).

21.3 THE PRINCIPLE THAT JUDGES MUST BE INDEPENDENT AND IMPARTIAL

The principle that a court of law should be independent and impartial is firmly embedded in any legal system and indisputably constitutes a general principle of law. It gives rise to one of the most fundamental human rights. As the ICTY Appeals Chamber held in *Furundžija* (*Appeal*),

> The fundamental human right of an accused to be tried before an independent and impartial tribunal is generally recognized as being an integral component of the requirement that an accused should have a fair trial. (§177.)[10]

The court derived a set of principles from this 'general rule' (§§189–90), adding that the relevant Rule (15(A))[11] fell to be interpreted in accordance with such principles (§191).

One may ensure the independence and impartiality of judges only by: (i) adopting selection mechanisms that make it possible to choose persons who are not only competent, of moral integrity, and unbiased, but also independent of any political or governmental authority; (ii) prohibiting judges from seeking or receiving instructions from outside authorities or being in any way involved in the interests or concerns of the parties; (iii) setting up monitoring procedures that prevent judges from showing or practising bias and, if they are found to be partial or slanted, remove judges from a case or even from the court.

proved, to substitute a conviction on that alternative charge. If, however, as in the present case, the Court finds that a material element constituting the offence has not been proved, we consider that the accused is entitled to a formal finding of not guilty in respect of the charge which has not been proved' (at 22).

[10] The Appeals Chamber also held that the national jurisprudence and the legislation it had surveyed evidenced the existence of a 'general rule', whereby 'a Judge should not only be subjectively free from bias, but also . . . there should be nothing in the surrounding circumstances which objectively gives rise to an appearance of bias' (§189).

[11] It provides that: 'A Judge may not sit on a trial or appeal in any case in which the Judge has a personal interest or concerning which the Judge has or has had any association which might affect his or her impartiality. The Judge shall in any such circumstance withdraw, and the President shall assign another Judge to the case.'

In international proceedings the authorities that might in some way interfere with the judges' impartiality are either the appointing authority or body, or States (in particular the judge's national State). Hence, election by a 'parliamentary' body is the best mechanism for appointing judges. This system is provided for in the Statutes of the ICTY and the ICTR (judges are elected by the UN General Assembly, upon proposal of the UN Security Council, which shortlists candidates nominated by member States). The Statute of the ICC provides for the election, by the Assembly of States parties to the Statute, of candidates nominated by each contracting State. A wise manner of further strengthening the independence of judges is the one envisaged in Article 36(9)(a) of the ICC Statute, whereby judges are not eligible for re-election after the expiry of their mandate.

Once judges have been elected, various means exist for ensuring that they remain independent. First, they are duty bound to refrain from engaging in activity that might jeopardize their independence or affect confidence in their independence (see for instance Article 40(1) of the ICC Statute). Secondly, they enjoy privileges and immunities including immunity from States' jurisdiction; such immunities are among other things designed to shield them from any undue interference by States. Thirdly, the internal regulations of the Tribunals provide for methods and procedures for ensuring judges' independence. These also apply to *specific* cases where a judge may feel that he may not be impartial, or may be seen as involved in, or concerned with, a particular case. These mechanisms are those for the disqualification, recusal, or self-recusal of judges.

A number of rules set out the standards and mechanisms for ensuring the disqualification of a judge from sitting on a particular case. In addition to ICTY Rule 15(A) (see above), a much more elaborate and detailed provision can be found in the ICC Rules (Rule 34).

Normally, if the judge does not disqualify himself, the matter may be brought to the Court or the relevant Chamber, or even to the Tribunal's Bureau (this holds true for the ICTY and the ICTR), where a majority of judges shall pronounce on the matter, in the absence of the judge concerned.[12]

[12] To date the issue of disqualification has been raised in a number of cases: *Delalić and others* (decisions of the Bureau of 4 September 1998 and 1 October 1999), *Kordić and Čerkez* (decision of the Bureau of 4 May 1998), *Brđanin and Talić* (*Decision*) of 18 May 2000, *Furundžija* (*Appeal*). It is notable that so far motions for recusal have never been granted.

In *Delalić and others* (decision of the Bureau of 4 September 1998), the Bureau held that the fact of having been elected second Vice-President of Costa Rica did not disqualify Judge Odio Benito because she had pledged not to assume any function in the Costa Rican Government before the completion of her mandate as a judge, and the commitment had been confirmed by the President of Costa Rica. Subsequently some of the defendants filed with the Appeals Chamber a motion for disqualification of three judges sitting on that Chamber on their appeal against conviction; they claimed that these judges, by participating in the plenary session of the ICTY judges which found that Judge Odio Benito was not disqualified from sitting on the case at the trial level, were disqualified from sitting on the appeal. The Tribunal's Bureau, by a decision of 25 October 1999, dismissed the motion. It found that the three judges had participated in an administrative decision concerning the general question of whether Judge Odio Benito was entitled to continue to exercise

21.4 THE PRINCIPLE OF FAIR AND EXPEDITIOUS TRIAL

That trials must be fair is by now a universally accepted principle of international law. It was laid down in human rights treaties (for instance, the UN Covenant on Civil and Political Rights (Articles 14(1) and 26) and in the European Convention on Human Rights and the American Convention on Human Rights), with regard to national trials. International case law, in particular that of the European Court of Human Rights, has fully upheld and spelled out the principle (see in particular such cases as *Artico* (§32), *Barberà, Messegué and Jabardo* (§67), *Edwards* (§36), *Raffineries grecques* (§49), including the more recent *Birutis and others* (§§26–35) and *Beckles* (§§48–66)).[13] The principle has then come to acquire a fundamental value also with regard to international proceedings. It was laid down in the Charter of the IMT (Article 16) and that of the IMTFE (Article 9); it is set forth in the Statutes of the ICTY (Article 21(2)), the ICTR (Article 20(2)), and the ICC (Article 67, also on the rights of the accused). It seems indisputable that by now it has come to belong to the category of customary norms of international law. The proposition is warranted that the principle is even endowed with the force of a peremptory norm, that is, may not be derogated from by treaty. Although there is no State practice supporting this proposition, the insistence of States through international treaties and the copious case law emphasizing the importance of the principle seem to corroborate the view that the principle has acquired *jus cogens* status.

The principle is articulated into three main standards: equality of arms; publicity of proceedings; and expeditiousness of proceedings.

21.4.1 EQUALITY OF ARMS

It should be noted at the outset that there are two different concepts of equality of arms.

First, there is the concept that has been developed in the case law of the European Court of Human Rights over the years. It implies that the accused may not be put at a serious procedural disadvantage with respect to the prosecutor. This principle applies

her functions as a judge; they had not participated in any judicial decision on the specific judicial question of whether Judge Odio Benito should be disqualified from sitting in *Delalić and others* (§14).

In *Furundžija (Appeal)* the appellant had recused Judge Mumba because, before being elected judge of the ICTY, she had been a delegate of her government in the UN Commission on the Status of Women, where the definition of rape (the offence submitted to the Trial Chamber in the case at issue) had been discussed; in addition she had met persons who later were involved in the trial, namely three authors of the *amicus curiae* briefs submitted in the case as well as one of the prosecutors. The Appeals Chamber found that the link of the judge with these person had been 'tenuous' (§194) and in addition her membership in the UN body, her sharing the goals of that body and her concern for the protection of the rights of women had not created any bias in her (§§195–215).

[13] The requisites of a fair trial in international law were discussed, with regard to war crimes, by the Supreme Court of Norway in *Latza and others* (at 52–85).

to the accused only: human rights treaties do not afford to the prosecutor a right to be put on the same footing with the defence. On the other hand, human rights treaties do not forbid, or even sometimes require, the accused to be put in a 'better' or more advantageous position than the prosecution in order to preserve an overall balance in the proceedings.

Secondly, equality of the parties is an essential ingredient of the adversarial structure of proceedings, based on the notion of the trial as a contest between two parties. Under this approach, it is indispensable for both parties to the proceedings to have the same rights; otherwise, there is no fair fight between the two 'contestants', and the spectators will not be convinced by the outcome. Here, fairness works both ways and it is, therefore, also the right of the prosecutor not to be put in a disadvantageous position. Similar worries do not exist in inquisitorial systems of justice, where proceedings are conceived of as an 'official inquiry'.[14]

Here, I shall focus on the first notion of equality of arms. The main consequences of this notion are as follows:

1. The defendant has the right to know full particulars specifying the charges preferred against him in the indictment.

2. In addition, with the shortest delay, the accused has the right to examine the evidence gathered by the prosecution in support of the charges. The 'discovery' process is regulated in detail so as to guarantee the defence as far as possible. The 'disclosure' of this evidentiary material must be done by the prosecutor within a set time-period (30 days after the initial appearance of the accused, under the Rules of the ICTY and ICTR); in addition, no later than 60 days before the date set for trial, the prosecutor must communicate to the defence 'copies of the statements of all witnesses whom the Prosecutor intends to call to testify at trial' (Rule 66(A)(ii) ICTY).[15] The defence has the right to inspect all books, documents, photographs, and tangible objects in the Prosecutor's custody upon request (Rule 66(B) ICTY), but if the defence makes this request, it triggers reciprocal disclosure obligations on the part of the prosecution (see Rule 67(C)).

3. The defendant has the right to appoint one or more defence counsel; if he is indigent, he has the right to a counsel appointed and paid by the Tribunal; in addition,

[14] It would seem that there is some confusion over the two concepts of procedural equality and some misunderstanding of the case law of the European Court of Human Rights in the case law of the ICTY, e.g. with regard to the admissibility of evidence and to disclosure of evidence. For instance, in *Zlatko Aleksovsi* (*Decision on Prosecutor's Appeal on Admissibility of Evidence*) (§§22–8), the Appeals Chamber in its decision of 16 February 1999 refused to apply more lenient standards of admissibility to (hearsay) evidence presented by the defence, stating that the prosecution is also entitled to a fair trial within the meaning of human rights conventions. This confusion in case law may be due to the fact that the two different conceptions of equality may, in certain situations, clash.

On the notion that the excessively succinct and summary nature of many defence witness statements violated the principle of equality of arms see the ICTY decision in *Kupreškić and others* of 11 January 1999, at 2.

[15] See among other things the *Decision in Kupreškić and others on Order of Presentation of Evidence*, of 21 January 1999, at 2–3.

he has the right to appoint or have appointed by the Tribunal, in case of indigence, one or more investigators for the purpose of collecting evidence.[16]

4. The defendant has the right to call witnesses and to cross-examine any witness called by the prosecution. The defence also has the right to request depositions. In addition, the defendant has the right to *obtain the attendance* of witnesses (for instance, by asking the Court to subpoena witnesses, or to call as court witnesses persons who would be reluctant to testify on behalf of the defence; this was repeatedly done, for instance, in *Kupreškić and others*).[17] Furthermore, the accused may request the granting of safe-conducts for witnesses who might fear for their liberty, as well as the taking of testimony by videoconference, whenever witnesses refuse to attend court proceedings at the Court's seat.

21.4.2 PUBLICITY OF PROCEEDINGS

That the proceedings must be public, subject to some exceptions, is a general principle of modern criminal law. Publicity of the hearings is clearly a means of better ensuring that the trial, being under public scrutiny, be fair, in particular that the rights of the accused are not infringed and that the court conduct the proceedings impartially. This requirement was not set out in the Charters of the IMT and the IMTFE. It is, however, laid down in the Statutes of the ICTY (Article 21(2)), the ICTR (Article 20(2)), and the ICC (Article 67(1)), as a fundamental right of the accused. It is also proclaimed with regard to national trials, in the European Convention on Human Rights (Article 6(1)), the UN Covenant on Civil and Political Rights (Article 14(1)), and the American Convention on Human Rights (Article 8(5)).

[16] It would seem that the court must also make sure that the accused is adequately defended by counsel. In this connection it is interesting to mention *Kottsiepen*, a case brought after the Second World War before a British Court of Appeal sitting in Germany. The Court held that defence counsel had not sufficiently assisted the accused and noted the following: 'The case came before the Court on 30th March. Counsel who appeared on behalf of the Appellant stated that he had only been instructed on the previous day, owing to the illness of Counsel who drew the Notice of Appeal. He was offered an adjournment by the Court, but he stated that he had read the papers, interviewed his client, and was ready to proceed. It soon became apparent, however, that Counsel had not read the Record of trial which had been supplied to the Appellant, and he did not appear to appreciate the nature of the proceedings before the Court of Appeal. In spite of repeated invitations to argue the questions of law raised in the Notice of Appeal, he persisted in irrelevancies (at 110). The Court noted that 'As no assistance was forthcoming from this source [the defence counsel], the Court called upon the Director of Prosecutions to deal with the questions of law involved, in the hope that Counsel would then appreciate what were the issues before the Court. Counsel was then again invited to argue these questions, but at that stage would only address the Court in mitigation of sentence. It such circumstances it was obviously unfair to the Appellant to proceed with the case, and it was adjourned to enable him to be adequately represented. . . . We cannot but deplore that a lawyer should be so lacking in respect for the Court or for his client's interests as to appear to argue a case without familiarizing himself with the issues involved, or with the procedure of the Court' (at 108–12). Since the Prosecutor was not opposing the quashing of the conviction made by the Trial Court, the Court quashed it, considering that 'on the findings of the learned Trial judge, the conviction on the charge as it was framed' could not be supported (at 112).

See also *Hermann*, generally on the rights of the defence, and more specifically on the right of the accused to a finding on an alternative charge (at 164–6). For more recent cases, see for instance the decision of an ICTY Trial Chamber in *Martić Milan* (*Decision on Appeal against Decision of Registry*), at 2–8.

[17] See for instance the *Decision on Defence Motion to Summon Witnesses*, of 6 October 1998 (at 2–3).

Nevertheless, the conduct of in camera hearings is provided for whenever this is required by the need to protect the victims and witnesses (Articles 22 (ICTY Statute), 21 (ICTR Statute), and 68 (ICC Statute)). The decision to hold hearings behind closed doors is taken by the Court, at the request of one of the parties or *proprio motu.*

21.4.3 EXPEDITIOUSNESS OF PROCEEDINGS

One of the obvious requirements of a fair trial is that trial proceedings be as speedy as possible. Plainly, as the accused enjoys the presumption of innocence until found guilty (see *supra*, 21.2), it is only rational and appropriate to establish whether he is innocent or guilty as rapidly as possible.

This principle, laid down both in treaties on human rights and in the Statutes of the ICTY, the ICTR, and the ICC, acquires special importance in international criminal proceedings, on the following ground. Very often, for practical reasons, it is difficult or inappropriate for international courts to release the accused person on bail; hence, frequently the accused is in prison, from his arrest until conviction or acquittal. This feature of international trials renders expeditiousness of proceedings all the more necessary. One should also add that often the defendants tend not to plead guilty (see *supra*, 20.2.5); were they to use this means, they would avoid commencement of trial proceedings proper, or terminate them, if the guilty plea is entered after commencement of trial. They do so either because they are innocent, or because, even if guilty, they prefer to take the chance of a lengthy trial. They hope that the evidence will be insufficient to establish their guilt; thus, being acquitted, they will avoid the stigma attaching to international crimes, which renders perpetrators more odious than authors of common offences. Pleading guilty being a relatively rare occurrence, it follows that in most cases the court must conduct trial proceedings proper to see whether or not the evidence establishes, beyond a reasonable doubt, the defendant's guilt.

It should be added that it would appear that in international proceedings entering a guilty plea is not necessarily part of, nor does it necessarily result from, a process of plea-bargaining (that is an agreement between prosecution and defence whereby the defendant pleads guilty to a reduced charge in exchange for the prosecution's undertaking to drop other charges or to seek a relatively lenient sentence).

In proceedings before the ICTY Trial Chamber, so far defendants have entered a guilty plea on a few occasions. In *Erdemović* the accused pleaded guilty to murder as a war crime (before he had pleaded guilty to murder as a crime against humanity), and was sentenced to five years' imprisonment (*Erdemović, Sentencing Judgment* of 5 March 1998).[18] In *Jelisić* the accused pleaded guilty to war crimes and crimes against

[18] The Court considered his entering a guilty plea as a mitigating circumstance. It stated that: 'An admission of guilt demonstrates honesty and it is important for the International tribunal to encourage people to come forth, whether already indicted or as unknown perpetrators. Furthermore, this voluntary admission of guilt which has saved the International Tribunal the time and effort of a lengthy investigation and trial is to be commended' (at 16).

humanity; he was convicted of plunder, cruel treatment, and inhumane acts as well as murder. The prosecution asked the Trial Chamber to pronounce a life sentence on the accused (§119). The court sentenced him to 40 years' imprisonment. (The Trial Chamber considered the guilty plea as a mitigating factor, but gave it relatively little weight since the accused had shown no remorse for his crimes: §127.) In *Todorović* the accused first pleaded not guilty to all charges. Subsequently, when he filed a motion challenging the legality of his arrest, he reached an agreement with the Prosecutor whereby he would: (i) plead guilty to some charges, (ii) withdraw all his motions including those concerning the legality of his arrest, and (iii) co-operate with the prosecution. Under the agreement, the Prosecutor undertook to recommend to the Trial Chamber a sentence of not less than 5 years' and not more than 12 years' imprisonment. Both parties undertook not to appeal against any sentence imposed by the Trial Chamber within that range.[19]

At the ICTR, guilty pleas, such as were entered in *Kambanda* (*Judgment and sentence*), in *Serushago* (*Sentence*), and in *Ruggiu*, have always been considered as a mitigating circumstance.[20]

It is notable that very often in international criminal trials both questions of fact and those relating to law prove extremely complex, thereby requiring much time for their proper consideration. In particular, it may prove necessary to call a great number of witnesses, coming from different countries. Furthermore, normally international courts must rely on State co-operation for investigations, the gathering of evidence, the apprehension of accused, and so on. All this necessarily complicates and slows down the whole process. In addition, language barriers prolong the proceedings, as normally the language of the witnesses and the accused is different from that of the court, and, on top of that, the court is bound to employ more than one official language. Often the defendant contributes to the length of proceedings by filing many

19 The Trial Chamber held that a guilty plea 'should, in principle, give rise to a reduction in the sentence that the accused would otherwise have received', adding that a guilty plea facilitates the work of the Tribunal by avoiding a possible lengthy trial with all the attendant difficulties, and 'relieves victims and witnesses of the necessity of giving evidence with the attendant stress which this may incur' (§80). It also stated that it was in no way bound by the agreements between the prosecution and the defence, noting that it was 'the Chamber's responsibility to determine an appropriate sentence in this case' (§79). The Trial Chamber sentenced Todorović to 10 years' imprisonment.

In *Sikirica and others* (*Sentencing judgment*) the three accused made a plea agreement with the prosecution after the prosecution case had ended and the defence case had commenced. The accused admitted a number of facts and the prosecution agreed to recommend a reduced sentence. The Trial Chamber sentenced Sikirica to 15 years' imprisonment, Dosen to 5 years, and Kolundžija to 3 years (§245).

20 Kambanda, after reaching an agreement with the prosecution, pleaded guilty to all counts in the indictment; the agreement entered into with the prosecution expressly stated that no agreements, understandings, or promises had been made between the parties with respect to sentence, which remained at the discretion of the Trial Chamber (*Kambanda*, §48). The court sentenced the accused to life imprisonment (§62). The Appeals Chamber confirmed the sentence (*Kambanda* (*Appeal*) (§126). In *Serushago* (*Sentence*), after entering into an agreement with the prosecution, the accused pleaded guilty to four of the five counts in the indictment (they included genocide and crimes against humanity). The Trial Chamber sentenced him to 15 years' imprisonment (§42). The sentence was confirmed by the Appeals Chamber (*Serushago* (*Appeal, reason for judgment*), §34).

procedural motions, as he is entitled to do, but which inevitably delay the outcome of the trial.

The ICTY has devised several mechanisms and procedures to reduce the length of proceedings. Among other things, (i) a pre-trial judge as well as pre-trial conferences have been provided for, (ii) time limits for the filing of procedural or preliminary motions have been set, and (iii) provision has been made for admission of written evidence and in particular for the filing of affidavits. Furthermore, (iv) the number of judges has been increased, in particular through the election of *ad litem* judges (that is, non-permanent judges, or not-full-time judges, who only sit in one or two cases), which required an amendment to the ICTY Statute by Security Council resolution no. 1329 (2000) of 30 November 2000 (a similar amendment has recently been adopted for the ICTR).

21.5 THE PRINCIPLE THAT THE ACCUSED MUST BE PRESENT AT HIS TRIAL

It is common knowledge that common law countries always require that the accused be present at trial, for trial proceedings to be commenced. As noted above (20.2.6), this requirement is chiefly dictated by the adversarial nature of the common law trial: being substantially a 'duel' between the prosecution and the defence, it must of necessity presuppose the attendance of both adversaries, so that each of them may gather evidence on their own behalf and cross-examine the witnesses called by the adversary. Probably it is also felt that a trial where the accused is absent may lend itself to abuses, particularly in authoritarian countries. (Indeed on many occasions undemocratic States have used trials *in absentia* to pronounce upon and sentence political dissidents living abroad.) Also international courts have emphasized the importance of the defendant's attendance at trial: as the European Court of Human Rights put it in *Poitrimol* v. *France* (and reiterated in *Krombach* v. *France* (§86)),

> It is of capital importance that a defendant should appear, both because of his right to a hearing and because of the need to verify the accuracy of his statements and compare them with those of the victim—whose interests need to be protected—and of the witnesses. (§35.)

In some countries constitutional reasons may also underpin this approach. For instance, in the United States, the Supreme Court ruled in *Gagnon* (at 1484) that the ban on trials *in absentia* was rooted in both the 'Confrontation Clause' of the Sixth Amendment and the 'Due Process Clause' of the Fourteenth Amendment (the former grants to every person the right 'to be confronted with the witnesses against him', while the latter provides that a State shall not 'deprive any person of life, liberty, or property, without due process of law'). Nevertheless, even countries banning trials *in absentia* do allow criminal trials to go on if, after appearing in court, the defendant deliberately absconds to avoid trial: this is for instance admitted by the US Supreme Court (see *Taylor* (at 17–29) and *Crosby* (at 748–53)).

In contrast, many civil law countries permit such trials (see 20.2.6). This institution is not connected with the inquisitorial system prevailing in civil law countries, as proved by the fact that such a country as Italy, which embraced the accusatorial system a few years ago, allows trials *in absentia*, whereas countries such as Spain and Germany, which have adopted the inquisitorial system, rule them out (probably because they regard the right of the accused to be present as an overriding human right, or because they consider it 'uneconomic' to hold trials that are not directed at attaining the ultimate purpose of any criminal trial, namely, to do justice, and therefore put the accused in jail, if convicted).[21]

The underlying basis for provisions permitting trials *in absentia* is that one should not allow justice to be thwarted by the accused, when he chooses to escape instead of standing trial. In these systems, the defendant has a legal entitlement to be present at his trial; if he absconds and flees the jurisdiction even before commencement of trial, he implicitly waives that entitlement. Were judges to be barred from proceeding by the accused's absconding, this would mean that ultimately criminal justice could be kept at bay by indictees. In addition, as the European Court of Human Rights put it in *Colozza* v. *Italy*,

> the impossibility of holding a trial by default may paralyse the conduct of criminal proceedings, in that it may lead, for example, to dispersal of the evidence, expiry of the time-limit for prosecution or a miscarriage of justice. (§29.)

Furthermore, in countries upholding a system whereby the evidence on behalf of the accused is gathered either by the investigating judge (or by the prosecutor), at least in principle the defendant is not put at a disadvantage. It is therefore felt that holding trial proceedings is not detrimental to the defendant, for his case may be made in court by a defence counsel (appointed by the court, if need be) on the basis of the evidence impartially collected by the investigating judge. Hence, under these systems, it is held admissible that criminal trials be conducted in the absence of the defendant, provided some basic safeguards, forcefully spelled out by the European Court of Human Rights, are respected: (i) the accused must have been formally notified of the charges against him; (ii) there is evidence that he is deliberately absenting himself from the proceedings; (iii) the accused has the right to appear in court at any moment and request that proceedings be commenced again, even if he has already been convicted; in other words, he has the right to obtain 'from a court which ha[s] heard him, a fresh determination of the merits of the charge' (*Colozza* v. *Italy*, §29; *Krombach* v. *France*, §§85, 87); (iv) the accused must be granted the right to be defended in court

[21] However, in Germany another ground is advanced: as C. Roxin (*Strafverfahrensrecht*, Munich: Beck, 1991, at 405) put it, 'the trial judge must personally see the accused in front of him, in order to arrive at the right picture of his personality'. See also B. Swart, 'La place des critères traditionnels de compétence dans la poursuite des crimes internationaux', in Cassese and Delmas-Marty, *Juridictions nationales*, 581–3.

by counsel (*Lala and Pelladoah* v. *The Netherlands*, §§33–4, 40–1; *Krombach* v. *France*, §§88–91).

As national legal systems differ on this matter, can one find an international rule prohibiting or allowing such trials? Indisputably, there is no international treaty provision prohibiting them. By the same token, the existing treaty rules on trial proceedings, contained in such treaties as the UN Covenant on Civil and Political Rights (Article 14(3)) and the European Convention on Human Rights (Article 6(1)) have been interpreted by the relevant international bodies as not ruling out trials *in absentia*.[22]

What must then be the condition of international criminal proceedings? The few international treaty rules on the matter are either silent or not consistent. Interestingly, the Charter of the IMT explicitly laid down in Article 12:

> the right [of the Tribunal] to take proceedings against a person charged with crimes set out in Article 6 of this Charter in his absence, if he has not been found or if the Tribunal, for any reason, finds it necessary, in the interests of justice, to conduct the hearing in his absence.

Indeed, one of the accused, Martin Borman, was tried and sentenced in his absence (vol. I, at 338–41).

The relevant provisions of the Statutes of the ICTY and the ICTR do not clarify the matter. They provide that the accused has the right 'to be tried in his presence' (Articles 21(4)(d) and 20(4)(d) respectively). However, nothing is said about the case where the accused implicitly waives this right by absconding before trial proceedings commence: one could easily construe this provision to the effect that the trial may be conducted in the absence of the accused if he, after being duly notified of the indictment and the charges contained therein, were to flee in order to evade criminal justice.

By contrast, the Statute of the ICC, at Article 63(1), seems clearly to require the presence of the accused as a basic requirement for the commencement of trials (with the exception, normally provided for in common law countries, that the accused's presence is not required if he disrupts the trial: see Article 63(2)).

Faced with the paucity and inconsistency of international rules, one ought to be

22 Thus, the UN Human Rights Committee held in *Daniel Mbenge* v. *Zaire* (1983) (§§13–14.2), in *Hiber Conteris* v. *Uruguay* (1985) (§§9.2–10) and in *Dieter Wolf* v. *Panama* (1992) (§6.5) that the relevant State had breached Article 14(3)(d), but only because trial proceedings had commenced without the accused having knowledge of the proceedings against him. In *Raphael Henry* v. *Jamaica* (1991) (§8.3) the Committee held that the State had not breached that provision because the accused had opted for representation by counsel and therefore could not claim that his absence during the appeal hearing constituted a violation of the Covenant. Furthermore in *Daniel Mbenge* v. *Zaire* the Committee stated that Article 14(3)(d) 'and other requirements of due process enshrined in Article 14 cannot be construed as invariably rendering proceedings *in absentia* inadmissible irrespective of the reasons for the accused person's absence. Indeed, proceedings *in absentia* are in some circumstances (for instance, when the accused person, although informed of the proceedings sufficiently in advance, declines to exercise his right to be present) permissible in the interest of the proper administration of justice' (§14.1).

The European Court of Human Rights held that the right of the accused to participate in the trial, although not expressly laid down in Article 6 of the European Convention on Human Rights, is a right 'whose existence is shown by the object and purpose of the Article taken as a whole' (*Colozza* v. *Italy*, §27, *Brozicek* v. *Italy*, §45). Nonetheless, the Court did not rule that trials *in absentia* were as such incompatible with Article 6: see, for instance, *Colozza* v. *Italy* (§§27–30), *Poitrimol* v. *France* (1993, §§30–39) and *Krombach* v. *France* (§§82–91).

able to find a convincing solution by drawing upon general principles and looking at the specificities of international criminal proceedings. In favour of trials *in absentia* one could argue that it would be contrary to law and justice to authorize the alleged perpetrators of gruesome crimes to make a mockery of international justice by preventing trials through their deliberate absence. Nonetheless, it would seem that at the international level the interests of justice would be better served if the contrary view were taken. In spite of the aforementioned international case law and the dubious interpretation of the relevant provisions of the Statutes of the ICTY and ICTR, the proposition is warranted that when international criminal proceedings are being held, the accused must be present at trial, before trial proceedings are commenced. The rationale behind this proposition is that the nature and the unique features of these proceedings make this requirement indispensable. In international trials the search for and collection of evidence may prove extremely difficult, because: (i) as a rule the court is headquartered in a country far away from the place of the crime, (ii) witnesses may be scattered over many countries; (iii) there is no investigating judge charged with collecting evidence on behalf of both the prosecution and defence; under the accusatorial system each party must search for and find the necessary evidence; (iv) the lack of an international body of investigators under the control of the prosecutor endowed with the power of freely going wherever the evidence may happen to be, to question witnesses and collect material evidence, makes investigations undertaken for the purpose of supporting or dismissing charges extremely complex; the same holds true for the defence, which may not count on the court's power to order investigators to collect evidence on the defence's behalf; (v) in most cases matters are further complicated by the fact that the crimes with which the accused is charged have been perpetrated years before the court proceedings start.

As a result of these characteristics of international criminal trials, it proves crucial for the fair conduct of proceedings that the accused be present. If present, he may, first, issue instructions to his defence counsel, or consult with them, on the evidence that could be collected to support his case. Instead, a trial in his absence, even if he were to be represented in court by able defence counsel appointed by the court, would be most likely to end up in a mistrial or a miscarriage of justice. Indeed, in most cases the defence counsel could not prove able to muster all the necessary evidence in rebuttal of the prosecution's case. Secondly, the presence of the accused is important for the cross-examination of prosecution witnesses, for he can suggest to his defence counsel points or issues on which to conduct cross-examination. Thirdly, the accused may prove of great importance for the court in its findings, because he may decide to testify in court, and in any case his behaviour and appearance may be of some relevance to the court in establishing whether he may be found guilty or innocent.

In sum the imperative of a fair trial, in conjunction with the specificities of international criminal proceedings, leads to the conclusion that, in such proceedings, trials may prove fair only if the accused is present. This proposition also holds true for the ICC, although one could argue that there, as the Prosecutor is duty bound to gather evidence for both the prosecution and the defence, one could dispense with the presence of the accused. However, various factors make for the need for the accused to be present at trial. In particular, one should mention the following factors: the complexity of international trials, the stigma attaching to international crimes coupled with the wide publicity the media give to allegations concerning such crimes, the consequent need to ensure that the presumption of innocence accruing to any accused person not be jeopardized by the failure of the accused to instruct his defence counsel for the preparation of his case.

The presence of the accused seems to be so important as to warrant the proposition that, if he escapes after the trial commences, proceedings should be stayed, until the indictee is arrested and brought to trial again, or voluntarily surrenders. In other words, the characteristics of international criminal proceedings emphasized above should rule out a solution normally adopted at the national level by countries that ban trials *in absentia*, that is, continuation of trial if the accused absconds after the initiation of proceedings (see for instance Rule 43 of the US Federal Court Rules of Procedure). At the national level, this solution is justified by the need both to safeguard the public interest in the dispensation of justice and to prevent individuals from evading adjudication. At the international level the need to ensure a fair trial and to avoid any miscarriage of justice should instead prevail.[23] In addition, there is not the problem of a statute of limitations (which is another rationale for holding trials *in absentia* in civil law countries), since international crimes do not fall under any statute of limitations.

It should be added that there may nevertheless be cases where *in absentia* proceedings may exceptionally appear warranted. The ICTY Appeals Chamber envisaged such a case in *Blaškić* (*Subpoena*). It held that if an individual does not comply with a subpoena or order issued by the Tribunal, he could be held in contempt of the

[23] When it seemed that States were intent on refusing to co-operate with the Tribunal and therefore no trial could be held for lack of indictees at The Hague, the ICTY adopted an imaginative measure designed to respect the principle whereby the accused must be present for a proper trial to be conducted, while at the same time taking some action to react to the lack of co-operation of States and their consequent refusal to detain persons accused of appalling crimes. This measure was Rule 61 of the Rules of Procedure and Evidence ('Procedure in Case of Failure to Execute a Warrant'). Under this Rule, if an arrest warrant has not been executed, the confirmation judge may order that the Prosecutor submit the indictment to the Trial Chamber of which the judge is a member. The Prosecutor then submits the indictment in open court, together with the evidence available, and may call and examine witnesses. The Trial Chamber may conclude that 'there are reasonable grounds for believing that the accused has committed all or any of the crimes charged in the indictment', whereupon it: (i) issues an international arrest warrant to be transmitted to all States; and (ii) may freeze the assets of the accused; if the absence of the accused is due to lack of co-operation of a State, it (iii) may request the Tribunal's President to notify the Security Council of the failure of the relevant State to comply with Article 29 of the ICTY Statute (on the obligation of States to co-operate). Clearly, this procedure is not a trial proper. It is a sort of fall-back, designed to stimulate States to arrest indictees, by making public and exposing the charges preferred by the Prosecutor against some persons.

The procedure was resorted to on five occasions between 1995 and 1996 (*Nicolić*; *Martić*; *Mrskić*, *Radić*, *and Šlijvančanin*; *Raijć*; *Karadžic and Mladić*). Since then it has not been relied upon, on account of the increasing number of arrests made either by States or by the NATO forces in Bosnia and Herzegovina, which enabled the Tribunal's Chambers to commence trials proper.

Tribunal and the specific contempt procedure could be set in motion. Should the individual also fail to attend these contempt proceedings, '*in absentia* proceedings should not be ruled out' (§59). The Appeals Chamber held that, although it was not appropriate to hold such proceedings against persons falling under the primary jurisdiction of the Tribunal (that is, accused of one of the international crimes over which the Tribunal had jurisdiction under its Statute),

> By contrast, *in absentia* proceedings may be exceptionally warranted in cases involving contempt of the International Tribunal, where the person charged fails to appear in court, thus obstructing the administration of justice. These cases fall within the ancillary or incidental jurisdiction of the International Tribunal. (§59.)[24]

SELECT BIBLIOGRAPHY

C. J. M. Safferling, *Towards an International Criminal Procedure* (Oxford: Oxford University Press, 2001), 226–68; S. Zappalà, *International Criminal Trials and Respect for Human Rights in International Criminal Proceedings* (Oxford: Oxford University Press, 2003), at 1–194.

24 The Appeals Chamber added, however, that all the necessary judicial safeguards should be offered to the absent defendant (§59).

It should be noted that the Chamber's judgment was unanimous; this means that the three judges from common law countries sitting on the Appeals Chamber concurred with the Chamber's ruling on the question of *in absentia* proceedings as well.

22

STAGES OF INTERNATIONAL PROCEEDINGS IN OUTLINE

(A) PROSECUTOR'S INVESTIGATIONS AND PRE-TRIAL PROCEEDINGS

22.1 GENERAL

It may prove useful to summarize the unfolding of international proceedings, from the investigations initiated by the Prosecutor to the appeal or revision proceedings. I will undertake the exposition of these proceedings on the basis of the relevant provisions of the Statutes and the Rules of Procedure and Evidence of the ICTY, the ICTR, and the ICC, as well as the judicial practice of the first two Tribunals.

22.2 THE SETTING IN MOTION OF INTERNATIONAL CRIMINAL INVESTIGATIONS

The Statutes of the ICTY and the ICTR provide that the Prosecutor alone decides whether or not to commence investigations:

> The Prosecutor shall initiate investigations ex officio or on the basis of information obtained from any source, particularly from Governments, United Nations organs, intergovernmental or non-governmental organizations. The Prosecutor shall assess the information received or obtained and decide whether there is sufficient basis to proceed. (Articles 18(1) ICTY Statute and 17(1) ICTR Statute.)

Thus, no formal right of complaint is granted to the alleged victims nor is the power of governments to set in motion investigations provided for, although both the victims and governments may submit information and allegations to the Prosecutor. Non-governmental organizations as well as inter-governmental bodies (such as, for instance, NATO) are endowed with a similar power.

The Prosecutor enjoys very broad discretion as to whether or not to initiate investigations and against whom. It is not clear why any decision as to the initiation of investigations into a specific case is left to the Prosecutor alone: the Reports of the Secretary-General accompanying the Statutes do not clarify the issue. It is plausible that the Secretary-General and the Security Council considered that: (i) the existence of numerous reports about the alleged crimes perpetrated in the two countries made it superfluous to grant a right of complaint proper; in addition (ii) such a right would have triggered the proceedings even when the alleged crimes were of minor importance and it was therefore not appropriate for them to be amenable to international justice; furthermore, (iii) to grant a right of complaint to governments might have enabled States to act on political grounds or at any rate prompted politically motivated States to make use of criminal justice for their own ends; this outcome was all the more probable because of the existence in the area (particularly in the former Yugoslavia) of States still opposed politically and ideologically.

In the case of the ICC it is provided that investigations may be initiated: (i) at the request of a *State party* to the Statute, or (ii) by the *Prosecutor proprio motu*, or (iii) at the request of the UN *Security Council* acting under Chapter VII of the UN Charter. The alleged victims of crimes or non-governmental organizations acting on their behalf have no right to refer a case to the Court, but the Prosecutor may make use of the information and allegations they might submit. Probably it was felt that to grant such a right would have resulted in the Court being flooded with innumerable complaints, most of them probably frivolous or unfounded. This should not apply to the right of a State to lodge a complaint: States are expected carefully to screen allegations of crimes made by the victims or by private organizations, with a view to ascertaining whether they are supported by reliable evidence.

A second notable feature of the ICC system is that the Statute clearly draws a distinction between preliminary investigations or, as we shall term them here, *inquiry*, and *investigation* proper. The need for an inquiry to precede investigations is provided for in Article 15 with exclusive regard to cases where the Prosecutor decides to take proceedings *proprio motu*. The inquiry consists of a search for information or the gathering of evidence about an alleged crime, for the purpose of establishing if there is 'a reasonable basis to proceed with an investigation'. The initiation of the inquiry by the Prosecutor on his own initiative is based on any relevant information he may have received from any reliable source, as well as 'written or oral testimony at the seat of the Court' (Article 15(1)). If and when he has established that such 'reasonable basis' exists, the Prosecutor must submit to the Pre-Trial Chamber a 'request for authorization of an investigation'. If the Pre-Trial Chamber grants the request, the Prosecutor may commence the investigation. By contrast, in the case of referral of a 'situation' by a State or by the Security Council, the Prosecutor's request to the Pre-Trial Chamber for the authorization of an investigation is not required. Clearly, it is assumed that the national authorities of the referring State have already undertaken an inquiry, and that the Security Council, through one of its subordinate bodies, has already made a first screening of information relating to the possible perpetration of crimes.

Article 14 ICC Statute provides for the initiation of investigations at the request of a State into a 'situation' in which one or more crimes under the Court's jurisdiction appear to have been committed. It stipulates that 'as far as possible' the State should 'specify the relevant circumstances' and provide the necessary 'supporting documentation'. Interestingly, the Statute does not set out any further requirements; in particular, it does not require that the requesting State be the national State of the victim or the alleged perpetrator, or the State on whose territory the crime has been allegedly committed. Hence, any contracting State, even a State that has no link whatsoever with the crime, may file the request. This regulation is clearly based on the principle that the crimes under the Court's jurisdiction are of universal concern; consequently any State possessing the relevant information may bring them to the attention of the Prosecutor.

Commencement of investigations at the request of the Security Council may be undertaken by the Prosecutor whenever that UN body, 'acting under Chapter VII of the UN Charter' (Article 13(b)), refers to the Prosecutor 'a situation in which one or more' crimes under the jurisdiction of the ICC appear to have been committed. Plainly, the Security Council may only submit to the ICC 'situations' involving serious crimes the perpetration of which amounts to a 'threat to the peace' (or a 'breach of the peace')—these are, however, broad notions involving a wide discretionary power of the Security Council in their interpretation.

22.3 CONDITIONS THE PROSECUTOR MUST FULFIL BEFORE INITIATING AN INVESTIGATION

In the ICTY and the ICTR system the Prosecutor not only has absolute freedom to decide whether or not to initiate investigations and against whom, but also is free to carry out investigations outside any judicial scrutiny (although he must of course comply with a set of obligations regarding the conduct of investigations and the rights of the suspects). Such judicial scrutiny is only made at the end of the investigations, when the Prosecutor submits an indictment to a reviewing judge, who may admit or dismiss it.

By contrast, in the ICC system the actions of the Prosecutor are subject to a set of conditions, whenever the initiation of investigations (i) has been requested by a State, or (ii) has been made by the Prosecutor on his own initiative. (These conditions do not apply when the investigations have been requested by the Security Council.)

In the case of a *State request*, as well as in the case of the Prosecutor acting *proprio motu*, the Prosecutor, as pointed out above, must first of all determine whether 'there would be a reasonable basis to commence an investigation' (Articles 18(1) and 53(1)). If he is satisfied that there is such a basis, he must notify 'all States Parties and those States which, taking into account the information available, would normally exercise jurisdiction over the crimes concerned' (Article 18(1), which formally speaking only applies to referrals by States). In case of referral by the Security Council, the Prosecutor may find other means of enabling States to become cognizant of the referral and of the possible initiation of court investigations. Only if no State concerned is investigating the alleged crime nor has the alleged author been brought to trial before a national judge, or instead a State concerned is investigating or conducting judicial proceedings, but is clearly 'unwilling or unable' to do justice, may the Prosecutor initiate investigations proper.

As stated above, in the case of preliminary investigations or inquiry initiated by the *Prosecutor proprio motu*, in addition to these conditions, it is necessary for the Prosecutor to submit to the Pre-Trial Chamber a request for authorization of an investigation, together with any supporting material collected. The Prosecutor may initiate investigation only after obtaining such judicial authorization (and if also the other conditions mentioned above are fulfilled).

The differentiation between the three instances of initiation of proceedings can be easily explained. In the case of referral to the Court by the Security Council, it has been considered that a ruling by the Pre-Trial Chamber was not necessary. The fact that the crimes submitted by the Security Council to the Court involve a threat or even a breach of the peace has been considered of paramount importance and at any rate sufficient to remove that condition.

The condition, imposed only for cases where the Prosecutor initiates the inquiry on his own motion, that the Pre-Trial Chamber should first authorize the conduct of investigation, is aimed at limiting the power of the Prosecutor. The same condition has not been regarded as necessary when the initiative is taken by a State. Clearly it has been thought that before submitting a case to the ICC a State party gives due consideration to the importance and significance of the step it takes in bringing the case before the Court.

It is however important to emphasize that, conversely, no distinction is made among the three categories of instances as far as the possibility of challenging the admissibility of a case is concerned. Whether the case is brought to the Court by a State or the Security Council, or is initiated by the Prosecutor, the accused or other persons involved as well as States have the right to challenge the admissibility of the case prior to the confirmation of the indictment containing the charges, that is during investigation (see Article 19).

22.4 CONDUCT OF INVESTIGATIONS BY THE PROSECUTOR

As stated above, in international trials before the ICTY and the ICTR the adversarial system prevails. Hence, the situation is different from that in civil law countries which still uphold the institution of an investigating judge (*juge d'instruction*). There, it is first the Prosecutor who, through his staff, conducts preliminary investigations and gathers the available evidence against the suspect; then, if he considers that he has a prima facie case, he hands the case over to the investigating judge. It falls to this judge to search out and collect evidence, both that against the accused and the evidence exculpating him. Conversely, in international proceedings the Prosecutor gathers evidence against the suspect in his investigation. It is primarily for the defence to look for and collect evidence aimed at refuting the charges (although if the Prosecutor finds exculpatory evidence, he is duty bound to disclose it to the defence).

In the conduct of investigations, the Prosecutor may need to have a suspect arrested. Under Rule 40(A) of the Rules of Procedure and Evidence (RPE) of the ICTY, he will have to request the relevant State to arrest the suspect and place him in custody. However, under Rule 40(B), if a State is prevented from keeping the suspect in custody or is unable or unwilling to take the measures necessary to prevent his escape, the Prosecutor may apply to a judge of the ICTY designated by the Tribunal's President for an order to transfer the suspect to the seat of the Tribunal or any other place decided upon by the Tribunal's Bureau. Rule 40 *bis* also provides for the possibility of the Prosecutor requesting a judge of the Tribunal to issue an order for the transfer to and provisional detention of a suspect in the detention unit of the Tribunal.

I have already mentioned above that in the ICC the system is in some respects closer to the inquisitorial model and perhaps more attuned than the ICTY and ICTR system to the specific requirements of international criminal trials. Indeed, under Article (54)(1)(a) of the ICC Statute, the Prosecutor is under the obligation to gather evidence both against and in favour of the suspect or accused. It is for the Pre-Trial Chamber to issue orders of arrest and other orders requested by the Prosecutor (see Article 58 of the ICC Statute).

Interestingly, under Article 56 of the ICC Statute, upon request of the Prosecutor and while the investigation is being conducted by the Prosecutor, the Pre-Trial Chamber may take measures to collect or preserve evidence, whenever such evidence might not be available subsequently for the purposes of trial.

22.4.1 THE NEED FOR CO-OPERATION BY STATES

Of course, the conduct of investigations involves the search for and collection of evidence. To do so, any international prosecutor perforce needs to rely upon the co-operation of States. Indeed, the suspects, the victims, or any witnesses may be on the territory of one or more sovereign States. The Prosecutor has no power or authority to carry out his functions on such territories. To discharge his mission he therefore needs the co-operation of all the relevant States. Such co-operation may take two different forms: (i) at the request of the Prosecutor, the national authorities (prosecutors or investigating judges, depending on the national legislation) may carry out all the actions required by the Prosecutor, for instance, question suspects, victims, or witnesses, conduct on-site investigations, seize documentary evidence or other evidentiary material; (ii) they may authorize the international prosecutor to carry out investigations on national territory, if need be with the assistance of specially designated national authorities (judges, prosecutors) or of the national authorities that are territorially competent. Clearly, the second form of co-operation is far more internationally oriented and favourable to the expansion of the Prosecutor's powers.

The choice between the two different modes of co-operation very much depends on the attitude of individual States. For instance, in the case of the ICTY, in their implementing legislation some States (such as Australia, France, Italy, New Zealand, and Spain) tend to attribute to national judicial authorities the power to collect evidence and perform other acts necessary for the Prosecutor's investigations. Other States, on the other hand, tend to authorize the Prosecutor to fulfil at least some parts of his mission autonomously on the national territory; this for instance holds true for Austria, Finland, Germany, and Switzerland.

In *Blaškić* (*Judgment on the request of Croatia*) the ICTY Appeals Chamber held that normally the International Tribunal must turn to the relevant national authorities for the collection of evidence, the seizure of evidentiary material, etc. However, the Tribunal's Prosecutor was authorized directly to carry out such activities on the territory of a State in two situations: (i) when the State was one of the former belligerents or entities of the former Yugoslavia (§53); and (ii) when such investigative activity was authorized by national implementing legislation (§55). In addition, according to the Appeals Chamber, the Tribunal was authorized to reach out directly to private individuals living on the territory of a State when such individuals were needed to testify in court or deliver a particular document and the State concerned had refused to comply with an order of the Tribunal; in such instances the Tribunal could directly summon a witness or order an individual to hand over evidence or appear in court (§§55–56).[1] It should be added that of course, whenever international police or military forces are available which are lawfully stationed on the territory of a State where evidence may be found, the Prosecutor may turn to them for assistance in the gathering of evidence. This happened in *Kordić and Cerkez* (*Decision on defence motion to suppress evidence*), where an ICTY Trial Chamber held that the search and seizure of documents in Bosnia and Herzegovina by

[1] The Appeals Chamber justified the first exception as follows: 'The first class encompasses States: (i) on the territory of which crimes may have been perpetrated; and in addition, (ii) some authorities of which might be implicated in the commission of these crimes. Consequently, in the case of those States, to go through the official channels of identifying, summoning and interviewing witnesses, or to conduct on-site investigations, might jeopardize investigations by the Prosecutor or defence counsel. In particular, the presence of State officials at the interview of a witness might discourage the witness from speaking the truth, and might also imperil not just his own life or personal integrity but possibly those of his relatives. It follows that it would be contrary to the very purpose and function of the International Tribunal to have State officials present on such occasions. The States and Entities of the former Yugoslavia are obliged to cooperate with the International Tribunal in such a manner as to enable the International Tribunal to discharge its functions. This obligation (which, it should be noted was restated in the Dayton and Paris Accords), also requires them to allow the Prosecutor and the defence to fulfil their tasks free from any possible impediment or hindrance' (§53).

As to the third exception, the Appeals Chamber found that it was justified on the following grounds: 'In the above-mentioned scenarios [that is, if the national authorities refuse to co-operate and therefore prevent an individual from testifying or handing over evidence] the attitude of the State or Entity may jeopardize the discharge of the International Tribunal's fundamental functions. It is therefore to be assumed that an inherent power to address itself to those individuals inures to the advantage of the International Tribunal. Were it not vested with such a power, the International Tribunal would be unable to guarantee a fair trial to persons accused of atrocities in the former Yugoslavia' (§55).

members of the Office of the Prosecutor accompanied by forces of SFOR was 'perfectly within the powers of the Prosecution provided for in the [ICTY] Statute' (at 4).

The problem of co-operation by States will prove *of special importance* in the case of the ICC, on various grounds. First, the provisions on co-operation are numerous and detailed (Articles 86–102) and, in essence, impose upon contracting States both general and specific obligations to co-operate. However, in case of refusal or failure to comply with such obligations, the Court can only 'make a finding to that effect' and refer the matter to the Assembly of States Parties (or to the UN Security Council, in cases that had been referred by this organ to the Court) (Article 87(7)). If the failure to co-operate comes from a State not party to the Statute that had entered into an ad hoc agreement or arrangement with the Court, the Court may inform the Assembly of States Parties or, depending on whether the matter had been referred to it by the Security Council, such organ.

Secondly, the general scheme of relations between the Court and States is substantially based on a 'horizontal' approach: States are not subordinate to the Court but on its level, as it were (see *supra*, 19.7). It follows that if a State decides not to co-operate, the Court can only fall back on the usual international law mechanisms for inducing compliance with international obligations. It lacks any special authority, or power, or means of putting into effect its orders, or generally discharging its mission, on the territory of a recalcitrant State party. However, under Article 57(3)(d) of the ICC Statute the Pre-Trial Chamber may authorize the Prosecutor:

> to take specific investigative steps within the territory of a State Party without having secured the cooperation of that State under Part 9 [on International Co-operation and Judicial Assistance] if, whenever possible having regard to the views of the State concerned, the Pre-Trial Chamber has determined in that case that the State is clearly unable to execute a request for cooperation due to the unavailability of any authority or any component of its judicial system competent to execute the request for cooperation under Part 9.

Thirdly, the Court acts upon the principle of complementarity. In other words it only adjudicates cases where national prosecutorial or judicial authorities are unable or unwilling to deal with a case (see *supra*, 19.5 and 7). One of the consequences of this main feature of the Court's activity is that, except where the relevant State consents to the exercise of the Court's jurisdiction, the Court *substitutes for* national authorities. Proceedings commence before the ICC only if national authorities have been labelled by the Court as 'unwilling or unable genuinely to prosecute', or as having held trial proceedings 'not conducted independently or impartially' or 'inconsistent with the intent to bring the person concerned to justice' (Article 17). Whenever this is so, it follows that those national authorities are most unlikely to be prepared to co-operate with the ICC, for instance in the collection of evidence, service of documents, execution of searches and seizures.

22.4.2 RIGHTS OF SUSPECTS AND OTHER PERSONS INVOLVED IN INVESTIGATIONS

Any person involved in investigations, for instance suspects (that is, any person about whom there are grounds to believe that he may have committed an international crime) or persons questioned as witnesses (whether or not they may become suspects) possesses under customary and treaty law a set of fundamental rights. Such rights are protected, albeit implicitly, in the Statutes of the ICTY and the ICTR, whereas they are laid down in much detail in the Statute of the ICC.

Under Article 55(1) of the ICC Statute these rights are granted to suspects even when investigations and other preliminary activities are carried out by State authorities at the request of the Prosecutor. These rights include the right: (i) to be questioned in a language that the person understands or to be assisted by an interpreter without payment; (ii) not to be subjected to any form of coercion or threat; (iii) not to be subjected to any form of cruel, inhuman, or degrading treatment; (iv) not to incriminate himself or to confess guilt; and (v) not to be arbitrarily deprived of his liberty.

Persons suspected of an international crime possess *in addition* the following rights (laid down in Article 55(2) of the ICC Statute as well as in customary law): (i) to be informed, prior to questioning, that there are grounds to believe that they have committed an international crime; (ii) to be cautioned that any statement the suspect makes shall be recorded and may be used in evidence; (iii) to remain silent, without their silence creating a presumption of guilt; (iv) to be legally assisted by a person freely chosen or assigned by the court's registry, at the court's expense; (v) to be questioned in the presence of counsel.

22.4.3 SUBMISSION OF THE INDICTMENT OR CHARGES

In the ICTY and ICTR system the outcome of investigations may be the drawing up, by the Prosecutor, of an indictment, containing 'a concise statement of the facts of the case and of the crime with which the suspect is charged'. The Prosecutor may proceed to take such a step whenever he 'is satisfied in the course of an investigation that there is sufficient evidence to provide reasonable grounds for believing that a suspect has committed a crime within the jurisdiction of the Tribunal' (Rule 47(B) of the ICTY RPE). The indictment must set forth the name and particulars of the suspect; it must also contain a concise statement of facts and an indication of the charges preferred against the suspect. The Prosecutor may withdraw the indictment without prior leave, at any time before its confirmation by a judge; thereafter, the withdrawal needs the leave of a judge or the Trial Chamber (see, for instance, Rule 51(A) of the RPE of the ICTY). Similarly, the Prosecutor may amend the indictment without prior leave, before confirmation, whereas thereafter he can do so only with the leave of a judge or, depending upon the case, of the competent Trial Chamber (see for instance Rule 50 of the RPE of the ICTY).

Under the ICC Statute, at the end of investigations the Prosecutor submits charges setting out the facts and the crimes of which the suspect is accused (see Article 61).

Interestingly, under the ICC Statute the Prosecutor does not enjoy a discretional power to conclude that, upon investigation of a case, there is insufficient basis for a prosecution. Whenever he reaches this conclusion, he must so inform the Pre-Trial Chamber, stating the reasons therefor, as well as, if it is a State or the Security Council that has referred a situation, that State or the Security Council (Article 53(1) and (2) of the ICC Statute). Either at the request of the State or the Security Council or, depending upon the case, on its own initiative, the Pre-Trial Chamber may review the Prosecutor's decision and request him to reconsider it (Article 53(3)).[2] This entails that the Prosecutor's discretionary power is not unqualified but subject to judicial scrutiny. This legal regulation appears to be meritorious by: (i) setting out the general standards by which the Prosecutor may decide whether or not to prosecute a case, (ii) obliging the Prosecutor to give reasons for his deciding not to prosecute and in addition (iii) empowering the Pre-Trial Chamber to reverse his decision, the otherwise unfettered powers of the Prosecutor are significantly restricted and any abuse is forestalled or, in any case, may be checked.

A question that has arisen many times is whether the charges made by the Prosecutor may be *cumulative* for the same act (for instance, the same murder is characterized and charged both as a war crime and as a crime against humanity). In *Akayesu* an ICTR Trial Chamber held that cumulative charges could be made in three instances (where the offences charged had different legal ingredients; where the relevant provisions protected different interests; and where it proved necessary to record a conviction for multiple offences in order fully to describe what the accused had done) (§§461–70). In a decision in *Tadić* an ICTY Trial Chamber held that the matter was only theoretical and had no practical relevance.[3] In *Kupreškić and others*, an ICTY Trial Chamber held that two seemingly conflicting requirements must be reconciled, namely 'the requirement that the rights of the accused be fully safeguarded' and the requirement that 'the Prosecutor be granted all the powers consistent with the [ICTY] Statute to enable her to fulfil her mission efficiently and in the interests of justice' (§724). In the light of these requirements, the Chamber concluded that the Prosecutor should make *cumulative* charges if the facts charged violated simultaneously two or more provisions of the Statute, and charge *in the alternative* when an offence appeared to be in breach of more provisions, one of them being special to the other (for instance, a murder could be charged as a crime against humanity and in the alternative, for the event of the widespread or

[2] However, under Article 53(3)(b) the Pre-Trial Chamber may on its own initiative review a decision of the Prosecutor not to proceed only if such decision has been made on the grounds that the prosecution would not serve the interests of justice on account of the gravity of the crime, or the interests of the victims, or the age or infirmity of the alleged perpetrator, and his or her role in the alleged crime.

[3] *Tadić* (*Decision on the Defence motion on the Form of the indictment*), at 10.

systematic practice not being proved, as a war crime) (§§720–7). However, both another Trial Chamber, in *Brđanin and Talić* (*Decision on the amended indictment*) (§§29–43), and the ICTY Appeals Chamber, in *Delalić and others* (§400), disallowed this view (see *supra*, 11.2).

22.4.4 CONFIRMATION PROCEEDINGS

The procedure for reviewing indictments adopted by the ICTY and the ICTR differs from that of the ICC. The Rules of Procedure and Evidence of these two Tribunals do not provide for what is considered an essential safeguard in all adversarial systems of justice, namely a 'preliminary hearing' in which the Prosecutor must, in an open and adversary hearing, establish that there is a prima facie case. This is probably due to the fact that originally the RPE envisaged confirmation of the indictment as the prerequisite for issuing an arrest warrant.

In the ICTY and ICTR system the Prosecutor must submit the indictment, together with the 'supporting material' (that is, all the material designed to corroborate the charges brought by the Prosecutor) to the judge on duty. The judge reviews the indictment and supporting material and may: (i) confirm the indictment; (ii) dismiss it; (iii) request the Prosecutor to present additional material; or (iv) adjourn the review so as to give the Prosecutor the opportunity to modify the indictment. The reviewing judge performs these alternative acts in a hearing that is *ex parte*, that is, without the suspect or his counsel, and is held in camera. Pursuant to Article 19(1) of the ICTY Statute, the standard for confirmation of the indictment is that there must be a prima facie case,[4] a standard that would seem to be more exacting than that required for the Prosecutor's appraisal (which is that 'there is sufficient evidence to provide reasonable grounds for believing that a suspect has committed a crime', Rule 47(B) ICTY RPE).[5] Upon confirmation of the indictment, the suspect acquires the status of an *accused*. In addition the judge may, at the request of the Prosecutor, issue one or more arrest warrants or any other order sought by the Prosecutor, which the judge deems appropriate to make in the interests of justice. (In the ICC system under Article 58 the Pre-Trial Chamber may issue arrest warrants even before a person is formally charged.)

In contrast, in the ICC system the Prosecutor submits the charges to the Pre-Trial Chamber, which holds a *public hearing in the presence of the 'person charged'* (unless

[4] Judge McDonald, in her decision in *Kordić and others* (*Review of the indictment*) held that, for the purposes of confirmation, the prima facie case standard meant that there was a credible case which would, if not contradicted by the defence, be a sufficient basis to convict the accused on the charge (at 1123).

[5] In his Separate Opinion in the decision in *Rajić* (*Review of the indictment*), Judge Sidhwa held that this requirement means that it is sufficient for the Prosecutor to point to 'such facts and circumstances as would justify a reasonably or ordinary prudent man to believe that a suspect has committed a crime' (at 1065).

For a detailed discussion of Rule 47(B), see D. Hunt, 'The Meaning of a *Prima Facie* Case', in *Essays on ICTY Procedure*, 137–49.

such person waives his right to attend, or absconds and may not be detained, and the Chamber decides nonetheless to hold the hearing), or his counsel. The purpose of the hearing is to enable the Chamber to 'determine whether there is sufficient evidence to establish substantial grounds to believe that the person committed each of the crimes charged' (Article 61(7)). The Pre-Trial Chamber may: (i) confirm the charges or some of them, and commit the person to a Trial Chamber for trial; (ii) decline to confirm the charges 'in relation to which it has determined that there is insufficient evidence'; or (iii) adjourn the hearing to enable the Prosecutor to submit further evidence or amend the charges (Article 61(7)).[6]

22.5 PRE-TRIAL PROCEEDINGS

Both in the ICTY and ICTR system and in the system of the ICC, pre-trial proceedings commence with the initial appearance of the accused and his entering a plea of guilty or not guilty.

In this initial hearing the Court reads the indictment or the charges previously confirmed by a reviewing judge (in the ICTY and ICTR systems) or by the Pre-Trial Chamber (in the ICC system) to the accused, satisfies itself that the accused understands the nature of the charges and is assisted by defence counsel, and then asks him whether he pleads guilty or not guilty.

In the ICTY and ICTR system, if the accused pleads guilty, the Trial Chamber enters a finding of guilt—provided the requisite conditions are met. (These conditions were first laid down jurisprudentially in the *Erdemović* (*Appeals*) judgment and then codified in paragraphs (i) to (iv) of Rule 62 *bis* RPE ICTY.) The Trial Chamber also instructs the Registrar to set a date for the sentencing hearing (Rule 62 *bis* RPE ICTY). If instead the accused pleads not guilty, the Trial Chamber: (i) shall ensure that the Prosecutor discloses to the defence, within the prescribed time limit (30 days after the initial appearance of the accused, under Rule 66(A)(i) of the ICTY RPE) the supporting material which accompanies the indictment or the charges at the time of confirmation; and (ii) appoints a pre-trial judge, charged with co-ordinating communication between the parties during the pre-trial phase. It may also convene a status conference to organize exchanges between the parties so as to ensure expeditious preparation for trial.

In the period before initiation of trial proper, the parties may file preliminary motions, namely motions which: (i) challenge the court's jurisdiction, or (ii) allege defects in the form of the indictment or charges, or (iii) seek severance of counts joined in one indictment or separate trials, or instead seek joinder of trials, or (iv) raise objections concerning the assignment of counsel. The parties may also file other motions that are not preliminary in nature (for instance, motions for the provisional release of the accused, for the disqualification or recusal of a judge, etc.).

[6] See also Rules 121–6.

Motions are considered and pronounced upon by the Trial Chamber and, subject to certain conditions, may be appealed to the Appeals Chamber.

In the ICTY and ICTR system, once the Prosecutor's disclosure of evidence is completed and preliminary motions, if any, are disposed of, the pre-trial judge orders the Prosecutor to file within a certain time limit: (i) a pre-trial brief addressing the factual and legal issues; (ii) admissions by the parties and a statement of matters which are not in dispute; (iii) a statement of contested matters of fact and law; (iv) a list of witnesses the Prosecutor intends to call, with among other things a summary of the facts on which each witness will testify; (v) a list of exhibits the Prosecutor intends to offer stating where possible whether the defence has any objection as to authenticity. The pre-trial judge may convene one or more status conferences, where measures are taken to ensure expeditious preparation for trial and in addition the status of the accused is reviewed.

Once the Prosecutor has completed all his filings and all the motions have been disposed of, the pre-trial judge submits to the Trial Chamber a *complete file* (which however may not be compared to the 'case file' of inquisitorial systems, where the court finds the evidentiary material for both the prosecution and the defence). This file includes all the documents filed by the parties, transcripts of the status conferences, and minutes of meetings held by the judge with the parties. This file enables the Trial Chamber to hold a *Pre-Trial Conference* where (if the Trial Chamber 'considers that an excessive number of witnesses are being called to prove the same facts', Rule 73 *bis* (C) of the ICTY RPE), it may call upon the Prosecutor to reduce the number of witnesses he intends to call, or to shorten the estimated length of the examination-in-chief for some witnesses.

With the assistance of the aforementioned 'complete file' the Trial Chamber is thus in a position to commence trial.

In the ICC system pre-trial proceedings unfold before the Pre-Trial Chamber. The Statute allots extensive powers to this Chamber. After the arrest of the accused and his surrender to the Court, the Chamber must satisfy itself that the accused has been informed of both the charges against him and his rights under the Statute (Article 60(1)). He has among other things the right to apply for interim measures pending trial. In particular, he may apply for provisional release. In this phase the Prosecutor may amend the charges after giving notice to the accused and provided that the Pre-Trial Chamber has authorized such amendment. It is also in this phase that the Prosecutor must proceed to the disclosure of the 'evidentiary' materials he has collected (this matter is regulated by Rules 76–84).

Interestingly, under Rule 121(10) the Registry must keep a 'full and accurate record' of the proceedings before the Chamber, 'including all documents transmitted to the Chamber', hence also the 'supporting material' on which the charges preferred by the Prosecutor are based. The Prosecutor, the person subject to an arrest warrant or to a summons, and victims and their legal representatives are entitled to consult this record. The record is then transmitted to the Trial Chamber before trial proceedings open (Rule 131). It would seem that in this way the ICC system goes much further than the two ad hoc Tribunals in making available 'evidentiary' material to the Trial Chamber before the trial. Thus, it would seem, an important feature of the inquisitorial system has been to some extent incorporated into the ICC procedure.

(B) TRIAL PROCEEDINGS

22.6 CASE PRESENTATION

In the ICTY and ICTR system normally the trial begins with an *opening statement of the Prosecutor*, where he sets out the main elements of charges and outlines his case. The defence may, if it so wishes, also make an opening statement, although normally defence counsel prefer to make such a statement when the Prosecutor's case rests, that is at the beginning of the defence case (Rule 84 ICTY RPE).

The accused has the right to make a statement 'under the control of the Trial Chamber', without taking an oath. This statement is not testimony, hence the accused is not examined and cross-examined upon it. However, the Trial Chamber may decide to give it probative value (Rule 84 *bis* ICTY RPE). Allowing the accused to make a statement that is not a piece of evidence is an exception to the normal scheme of the adversarial system, where the accused may, if he so wishes, give evidence on his own behalf, but is then examined and cross-examined. The IMT Charter, in Article 24(j), had already envisaged this departure; however, that rule provided for the defendants to make a statement at the end of the trial, after the closing statements of the prosecution and defence—this was of course in addition to their testifying as witnesses. (Thus defendants effectively spoke *after* the case was closed, that is, after the trial had finished and all the evidence had been produced; so the IMT could probably tolerate this departure because in effect it was happening 'outside the trial proper'.) The reason behind this departure from most common law systems is that this is the only opportunity for defendants freely—that is, without being cross-examined—to set out their general views and explain their motivations or why they consider they are innocent.

The Prosecutor then presents his case. To this end, he calls witnesses and produces exhibits. Witnesses are first examined-in-chief by the Prosecutor, then cross-examined by defence counsel, and subsequently re-examined by the Prosecutor.[7]

The usual rules on the nature and limits of *examination-in-chief* (or direct examination, in American terminology), *cross-examination*, and *re-examination* (or redirect,

[7] As happens in the practice of some common law countries (but not in England, where it is strictly forbidden), also in international criminal tribunals before examining witnesses in court, each party is entitled to undertake 'witness preparation', that is, to rehearse the examination-in-chief, by asking the witness all the necessary questions. In this way the whole testimony is rehearsed. It is commonly stated that, as a rule of thumb, a prosecutor or defence counsel should never ask a question in examination-in-chief or cross-examination without previously knowing the answer. This practice, which could sound odd or unfair to

in American terminology) apply. Thus, in examining witnesses in chief the Prosecutor or the Defence must refrain from asking *leading questions* (that is, questions that suggest the answer, such as: 'Was the car yellow?'), whereas such questions may be put in cross-examination.[8]

The traditional reason behind the prohibition of leading questions in examination-in-chief is that in criminal trials held in common law countries the jury is required to hear the full information, or the account of events, directly from the witness, without any interference from prosecutors or defence counsel. In short, jurors are expected to hear information about facts not through the prosecutor or defence counsel but as directly as possible from the witness. In contrast, in cross-examination the prosecutor and defence counsel are allowed to ask leading questions so as to put their case to the witness and to cast doubt on the acceptability or credibility of the witness.

However, judges sitting on international courts tend to be more flexible or at any rate not bound by strict rules. They may therefore allow leading questions in examination-in-chief, thereby overruling objections by the other party, if they consider that such questions may justifiably be put in the interests of justice, in particular to speed up the proceedings. Even in common law systems, leading questions are allowed where the witness is dealing with matters that are not contentious, or are agreed between the parties, and it seems appropriate to apply a similar rule to international tribunals.

Cross-examination 'shall be limited to the subject-matter of the evidence-in-chief and matters affecting the credibility of the witness and, where the witness is able to give evidence relevant to the case for the cross-examining party, to the subject matter of that case' (Rule 90(H)(i) of the ICTY RPE). A further requirement is set out for cross-examination: under Rule 90(H)(ii) of the ICTY RPE,

> In the cross-examination of a witness who is able to give evidence relevant to the case for the cross-examining party, counsel shall put to that witness the nature of the case of the party for whom that counsel appears which is in contradiction of the evidence given by the witness.

lawyers in civil law countries, is among other things aimed at: (i) focusing, in the questions and answers, on the key issues of testimony, (ii) reducing the witness's anxiety about his testimony in court and at the same time building in him a feeling of security and confidence, and (iii) putting the witness in a proper frame of mind to be effective in his testimony or with a view to avoiding receiving a surprising answer which could be damaging to one's client (especially in cross-examination, although in examination-in-chief it could be partly also a way of making the witness comfortable). It is also important to 'control' the witness, for instance asking short, specific questions, so that the witness does not go ranting off on other subjects.

Often, prosecutors and defence counsel also simulate cross-examination, so as to better prepare the witness to questions from the other side.

In *Kupreškić and others* (*Decision on communications between the parties and their witnesses*) the Trial Chamber ruled that, once a witness had made the 'solemn declaration' provided for in Rule 90(1) he could no longer communicate with the party that had called him, except with the leave of the Chamber (at 3).

[8] A legal provision on leading questions can be found in Rule 611(C) of the 2001 US Federal Rules of Evidence ('Leading questions should not be used on the direct examination of a witness except as may be necessary to develop the witness' testimony. Ordinarily leading questions should be permitted on cross-examination. When a party calls a hostile witness, an adverse party, or a witness identified with an adverse party, interrogation may be by leading questions').

This is an important requirement. For example, a witness may testify that he saw the accused commit a killing and the defence does not put to the witness in cross-examination that he could have been mistaken; then in his closing speech the defence argues that the witness could have been mistaken as it was night-time at the time of the killing. There is then a basic unfairness. The witness should have been given the opportunity to respond to that suggestion when he was on the witness stand, when he might have been able to give a convincing rebuttal (e.g. 'Nonsense, it was broad daylight' or 'But I was standing only a metre away').

A party may also ask the Trial Chamber to authorize questions relating to additional matters, that is, matters not raised in examination-in-chief.[9]

Judges may at any stage put questions to the witnesses (Rule 85(B) ICTY RPE). In the practice of the ICTY, if judges ask questions at the end of re-examination and these questions are not directly related to matters raised in examination-in-chief or cross-examination, then the parties are authorized to examine and cross-examine the witness on those specific matters.

Generally speaking, judges have broad powers in directing the examination of witnesses. Their guiding principle is that they must conduct business in the interest of justice so as to ensure a fair trial. They therefore enjoy considerable latitude. They exercise their powers by ruling on possible objections by the counter-party to specific questions put by the Prosecutor or defence counsel, as the case may be. Also, and more generally, they direct the case presentation by deciding what measures should be taken to facilitate the testimony of vulnerable witnesses, by ruling on the admissibility or relevance of evidence, controlling the manner of questioning to avoid any harassment or intimidation of the witness, and by deciding on written or oral motions submitted by the parties with respect to the questioning of witnesses.[10]

After the close of the Prosecution's case, the pre-trial judge orders the defence to file a list of the witnesses it intends to call, with a summary of the facts on which each witness will testify and the estimated length of time required for each witness, plus a list of exhibits (Rule 65 *ter* (G) of the ICTY RPE). In addition, the Trial Chamber may hold a Pre-Defence Conference, where it may call upon the defence to reduce the number of witnesses it intends to call to prove the same facts or to shorten the estimated length of the examination-in-chief for some witnesses (Rule 73 *ter* ICTY RPE). The defence then makes an opening statement and calls witnesses, who are questioned in accordance with the rules set forth above, and may of course also produce exhibits.

At the end of the defence case, the Prosecutor may present *evidence in rebuttal*, then

[9] Under Rule 90(H)(iii) ICTY RPE, 'The Trial Chamber may, in the exercise of its discretion, permit enquiry into additional matters'. See also ICTY, *Decision in Kupreškić and others on limitation of scope of cross-examination of character witnesses*, at 2.

[10] Under Rule 90(F) of the ICTY RPE, 'The Trial Chamber shall exercise control over the mode and order of interrogating witnesses and presenting evidence so as to (i) make the interrogation and presentation effective for the ascertainment of the truth; and (ii) avoid needless consumption of time'.

the defence may present *evidence in rejoinder*, and the Court may have evidence ordered by it to be presented (*court evidence*). Normally witnesses called by the court are questioned first by the judges, then cross-examined by the Prosecutor and subsequently by defence counsel; this sequence is established in the interest of the defence, which has thus the opportunity to first hear the questioning by the judges and the prosecution. The Court may then re-examine the witnesses, with the usual caveat that if in so doing it raises matters not previously considered in examination or cross-examination, the Prosecutor and the Defence have the right to cross-examine on such matters.

Once all the evidence has been presented, the Prosecutor makes a *closing argument*, followed by a closing statement by the Defence. In these arguments both parties, in addition to summing up their appraisal of the evidence and setting out their main arguments on points of fact and law, are *obliged* to address sentencing matters in their closing speeches (ICTY Rule 86(C)).[11]

A similar system is envisaged for the ICC. Under Rule 141(2) of the ICC, 'the defence shall always have the opportunity to speak last'. Furthermore, it has wisely been provided that matters relating to sentencing be separately addressed by the parties, before the end of trial, in 'additional hearings' (see Article 76 and Rule 143).

22.7 RULES OF EVIDENCE

The most fundamental principle relating to the taking of evidence in international trials is common to all systems based on the adversarial model and is indeed inherent in this model. Under this principle any written or oral testimony, documents, or other piece of documentation only become evidence *if admitted in court* after being the subject of arguments by the parties. In other words, no evidence exists outside court proceedings. Also affidavits and any exhibit or evidentiary material may only become a piece of evidence after being presented in a court hearing by the party concerned, being discussed or agreed between the parties, and declared admissible by the court.

A second fundamental principle, which is not shared with common law systems and is unique to international proceedings, is that *courts are not bound by strict and 'technical' rules of evidence* but enjoy great flexibility and should be guided, rather than by formal standards, by general principles of fairness.

That in international trials rules of evidence should be simplified as much as

[11] This rule has been much attacked by the defence, who say: how can we address sentencing matters when (a) our position at that point is that the accused is completely innocent ('Your Honours, my client is completely innocent, but if you find him guilty, please bear in mind that he only beat the victims with his fists and not with a stick'!), and (b) we do not know what factual findings the Chamber will make. It is like the old schoolboy plea, when charged with breaking the window in the headmaster's study: (i) first, there is no witness in the headmaster's study, (ii) if there is a window, it is not broken, (iii) if it is broken, I did not do it, (iv) if I did it, it was an accident. This does not sound very convincing as a closing speech—the protestation of innocence is undercut by what sounds like admissions by the accused.

possible was first proposed in 1945 by the US delegate to the London Conference. In illustrating paragraphs 17 and 18 of the American draft of the Proposed Agreement[12] to the representatives of the other three Powers, Justice Robert H. Jackson, the US representative, stated:

> We do not want technical rules of evidence designed for jury trials to be used in this case to cut down what is really and fairly of probative value, and so we propose to lay down as a part of the statute [of the future IMT] that utmost liberality shall be used . . . The idea may have more significance to British and American lawyers than it does to Continental lawyers.[13]

As provided in Article 19 of the IMT Charter, an international court may adopt and apply 'to the greatest possible extent expeditious and non-technical procedure', and admit 'any evidence which it deems to have probative value'. This regulation of the administration of evidence is premised on the notions that: (i) there is no jury consisting of lay people without any expert knowledge; the court is made up of professional judges, who are in a position to appraise the probative value of each piece of evidence; (ii) the specific features of international criminal proceedings require courts to be flexible and to be guided primarily by the need to ensure a fair and expeditious trial. It follows from this principle that, among other things, a Trial Chamber 'may exclude evidence if its probative value is substantially outweighed by the need to ensure a fair trial' (Rule 89(D) of the ICTY RPE).[14]

Within this general context, some specific rules on certain matters have evolved and may be held to be customary in nature; consequently, under general principles of international law, they may be derogated from by courts if their statutes or rules of procedure and evidence so require (see *supra*, 2.4.1–3).

In international criminal proceedings it now seems accepted that the standard of proof should be that judges must be convinced *beyond a reasonable doubt* of the guilt of the accused before they may convict. This standard (on which see *infra*) is laid down in Rule 87(A) of the ICTY RPE and in Article 66(3) of the ICC Statute. It has also been upheld in the ICTY case law.[15] Courts are authorized to exclude evidence that has been gathered in breach of fundamental principles of law, for instance in violation of fundamental human rights safeguards (for example, evidence obtained from a person who has previously been subjected to inhuman or degrading treatment), or by dubious or devious methods (for example, by surreptitiously obtaining the piece of evidence at issue).[16]

[12] International Conference on Military Trials, at 59.

[13] Ibid., at 83.

[14] In *Blaškić* a Trial Chamber insisted on the general principle of liberal admission of evidence: 'The principle embodied by the case-law of the Trial Chamber on the issue is the one of extensive admissibility of evidence—questions of credibility or authenticity being determined according to the weight given to each of the materials by the Judges at the appropriate time' (§34).

[15] See for instance *Jelisić* (§108), *Kunarac* (*Decision on motion for acquittal*) (§3), *Kvočka* (*Decision on defence motions for acquittal*) (§12), *Delalić and others* (*Appeal*) (§434), *Jelisić* (*Appeal*) (§§34–7).

[16] As stated in Rule 95 of the ICTY RPE, 'No evidence shall be admissible if obtained by methods which cast substantial doubt on its reliability or if its admission is antithetical to, and would seriously damage, the integrity of the proceedings.' See also Article 69(7) of the ICC Statute.

Other rules are designed to expedite trial proceedings and avoid waste of time. For instance, international courts may take *judicial notice* of facts of common knowledge or of public documents (such as UN records, records of other proceedings of the same court, etc.). That means that neither party is required to provide evidence that such facts occurred or that the documents are authentic (for a case where the court took judicial notice of UN reports, see for instance *Akayesu*, §157). Furthermore, instead of calling expert witnesses, their statements may be filed with the court, so that, if the other party does not object to the statement and does not wish to cross-examine the expert witness, the statement is admitted into evidence without calling the witness to testify in person (see Rule 92 *bis* of the ICTY RPE).[17] In addition *affidavits* (that is, formal written statements signed by a witness in front of a public official or in accordance with another procedure provided for in national legislation) may be admitted into evidence. They may be so admitted, but only: (i) in order to corroborate the testimony of a witness who appears in court, (ii) if the affidavit is filed prior to the testimony of that witness, and (iii) if the opposing party does not object to the filing of such affidavit.[18]

There are also rules on evidence relating to *cases of sexual assault*. In such cases, in light of current practices, rules of evidence tend to protect the victim. Consequently: (i) no corroboration of the victim's testimony is required; (ii) consent of the victim is not allowed as a defence if the victim was subjected to or threatened with or had reason to fear violence, duress, detention, or psychological oppression, or reasonably believed that if she or he did not submit, another person might be so subjected, threatened, or put in fear; (iii) the prior sexual conduct of the victim may not be admitted into evidence (see Rule 96 of the ICTY RPE).

Rules also require that *communications between lawyer and client* be treated as 'privileged'. Consequently they require that such communications are not subject to disclosure at trial, with some exceptions (if the client consents to such disclosure or has voluntarily disclosed the content of such communications to a third party, and such party then gives evidence of that disclosure); see Rule 97 of the ICTY RPE.[19]

Finally, special rules deal with the delicate question of *evidence affecting national security of States*. Plainly, in international trials, particularly when crimes linked to armed conflict are at stake, important evidence may be in the possession of military officers or other State agents who rely upon sources affecting national security. Courts have therefore to strike a balance between the need to respect the legitimate security concerns of States and the demands of justice. This in particular applies to States

[17] See on this Rule the Trial Chamber's Decision in *Milošević* on *Prosecutor's request to have written statements admitted*, §§4–30, the decision in *Milošević* on *Prosecution application to admit evidence pursuant to Rule 92 bis without cross-examination*, at 2. See also the Trial Chamber's decision in *Galić* on the *Prosecution request for admission of Rule 92 bis statements*, at 4–19, as well as on *Admission into evidence of a written statement by a deceased witness*, at 2–6.

[18] On the legal value of affidavits and the need to consider them carefully see among other cases, *Josef Kramer and others* (the *Belsen* trial), at 636.

[19] On this matter see the decision of 27 November 1996 in *Tadić* (*Decision on prosecution motion for production of defence witness statements*), at 2, and Separate Opinion of Judge Stephen, at 3–7.

when the documents raising national security concerns are in their custody: as the ICTY Prosecutor rightly argued in her Brief in *Blaškić* (*Judgment on the request of Croatia*), to grant a State a blanket right to withhold, for security purposes, documents necessary for trial might jeopardize the very function of an international criminal tribunal and 'defeat its essential object and purpose' (§§70–3).[20]

The ICC Statute contains a provision (Article 72) which regulates the matter in detail. It emphasizes the need for the parties concerned to take 'all reasonable steps . . . to resolve the matter through cooperative means', so as to achieve solutions acceptable to both the parties and the Court. If solutions cannot be agreed and the Court holds that the documents are relevant and necessary for establishing the guilt or innocence of the accused, provision is made for such measures as hearings in camera and *ex parte*, the drawing of inferences, as well as orders for disclosure.

A related problem may arise when the *source of information is confidential* and a witness provides documents or information only on condition that the source not be disclosed. This is a frequent occurrence in the case of international criminal proceedings, for intelligence organizations may hold documents and other information of great relevance to a trial, but may not be prepared to 'go public'. In these cases, the possibility that the person could be compelled by the court to disclose his source may prompt him to refuse to testify. The ICTY RPE takes this possibility into consideration in Rule 70.[21]

Regard is also taken of some categories of potential witnesses who could not testify without breaching their official duties of confidentiality (this in particular applies to staff members of the International Committee of the Red Cross). These staff members, if called by either party to testify, may decline to do so, and the court will not compel them to give evidence. This right for officials of the ICRC, envisaged in *Simić*[22] is formally set out in Rule 73(4–6) of the ICC RPE.

[20] In *Blaškić* (*Judgment on the request of Croatia*) the Appeals Chamber suggested some general criteria for the situation where the documents are in a State's custody. In its view: (i) the Court must establish whether the State is acting in good faith; (ii) (Judge Karibi-Whyte dissenting) the State at issue may be invited to submit the relevant documents to the scrutiny of one judge designated by the Trial Chamber; this measure 'should increase the confidence of the State that its national security secrets will not accidentally become public'; (iii) if the documents need to be translated into one of the working languages of the Tribunal, such translation may be carried out by the State itself; (iv) the documents will then be scrutinized by the judges in camera, in *ex parte* proceedings, and no transcript is made of the hearing; (v) the documents considered not relevant will be returned to the State, whereas those that are material to the case may be redacted by the State concerned. The Chamber added that in exceptional cases a State may be allowed, subject to some stringent conditions, to withhold documents of great relevance to national security while at the same time of scant relevance to the trial proceedings (§68).

[21] This Rule provides that: (i) the Trial Chamber may not order the party to produce additional evidence received from the entity or person providing the initial information; (ii) it may not summon (or compel to appear in court) the person or a representative of the entity for the purpose of obtaining that additional evidence; in addition, (iii) if the party concerned calls a witness to introduce the information at issue, the Trial Chamber may not compel him to answer questions relating to the information or its origin, if the witness declines to answer on grounds of confidentiality. However, (iv) the Rule in no way detracts from the power of the Trial Chamber to exclude evidence 'if its probative value is substantially outweighed by the need to ensure a fair trial'.

[22] *Simić* (*Decision on the prosecution motion under Rule 73 for a ruling concerning the testimony of a witness*), 27 July 1999, §§34–80.

22.8 CONTROL OF PROCEEDINGS

International courts, like any court, have an inherent power to control their proceedings. This among other things entails that Trial Chambers are authorized to decide when an exception should be made to the basic principle whereby proceedings are public. Whenever the need to protect victims or witnesses, public order or morality, security, or the interests of justice so require, a Trial Chamber may, either on its own initiative or at the request of either party, order that a hearing or part thereof be held in closed session (see e.g. Rule 79 of the ICTY RPE). It may also order that, for the sake of protecting witnesses, witnesses give testimony though image- or voice-altering devices or closed circuit television (see, for instance, Rule 75(B) of the ICTY RPE).

In addition, the Trial Chamber may order that a person be excluded from the courtroom whenever this proves necessary to ensure a fair trial to the accused or to maintain the dignity and decorum of the proceedings; it can also order the removal of the accused if he engages in disruptive conduct (see for instance Rule 80 of the ICTY RPE).

The Court may also initiate *contempt proceedings* against a witness when he or she 'contumaciously refuses or fails to answer a question' (Rule 77(A) of the ICTY RPE).

In the ICC system the powers of the Court to control proceedings are regulated by Article 64. Detailed provisions are contained in Article 70 on the issue of offences against the administration of justice and in the relevant Rules of the ICC RPE implementing or spelling out the Statute's provisions.

22.9 DELIBERATIONS

When both parties have completed their presentation of the case, the Court declares the hearings closed and retires to deliberate in private.

A major issue is that of the *standard of proof* required for a court to determine whether the accused is guilty. It is common knowledge that in common law systems the standard of proof varies depending on whether the proceedings are criminal or civil, whereas in countries of Roman-Germanic tradition the standard of proof in criminal cases is rather loose, but is formally pre-established by law for civil litigation.

In common law countries the standard normally required in criminal proceedings is that facts must be proved 'beyond a reasonable doubt'. This means that the facts must be proved in such a way that a court satisfies itself without hesitation that the accused is guilty; in other words, the court must find that the accused is guilty without entertaining a doubt that would cause any reasonable and prudent person to hesitate before reaching a definite conclusion. As the European Court of Human Rights put it in *Barberà, Messegué and Jabardo*, 'any doubt should benefit the accused' (§77). In 1947 Lord Denning set out a clear definition of the standard of proof under discussion in *Miller* v. *Minister of Pensions*. He pointed out that:

the degree of cogency as is required in a criminal case before an accused person is found guilty . . . is well settled. It need not reach certainty, but it must carry a high degree of probability. Proof beyond reasonable doubt does not mean proof beyond the shadow of a doubt. The law would fail to protect the community if it admitted fanciful possibilities to deflect the course of justice. If the evidence is so strong against a man as to leave only a remote possibility in his favour which can be dismissed with the sentence 'of course it is possible, but not in the least probable', the case is proved beyond reasonable doubt, but nothing short of that will suffice. (At 3.)

In contrast, less stringent requirements are provided for in non-criminal proceedings, that is, civil actions, for instance tort cases: issues must be proved 'by a preponderance of the evidence' (that is, evidence showing, as a whole, that the fact sought to be proved is more probable than not, evidence that is more convincing than that offered in opposition to it), or, under a test requiring a higher degree of proof, 'by clear and convincing evidence' (that is, by evidence that is clear and explicit and is sufficient to make out a prima facie case). The upholding of different standards of proof for criminal and civil proceedings accounts for the possibility that trial proceedings may be terminated with the acquittal of the defendant and be followed by proceedings for damages in tort law (as for instance in the famous *O. J. Simpson* case). It should however be noted that in some instances a rule different from that prevailing is applied even in criminal proceedings: for instance, under Rule 850(a)(b) of the US Uniform Code of Military Justice, 'The accused has the burden of proving the defense of lack of mental responsibility by clear and convincing evidence'.[23]

Also in many countries of continental Europe and most other civil law countries the law draws a distinction between private law proceedings and criminal proceedings. For the former category the law defines both the classes of admissible evidence and the requirements for their admissibility, and their respective probative value. In contrast, in criminal proceedings, the principle of the free evaluation of evidence obtains: the court freely evaluates the evidence and freely decides what weight to give to each piece of evidence. What matters is that the judge reaches the 'conviction' that the accused is guilty or innocent.[24]

23 The standard of proof, even under Rule 850, is still 'beyond a reasonable doubt', e.g. if the accused is charged with murder under the US Uniform Code, the prosecution will have to prove that he committed the murder beyond a reasonable doubt. The question is—what happens if the accused then turns around and says, yes I killed intentionally, but I was insane or otherwise deranged at the time? It would be very hard for the prosecution to prove '*beyond a reasonable doubt*' that the person is not insane. So what the law does instead is put a burden on the defence to prove that he was insane. But it would equally be too harsh on a defendant to require him to prove '*beyond a reasonable doubt*' that he was insane. Insanity is a tricky question and no certainties exist. Therefore the law imposes on the defendant this intermediate standard of 'clear and convincing evidence'. This is known as a reversible burden of proof and is often imposed for 'special defences'.

Interestingly, the ICC Statute forbids any reversing of burdens of proof. See Article 67(1)(i) of the Rome Statute.

24 For instance, in French law Articles 1315 ff. and 1341–8 of the Civil Code set out the modes of evidence and the probative force of each class of admissible evidence in civil proceedings, whereas Articles 353, 427, and 536 of the Code of Criminal Procedure lay down the standards of the '*intime conviction*' of the judges and

It would seem that the two standards of proof required in common law and civil law countries respectively (the 'beyond reasonable doubt' test and the test of the '*intime conviction*' of the judge) are not identical, the latter being more loose and, it would seem, broader. (Other commentators[25] have advanced a contrary view.)[26]

The judgment given at the ICTY, the ICTR, and the ICC must provide a statement of the facts as found by the court and the legal reasons for its findings. Judges who do not concur with the majority may append to the judgment their separate or dissenting opinions. On this score, criminal courts uphold the system prevailing in both common law systems and international 'civil' (that is, interstate) courts such as the International Court of Justice.

22.10 SENTENCING

Whenever sentencing does not constitute a procedure per se as a result of the accused entering a guilty plea, the sentence is part of the verdict.

Penalties are not provided for in an accepted tariff of penalties. International provisions only rule out the death sentence. Otherwise they provide very general indication to courts. For instance, the ICTY Statute provides that 'in determining the terms of imprisonment, the Trial Chambers shall have recourse to the general practice

provide that the court need not explain why they have attached value to one piece of evidence rather than to another. Article 192(1) of the Italian Code of Criminal Procedure is stricter: 'The judge appraises evidence and gives account in the judgment's legal grounds of the conclusions reached and the criteria adopted'.

Arguably the provisions in French law on standards of proof in criminal trials do not force the jury or the court to convict a person whenever a certain amount of evidence is available (hence the word 'intime'); on the other hand, as a matter of principle, they may, in reaching a decision of guilty, use all evidence available, unless otherwise provided by law, and attach to it the value it deserves in their eyes (this is called in German legal literature '*freie Beweiswürdiging*').

In the Netherlands and Germany the courts must be convinced beyond reasonable doubt.

25 For, instance, Pradel (at 474). Indeed, the question arises of whether one can really have an '(*intime*) *conviction*' if one is not convinced beyond reasonable doubt that the accused is guilty.

26 In *Heinz Heck and others* (the *Peleus* trial) the Judge Advocate in his summing up explained the 'beyond a reasonable doubt' test as follows: 'A reasonable doubt does not mean some fanciful or imaginary doubt such as a weak mind may grasp if it is struggling to avoid an honest conclusion on evidence that is plain. It means the kind of doubt that might affect you in the conduct of some important affair of your own. If, having considered this case as I know you will, most anxiously, you are left with a reasonable doubt such as I have described, then it is your duty to give to any accused person as to whom you entertain such a doubt the benefit of it and to acquit him. If, on the other hand, the evidence that you have heard drives your minds to the conclusion that he is guilty, it is equally your duty to say so without regard to the consequences of this finding' (at 123). In *Wolfgang Zeuss and others* (the *Natzweiler* trial) the Judge Advocate, in his summing up, stated that 'reasonable doubt means just such an inquiry as you would make into any affairs of your own in your everyday life. Probably there are few things in the world about which we can be utterly and completely certain. In most things there is some doubt—some little doubt—in one's mind, but you are not obliged to take into account any sensitive doubt—anything which would not affect your judgment in you own affairs. What you have to do is to be satisfied beyond reasonable doubt. That means you must not be left, having decided that a person is guilty, feeling that perhaps you were wrong about that' (at 199).

In its decision of 6 December 1988 in *Barberà, Messegué and Jabardo* v. *Spain*, the ECHR held that 'all reasonable doubts must be silenced' (Series A146, §77). See also Safferling, at 259–60.

regarding prison sentences in the courts of the former Yugoslavia' (Article 24(1)). The ICTR Statute provides similarly in Article 23(1), referring of course to the courts of Rwanda. Articles 77 and 78 of the ICC Statute, although less terse, do not provide any definite guideline to the ICC Trial Chambers with regard to the determination of sentence.

It is therefore for each Trial Chamber to establish the prison sentence it considers appropriate, in view of the gravity of the crime.

In *Delalić and others* (*Appeal*) (§806) and in *Aleksovski* (*Appeal*) (§185) the ICTY Appeals Chamber held that *retribution* and *deterrence* ought to constitute the main guiding principles in sentencing for international crimes. Trial Chambers have normally taken the same approach (see, for instance, *Furundžija* (§288)). Thus, for example, in *Todorović* (*Sentencing judgment*) an ICTY Trial Chamber took the view that those two notions or, as it termed them, 'purposive considerations', merely formed the backdrop against which the sentence of an individual accused must be determined (§28).[27]

In other cases, ICTY Trial Chambers have also considered *reprobation* and *stigmatization* as among the main purposes of sentencing: see, for instance, *Erdemović* (*Sentencing judgment*) (§65), *Furundžija* (§289), and *Blaškić* (§§763–4).[28]

In some cases Trial Chambers have also mentioned the purpose of *rehabilitating the accused*, particularly when he was of young age.[29]

27 The Chamber went on to say that the principle of retribution 'must be understood as reflecting a fair and balanced approach to the exaction of punishment for wrongdoing. This means that the penalty imposed must be proportionate to the wrongdoing: in other words that the punishment be made to fit the crime' (§29). As for deterrence, it held that it meant that 'the penalties imposed by the International Tribunal must, in general, have sufficient deterrent value to ensure that those who would consider committing similar crimes will be dissuaded from doing so'. The Chamber went on to say that, 'Accordingly, while the Chamber recognises the importance of deterrence as a general consideration in sentencing, it will not treat deterrence as a distinct factor in determining sentence in this case' (§30).

28 In *Erdemović* (*Sentencing judgment*) the ICTY Trial Chamber held that: 'The International Tribunal sees public reprobation and stigmatisation by the international community, which would thereby express its indignation over heinous crimes and denounce the perpetrators, as one of the essential functions for a prison sentence for a crime against humanity' (§65).

29 For instance, in *Furundžija* (§291) an ICTY Trial Chamber stated that none of the various purposes of punishment such as retribution, deterrence, and stigmatization was to detract 'from the Trial Chamber's support for rehabilitative programmes in which the accused may participate while serving his sentence; the Trial Chamber is especially mindful of the age of the accused in this case'.

In the same case the Trial Chamber also stated that it was to be guided in its determination of the sentence by the principle proclaimed as early as 1764 by Cesare Beccaria (*An Essay on Crimes and Punishment*, 1775, reprinted (Brookline Village, Ma: Brandon Press Inc., 1983)), namely that 'punishment should not be harsh, but must be inevitable'. It went on to state that 'It is the infallibility of punishment, rather than the severity of the sanction, which is the tool for retribution, stigmatisation and deterrence. This is particularly the case for the international tribunal; penalties are made more onerous by its international stature, moral authority and impact upon world public opinion, and this punitive effect must be borne in mind when assessing the suitable length of sentence' (§290). This proposition, while it seems correct in that it stresses the particular stigma attaching to punishment by an international tribunal as well as the need for the penalties not to be excessively harsh, could appear questionable in another respect: it does not seem that inevitability of punishment is a major feature of international courts; these courts must of necessity concentrate on major instances of gross violations of international criminal law and therefore cannot but be selective; it follows that in many instances perpetrators will not be punished, unless they are brought before national courts.

Some courts have tried to set out some general considerations warranting their sentencing policy. For instance, in *Nadler and others* a British Court of Appeal acting under Control Council Law no. 10 stated that:

Upon the conviction of any person of a crime against humanity under Law 10, a capital sentence is, in the opinion of this Court, the appropriate sentence where such person has unlawfully and maliciously killed another or where the inhumane conduct of such person has materially contributed to the death of another. While in cases that fall within neither of these two classes a sentence of death will usually be excessive, there may, nevertheless, be other cases where the conduct of the convicted person is so grossly or persistently inhumane, on such a scale or so serious in its consequences that a capital sentence is proper although it is not proved that such conduct has either caused or contributed to a death. (At 134–6.)

It should be emphasized that the Statute of the ICC makes much headway also in the area of penalties. For, in addition to providing for imprisonment, it also stipulates, in Article 77(2), that besides imprisonment the Court may order 'a fine under the criteria provided for in the Rules of Procedure and Evidence' and 'a forfeiture of proceeds, property and assets derived directly or indirectly from the crime, without prejudice to the rights of bona fide third parties'. The Court may order that money and other property collected through fines or forfeiture be transferred to a trust fund established by decision of the Assembly of States Parties for the benefit of the victims or their families (Article 79).

22.11 REPARATION OR COMPENSATION TO VICTIMS

The ICTY and ICTR Statutes only provide for the right of victims to *restitution*. Articles 24(3) of the ICTY Statute and 23(3) of the ICTR Statute stipulate that in addition to imprisonment, a Trial Chamber 'may order the return of any property and proceeds acquired by criminal conduct, including by means of duress, to their rightful owners'. Nonetheless, the Rules of Procedure and Evidence make allowance for compensation.[30]

[30] Rule 105 of the ICTY RPE regulates restitution in detail. It stipulates that after a judgment of conviction containing a specific finding of unlawful taking of property, at the request of the Prosecutor or *proprio motu* the Trial Chamber may hold a special hearing on the question of restitution. If such property or its proceeds are in the hands of third parties not otherwise connected with the crime, they will be summoned before the Trial Chamber and given the opportunity to justify their claim to the property or its proceeds. The Trial Chamber, if it is able to determine the rightful owner 'on the balance of probabilities', orders its restitution or the restitution of its proceeds. If instead it is unable to determine ownership, it requests the competent national authorities to do so, and orders thereafter the restitution of the property or of its proceeds.

Rule 106, on compensation to victims, cannot of course grant to victims a right to compensation, absent any provision on the matter in the Statute. Nonetheless it provides that the Registrar shall transmit to the relevant national authorities the judgment finding the accused guilty of a crime that has caused injury to a victim. It will be for the victim to claim compensation before the competent national court. For this purpose, 'the judgment of the Tribunal shall be final and binding as to the criminal responsibility of the convicted person for such injury'. (The final and binding nature of the Tribunal's findings seems to be an aspect of the ICTY's primacy.)

The ICC Statute is more favourable to victims. First, in Article 75 it provides for various forms of reparations (restitution, compensation, and rehabilitation). Secondly, as pointed out above, Article 79 stipulates that the Assembly of States Parties shall establish a trust fund for the benefit of the victims and their families. Rules 94–9 of the ICC RPE regulate the matter in some detail.

It appears from Article 75 and the Rules just mentioned that the proceedings for determining reparations may be initiated either by a victim, under Rule 94, or by the Trial Chamber on its own motion, pursuant to Article 75(1) and Rule 95. Victims and the convicted persons may take part in the proceedings and be heard by the court. The Trial Chamber may appoint experts to assist it in determining the damage, loss, or injury and suggesting 'the appropriate types and modalities of reparation'. Interestingly, under Rule 97(2), 'The Court shall invite, as appropriate, victims or their legal representatives, the convicted person as well as interested persons and interested States to make observations on the reports of experts'. The Trial Chamber grants reparation by ordering an 'award against a convicted person'.

(C) APPELLATE AND REVIEW PROCEEDINGS

22.12 GENERAL

The right of defendants to appeal against conviction or sentence is normally regarded as a fundamental human right. Subject to some exceptions, it is basically predicated on the notion of fair trial. At present this right is laid down in numerous international treaties on human rights as well as the Statutes of international courts. (Before the blossoming of the human rights approach, the right was not considered fundamental, as evidenced by the fact that the Statutes of the IMT and the Tokyo Tribunal did not contemplate a right of appeal.) Alongside this right in some legal systems provision may also be made for the power of Prosecutors to appeal against acquittals. Clearly, here the rationale is no longer to reaffirm a fundamental human right, but rather to ensure the proper administration of justice, by enabling the Prosecutor to file an appeal to a higher court when he considers that the acquittal of the accused amounts to a miscarriage of justice.

The notion and purpose of appellate proceedings vary however in national systems (see *supra*, 20.2.10). Subject to a number of specifications and exceptions, in *civil law countries* these proceedings amount largely to a retrial by a court of appeal. Very often both law and facts are brought before this court, for the appellant may claim that the trial court has both misapplied or misunderstood the relevant law, and wrongly established the facts. Hence the court of appeal hears the case anew, if need be by admitting or calling the same or new witnesses, and confirms, reverses, or quashes the trial court's judgment or sentence. The right of appeal inures to both the convicted or sentenced and the Prosecutor, who may also appeal against sentence. (However usually any increase in the sentence by the appeals court, or *reformatio in pejus*, is only admitted within strict limits.)

In contrast, in most *common law countries* appellate proceedings do not lead to a retrial, for the appellate court consists of professional judges who may not substitute themselves for a jury, the only body entitled to make findings of fact. Hence appeals courts do not review the facts. Normally the court of appeal, without any jury, decides on the basis of the trial record. Only exceptionally does it receive evidence, provided it would have been admissible at trial and was not adduced at that stage (for instance, because it was not then available). The reason why courts of appeal only exceptionally hear evidence is that the jury is the sole trier of fact and all the relevant evidence must be put before, and evaluated by, the trial court. The court of appeal may dismiss the appeal, quash the judgment, or request a retrial by a trial court.

In addition appellate proceedings in common law jurisdictions normally exhibit two features designed to reduce the number of appeals and thus shorten the total length of proceedings. First, normally the Prosecutor may not appeal against acquittal. (It is felt that such an appeal would compromise the acquitted defendant's right to be tried by a jury.) Nor is he allowed to appeal against sentence. Secondly, subject to an exception to be mentioned below, the accused may not appeal automatically against conviction or sentence, but only if granted leave to appeal by a judge sitting on the appeals court. This applies to the vast majority of appeals, those made on grounds of *mixed law and fact* (for instance, that the trial judge issued wrong instructions to the jury, misdirecting it in his summing up about the elements of the offence). The purpose of requesting that the defendant be granted leave to appeal is to avoid frivolous, vexatious, or unmeritorious appeals: the single judge that pronounces upon the request for leave to appeal functions as a sort of filter, for he grants leave only if he holds that there is an arguable point in the appeal. However, no leave to appeal is required when the appellant challenges the conviction or sentence on the ground of *pure law*. (Examples include, that the indictment was defective on its face; that the trial court lacked jurisdiction to try the offence, because the offence had been committed abroad; that the facts and evidence relied upon by the prosecutor did not amount to the offence of which the appellant had been convicted; that a defence submission of no case to answer had been wrongly rejected by the judge; or that admissible evidence had been excluded, etc.) When appealing on the ground of pure law the appellant may bring the case before the court of appeal as of right.

In international criminal proceedings neither the common law system nor the civil law model has been upheld. Rather, a mixed system has been accepted, as we shall see below.

22.13 APPEALS AGAINST INTERLOCUTORY DECISIONS

International criminal courts, like their national counterparts, may issue interlocutory decisions, either on preliminary motions (for instance, those which challenge the jurisdiction of the court; see *supra*, 22.5) or on any other motion (for instance, motions for provisional release; see 22.5). Either party may lodge an appeal against such decisions (see Rule 72 of the ICTY RPE and of the ICTR RPE, as well as Article 82 of the ICC Statute).

In drafting the Rules of Procedure on appeals against interlocutory decisions, judges of the ICTY and the ICTR went through different stages. In a first phase they took a rather restrictive approach in providing for such interlocutory appeals; they subsequently broadened the range of cases where such appeals could be lodged; finally, faced with an increasing number of such appeals and fearing that they might unduly delay trial proceedings, they adopted a restrictive attitude aimed at significantly limiting the number of appeals likely to be filed.

Only for interlocutory decisions on jurisdiction does the appeal lie as of right. In all other cases the appellant must first request leave to appeal. A bench of three judges of the Appeals Chamber may grant or refuse leave, depending on whether the appellant has shown 'good cause' (see Rule 72(B) of the ICTY RPE; see also Rule 72 of the ICTR RPE).[31]

For some of these appeals, if leave to appeal is granted by the bench of three judges, the Appeals Chamber may decide to apply an 'expedited appeals procedure', which among other things involves that the appeal is determined entirely on the basis of: (i) the original records of the Trial Chamber; (ii) written submissions by each party, without a second exchange of briefs in reply; and (iii) without any hearing (see Rule 116 *bis* of the ICTY RPE and Rule 117 of the ICTR RPE).

Recently, judges amended Rule 73 of the ICTY RPE relating to motions (other than preliminary motions). They have provided that, to appeal against a Trial Chamber's decision on any such motion, it is necessary for the relevant Trial Chamber, upon request of a party, to 'certify' that the decision involves 'an issue that would significantly affect the fair and expeditious conduct of the proceedings or the outcome of the Trial, and for which . . . an immediate resolution by the Appeals Chamber may materially advance the proceedings'. The request must be submitted within seven days of the issuing of the decision. If the certification is granted, the relevant party may appeal to the Appeals Chamber without leave within seven days of the filing of the certification.[32]

31 Or, in the case of other motions, not preliminary in nature, if 'the decision impugned would cause such prejudice to the case of the party seeking leave as could not be cured by the final disposal of the trial including post-judgment appeal', or 'if the issue in the proposed appeal is of general importance to proceedings before the Tribunal or in international law generally' (Rule 73(B)(i) and (ii) of the ICTY RPE; Rule 73(B) of the ICTR RPE instead always excludes appeals).

32 This 'certification' system may be criticized since a Trial Chamber, fearing reversal by the Appeals Chamber, may simply decide not to certify the appeal, in which case the avenue of appeal is completely cut off. Probably the reply would be that ultimately the issue can be resolved by final Appeals, after the Trial Chamber judgment has been rendered.

In the ICC system interlocutory appeals are regulated in a detailed manner in Article 82.

22.14 APPEALS AGAINST JUDGMENT OR SENTENCE

As in common law systems, international appellate proceedings *do not involve a re-trial.* On many occasions the ICTY Appeals Chamber has emphasized that an appeal is not an opportunity for the parties to re-argue their cases. On appeal, parties must limit their arguments to matters that fall within the scope of the grounds of appeal, namely an error of law invalidating the judgment or an error of fact involving a miscarriage of justice (see *Furundžija* (*Appeal*), §40, *Kupreškić and others* (*Appeal*) (§22)).

However, the relevant provisions of the Statutes confer the right of appeal on both the defendant and the Prosecutor, thus departing from the common law system. Both parties may appeal against conviction or sentence, and the Prosecutor may appeal against acquittal.

Another departure lies in the fact that the range of grounds on which one may appeal is much broader. These grounds are: (i) an error of law so serious as to invalidate the judgment; (ii) an error of fact so serious as to entail a miscarriage of justice. Under Article 81 of the ICC Statute, an appeal may also be lodged on the ground of a 'procedural error' or 'on any other ground that affects the fairness or reliability of the proceedings or decision'. Furthermore, either party may appeal against a sentence 'on the ground of disproportion between the crime and the sentence'.

A third departure from the common law system is that the possibility to hear fresh evidence is much wider. Under Rules 115 of the ICTY and ICTR RPE a party to the appellate proceedings may lodge a motion asking that additional evidence, which was not available to this party at trial, be presented. The Appeals Chamber may authorize the presentation of such evidence 'if it considers that the interests of justice so require'. Plainly, if such authorization is granted, the Appeals Chamber will have to hear the new evidence and may therefore have to reconsider some of the facts. Of course, the same rules governing the presentation of evidence before Trial Chambers will also apply before the Appeals Chamber.[33]

[33] In *Tadić* (*Appeal, decision on admissibility of additional evidence*) (§§27–74) the Appeals Chamber held that the unavailability of the evidence at trial must not result from lack of due diligence on the part of relevant defence counsel; in addition, the interests of justice required admission of evidence only if the evidence: (i) was relevant to a material issue; (ii) was credible; and (iii) was such that it would probably show that the conviction was unsafe. See also *Delalić and others* (*Appeal, order on motion of Landzo*), at 2–3, *Jelisić* (*Appeal, decision on additional evidence*) at 3, as well as *Kupreškić and others* (*Appeal*) (§§48–76).

On many occasions the ICTY Appeals Chamber has rejected motions for the admission of additional evidence. This, for instance, happened in *Tadić* (*Appeal, decision on the admission of additional evidence*), as well as in *Jelisić* (*Appeal*) (§§20–1). In other cases additional evidence has been admitted. See for instance *Delalić and others* (*Order on motion for the extension of the time-limit an admission of new evidence*, of 31 May

The Appeals Chamber may dismiss the appeal, or acquit the appellant, or order that the accused be retried, or change the sentence.

The ICC Statute provides that appeals may be lodged both by the convicted persons and by the prosecutor. They may appeal against either the judgment or the sentence, or both (Articles 81 and 83).

22.15 REVIEW OF JUDGMENT OR SENTENCE

Under Article 26 of the ICTY Statute, Article 25 of the ICTR Statute, and Article 84 of the ICC Statute, whenever a new fact is discovered which (i) was not known to the party concerned at the time of trial or appellate proceedings, and (ii) could have been 'a decisive factor in reaching the decision', the convicted person or the Prosecutor may apply for review of the judgment. Rule 119 of the ICTY RPE and Rule 120 of the ICTR RPE add a further condition: the new fact 'could not have been discovered through the exercise of due diligence'.

The rationale behind this review procedure is evident: although a judgment or sentence may be endowed with the legal force of *res judicata* (that is, the force of a binding and final judicial decision), it would be contrary to elementary principles of justice not to revise it any time a new fact emerges that was unknown at the time of trial and which, if known, would have led to a totally different decision. In the case of review proceedings, what must be new is a *fact, not evidence* of a fact known at the time of trial. As the ICTY Appeals Chamber rightly held in *Tadić* (*Appeal on admission of additional evidence*), 'The mere subsequent discovery of evidence of a fact which was known at trial is not itself a new fact within the meaning of Rule 119 of the Rules' (at §32).

Under the ICTY and ICTR systems the convicted person may at any time file an application for review, while the Prosecutor has a time limit of 'one year after the final judgment has been pronounced'. The motion for review does not automatically lead to a new trial: it is necessary for the Chamber which delivered the judgment to conclude that the new fact, if proved, could have been 'a decisive factor in reaching the decision'. This examination is 'preliminary' in nature. If the Chamber's conclusion is affirmative, then the relevant Chamber commences a new trial, and its judgment may then be appealed (Rules 120–1 of the ICTY RPE and Rules 121–2 of the ICTR RPE).

The ICC system *broadens the category of persons* entitled to apply for review. It grants the right to apply not only to the convicted person and the Prosecutor (who must only act on behalf of the convicted person, hence may not seek review *contra reum*) but also, after the death of this person, to spouses, children, parents, or 'one person alive at the time of the accused's death who has been given express written

2000, at 8–9, and of 14 February 2000, at 2–3), in *Kupreškić and others* (*Appeal, decision on the motions of Drago Josipović and others*), at 7). See also *Akayesu* (*Appeal, decision of 22 August 2000*) (at 5–6). In *Kupreškić and others* (*Appeal*) the ICTY Appeals Chamber, after considering and weighing additional evidence (§§263–302) concluded that the findings of the Trial Chamber had resulted in a miscarriage of justice (§§303–4).

instructions from the accused to bring such a claim'. In addition, the Statute *broadens the classes of requirements* necessary for applying for review. These conditions include not only (i) the discovery of a decisive fact, but also (ii) the discovery that decisive evidence was false, forged, or falsified, and (iii) the fact that one or more judges sitting on trial committed an act of serious misconduct or a serious breach of duty justifying the removal of that or those judges from office pursuant to Article 46 of the ICC Statute. Under the same Statute, the motion for review is submitted to the Appeals Chamber, which, if it considers it meritorious, may (i) reconvene the original Trial Chamber, or (ii) constitute a new Trial Chamber, or (iii) retain jurisdiction over the matter.

22.16 REVIEW OF OTHER FINAL DECISIONS

In *Barayagwisa* (*Appeal on request for review or reconsideration*) the question arose of whether a decision of the ICTR Appeals Chamber of 3 November 1999, which dismissed the indictment against the appellant and terminated the proceedings, could be the object of review before the Appeals Chamber at the request of the Prosecutor. The defence submitted that Articles 24 (on appellate proceedings) and 25 (on review proceedings) of the ICTR Statute, in granting the right of appeal or review to a convicted person (besides the Prosecutor) presupposed that the right to request review was only available after conviction. The Appeals Chamber dismissed the argument. It noted that:

> If the Appellant were correct that there could be no review unless there has been a conviction, it would follow that there could be no appeal from acquittal for the same reason. Appeals from acquittals have been allowed before the Appeals Chamber of the ICTY. The Appellant's logic is not therefore correct. (§47.)

Furthermore, the Chamber stated that it considered it important to note:

> that only a final judgment may be reviewed pursuant to Article 25 of the Statute and to Rule 120. The parties submitted pleadings on the final or non-final nature of the Decision [of 3 November 1999] in connection with the request for reconsideration. The Chamber would point out that a final judgment in the sense of the above-mentioned articles is one which terminates the proceedings; only such a decision may be subject to review. Clearly, the Decision of 3 November 1999 belongs to that category, since it dismissed the indictment against the Appellant and terminated the proceedings. (§49.)

Hence, according to this case law, in the ICTY and ICTR systems a review motion may be filed even against a decision that is not *stricto sensu* a judgment, provided such decision puts an end to the proceedings.

(D) ENFORCEMENT OF SENTENCES

22.17 PLACE OF IMPRISONMENT

International courts do not have any prison available in which to detain convicted persons. Consequently they must of necessity turn to States to see whether they may hold those persons in jail. Article 27 of the ICTY Statute provides that 'imprisonment shall be served in a State designated by the International Tribunal from a list of States which have indicated to the Security Council their willingness to accept convicted persons'. Article 26 of the ICTR has a similar tenor.[34]

Similarly, Article 103(1)(a) of the ICC Statute provides that 'a sentence of imprisonment shall be served in a State designated by the Court from a list of States which have indicated to the Court their willingness to accept sentenced persons'.

So far the ICTY and the ICTR have entered into agreements with individual States, which have agreed to hold persons convicted by the Tribunals in their national prisons.[35]

22.18 CONDITIONS OF DETENTION

Of course, imprisonment of convicted persons must be in conformity with the general laws and regulations applicable in the relevant State. However, conditions of detention of those persons must accord with international standards. This requirement, although not explicitly laid down in the Statutes of the ICTY and the ICTR, is implicit in the whole system of international courts: these courts are bound to respect international standards on human rights and in particular to comply fully with these standards as far as the rights of the accused and victims and witnesses are concerned.[36]

[34] It provides that 'Imprisonment shall be served in Rwanda or any of the States on a list of States which have indicated to the Security Council their willingness to accept convicted persons, as designated by the International Tribunal for Rwanda. Such imprisonment shall be in accordance with the applicable law of the State concerned, subject to the supervision of the International Tribunal for Rwanda'.

[35] The UN has made agreements for the ICTY with Italy (signed on 6 February 1997), Finland (7 May 1997), Norway (24 April 1998), Sweden (23 February 1999), Austria (23 July 1999), France (25 February 2000), and Spain (28 March 2000). The agreement with Spain differs in many respects from the other agreements. Among other things, it provides that Spain will only consider the enforcement of sentences pronounced by the ICTY where the duration of the sentence imposed does not exceed the highest maximum sentence for any crime under Spanish law (currently 30 years). The UN has entered into agreements for the ICTR with Mali, Benin, and Swaziland.

[36] In the various Agreements concluded by International Tribunals with States for the enforcement of sentences it is provided that 'conditions of detention shall be compatible with the Standard Minimum Rules for the Treatment of Prisoners, the Body of Principles for the Protection of All Persons under Any Form of Detention or Imprisonment and the Basic Principles of the Treatment of Prisoners' (Article 3(5) of the various Agreements).

The ICC Statute makes this requirement explicit. Article 106(2) provides that 'the conditions of imprisonment . . . shall be consistent with widely accepted international treaty standards governing treatment of prisoners'.

22.19 REDUCTION OR COMMUTATION OF SENTENCE AND PARDON

International provisions stipulate that the State where the convicted person serves his sentence is not allowed to reduce or change the penalty or release the person before expiry of the sentence pronounced by the International Court (see, for instance, Article 110(1) and (2) of the ICC Statute). Only the International Court may decide upon any change in the sentence.

However, conflicts may arise between the general legislation of the State enforcing the penalty and international prescriptions. It may happen that in the State at issue detainees are entitled to a reduction of sentence, or to early release, or to special treatment (for instance, parole) after serving the sentence for a certain number of years, or in case of good behaviour. If, however, these conditions are not applied to persons convicted by the International Tribunal, this may be deemed to constitute discrimination against these international convicts.

This difficult issue has been settled in a flexible manner in agreements concluded between the Tribunals and States. For instance, in the first such agreement with the ICTY, which also served as a model for subsequent agreements, that with Italy of 6 February 1997, it is provided that 'if pursuant to the applicable national law of the requested State, the convicted person is eligible for non-custodial measures or working activities outside the prison, or is entitled to benefit from conditional release, the Minister of Justice shall notify the President of the Tribunal' (Article 3(3)). The provision then stipulates that, if the President of the Tribunal, in consultation with the judges, does not consider those national measures appropriate, the convicted person shall be transferred to the International Tribunal, presumably for the purpose of being transferred to another State willing to have him serve the remainder of his sentence. A similar provision (Article 8) covers the issue of pardon or commutation of sentence.

The question of *pardon* is particularly difficult. In most States only the Head of State may grant pardon. States are extremely jealous of this prerogative of their supreme national organ. Article 28 of the ICTY Statute (and the corresponding Article 27 of the ICTR Statute) provides that:

> If, pursuant to the applicable law of the State in which the convicted person is imprisoned, he or she is eligible for pardon or commutation of sentence, the State concerned shall notify the International Tribunal accordingly. The President of the Tribunal, in consultation with the judges, shall decide the matter on the basis of the interests of justice and the general principles of law.

On the face of it, the matter is 'decided' by the President of the Tribunal in consultation with judges. The power of pardon would thus seem ultimately to belong to the international body, in contrast to the regulation of most national constitutions.

The judges of the ICTY skilfully smoothed out the problem in the Rules of Procedure and Evidence. Under Rule 123 ICTY, if the person is eligible for pardon or commutation of sentence under national legislation, the State concerned shall notify the International Tribunal, and then the Tribunal's president, in consultation with the judges 'shall . . . determine whether pardon or commutation is appropriate' (Rule 124), on the basis of a set of criteria laid down in Rule 125. Thus, the international body only decides on the appropriateness of pardon (or commutation), and the final decision is left to the relevant national authority (Rules 124–6 of the ICTR RPE are identical in content).

The ICC Statute does not make any provision for the granting of pardon. Under Article 110 it is for the Court alone to take any decision on the *reduction* of sentences (whereas Rule 211(2) makes provision for the eligibility, under national law, for a prison programme, or benefit entailing 'some activity outside the prison facility', and simply provides that the Court must be notified and shall exercise its supervisory activity). It is therefore probable that a solution similar to that set out by the ICTY and ICTR in their Rules will be opted for, the more so because Article 104 of the ICC Statute provides that the Court 'may, at any time, decide to transfer a sentenced person to a prison of another State'.

22.20 SUPERVISION OF IMPRISONMENT

The Statutes of the ICTY and the ICTR provide that imprisonment served in a State designated by the Tribunal shall be 'subject to the supervision of the International Tribunal' (Articles 27 and 26, respectively). The ICTY entered into an agreement with the International Committee of the Red Cross, authorizing the Committee to make inspections not only in the Detention Unit in The Hague (where accused are held pending trial or appeal) but also, subject to the consent of the relevant State, in the country where the sentence is enforced.

Indeed, almost all Agreements on the enforcement of sentences provide for inspection by the ICRC.[37]

Under Rule 211 of the ICC RPE the Court's Presidency 'may . . . request any information, report or expert opinion from the State of enforcement or from any

[37] For instance, the Agreement with Italy of 6 February 1997 stipulates in Article 6(1) that the ICRC may carry out inspections 'at any time and on a periodic basis'; 'the frequency of visits [is] to be determined by the ICRC'. The ICRC submits a 'confidential report based on the findings of these inspections' to the Italian Minister of Justice and the President of the ICTY, who will consult each other on those findings. The Tribunal's President may then request the Italian Minister of Justice 'to report to him any changes in the conditions of detention suggested by the ICRC'.

The Agreement with Spain differs from the other Agreements on the enforcement of sentences in that it provides for inspections of the conditions of detention and treatment of the convicted persons by a Parity Commission instead of by the ICRC.

reliable source'. The Presidency may also delegate a judge or a staff member of the court to supervise the conditions of detention.[38]

(E) THE SPECIFICITY OF INTERNATIONAL TRIALS

22.21 THE UNIQUE TRAITS OF INTERNATIONAL CRIMINAL TRIALS

It may now be appropriate briefly to sum up the main traits of international criminal proceedings.

1. It is the *Prosecutor who sets proceedings in motion.* (However, in the ICC system, the Prosecutor may also act at the request of a State or the UN Security Council.) The Prosecutor is not duty bound to initiate proceedings any time he becomes cognizant of an international crime. He enjoys broad *discretionary power* in selecting the crimes on which to concentrate. In this respect, it is for him to decide which crimes under the jurisdiction of the relevant international court are so serious as to deserve to be brought before an international court (however, in the ICC system the Prosecutor acts under the scrutiny of the Pre-Trial Chamber).

2. There is *no international body such as an investigating judge* charged with the collection of evidence on behalf of both the accusation and the defence. Rather, the Prosecutor, before preferring the charges against the accused, looks for and gathers the evidence. It is for the defence to search for evidence to refute the accusation's charges.

3. Nonetheless, unlike his counterpart in many national law systems, the Prosecutor is not merely a party to the trial. At least under the ICC Statute, he is also bound to search for, gather, and pass on to the defence any evidence exonerating the accused.[39] In other words, he acts as an '*organ of justice*' rather than a mere party to the trial.

4. Legally speaking, in order to collect evidence (interview witnesses, search premises, seize material evidence, arrest suspects, etc.) both the Prosecutor and the Defence must turn to national authorities, in particular to the authorities of the State where the witness, or material evidence, or the suspect are located. Without State co-operation international trials become deadlocked or come to a standstill. However, in fact both the prosecution and the defence often may interview witnesses without

[38] Under Rule 211(1)(c) the judge or the staff member 'will be responsible, after notifying the State of enforcement, for meeting the sentenced person and hearing his or her views, without the presence of national authorities'.

[39] Under Rule 68 of the ICTY and ICTR Rules, the prosecutor is only obliged to hand over to the defence any exculpatory evidence he may have found.

having to turn to any national authorities.[40] The same is true of gathering evidence—certain evidence may be gathered without turning to national authorities at all. However, anything involving *coercive powers* depends on help from the authorities, as does consulting archives, etc. which *belong to a State.*

5. There is no *jury* responsible for evaluating the facts. International courts consist only of *professional* judges. The underlying reasons for this regulation are that: (i) it would be difficult to establish the criteria for appointing jurors;[41] (ii) international crimes are complex offences; their appraisal requires extensive legal knowledge of both public international law and criminal law. In addition the facts are often extremely complicated and the evidence may prove difficult to evaluate. In short, only experienced judges possessing wide legal expertise may be in a position to adjudicate these crimes.

6. Trials *in absentia* may not be conducted. The presence of the accused is always required, except for cases where he explicitly waives his right to be present after appearing in court.

7. The guilty-plea procedure, adopted at the international level, does not yield the same results as in common law systems, where it often makes it possible to drastically cut the number of criminal trials. At the international level various factors tend to discourage accused persons from making use of this procedural mechanism. Nevertheless, there seems to be an increasing trend towards greater resort to the guilty-plea procedure and the plea-bargaining scheme underlying it. Among the reasons behind this recent tendency one may perhaps discern the need to reduce the number of trials and streamline the rather cumbersome international criminal procedure.

8. International trials are not a contest between two parties, overseen by a neutral and passive referee. International courts play *an active role in directing the proceedings.* In particular, they possess *extensive powers* with regard to evidence. They may call witnesses. They may also summon as court witnesses persons that a party would like to call to testify in court, but who are loath to do so on a number of grounds (see *supra*, 21.4.1).

9. Victims do not play a major role. However, in the ICC system they may set forth their views and concerns in court, and, although they may not call witnesses, they are entitled to examine or cross-examine witnesses called by either party (however, they have no access to the evidence gathered by the parties, nor can they lodge an appeal).

10. As the principle *nulla poena sine lege* finds only limited application at the international level, courts enjoy broad powers in sentencing convicted persons.

11. As a rule appellate proceedings are not aimed at a retrial, but are designed to verify whether the trial court erred in law or misapprehended facts in such a serious manner as to bring about a miscarriage of justice (however, in some limited cases courts of appeal may hear new evidence).

[40] Often they simply telephone them or send them an e-mail.

[41] For instance, what nationality should they be? How could they be selected? And so on.

22.22 THE MERITS OF INTERNATIONAL CRIMINAL JUSTICE

International tribunals present a number of advantages or merits over domestic courts, particularly those sitting in the territory of the State where atrocities have been committed.

It is a fact that national courts are not inclined to institute proceedings for crimes that lack a territorial or national link with the State. As noted above, until 1994, when the establishment of the International Criminal Tribunal for the former Yugoslavia gave a great impulse to the prosecution and punishment of alleged war criminals, the criminal provisions of the 1949 Geneva Conventions had never been applied. National courts are still State oriented and loath to search for, prosecute, and try foreigners who have committed crimes abroad against other foreigners. For them, the short-term objectives of national concerns seem still to prevail. This is also due in part to the failure of national parliaments to pass the necessary legislation granting courts universal jurisdiction over international crimes. In this respect the implementation in the USA of the 1949 Geneva Conventions is indicative: as noted above (see 16.3.2) the relevant US Statute only provides for jurisdiction over grave breaches of those Conventions where the perpetrator or the victim has US nationality; in this manner the universality principle proclaimed in the Conventions has been deprived of its enormous innovative scope within the US legal system. Faced with this and other similar national legal conditions, international courts are obviously called upon to play the crucial role of *replacing national courts.*

Secondly, the crimes at issue being international, that is, serious breaches of international law, international courts are the most appropriate bodies to pronounce on them. They are in a better position to understand and apply international law.

Thirdly, international judges may be in a better position to be impartial, or at any rate more even-handed, than national judges who have been caught up in the milieu in which the crime in question was perpetrated. The punishment by international tribunals of alleged authors of international crimes normally meets with less resistance than national punishment, as it injures national feelings to a lesser degree.

Fourthly, international courts, more easily than national judges, are able to investigate crimes with ramifications in many countries. Often witnesses reside in different countries, and other evidence needs to be collected, requiring the co-operation of several States. In addition, special expertise is needed to handle the often tricky legal issues arising from the various national legislations involved.

Fifthly, trials by international courts may ensure some kind of uniformity in the application of international law, whereas proceedings conducted before national courts may lead to disparity both in the interpretation and application of that law and the penalties given to those found guilty.

Finally, as international trials are by definition more visible than national criminal proceedings, holding international trials signals the will of the international community to break with the past, by punishing those who have deviated from acceptable standards of human behaviour. In delivering punishment, the international community's purpose is not so much retribution as stigmatization of the deviant behaviour, in the hope that this will have a deterrent effect.

22.23 THE MAIN PROBLEMS OF INTERNATIONAL CRIMINAL PROCEEDINGS

However, one should not be blind to the numerous and grave problems which beset international trials.

The crucial problem international criminal courts face is the *lack of enforcement agencies* directly available to those courts, for the purpose of collecting evidence, searching premises, seizing documents, or executing arrest warrants and other judicial orders. It follows that, as I have already emphasized many times, international courts must rely heavily on the co-operation of States. As long as States refuse outright to assist those courts in collecting evidence or arresting the indictees, or do not provide sufficient assistance, international criminal justice can hardly fulfil its role. This of course also applies to those cases, such as that of the ICTY, where a multilateral force established under the aegis of the UN provides assistance in executing arrest warrants (I am referring of course to the NATO forces operating in Bosnia and Herzegovina and, more recently, in Kosovo).

In addition, there exists a need for international criminal courts to *amalgamate* different judges, each with a varied cultural and legal background. (Some come from common law countries, others from States with a civil law tradition. Some are criminal lawyers, others are primarily familiar with international law. Some have previous judicial experience, others do not.)

Another serious problem is the *length* of international criminal proceedings. It results primarily from the adoption of the adversarial system, which requires that all the evidence be scrutinized orally through examination and cross-examination (whereas in the inquisitorial system the evidence is selected beforehand by the investigating judge). It should also be noted that the adversarial system was conceived of, and adopted, in most common law countries, as a fairly exceptional alternative to the principal policy choice, namely avoidance of trial proceedings through plea-bargaining. In fact, on account of this feature, the adversarial model works sufficiently well in most countries. However, in international criminal proceedings defendants tend not to plead guilty, because of, among other things, the serious stigma attached to international crime. They prefer to stand trial in spite of the time involved in examination and cross-examination of witnesses.

Additionally, the protracted nature of the proceedings is often accentuated by the need to prove some ingredient of the crime (for instance, the existence of a widespread or systematic practice, in the case of crimes against humanity) or by the need to look into the historical or social context of criminal conduct.

The question of the length of international trials is further complicated by language problems. At the national level proceedings are normally conducted in only one language; before international courts in at least two, and possibly in three or more languages, with the consequence that documents and exhibits need to be translated. This factor, coupled with the frequent need—as I have already emphasized—to uphold what is a typical feature of the inquisitorial system, namely keeping the accused in custody both in the pre-trial phase and during trial and appeal, makes for a state of affairs that is hardly consistent with the right to a 'fair and expeditious trial' and the presumption of innocence accruing to any defendant.

SELECT BIBLIOGRAPHY

GENERAL

Comparative law

M. Delmas-Marty, *Procédures pénales d'Europe* (Paris: PUF, 1995); G. Stefani, G. Levasseur, and B. Bouloc, *Procédure pénale*, 16th edn (Paris: Dalloz, 1996); A. Ashworth, *The Criminal Process—An Evaluative Study*, 2nd edn (Oxford: Oxford University Press, 1998); S. Guinchard, M. Bandra, X. Lagarde, and M. Douchy, *Droit processuel—Droit commun du procès* (Paris: Dalloz, 2001); M. Delmas-Marty and J. R. Spencer (eds), *European Criminal Procedures* (Cambridge: Cambridge University Press, 2002).

International law

D. Weissbrodt and R. Wolfrum (eds), *The Right to a Fair Trial* (Berlin: C. 1997); E. J. Wallach, 'The Procedural and Evidentiary Rules of the Post-World War II War Crimes Trials: Did They Provide an Outline for International Legal Procedure?', 37 *Columbia Journal of Transnational Law* (1999), 851–83; L. Arbour and others (eds), *The Prosecutor of a Permanent International Criminal Court* (Freiburg im Breisgau: Edition Iuscrim, 2000); L. C. Vohrah, 'Pre-Trial Procedures and Practices', in G. Kirk McDonald and O. Swaak-Goldman (eds), *Substantive and Procedural Aspects of International Criminal Law I* (The Hague, London, Boston: Kluwer, 2000), 479–545; G. Kirk McDonald, 'Trial Procedures and Practices', ibid., 547–622; A. G. Karibi-Whyte, 'Appeal Procedures and Practices', ibid., 623–68; C. J. M. Safferling, *Towards an International Criminal Procedure* (Oxford: Oxford University Press, 2001); R. May and others (eds), *Essays on ICTY Procedure and Evidence* (The Hague, London, Boston: Kluwer, 2001); S. Zappalà, *Human Rights in International Criminal Proceedings* (Oxford: Oxford University Press, 2003).

RULES OF EVIDENCE

Comparative law

Pradel, 471–5; G. P. Fletcher, *Basic Concepts*, 14–17

International law

A. M. La Rosa, 'Réflexions sur l'apport du Tribunal Pénal international pour l'ex-Yougoslavie au droit au procès équitable', 101 RGDIP (1997), 945–86; Y. Nouvel, 'La preuve devant le Tribunal Pénal pour l'ex-Yougoslavie', 101 RGDIP (1997), 905–44;

R. May and M. Wierda, 'Trends in International Criminal Evidence: Nuremberg, Tokyo, The Hague and Arusha', 37 *Columbia Journal of Transnational Law* (1999), 725–65; A. M. La Rosa, 'La preuve', in Ascensio, Decaux, and Pellet (eds), *Droit international pénal*, 763–78; R. May and M. Wierda, 'Evidence before the ICTY', in R. May and others (eds), *ICTY Procedure and Evidence*, 249–61: G. Boas, 'Admissibility of Evidence', ibid., 263–74; E. O'Sullivan, 'Judicial Notice', ibid., 329–39; P. Wald, 'To Establish Incredible Events by Credible Evidence: the Use of Affidavit Testimony in Yugoslavia War Crimes Tribunal Proceedings', 42 HILJ (2001), 535–53; G. Sluiter, *International Criminal Adjudication and the Collection of Evidence: Obligations of States* (Antwerp, Oxford, New York: Intersentia, 2002).

Sentencing

K. Ambos and S. Wirth, 'Sentencing, Cumulative Charging, Genocide and Crimes against Humanity', in A. Klip and G. Sluiter (eds), *Annotated Leading Cases of International Criminal Tribunals II* (2001); J. C. Nemitz, 'Sentencing in the Jurisprudence of the International Criminal Tribunals for the former Yugoslavia and Rwanda, in Fischer, Kress, and Lüder (eds), *International and National Prosecution*, cit., 605–25

23

THE OUTLOOK FOR INTERNATIONAL CRIMINAL JUSTICE

23.1 THE IMPORTANCE OF REACTING TO WIDESPREAD ATROCITIES

The First World War was dubbed 'the war to end all wars'. However, the Great War, as it was also called, brought to an end neither warfare nor man's inhumanity to man. Its legacy was slaughter on a scale never seen before and the disappearance of a whole generation of men from Europe. When it was over, it was generally felt that those responsible for starting the war or for committing atrocities should be brought to trial and punished. In addition to adopting in the peace treaties clauses designed to provide for the trial of the major figures responsible for the war and the crimes committed during its course, proposals were put forward for the establishment of a permanent criminal court. It was a dream, and it did not come true. The war's aftermath contained the seeds from which the Second World War would later erupt. Since then, some 250 conflicts of an international and non-international character have occurred. It has been estimated that, along with the death toll produced by authoritarian regimes, these conflicts have brought about the death or injury of more than 170 million persons as well as other inestimable harmful consequences.[1] In the course of these conflicts vicious crimes, in particular war crimes, were perpetrated. Furthermore, appalling offences such as genocide, crimes against humanity, and torture have been committed in time of peace. It would be facile to blame all these misdeeds on human wickedness and recall that since time immemorial man has been inhuman to man. It is a fact that the worst planners, perpetrators, or instigators of these crimes, including decision-makers, military leaders, and senior executors, have seldom been brought to account for their misdeeds. It is however also a fact that the frustration and dismay with which we witness all these horrors is accompanied by indignation and the feeling that it is imperative to react to inhumanity.

[1] See J. Balint, 'An Empirical Study of Conflict, Conflict Victimization and Legal Redress', in C. Joyner and C. Bassiouni (eds), 14 *Nouvelles Études Pénales* (1998), at 101.

The failure of States forcefully to respond to crimes is all the more striking because in the meantime the international community, chiefly through the United Nations, has proclaimed and laid down in international instruments a set of fundamental values such as peace, respect for human rights, and self-determination of peoples. To be consistent, any gross denial of such values, in particular international crimes, ought to have been repressed by bringing the alleged authors to trial. The astounding 'silence' of international criminal justice has once again brought to the fore one of the typical flaws of the present world community: the gulf between normative values and harsh realities, in other words the fact that the rich potential of international legal standards is not matched by their implementation.

Let us briefly ask ourselves why resort to criminal justice to suppress appalling international crimes has so far proved a relative failure.

Bringing to book the alleged perpetrators of international crimes in many cases proves to be in conflict with State sovereignty. The sovereign State tends to follow its own short-term interests, too often to the detriment of the general interests of the international community. It also tends to protect its nationals even when they have infringed fundamental values of the international community. It does so especially where the person in question has acted as a State agent (Head of State, member of cabinet, military official, etc.). In other words, faced with war crimes, crimes against humanity, genocide, torture, or international terrorism, sovereign States too often protect their nationals at all costs. They refrain from either exercising their territorial jurisdiction or acting upon the active nationality principle, and also refuse to extradite their nationals to other States, or to hand them over to international authorities. By the same token, as States are self-centred and loath to look into possible misdeeds committed in a foreign country and primarily affecting the human community living there, they tend to shy away from prosecuting foreigners who have allegedly engaged in criminal activity abroad.

Since however there can be no doubt that the sovereign State is still indispensable, as is shown by the anarchy that reigns in States lacking any central authority capable of protecting the general interests of the population and exercising effective control over it,[2] it proves necessary to reconcile the needs of State sovereignty with the demands of international criminal justice.

23.2 CURRENT TRENDS IN THE REACTION TO WIDESPREAD ATROCITIES

We should ask ourselves what could be done realistically to improve international criminal justice. However, before doing so, I shall briefly outline some interesting and

[2] Such States are dominated by clans, tribes, criminal organizations, or even terrorist groups. They are therefore incapable of acting as valid representatives of the State in relations with other members of the international community.

innovative trends that—in spite of the general hostility towards justice in the international environment, as noted above—are emerging in the international community as a result of the staggering upsurge in international criminality, noted most recently in the area of terrorism.

It seems that a few trends stand out. First, resort to the legal arsenal concerning *State* responsibility is increasingly yielding in importance, at least in the area of respect for individuals' fundamental rights, to actions and mechanisms for the enforcement of *individual* liability. No doubt in interstate relations the legal rules and machinery for invoking and enforcing State responsibility, that is, for reacting to wrongful acts of States, still possess considerable significance and are used by States, particularly in the area of commercial or territorial disputes and in other similar matters. Nevertheless, one can discern a tendency to shift attention from the interstate to the inter-individual level and to react to gross breaches and atrocities more by attempting to prosecute and punish individuals rather than by invoking the responsibility of the State for which they may have acted as State agents. It is indicative of this tendency that the provisions of the 1949 Geneva Conventions on compensation by States for grave breaches have remained a dead letter, whereas there is increasing resort to the criminal provisions of the Conventions.

Secondly, when resort is made to mechanisms for enforcing compliance by States with international law or at any rate for inducing them to respect international law, there is an increasing tendency to target *individuals* (sometimes in addition to States), and in certain cases even to use tools of international *criminal* justice. Two examples may help to clarify this point. In recent times the UN Security Council when adopting resolutions under Chapter VII of the UN Charter, in particular for the purpose of reacting to threats to peace, issued sanctions not against a State but against an individual or groups of individuals who, according to the Security Council, were responsible for promoting or carrying out the acts amounting to that threat. For instance, in some resolutions the Security Council has requested States 'to freeze without delay funds and other financial assets of Usama Bin Laden and individuals and entities associated with him' (see for instance SC resolutions 1333(2000), at §8(c), and 1390(2002), at §2(a)). It is notable that these enforcement actions include interim measures typical of criminal justice, namely the freezing of private assets belonging to an individual. Another example can be drawn from the practice of the European Union (EU). Recently, faced with the 'escalation of violence and intimidation of political opponents and the harassment of the independent press' in Zimbabwe, the Council of the EU, noting that Zimbabwe had engaged in 'serious violations of human rights and of the freedom of opinion, of association and of peaceful assembly', decided to take sanctions not only against the Government of Zimbabwe but also against 'those who bear a wide responsibility for such violations', namely a number of State officials starting with the Head of State, R. G. Mugabe. By legally binding acts the Council has requested member States among other things to freeze the private assets of those State

[3] These examples show that the international institutionalized response to iolations of human rights is in some respects moving away from the concept of e responsibility' towards the more realistic and modern concept of 'individual accountability': in addition to holding accountable the State as such, resort has been made to the tools normally used for enforcing criminal liability in order to target the groups and individuals who act within and on behalf of the State; in other words, taking sanctions to target not only the State but also groups and individuals within that State.

This example provides a good opportunity to stress a further significant development. As noted above, when the Council of the European Union adopted a binding decision enjoining the 15 member States to take sanctions against both Zimbabwe and some of its leaders, the sanctions imposed included the freezing of the personal assets of the Head of State, R. Mugabe. This is the first time States have *disregarded* the customary rules on the *personal immunity* of foreign Heads of State. It is significant that the 15 European States have jointly brought about this notable deviation from universally accepted international standards for the purpose of enforcing effectively respect for human rights by a State and its leader. It is also notable that, so far, neither Zimbabwe nor any other State has contested the international legality of those sanctions. We may therefore be witnessing a gradual erosion—at least in connection with and as a reaction to systematic and large-scale breaches of human rights—of the authority of traditional international customary rules on the personal immunities of senior State officials. It may well be that this European decision is a signal of a change in international attitudes and behaviour. Indeed, if supported by future State practice, that decision may be destined to generate, at the normative level, an exception to those customary international law rules. Such exceptions could provide that the personal immunities of Heads of State and other senior State dignitaries may be disregarded as a result of collective decisions by groups of States or international organizations, whereas individual States would not be allowed on their own to set those immunities aside for risk of abuse.

Another interesting development, which occurred in the United States, evinces the increasing importance of legal tools proper to criminal justice. In some recent civil law cases, the US courts concerned resorted to *criminal law notions* as set out in the recent case law of international criminal tribunals, to settle issues relating to civil litigation (see for instance *Kadić* v. *Karadzić*, at 25–30, *Garcia J. G. and Vides Casanova C. E.*, at 3–7,[4] as well as *Doe* v. *Lumintang*, at 17–19). This development is indicative

[3] See Council Common Position of 18 February 2002 concerning restrictive measures against Zimbabwe (2002/145/CFSP), in *Official Journal of the European Communities*, 21.32.2002, L50/1; Council Regulation (EC) No. 310/2002 of 18 February 2002 on the same matter, ibid., L50/4; Council Common Position of 22 July 2002 amending Common Position 2002/145/CFSP, ibid., L195/1, Commission Regulation no. 1643/2002 of 13 September 2002, ibid., L247/22; and Council decision of 14 September 2002 implementing Common Position 2002/145/CFSP, ibid., L247/56.

[4] In this case the two defendants, the former Defence Minister and former Director of the Salvadoran National Guard, both living in Florida, were sued for damages for their command responsibility in the killing of various persons in Salvador by members of the Salvadoran National Guard. Command responsibility is provided for in the US Torture Victim Protection Act of 1991. Nonetheless, the US courts that pronounced on this case relied heavily on not only *Yamashita*, but also on ICTY case law (see decision of 30 April 2002, at 3–7). See also the Instructions of the judge to the jury of the District Court, at 6–9.

both of an increasing osmosis between civil and criminal litigation and also of the greater and greater importance being acquired by legal tools proper to criminal law.

Finally, there is an area where current trends would seem at first sight to go in a direction contrary to the trends underscored so far, but which in fact bear out the increasing emergence of individuals on the international scene and, more importantly from our viewpoint, offer potential for the future development of criminal justice. There have been many cases where, on practical or legal grounds, individuals have been unable to vindicate rights breached by foreign State officials, through criminal action brought either in their own State or in the foreign State whose agents perpetrated the offence. In many of these instances individuals have turned to *civil litigation* and brought a claim against the *State* on whose behalf those allegedly responsible had acted (or, in the unique case of the United States, against the individuals allegedly responsible). For instance, Dutch nationals sued the Japanese Government for ill-treatment in civilian internment camps in the Dutch East Indies during the Second World War (*Sjoerd Albert Lapre and others*, at 12–38); nationals of the Federal Republic of Yugoslavia brought a case in Italy against the Italian State for alleged breaches of the laws of warfare in 1999 in Belgrade (*Marković*, at 3–6); Chinese nationals brought a claim against Japan before the Tokyo District Court for the use by Japanese forces of bacteriological weapons in China during the Second World War (*Germ warfare* case); a case was brought in the United Kingdom against Kuwait for acts of torture allegedly perpetrated in Kuwait (*Al-Adsani* v. *Kuwait* at 537–51; the case was subsequently brought before the European Court of Human Rights: see *Al-Adsani* v. *United Kingdom*); Greek nationals filed claims for compensation against Germany in Greece for crimes committed during the Second World War (*Prefecture of Voiotia* v. *FRG*, at 511–14); and the same has happened in the United States (see *Princz* v. *FRG*, at 604–12) . In all these cases individuals have ultimately relied upon a scheme typical of interstate relations: bringing before national courts claims for compensation against the State allegedly responsible. True, most of these claims have been dismissed: in essence they have stumbled against the obstacle of sovereign State immunity.[5] Nonetheless, these cases show the emergence of individuals on the international level. In other words, individuals no longer accept that their interests, legal claims, and human concerns be managed by their national States in diplomatic dealings. They no longer accept that their interests must be channelled through the diplomatic action their State may undertake at the interstate level. They wish to take their rights in their own hands. Therefore to vindicate their claims they turn either directly to courts of their own State or to those of the foreign State allegedly responsible. Clearly, there

[5] This also holds true for *Marković*, where the action against the State allegedly responsible for a breach of an international rule had been brought before the courts of that State. See *Marković*, at 6–9 (the Court held that war acts are a typical expression of governmental acts over which no judicial review is admissible; according to the Court, legal questions relating to the legality of such acts may only be settled at the international level, through negotiations between States).

An exception is established by *Prefecture of Voiotia* v. *FRG*, where the Greek Court of Cassation held Germany responsible for the killing of Greek civilians in June 1944 and awarded damages to the relatives of the victims (at 511–14).

is huge potential here for recourse to criminal justice. As in most of these cases individuals are more interested in international stigmatization of misconduct and retribution than in monetary compensation for past misdeeds, it would be appropriate for them to turn to criminal courts, provided such courts have the jurisdiction and power to enforce their judgments. This is therefore an area where criminal justice could develop and expand, provided one finds a realistic path and offers viable legal options.

The trends highlighted above may seem disparate and heterogeneous, yet a common thread unites them. This is the forceful emergence of individuals on the international level, either as the authors of international crimes or of gross and large-scale breaches of human rights, or as the victims of those crimes or breaches. The international community is gradually realizing that it must deal directly with perpetrators of serious crimes by authorizing national courts to prosecute and punish them through the establishment of international tribunals or by taking sanctions that directly target individuals even if they are very high ranking State officials. By the same token, the international community cannot any longer allow claims and complaints of victims to be 'filtered' through State channels and machinery. It is therefore trying to ensure that these victims are able to appear before national or international courts in order to vindicate their rights directly and without any intermediary.

The Statute of the ICC to a large extent compounds and encapsulates most of these trends, for it also envisages the prosecution of alleged authors of serious crimes, and allows victims both to promote international justice—hence stigmatization of criminality and retribution (see however 22.2)—and to appear before international bodies to claim compensation for any damage suffered from international crimes.

23.3 RESORTING TO IMPROVED TRUTH AND RECONCILIATION COMMISSIONS

I shall now briefly canvass the possible avenues open to those eager to ensure that the promise of justice is fulfilled. I shall also underline the possible merits of each possible option.

It should be admitted that on many occasions, depending on special historical, political, or social circumstances, it may prove appropriate to respond to the widespread perpetration of international crimes not only by resort to judicial process, but also by a different response. In addition to bringing to trial at least some of the alleged authors, it may prove helpful to establish Truth and Reconciliation Commissions. This may be done, in particular, when there are too many perpetrators, and therefore it would prove too difficult, costly, or time consuming to institute trial proceedings for all, or when the former government is still strong and any major trial of all the persons who orchestrated or ordered atrocities would be likely to jeopardize the stability and viability of the new democratic government. We have, however, seen above (1.2.3(D)) the major flaws of such Commissions. It is therefore not necessary to dwell on them now. Rather, it is fitting to set out the conditions on which the Commissions may be accepted as a useful and appropriate supplement to criminal justice. To be effective, the Commissions should be entrusted with the following tasks:

1. Deal with alleged war crimes, crimes against humanity, torture, or terrorism committed by *low- or middle-level offenders*. As for genocide, the extreme gravity of this crime and the need to protect groups against their extermination seem always to impose a judicial response, so that the alleged perpetrators are brought to book and duly punished. Similarly, those who have allegedly planned, instigated, masterminded, or ordered the commission of such crimes (i.e. the military and political leaders) should be prosecuted and tried either by a national criminal court or at the international level.

2. The aforementioned low- or middle-level perpetrators should, either on their own initiative, or at the request of the national authorities (or at the behest of the victims or at the suggestion of an international tribunal), be brought before the Commission to admit their crimes in *public hearings* and give evidence about crimes committed by others. *Victims* should be allowed to air their grievances fully.

3. The Commissions should not only discover facts and elements of criminal liability, but also *shed light on the social, political, ideological, and historical causes of the conflict*, so as to contribute to indicating to the appropriate State authorities the ways of removing those causes to the extent that this is possible.

4. If the Commissions are satisfied that full disclosure has been made and, if need be, reparation (as determined by the Commissions) has been paid to the victims, they might grant individual *pardon* to the persons concerned (alternatively and depending on the constitutional mechanisms of the relevant State, the Commission could *propose to the Head of State the granting of a pardon*). Pardon would entail exemption, for the individual on whom it is bestowed, from the punishment the law inflicts for the crime he has committed, *not obliteration of the crime*. Such obliteration could only follow from amnesty; however, the ICTY, in *Furundžija* (§155), held in 1998 that amnesty for international crimes is contrary to international *jus cogens*. Other courts have taken the same stand (see *supra*, 17.1).

5. If the Commissions consider that the persons asking for pardon have not fully disclosed their own crimes or the crimes perpetrated by others with whom they were connected, or, although not indigent, have failed to pay full compensation to the victims, they might turn over the file to a criminal court of the relevant State (if the judiciary of such State is independent and fully upholds all the principles of democracy and fair justice), or, alternatively, to an international tribunal. The same should hold true for cases where the Commissions find that the atrocities committed

by the applicant are so extensive and appalling as to render pardon unwarranted. (Where the crimes are not political in nature but private, there should also be no amnesty.)[6]

6. The Commissions should co-operate with national criminal courts or the appropriate international tribunal. In particular, they could hand over to those courts or to an international tribunal any evidence they collect against military or political leaders (so that those persons could then be prosecuted in court), in addition to submitting to them the files of those persons who have not met the standards set by the Commissions for the granting of judicial pardon.

23.4 ENHANCING THE ROLE OF NATIONAL COURTS

National courts should play an even greater role in prosecuting and punishing international crime. Clearly, international courts, whenever they are established (and this is not a frequent occurrence, to say the least) *cannot* pronounce on all crimes against humanity or gross breaches of human rights or humanitarian law occurring on a daily basis in so many parts of the world. They may have no jurisdiction over some of these crimes. Or, if they do have jurisdiction, prosecution and trial proceedings may turn out to be protracted, if only because of the difficulty in collecting the necessary evidence. By and large, the principle of 'complementarity' (or 'subsidiarity') enshrined in the Rome Statute of the ICC seems sound: as a rule it is for *national* courts to adjudicate on international crimes.

To this end, national legislatures should provide those courts with the necessary legal tools to enable them to exercise criminal jurisdiction.

In particular, more use should be made of courts endowed with *territorial* jurisdiction, for they are the courts best fitted to try this category of crimes (but we saw above why often such courts refrain from pronouncing upon crimes). Also, more extensive use of the principle of *active or passive nationality* would prove helpful. The State of nationality of the alleged perpetrator would seem to have at least a moral duty to institute proceedings. In spite of the limitations inherent in the passive nationality principle, the State of nationality of the victims should also be sympathetic to victims who have suffered, and replace revenge by impartial and fair justice. These States, however, seldom take action, either for lack of the necessary legal wherewithal or for lack of 'political' will.[7]

It is therefore imperative to prompt States: (i) to pass legislation providing for

[6] That was the position at the South African Truth and Reconciliation Commission: if a person was killed or tortured for reasons wholly unrelated to apartheid, the crime did not fall within the ambit of the Commission's powers of amnesty.

[7] Two cases in point are the recent decisions of Australian courts on the alleged acts of genocide against Australian aborigines ordered or connived at by Australian State officials (see Federal Court of Australia, *Nulyarimma* v. *Thompson*, and *Buzzacott* v. *Hill*, 2 September 1999, in 39 ILM (2000), 20 ff.). Although Australia was bound both by customary rules on genocide and the 1948 Convention on genocide, the courts were unable to pronounce on the alleged genocidal acts for lack of the necessary implementing legislation.

jurisdiction over international crimes; (ii) to implement such legislation; (iii) in particular, to enact legislation necessary for the implementation of the relevant 'criminal' provisions of the four 1949 Geneva Conventions and the two Additional Protocols of 1977, and bring these provisions into effect; and (iv) to ratify international treaties designed to impose the obligation to prosecute authors of some categories of crimes (for instance, the 1984 Convention on torture and the various treaties on terrorism) and bring them into effect.

23.4.1 RESORT TO UNIVERSAL JURISDICTION

Another means of reconciling respect for the current structure of the international community, based on a plurality of sovereign States and the need for effective criminal justice, might involve expanding the jurisdiction of State criminal courts by extending their jurisdiction to all international crimes, wherever the crime is committed and whatever the nationality of the alleged author or victim. This would involve enlarging the *universal* criminal jurisdiction of States.

As was pointed out above (see *supra*, 15.5.1) there are two categories of universal jurisdiction: *absolute* jurisdiction (where national prosecution may be commenced even if the suspect is not on the territory of the prosecuting State) and *conditional* jurisdiction (where the presence of the suspect on the territory of the State is a necessary condition for instituting criminal proceedings).

Resort to a broad conception of universality entails among other things that courts may entertain criminal proceedings against foreign Heads of State or foreign senior State officials, provided only that someone lodges a complaint.[8] This however may involve the risk of abuse as well as friction in international relations, particularly when the foreign State official, because of the initiation of criminal proceedings against him, may end up being hindered in the exercise of his functions, being de facto barred from travelling abroad for fear of prosecution or even arrest. Admittedly, the risk of abuses may be tempered by the existence of personal immunities accruing to senior State officials on official missions abroad, as well as to diplomatic and consular agents (see 14.2). Nonetheless, it would be judicious for prosecutors, investigating judges, and courts to invoke this broad notion of universal jurisdiction with great caution, and only if they are fully satisfied that compelling evidence is available against the accused. Generally speaking it would seem harmful or at least illusory to transform national judges into some sort of 'knights errant of human nature', in the words attributed to Beccaria,[9] charged with righting the most serious wrongs throughout the world.

It would seem therefore appropriate to opt for *conditional* universal jurisdiction

[8] For example, Belgian judges have received complaints against several well-known personalities, including Augusto Pinochet and Fidel Castro, the Israeli prime minister Ariel Sharon, a current foreign minister (of the Congo), the former leaders of the Khmer Rouge, a former Moroccan minister, and a former Iranian prime minister.

[9] This image does not appear in the Harlem edition, the last edition revised by Beccaria; however, it does appear in some translations, for example, the English translation of 1775. (See C. Beccaria, *An Essay on Crimes and Punishment*, reprinted (Brookline Village, Ma.: Branden Press Inc., 1983), at 64, 'as if judges were to be the knights errant of human nature in general'.)

whenever the suspect or accused is an incumbent senior foreign State official not enjoying personal immunities under international law, or a former State official (to whom personal immunities, if any, no longer accrue because he has left office). Arguably, it would be realistic and practical for national lawmakers to deal with universal jurisdiction over foreign State officials by promulgating a law akin to that in force in Germany,[10] and in France,[11] or even to improve upon them. For example, they could decide that whenever an international crime is prohibited by a treaty ratified by the State, or by a rule of customary international law, the State on the territory of which the suspect or accused is found is authorized to initiate criminal proceedings and exercise criminal jurisdiction subject to some strict conditions: (i) that the State where the crime was committed neither exercises its jurisdiction nor requests the extradition of the suspect or accused, or, if the territorial State does request extradition, (ii) that it is clearly incapable of, or for any reason cannot ensure a fair, expeditious, and effective trial. A further condition should be that (iii) the foreign State official does not enjoy, or no longer enjoys, the personal immunities from criminal prosecution provided for in international law for some senior dignitaries or diplomats.[12]

Of course, in addition to the possible adoption of general legislation, any time a State has ratified a treaty on international crimes (for instance, the 1984 Convention on Torture) laying down the *forum deprehensionis* principle, the State will apply that principle and accordingly exercise universal jurisdiction on the strength of the national rules implementing the relevant provisions of the treaty.[13]

[10] See para. 6, Ch. 9 of the Criminal Code (*Strafgesetzbuch*), which stipulates that German law applies with regard to all acts committed in foreign countries that Germany is obliged to punish by virtue of an international treaty incorporating the principle of universal jurisdiction. Although German case law normally requires some connecting factor (*Anknüpfungspuntkt*) between the crime and Germany, such as residence of the accused in Germany, the Federal Court held, in its judgment of 21 February 2001 in the *Sokolović* case (not yet published), that a connecting factor is not indispensable. (In this case, the accused had resided in Germany for twenty years and returned there regularly to receive his retirement pension.)

On the German system in general, see R. Roth and Y. Jeanneret, 'Droit allemand', in Cassese and Delmas-Marty (eds), *Juridictions nationales*, at 19–22. On the case law concerning Article 6(1) of the German Criminal Code, especially the crime of genocide, see in particular A. Eser, 'Völkermord und deutsche Strafgewalt—Zum Spannungsverhältnis von Weltrechtsprinzip und legitimierendem Inlandsbezug', in *Strafverfahrensrecht in Theorie und Praxis, Festschrift für Lutz Meyer-Gossner* (Munich: Beck, 2001), at 3–31 (this paper was written prior to the judgment in the aforementioned *Sokolović* case of 21 February 2001).

[11] Article 689–1 of the French Code of Criminal Procedure provides that 'pursuant to the international conventions referred to in the following articles [that is, Articles 689–2 to 689–7, referring to treaties on torture and various forms of terrorism] any person guilty of any of the offences listed in those articles . . . may be prosecuted and tried by French courts if that person is present in France'.

[12] See also the conditions set out in the Joint Separate Opinion of Judges R. Higgins, P. Kooijmans, and T. Buergenthal in *Case Concerning the Arrest Warrant of 11 April 2000* (Judgment of the International Court of Justice of 14 February 2002), at §§59–60.

[13] Plainly, the conditional universality principle may be tainted by a serious limitation. When applied to a former Head of State or government or senior member of cabinet or diplomat, the principle may result in these persons never being brought to trial if they are prudent enough to avoid travelling to a country where they could become amenable to judicial process. Similarly, a foreign State requesting their extradition on the basis of the absolute universality principle is likely to come up against a blunt refusal by the national authorities to hand over the former senior official (unless this official is out of favour with the new government). It would however appear that the need to forestall possible abuses should make this eventuality acceptable, however seriously it may run counter to the fundamental imperatives of international justice.

As stated above (15.5.1(B)), a different category of universal jurisdiction could be adopted for international crimes allegedly perpetrated by *low-ranking* military officers or other junior State agents, or even *civilians*. As I have already noted (*supra*), normally these persons are not well known, and their travels abroad do not make news. Therefore, issuing arrest warrants against them even when they are abroad would make it possible for them to be apprehended as soon as they enter the territory of the prosecuting State.

23.5 NATIONAL CRIMINAL JUDGES AND INTERNATIONAL COURTS

A crucial question is that of the relationship between national criminal judges and international courts. In my opinion, resort to national courts exercising territorial, national, or universal jurisdiction offers an advantage compared with international criminal courts. National judges have all the coercive arms of the State at their disposal. Normally—and I emphasize the word 'normally'—they can therefore render justice more effectively.

However, by pleading for a widening of the criminal jurisdiction of national courts, I do not intend to underestimate the merits of international criminal courts. On the contrary, I consider that these courts can play an essential role in at least four ways.

First of all, they can incite national judges to broaden their jurisdiction, or at least to exercise it under their traditional grounds of jurisdiction. Indeed, as I have already pointed out above, for over forty years after the entry into force of the 1949 Geneva Conventions national courts have not used the universal jurisdiction they derived from these Conventions. They have only begun to discover that they are endowed with such jurisdiction since the establishment by the United Nations of the two ad hoc criminal tribunals in 1993 and 1994.

Secondly, international courts can replace national judges whenever these judges are unable or unwilling to render justice in a fair, impartial, and efficient manner.

Thirdly, on many occasions international courts and tribunals may prove more impartial than national courts, particularly those of the State where the crime was perpetrated, and therefore where tensions, animosity, and popular resentment may exist jeopardizing the fairness of a trial.

Finally, only international courts can take adequate and appropriate judicial action when a case involves very complex international crimes. This is particularly so either when these crimes implicate powerful political and military leaders, or when the evidence is widely scattered over many countries, as the investigation then requires powers going beyond those at the disposal of the national judge.

It should nevertheless be added that at present a number of major Powers appear reluctant to accept the jurisdiction of international tribunals and even to submit to the ICC. It is a matter of regret that such States as the USA, Russia, and China oppose the Court, and the Superpower is actively trying even to shun its jurisdiction over US nationals that possibly commit crimes in a State party to the ICC Statute.[14] It is to be hoped that this negative attitude, inconsistent with the ideals firmly embedded in the US Constitution and the American historical tradition, will gradually wane and eventually disappear.

23.6 USING MIXED CRIMINAL COURTS AND TRIBUNALS FOR INTERNATIONAL CRIMES

On some occasions the establishment of mixed or 'internationalized' courts such as those set up in East Timor, in Kosovo, or in Sierra Leone, may appear to be a better solution than resort to national courts or to international criminal tribunals.

Plainly, there are situations where the *national judicial system* has collapsed due to civil strife or protracted internal commotion. Think for instance of what has happened in Colombia. There, resort to national courts would be of no avail. Other cases are those where, although a judicial system does exist and works fairly smoothly, ethnic or religious tensions are so strong that the judiciary is also 'contaminated' and proves therefore unable to administer justice when faced with international crimes grounded on ethnic or religious divides. Think for instance of such situations as Bosnia and Herzegovina. The system of 'internationalized' courts could prove very effective also when the ICC is firmly established: indeed, it may ensure a proper functioning of the complementarity mechanism and prevent the Court from being flooded with hundreds of cases because of the inadequacy of national systems due to the collapse of the local judiciary. Mixed or 'internationalized' courts will prove even more important whenever the collapsing official apparatus is that of a State that is not party to the ICC Statute.

Similarly, the appalling terrorist acts perpetrated against US territory in 2001 would probably be the appropriate subject matter for 'internationalized' courts. Adjudication of those crimes in US courts might lead observers to believe that the fundamental principle of presumption of innocence could hardly be respected. In addition, as those courts may impose death sentences, European States that apprehend alleged culprits may be obliged to refuse to hand them over to US courts on human rights grounds. Furthermore, these crimes have wide ramifications in many countries; the

[14] As is well known, the USA is pursuing this purpose both by entering into bilateral agreements with States that are, or may become, parties to the ICC Statute, and by having the Security Council adopt resolutions exonerating US personnel from the Court's jurisdiction. See in this respect resolution 1422(2002) adopted by the Security Council on 12 July 2002. Under para. 1, the Security Council '*requests*, consistent with the provisions of Article 6 of the Rome Statute, that the ICC, if a case arises involving current or former officials or personnel from a contributing State [i.e. contributing to peace-keeping or peace-enforcing operations established or authorized by the UN Security Council] not a Party to the Rome Statute over acts or omissions relating to a United Nations established or authorized operation, shall for a twelve-month period starting 1 July 2002 not commence or proceed with investigation or prosecution of any such case, unless the Security Council decides otherwise.' Para. 3 stipulates that 'Member States shall take no action inconsistent with paragraph 1 and with their international obligations'.

prosecution may therefore have to search for and collect the evidence in many States and will therefore need the co-operation of those States. Also in this respect a mixed or 'internationalized' tribunal would seem to be the proper forum. In addition, trials conducted before such tribunals would expose the terrorist acts and their context much better than trials before an 'ordinary' national court.

Other instances where the national judicial system is inadequate and needs to be bolstered by an international component is that of Palestine, where courts could be beefed up by international prosecutors and judges, so as to prosecute and try serious crimes of terrorism in a fair, effective, and expeditious manner.

In addition, one may bring before 'internationalized' courts crimes against humanity, torture, or genocide perpetrated in some authoritarian countries, where the political system still protects the alleged perpetrators, while neighbouring countries refuse on political grounds to take action against them.

23.7 SOME TENTATIVE CONCLUSIONS: THE NEED TO WORK FOR CRIMINAL JUSTICE ON VARIOUS FRONTS

Human rights have by now become a *bonum commune humanitatis* (a common asset of whole humankind), a core of values of great significance for the whole of humankind. It is only logical and consistent to grant the courts of all States the power and also the duty to prosecute, bring to trial, and punish persons allegedly responsible for intolerable breaches of those values. By so doing, national courts would eventually act as 'organs of the world community'. That is to say, they would operate not on behalf of their own authorities but in the name and on behalf of the whole international community. Thus, at long last the theoretical construct put forward in the 1930s by the great French international lawyer Georges Scelle, the construct he termed *dédoublement fonctionnel* (role-splitting), for long a Utopian doctrine, would be brought to fruition and translated into reality.[15] Scelle emphasized that, since the international legal order lacks legislative, judicial, and enforcement organs acting on behalf of the whole community, national organs may perforce have to fulfil a dual role: they may act as State organs whenever they operate within the national legal system; they may act qua international agents when they operate within the international legal system. In a way, for Scelle, national officials exhibit a sort of 'split personality'. That is to say, although from the point of view of their legal status they are and remain State organs, they can function either as national or as international agents.

As a result of the present state of affairs and the trends emerging in the world community, Scelle's doctrine has come to acquire an enhanced vitality, at least as far

[15] See G. Scelle, *Précis de droit des gens. Principes et systématique*, I (Paris: Librairie du Recueil Sirey, 1932), at 43, 54–6, 217; II, at 10, 319, 450; Idem, 'Théorie et pratique de la fonction exécutive en droit international', 55 HR (1936), 91–106. On this doctrine see A. Cassese, 'Remarks on Scelle's Theory of Role Splitting (*dédoublement fonctionnel*) in International Law', 1 EJIL (1990), 210 ff.

as the social function of law enforcement is concerned, and in spite of the growing tendency of States to institute international or mixed criminal tribunals and courts.

However, as we have seen above, resort to national courts is not free from deficiency, any more than are the other available means of reacting to atrocities and other gross violations of human rights, namely the establishment of Truth and Reconciliation Commissions, of international criminal tribunals, or of mixed or 'internationalized' courts. None of these avenues is flawless. Probably the best response to atrocities lies in a prudent and well-thought-out combination of the various approaches, seen not as alternatives but as a joint reaction to the intolerable suffering we are obliged to witness every day.

In conclusion, I consider it is the *combination of more incisive action* by the most effective societal and institutional devices of the many available to lawmakers that could send a shock-wave through the practice of impunity. Let me repeat again that international criminal law is a branch of law that, more than any other, is about human wickedness and aggressiveness. It also deals with how society faces up to violence and viciousness to try to stem them to the extent that this is possible. Clearly, given the magnitude of the task, there is *no single response* to the multifarious aspects of international criminality. One must perforce resort to a whole gamut of responses, each most suited to a specific condition, effectively to stem international crimes.

INDEX

F

G

H

I

R

S

T